Takeovers
Volume II

The International Library of Management
Series Editor: Keith Bradley

Titles in the Series:

Takeovers
Volume II

Edited by

Andy Cosh

Queens' College, Cambridge
ESRC Centre for Business Research, University of Cambridge

and

Alan Hughes

Sidney Sussex College, Cambridge
ESRC Centre for Business Research, University of Cambridge

Ashgate

DARTMOUTH

Aldershot • Brookfield USA • Singapore • Sydney

Published by
Dartmouth Publishing Company Limited
Ashgate Publishing Limited
Gower House
Croft Road
Aldershot
Hants GU11 3HR
England

Ashgate Publishing Company
Old Post Road
Brookfield
Vermont 05036
USA

British Library Cataloguing in Publication Data
Takeovers. – (The international library of management)
  1. Consolidation and merger of corporations
  I.Cosh, Andy II.Hughes, Alan
  658.1'6

Library of Congress Cataloging-in-Publication Data
Takeovers / edited by Andy Cosh and Alan Hughes.
        p. cm. – (The international library of management)
  Includes bibliographical references and indexes.
  ISBN 1–85521–556–X (hb)
  1. Consolidation and merger of corporations. I. Cosh, A. D.
II. Hughes, Alan. 1946–   III. Series.
HD2746.5.T35 1998
658.1'6–dc21

                                                98–3786
                                                 CIP

ISBN 1 85521 556 X

Printed in Great Britain by Galliard (Printers) Ltd, Great Yarmouth

Contents

PART IV   THE IMPACT OF TAKEOVERS ON COMPANY PERFORMANCE

Share Price Studies

Financial Accounts and Other Studies

PART V   MANAGERS AND SHAREHOLDERS IN THE TAKEOVER PROCESS

Acknowledgements

The editors and publishers wish to thank the following for permission to use copyright material.

American Accounting Association for the essay: Victor Pastena and William Ruland (1986), 'The Merger/Bankruptcy Alternative', *Accounting Review*, **LXI**, pp. 288–301.

American Economic Association for the essay: Gregg A. Jarrell, James A. Brickley and Jeffrey M. Netter (1988), 'The Market for Corporate Control: The Empirical Evidence Since 1980', *Journal of Economic Perspectives*, **2**, pp. 49–68.

American Finance Association for the essays: George P. Baker (1992), 'Beatrice: A Study in the Creation and Destruction of Value', *Journal of Finance*, **XLVII**, pp. 1081–119; Anup Agrawal, Jeffrey F. Jaffe and Gershon N. Mandelker (1992), 'The Post-Merger Performance of Acquiring Firms: A Re-examination of an Anomaly', *Journal of Finance*, **XLVII**, pp. 1605–21; René M. Stulz, Ralph A. Walkling and Moon H. Song (1990), 'The Distribution of Target Ownership and the Division of Gains in Successful Takeovers', *Journal of Finance*, **XLV**, pp. 817–33; Randall Morck, Andrei Shleifer and Robert W. Vishny (1990), 'Do Managerial Objectives Drive Bad Acquisitions?', *Journal of Finance*, **XLV**, pp. 31–48.

Blackwell Publishers for the essays: David J. Ravenscraft and F. M. Scherer (1987), 'Life After Takeover', *Journal of Industrial Economics*, **XXXVI**, pp. 147–56; Alexander R. Slusky and Richard E. Caves (1991), 'Synergy, Agency, and the Determinants of Premia Paid in Mergers', *Journal of Industrial Economics*, **XXXIX**, pp. 277–96.

Elsevier Science BV for the essays: Julian R. Franks and Robert S. Harris (1989), 'Shareholder Wealth Effects of Corporate Takeovers: The U.K. Experience 1955–1985', *Journal of Financial Economics*, **23**, pp. 225–49. Copyright © 1989 Elsevier Science Publishers BV; Rolf Bühner (1991), 'The Success of Mergers in Germany', *International Journal of Industrial Organization*, **9**, pp. 513–32. Copyright © 1991 Elsevier Science Publishers BV. All rights reserved; David J. Ravenscraft and F. M. Scherer (1989), 'The Profitability of Mergers', *International Journal of Industrial Organization*, **7**, pp. 101–16. Copyright © 1989 Elsevier Science Publishers BV; Paul M. Healy, Krishna G. Palepu and Richard S. Ruback (1992), 'Does Corporate Performance Improve After Mergers?', *Journal of Financial Economics*, **31**, pp. 135–75. Copyright © 1992 Elsevier Science Publishers BV. All rights reserved; George P. Baker and Karen H. Wruck (1989), 'Organizational Changes and Value Creation in Leveraged Buyouts: The Case of the O. M. Scott & Sons Company', *Journal of Financial Economics*, **25**, pp. 163–90. Copyright © 1989 Elsevier Science Publishers BV; B. Espen Eckbo and Herwig Langohr (1989), 'Information, Disclosure, Method of Payment,

Series Preface

The International Library of Management brings together in one series the most significant and influential articles from across the whole range of management studies. In compiling the series, the editors have followed a selection policy that is both international and interdisciplinary. The articles that are included are not only of seminal importance today, but are expected to remain of key relevance and influence as management deals with the issues of the next millennium.

The Library was specifically designed to meet a great and growing need in the field of management studies. Few areas have grown as rapidly in recent years, in size, complexity, and importance. There has been an enormous increase in the number of important academic journals publishing in the field, in the amount published, in the diversity and complexity of theory and in the extent of cross-pollination from other disciplines. At the same time, managers themselves must deal with increasingly complex issues in a world growing ever more competitive and interdependent. These remarkable developments have presented all those working in the field, whether they be theorists or practitioners, with a serious challenge. In the absence of a core series bringing together this wide array of new knowledge and thought, it is becoming increasingly difficult to keep abreast of all new important developments and discoveries, while it is becoming ever-more vital to do so.

The International Library of Management aims to meet that need, by bringing the most important articles in management theory and practice together in one core, definitive series. The Library provides management researchers, professors, students, and managers themselves, with an extensive range of key articles which, together, provide a comprehensive basis for understanding the nature and importance of the major theoretical and substantive developments in management science. The Library is the definitive series in management studies.

In making their choice, the editors have drawn especially from the Anglo-American tradition, and have tended to exclude articles which have been widely reprinted and are generally available. Selection is particularly focused on issues most likely to be important to management thought and practice as we move into the next millennium. Editors have also prefaced each volume with a thought-provoking introduction, which provides a stimulating setting for the chosen articles.

The International Library of Management is an essential resource for all those engaged in management development in the future.

KEITH BRADLEY
Series Editor
The International Library of Management

sample of more than 1,800 U.K. acquisitions spanning a 30-year period (1955-85). A central objective is to conduct tests that can be performed on U.S. data to see whether particular findings emerge for the U.K. Such country results may be unique because of special institutional and regulatory circumstances. Indeed, unlike the U.S. data, ... the market for corporate control is reasonably competitive ... institutional differences. The U.K. ... independent tests of many issues ...

2. Background and methodology of the paper

This paper ... acquisitions as value-enhancing transactions ... work ... value creation ... may arise for a number of reasons ... including cost savings, use of increased monopoly power, or replacement of inefficient management. In contrast, managerial theories (Mueller (1969)) view takeovers as extensions of managerial ... self-interest, undertaken for the purpose of increasing their own wealth or prestige by managing a larger postmerger entity.

... empirical work in the U.S. (Jensen and Ruback (1983), Mandelker (1974) ... Bradley, Desai and Kim (1983)) ... largely supported the contention that successful acquisitions create value for shareholders, although ... evidence to the contrary (see Malatesta (1983) and Roll (1986)).

Jensen and Ruback (1983) report returns to targets of 20% in tender offers and ... in mergers ... the abnormal returns to bidders ... in tender offers ... the distribution of value gains between the two ... bidder is subject to more controversy. Some U.S. studies show essentially no gains going to the targets (Dodd (1980), Mandelker (1974), Asquith (1983), Langetieg (1978)) in contrast, find ... gains split evenly between merging parides, and others (Asquith, Bruner and Mullins (1983), Dodd and Ruback (1977)) show ... bidding-firm shareholders earning positive and statistically significant gains from successful takeovers.

See also Langetieg (1978), Firth (1980), Halpern (1973), Bradley (1980) and Kummer (1978), ... Asquith, Bruner and Mullins (1983), Halpern (1983) and Firth (1980), and Varaiya (1986). Bradley and Sunder (1988) argue that shareholder gains may be illusory in all respects or it may simply be a redistribution of wealth from one party to another. In studying joint gains, one relies on stock price data and in so doing faces potentially difficult problems in evaluating nonstockholder claims such as manager, bondholder, labour, and tax claims ... to various classes of securities (e.g., preferred stock, common stock, and convertibles).

Introduction

In Volume I of these essays our primary concern was with the extent, industrial direction, and motivation for acquisitions and mergers. The essays which we presented inevitably touched on the effects of acquisition and merger activity on company performance. The interest in performance in Volume I lay primarily in the extent to which it reflected the motivations of those involved or, in the context of the market for corporate control, the way in which resource reallocation affected the efficient use of the merged assets, or was affected by various institutional and bidding characteristics. In this volume we focus on the performance effects of merger as an end in itself. The essays do, of course, contain references to the literature on the market for corporate control and to the industrial direction of merger. Our emphasis in presenting them here is, however, primarily to assess private performance impacts. The essays measure performance in terms of accounting profitability and shareholder wealth creation, and our selection is motivated by a concern to illustrate the nature and extent of the private gains to shareholders arising from merger and acquisition. Within that remit we have also chosen essays which analyse the distribution of these gains between the shareholders of the bidding company and those of the company acquired, as well as analyses of the determinants of that distribution.

Volume III has a wider focus which goes beyond shareholder welfare. It includes essays on the internal management and human resource aspects of acquisitions and mergers, as well as their labour productivity and public policy implications.

The Impact of Takeovers on Company Performance

Share Price Studies

The vast majority of studies examining the consequences of takeover activity have been based on the analysis of movements in the share prices of the bidder and target. Such studies compare the share returns of the participants surrounding the bid with some counterfactual proposal of what these returns might have been in the absence of the takeover, or takeover bid. The difference between the actual and counterfactual returns over any time interval is then termed an 'abnormal' return attributable to the 'information' imparted by the bid. These 'abnormal' returns can be accumulated over several time intervals (for example, months) to give 'cumulative abnormal returns' or CARs. Positive CARs show that the market places a positive evaluation on the likely merger outcome, and the reverse is true for negative CARs. The models used for the counterfactual are usually based on the CAPM model of which the most common form is the market model. In this model the firm's share return is taken to be linearly related to the market return and the parameters of the model are evaluated empirically for a supposedly merger-clean period, usually taken some time before the takeover bid announcement. There are other variants of this approach, notably one closer to the CAPM itself in which the intercept is taken from a measure of the risk-free interest rate, and another – the index model – in which the firm's share return is assumed to track the return for the market portfolio.

An essential feature of these approaches is that they make strong assumptions about the nature of stock market pricing (see, for example, Hughes, 1993). In particular, the demand curve for stocks is assumed to be perfectly elastic. The marginal price reflects average opinion, and any individual can buy and sell any amount of stock without affecting the price. If sharp 'abnormal' movements in price occur in association with an event, such as a takeover, they reflect the new average market sentiment produced by that event. The distribution of these gains between target and bidder shareholders is then determined by institutional factors governing, for instance, the competitiveness of the bid market, and the protection of different classes of shareholder, or the tactics which can be employed in the bid process by the various parties involved. An alternative view of market pricing is, however, possible. If there are divergences of expectations and opinion in the stock market, and market demand curves slope downwards and to the right, then some stockholders will be intramarginal and will require a premium to be bought out (Hughes, Mueller and Singh, 1980; Mayshar, 1983; Black, 1986; Miller, 1977). This premium will not necessarily, therefore, reflect any new average sentiment based on new information about the efficiency impact of the merger. The CARs will still represent private gains, but in this case will reflect the fact that for *some* reason bidders felt willing to pay the price necessary to buy out all the intramarginal shareholders. Volume I, for instance, included Gort's model of takeovers which exploited similar reasoning to explain takeovers as a result of the differing stability of expectations between classes of stockholders in the face of exogenous informational shocks. Further reasons for valuation differences and the size of bid premia and CARs are explored in a number of the essays which follow. For instance, the use of cash as a means of payment may be hypothesized to raise bid premia because they are made as part of a pre-emptive high valuation signal to ward off competing bids (see Fishman, Volume I, Chapter 30). Equally, bid premia may reflect the ability of managers of mature corporations with free cash flow to pursue their own interests at the expense of shareholder value (Mueller, Jensen, Chapters 12 and 20, Volume I). Whilst these and related issues should cause concern when seeking to interpret 'event study' merger outcomes in terms of social efficiency, they do not carry the same implication when seeking to gauge private gains and losses to shareholders.

Conn (Chapter 5) provides a further critique of the event study methodology on its own terms. The main concern that he raises is the instability of the betas (the estimated coefficient on the companies' stocks in the relevant share price model being used) of the bidder and target firms during takeover. This instability may be either due to a change in the systematic risk of the merging firms themselves or to the general changes in economic activity. If the takeover leads to a rise in the bidder's beta due to changing operating and financial risk then the abnormal gain calculated by the usual event study methodology will tend to be overstated. Some evidence for this sort of effect is found in Mandelker (1974). Furthermore, the association of increases in merger activity with rising stock markets and economic activity would also impart a bias if economic booms bring with them rising betas. Conn does not provide conclusive evidence but suggests that the gains (losses) found for bidder shareholders may have been over- or understated. He suggests that the period chosen for estimating the CAPM-based model should fall within the new equilibrium period after the acquisition.

Jensen (Chapter 3) provides both a succinct summary of his earlier joint review of studies of the share price effects of takeovers (Jensen and Ruback, 1983) and evidence for his free cash flow theory. Takeovers are the mechanism through which the market for corporate control operates, with management teams competing for the control of resources. Jensen sees the market for corporate control as a key agent of structural change and a mechanism for the external control of management. He argues that the evidence supports this benign view of takeovers which bring substantial net gains to the participants. Target firm shareholders gain substantially whilst the returns to bidding firms are smaller, but positive, for tender offers, and neutral for other acquisitions. The difference between tender offers and other forms of offer may be due to the former being predominantly cash offers and therefore representing managers' use of free cash flow without the agency control required by the issue of stock which is more characteristic of other acquisition forms.

Whilst not underestimating the importance of the variety of factors driving takeover activity (such as deregulation, synergies, economies of scale and scope, taxes, managerial incompetence and globalization), Jensen stresses the importance of the conflict between shareholders and management over the payout of free cash flow. Free cash flow is defined somewhat elusively as the excess of cash flow over that required for projects which have a positive net present value. The proposed solution to this problem is the exchange of equity into debt because the increased leverage commits management to meeting future interest and principal payments. Takeovers can represent not only a means by which management, unfettered by debt, may misuse free cash flow, but also a mechanism by which such abuse can be controlled. Thus firms with high free cash flows and low debt, operating in stagnant or declining industries, may engage in diversification acquisition with low returns for their shareholders. On the other hand, the growth of highly leveraged, hostile takeovers of large companies can be seen as a response to this sort of problem. Indeed, Jensen sees such takeovers as the main corrective force, since board-level control mechanisms are often inadequate. In view of this, he then argues for the avoidance of legislation or poison pill defences which hamper the efficiency of the market for corporate control.

This view is explored further in Baker and Wruck's case study analysis of the response of O.M. Scott & Sons to its leveraged buyout (Chapter 20). The agency benefits of high leverage and management ownership identified by Jensen are observed in this case; but it also shows the importance of the processes by which these benefits are realized. Baker and Wruck highlight the importance of incentive structures and external monitoring in providing the environment for internal organizational changes. They also show how debt covenants were used to avoid management becoming tempted to achieve short-term cash generation at the expense of long-term value.

The 1980s merger boom in the USA also provides the focus for the review by Jarrell, Brickley and Netter (Chapter 4). They find premiums of about 30 per cent being paid to target shareholders and also that target share prices rise even before the formal announcement of an offer, partly due to the pre-bid tactic of accumulating toehold stakes. This suggests that, where abnormal returns are measured from the announcement date, they may underestimate the total premium. They will thus overstate the benefits to bidders of acquiring toehold stakes in order to lower the premium. They draw on Jarrell and Poulsen (1987) to show that the abnormal returns to bidders around the bid changed from significantly positive in the 1960s to insignificantly negative in the 1980s. They examine a number of possible sources of takeover gains, reject the view that they derive from undervalued targets and conclude that they come from 'the beneficial reshuffling of productive assets'. They attribute the shift in the division of the gains in favour of the target shareholders as due, in part at least, to the increase in takeover defences which they document. However, along with Jensen, Jarrell *et al.* are generally critical about the increased use of such defences because they inhibit the efficiency of the market for corporate control.

The consensus view about the outcomes for the USA is generally that they are privately beneficial (see, for example, Jensen and Ruback, 1983). Target shareholders gain significantly and the shareholders of the bidding firms either gain modestly or are unaffected. In contrast, Firth's studies of UK takeovers (Firth, 1979, 1980) concluded that the losses to bidder shareholders outweighted the gains to target shareholders so that, in aggregate, there were shareholder private losses. In Chapter 2 Franks and Harris address this conflict of results by drawing on a large sample of UK takeovers in the period 1955–85 which includes over 1000 acquirers and over 1800 acquired firms. Using the index model, in which the abnormal return to a share in any month is the simple difference from the market return, Franks and Harris find large positive gains to target shareholders in the six months around the acquisition. The gains estimated for their whole period are smaller, but still significantly positive, when calculated by reference to the market model with parameters estimated over the five-year period beginning six years prior to the acquisition. But, in contrast to Firth's results, they also find small, but significantly positive, gains for bidder shareholders on average. This remains true when they estimate results for the same period as did Firth and using the same, market, model. Their sample is, however, smaller than Firth's for this period because it is restricted to larger companies with share price data on the London Business School Price Database.

Franks and Harris also examined a number of other issues which have been addressed by US studies. They found that tender offers were more likely to bring larger gains, particularly for target shareholders, than other acquisition methods. Contested bids brought higher returns to target shareholders and lower returns to those of bidding firms, but the reverse was true for bids in which the bidder held a significant pre-bid stake in the target firm. These findings supported those of earlier studies for the USA. Franks and Harris also report on the share returns of bidding firms during the two years after the acquisition, but obtain mixed findings. Using the market model there is a significant deterioration in shareholder returns during this period, but the index model and the CAPM model suggest that the acquirers continue to outperform the market.

Further evidence for the UK is provided by Limmack (Chapter 1) who studied over 500 bid announcements in the period 1977–86, of which about 85 per cent were subsequently completed. His study addresses the impact on shareholder returns for both the bidder and the target around the announcement and completion dates. When considering only the bid period – from announcement to outcome – he finds substantial gains for target shareholders and no significant abnormal returns for bidder shareholders. This lends support to Franks and Harris but differs from the findings of Firth for the earlier period, 1969–75. However, when the two-year period after the bid outcome is included in the assessment of returns, bidder shareholders suffer significant losses. In contrast to the findings of Franks and Harris, this outcome, whilst stronger when using the market model, is also found to be the case when using the index model and a model based on adjusted beta values. Limmack concludes discrepancies and the hubris of managers in following them through. Thus some value-destroying acquisitions will occur not because the management team carries them out for their own ends in the knowledge that they are inconsistent with shareholder interests, but, rather, because they believe that they are capable of making them work (despite all evidence to the contrary).

Divergences of characteristics between shareholders can also affect merger outcomes. Shareholders are not atomistic and homogeneous. The relative size of shareholders' various types of holding can be therefore be influential on the outcomes of bids. Stulz, Walkling and Song (Chapter 14) identify the holdings of three groups – target management, institutions and the bidder – as being of particular importance. Examining the bid period CARs for 104 US successful tender offers in the period 1968–86, they find that the target's gain is negatively related to bidder's pre-bid holdings and institutional ownership in the target. They suggest that the latter is due to the preferential tax position of the institutional investor. They also hypothesize that, where target management places a high value on incumbency, it is likely to use its stake to reduce the probability of success. More controversially, they argue that firms which receive multiple offers are those where the value of incumbency is high. They find higher target returns in multiple bids and that target management holdings in such bids are positively associated with the size of these returns. The size of the target management's holding is not found to have any effect in single bidder tender offers.

Yen (Chapter 15) also tackles the question of whether managerial resistance is in the interest of target shareholders. This is done by examining 30 US merger proposals in the 1970s, of which 16 were accepted and 14 were rejected. The target shareholder gains for each group is measured and, in the case of the rejected offers, the would-be average wealth gain is measured. He finds a much lower wealth gain in the rejected group and also shows that the latter group would have had higher returns than the accepted group had they accepted the offer. He concludes that managerial resistance is contrary to shareholder interests.

An alternative approach is adopted by Slusky and Caves (Chapter 17) who take as their starting point the presumption that most of the gains from takeovers accrue to the target shareholders. This leads them to argue that an analysis of the determinants of target premia will provide an understanding or the sources of takeover gains. They test this hypothesis by using a sample of 100 larger merger transactions among US non-financial companies between 1986 and 1988. They examine the relationships between target premia and measures of operating and financial synergy, agency factors, the method of payment and whether there is a rival bid. In common with other studies they conclude that the latter two measures have a strong positive impact on the size of the premium. They find no evidence to show that operating synergies boost premia, but do find some evidence for financial synergy. A large part of Slusky and Caves' model's explanatory power is provided by the agency factors. In particular, they find that bidder management shareholdings in their company reduce the premium paid in uncontested bids, but that their effect is muted and insignificant in contested bids. By contrast, target management shareholdings have an insignificant negative impact on the premium in uncontested bids, but a positive, though insignificant, impact in contested bids. The latter finding lends some support to the entrenchment findings of Stulz, Walkling and Song in Chapter 14.

A critique of the methodology used to assess both the overall gains to the shareholders of merging firms and the division of these gains between them is provided by Magenheim and

Mueller (Chapter 23). Drawing on their own sample of 78 acquisitions in the years 1976–81 and a review of other studies they demonstrate that the findings depend on the period over which the abnormal returns are measured and the benchmark against which normality is judged. They show that studies which measure abnormal returns over longer periods than simply the bid period yield much more pessimistic findings about the impact on bidder shareholders.

The most uncomfortable finding for proponents of market efficiency from the share price studies of mergers is that significant negative returns accrue to acquirers in the few years after merger. This finding is uncomfortable because the event study methodology itself is based on the view that the market is efficient in an informational sense and that it is not possible to beat it on the basis of public information. Hence the reliance on the worth of a merger being based on the share price change which the new information 'reveals'. As one leading researcher has written:

> I do not believe there is an explanation for this phenomenon that is consistent with market prices ... whatever you call it, this finding can be used to make money. I can tell when a merger is completed. I can sell short. That gains me supernormal returns. And that violates market efficiency. (Ruback, 1988)

This issue is explored in depth by Agrawal, Jaffe and Mandelker (Chapter 13) who use a sample of 937 mergers and 227 tender offers by NYSE firms over the period 1955–87. They show larger negative cumulative returns over the five years after merger completion and that the negative returns of conglomerate mergers are not so bad as those of non-conglomerate mergers. They demonstrate that these negative returns are not associated with the relative size of the merging firms, nor with their industrial location. They do find one sub-period, 1975–79, when the post-merger performance is significantly positive. It is also important to note that, whilst their sample exhibits significant negative CARs, about 45 per cent of the sample display positive CARs. These findings suggest that outcomes may be sample- and period-specific and also give some understanding of why it may not be so easy to make money as Ruback suggests.

The view that takeovers may be as much the outcome of the agency problem as a solution to it is examined by Firth in Chapter 18. For a sample of 254 UK takeover bids in the period 1974–80, he examined the consequences for both bidder shareholders and bidder management. More than two-thirds of the sample suffered negative abnormal returns in the bid period. However, even in this sample, the bidder company's CEO increased his remuneration, albeit somewhat less than the increase in those companies with positive abnormal returns. When the overall wealth impact on the CEO is assessed by combining the stockholding changes with six years' remuneration increase (discounted at 4 per cent), the CEOs of unsuccessful acquirers were substantially better off, on average. Firth concludes that this supports the managerial motive for mergers hypothesis.

An alternative view of the acquisition process is provided by the company failure literature in which acquisition is seen as an alternative to bankruptcy. Pastená and Ruland (Chapter 19) show that here, too, agency factors influence outcomes. They argue that, in addressing the acquisition/failure choice, creditors and shareholders will favour acquisition but management with low ownership stakes may favour bankruptcy since this option enhances their prospects of continued control of the company. They find that distressed firms with high ownership concentration show a higher tendency to merge rather than enter bankruptcy than do firms where managerial interests dominate.

Eckbo and Langohr (Chapter 21) provide a study of French acquisitions surrounding the introduction of new information disclosure provisions in 1970. They also analyse the impact of the medium of exchange on the share returns of the merging companies, showing that, following the new disclosure provisions, the premium on cash tender offers rose sharply. They find no merger impact on bidder returns either for cash equity offers, or before or after the new disclosure provisions. Their finding that bidder returns are unchanged but target returns are increased suggests that the disclosure provisions shifted the division of the returns towards targets. Finally, in keeping with the agency and free cash flow arguments advanced earlier, they find much larger bid premia for all cash than for all stock offers.

Franks, Harris and Mayer (Chapter 22) are also concerned with the impact of the method of payment on merger share price outcomes. Their study draws upon 954 UK acquisitions and 1555 US acquisitions in the years 1955–85. They show that, over these three decades, the method of financing US acquisitions changed from being dominated first by equity, then by convertibles, and then finally by all cash offers. The latter represented just under 80 per cent of all offers during 1980–84. Financing of acquisitions in the UK was more balanced between cash and equity throughout this time, with an increased use of mixed finance in the later period.

Franks *et al.* find that target shareholders receive larger wealth gains in cash takeovers than in those involving all equity. This is also true for bidder shareholders, but the gains over the six-month bid period are small and generally insignificant. For the US sample they provide some further analysis by partitioning their data between mergers and tender offers and by whether contested or not. The results suggest that both the medium of exchange and the form of offer influence premiums and that a significant proportion of the difference in premium between tender and merger offers is attributable to the predominant use of cash in the former. They also show that the impact of a contested bid is significant only for tender offers, independent of how they are financed. Finally, Franks, Harris and Mayer find evidence for negative post-merger returns for the acquiring companies. The returns are lower for equity offers than cash offers, but are sensitive to the choice of model used for the calculations.

This volume concentrates on the consequences of mergers and acquisitions for managers and shareholders. In Volume III we explore wider shareholder issues and the policy stance of the state to the takeover process.

References

Black, F. (1986), 'Noise', *Journal of Finance*, **41**, 529–43.
Firth, M. (1979), 'The Profitability of Takeovers and Mergers', *Economic Journal*, **89**, 316–28.
Firth, M. (1980), 'Takeover, Shareholder Returns, and the Theory of the Firm', *Quarterly Journal of Economics*, **94**, 235–60.
Hughes, A., Mueller, D. C. and Singh, A. (1980), 'Hypotheses about Mergers' in D. C. Mueller (ed.), *The Determinants and Effect of Mergers*, Cambridge, Mass.: Oelgeschlager, Gunn and Hain.

Jarrell, G. and Poulson, A. B. (1987), 'The Return to Acquiring Firms: Evidence from Three Decades', University of Rochester Working Paper.

Jensen, M. C. and Ruback, R. S. (1983), 'The Market for Corporate Control: The Scientific Evidence', *Journal of Economics*, **11**, 5–50.

Mandelker, G. (1974), 'Risk and Return: The Case of Merging Firms', *Journal of Financial Economics*, **1**, 303–35.

Mayshar, J. (1983), 'On Divergence of Opinion and Imperfections in the Capital Market', *American Economic Review*, **73**, 114–28.

Meeks, G. (1977), *Disappointing Marriage: A Study of the Gains from Merger*, Cambridge: Cambridge University Press.

Miller, E. (1977), 'Risk, Uncertainty and Divergence of Opinion', *Journal of Finance*, **32**, 1151–68.

Mueller, D. C. (ed.) (1980), *The Determinants and Effects of Mergers: An International Comparisons Study*, Cambridge Mass.: Oelgeschlager Gunn and Hain.

Ruback, R., (1988), 'Do Target Shareholders Lose in Unsuccessful Control Contests?' in A. Auerbach (ed.), *Corporate Takeovers: Causes and Consequences*, Chicago: University of Chicago Press for NBER.

Part IV
The Impact of Takeovers on Company Performance

Share Price Studies

[1]

Accounting and Business Research, Vol. 21, No. 83, pp. 239–251, 1991

Corporate Mergers and Shareholder Wealth Effects: 1977–1986

R. J. Limmack*

Abstract—The paper investigates the distribution of returns to shareholders of UK companies involved in acquisitions during the period 1977–1986. Three control models were used in the analysis: the market model with parameters identified through OLS regression, a model based on adjusted betas, and finally an index-relative model. Abnormal returns were identified around both bid announcement and outcome dates for bidders and targets in completed and abandoned bids. Examination was also made of the distribution of wealth changes for bidders and targets separately and for both in combination. The results demonstrate that, although there is no net wealth decrease to shareholders in total as a result of takeover activity, shareholders of bidder firms do suffer wealth decreases. By contrast, shareholders in target firms obtained significant, positive wealth increases in both completed and abandoned bids.

Introduction

Neo-classical economic theory assumes that corporate management acts to maximise the wealth of shareholders. Takeovers are seen as devices by which inefficient management teams may be replaced (Manne, 1965) and which facilitate the redeployment of capital to more efficient, i.e. 'profitable' users (Williamson, 1970; Weston, 1970). It follows, therefore, that if management pursues policies of shareholder wealth maximisation then shareholders should not suffer wealth decreases as a result of their company acquiring other companies. Additionally, in a competitive acquisitions market, competition amongst potential acquirers will raise the price to be paid for the target until the acquiring firm obtains no excess rate of return (Mandelker, 1974). In such a market the acquisition of one company by another may, therefore, be viewed as a zero net present value investment decision.

Studies which have addressed the question of the efficiency of the takeover mechanism as a device for controlling the actions of management have tended to fall into two groups. Early studies focused on the profitability and other financial characteristics of the companies involved and drew inferences about their relative efficiency (for

example Singh, 1971; Meeks, 1977). Accounting-based studies have been criticised on a number of grounds, including the downward bias introduced to post-merger measures of profitability (Appleyard, 1981) and the lack of adjustment for any consequent change in the risk profile of the acquiring firm (Weston *et al.*, 1988, p. 793). The second group of studies have evaluated the impact of acquisition activity on the wealth of the shareholder groups involved by examining security returns around and within the period in which the acquisition occurs.

While there is a wealth of evidence from US studies to support the contention that acquisitions are value-creating activities for shareholders (see Jensen and Ruback, 1983; and Jarrel *et al.*, 1988 for a review of the evidence), evidence on acquisition activity in the UK is less plentiful and the conclusions are ambiguous. The primary aim of the current paper is to provide further evidence on the impact of acquisition activity on the wealth of shareholders by an analysis of those takeover bids involving UK quoted companies which were initiated during the period 1 January 1977 to 31 December 1986. The study examines security returns and wealth changes to shareholders both for those bids which were completed ('successful' bids) and for those bids which were abandoned ('unsuccessful' bids). Evidence is provided on the efficiency of the market for corporate control in the UK. Whereas previous studies of UK acquisition activity have focused on the bid announcement date, the current study provides an analysis of returns around both bid and outcome announcement dates. It is suggested that the latter practice captures more completely the wealth changes arising from acquisition activity (Asquith, 1983).

*The author is lecturer in accountancy at the University of Stirling. Financial support for the research programme, for which the current paper provides a preliminary report, was provided by the Economic and Social Research Council (Ref. No. F00232424) and the Centre for Investment Management, University of Stirling. Assistance in data collection was provided by Beverley Allan, Jill Reid, and Elizabeth Roberts. The author acknowledges helpful comments provided by Professor Charles Ward and by two anonymous referees. The current paper is a revised version of an earlier paper presented at the Ninth International Finance Conference, Paris 1989.

Previous studies

In a study of UK mergers in the brewing and distilling industry over the period 1955–72, Franks, Broyles and Hecht (1977) found net gains to shareholders in the companies involved, although most of the gains appeared to accrue to the shareholders of target companies. Their conclusions suggest no significant loss to shareholders of acquiring companies. By contrast, studies by Firth (1979, 1980) of mergers involving a larger sample of UK quoted companies over the period 1969–75 found that gains obtained by shareholders of target companies were more than offset by losses to shareholders of acquiring firms. In the case of completed bids Firth also reported a post-merger adjusted loss to shareholders of acquiring companies. In studies involving relatively small samples of companies, Barnes (1984) and Dodds and Quek (1985) found negative adjusted returns for acquiring companies following the announcement of the bid. By contrast to the above, in a recent comprehensive study of UK mergers undertaken over the period 1955–85, Franks and Harris (1989) report positive adjusted returns to shareholders of both acquiring and acquired firms over a six month period commencing four months before the bid announcement, but also provide evidence of subsequent post-merger losses to shareholders of bidding firms. In summary, previous studies of UK merger activity disagree as to whether the returns to shareholders of bidding firms are zero or negative and whether there is an overall wealth increase or decrease arising from acquisition activity.

The next two sections describe the data and methodology used in the current study before presenting the results. Reported results include the return to shareholders of target and bidder companies in both completed and abandoned bids. In addition, the wealth gain (or loss) to each group of shareholders is calculated, together with the combined net effect on shareholder wealth for a sub-sample of completed bids.

Data

The data examined in the current study were drawn from the set of all bids announced within the period 1 January 1977 to 31 December 1986 involving companies quoted on the International Stock Exchange, London (ISE). Data requirements placed the following additional constraints on the companies to be examined:

(i) the bid outcome was announced by 31 December 1986;
(ii) the company had to be listed on the London Share Price Database (LSPD) throughout the periods prior to and during the bid;

(iii) daily share price data was available, either from Datastream or newspaper sources, for the period surrounding the bid and outcome announcement days.

Examination was made of the relevant pages in the *Financial Times*[1] over the whole period 1 January 1977 to 31 December 1986 to identify the date of formal announcement of each bid. The progress of the bid was then monitored in order to identify the outcome, i.e. whether completed or abandoned, and the date on which the outcome was announced. Bids in which the offer price was subsequently raised have been treated as one single bid.

Table 1 provides details of the impact of the above constraints on sample size and characteristics. In general, lack of data led to the elimination of smaller companies. In addition the use of the adjusted beta control model was restricted to those bids which were initiated from January 1979 onwards, as the Risk Measurement Service was not available before that date. Results reported throughout the paper are for those companies for which data was available for the period from six months prior to the bid month through to the end of the outcome month. However analysis was also undertaken on the full data set available for each sub-period without revealing any significant difference from the published results. In order to include a company in that part of the analysis involving the market model, an additional constraint was placed, namely that observations were to be available for at least 40 months of the pre-bid estimation period. In order to minimise 'survivor' bias no constraint was placed on the number of months for which bidder companies' returns were available following the outcome of the bid. The result of this latter condition was that returns for bids with outcome dates after 31 December 1985[2] were not recorded for the full 24 month post-outcome period. Throughout the remainder of the paper results are reported only for the application of the adjusted beta control model unless significantly different results were obtained using either of the other models.

The full data set was sub-divided into two groups, according to whether the bid was completed or abandoned. A bid was identified as abandoned if no further bid was made by the original bidder within six months following the abandonment date. The equity market value for each bidding and target company in the sample was identified as at the beginning of the month six months prior to the month of formal announcement of the bid.

[1]Alternative newspaper sources were consulted when the *Financial Times* was unavailable for any period.
[2]Monthly data was available only to 31 December 1987.

Table 1
Impact of data constraints on sample sets used with adjusted betas control model

	Bidders		Targets	
	N	Average Size (£M)	N	Average Size (£M)
Bids identified	1284	—	1284	—
Post-1986 outcome	23		23	
	1261		1261	
No data	460		177	
	801	234	1084	43
No RMS betas	235		282	
Pre-bid data	566	270	802	49
No daily data	29		207	
Bid-outcome data	537	271	595	56
Partial data sets	8		43	
Final data sets	529	275	552	59

Composition of Final Data Sets

	N	Average Size (£M)	N	Average Size (£M)
Completed bids	448	273	462	49
Abandoned bids	81	286	90	106

Following Asquith (1983) the study is concerned with security returns around two event dates; the 'announcement date' and the 'outcome date'. The announcement date is here identified as the day identified in the *Financial Times*. Similarly the outcome date is the first day on which the bid was described in the *Financial Times* as unconditional in the case of completed bids, or as lapsed or withdrawn in the case of abandoned bids.

The analysis of security price changes around the two event dates provides evidence of stock market reaction to partially anticipated events (see Malatesta *et al.*, 1985). The bid outcome, the partially anticipated event, is known with certainty in relatively few bids at the bid announcement date. The disclosure of new information concerning the bid will relate both to the likely stream of benefits to shareholder groups and the probability of these being obtained, i.e. the likelihood of the bid succeeding. As the likelihood of the bid succeeding changes, an efficient securities market will adjust share prices accordingly. Examination of security price changes between the two event dates reflects the market's perception of the result of the bid.

Methodology

In order to assess the impact of mergers on security prices, abnormal returns have been identified using three control methods. The first control model, the Market Model developed by Fama, Fisher, Jensen and Roll (1969), was applied in the form:

$$\log_e(1 + R_{j,t}) = \alpha_j + \beta_j \log_e(1 + R_{m,t}) + U_{j,t} \quad (1)$$

where

$R_{j,t}$ = return on security$_j$ period$_t$
$R_{m,t}$ = return on the market for period$_t$
α_j, β_j are parameters for security$_j$
and $U_{j,t}$ is the residual error term

In order to estimate the parameters for each security, monthly share price returns data were collected for the period month -67 through to month -7, where month 0 represents the month of announcement of the bid. The period from month -6 to month -1 was excluded because prior UK studies had commented that the pattern of residuals for bidding companies suggests that 'the market is beginning to anticipate mergers on average at least 3 months prior to the announcement date' (Franks *et al.*, 1977). Inclusion of this period would therefore have been a source of potential bias in parameter estimation. Contemporaneous returns on the FT All Share Index were collected in order to provide a proxy for the returns on the market.

One possible criticism of the use of the pre-bid period for identification of the market model parameters is that the characteristics of bidders' security returns may change as a result of the bid. Post-outcome returns would reflect these changes and bias the results. Another serious problem arises, however, as a consequence of the fact that many securities quoted on the ISE are traded infrequently. This 'thinness of trade' means that data provided in the LSPD tapes do not all represent end-of-month transactions. One consequence of infrequent trading is that the alphas and betas calculated on the basis of the above OLS regressions may be mis-specified.

Available evidence for the UK suggests that the share prices of many quoted companies exhibit the characteristics of infrequently traded securities. In particular, OLS estimates of the market model parameters for thinly-traded securities are likely to produce an overstatement of alpha values and a corresponding understatement of beta values (see Dimson, 1979). Results of the regressions undertaken to identify market model coefficients suggest that these characteristics are also present in the merger data set. The mean alpha values for all bidder companies in the sample was found to be 0.006, while the mean beta value was 0.86. For all target companies the mean alpha value was found to be 0.002 while the mean beta was 0.71. Because of this problem, the validity of results obtained using OLS estimates of market model parameters must be questioned. The current study incorporates results obtained using this control model, however, in order to provide a basis for comparison with previous studies and the other control models adopted.

A number of procedures have been devised for correcting the thin-trading bias (Scholes and Williams, 1977; Dimson, 1979; Cohen *et al.*, 1983). Application of these procedures in studies involving daily data (see Brown and Warner, 1985; and Dyckman, Philbrick and Stephan, 1984) suggests that while the procedures reduce the bias in OLS estimates of beta they lead to no improvement in the power of event study tests.

In order to test for possible bias in the results, the analysis was repeated using the adjusted betas supplied by the London Business School Risk Measurement Service (RMS). RMS betas are estimated on the basis of regressing trade-to-trade security returns on the market returns observed over identical periods of time. The betas so calculated are then Bayesian-adjusted following Vasicek (1973). (The method is described more fully in Dimson and Marsh, 1979; and Marsh, 1980.) The RMS provide a readily available source of adjusted betas which have been found to be superior to those obtained using other methods (see Dimson, 1979). Accordingly, beta values were obtained from the Risk Measurement Service for a date approximately six months prior to the bid

announcement month.[3] Alpha values to correspond with the relevant RMS betas were estimated as follows:

Let Rj be the mean return of firm j over the market model estimation period, and Rm be the mean market return over the same period. Then

$$\hat{\alpha}_{j,RMS} = \bar{R}_j - \hat{\beta}_{j,RMS}\,\bar{R}_m \qquad (2)$$

where

$$\beta_{j,RMS} = \text{the RMS } \beta$$

and

$$\alpha_{j,RMS} = \text{the estimated } \alpha \text{ value}$$

The relevant RMS alphas and betas averaged 0.005 and 0.96 respectively for bidder companies and -0.002 and 0.90 for target companies.

Abnormal returns were then calculated for all relevant periods using the RMS beta values and estimated alpha values.[4] As the RMS did not commence until 1979, this necessarily involved a reduction in sample size.

For the third control model, residuals were calculated using an Index Model, that is by assuming an alpha of zero and beta of one for all securities, i.e.

$$\log_e(1 + R_{j,t}) = \log_e(1 + R_{m,t}) + U_{j,t} \qquad (3)$$

In order to provide continuity of results and comparability with previous studies of UK data the results are reported in four stages:

(a) pre-announcement,
(b) announcement to outcome,
(c) post-outcome,
(d) overall.

Abnormal returns are reported only for those companies for which a complete set of data was available from month -6 through to the outcome month. An analysis of abnormal returns for data sets available for sub-periods confirmed that, while the above constraint reduced the reported number of observations, it had no significant impact on the results obtained. Analysis was extended for all bidders and for targets in abandoned bids for a period of up to 24 months following the outcome announcement month. The periods for which analysis was undertaken are illustrated in Figures 1 and 2.

---

[3]As the Risk Measurement Service is provided quarterly the beta values were collected over a period from 7.5 to 4.5 months prior to the bid announcement.

[4]Returns obtained using the Adjusted Betas control model were revised to incorporate the estimated alpha values following a suggestion made by one of the referees, The returns subsequently obtained, however, were not significantly different from those reported in earlier drafts of the paper which had assumed an alpha value of zero for all securities.

have identified an Abnormal Performance Index (API) where:

$$\text{API}_t = \frac{1}{N} \sum_{j=1}^{j=N} \prod_{t=1}^{t=6} (1 + \overline{A_{j,t}}) \qquad (9)$$

While the CAR measure represents the abnormal return on a portfolio which is rebalanced every period to give equal weighting to each security, the API identifies the abnormal return from investing an equal amount in each security at the beginning of the period but without subsequent rebalancing.

Value Weighted Returns (VWR) were calculated to represent the return which would be obtained by an investor in a value-weighted portfolio of companies. Weights were identified by reference to the total equity market value of each company six months prior to the bid, that is:

$$\text{VWR}_j = \text{MV}_{j,t} \left[\left(\prod_{t=-6}^{t=-1} (1 + A_{j,t}) \right) - 1 \right] \qquad (10)$$

and

$$\overline{\text{VWR}} = \sum_{j=1}^{j=N} \frac{\text{VWR}_j}{\text{MV}_{t-6}} \qquad (11)$$

where $\overline{\text{MV}_{t-6}}$ is the mean size at $t-6$.

The statistical significance of the results is assessed after calculating standard errors of the mean.

The results for bidding and target companies in completed and abandoned bids are tabulated in Table 2. Reported results include standard errors, together with the proportion of observations that were positive.

Figure 1
Sub-periods included in the analysis

Estimation Period	Month −67[a] to Month −7[a]
Pre-Bid Period	Month −6[a] to Month −1[a]
Bid Period (see Figure 2)	Bid month to Outcome Month
Post-Outcome Period	Month +1[b] to Month +24[b]

[a] Relative to bid month
[b] Relative to outcome month

(a) Pre-announcement

Using each of the models identified in equations (4) to (6) below, monthly abnormal returns $(AR_{j,t})$ were first identified for each company over the period −6 through −1 where month 0 corresponds to the bid announcement month.

Model 1: OLS Market Model

$$A_{j,t} = \log_e(1 + R_{j,t})$$
$$- [\alpha_{j,\text{OLS}} + \beta_{j,\text{OLS}} \log_e(1 + R_{m,t})] \qquad (4)$$

Model 2: Adjusted Beta Model

$$AR_{j,t} = \log_e(1 + R_{j,t})$$
$$- [\alpha_{j,\text{RMS}} + \beta_{j,\text{RMS}} \log_e(1 + R_{m,t})] \qquad (5)$$

Model 3: Index Model

$$A_{j,t} = \log_e(1 + R_{j,t}) - \log_e(1 + R_{m,t}) \qquad (6)$$

The abnormal returns (residual effect) for each security are averaged over each month prior to the announcement month:

$$\overline{AR}_t = \frac{1}{N} \sum_{j=1}^{N} AR_{j,t} \qquad (7)$$

where N is the number of securities in month t.

The average abnormal returns (residuals) are then cumulated to identify the Cumulative Abnormal Return (CAR) over the reported period:

$$\text{CAR}_t = \sum_{t=1}^{t=N} \overline{AR}_t \qquad (8)$$

As an alternative to the calculation of Cumulative Abnormal Returns (CAR), a number of studies

(b) Announcement to outcome

Abnormal returns were calculated for bidding and target companies over each of the following periods separately:

(i) From the end of month prior to bid announcement up to and including the announcement date (pre-bid period).

(ii) The day following bid announcement to the day preceding the outcome announcement (post-bid period).

(iii) The outcome announcement day to the end of month in which the outcome was announced (post-outcome period).

(iv) From the end of month prior to the bid announcement date to the end of the month in which the outcome was announced (bid period).

Inclusion of the identified announcement day in period (i) above, and outcome date in period (iii), ensures that period (ii) encompasses the period of 'uncertainty' concerning the bid outcome. The above periods are illustrated by means of the diagram in Figure 2.

Table 2
Abnormal returns for the period prior to the bid announcement month for bids undertaken during the years 1977–1986. Results reported using adjusted betas

	Bidders		Targets	
	(i)	(ii)	(iii)	(iv)
	Completed	*Abandoned*	*Completed*	*Abandoned*
Month	*Bids*	*Bids*	*Bids*	*Bids*
	%	%	%	%
−6	1.27**	2.11*	0.41	−1.31
	(0.48, 53)	(1.04, 59)	(0.47, 58)	(1.06, 48)
−5	1.37**	1.61	0.78	0.12
	(0.52, 52)	(1.30, 53)	(0.50, 59)	(1.17, 49)
−4	0.32	1.69	−0.28	0.23
	(0.51, 49)	(1.25, 51)	(0.48, 54)	(1.22, 57)
−3	0.66	1.55	0.41	1.39
	(0.49, 47)	(1.35, 52)	(0.47, 53)	(1.26, 63)
−2	2.70***	2.14**	1.71***	0.58
	(0.64, 57)	(1.00, 57)	(0.55, 64)	(1.11, 58)
−1	0.22	−0.59	3.64***	5.40***
	(0.48, 48)	(1.27, 51)	(0.66, 68)	(1.83, 66)
Cumulative Months				
−6 *to* −1				
CAR (%)	6.53***	8.51***	6.67***	6.41**
	(1.23, 58)	(2.59, 65)	(1.48, 60)	(3.03, 63)
API	1.06***	1.08***	1.08***	1.06**
	(0.01, 55)	(0.03, 56)	(0.02, 58)	(0.03, 61)
Value				
Weighted (%)	−0.18	10.40**	15.31**	5.20
	(2.35, 55)	(4.06, 56)	(7.50, 58)	(5.73, 59)
Size				
(£ Millions)	273	286	49	106
Observations	448	81	462	90

Note: Figures in parentheses represent standard errors followed by percentage positive.
  *Indicates significant at 10% level.
 **Indicates significant at 5% level.
***Indicates significant at 1% level.

(c) *Post-outcome*

Monthly abnormal returns were calculated for bidding companies for the 24 month period follow-ing the outcome month, month 0, (or until data were no longer available if earlier). As monthly data were available only to 31 December 1987, the results reported in this section do not include full data for bids announced in 1986. Summarised results are reported in Table 4 for bidders in both completed and abandoned bids. Post-outcome abnormal returns for targets in aban-doned bids are also reported in Table 4.

(d) *Overall*

One of the problems in calculating the overall returns to companies involved in takeover bids is to identify the period over which share prices are affected by the bid. In their recent study Franks and Harris (1989) identify returns initially over a period of six months beginning four months prior to the month in which they first identify a

Figure 2
Time diagram identifying the relevant sub-periods within the bid-outcome period

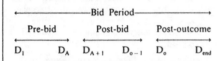

D_1 = beginning of announcement month
D_A = bid announcement day
D_o = outcome announcement day
D_{end} = end of outcome month

Table 3
Abnormal returns for the period from the beginning of the bid month to the end of the outcome announcement month for bids undertaken during the years 1977–1986. Results reported using adjusted betas

	Bidders		Targets	
	(i)	*(ii)*	*(iii)*	*(iv)*
	Completed	*Abandoned*	*Completed*	*Abandoned*
Month	*Bids*	*Bids*	*Bids*	*Bids*
	%	%	%	%
Pre-bid[1]	0.08	−0.55	24.29***	23.87***
	(0.49, 57)	(1.06, 41)	(1.26, 87)	(3.26, 83)
Post-bid	−0.00	−3.99**	6.16***	−3.29
	(0.72, 45)	(1.58, 39)	(0.92, 57)	(2.16, 33)
Post-outcome[2]	0.15	−1.28*	−0.14	−0.30
	(0.45, 41)	(0.69, 31)	(0.27, 41)	(9.60, 39)
Bid period	−0.20	−6.02***	31.38***	19.87***
	(0.93, 46)	(1.81, 28)	(1.64, 85)	(4.26, 70)
Value-weighted overall	−2.55*	−5.40*	32.98***	10.06
	(1.33, 46)	(3.15, 24)	(4.94, 85)	(6.44, 69)

Note: Figures in parentheses represent standard errors followed by percentage positive.
[1]Includes announcement day.
[2]Includes outcome day.
*Indicates significant at 10% level.
**Indicates significant at 5% level.
***Indicates significant at 1% level.

bid.[5] It is not clear, however, that returns to bidder companies prior to the formal bid anticipate the bid announcement rather than reflecting other information concerning the bidder. Overall returns to bidder companies are, therefore, reported using as a base month the date of the formal announcement of the bid. For target companies the behaviour of pre-bid returns may be more readily identified as reflecting investors' expectations of the likelihood of a bid. Returns to shareholders of target companies were therefore measured over the period beginning three months prior to formal announcement of the bid. Additional tests were also conducted for targets using a base date six months prior to the bid month, but without significantly affecting the results. Summarised results for the overall period of analysis are reported for bidders in Table 5 and for targets in Table 6.

---

[5]Four key months are identified by Franks and Harris including the first approach date, first bid date, unconditional date, or date of removal from LSPD tapes. For around 73% of the bids, the appropriate key date was the date of the first formal merger offer, the date that coincided with that used in the current study.

Analysis of results

(a) Pre-bid

Bidder Companies. As reported in Table 2, bidder companies obtain significantly positive abnormal returns in the months immediately preceding formal announcement of the bid. As the results obtained were not sensitive to the choice of control model, reporting is restricted to the results obtained from application of the adjusted betas model, i.e. model 2 from equation (5). The returns obtained by bidders were also found to be independent of the ultimate outcome of the bid. The results are contrary to those reported by Firth (1980) who identified 'no significant abnormal security price behaviour associated with bidding firm', but they are consistent with those reported by Franks, Broyles and Hecht (1977). Value-weighted returns were significantly lower than equally weighted returns for bidders in completed bids, indicating that larger bidders on average earned a lower pre-bid abnormal return than smaller bidders.

In an analysis of the characteristics of companies involved in abandoned takeover bids over the period 1965–75, Pickering (1983) found that bids

Table 4
Abnormal returns for the 24 months following outcome announcement month for bids undertaken during the years 1977–1986. Results reported using adjusted betas

	Bidders		Targets
	(i) *Completed Bids*	*(ii)* *Abandoned Bids*	*(iii)* *Abandoned Bids*
	%	%	%
CAR			
Month 1–12	−1.47	−10.10***	5.16
	(1.77, 51)	(3.45, 33)	(5.51, 49)
Month 13–24	−3.00*	−10.13**	−2.48
	(1.66, 48)	(3.92, 29)	(3.81, 42)
Month 1–24	−4.47**	−20.23***	2.68
	(2.24, 49)	(5.66, 30)	(7.05, 44)
Value-weighted			
Month 1–12	2.60	−3.10	−7.24
	(13.5, 46)	(24.8, 29)	(5.24, 44)
Month 13–24	−2.40	−0.30	−12.29**
	(16.2, 39)	(25.1, 30)	(5.04, 40)
Month 1–24	0.80	−4.30	−17.00**
	(14.9, 44)	(25.2, 30)	(8.28, 38)

Note: Figures in parentheses represent standard errors followed by percentage positive.
  *Indicates significant at 10% level.
 **Indicates significant at 5% level.
***Indicates significant at 1% level.

were made by both very strong and very weak companies. In the current study, the variation of pre-announcement returns obtained by bidders in abandoned bids (Table 2) is greater than that for completed bids. However, the difference in abnormal returns obtained by the two groups of bidders was not found to be statistically significant. It was not possible to infer from this analysis that bidders in abandoned bids were 'weaker' than those in completed bids.

There are at least two possible explanations for the positive abnormal returns for bidder firms in the pre-bid period. The first is that news of the bid is leaked to the market prior to the date of formal announcement. However, this explanation is only plausible if news of the bid is, on average, perceived positively, with the expected gains from completed bids outweighing the potential loss on abandoned bids. Further support for this explanation would therefore be available if, following bid announcement, bidders in completed bids obtained positive abnormal returns while bidders in abandoned bids obtained negative abnormal returns (see Table 3 in the next section).

The second possible explanation for the pre-bid abnormal return is that companies undertake acquisitions during a period of relatively good performance. Although some support is available for

the first explanation in that merger talks are often initiated some weeks prior to the formal announcement of the bid, it is unlikely that this completely explains the consistent pattern of positive pre-announcement abnormal returns. Acceptance of the second of the above explanations, however, provides tentative support for the hypothesis that takeovers involve a reallocation of resources to the more profitables firms.

Target Companies. Target companies also achieve significantly positive abnormal returns prior to the formal announcement of the bid, as reported in Table 2, columns (iii) and (iv). In addition value-weighted returns for targets in completed bids were higher than the unweighted returns. Significantly positive abnormal returns are obtained by target companies over a period beginning two to three months prior to formal announcement of the bid. This result again conflicts with the earlier finding of Firth (1980) who reported no evidence of 'successful anticipation of, or leaking of, the bid announcement' for a period up to and including two months prior to the bid announcement. The results are, however, consistent with those obtained by Franks *et al.* (1977) who suggested that the stock market 'is beginning to anticipate mergers on average at least 3 months prior to the announcement date'.

Table 5
Overall returns for bidders in completed and abandoned bids from bid month to 12, 24 months following outcome month

	Control Model		
	Adjusted Betas	Market Model	Index Model
	%	%	%
(a) Completed bids			
(i) *CARs*			
Bid month	−1.66	−5.55***	−2.15
to month +12	(2.08, 51)	(1.87, 44)	(1.67, 49)
Bid month	−4.67*	−14.96***	−7.43***
to month +24	(2.65, 48)	(2.81, 43)	(2.19, 48)
(ii) *Value-weighted returns*			
Bid month	−4.42	−9.32**	−4.54
to month +12	(3.33, 46)	(4.04, 39)	(3.76, 44)
Bid month	−2.48	−10.31*	−2.34
to month +24	(3.84, 42)	(5.52, 35)	(4.83, 36)
(b) Abandoned bids			
(i) *CARs*			
Bid month	−16.12***	−11.68***	−5.79*
to month +12	(4.02, 33)	(4.07, 38)	(3.19, 41)
Bid month	−26.25***	−24.20***	−7.38*
to month +24	(6.00, 29)	(5.90, 35)	(4.37, 39)
(ii) *Value-weighted returns*			
Bid month	−17.40	−14.11**	−9.61**
to month +12	(22.30, 19)	(5.63, 33)	(4.28, 36)
Bid month	−19.10	−20.49**	−14.54**
to month +24	(22.40, 18)	(9.75, 28)	(6.04, 33)

Note: Figures in parentheses represent standard errors followed by percentage positive.
*Indicates significant at 10% level.
**Indicates significant at 5% level.
***Indicates significant at 1% level.

Although a comparison of the results for targets in completed and abandoned bids (Table 2 columns (iii) and (iv)) reveals no significant difference in the overall pattern of returns, the results indicate that completed bids were anticipated earlier than abandoned bids. It is possible that in completed bids the pre-merger returns reflect the acquisition of 'toe-hold' interests by bidders and that this acquisition contributes towards a sucessful takeover strategy (see also Franks and Harris, 1989).

(b) Announcement to Outcome

Table 3 reports the abnormal returns to the shareholders of both bidder and target companies over the period surrounding the announcement and outcome dates. As previously, the results obtained were insensitive to the choice of control model. Results are therefore reported only for the application of the adjusted betas control model.

Bidder Companies. As shown in column (i) of Table 3, bidders in completed bids achieve abnormal returns over the bid period of −0.20% (not significantly different from zero), when measured on an equally weighted basis. This result, if considered in isolation, provides evidence to support the hypothesis of a perfectly competitive acquisitions market with takeovers taking the characteristics of a zero net present value investment decision. Further support for the hypothesis of a perfectly competitive acquisitions market is found in the behaviour of returns to shareholders of bidding companies in abandoned bids. Over the sub-period which includes announcement of bid abandonment, shareholders of the failed bidding firms suffer a significantly negative wealth decrease of −1.28%. Indeed, in the period following announcement of the bid but prior to formal announcement of abandonment, bidding firm shareholders suffer a wealth decrease of −3.99% Not only does the market appear to view abandonment of the bid as detrimental to the interests of

Table 6
Overall returns for targets in completed and abandoned bids undertaken over the period 1977–1986. Results reported following the application of adjusted betas control model

	CAR %	Value-Weighted Return %
(a) Completed bids		
Month −3 to outcome	37.15*** (1.80, 85)	34.41*** (5.42, 84)
(b) Abandoned bids		
Month −3 to outcome	27.23*** (5.15, 62)	18.79** (7.79, 68)
Month −3 to month +12	32.39*** (8.30, 68)	10.58* (5.44. 61)
Month −3 to month +24	29.91*** (9.81, 63)	−0.43 (7.26, 57)

Note: Figures in parentheses represent standard errors followed by percentage positive.
 *Indicates significant at 10% level.
 **Indicates significant at 5% level.
 ***Indicates significant at 1% level.

the shareholders of the bidding firm, but the outcome of the bid is also anticipated before final announcement.

In part (a) of this section, one possible explanation of positive pre-bid abnormal performance to bidders was identified as information leaked to the market prior to formal bid announcement. In the pre-bid period, however, the ultimate bid outcome cannot be known with certainty. Therefore for this hypothesis to be valid any pre-bid returns would be weighted by the probability of the bid proving to be successful. Following bid outcome, returns to successful bidders would be expected to rise further, while returns to unsuccessful bidders would fall. While the results reported in Table 3 show that bidders in abandoned bids obtain significantly negative abnormal returns following bid announcement, the absence of positive abnormal returns to bidders in completed bids leads to rejection of the 'information leakage' hypothesis to explain positive pre-bid performance.

When computed on a value-weighted basis, returns to shareholders of bidding firms were found to be significantly negative (at the 10% level), for both completed and abandoned bids. Larger companies in completed bids, on average, earn lower returns than smaller companies both in the period prior to the bid month (see Table 2 earlier) and in the bid period itself.

Target Companies. The results obtained for target companies over the bid period reveal large, significant wealth gains to shareholders in both completed and abandoned bids. In completed bids shareholders of target companies obtain average wealth increases of over 30%, whether measured on an equally weighted or a value weighted basis. In the sub-period which includes formal announcement of the bid, target company shareholders obtain abnormal returns of around 24%, irrespective of the ultimate outcome of the bid. However, in the period of uncertainty prior to formal announcement of the outcome, shareholders of targets in completed bids obtain abnormal returns which are significantly higher (6.16% v. −3.29%) than their counterparts in abandoned bids. This result provides further evidence that the market anticipates the outcome of the bid prior to formal announcement.

The negative abnormal returns for bidders in abandoned bids was first reported for the US by Asquith (1983). His results differ for targets in abandoned bids, however, in that most of the previously obtained gains disappeared in the post-bid period. The results obtained in the current study indicate that the price of shares in target companies in abandoned bids do not, on average, fall back to their pre-bid level. As reported in the next section, this result holds even when the target company remains independent for a period of at least two years following abandonment of the bid.

(c) Post-outcome

Bidder Companies. Table 4 columns (i) and (ii) describes the distribution of returns to shareholders in bidder companies over the 24 month period following the month of announcement of the bid outcome. For both completed and abandoned bids there is a downward drift in returns over the whole period. Examination of the monthly pattern of average abnormal returns (not reported here) reveals that this pattern is not confined to any individual month of the post-outcome period. This result is consistent whichever control model was applied, with a 24 month bidder CAR using the market model of −14.08%, and −6.87% using the index model. A similar result was also reported by Franks and Harris (1989).

When the post-outcome abnormal returns are calculated on a value-weighted basis, however, a different pattern emerges, with the post-outcome abnormal returns based on application of the adjusted beta control model and the index model not significantly different from zero. While application of the market model produces a value-weighted CAR of −8.46% this is not significantly different from zero at the 10% level. These results taken together suggest that, while the market takes a considerable period to adjust to bids made by smaller companies, market reaction to bids undertaken by larger companies is more rapid and takes place in the period immediately surrounding the bid. While the results reported using value-weighted returns also suggest that the downward reappraisal of takeover benefits is largely confined to smaller bidders, this conclusion should be treated with caution. It is possible that, because of the relative size of bidder and target, any downward reappraisal of the benefits of the bid to large bidders may be swamped by the absolute size of the bidder.

Franks and Harris (1989) report a similar pattern of post-outcome CARs measured using the market model but attribute this to bias in the calculation of alpha values. They suggest that the high pre-bid alphas represent the achievement of positive abnormal returns prior to the bid, and that the failure to repeat this performance over the post-bid period is responsible for the post-merger pattern of returns. In the current study, bidder company alpha values averaged around 0.6% (as against 0.95% reported by Franks and Harris), and may partly explain the pattern of post-merger returns, at least for those results reported using the market model. However, as described above, the results obtained in the current study using the other two control models also indicate a similar downward tendency. In addition the post-outcome results both in the current study and that of Franks and Harris may also include an upward bias through the inclusion of positive abnormal returns obtained by those bidder companies who themselves become targets for bids in the 24 month post-outcome period.

By comparison with bidders in completed bids, those bidders who are unsuccessful obtain significantly negative CARs of −20.23% over the 24 months following the bid outcome. It appears that while the market may be ambivalent in its attitude to successful bids, it has no sympathy with 'losers'.

Target Companies. Table 4 also includes data on the post-outcome returns to targets in abandoned bids. Reported CARs for the 24 month period are not significantly different from zero. This result is consistent with that reported by Firth (1980). When abnormal returns to targets in abandoned bids were recalculated on a value-weighted basis, however, a different pattern emerges, with most of the previously obtained wealth gains disappearing. The retention of bid premium is therefore confined largely to smaller targets.

(d) Overall

Bidder Companies. Table 5(a) reports the abnormal returns to bidder companies from bid month through the 12 and 24 months following the outcome month. Results are reported both on an equally weighted and a value-weighted basis for all three control models. Reported CARs display a consistent (although not always statistically significant) pattern of negative returns to bidders, whether in completed or abandoned bids. A similar

consistent pattern emerges when abnormal returns were calculated on a value-weighted basis, although only the returns obtained following application of the market model were found to be significantly different from zero. The overall results reported in Table 5(a) suggest that, contrary to the impression made when examining returns around the bid period only, acquisitions are negative, rather than zero, net present value investment decisions.

The CARs reported in Table 5(b) demonstrate that failure to complete the bid also produces significantly negative wealth changes to bidders in abandoned bids. The results appear to be inconsistent in that, if the stock market views a successful bid as detrimental to the interests of the shareholders of the bidding company, then one would expect a favourable reaction to bid abandonment. It is possible, however, that the adverse reaction to bid abandonment may in part be due to the subsequent acquisition of valuable resources (the target company) by a competitor.

Target Companies. Table 6(a) reports the pattern of CARs to targets in completed bids, following application of the adjusted betas control model. The other control models also produced a similar pattern of large, significantly positive wealth increases of between 35% and 40%. Table 6(b) summarises the returns obtained by targets in abandoned bids from a base date three months prior to formal announcement of the bid. Reporting is again restricted to the results obtained following application of the adjusted betas control model, with the other models producing similar results. As found previously, by Firth (1980) and Parkinson and Dobbins (1988) for the UK, and Bradley *et al.* (1983) for the US, targets in abandoned bids on average retain a significant portion of the bid premium over the two years following the abandonment of the bid. However, when abnormal returns were recalculated, on a value-weighted basis, the bid premium disappeared and the market value of the targets reverted to their pre-bid level.

Wealth changes

While the above results demonstrate that shareholders of target companies make significant gains from takeovers, it is not clear whether these gains are solely as a result of a transfer of wealth from the shareholders of the bidding company or whether there is also a net wealth increase, indicating possible synergistic benefits. While the finding of a net wealth gain would not of itself support the argument of efficiency gains from mergers, as the gains may for example arise from the exercise of monopoly power, the presence of a net wealth loss would be a powerful economic argument against merger activity. In this final section of the analysis,

ACCOUNTING AND BUSINESS RESEARCH

Table 7
Mean wealth effects on shareholders of companies involved in completed acquisitions, 1977–1986 (£millions). Results reported using adjusted betas

	Bidder[a]	Target[b]	Combined
Bid period	−13.19**	19.02***	5.84
	(5.76, 40)	(3.69, 87)	(5.09, 65)
Bid period to month +12	−13.00		6.02
	(12.30, 43)		(12.0, 56)
Bid period to month +24	−18.20		0.80
	(15.70, 40)		(15.30, 50)

Note: Figures in parentheses represent standard errors followed by percentage positive.
[a]From bid month.
[b]From month − 3.
**Indicates significant at 5% level.
***Indicates significant at 1% level.

---

therefore, the hypothesis was tested that completed acquisitions produce no net wealth increase to shareholders of the companies involved. For each completed bid for which data was available for both target and bidder, the wealth change to each group of ordinary shareholders was calculated:

$$\text{Wealth Change} = MV_{j,t-6}\left[\left(\prod_{t=1}^{t=n}(1 + A_{j,t})\right) - 1\right] \quad (12)$$

Wealth changes are calculated by applying the relevant abnormal return to the equity market value of each company six months prior to the bid.[6]

Abnormal returns for shareholders of bidder companies are calculated from the bid month while those for shareholders of target companies are calculated from month −3. Table 7 describes the mean wealth changes to bidder and target companies, as well as the net wealth change following application of the adjusted betas control model. While the wealth changes obtained, on average, by target company shareholders are significantly positive, the combined wealth effect indicates that this gain is achieved at the expense of shareholders of bidding companies. Combined wealth changes are not, on average, significantly different from zero.

The results reported in Table 7 do however suggest that, at worst, acquisitions are not value reducing activities and that acquisitions should not be opposed simply on those grounds. Bidder company shareholders do appear, however, to suffer wealth losses with too high a price paid for the

---

[6]The analysis was also repeated using alternative base dates, but without altering the results significantly.

benefits obtained from the acquisition which appears to involve a transfer of wealth to target company shareholders (see also Firth, 1980).

Summary and conclusions

The current study examines the distribution of returns and wealth changes to shareholders of target and bidder firms in takeover bids over the period 1977 to 1986. The results provide conflicting evidence depending on the period included in the analysis of abnormal returns and the control model used. Results reported using OLS estimates of market model parameters are subject to criticism, both on the basis of bias due to infrequent trading and also possible post-bid changes in the risk-return profile of surviving companies, and must therefore be treated with caution. A number of conclusions may, however, be drawn from the results reported in the study.

If analysis of acquisitions considers only the period surrounding the bid, i.e. bid month to outcome month (Table 3), it appears that target company shareholders gain substantially from bids, and bidder company shareholders do not lose. If the post-outcome period is included in the analysis of returns and wealth changes to bidder companies, then substantial losses are experienced, on average, over a period of two years following the bid. This conclusion is most apparent using the market model but is consistent with results obtained using the other control models also. Both bidder companies and the market appear to overestimate the likely benefits to be obtained from acquisitions. The results obtained with value-weighted returns indicate that the market adjusts the price of shares of large bidders in the period immediately surrounding the bid but that the market adjustment for smaller bidders is less immediate with wealth losses obtained over a period of up to two years following the outcome of the bid. For target companies in abandoned bids, the gains made during the bid period remain for a period of at least two years subsequent to the bid. This result may reflect one or more of a number of factors, including the prospect of future bids. Further research into this issue is recommended.

The results obtained also suggest that the gains made by target company shareholders are at the expense of shareholders of bidder companies. There is no evidence of a net wealth increase resulting from takeover activity over the period 1977–1986. One implication of this result however is that, despite the losses to shareholders of bidder companies, investors holding well-diversified portfolios will suffer no wealth decrease as a result of acquisition activity.

The results obtained identified a wide variation in the pattern of returns obtained across the sample of bidder companies. One direction which current research is taking is to examine whether there are characteristics which discriminate between those bids which produce positive abnormal returns to shareholders of bidding companies and those which produce negative abnormal returns (see Limmack, 1990; and Morck *et al.*, 1990).

References

Appleyard, A. R. (1980), 'Takeovers: Accounting Policy, Financial Policy and the Case against Accounting Measures of Performance' (1980), *Journal of Business Finance and Accounting*, 7, pp. 541–554.

Asquith, P. (1983), 'Merger Bids, Uncertainty, and Stockholder Returns', *Journal of Financial Economics*, 11, pp. 51–83.

Barnes, P. (1984), 'The Effect of a Merger on the Share Price of the Attacker, Revisited', *Accounting and Business Research*, 15, pp. 45–49.

Brown, S. J. and Warner, J. B. (1985), 'Using Daily Stock Returns: The Case of Event Studies', *Journal of Financial Economics*, 14, pp. 3–31.

Bradley, M., Desai, A. and Kim, E. H. (1983), 'The Rationale Behind Interfirm Tender Offers: Information or Synergy?' *Journal of Financial Economics*, 11, pp. 183–206.

Bradley, M., Desai, A. and Kim, E. H. (1988), 'Synergistic Gains from Corporate Acquisitions and their Division Between the Stockholders of Target and Acquiring Firms', *Journal of Financial Economics*, 21, pp. 3–40.

Cohen, K. J., Hawawini, G. A., Maier, S. F., Schwartz, R. A. and Whitcomb, D. K. (1983), 'Friction in the Trading Process and the Estimation of Systematic Risk', *Journal of Financial Economics*, 12, pp. 263–278.

Dimson, E. (1979), 'Risk Measurement When Shares Are Subject to Infrequent Trading', *Journal of Financial Economics*, 17, pp. 197–226.

Dimson, E. and Marsh, P. R. (1979), 'Risk Measurement Service', London Business School, unpublished paper.

Dimson, E. and Marsh, P. R. (1983), 'The Stability of UK Risk Measures and the Problem of Thin Trading', *Journal of Finance*, 38, pp. 753–783.

Dodd, P. and Ruback, R. (1977), 'Tenders Offers and Stockholder Returns: an Empirical Analysis', *Journal of Financial Economics*, 5, pp. 351–373.

Dodds, J. and Quek, J. (1985), 'Effects of Mergers on the Share Price Movement of the Acquiring Firms: A UK Study', *Journal of Business Finance and Accounting*, 12, pp. 285–296.

Dyckman, T., Philbrick, D. and Stephan, J. (1984), 'A Comparison of Event Study Methodologies Using Daily Stock Returns: A Simulation Approach', Supplement to *Journal of Accounting Research*, 22, pp. 1–30.

Firth, M. (1979), 'The Profitability of Takeovers and Mergers', *Economic Journal*, 89, pp. 316–328.

Firth, M. (1980), 'Takeovers, Shareholder Returns and the Theory of the Firm', *Quarterly Journal of Economics*, 94, pp. 235–260.

Franks, J. R., Broyles, J. E. and Hecht, M. (1977), 'An Industry Study of the Profitability of Mergers in the UK', *Journal of Finance*, 32, pp. 1513–1525.

Franks, J. and Harris, R. (1989), 'Shareholder Wealth Effects of Corporate Takeovers: The UK Experience 1955–1985', *Journal of Financial Economics*, 23, 225–249.

Jarrell, G. A., Brickley, J. A. and Netter, J. M. (1988), 'The Market for Corporate Control: The Empirical Evidence Since 1980', *Journal of Economic Perspectives*, 2, pp. 49–68.

Jensen, M. C. and Ruback, R. (1983), 'The Market for Corporate Control: The Scientific Evidence', *Journal of Financial Economics*, 11, pp. 5–50.

Limmack, R. J. (1990), 'Takeover Activity and Differential Returns to Shareholders of Bidding Companies', *Hume Occasional Paper No.*, 19, David Hume Institute.

Malatesta, P. H. and Thompson, R. (1985), 'Partially Anticipated Events: A Model of Stock Price Reactions with an Application to Corporate Acquisitions', *Journal of Financial Economics*, 14, pp. 237–250.

Mandelker, G. (1974), 'Risk and Return: the Case of Merging Firms', *Journal of Financial Economics*, 1, pp. 303–335.

Manne, H. G. (1965), 'Mergers and the Market for Corporate Control', *Journal of Political Economy*, 73, pp. 110–120.

Marris, R. and Mueller, D. C. (1980), 'The Corporation, Competition, and the Invisible Hand', *Journal of Economic Literature*, 18, pp. 32–63.

Meeks, G. (1977), *Disappointing Marriage: A Study of the Gains of Merger*, Cambridge University Press.

Morck, R. A., Shleifer, A. and Vishny, R. W. (1990), 'Do Managerial Objectives Drive Bad Acquisitions?', *Journal of Finance*, 45, pp. 31–48.

Pickering, J. (1983), 'The Causes and Consequences of Abandoned Mergers', *Journal of Industrial Economics*, 31, pp. 267–281.

Scholes, M. and Williams, J. (1977), 'Estimating Betas from Nonsynchronous Data', *Journal of Financial Economics*, 5, pp. 309–327.

Singh, A. (1971), *Takeovers: Their Relevance to the Stockmarket and the Theory of the Firm*, Cambridge University Press.

Singh, A. (1975), 'Takeovers, Economic Natural Selection, and the Theory of the Firm: Evidence from the Postwar United Kingdom Experience', *Economic Journal*, 85, pp. 497–515.

Strong, N. C. (1989), 'Modelling Abnormal Returns', Paper presented to the Accounting Research Methods Summer School on Market-Based Accounting Research, University of Strathclyde.

Vasicek, O. A. (1973), 'A Note on Using Cross-Sectional Information in Bayesian Estimation of Security Betas', *Journal of Finance*, 28, pp. 1233–1239.

Weston, J. Fred (1970), 'The Nature and Significance of Conglomerate Firms', *St. John's Law Review*, 44, Special Edition, pp. 66–80.

Weston, J. E. and Copeland, T. E. (1988), *Managerial Finance*, 2nd UK Edition, adapted by A. F. Fox and R. J. Limmack, Cassell, London.

Williamson, O. E. (1964), *The Economics of Discretionary Behaviour: Managerial Objectives in a Theory of the Firm*, Prentice-Hall, Englewood Cliffs, NJ.

[2]

Journal of Financial Economics 23 (1989) 225-249. North-Holland

SHAREHOLDER WEALTH EFFECTS OF
CORPORATE TAKEOVERS
The U.K. Experience 1955-1985*

Julian R. FRANKS

London School of Business, London, England

Robert S. HARRIS

University of Virginia, Charlottesville, VA 22906, USA

Received November 1986, final version received January 1989

This paper examines the effects of over 1,800 U.K. takeovers on shareholder wealth in the period 1955-1985. It shows that around the merger announcement date targets gain 25 to 30 percent and bidders earn zero or modest gains. The U.K. data allow independent tests of many issues addressed in studies of U.S. takeovers. Target gains are higher in the U.K. after 1968, suggesting that increases in U.S. target gains at the same time may not be attributable to the Williams Act. Postmerger share-price performance suggests that acquisitions follow favorable developments in bidders' equity prices.

1. Introduction

In their review of the empirical evidence on shareholder wealth effects of U.S. takeovers, Jensen and Ruback (1983) conclude that targets clearly gain and bidders gain, or at least do not lose. There is no such consensus about the U.K. experience. For example, Firth's (1979, 1980) U.K. studies find gains to targets are more than offset by losses to bidders. Franks, Broyles, and Hecht (1977), in contrast, report gains to both parties. Like other U.K. studies, however, these papers suffer from either small samples or samples confined to short periods of calendar time.

An objective of this paper is to resolve the conflicting evidence in the U.K. by providing a comprehensive study of wealth gains to stockholders. We use a

*We thank Mike Staunton for collecting some of the data, Nick Grattan and Ed Bachman for programming assistance, and the Leverhulme Trust for financial support. We thank the participants at Seminars at the London Business School, NBER, the Institute of Fiscal Studies, the University of Colorado at Boulder, the University of Virginia and the University of North Carolina at Chapel Hill, particularly Alan Auerbach, Mark Flannery, Oliver Hart, David Hirshleifer, Colin Mayer, Stewart Myers, Stan Ornstein, Michael Rothschild, and Ailsa Roell. We also wish to thank Wayne Mikkelson, the referee, and Richard Ruback and Michael Jensen, the editors.

sample of more than 1,800 U.K. acquisitions covering a 30-year period (1955–85). A second objective is to replicate tests that have been performed on U.S. data to see whether parallel findings emerge for the U.K. Each country's results may be unique because of different institutional and regulatory conditions. Alternatively, similar results may occur if the market for corporate control is reasonably competitive in both countries and robust to specific institutional differences. The U.K. data allow independent tests of many issues addressed in the U.S., such as the relative wealth effects of tender offers and mergers, the impact of the Williams Act, the influence of revised and contested bids, and the role of toehold interests. The paper also provides an opportunity to compare the postmerger share-price performance of U.K. and U.S. bidders, a subject of continuing controversy in the empirical literature.

2. Background and organization of the paper

Economic theory generally offers two competing thoughts about the efficacy of takeovers for corporate shareholders. Neoclassical theory [Manne (1965)] views corporate acquisitions as value-enhancing activities in which managers work to maximize shareholder wealth. This value creation may come from numerous sources, including cost savings, exercise of increased monopoly power, or replacement of inefficient management. In contrast, managerial theories [Mueller (1969)] view takeovers as extensions of managers' own personal interests, undertaken for the purpose of increasing their own wealth or prestige by managing a larger postmerger entity.

Empirical work in the U.S. [Halpern (1973), Mandelker (1974), Asquith (1983), and Bradley, Desai, and Kim (1988)] has largely supported the contention that successful acquisitions create value for shareholders, although there is some evidence to the contrary [see Malatesta (1983) and Roll (1986)]. Jensen and Ruback (1983) report returns to targets of 29% in tender offers and 16% in mergers; for bidders the abnormal returns are 4% in tenders and zero in mergers. The distribution of value gains between the target and bidder is subject to more controversy. Some U.S. studies show essentially all gains going to the target [Dodd (1980), Mandelker (1974), Asquith (1983)]. Halpern (1973), in contrast, finds dollar gains split evenly between merging parties, and others [Asquith, Bruner, and Mullins (1983), Dodd and Ruback (1977)] show bidding-firm shareholders earning positive and statistically significant gains from successful takeovers.[1]

---

[1] See also Langetieg (1978), Kummer and Hoffmeister (1978), Bradley (1980), and Eckbo (1983), as well as survey articles by Jensen and Ruback (1983), Halpern (1983), and Jarrell, Brickley, and Netter (1988). Shleifer and Summers (1988) note that shareholder gains may be incremental to all parties to a merger or may simply be a redistribution of wealth from one party to another. In studying gains and losses to stockholders, we ignore gains and losses to other security holders such as bondholders and to stakeholders with nontraded claims such as managers or employees. Dennis and McConnell (1986) examine returns to various classes of securities, including bonds, preferred stock, common stock, and convertibles.

Existing evidence in the U.K. is far less conclusive. The sample chosen by Franks, Broyles, and Hechts (1977) (hereafter FBH) includes only 74 acquisitions in the breweries and distilleries industry. FBH find significant positive gains to targets with no offsetting losses to bidders. Firth examines samples of acquisitions over the period 1969–1975 but finds, in sharp contrast to FBH, that any gains to target shareholders are more than offset by losses to bidders. Firth concludes that mergers are most likely 'motivated by maximization of management utility reasons' (1980, p. 235). Smaller samples were studied by Barnes (1984) and Dodds and Quek (1985), who only added to the controversy by providing contradictory conclusions.

After discussing our sample and method in the third section of the paper, we present our empirical results in section 4. The empirical findings are divided into seven parts. In the first, the overall percentage wealth gains to bidders and targets are measured on an equally weighted and value-weighted basis. In addition, the total sterling gains and losses are provided, as well as the proportion of acquisitions in which the aggregate wealth gains of the two parties are positive. Because bidders are on average eight times larger than targets, the relative size of the bidder and target is controlled for in the second part. This helps us detect the impact of the acquisition on the bidder's share price.

In the third part, we control for the form of acquisition and compare results from the U.K. with results for U.S. tenders and mergers. This comparison provides a more robust test of how institutional and regulatory factors can affect the bidding process and wealth gains. For example, results for the U.S. suggest that the 1968 Williams Act, which provided for regulation of and mandatory information disclosure in cash tender offers, increased the competitiveness of the acquisitions market. The act was amended in 1970 to expand the types of offers covered and to extend the rule-making powers of the Securities and Exchange Commission (SEC). One amendment increased the minimum time a tender offer must remain open to 20 business days and required that an offer must remain open for 10 business days after any increase in the offer amount. Such increases in length of the tender offer process may well increase the likelihood of a competing bid. Studying U.S. tender offers, Bradley, Desai, and Kim (1988) find that after the act was passed gains to target shareholders increased and gains to bidders were reduced. Because no comparable act was passed in the U.K., the U.K. data provide an opportunity to assess whether the trend in wealth effects in the U.S. before and after 1968 was repeated in the U.K.

In the fourth part of section 4, we compare wealth gains from revised and unrevised bids. We also separate revised bids into single-bidder and multiple-bidder cases. This comparison enables us to determine how the distribution of gains between bidder and target is altered as a result of competition in bidding. The U.K. results are compared with those for the U.S. after controlling for the form of offer.

In the next part, we analyze wealth gains arising from toehold interests. Shleifer and Vishny's (1986) proposition that bid premiums decline as toeholds increase is tested. By studying both toeholds and the nature of the subsequent bid, we examine whether toeholds are important preparations for what is expected to be a competitive bidding process.

In part six, we analyze both target and bidder gains cross-sectionally to distinguish among the variables that might explain shareholder gains. For example, we examine whether wealth effects related to the form of acquisition can be attributed to differences in the nature of the bidding contest or the date of the bid, whether before or after 1968.

In the last part, we examine the performance of successful bidding firms during the two years after merger. A puzzling result in U.S. evidence noted by Jensen and Ruback is 'that the post-outcome abnormal returns for the merger studies reported...provide evidence of systematic reductions in stock prices' for successful bidders. Langetieg (1978) and Asquith (1983) report significant negative abnormal returns in the year following the merger announcement. Malatesta (1983) finds significant negative performance postmerger for smaller bidders and for bidders in mergers after 1970. In comparison, Firth (1980) finds no marked evidence of nonzero postmerger performance in the U.K. The U.K. data provide an opportunity to replicate the U.S. tests on a large independent sample over an equivalent calendar period.

3. Data and method

3.1. Sample

Our initial sample contains 1,898 target firms and 1,058 acquirers (bidders) in U.K. acquisitions. This sample represents an exhaustive set of acquisitions as recorded in the London Share Price Database (LSPD) for the period January 1955 to June 1985. LSPD includes all U.K. companies listed in London since 1975. Before 1975, approximately two-thirds of U.K.-listed companies are recorded, with a bias in favor of larger companies. Bidders not included in our sample are either (a) unlisted private U.K. companies, (b) unlisted nationalized U.K. companies, (c) listed U.K. firms not in LSPD, or (d) non-U.K. companies. Where several acquisitions were made by the same bidder, the bidder is counted separately for each acquisition. In our sample, 272 bidders have acquired more than one company and 58 have acquired four or more companies.

In the U.K., publicly listed companies are acquired or merged through two types of transactions. The more popular method is through an offer for shares made directly to the target's shareholders, and the offer is usually made contingent on acceptance by 90% or more of shares outstanding. If less than the stated minimum number of shares is tendered, the offer lapses; all

J.R. Franks and R.S. Harris, Wealth effects of takeovers in the U.K. 229

Table 1

Key dates for U.K. acquisitions.

Earliest date	Number of acquisitions	Lag from prior date (days)
First approach	332	0
First bid	1,410	55
Unconditional	31	86
LSPD	125	110

tendered shares are returned. The minimum of 90% is chosen because section 209 of the 1948 Companies Act permits companies with over 90% ownership interest to compulsorily buy out any outstanding minority shareholders at the original offer price. Thus bidders may avoid in part the free-rider problems described by Grossman and Hart (1980) and Yarrow (1985). The offer to purchase, described above, characterizes about 91% of our sample. In the remaining cases, virtually all mergers are completed by a 'scheme of arrangement' under sections 206–208 of the 1948 act. Here a shareholders' meeting is convened under a court's direction, and the merger can be consummated if more than 75% of votes by those voting are cast in favor [see Röell (1986) for a discussion].[2]

For each acquisition, we have up to four key dates. The *first approach date* is the date when the Stock Exchange is initially informed that merger talks are under way. The *first bid date* is the date of the first formal merger offer. This is followed by an *unconditional date*, when a sufficient proportion of shares has been pledged to the bidder to guarantee legal control. Finally, the *LSPD date* shows the last date for which stock return data are available for the target, usually the delisting date. The first three dates are taken from the records of the EXTEL Company, a British vendor of financial data.

There may not be four distinct dates for all acquisitions. For example, the first bid date may not be preceded by a formal announcement of talks. Table 1 shows the distribution of acquisitions by the earliest distinct date available, as well as the average lags between the dates when they differ.

For each acquisition, we also search EXTEL records for revised or contested bids and premerger equity ownership in the target (toehold interest) held by a bidder. Toehold interests are taken from offer documents of the bidding

---

[2] Of the 174 mergers in our sample concluded by a 'scheme of arrangement', 57 cases involved acquiring companies with toehold equity interests (averaging 63% of the target shares). It seems reasonable to assume that, in these cases, a transfer of managerial control preceded the merger. Why are schemes of arrangement not more popular? The scheme of arrangement requires the agreement of boards of directors of both bidder and target and that of the court. Such delays induced by the court proceedings increase the potential for competing bids [a point made by Röell (1986)].

companies. The dates of purchase are not disclosed. Toehold interests are recorded for 386 target companies, although only 283 of the toehold bidders are in our sample. In 211 cases, the toehold is less than 30%. Finally, in 187 acquisitions there are revised bids, although in only 84 cases is the bid contested.

Our sample does not include failed bids, since these are not recorded in LSPD. A possible consequence of excluding failed mergers is to introduce a bias, since investors must buy shares without knowledge of the bid outcome. The direction of the bias will depend, however, on the nature of failed bids. If share-price gains on merger announcements are due to anticipation of real asset changes on merger, they should erode if no takeover occurs. On the other hand, if a bid is based purely on superior information held by the bidder and no operational change is required to realize increased value, the increase in target share price around the bid announcement will be due to revelation of new information. The gain should not erode when the bid fails if the private information has become public.

3.2. Share-price data

Monthly rates of return are based on prices taken from LSPD. These returns are calculated in two ways: on the basis of jobbers' (i.e., market makers) price quotes and on traded prices. For each month, jobbers' price quotes (average of bid and ask) are taken at the end of the last day on which the stock is traded. Although traded prices are available, their order during a day is not recorded in LSPD (or by the Stock Exchange, prior to 1986) so that end-of-day traded prices cannot be identified. As a result, for each month LSPD uses a price selected at random from the price series taken on the last day on which the stock is traded. Since jobbers' quotes are available at the close of day, our reported results are based on these prices; the results are not appreciably affected, however, when we use traded prices. For the purpose of calculating abnormal returns, weighted by the equity capitalization of individual companies, we use shares outstanding at the end of the calendar year prior to the merger. For some targets, share-price data are unavailable around the event date, reducing our usable sample to 1,814 targets.

3.3. Abnormal returns and tests

To assess the effects of mergers on share prices, we use variations of event-study methodology. Specifically, for any company j, we define an abnormal return (ar_{jt}) as

$$ar_{jt} = r_{jt} - c_{jt}, \tag{1}$$

where r_{jt} is the continuously compounded realized return (log form) in month t (dividends plus capital gains) and c_{jt} is a control return that calculates an estimate of what shareholder returns would have been in the absence of a merger. Time, t, is defined in relation to an event date, which, as discussed above, could be the first approach date, the first bid date, or the unconditional date.

Brown and Warner's simulation results (1980, 1985) on both monthly and daily data suggest that, in many cases, relatively straightforward procedures are as powerful as more elaborate tests in detecting abnormal returns. To see whether the specification of control returns affects our results, we use three alternate models to determine c_{jt} using the following equation:

$$c_{jt} = \alpha_j + \beta_j rm_t.$$

In the first model, the market model, values for α and β are estimated by regressing r_{jt} on rm_t for the 60-month period beginning at $t = -71$.[3] In the second model, we set $\alpha = 0$ and $\beta = 1$ for all firms. The third model is based on the Capital Asset Pricing Model (CAPM) and sets $c_{jt} = r_{ft} + \beta_j(r_{mt} - r_{ft})$ where β is from the market model and r_{ft} is the yield on three-month Treasury obligations converted to a one-month-yield basis.

Although infrequent trading will produce some bias in measured parameters in our first and third models [see Dimson (1979, 1985) and Dimson and Marsh (1983) for a discussion], simulation studies by Brown and Warner (1980) suggest the impact on the results is small. We also examine directly the effects of thin trading.

Company abnormal returns calculated in eq. (1) are then aggregated to form a portfolio abnormal return (AR_t) defined as

$$AR_t = \frac{1}{N} \sum_{j=1}^{N} ar_{jt},\qquad(2)$$

where N is the number of companies in a particular portfolio, e.g., the portfolio of targets. The statistical significance of AR_t is assessed with the statistic $T_t = AR_t/\sigma$, where σ is the standard deviation of the AR_t's (assumed to be normally distributed) for a period assumed to be unaffected by the merger. In reported results, σ is calculated for the 60-month period beginning at $t = -71$. Given these procedures, T_t is distributed according to Student's t distribution with 59 degrees of freedom. This procedure is the crude adjust-

[3] During the earliest years of our analysis, sufficient data were unavailable to calculate α and β. In these cases, companies were assigned $\alpha = 0$, $\beta = 1.0$. Malatesta (1986) provides evidence that standard event methodologies are in many cases more powerful than more elaborate techniques which estimate systems of equations.

ment for cross-sectional dependence as discussed by Brown and Warner (1980). Alternatively, the statistical significance of AR_t is tested nonparametrically using the percentage of the ar_{jt} that is positive.[4]

Although cumulations of AR are frequently used for assessing multiperiod returns, they can be unsatisfactory when companies disappear from the analysis as a result of nontrading, delisting, or suspension close to the bid date. As an alternative to cumulative portfolio returns, we construct company-specific 'total abnormal returns' (tar_t) that are then aggregated into average total abnormal return (TAR_t) for a sample defined as

$$TAR_t = \frac{1}{N} \sum_{j=1}^{N} tar_{jt} = \frac{1}{N} \sum_{j=1}^{N} \sum_{i=t_b}^{t} ar_{ji}, \qquad (3)$$

where the cumulation process begins at time t_b and includes those monthly abnormal returns that are observed up to and including month t, and N is the number of companies in a sample. For example, if in month $+1$ two companies obtain an average residual of 10% and in month $+2$ only one survives (or is traded) and obtains a residual of 5%, TAR for the two months according to (3) is 12.5%, compared with 15% if the cumulation is based on averages across companies each month. In addition to the equally weighted TAR shown in (3), we calculate TAR on a market-value-weighted basis. We assess the statistical significance of TAR_t using the statistic $TTAR_t = TAR_t/\sigma_{TAR}$, where $\sigma_{TAR} = \sqrt{M}\,\sigma$ and M is the average (across companies) number of months for which return data are available to form TAR_t. The statistic $TTAR_t$ is approximately a standard normal variate under the assumptions that TAR_t has a zero mean and the AR_t are independent.

4. Empirical findings

4.1. Overall wealth gains

Table 2 reports shareholder wealth effects for the total sample. All results are based on our simplest model ($\alpha = 0$, $\beta = 1$), and returns are reported on both an equally weighted and a value-weighted basis.

In month 0, target shareholders average statistically significant positive total abnormal returns of about 23%. Given possible arrival of information before the measured event date and possible anticipation of news by the market, we also examine results over the six-month period (-4 to $+1$). Over this period, target abnormal returns average 25.8% or 29.7%, depending on whether the

---

[4] This is accomplished by comparing the positive percentage to a binomial distribution when the probability of a positive return is 0.50 as would be the case if any merger had an equal chance of producing positive or negative returns.

J.R. Franks and R.S. Harris, Wealth effects of takeovers in the U.K. 233

Table 2

Percentage total abnormal returns (*TAR*) for the total sample of 1,814 targets and 1,058 bidders in completed U.K. acquisitions during the period 1955–1985.

TAR is defined as the difference between the return on the stock and the return on an equally weighted portfolio of all stocks in the London Share Price Database (LSPD). Month 0 is the earliest available of the first approach, first bid, unconditional, or LSPD dates.[a] Entries are average *TAR*s and the numbers in parentheses are the *t*-statistic and percentage positive.

Period of return	Targets	Bidders
Month 0 (equal weighting)	23.3 (60.60,87)	1.0 (2.30,51)
Months −4 to +1 (equal weighting)	29.7 (31.50,85)	7.9 (7.50,65)
Months −4 to +1 (value weighting)	25.8 (27.40,85)	2.4 (2.28,65)
Average size, in millions of pounds of equity market value	14.05	107.91

[a] The first approach date is the date the Stock Exchange is initially informed of merger talks. The first bid date is the date of the first formal bid, which is followed by the unconditional date, when enough shares have been pledged to the bidder to guarantee legal control. The LSPD date is the last date for which share returns are available (usually the delisting date).

results are value-weighted or equally weighted. The smaller gains when we use value weightings suggest that smaller targets obtain higher percentage premiums in takeovers.

Bidders earn positive but small abnormal returns in month 0 (about 1%). Over the period −4 to +1, however, there are total abnormal returns to bidders of 2.4% and 7.9% on a value- and equal-weighted basis, both of which are significantly greater than zero.

Since value-weighted returns to both targets and bidders are positive, the U.K. evidence supports the hypothesis that there are positive total shareholder gains in takeovers. For example, using the data in table 2 for an average size target, the gain is £3.62 million over the period −4 to +1. For an average size bidder, the pound gain is £2.63 million for the same six-month period.[5] To provide a more refined calculation of pound takeover gains, we examine 721 pairs of target and bidding firms for which we have high-quality market-value data for both firms. This is analogous to Bradley, Desai, and Kim's (1988) sample restriction in their study of U.S. tenders. Using the same procedures as in table 2 to compare abnormal returns and analyzing the period −4 to +1,

[5] We calculate this gain as the value-weighted percentage gain multiplied by the average market value of a target. The gain is $0.258 \times 14.05 = 3.62$. This procedure is equivalent to dividing total pound gains to targets by the number of targets, since we use value-weighted returns. The same procedure is used for bidders.

we find that the average gain for these target–bidder pairs is £7.05 million and 74% of the pairs experience positive gains.[6] On average, bidders receive about half of the pound gains (£3.49 million). For month 0, the picture is a little different. The average gain is £2.37 million and 68% of the merger pairs experience positive gains. On average, bidders lose £0.57 million (49% are positive) and targets receive £2.94 million (93% are positive). The bidders' losses are less than 0.5% of their market capitalization. If the distribution of gains is measured on the basis of month 0, all the wealth gains accrue to targets, whereas if the basis is months −4 to +1, the wealth gains are evenly distributed.

We examine the sensitivity of our results to the choice of control return. The abnormal returns are largely insensitive to the choice of the three models used for control returns, except for bidders over the six-month period. Using the market model, the six-month (−4 to +1) total abnormal return for bidders is 3.5%, compared with over 7% using either of the other models. For all models, however, the six-month TAR to bidders is significantly positive. Further, the results of our models are not affected materially when we adjust our parameter estimates for thin trading. Changes in *TAR* estimates are less than 1%.[7]

We also examine the effects of a number of sample restrictions. In the restricted cases, companies are excluded if any of the following criteria are met: (i) the LSPD date is the only event date available, (ii) the firm's stock is suspended from trading any time in the twelve months prior to the event date, or (iii) the merger announcement occurs on or after the 26th day of the month. Mergers in (i) are excluded because the delisting date (LSPD) does not correspond with the arrival of merger information in the market; 125 companies are excluded on these grounds. The second criterion, which removes 37 companies from the sample, assures that our results are not contaminated by returns actually earned over a series of nontraded months that are erroneously allocated to the single month following resumption of trading. Finally, the third criterion assures that if the bid was announced on the last trading day of the month it is not incorrectly allocated to the following month. For example, if a merger announcement becomes public after the market closes on the last day of the month, the information would be covered in the *Financial Times* at the beginning of the subsequent month, and would be so recorded in LSPD.

[6]For each firm, the gain is the market value of the company in the month before the measurement period multiplied by the *TAR* over the measurement period. For this calculation, it is necessary to construct monthly market values for LSPD companies, adjusting for stock splits and rights issues.

[7]Specifically, for our sample of mergers in 1983, we compared our estimates of beta with those reported by the London Business School's Risk Measurement Service (RMS), where betas are adjusted for thin trading using Dimson's (1979) method. Adjusted betas for bidders average 0.920, compared with the average of unadjusted betas of 0.897. For targets, comparable figures are 0.854 and 0.706, respectively. *TAR*s are substantially the same. For example, using the CAPM, the difference in the *TAR* (months −4 to +1) is 0.7% for targets and 0.3% for bidders.

J.R. Franks and R.S. Harris, Wealth effects of takeovers in the U.K. 235

Results for both targets and bidders are essentially unchanged when the restricted sample is used, so we do not report the results. Results are also essentially unchanged if we define month 0 as the earliest available date among the first bid, unconditional, or LSPD dates.

The evidence in table 2 strongly supports the contention that target shareholders gain substantially in mergers. The data on the bidders are more difficult to interpret. Abnormal returns before the bid may result from anticipation of possible merger benefits or from unexpected good news about earnings. In particular, bidders may time mergers to occur when their share prices and earnings are strong. Indeed, good earnings and share price performance may provide a motivation for the bid. For example, Jensen (1986) discusses how free cash flow generated by exceptionally good performance may lead to an acquisition.

Comparing wealth effects in table 2 with results of earlier U.K. studies, our findings are quite similar to those of Franks, Broyles, and Hecht (1977). FBH found gains to targets of about 26% for months -3 to 0 and positive though small abnormal returns to bidders. Our findings are strikingly different, however, from those of Firth (1979, 1980), who studied seven years (1969–1975) of U.K. merger activity. Using equal weighting, Firth found target gains of 37% in the period -4 to $+1$ and 28% in month 0. Both figures are higher than our results. The most notable differences between our results and Firth's are for bidders: Firth shows statistically significant negative abnormal returns of -6.3% in month 0 and -9.1% for the period -4 to $+1$. Firth concludes that the losses to bidders more than offset value gains to targets. We have attempted to replicate Firth's results for the period 1969–1975 using our own data set. After excluding mergers in which premerger equity interests exceed 30% and using the market model (as did Firth) on a sample of 302 mergers, we find abnormal returns to bidders of -0.1% in month 0 and 4.2% for months -4 to $+1$. The six-month TAR has a t-statistic of 2.02 and is significantly positive at the 5% level. It is possible that the difference in sample size (302 compared with Firth's 434) is because, before 1975, LSPD includes only two-thirds of listed companies, with a bias in favor of larger companies.

4.2. Relative size of target and bidder

A potential difficulty in measuring effects of mergers on bidders is that the large size of the bidder in relation to the target may obscure the gains or losses anticipated from merger. Table 2 shows that, in our sample, bidders are on average about eight times as large as targets. Table 3 partitions our sample by the relative market values of the merging firms.

When targets are relatively large in comparison with bidders, there is no evidence that bidders lose. Although the six-month returns for bidders appear

Table 3

Percentage total abnormal returns (*TAR*) for targets and bidders partitioned by the relative size of
the equity market value of the merging firms.

TAR is calculated as the difference between the return on the stock and a control return using
premerger market-model parameters. Month 0 is the earliest available of first approach, first bid,
unconditional, or LSPD dates.[a] Entries are equally weighted *TAR*s and the number in parentheses
is the percentage positive. The sample period is 1955–1985.

Relative size of target to bidder	N	Month 0		Months −4 to +1	
		Target	Bidder	Target	Bidder
All mergers	844	23.5[b] (87)	0.1 (46)	29.7[b] (88)	3.5[b] (65)
Less than 50%	439	28.1[b] (92)	−0.1 (45)	35.5[b] (89)	2.3 (54)
Between 50% and 100%	124	21.5[b] (87)	2.1 (48)	23.7[b] (84)	5.8[b] (61)
Greater than 100%	62	20.2[b] (88)	−1.2 (39)	27.6[b] (86)	6.0 (52)

[a] The first approach date is the date the Stock Exchange is initially informed of merger talks.
The first bid date is the date of the first formal bid, which is followed by the unconditional date,
when enough shares have been pledged to the bidder to guarantee legal control. The LSPD date is
the last date for which share returns are available (usually the delisting date).
[b] Significantly different from zero at 5% level based on *t*-test (two-tailed).

somewhat higher when the target is relatively large, the differences are not
statistically significant.[8] Moreover, month 0 abnormal returns for bidders are
virtually unchanged for different size ratios of target and bidder. In contrast,
target abnormal returns do appear higher when the target is small in relation
to the bidder. For example, when the target is less than half the size of the
bidder, the 28.1% *TAR* in month 0 is significantly higher than the 21.5% when
the target is smaller than the bidder but over half its size (*t*-statistic of 3.16).

4.3. U.K. and U.S. results: Form of offer and the Williams Act

Empirical work in the U.S. shows that shareholders experience larger wealth
gains in tenders than in mergers. For example, for the interval comparable to
months −1 and 0 in our work, Jensen and Ruback (1983) report abnormal
returns to target shareholders of 29% in tenders versus only 16% in mergers.
For bidders, Jensen and Ruback show 4% gains in tenders and no gains in
mergers; more recently, however, Bradley, Desai, and Kim (1988) suggest that

[8] Significance tests for differences in two cell means (M_1 and M_2) are based on a *t*-test
calculated at $t = (M_1 - M_2)/SD$, where $SD = \sqrt{S_1^2/N_1 + S_2^2/N_2}$, N is the number of observations averaged in cell mean, and S is the cross-sectional standard deviation about the cell mean.

Table 4

Percentage total abnormal returns (*TAR*) to merging firms in the U.S. and U.K., partitioned by the form of offer.

TAR is calculated as the difference between the returns on the stock and a control return using premerger market model parameters. The *TAR* is an equally weighted average and the figures in parentheses are the percentage positive. In the U.K., month 0 is the earliest available of first approach, first bid, unconditional, or LSPD dates. In the U.S., month 0 is the announcement month as gathered from the *Wall Street Journal*. The sample period is 1955–1985.

	Month 0		Months −4 to +1	
	U.K.	U.S.[a]	U.K.	U.S.[a]
Panel A: Targets				
Tenders	24.0[c]	23.3[c]	30.1[c]	34.9[c]
	(88)	(90)	(85)	(86)
	N = 1,693	N = 229		
Other[b]	14.8[c]	14.7[c]	20.0[c]	20.7[c]
	(73)	(81)	(79)	(79)
	N = 121	N = 1,210		
Panel B: Bidders				
Tenders	1.2[c]	1.0	8.0[c]	0.7
	(51)	(54)	(65)	(52)
	N = 1,012	N = 164		
Other[b]	−3.6[c]	0.1	5.2	1.5
	(40)	(49)	(59)	(52)
	N = 46	N = 861		

[a] Based on U.S. sample covering the period 1955–1984 as discussed in Franks and Harris (1987) and Franks, Harris, and Mayer (1988).
[b] In the U.S., the 'other' category includes all offers that are not tenders. In the U.K., 'other' comprises schemes of arrangement.
[c] Significantly different from zero at the 5% level based on a *t*-test (two-tailed).

bidder gains in tenders have decreased in recent years, even showing losses in the 1980s.

Table 4 provides a direct comparison between the U.S. and U.K. using unpublished results from Franks and Harris (1987), who study U.S. acquisitions covering the same period as our U.K. sample. Results are partitioned by the form of offer. The 'other' category includes combinations consummated by schemes of arrangements in the U.K. and mergers (i.e., offers that are not tenders) in the U.S. Although both schemes and mergers involve a vote by shareholders, the former is convened under a court's direction and requires a 75% vote in favor as well as the approval of both boards of directors.

Panel A shows our estimates of gains to targets in month 0 and for the six-month period from −4 to +1. Both sets of estimates show that, for a given form of offer (tender or other), target wealth gains are strikingly similar in the two countries. Furthermore, consistent with U.S. results, U.K. evidence shows

Table 5

Target wealth gains in U.K. acquisitions before and after 1968.

Three-year periods		Entire sample period	
Year of takeover	Average TAR	Year of takeover	Average TAR
1965–1967	26.10%	1955–1968	26.08%
1969–1971	31.60%	1969–1984	33.56%

that target gains are substantially higher in tender offers. For example, in month 0, the 24% target abnormal return in tender offers is significantly higher than the 14.8% gain in other offers ($t = 7.23$).

Turning to wealth effects for bidders, panel B suggests that in both countries bidders in tenders do better than those using other types of offers. In month 0, U.K. bidders have a 1.2% wealth increase in tenders, which is significantly higher than the 3.6% loss in other offers ($t = 2.95$). Using the six-month $TARs$, there is some evidence that U.K. bidders using tender offers appear to do better than bidders using tenders in the U.S. As discussed earlier, however, abnormal returns to bidders before the bid may, at least in part, reflect bidders' timing of takeovers to coincide with their own favorable share-price performance.

Work on tenders in the U.S. [Jarrell and Bradley (1980) and Bradley, Desai, and Kim (1988)] concludes that target gains increased after the passage of the Williams Act in 1968, presumably as a result of increased competitiveness in the bidding market. Table 5 shows the target wealth gains (months -4 to $+1$) for our U.K. sample before and after 1968. Gains to U.K. targets are higher after 1968, whether measured over three-year subperiods (1965–1967 vs. 1969–1971) or for all years in our sample. That target shareholder gains are also higher in the U.K. after 1968 suggests that increases in U.S. bid premiums may not be attributable to specific U.S. legislation such as the Williams Act. The only significant regulatory change in the U.K. around this time was a small modification in disclosure rules on toehold interests. We do not believe this modification could have significantly increased the competitiveness of the U.K. bidding market.

4.4. Revised and contested bids

We expect that multiple bids for a target will reflect less uniqueness in the market for merger benefits and, as a result, smaller gains for bidders and larger gains for targets. Alternatively, multiple bids might indicate larger aggregate merger benefits and little about their uniqueness. In this case we would expect to see higher gains to target companies than in the single-bid case, but with no

Table 6

A comparison of percentage total abnormal returns (*TAR*) arising from single, multiple, and contested bids.

TAR is calculated as the difference between the return on the stock and a control return using premerger market-model parameters. Month 0 is the earliest available of the date of the first formal bid or the date when the bidder has enough shares to guarantee control (the unconditional date). The sample period is 1955–1985.

	N^a	*Panel A: Equally weighted TARs (t-statistics in parentheses)*			
		Month 0		Months -4 to $+1$	
		Target	Bidder	Target	Bidder
1. All firms	1,445	21.9	0.0	29.7	3.0
		(61.88)	(.08)	(34.25)	(2.80)
2. Single bids (unrevised and uncontested)	1,238	20.6	0.0	27.4	3.3
		(54.58)	(.05)	(28.54)	(2.82)
3. Multiple bids a) Revised bids (uncontested)	123	28.7	0.3	40.5	0.5
		(23.80)	(.18)	(13.70)	(.18)
b) Contested bids	84	29.1	-0.4	46.6	2.6
		(23.30)	($-.35$)	(15.22)	(.87)

Panel B: t-statistics on the differences in returns[b]	Month 0	Months -4 to $+1$
Single bids versus revised bids (uncontested)	4.05	3.79
Single bids versus contested bids	3.42	4.76
Revised bids (uncontested) versus contested bids	.13	1.18

[a] N is number of targets.

[b] The calculated t-statistics test the hypothesis that the *TARs* are equal and are calculated as $t = (M_1 - M_2)/SD$, where M stands for cell mean, $SD = \sqrt{S_1^2/N_1 + S_2^2/N_2}$, N is the number of observations averaged in a cell mean, and S is the cross-sectional standard deviation about the cell mean.

compensatory fall in bidder returns. Table 6 reports wealth effects partitioned into takeovers with single bids (unrevised and uncontested) and multiple bids (revised or contested). The evidence suggests two conclusions for target firms. First, in panel A target shareholders obtain larger gains with multiple bids (by one or more bidders). Target abnormal returns are one-third to two-thirds higher when there are multiple bids. These differences are significantly different from zero at the 1% level, as shown by the large t-statistics in panel B. Second, target wealth effects are essentially the same whether there is a revised (but uncontested) bid or whether the bid is contested by a third party. The last row of panel B shows the small and insignificant t-statistics. This second result suggests that revised bids may reflect potential competition acting as a discipline in the bidding market.

240   *J.R. Franks and R.S. Harris, Wealth effects of takeovers in the U.K.*

Table 7

Wealth effects in U.S. acquisitions.

	Tenders plus mergers		Tenders only	
	Target	Bidder	Target	Bidder
Single bids	21.6%	1.8%	28.1%	0.7%
Revised bids (uncontested)	20.9%	−1.6%	35.8%	3.7%
Contested bids	29.4%	1.4%	41.5%	−0.2%

A further hypothesis is that gains to bidding firms will be smaller with multiple bids. As table 6 shows, the gains to bidders are slightly smaller with multiple bids, but the differences are not statistically significant.

Since bidders and targets may experience value gains a number of months after the first bid date as a result of the bid process, we repeat the analysis in table 6 using the unconditional date as month 0. At this date the acquirer's bid is known to succeed. TARs (-4 to $+1$) display patterns similar to those reported in table 6.

The evidence in table 6 thus suggests that, in the U.K., multiple bids reflect larger gains to the merging process, with the target receiving all the benefits. This evidence is consistent with a competitive bidding market channeling essentially all gains to target firms. As Ruback (1983) points out, however, a full investigation of the competitive state of the acquisitions market involves analyzing possible gains to all potential acquirers of a given target.

Our U.K. results for targets are quite consistent with .Bradley, Desai, and Kim's (1988) U.S. finding that multiple bidders result in abnormal returns of over 40% to target shareholders, compared with less than 30% in the single-bidder case. An even more direct comparison between the two countries is available using data from Franks and Harris (1987). Of their 1,439 takeovers, 229 are tender offers. They find table 7's wealth effects (TAR) measured over the six months beginning four months before the bid (months -4 to $+1$).[9] When these results are compared with those in table 6, four conclusions stand out. First, contested bids lead to higher target wealth effects in both countries. Second, in the U.S., revised but uncontested bids appear to be associated with higher target abnormal returns only in tender offers. Bid revisions in many mergers (nontenders) may be negotiated changes in the terms of exchange that are a natural part of a bargaining process between two management teams rather than an anticipation of other potential bidders. Third, the impact of multiple bids on target wealth effects is similar for U.S. tenders and U.K.

[9]The results use market-model control returns and cover 1,439 targets, of which 28% are multiple bids. Of the acquisitions, 229 are tenders, of which 57% are multiple bids. We report results for months -4 to $+1$, since there is often a run-up in share price prior to the bid that appears more pronounced in multiple bids.

J.R. Franks and R.S. Harris, Wealth effects of takeovers in the U.K. 241

takeovers. Since the vast majority of U.K. acquisitions are tenders, this demonstrates the importance of controlling for institutional differences such as the form of acquisition in the two countries. Fourth, while Bradley, Desai, and Kim's (1988) results on U.S. tenders provide some indication of smaller bidder returns in the multiple-bid case, our data provide no strong evidence that bidders earn substantially less in this case.

The evidence from the U.K. and U.S. thus appears consistent in supporting the view that multiple bids reflect larger total gains to the acquisition process.

4.5. Premerger equity interests

In the U.K. before 1967, companies could purchase shares in other companies, often termed toehold interests, before launching a bid, revealing those toeholds only when they exceeded 10% of the target's equity capitalization. After 1967, the threshold was lowered to 5%. Grossman and Hart (1981) have provided one important motivation for toeholds. They argue that, in a diffusely held firm, potential bidders would not have an incentive to pay the search costs for information on merger benefits because of the free-rider problem. Toehold positions can circumvent this free-rider problem if a capital gain accrues to the shares held when the bid is revealed. The share-disclosure laws in the U.K., however, would appear to constrain severely the size of the potential capital gain.

Shleifer and Vishny (1986) provide specific predictions about the effects of large premerger ownership positions. Their model assumes a firm owned by one large shareholder – the prospective bidder – and a large group of small shareholders. The large stake provides an incentive for the major shareholder (L) to monitor the target. In their model, the gains to L are limited to the capital gains on its premerger interest in the target. As the proportion of the firm's share held by L rises, a takeover becomes more likely and the price of the firm's shares increases. When the takeover does occur, the premium over the prevailing stock price paid to tendering shareholders (the takeover premium) is actually lower. Thus Shleifer and Vishny's proposition 1 states: 'An increase in the proportion of shares held by L results in a decrease in the take-over premium but an increase in the market value of the [target] firm' (p. 470).

We have partitioned toeholds at a 30% threshold, since the U.K. Takeover Panel requires a bid for the entire company when a bidder's toehold interest exceeds this figure. This rule was introduced in the early 1970s presumably because it was thought that toeholds greater than 30% conveyed a purchasing advantage. Panel A of table 8 shows that target shareholders actually receive larger gains when the bidder has a premerger interest. These larger gains occur, however, when the toehold is less than 30%. When the toehold is greater than 30%, the wealth effects are lower and about the same as those obtained in

Table 8

Percentage total abnormal returns (*TAR*s) in acquisitions partitioned by the size of the bidder's premerger equity interest (toehold).

*TAR*s are calculated as the difference between the return on the stock and a control return using premerger market-model parameters. Month 0 is the earliest available of the first bid, unconditional, or LSPD date.[a] Figures in parentheses are *t*-statistics. The sample period is 1955–1985.

		Month 0		Months −4 to +1	
	N	Target	Bidder	Target	Bidder
Panel A: All bids					
1. Without toehold	1,061	20.9	−0.5	28.5	2.7
		(54.57)	(−0.88)	(30.38)	(2.15)
2. With toehold below 30%	173	27.5	0.3	38.3	3.3
		(25.28)	(0.23)	(14.75)	(1.23)
3. With toehold above or equal to 30%	207	22.1	2.2	28.6	3.7
		(19.29)	(2.07)	(10.20)	(1.41)
Panel B: Unrevised and uncontested bids					
1. Without toehold	927	19.8	−0.3	26.4	3.1
		(43.49)	(−0.55)	(23.64)	(2.29)
2. With toehold below 30%	126	23.9	0.1	33.4	3.3
		(18.46)	(0.08)	(10.54)	(1.18)
3. With toehold above or equal to 30%	183	22.2	2.0	28.3	3.8
		(19.75)	(1.73)	(10.29)	(1.34)

[a] The first bid date is the date of the first formal bid, which is followed by the unconditional date, when enough shares have been pledged to the bidder to guarantee legal control. The LSPD date is the last date for which share returns are available (usually the delisting date).

bids where there are no toeholds. For month 0, the equally weighted *TAR* is 27.5% when toeholds of less than 30% are present versus about 20% in takeovers where no toehold exists. As a result, there is no apparent discrimination against remaining shareholders when the bidder has a toehold position. These conclusions contrast with the findings of Franks (1978), who showed higher returns to bidders with toeholds for any industry sample of mergers. Our findings that target gains are smaller in toeholds above 30% does, however, provide modest support for Shleifer and Vishny's proposition 1.

Given our prior results showing increases in target wealth gains associated with revised and contested bids, panel B focuses on toeholds when there is only a single bid. Toeholds of less than 30% are still associated with higher target wealth effects: *TAR*s are 33.4% for months −4 to +1, compared with 26.4% where no toeholds exist (the *t*-value for the difference of means is 2.27). The difference in target wealth effects associated with toeholds is, however, lower in panel B, where there are only single bids, than in panel A. The results suggest that toeholds are associated with higher target gains, but part of that difference reflects the increased probability of a revised or contested bid. Of the toeholds under 30%, 27% are accompanied by multiple bids, whereas for firms without toeholds (or with toeholds above the 30% threshold) only 15% are accompanied by multiple bids. This suggests that toeholds are often evidence of a bidder's preparation for what is expected to be a competitive bidding process.

Turning to changes in bidder shareholder wealth, panels A and B show about the same wealth effects for bidders with toeholds of less than 30% and bidders without toeholds. Bidders with toeholds of more than 30% obtain abnormal returns of about 2% in month zero; the abnormal returns are not very different, however, during the period -4 to $+1$. These results provide little indication that toeholds increase (or reduce) the competitiveness of bidding, or allow bidders to use a purchasing advantage to reap large profits at the expense of other ('nontoehold') owners of the target firm.

Our procedures may underestimate abnormal returns in takeovers where toeholds are taken if, as U.S. evidence suggests [Madden (1981) and Mikkelson and Ruback (1985)], part of the gain to targets occurs at the initiation of the toehold, which may be well before our month zero. Unfortunately, takeover offer documents, from which we gather our information on toeholds, do not disclose the dates of toehold purchase.

4.6. Cross-sectional analysis

To distinguish the effects on shareholder gains of different variables, a cross-sectional regression analysis is used on the sample of 721 pairs of target and bidding firms. For this sample, we have high-quality market-value data that allow us to control for the relative size of the merging firms, as well as the form of acquisition, the contested nature of the bid, its calendar date, and the presence of a toehold.

The following multiple regression is estimated:

$$tar_j = \beta_0 + \beta_1 \alpha_{1j} + \beta_2 \alpha_{2j} + \beta_3 \alpha_{3j} + \beta_4 \alpha_{4j} + \beta_5 \alpha_{5j} + \beta_6 \alpha_{6j} + U_j.$$

The bid premium tar_j for firm j (months -4 to $+1$) is defined in eq. (3). The α variables are coded according to the characteristics of the acquisition. Suppressing the company subscripts, the definitions are:

$\alpha_1 = 1$ if the form of acquisition is a scheme of arrangement, 0 otherwise;
$\alpha_2 = 1$ if there are multiple bids (revised or contested), 0 otherwise;
$\alpha_3 = 1$ if the announcement is after 1968, 0 otherwise;
$\alpha_4 = 1$ if there is a toehold below 30%, 0 otherwise;
$\alpha_5 = 1$ if there is a toehold equal to or above 30%, 0 otherwise;

Table 9

Coefficient estimates for cross-sectional analysis of wealth gains in U.K. acquisitions.

	Intercept	α_1	α_2	α_3	α_4	α_5	α_6	R^2
Targets	21.97	2.36	8.44	8.91	0.84	−5.1	−0.13	2.6%
	(8.32)	(0.37)	(2.41)	(2.94)	(0.22)	(−1.30)	(−1.02)	
Bidders	4.87	4.80	2.50	−2.60	−3.82	0.55	0.00	0.9%
	(2.75)	(1.15)	(1.05)	(−1.33)	(−1.48)	(0.21)	(0.00)	

α_6 is the ratio of the market value of the equity of the target to that of the bidder;

U_j is an error term assumed to be normally distributed with zero mean and constant variance.

The coefficient estimates are given in table 9 (*t*-statistics in parentheses). For targets, the coefficients are significant for multiple bids (α_2) and for the calendar date of the acquisition (α_3). After the other variables are controlled for, multiple bids are associated with higher target gains, confirming earlier results in table 6. Target gains are also higher for acquisitions announced after 1968. None of the other variables appear strongly related to target gains. Interestingly, the regression results suggest that the lower target gains in schemes of arrangement documented in table 4 appear to result from the uncontested nature of these bids and their calendar time (before rather than after 1968). These results reinforce an earlier conclusions that the post-1968 increase in U.S. target gains coincide with a similar increase in the U.K. As a result, factors others than the Williams Act appear to be at work in explaining the rising trend of target gains.

Turning to the results for bidders, none of the coefficients are significant. This is consistent with prior results.

4.7. Postmerger performance of bidders

We measure postmerger performance beginning at the unconditional date to avoid any contamination of the returns by changes in value accompanying speculation about the success of the offer. Table 10 shows very different results for postmerger performance of bidders depending on how control returns are constructed. Using the market model, the results in panel A indicate that bidder postmerger performance is negative, cumulating to about −13% by two years after the merger. These losses are more than enough to offset the small positive wealth effects for bidders shown earlier. The negative drift in bidder share prices is consistent with U.S. findings in earlier studies.

Table 10

Postmerger performance of 1,048 successful bidders in U.K. takeovers during the period
1960–1985.

Percentage total abnormal returns (*TARs*) are measured in the months after the unconditional
date, at which the bidder has enough shares to guarantee control of the target. Figures in
parentheses are *t*-statistics.

*Panel A: TARs beginning after the unconditional date and ending at various times using
different methods of forming control returns*

Model for control returns	Months after unconditional date			
	+6	+12	+18	+24
1. $\alpha = 0$, $\beta = 1.0$	3.6	3.8	5.4	4.8
	(3.80)	(2.84)	(3.29)	(2.53)
2. Market model	−0.6	−4.8	−7.3	−12.6
	(−.65)	(−3.70)	(−4.60)	(−6.88)
3. CAPM	3.6	3.8	0.5	4.5
	(3.99)	(2.98)	(.32)	(2.50)

Panel B: Total abnormal returns for months +1 to +24

	Control returns use bidder parameters			Control returns use weighted average of target and bidder parameters[a]		
	Mean	Standard error	(t)[b]	Mean	Standard error	(t)[b]
1. $\alpha = 0$, $\beta = 1.0$	4.6	1.5	(3.07)	5.5	1.8	(3.06)
2. Market model	−11.7	1.8	(−6.50)	−9.5	2.2	(−4.32)
3. CAPM	4.4	1.6	(2.75)	5.1	1.9	(2.68)

[a] α and β parameters are weighted (by market value of equity) averages of bidder and target
parameters. If either market value is missing, we exclude the observation. Therefore, results for the
$\alpha = 0$, $\beta = 1.0$ model are slightly different in the weighted and unweighted cases.
[b] The reported *t* is the mean divided by the standard error of the mean and is distributed
approximately standard normal for these sample sizes.

The other two models' results in panel A show a quite different fate for
bidders. Both show positive returns of about 4% for the two years following
the takeover. In summary then, these two models give a much different picture
and suggest that after mergers, bidder shareholders match or slightly outperform the market in general. The differences in model results are directly
attributable in this case to the cumulative effects of subtracting the α values
from the realized returns of bidding companies when the market model is
used. The average bidder α is 0.0095 per month (average $\beta = 0.92$), which
indicates that bidding firms (premerger) were outperforming the market by
almost 1% per month. A failure to repeat this performance after the merger
would show abnormal losses of over 20% over a 24-month period. The average
bidder α is substantially higher than the average of 0.0044 for targets.

A number of possible explanations exist for high premerger α's. First, the high α values may reflect problems in estimation. We have already discussed thin trading, and noted how little the adjustments affected our results (see footnote 7). Another possibility is that the bidder's premerger α and β are inappropriate control returns for the postmerger company, given that it is a portfolio combination of two firms. Panel B shows, however, that even when α and β values of the target and bidder are averaged to reflect this portfolio effect (using the premerger equity market values as weights for the merging firms), our results are not materially changed. Another interpretation is more behavioral. If bidders time mergers to take advantage of recent abnormal returns in their own stock prices, we would expect positive α's for bidders when α is measured over a premerger period. Such positive α's, if unsustainable, would introduce a negative drift in abnormal returns, which could be interpreted as too 'high' a control return rather than poor performance by bidders.[10]

The share-price results using a market model with premerger α's are consistent with the results of accounting studies in the U.S. [Ravenscraft and Scherer (1987)] and the U.K. [Meeks (1977)]. These studies generally show declines in accounting measures of profitability, such as return on investment (ROI), subsequent to merging. If the acquiring companies time mergers to coincide with ROIs that are historically high, the postmerger decline may be an inevitable deterioration that has nothing to do with the takeover.

Since bidders are typically larger firms (which also increase in size as a result of the takeover), it is also possible that our postmerger performance results are related to a size effect [Malatesta (1983) and Dimson and Marsh (1986)]. When we construct a size measure, however, we still find indications of postmerger losses to bidders.

All securities in LSPD are placed into decile portfolios each year based on size of equity market capitalization. Bidders are allocated to decile portfolios based on the combined equity market capitalization of the two merging firms at the time of the bid. Using the unconditional acceptance date, we calculate abnormal returns for the postmerger period $+1$ to $+24$. The monthly abnormal returns are the difference between the returns to the bidder and the returns (equally weighted) on the decile portfolio. Decile 1 contains the smallest firms, and the results are given in table 11.

Two points are worth noting. First, bidders are relatively large, since they are concentrated in the higher size deciles. Second, in all size groups, bidders (including larger bidders) do not perform as well as other firms of comparable

---

[10] If mergers are frequently financed by stock issues, these results are consistent with both U.S. and U.K. evidence indicating that firms issue stock after especially favorable movements in their own stock price [Jalilvand and Harris (1984), Marsh (1982)]. Further investigation of this conjecture requires control for whether takeovers are cash or equity bids [Franks, Harris, and Mayer (1988)].

Table 11

Postmerger performance in U.K. acquisitions controlling for firm size.

Decile	Sample size	Postmerger performance	Decile	Sample size	Postmerger performance
1	18	− 20.8%	6	76	− 17.9%
2	35	− 3.7%	7	97	− 8.1%
3	46	− 12.2%	8	118	− 18.7%
4	48	− 8.7%	9	209	− 14.2%
5	66	− 10.9%	10	395	− 11.7%

size. Further research might investigate performance benchmarks based on factors in addition to firm size [see Lehmann and Modest (1987) and Grinblatt and Titman (1987)].

5. Summary and conclusion

Existing evidence in the U.K. gives conflicting answers on whether mergers create value for shareholders. In a comprehensive study of U.K. acquisitions for the period 1955–1985, we find that mergers have, on average, been value-creating for shareholders as measured by equity market prices around the merger announcement date. Shareholders of targets gain, and bidder shareholders gain or do not lose. Target shareholder gains and merger benefits appear to be higher in revised or contested bids. This evidence is similar to that found in many U.S. studies. We also find higher target wealth gains when bidders hold a premerger equity interest. There is no strong evidence, however, that revised bids, contested bids, or premerger equity interests affect bidder gains around the merger date.

The postmerger performance of bidders depends on the benchmark returns against which bidders are evaluated. Bidders may time takeovers to coincide with favorable performance by their own stock. The timing of acquisitions in relation to the stock price performance of the bidding (or target) company should be, we believe, a subject for further research.

By directly comparing our U.K. results with those for the U.S., we examine the importance of institutional differences between the two countries, as well as provide insight into the generality of U.S. results. Two findings stand out. First, target wealth gains in both the U.K. and U.S. increased after 1968; this evidence casts doubt on the interpretation that the increase in the U.S. results from provisions of the Williams Act. Second, after the form of offer (tender or other) is controlled for, gains to U.S. targets are strikingly similar to those in the U.K., suggesting that the wealth effects of takeover are quite comparable in the two countries.

References

Asquith, Paul, 1983, Merger bids, uncertainty, and stockholder returns, Journal of Financial Economics 11, 51–86.

Asquith, Paul, Robert F. Bruner, and David W. Mullins, Jr., 1983, The gains to bidding firms from merger, Journal of Financial Economics 11, 121–139.

Barnes, Paul, 1984, The effect of a merger on the share price of the attacker, revisited, Accounting and Business Research 15, 45–49.

Bradley, Michael, 1980, Inter-firm tender offers and the market for corporate control, Journal of Business 53, 345–376.

Bradley, Michael, Anand Desai, and E. Han Kim, 1988, Synergistic gains from corporate acquisitions and their division between the stockholders of target and acquiring firms, Journal of Financial Economics 21, 3–40.

Brown, Stephen J. and Jerold B. Warner, 1980, Measuring security price performance, Journal of Financial Economics 8, 205–258.

Brown, Stephen J. and Jerold B. Warner, 1985, Using daily stock returns: The case of event studies, Journal of Financial Economics 14, 3–31.

Dennis, Debra K. and John J. McConnell, 1986, Corporate mergers and security returns, Journal of Financial Economics 16, 143–187.

Dimson, Elroy, 1979, Risk measurement when shares are subject to infrequent trading, Journal of Financial Economics 7, 197–226.

Dimson, Elroy, 1985, Friction in the trading process and risk measurement, LBS working paper, Economics Letters 18, 251–254.

Dimson, Elroy and Paul Marsh, 1983, The stability of U.K. risk measures and the problem of thin trading, Journal of Finance 38, 735–783.

Dimson, Elroy and Paul Marsh, 1986, Event study methodologies and the size effect: The case of UK press recommendations, Journal of Financial Economics 17, 113–142.

Dodd, Peter, 1980, Merger proposals, management discretion and stockholder wealth, Journal of Financial Economics 8, 105–138.

Dodd, Peter and Richard Ruback, 1977, Tender offers and stockholder returns: An empirical analysis, Journal of Financial Economics 4, 351–374.

Dodds, J.C. and J.P. Quek, 1985, Effect of mergers on the share price movement of the acquiring firms: A UK study, Journal of Business Finance and Accounting, Summer, 285–296.

Eckbo, Espen, 1983, Horizontal mergers, collusion and stockholder wealth, Journal of Financial Economics 11, 241–273.

Firth, Michael, 1979, The profitability of takeovers and mergers, Economic Journal 89, 316–328.

Firth, Michael, 1980, Takeovers, shareholder returns and the theory of the firm, Quarterly Journal of Economics 94, 235–260.

Franks, Julian R., 1978, Insider information and the efficiency of the acquisitions market, Journal of Banking and Finance 2, 379–393.

Franks, Julian R. and Robert S. Harris, 1986, The role of the Mergers and Monopolies Commission in merger policy: Costs and alternatives, Oxford Review of Economic Policy 2, 58–78.

Franks, Julian R. and Robert S. Harris, 1987, Takeovers in the U.S. and U.K., Unpublished manuscript (University of North Carolina, Chapel Hill, NC).

Franks, Julian R., Jack E. Broyles, and Michael J. Hecht, 1977, An industry study of the profitability of mergers in the U.K., Journal of Finance 32, 1513–1525.

Franks, Julian R., Robert S. Harris, and Colin Mayer, 1988, Means of payment in takeover: Results in the UK and US, in: A. Auerbach, ed., Corporate takeovers: Causes and consequences (University of Chicago Press, Chicago, IL).

Grinblatt, Mark and Sheridan Titman, 1987, A comparison of measures of abnormal performance on a sample of monthly mutual fund returns, Mimeo. (University of California at Los Angeles, Los Angeles, CA).

Grossman, Sanford and Oliver Hart, 1980, Takeover bids, the free-rider problem, and the theory of the corporation, Bell Journal of Economics 11, 42–64.

Grossman, Sanford and Oliver Hart, 1981, The allocational role of takeover bids in situations of asymmetric information, Journal of Finance 36, 253–270.

Halpern, Paul J., 1973, Empirical estimates of the amount of distribution of gains to companies in mergers, Journal of Business 46, 554–575.

Halpern, Paul J., 1983, Corporate acquisitions: A theory of special cases? A review of event studies applied to acquisitions, Journal of Finance 38, 297–317.

Jalilvand, Abolhassan and Robert S. Harris, 1984, Corporate behavior in adjusting to capital structure and dividend targets, Journal of Finance 39, 127–145.

Jarrell, Greg and Michael Bradley, 1980, The economic effects of federal and state regulation of cash tender offers, Journal of Law and Economics 23, 371–407.

Jarrell, Greg, James Brickley, and Jeffrey Netter, 1988, The market for corporate control: The empirical evidence since 1980, Journal of Economic Perspectives 2, 49–68.

Jensen, Michael C., 1986, Agency costs of free cash flow, corporate finance and takeovers, American Economic Review 76, 323–329.

Jensen, Michael C. and Richard Ruback, 1983, The market for corporate control: The scientific evidence, Journal of Financial Economics 11, 5–50.

Kummer, Donald R. and G. Ronald Hoffmeister, 1978, Valuation consequences of cash tender offers, Journal of Finance 33, 505–516.

Langetieg, Terrence, 1978, An application of a three-factor performance index to measure stockholder gains from merger, Journal of Financial Economics 6, 365–384.

Lehmann, Bruce and David Modest, 1987, Mutual fund performance evaluation: A comparison of benchmarks, Journal of Finance 42, 233–265.

Madden, Gerald P., 1981, Potential corporate takeovers and market efficiency: A note, Journal of Finance 36, December, 1191–1198.

Malatesta, Paul H., 1983, The wealth effect of merger activity and the objective functions of merging firms, Journal of Financial Economics 11, 155–181.

Malatesta, Paul H., 1986, Measuring abnormal performance: The event parameter approach using joint generalized least squares, Journal of Financial and Quantitative Analysis 21, 27–38.

Mandelker, Gershon, 1974, Risk and return: The case of merging firms, Journal of Financial Economics 1, 303–335.

Manne, Henry G., 1965, Mergers and the market for corporate control, Journal of Political Economy 73, 110–120.

Marsh, Paul, 1982, The choice between equity and debt: An empirical study, Journal of Finance 37, 121–144.

Meeks, G., 1977, Disappointing marriage: A study of the gains from mergers, Occasional paper 51 (Cambridge University Press, London).

Mikkelson, Wayne and Richard Ruback, 1985, An empirical study of the inter-firm equity investment process, Journal of Financial Economics 14, 523–554.

Mueller, Dennis, 1969, A theory of conglomerate mergers, Quarterly Journal of Economics 83, 643–659.

Ravenscraft, David and Frederick Scherer, 1987, Mergers, sell-offs and economic efficiency (The Brookings Institution, Washington, DC).

Röell, Ailsa, 1986, Allocative effects of take-overs under U.K. rules, Unpublished working paper (London School of Economics and NBER).

Roll, Richard, 1986, The Hubris hypothesis of corporate takeovers, Journal of Business 59, 197–216.

Ruback, Richard, 1983, Assessing competition in the market for corporate acquisitions, Journal of Financial Economics 11, 141–153.

Shleifer, Andrew and Lawrence Summers, 1988, Breach of trust in hostile takeovers, in: A. Auerbach, ed., Corporate takeovers: Causes and consequences (University of Chicago Press for NBER, Chicago, IL).

Shleifer, Andrew and Robert W. Vishny, 1986, Large shareholders and corporate control, Journal of Political Economy 94, 461–487.

Yarrow, G.K., 1985, Shareholder protection, compulsory acquisition and the efficiency of the takeover process, Journal of Industrial Economics 34, 3–16.

[3]

The Takeover Controversy: Analysis and Evidence*

Michael C. Jensen,
*University of Rochester and
Harvard Business School*[1]

Introduction

The market for corporate control is fundamentally changing the corporate landscape. Transactions in this market in 1985 were at a record level of $180 billion, 47 percent above the $122 billion in 1984. The purchase prices in 36 of the 3,000 deals exceeded a billion dollars in 1985, compared with 18 in 1984.[2] These transactions involve takeovers, mergers, and leveraged buyouts. Closely associated are corporate restructurings involving divestitures, spinoffs, and large stock repurchases for cash and debt.

The changes associated with these control transactions are causing considerable controversy. Some argue that takeovers are damaging to the morale and productivity of organizations and therefore damaging to the economy. Others argue that takeovers represent productive entrepreneurial activity that improves the control and management of assets and helps move assets to more productive uses.

The controversy has been accompanied by strong pressure on regulators and legislatures to enact restrictions that would curb activity in the market for corporate control. In the spring of 1985 there were over 20 bills under consideration in Congress that proposed new restrictions on takeovers. Within the past several years the legislatures of New York, New Jersey, Maryland, Pennsylvania, Connecticut, Illinois, Kentucky, and Michigan have passed antitake-

over laws. The Federal Reserve Board entered the fray early in 1986 when it issued its controversial new interpretation of margin rules that restricts the use of debt in takeovers.

Through dozens of studies, leading financial economists have accumulated considerable evidence and knowledge about the effects of the takeover market. Since most of the results of the work completed prior to 1984 are well summarized elsewhere,[3] I focus here on current aspects of the controversy and on new results. In a nutshell, the previous work tells us the following:

- Takeovers benefit target shareholders—premiums in hostile offers historically exceed 30 percent on average. and in recent times have averaged about 50 percent.
- Acquiring-firm shareholders on average earn about 4 percent in hostile takeovers and roughly zero in mergers.
- Takeovers do not waste credit or resources; they generate substantial gains—historically 8.4 percent of the total value of both companies. Recently the gains seem to have been even larger.
- Actions by managers that eliminate or prevent offers or mergers are most suspect as harmful to shareholders.
- Golden parachutes for top-level managers do not, on average, harm shareholders.
- The activities of takeover specialists such as Icahn,

* This article is a somewhat shortened version of Michael C. Jensen's "The Takeover Controversy: Analysis and Evidence," which will appear in the forthcoming volume. *Takeovers and Contests for Corporate Control* (Oxford University Press, 1987), edited by John Coffee. Louis Lowenstein, and Susan Rose-Ackerman. It is printed here with permission of the publisher.

1. Michael Jensen holds a joint appointment as Professor of Business Administration, Harvard Business School, and LaClare Professor of Finance and Business Administration and Director of the Managerial Economics Research Center at the University of Rochester's Graduate School of Management. This research is supported by the Division of Research, Harvard Business School, and the Managerial Economics Research Center, University of Rochester.

2. W. T. Grimm, *Mergerstat Review* (1985).

4. A detailed summary of this evidence is available in Michael C. Jensen and Richard S. Ruback, "The Market for Corporate Control: The Scientific Evidence," *Journal of Financial Economics* 11 (April, 1983); and in Michael C. Jensen, "Takeovers: Folklore and Science", *Harvard Business Review* (November/December 1984). See also Paul J Halpern., "Empirical Estimates of the Amount and Distribution of Gains to Companies in Mergers," *Journal of Business*, V. 46, No. 4 (October, 1973) pp 554-575.

Posner, Steinberg, and Pickens, on average, benefit shareholders.[5]
• Takeover gains do not come from the creation of monopoly power.

This paper analyzes the controversy surrounding takeovers and provides both theory and evidence to explain the central phenomena at issue. The paper is organized as follows. Section 2 contains basic background analysis of the forces operating in the market for corporate control—analysis which provides an understanding of the conflicts and issues surrounding takeovers and the effects of activities in this market. Section 3 discusses the conflict between managers and shareholders over the payout of free cash flow and how takeovers represent both a symptom and a resolution of the conflict. Sections 4, 5, and 6 discuss the relatively new phenomena of, respectively, junk-bond financing, the use of golden parachutes, and the practice of greenmail. Section 7 analyzes the problems the Delaware court is having in dealing with the conflicts that arise over control issues and its confused application of the business judgment rule to these cases.

The following topics are discussed:
• The reasons for takeovers and mergers in the petroleum industry and why they increase efficiency and thereby promote the national interest.
• The role of debt in bonding management's promises to pay out future cash flows, to reduce costs, and to reduce investments in low-return projects.
• The role of high-yield debt (junk bonds) in helping to eliminate mere size as a takeover deterrent.
• The effects of takeovers on the equity markets and claims that managers are pressured to behave myopically.
• The effects of antitakeover measures such as poison pills.
• The misunderstandings of the important role that "golden parachutes" play in reducing the conflicts of interests associated with takeovers and the valuable function they serve in alleviating some of the costs and uncertainty facing managers.
• The damaging effects of the Delaware court decision in Unocal vs. Mesa that allowed Unocal to make

a self-tender offer that excluded its largest shareholder (reverse greenmail).
• The problems the courts are facing in applying the model of the corporation subsumed under the traditional business judgment rule to the conflicts of interest involved in corporate control controversies.

The Market for Corporate Control — Background

The Benefits of Takeovers

The market for corporate control is creating large benefits for shareholders and for the economy as a whole. The corporate control market generates these gains by loosening control over vast amounts of resources and enabling them to move more quickly to their highest-valued use. This is a healthy market in operation, on both the takeover side and the divestiture side.

Gains to target firms. Total benefits created by the control market have been huge, as reflected in gains of $40 billion to stockholders of acquired firms in 260 tender offers alone in the period from January 1981 through May 1985.[6] This figure does not include the gains from other control transactions such as mergers, leveraged buyouts, or divestitures. Nor does it include the gains from reorganizations such as those of Phillips, Unocal and others that have been motivated by takeover attempts. (The Phillips, Unocal and ARCO reorganizations created gains of an additional $6.6 billion.) One study estimates the total premiums received by shareholders of target firms to have been approximately $75 billion in $239 billion of merger and acquisition deals in 1984 and 1985.[6a]

Gains to bidding firms. The evidence on the returns to bidding firms is mixed. The data indicate that prior to 1980 shareholders of bidding firms earned on average about zero in mergers (which tend to be voluntary) and about 4 percent of their equity value in tender offers (which tend to be hostile).[7] These differences in returns are associated with the form of payment rather than the form of the

5. Clifford G. Holderness and Dennis P. Sheehan, "Raiders or Saviors? The Evidence on Six Controversial Investors," *Journal of Financial Economics* 14 (December, 1985); and Wayne H. Mikkelson and Richard S. Ruback, "An Empirical Analysis of the Interfirm Equity Investment Process," *Journal of Financial Economics* 14 (December, 1985).

6. As estimated by the Office of the Chief Economist of the SEC and provided to the author in private communication.
6a. John D. Paulus, "Corporate Restructuring, 'Junk,' and Leverage: Too Much or Too Little?" (Morgan Stanley, February 1986).
7. See Jensen and Ruback [1983, Tables 1 and 2], cited earlier in note 4.

8

*Major changes in energy markets have required a radical restructuring
of and retrenchment in that industry; and takeovers have played an
important role in accomplishing these changes.*

offer (tender offers tend to be for cash and mergers tend to be for stock).[8]

Although there are measurement problems that make it difficult to estimate the returns to bidders as precisely as the returns to targets,[12] it appears the bargaining power of target managers, coupled with competition among potential acquirers, grants much of the acquisition benefits to selling shareholders. In addition, federal and state regulation of tender offers appears to have strengthened the hand of target firms; premiums received by target-firm shareholders increased substantially after introduction of such regulation.[13]

Causes of Current Takeover Activity

The current high level of takeover activity seems to be caused by a number of factors:
• the relaxation of restrictions on mergers imposed by the antitrust laws;
• the withdrawal of resources from industries that are growing more slowly or that must shrink;
• deregulation in the financial services, oil and gas, transportation, and broadcasting markets that is bringing about a major restructuring of those industries;
• and improvements in takeover technology, including a larger supply of increasingly sophisticated legal and financial advisers, and improvements in financing technology (for example, the strip financing commonly used in leveraged buyouts and the original issuance of high-yield non-investment-grade bonds).

Each of these factors has contributed to the increase in total takeover and reorganization activity in recent times. Moreover, the first three factors (antitrust relaxation, exit, and deregulation) are generally consistent with data showing the intensity of takeover activity by industry. For example, the value of merger and acquisition transactions by industry in the period 1981-84 (see Table 1) indicates that acquisition activity was highest in oil and gas, followed by banking and finance, insurance, food processing,

and mining and minerals. For comparison purposes, the last column of the table presents data on industry size measured as a fraction of the total value of all firms. All but two of the industries, retail and transportation, represent a larger fraction of total takeover activity than their representation in the economy as a whole.

Many areas of the U.S. economy have been experiencing slowing growth and, in some cases, even retrenchment—a phenomenon that has many causes, including substantially increased competition from foreign firms. This has increased takeover activity because takeovers play an important role in facilitating exit from an industry or activity. Major changes in energy markets have required a radical restructuring of and retrenchment in that industry; and, as discussed in detail below, takeovers have played an important role in accomplishing these changes. Deregulation of the financial service market is consistent with the high ranking in Table 1 of banking and finance and insurance. Deregulation has also been important in the transportation and broadcasting industries. Mining and minerals has been subject to many of the same forces affecting the energy industry, including the changes in the value of the dollar.

Takeovers Provide Competition for Top-level Management Jobs

The market for corporate control is best viewed as a major component of the managerial labor market. It is the arena in which different management teams compete for the rights to manage corporate resources.[14] Understanding this is crucial to understanding much of the rhetoric about the effects of hostile takeovers.

Managers formerly protected from competition for their jobs by antitrust constraints that prevented takeover of the nation's largest corporations are now facing a more demanding environment and a more uncertain future.

The development of innovative financing

8. See Yen-Sheng Huang and Ralph A. Walkling, "Differences in Residuals Associated with Acquisition Announcements: Payment, Acquisition Form, and Resistance Effects" (Manuscript, Georgia Institute of Technology and Ohio State University, November, 1985).
12. See B. Espen Eckbo, "Do Acquiring Firms Gain From Merger?" (unpublished manuscript, University of British Columbia, June, 1985). Eckbo concludes that the zero returns to U.S. bidding firms is due to difficulties in measuring the gains to bidding firms when the bidder is substantially larger than the target firm. In his sample the average Canadian bidder was approximately the same size as the average target while the average U.S. bidder is approximately 8 times the size of the average Canadian target. See also Jensen and Ruback [1983, pp 18ff.], cited earlier in note 4.
13. See Gregg Jarrell and Michael Bradley, "The Economic Effects of Federal and State Regulation of Cash Tender Offers," *Journal of Law and Economics* 23 (1980), pp. 371-40".
14. See Jensen and Ruback [1983], cited earlier in note 4.

*When the internal processes for change in large corporations are too
slow, costly, and clumsy to bring about the required restructuring or
management change, the capital markets are doing so through the
operation of the market for corporate control.*

**TABLE 1
Intensity of Industry
Takeover Activity:
1981–1984**

Intensity of industry takeover activity as measured by the value of merger and acquisition transactions in the period 1981–84 (as a percent of total takeover transactions for which valuation data are publicly reported) compared to industry size (as measured by the fraction of overall corporate market value).

Industry classification of seller	Percent of total takeover activity*	Percent of total corporate market value**
Oil and gas	26.3%	13.5%
Banking and finance	8.8	6.4
Insurance	5.9	2.9
Food processing	4.6	4.4
Mining and minerals	4.4	1.5
Conglomerate	4.4	3.2
Retail	3.6	5.2
Transportation	2.4	2 7
Leisure and entertainment	2.3	.9
Broadcasting	2.3	.7
Other	39.4	58.5

*Source: W. T. Grimm, *Mergerstat Review* (1984), p. 41.
**As of 12/31/84. Total value is measured as the sum of the market value of common equity for 4,305 companies, including 1,501 companies on the NYSE, 724 companies on the ASE plus 2,080 companies in the Over-The-Counter market. Source: *The Media General Financial Weekly*, (December 31, 1984), p. 17.

vehicles, such as high-yield, non-investment-grade bonds ("junk" bonds), has removed size as a significant impediment to competition in this market. Although they have not been widely used in takeovers yet, these new financing techniques permit small firms to obtain resources for acquisition of much larger firms by issuing claims on the value of the venture (that is, the target firm's assets) just as in any other corporate investment activity. It is not surprising that many executives of large corporations would like relief from this new competition for their jobs, but restricting the corporate control market is not the efficient way to handle the problems caused by the increased uncertainty in their contracting environment.

Takeovers Provide External Control

The internal control mechanisms of corporations, which operate through the board of directors, generally work well. On occasion, however, they break down. One important source of protection for investors in these situations is the takeover market. Other management teams that recognize an opportunity to reorganize or redeploy an organization's

assets and thereby create new value can bid for the control rights in the takeover market. To be successful, such bids must be at a premium over current market value. This gives investors an opportunity to realize part of the gains from reorganization and redeployment of the assets.

The Market for Corporate Control Is an Agent for Change

Takeovers generally occur because changing technology or market conditions require a major restructuring of corporate assets. In some cases takeovers occur because incumbent managers are incompetent. When the internal processes for change in large corporations are too slow, costly and clumsy to bring about the required restructuring or management change in an efficient way, the capital markets are doing so through the operation of the market for corporate control. In this sense, the capital markets have been responsible for bringing about substantial changes in corporate strategy in recent times.

Managers often have difficulty abandoning strategies they have spent years devising and im-

10

Some firms in the oil industry have to go out of business. This is cheaper to accomplish through merger and the orderly liquidation of marginal assets of the combined firms than by a slow, agonizing death in a competitive struggle in an industry with overcapacity.

plementing, even when those strategies no longer contribute to the organization's survival. Such changes often require abandonment of major projects, relocation of facilities, changes in managerial assignments, and closure or sale of facilities or divisions. It is easier for new top-level managers with no ties with current employees or communities to make such changes. Moreover, normal organizational resistance to change commonly lessens significantly early in the reign of new top-level managers. For example, the premium Carl Icahn was able to offer for TWA, and his victory over Texas Air in the battle for control of TWA, were made possible in part by the willingness of the TWA unions to negotiate favorable contract concessions with Icahn—concessions that TWA itself was unable to attain prior to the takeover conflict. Such organizational factors that make change easier for newcomers, coupled with a fresh view of the business, can be a major advantage to new managers after a takeover. On the other hand, lack of detailed knowledge about the firm also poses risks for new managers and increases the likelihood of mistakes.

Takeovers are particularly important in bringing about efficiencies when exit from an activity is required. The oil industry is a good example. Changing market conditions mandate a major restructuring of the petroleum industry, and none of this is the fault of management. Management, however, must adjust to the new energy environment and recognize that many old practices and strategies are no longer viable. It is particularly hard for many managers to deal with the fact that some firms in the oil industry have to go out of business. This is cheaper to accomplish through merger and the orderly liquidation of marginal assets of the combined firms than by a slow, agonizing death in a competitive struggle in an industry with overcapacity. The end of the latter process often comes in the bankruptcy courts, with high losses and unnecessary destruction of valuable parts of organizations that could be used productively by others.

In short, the external takeover market serves as a court of last resort that plays an important role in (1) creating organizational change, (2) motivating the efficient use of resources, and (3) protecting shareholders when the corporation's internal controls and board-level control mechanisms are slow, clumsy, or defunct.

Divestitures Are the Subject of Much Erroneous Criticism

If assets are to move to their most highly valued use, acquirers must be able to sell off assets to those who can use them more productively. Therefore, divestitures are a critical element in the functioning of the corporate control market, and it is thus important to avoid inhibiting them. Indeed, over 1200 divestitures occurred in 1985, a record level.[15] Labeling divestitures with emotional terms such as "bustups" is not a substitute for analysis or evidence.

Moreover, it is important to recognize that divested plants and assets do not disappear; they are reallocated. Sometimes they continue to be used in similar ways in the same industry, and in other cases they are used in very different ways and in different industries. But in all cases they are moving to uses that their new owners believe are more productive. This process is beneficial to society.

Finally, it is useful to recognize that the takeover and divestiture market provides a private market constraint against bigness for its own sake. The potential gains available to those who correctly perceive that a firm can be purchased for less than the value realizable from the sale of its components provide incentives for entrepreneurs to search out these opportunities and to capitalize on them by reorganizing such firms into smaller entities.

The mere possibility of such takeovers also motivates managers to avoid putting together uneconomic conglomerates and to break up existing ones. This is now happening. Recently it has appeared that many firms' defenses against takeovers have led to actions similar to those proposed by potential acquirers. Examples are the reorganizations occurring in the oil industry, the sale of "crown jewels," and divestitures brought on by the desire to liquidate large debts incurred to buy back stock or to make other payments to stockholders. Unfortunately, the basic economic sense of these transactions is often lost in a blur of emotional rhetoric and controversy.

The sale of a firm's crown jewels, for example, benefits shareholders when the price obtained for the division is greater than the present value of the future cash flows to the current owner. A takeover bid motivated by the desire to obtain such an underused division can stimulate current managers to re-

---

15. W. T. Grimm, *Mergerstat Review* (1985).

It is important to recognize that divested plants and assets do not disappear; they are reallocated...to uses that their new owners believe are more productive. This process is beneficial to society.

examine the economics of the firm's current structure and to sell one or more of its divisions to a third party who is willing to pay even more than the initial offerer. Brunswick's sale of its Sherwood Medical Division to American Home Products after a takeover bid by Whittaker (apparently motivated by a desire to acquire Sherwood) is an example of such a transaction. The total value to Brunswick shareholders of the price received for selling Sherwood to American Home Products plus the remaining value of Brunswick without Sherwood (the proceeds from the sale of Sherwood were distributed directly to Brunswick's shareholders) was greater than Whittaker's offer for the entire company.[16]

Managers May Behave Myopically But Markets Do Not

It has been been argued that growing institutional equity holdings and the fear of takeover cause managers to behave myopically and therefore to sacrifice long-term benefits to increase short-term profits. The arguments tend to confuse two separate issues: 1) whether *managers* are shortsighted and make decisions that undervalue future cash flows while overvaluing current cash flows (myopic managers); and 2) whether *security markets* are shortsighted and undervalue future cash flows while overvaluing near-term cash flows (myopic markets).

There is little formal evidence on the myopic managers issue, but I believe this phenomenon does occur. Sometimes it occurs when managers hold little stock in their companies and are compensated in ways that motivate them to take actions that increase accounting earnings rather than the value of the firm. It also occurs when managers make mistakes because they do not understand the forces that determine stock values.

There is much evidence inconsistent with the myopic markets view and none that supports it:

● Even casual observation of the equity markets reveals that the market values more than current earnings. It values growth as well. The mere fact that

price/earnings ratios differ widely among securities indicates the market is valuing something other than current earnings. Indeed, the essence of a growth stock is one that has large investment projects yielding few short-term cash flows but high future earnings and cash flows.
● The continuing marketability of new issues for start-up companies with little record of current earnings—the Genentechs of the world—is also inconsistent with the notion that the market does not value future earnings.
● A recent study provides evidence that (except in the oil industry) stock prices respond positively to announcements of increased investment expenditures, and negatively to reduced expenditures.[17] This evidence is inconsistent with the notion that the equity market is myopic.
● The vast evidence on efficient markets indicating that current stock prices appropriately incorporate all currently available public information is also inconsistent with the myopic markets hypothesis. Although the evidence is not literally 100 percent in support of the efficient market hypothesis, there is no better documented proposition in any of the social sciences.[18]

The evidence indicates, for example, that the market appropriately interprets the implications of corporate accounting changes that increase reported profits but cause no change in corporate cash flows.[19]

Additional evidence is provided by the 30 percent increase in ARCO's stock price that occurred when it announced its major restructuring in 1985. This price increase is inconsistent with the notion that the market values only short-term earnings. Even though ARCO simultaneously revealed that it would have to take a $1.2 billion write-off as a result of the restructuring, the market still responded positively.
● Recent versions of the myopic markets hypothesis emphasize increasing institutional holdings and the pressures institutional investors face to show high returns on a quarter-to-quarter basis. It is argued that these pressures on institutions are a major cause of pressures on corporations to generate high current

16. See the analysis in Jensen [1984, p. 119], cited in note 4.

17. John J. McConnell and Chris J. Muscarella, "Corporate Capital Expenditure Decisions and the Market Value of the Firm," *Journal of Financial Economics* 14, No. 3 (1985).

18. For an introduction to the literature and empirical evidence on the theory of efficient markets, see E. Elton and M. Gruber, *Modern Portfolio Theory and Investment Analysis*, (New York: Wiley, 1984). Chapter 15, p. 375ff. and the 167 studies referenced in the bibliography.

19. Examples are switches from accelerated to straight-line depreciation techniques and adoption of the flow-through method for reporting investment tax credits. Here the evidence indicates that "security prices increase around the date when a firm first announces earnings inflated by an accounting change. The effect appears to be temporary; and, certainly by the subsequent quarterly report, the price has resumed a level appropriate to the true economic status of the firm." See R. Kaplan and R. Roll, "Investor Evaluation of Accounting Information: Some Empirical Evidence," *Journal of Business*, (April, 1972), 225-257

12

---

*I believe this phenomenon [myopic managerial behavior] does occur.
Sometimes it occurs when managers hold little stock in their companies
and are compensated in ways that motivate them to take actions that
increase accounting earnings rather than the value of the firm.*

earnings on a quarter-to-quarter basis. The institutional pressures are said to lead to increased takeovers of firms (because institutions are not loyal shareholders) and to decreased research and development expenditures. It is argued that because R&D expenditures reduce current earnings, firms making them are therefore more likely to be taken over, and that reductions in R&D are leading to a fundamental weakening of the corporate sector of the economy.

A recent study of 324 firms by the Office of the Chief Economist of the SEC finds substantial evidence that is inconsistent with this version of the myopic markets argument.[20] The evidence indicates the following:
• increased institutional stock holdings are not associated with increased takeovers of firms;
•increased institutional holdings are not associated with decreases in research and development expenditures;
• firms with high research and development expenditures are not more vulnerable to takeovers;
• stock prices respond positively to announcements of increases in research and development expenditures.

Those who make the argument that takeovers are reducing R&D spending also have to come to grips with the aggregate data on such spending, which is inconsistent with the argument. Total spending on R&D in 1984, a year of record acquisition activity, increased by 14 percent according to *Business Week's* annual survey of 820 companies. (The sample companies account for 95 percent of total private-sector R&D expenditures.) This represented "the biggest gain since R&D spending began a steady climb in the late 1970s."[21] All industries in the survey increased R&D spending with the exception of steel. Moreover, R&D spending increased from 2 percent of sales, where it had been for five years, to 2.9 percent.

An Alternative Hypothesis

There is an alternative hypothesis that explains the current situation, including the criticisms of management, quite well.

Suppose that some managers are simply mistaken—that is, their strategies are wrong—and that the financial markets are telling them they are wrong. If they don't change, their stock prices will remain low. If the managers are indeed wrong, it is desirable for the stockholders and for the economy to remove them to make way for a change in strategy and more efficient use of the resources.

Free Cash Flow Theory of Takeovers[22]

More than a dozen separate forces drive takeover activity, including such factors as deregulation, synergies, economies of scale and scope, taxes, managerial incompetence, and increasing globalization of U.S. markets.[23] One major cause of takeover activity are the agency costs associated with conflicts between managers and shareholders over the payout of corporate free cash flow. Though this has received relatively little attention, it has played an important role in acquisitions over the last decade.

Managers are the agent of shareholders, and because both parties are self-interested, there are serious conflicts between them over the choice of the best corporate strategy. Agency costs are the total costs that arise in such cooperative arrangements. They consist of the costs of monitoring managerial behavior (such as the costs of producing audited financial statements and devising and implementing compensation plans that reward managers for actions that increase investors' wealth) and the inevitable costs that are incurred because the conflicts of interest can never be resolved perfectly. Sometimes these costs can be large and, when they are, takeovers can reduce them.

Free Cash Flow and the Conflict Between Managers and Shareholders

Free cash flow is cash flow in excess of that required to fund all projects that have positive net values when discounted at the relevant cost of capital. Such free cash flow must be paid out to share-

---

20. Office of the Chief Economist, Securities and Exchange Commission, "Institutional Ownership, Tender Offers, and Long-Term Investments," April 19, 1985.

21. "R&D Scoreboard: Reagan & Foreign Rivalry Light a Fire Under Spending", *Business Week*, July 8, 1985), p. 86 ff.

22. This discussion is based on my article, "Agency Costs of Free Cash Flow, Corporate Finance and Takeovers," forthcoming in *American Economic Review*, (May, 1986)

23. Richard Roll discusses a number of these forces in "Empirical Evidence on Takeover Activity and Shareholder Wealth," (presented at the Conference on Takeovers and Contests for Corporate Control, Columbia University, November, 1985)

*Free cash flow [that which cannot be profitably reinvested by
management inside the firm] must be paid out to shareholders if the
firm is to be efficient and to maximize value for shareholders.*

holders if the firm is to be efficient and to maximize
value for shareholders.

Payment of cash to shareholders reduces the
resources under managers' control, thereby reducing managers' power, and potentially subjecting
them to the monitoring by the capital markets that
occurs when a firm must obtain new capital. Financing projects internally avoids this monitoring and the
possibility that funds will be unavailable or available
only at high explicit prices.

Managers have incentives to expand their firms
beyond the size that maximizes shareholder
wealth.[24] Growth increases managers' power by increasing the resources under their control. In addition, changes in management compensation are
positively related to growth.[25] The tendency of firms
to reward middle managers through promotion
rather than year-to-year bonuses also creates an organizational bias toward growth to supply the new
positions that such promotion-based reward systems
require.[25a]

The tendency for managers to overinvest
resources is limited by competition in the product
and factor markets, which tends to drive prices toward
minimum average cost in an activity. Managers must
therefore motivate their organizations to be more efficient to improve the probability of survival. Product
and factor market disciplinary forces are often weaker
in new activities, however, and in activities that involve substantial economic rents or quasi-rents.[26] In
these cases, monitoring by the firm's internal control
system and the market for corporate control are more
important. Activities yielding substantial economic
rents or quasi-rents are the types of activities that generate large amounts of free cash flow.

Conflicts of interest between shareholders and
managers over payout policies are especially severe
when the organization generates substantial free
cash flow. The problem is how to motivate managers

to disgorge the cash rather than invest it at below the
cost of capital or waste it through organizational
inefficiencies.

Some finance scholars have argued that financial flexibility (unused debt capacity and internally
generated funds) is desirable when a firm's
managers have better information about the firm
than outside investors.[26a] Their arguments assume
that managers act in the best interest of shareholders. The arguments offered here imply that such
flexibility has costs: financial flexibility in the form of
free cash flow, large cash balances, and unused
borrowing power provides managers with greater
discretion over resources that is often not used in the
shareholders' interests.

The theory developed here explains (1) how
debt-for-stock exchanges reduce the organizational
inefficiencies fostered by substantial free cash flow,
(2) how debt can substitute for dividends, (3) why
"diversification" programs are more likely to be associated with losses than are expansion programs in
the same line of business, (4) why mergers within an
industry and liquidation-motivated takeovers will
generally create larger gains than cross-industry
mergers, (5) why the factors stimulating takeovers in
such diverse businesses as broadcasting, tobacco, cable systems and oil are essentially identical, and (5)
why bidders and some targets tend to show abnormally good performance prior to takeover.

The Role of Debt in Motivating Organizational Efficiency

The agency costs of debt have been widely discussed,[27] but the benefits of debt in motivating
managers and their organizations to be efficient have
largely been ignored. I call these effects the "control
hypothesis" for debt creation.

24. See Gordon Donaldson, *Managing Corporate Wealth*, (Praeger: 1984).
Donaldson, in a detailed study of 12 large Fortune 500 firms, concludes that
managers of these firms were not driven by maximization of the value of the firm,
but rather by the maximization of "corporate wealth." He defines corporate
wealth as "*the aggregate purchasing power available to management for
strategic purposes during any given planning period* ... this wealth consists of
the stocks and flows of cash and cash equivalents (primarily credit) that management can use at its discretion to implement decisions involving the control of
goods and services." (p. 3, emphasis in original) "In practical terms it is cash,
credit, and other corporate purchasing power by which management commands
goods and services." (p.22).
25. Where growth is measured by increases in sales See Kevin J. Murphy,
"Corporate Performance and Managerial Remuneration An Empirical Analysis,"
Journal of Accounting and Economics 7, Nos. 1-3 (April. 1985). pp. 11-42 This
positive relationship between compensation and sales growth does not imply,
although it is consistent with, causality.

25a. See George Baker, "Compensation and Hierarchies" (unpublished,
Harvard Business School, January, 1986).
26. Rents are returns in excess of the opportunity cost of the resources
committed to the activity. Quasi-rents are returns in excess of the short-run
opportunity cost of the resources to the activity.
26a. See Stewart C. Myers and Nicholas S. Majluf, "Corporate Financing and
Investment Decisions When Firms Have Information That Investors Do Not
Have,' *Journal of Financial Economics* 13 (1984), pp. 187-221.
27. See Michael C. Jensen and William H. Meckling, "Theory of the Firm:
Managerial Behavior, Agency Costs and Ownership Structure," *Journal of Financial Economics*, V. 3 (1976), pp. 305-360; Stewart C. Myers, "Determinants of
Corporate Borrowing," *Journal of Financial Economics*, V. 5, No. 2 (1977), pp.
147-175; and Clifford W. Smith, Jr. and Jerold B. Warner, "On Financial Contracting: An Analysis of Bond Covenants," *Journal of Financial Economics*, V. 7 (1979),
pp. 117-161.

14

The control function of debt is more important in organizations that generate large cash flows but have low growth prospects, and it is even more important in organizations that must shrink.

Managers with substantial free cash flow can increase dividends or repurchase stock and thereby pay out current cash that would otherwise be invested in low-return projects or otherwise wasted. This payout leaves managers with control over the use of future free cash flows, but they can also promise to pay out future cash flows by announcing a "permanent" increase in the dividend.[28] Because there is no contractual obligation to make the promised dividend payments, such promises are weak. Dividends can be reduced by managers in the future with little effective recourse to shareholders. The fact that capital markets punish dividend cuts with large stock price reductions is an interesting equilibrium market response to the agency costs of free cash flow.[29]

Debt creation, without retention of the proceeds of the issue, enables managers effectively to bond their promise to pay out future cash flows. Thus, debt can be an effective substitute for dividends, something that is not generally recognized in the corporate finance literature.[30] By issuing debt in exchange for stock, managers bond their promise to pay out future cash flows in a way that simple dividend increases do not. In doing so, they give shareholder-recipients of the debt the right to take the firm into bankruptcy court if they do not keep their promise to make the interest and principal payments.[31] Thus, debt reduces the agency costs of free cash flow by reducing the cash flow available for spending at the discretion of managers.

Issuing large amounts of debt to buy back stock sets up organizational incentives to motivate managers to pay out free cash flow. In addition, the exchange of debt for stock also helps managers overcome the normal organizational resistance to retrenchment that the payout of free cash flow often requires. The threat of failure to make debt-service payments serves as a strong motivating force to make

such organizations more efficient. Stock repurchase for debt or cash also has tax advantages. Interest payments are tax-deductible to the corporation; the part of the repurchase proceeds equal to the seller's tax basis in the stock is not taxed at all, and that which is taxed is subject to capital-gains rates.

The control hypothesis does not imply that debt issues will always have positive control effects. For example, these effects will not be as important for rapidly growing organizations with large and highly profitable investment projects but no free cash flow. Such organizations will have to go regularly to the financial markets to obtain capital. At these times the markets will have an opportunity to evaluate the company, its management, and its proposed projects. Investment bankers and analysts play an important role in this monitoring, and the market's assessment is made evident by the price investors pay for the financial claims.

The control function of debt is more important in organizations that generate large cash flows but have low growth prospects, and it is even more important in organizations that must shrink. In these organizations the pressures to waste cash flows by investing them in uneconomic projects are most serious.

[The original paper contains a section here entitled "Evidence from Financial Transactions in Support of the Free Cash Flow Theory of Mergers," which appears in the "Appendix" to this article.]

The Evidence from Leveraged Buyout and Going-Private Transactions

Many of the benefits of going-private and leveraged buyout transactions seem to be due to the control function of debt. These transactions are creating a new organizational form that competes

28. Interestingly, Graham and Dodd, in their treatise, *Security Analysis*, placed great importance on the dividend payout in their famous valuation formula: V = M (D + .33E),(p.454). V is value, M is the earnings multiplier when the dividend payout rate is a "normal two-thirds of earnings," D is the expected dividend, and E is expected earnings. In their formula, dividends are valued at three times the rate of retained earnings, a proposition that has puzzled many students of modern finance (at least of my vintage). The agency cost of free cash flow that leads to overretention and waste of shareholder resources is consistent with the deep suspicion with which Graham and Dodd viewed the lack of payout. Their discussion (chapter 34) reflects a belief in the tenuous nature of the future benefits of such retention. Although they do not couch the issues in terms of the conflict between managers and shareholders, the free cash flow theory explicated here implies that their beliefs, sometimes characterized as "a bird in the hand is worth two in the bush," were perhaps well founded. See Chapters 32, 34, and 36 in Benjamin Graham and David L. Dodd, *Security Analysis: Principles and Technique* (New York, McGraw-Hill, 1951).

29. See Guy Charest, "Dividend Information, Stock Returns, and Market Efficiency-II, *Journal of Financial Economics* 6, (1978), pp. 297-330; and Joseph Aharony and Itzhak Swary, "Quarterly Dividend and Earnings Announcements and Stockholder's Returns: An Empirical Analysis," *Journal of Finance* 35 (1980), pp. 1-12.

30. Literally, principal and interest payments are substitutes for dividends. However, because interest is tax-deductible at the corporate level and dividends are not, dividends and debt are not perfect substitutes.

31. Two studies argue that regular dividend payments can be effective in reducing agency costs with managers by assuring that managers are forced more frequently to subject themselves and their policies to the discipline of the capital markets when they acquire capital. See Frank H. Easterbrook, "Managers' Discretion and Investors' Welfare: Theories and Evidence," *Delaware Journal of Corporate Law*, V. 9, No. 3 (1984b), pp. 540-571; and Michael Rozeff, "Growth, Beta and Agency Costs as Determinants of Dividend Payout Ratios", *Journal of Financial Research*, V 5 (1982), pp. 249-59.

*If managers [of companies with strip financing] withhold dividends to
invest in value-reducing projects or if they are simply incompetent, strip
holders have recourse to remedial powers not available to the equity
holders [in firms without strip financing].*

successfully with the open corporate form because
of advantages in controlling the agency costs of free
cash flow. In 1984, going-private transactions totaled
$10.8 billion and represented 27 percent of all
public acquisitions.[36] The evidence indicates
premiums paid averaged over 50 percent.[37]

Desirable leveraged buyout candidates are
frequently firms or divisions of larger firms that have
stable business histories and substantial free cash
flow (that is, low growth prospects and high potential for generating cash flows)—situations where
agency costs of free cash flow are likely to be high.
Leveraged buyout transactions are frequently financed with high debt; ten-to-one ratios of debt to
equity are not uncommon. Moreover, the use of strip
financing and the allocation of equity in the deals
reveal a sensitivity to incentives, conflicts of interest,
and bankruptcy costs.

Strip financing, the practice in which risky non-
equity securities are held in approximately equal
proportions, limits the conflict of interest among such
security holders and therefore limits bankruptcy
costs. A somewhat oversimplified example illustrates
the point. Consider two firms identical in every
respect except financing. Firm A is entirely financed
with equity, and Firm B is highly leveraged with senior subordinated debt, convertible debt, and preferred as well as equity. Suppose Firm B securities are
sold only in strips—that is, a buyer purchasing X percent of any security must purchase X percent of all
securities, and the securities are "stapled" together so
they cannot be separated later. Security holders of
both firms have identical unlevered claims on the
cash flow distribution, but organizationally the two
firms are very different. If Firm B managers withhold
dividends to invest in value-reducing projects or if
they are simply incompetent, strip holders have recourse to remedial powers not available to the equity
holders of Firm A. Each Firm B security specifies the
rights its holder has in the event of default on its
dividend or coupon payment—for example, the right
to take the firm into bankruptcy or to have board representation. As each security above equity goes into
default the strip holder receives new rights to inter-
cede in the organization. As a result, it is quicker and
less expensive to replace managers in Firm B.

Moreover, because every security holder in the
highly levered Firm B has the same claim on the
firm, there are no conflicts between senior and junior claimants over reorganization of the claims in the
event of default; to the strip holder it is a matter of
moving funds from one pocket to another. Thus,
Firm B need never go into bankruptcy. The reorganization can be accomplished voluntarily, quickly, and
with less expense and disruption than through bankruptcy proceedings.

Securities commonly subject to strip practices
are often called "mezzanine" financing and include
securities with priority superior to common stock
yet subordinate to senior debt. This seems to be a
sensible arrangement. Because of several other
factors ignored in our simplified example, IRS
restrictions deny tax deductibility of debt interest in
such situations and bank holdings of equity are
restricted by regulation. Riskless senior debt need
not be in the strip because there are no conflicts with
other claimants in the event of reorganization when
there is no probability of default on its payments.

It is advantageous to have top-level managers
and venture capitalists who promote the transactions
hold a larger share of the equity. Top-level managers
frequently receive 15 to 20 percent of the equity, and
venture capitalists and the funds they represent generally retain the major share of the remainder. The
venture capitalists control the board of directors and
monitor managers. Managers and venture capitalists
have a strong interest in making the venture
successful because their equity interests are
subordinate to other claims. Success requires,
among other things, implementation of changes to
avoid investment in low-return projects in order to
generate the cash for debt service and to increase the
value of equity. Finally, when the equity is held primarily by managers or generally by a small number
of people, greater efficiencies in risk bearing are
made possible by placing more of the risk in the
hands of debt holders when the debt is held in well-
diversified institutional portfolios.

Less than a handful of these leveraged buyout
ventures have ended in bankruptcy, although more
have gone through private reorganizations. A thorough test of this organizational form requires the
passage of time and another recession.

Some have asserted that managers engaging in a

36. By number. See W. T. Grimm, Mergerstat Review (1985), Figs. 36 and 37.
37. See H. DeAngelo, L. DeAngelo and E. Rice, "Going Private: Minority
Freezeouts and Stockholder Wealth," *Journal of Law and Economics*, V. 27, No. 2
(October, 1984), pp. 367-401; and Louis Lowenstein, "Management Buyouts,"
Columbia Law Review, V. 85 (May, 1985), pp. 730-784. Lowenstein also
mentions incentive effects of debt but argues tax effects play a major role in
explaining the value increase.

16

Because the venture capitalists are generally the largest shareholder and control the board of directors, they have both greater ability and stronger incentives to monitor managers than directors representing diffuse public shareholders in the typical public corporation.

buyout of their firm are insulating themselves from monitoring. The opposite is true in the typical leveraged buyout. Because the venture capitalists are generally the largest shareholder and control the board of directors, they have both greater ability and incentives to monitor managers effectively than directors representing diffuse public shareholders in the typical public corporation.

Evidence from the Oil Industry

The oil industry is large and visible. It is also an industry in which the importance of takeovers in motivating change and efficiency is particularly clear. Therefore, detailed analysis of it provides an understanding of how the market for corporate control helps motivate more efficient use of resources in the corporate sector.

Reorganization of the industry is mandatory. Radical changes in the energy market from 1973 through the late 1970s imply that a major restructuring of the petroleum industry had to occur. These changes are as follows:

• a ten-fold increase in the price of crude oil from 1973 to 1979;
• reduced annual consumption of oil in the U.S.;
• reduced expectations of future increases in the price of oil;
• increased exploration and development costs;
• and increased real interest rates.

As a result of these changes the optimal level of refining and distribution capacity and crude reserves fell over this period, and since the late 1970s the industry has been plagued with excess capacity. Reserves are reduced by reducing the level of exploration and development, and it pays to concentrate these reductions in high-cost areas such as the United States.

Substantial reductions in exploration and development and in refining and distribution capacity meant that some firms had to leave the industry. This is especially true because holding reserves is subject to economies of scale, whereas exploration and development are subject to diseconomies of scale.

Price increases created large cash flows in the industry. For example, 1984 cash flows of the ten largest oil companies were $48.5 billion, 28 percent of the total cash flows of the top 200 firms in Dun's Business Month [1985] survey. Consistent with the agency costs of free cash flow, management did not pay out the excess resources to shareholders. Instead, the industry continued to spend heavily on exploration and development even though average returns on these expenditures were below the cost of capital.

Paradoxically, the profitability of oil exploration and drilling activity can decrease even though the price of oil increases if the value of reserves in the ground falls. This can happen when the price increase is associated with reductions in consumption that make it difficult to market newly discovered oil. In the late 1970s the increased holding costs associated with higher real interest rates, reductions in expected future oil price increases, increased exploration and development costs, and reductions in the consumption of oil combined to make many exploration and development projects uneconomic. The industry, however, continued to spend heavily on such projects.

The hypothesis that oil-industry exploration and development expenditures were too high during this period is consistent with the findings of the earlier-mentioned study by McConnell and Muscarella.[38] Their evidence indicates that announcements of increases in exploration and development expenditures by oil companies in the period 1975-1981 were associated with systematic decreases in the announcing firms' stock prices. Moreover, announcements of decreases in exploration and development expenditures were associated with increases in stock prices. These results are striking in comparison with their evidence that exactly the opposite market reaction occurs with increases and decreases in investment expenditures by industrial firms, and with SEC evidence that increases in research and development expenditures are associated with increased stock prices.[38a]

Additional evidence of the uneconomic nature of the oil industry's exploration and development expenditures is contained in a study by Bernard

---

38. John J. McConnell and Chris J. Muscarella, "Corporate Capital Expenditure Decisions and the Market Value of the Firm," *Journal of Financial Economics*, V. 14, No. 3 (1985).
38a. Office of the Chief Economist, Securities and Exchange Commission, "Institutional Ownership, Tender Offers, and Long-Term Investments," April 19, 1985.

Wall Street was not undervaluing the oil; it was valuing it correctly, but it was also correctly valuing the wasted expenditures on exploration and development that oil companies were making.

Picchi of Salomon Brothers. His study of rates of return on exploration and development expenditures for 30 large oil firms indicated that on average the industry did not earn "even a 10% return on its pretax outlays" in the period 1982-84. Estimates of the average ratio of the present value of future net cash flows of discoveries, extensions and enhanced recovery to expenditures for exploration and development for the industry ranged from less than .6 to slightly more than .9, depending on the method used and the year. In other words, even taking the cost of capital to be only 10 percent on a pretax basis, the industry was realizing on average only 60 to 90 cents on every dollar invested in these activities. Picchi concludes:

For 23 of the [30] companies in our survey, we would recommend immediate *cuts of perhaps 25%-30% in exploration and production spending. It is clear that much of the money that these firms spent last year on petroleum exploration and development yielded subpar financial returns—even at $30 per barrel, let alone today's $26-$27 per barrel price structure."[39]*

The waste associated with excessive exploration and development expenditures explains why buying oil on Wall Street was considerably cheaper than obtaining it by drilling holes in the ground, even after adjustment for differential taxes and regulations on prices of old oil. Wall Street was not undervaluing the oil; it was valuing it correctly, but it was also correctly valuing the wasted expenditures on exploration and development that oil companies were making. When these managerially imposed "taxes" on the reserves were taken into account, the net price of oil on Wall Street was very low. This provided incentives for firms to obtain reserves by purchasing other oil companies and reducing expenditures on non-cost-effective exploration.

High profits are not usually associated with retrenchment. Adjustment by the energy industry to the new environment has been slow for several reasons. First, it is difficult for organizations to change operating rules and practices like those in the oil industry that have worked well for long periods in the past, even though they do not fit the new situation. Nevertheless, survival requires that organizations adapt to major changes in their environment.

Second, the past decade has been a particularly puzzling period in the oil business because at the same time that changes in the environment have required a reduction of capacity, cash flows and profits have been high. This is a somewhat unusual condition in which the average productivity of resources in the industry increased while the marginal productivity decreased. The point is illustrated graphically in Figure 1.

As the figure illustrates, profits plus payments to factors of production other than capital were larger in 1985 than in 1973. Moreover, because of the upward shift and simultaneous twist of the marginal productivity of capital schedule from 1973 to 1985, the optimal level of capital devoted to the industry fell from Q_1 to Q_2. Thus, the adjustment signals were confused because the period of necessary retrenchment coincided with substantial increases in value brought about by the tenfold increase in the price of the industry's major asset, its inventory of crude oil reserves.

The large cash flows and profits generated by the increases in oil prices both masked the losses imposed on marginal facilities and enabled oil companies to finance major expenditures internally. Thus, the normal disciplinary forces of the product market have been weak, and those of the capital markets have been inoperative, during the past decade.

Third, the oil companies' large and highly visible profits subjected them to strong political pressures to reinvest the cash flows in exploration and development to respond to the incorrect, but popular, perception that reserves were too low. Furthermore, while reserves were on average too high, those firms which were substantially short of reserves were spending to replenish them to avoid the organizational consequences associated with reserve deficiencies. The resulting excessive exploration and development expenditures by the industry and the considerable delays in retrenchment of refining and distribution facilities wasted resources.

In sum, the stage was set for retrenchment in the oil industry in the early 1980s. Yet the product and capital markets could not force management to change its strategy because the industry's high internal cash flows insulated it from these pressures.

The fact that oil industry managers tried to invest funds outside the industry is also evidence that they could not find enough profitable projects within the industry to use the huge inflow of resources

39. Bernard J. Picchi, "The Structure of the U.S. Oil Industry: Past and Future" (Salomon Brothers Inc.) July, 1985, emphasis in original.

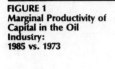

Partly as a result of Mesa's efforts, firms in the [oil] industry were led to merge, and in the merging process they paid out large amounts of capital to shareholders, reduced excess expenditures on exploration and development, and reduced excess capacity in refining and distribution.

FIGURE 1
Marginal Productivity of Capital in the Oil Industry:
1985 vs. 1973

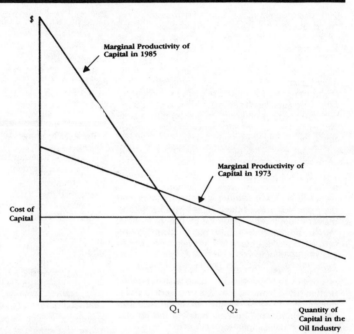

efficiently. Unfortunately these efforts failed. The diversification programs involved purchases of companies in retailing (Marcor by Mobil), manufacturing (Reliance Electric by Exxon), office equipment (Vydec by Exxon), and mining (Kennecott by Sohio, Anaconda Minerals by ARCO, Cyprus Mines by Amoco). These acquisitions turned out to be among the least successful of the last decade, partly because of bad luck (e.g., the collapse of the minerals industry) and partly because of a lack of managerial expertise outside the oil industry.

The effects of takeovers. Ultimately the capital markets, through the takeover market, have begun to force managers to respond to the new market conditions. Unfortunately, there is widespread confusion about the important role of takeovers in

bringing about the difficult but necessary organizational changes required in the retrenchment.

Managers, quite naturally, want large amounts of resources under their control to insulate them from the uncertainties of markets.[40] Retrenchment requires cancellation or delay of many ongoing and planned projects. This affects the careers of the people involved, and the resulting resistance means that such changes frequently do not get made without the major pressures associated with a crisis. A takeover attempt can create the crisis that brings about action where none would otherwise occur.

T. Boone Pickens of Mesa Petroleum perceived early that the oil industry must be restructured. Partly as a result of Mesa's efforts, firms in the industry were led to merge, and in the merging process they

40. See Gordon Donaldson. *Managing Corporate Wealth* (Praeger: 1984).

*Horizontal mergers for cash or debt in declining industries generate
gains by encouraging exit of resources (through payout to shareholders)
and by substituting existing capacity for investment in new facilities by
firms that are short of capacity.*

paid out large amounts of capital to shareholders, reduced excess expenditures on exploration and development, and reduced excess capacity in refining and distribution.

The result has been large gains in efficiency. Total gains to the shareholders in the Gulf-Chevron, Getty-Texaco and Dupont-Conoco mergers, for example, were over $17 billion. Much more is possible. A study by Allen Jacobs estimates that, as of December 1984, the total potential gains from eliminating the inefficiencies in 98 petroleum companies amounted to roughly $200 billion.[41]

Recent events indicate that actual takeover is not necessary to bring about the required adjustments:

• The Phillips restructuring plan, in response to the threat of takeover, has involved substantial retrenchment and return of resources to shareholders: and the result was a $1.2 billion (20%) gain in Phillips' market value. It repurchased 53 percent of its stock for $4.5 billion in debt, raised its dividend 25 percent, cut capital spending and initiated a program to sell $2 billion of assets.

• Unocal's defense in the Mesa tender offer battle resulted in a $2.2 billion (35%) gain to shareholders from retrenchment and return of resources to shareholders. It paid out 52 percent of its equity by repurchasing stock with a $4.2 billion debt issue and will reduce costs and capital expenditures.

• The voluntary restructuring announced by ARCO resulted in a $3.2 billion (30%) gain in market value. ARCO's restructuring involves a 35 to 40 percent cut in exploration and development expenditures, repurchase of 25 percent of its stock for $4 billion, a 33 percent increase in its dividend, withdrawal from gasoline marketing and refining east of the Mississippi, and a 13 percent reduction in its work force.

• The announcement of the Diamond-Shamrock reorganization in July 1985 provides an interesting contrast to the others and further support for the theory because the company's market value *fell* 2 percent on the announcement day. Because the plan results in an effective increase in exploration and capital expenditures and a reduction in cash payouts to investors, the restructuring does not increase the value of the firm. The plan involved reducing cash

dividends by $.76/share (−43%), creating a master limited partnership to hold properties accounting for 35 percent of its North American oil and gas production, paying an annual $.90/share dividend in partnership shares, repurchasing 6 percent of its shares for $200 million, selling 12 percent of its master limited partnership to the public, and *increasing* its expenditures on oil and gas exploration by $100 million per year.

Free Cash Flow Theory of Takeovers

Free cash flow is only one of approximately a dozen theories to explain takeovers, all of which are of some relevance in explaining the numerous forces motivating merger and acquisition activity.[41a] The agency cost of free cash flow is consistent with a wide range of data for which there has been no consistent explanation. Here I sketch some empirical predictions of the free cash flow theory for takeovers and mergers, and what I believe are the facts that lend it credence.

The positive market response to debt creation in oil and other takeovers is consistent with the agency costs of free cash flow and the control hypothesis of debt.[41b] The data is consistent with the notion that additional debt has increased efficiency by forcing organizations with large cash flows but few high-return investment projects to pay out cash to investors. The debt helps prevent such firms from wasting resources on low-return projects.

Acquisitions are one way managers spend cash instead of paying it out to shareholders. Therefore, free cash flow theory predicts which kinds of mergers and takeovers are more likely to destroy rather than to create value. It shows how takeovers are both evidence of the conflicts of interest between the shareholders and managers and a response to the problem. The theory implies that managers of firms with unused borrowing power and large free cash flows are more likely to undertake low-benefit or even value-destroying mergers. Diversification programs generally fit this category, and the theory predicts they will generate lower total gains. The major benefit of such diversifying transactions may be that they involve less waste of resources than if the funds had been invested

41. Allen Jacobs. "The Agency Cost of Corporate Control: The Petroleum Industry." (MIT, unpublished paper. March. 1986.)

41a. See Roll. 1986, cited earlier.
41b. See Robert Bruner. "The Use of Excess Cash and Debt Capacity as a Motive for Merger." (unpublished. Colgated Darden Graduate School of Business, December. 1985.)

20

Firms with a mismatch between growth and resources—firms with high growth, low liquidity, and high leverage, and firms with low growth, high liquidity, and lower leverage—are more likely to be taken over.

internally in unprofitable projects.[41c]

Low-return mergers are more likely to occur in industries with large cash flows where the economics dictate retrenchment. Horizontal mergers (where cash or debt is the form of payment) within declining industries will tend to create value because they facilitate exit; the cash or debt payments to shareholders of the target firm cause resources to leave the industry directly. Mergers outside the industry are more likely to have low or even negative returns because managers are likely to know less about managing such firms.

Oil fits this description and so does tobacco. Tobacco firms face declining demand as a result of changing smoking habits, but they generate large free cash flow and have been involved in major diversifying acquisitions recently—for example, the $5.6 billion purchase of General Foods by Philip Morris. The theory predicts that these acquisitions in non-related industries are more likely to create negative productivity effects—though these negative effects appear to be outweighed by the reductions in waste from internal expansion.

Forest products is another industry with excess capacity and acquisition activity, including the acquisition of St. Regis by Champion International and Crown Zellerbach by Sir James Goldsmith. Horizontal mergers for cash or debt in such an industry generate gains by encouraging exit of resources (through payout) and by substituting existing capacity for investment in new facilities by firms that are short of capacity.

Food-industry mergers also appear to reflect the expenditure of free cash flow. The industry apparently generates large cash flows with few growth opportunities. It is therefore a good candidate for leveraged buyouts, and these are now occurring; the $6.3 billion Beatrice LBO is the largest ever.

The broadcasting industry generates rents in the form of large cash flows on its licenses and also fits the theory. Regulation limits the overall supply of licenses and the number owned by a single entity. Thus profitable internal investments are limited and the industry's free cash flow has been spent on organizational inefficiencies and diversification programs, making these firms takeover targets. The CBS debt-for-stock exchange and restructuring as a defense against the hostile bid by Turner fits the theory, as does the $3.5 billion purchase of American Broadcasting Company by Capital Cities Communications. Completed cable systems also create agency problems from free cash flows in the form of rents on their franchises and quasi-rents on their investment, and are thus likely targets for acquisition and leveraged buyouts.

Large cash flows earned by motion picture companies on their film libraries also represent quasi-rents and are likely to generate free cash flow problems. Similarly, the attempted takeover of Disney and its subsequent reorganization is consistent with the theory. Drug companies with large cash flows from previous successful discoveries and few potential future prospects are also likely candidates for large agency costs of free cash flow.

The theory predicts that value-increasing takeovers occur in response to breakdowns of internal control processes in firms with substantial free cash flow and organizational policies (including diversification programs) that are wasting resources. It predicts hostile takeovers, large increases in leverage, the dismantling of empires with few economies of scale or scope to give them economic purpose (e.g. conglomerates), and much controversy as current managers object to loss of their jobs or changes in organizational policies forced on them by threat of takeover.

The debt created in a hostile takeover (or takeover defense) of a firm suffering severe agency costs of free cash flow need not be permanent. Indeed, sometimes it is desirable to "over-leverage" such a firm. In these situations, levering the firm so highly it cannot continue to exist in its old form yields

---

41c. Acquisitions made with cash or securities other than stock involve payout of resources to (target) shareholders, and this can create net benefits even if the merger creates operating inefficiencies. To illustrate the point, consider an acquiring firm, A, with substantial free cash flow that the market expects will be invested in low-return projects with a negative net present value of $100 million. If Firm A makes an acquisition of Firm B that generates zero synergies but uses up all of Firm A's free cash flow (and thereby prevents its waste) the combined market value of the two firms will *rise* by $100 million. The market value increases because the acquisition eliminates the expenditures on internal investments with negative market value of $100 million. Extending the argument, we see that acquisitions that have *negative* synergies of up to $100 million in current value will still increase the combined market value of the two firms. Such negative-synergy mergers will also increase social welfare and aggregate productivity whenever the market value of the negative productivity effects on the two merging firms is less than the market value of the waste that would have occurred with the firms' investment programs in the absence of the merger. The division of the gains between the target and bidding firms depends, of course, on the bargaining power of the two parties. Because the bidding firms are using funds that would otherwise have been spent on low- or negative-return projects, however, the opportunity cost of the funds is lower than their cost of capital. As a result, they will tend to overpay for the acquisition and thereby transfer most, if not all, of the gains to the target firm's shareholders. In extreme cases they may pay so much that the bidding-firm share price falls, in effect giving the target-shareholders more than 100 percent of the gains. These predictions are consistent with the evidence.

*The abolition of mere size as a deterrent to takeover...has made
possible the realization of large gains from reallocating larger
collections of assets to more productive uses.*

benefits. It creates the crisis to motivate cuts in expansion programs and the sale of those divisions that are more valuable outside the firm. The proceeds are used to reduce debt to a more normal or permanent level. This process results in a complete rethinking of the organization's strategy and structure. When it is successful, a much leaner, more efficient, and competitive organization results.

Some Evidence from Merger Studies

Consistent with the data, free cash flow theory predicts that many acquirers will tend to perform exceptionally well prior to acquisition. That exceptional stock price performance will often be associated with increased free cash flow which is then used for acquisition programs. The oil industry fits this description. Increased oil prices caused large gains in profits and stock prices in the mid-to-late 1970s. Empirical evidence from studies of both stock prices and accounting data also indicates exceptionally good performance for acquirers prior to acquisition.[42]

Targets will tend to be of two kinds: firms with poor management that have done poorly before the merger, and firms that have done exceptionally well and have large free cash flow that they refuse to pay out to shareholders....In the best study to date of the determinants of takeover, Palepu [1986] finds strong evidence consistent with the free cash flow theory of mergers. He studied a sample of 163 firms that were acquired in the period 1971-1979 and a random sample of 256 firms that were not acquired. Both samples were in mining and manufacturing and were listed on either the New York or American Stock Exchange. He finds that target firms were characterized by significantly lower growth and lower leverage than the nontarget firms, although there was no significant difference in their holdings of liquid assets. He also finds that poor prior performance (measured by the net-of-market returns in the four years before the acquisition) is significantly related to the probability of takeover, and, interestingly, that accounting measures of past performance such as

return on equity are unrelated to the probability of takeover. He also finds that firms with a mismatch between growth and resources are more likely to be taken over. These are firms with high growth (measured by average sales growth), low liquidity (measured by the ratio of liquid assets to total assets) and high leverage, and firms with low growth, high liquidity, and low leverage. Finally, Palepu's evidence rejects the hypothesis that takeovers are due to the undervaluation of a firm's assets as measured by the market-to-book ratio.[42a]

High-Yield ("Junk") Bonds

The last several years have witnessed a major innovation in the financial markets with the establishment of active markets in high-yield bonds. These bonds are rated below investment grade by the bond rating agencies and are frequently referred to as junk bonds, a disparaging term that bears no relation to their pedigree. They carry interest rates that are 3 to 5 percentage points higher than the yields on government bonds of comparable maturity. High-yield bonds are best thought of as commercial loans that can be resold in secondary markets. By traditional standards they are more risky than investment-grade bonds and therefore carry higher interest rates. An early study finds the default rates on these bonds have been low and the realized returns have been disproportionately higher than their risk.[43a]

High-yield bonds have been attacked by those who wish to inhibit their use, particularly in the financing of takeover bids. The invention of high-yield bonds has provided methods to finance takeover ventures like those companies use to finance more traditional ventures. Companies commonly raise funds to finance ventures by selling claims to be paid from the proceeds of the venture; this is the essence of debt or stock issues used to finance new ventures. High-yield bonds used in takeovers work similarly. The bonds provide a claim on the proceeds of the venture, using the assets and cash flows of the target

42. See the following two papers which were presented at the Conference on Takeovers and Contests for Corporate Control, Columbia University, November, 1985: Ellen B. Magenheim and Dennis Mueller, "On Measuring the Effect of Acquisitions on Acquiring Firm Shareholders or Are Acquiring Firm Shareholders Better Off After an Acquisition Than They Were Before?"; and Michael Bradley and Gregg Jarrell, "Evidence on Gains from Mergers and Takeovers." See also Paul R. Asquith and E. Han Kim, "The Impact of Merger Bids on the Participating Firms' Security Holders," *Journal of Finance,* 37, 1209-1228; Gershon Mandelker, "Risk and Return: The Case of Merging Firms," *Jour-*

nal of Financial Economics, V. 1, No. 4 (December, 1974), pp. 303-336; and T.C. Langetieg, "An Application of A Three-Factor Performance Index to Measure Stockholder Gains from Merger" *Journal of Financial Economics,* V. 6 (December, 1978), pp. 365-484.

42a. Palepu (1986), presented at the Conference on Takeovers and Contests for Corporate Control, Columbia University, November, 1985.

43a. Marshall E. Blume and Donald B. Keim, "Risk and Return Characteristics of Lower-Grade Bonds" (unpublished paper, The Wharton School, December, 1984).

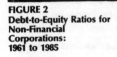

22

*The Federal Reserve System's own data are inconsistent with the
reasons given for its restrictions on the use of debt.*

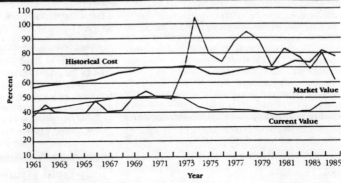

**FIGURE 2
Debt-to-Equity Ratios for
Non-Financial
Corporations:
1961 to 1985**

Source: Federal Reserve System [1986]

plus the equity contributed by the acquirer as collateral. This basic structure is the common way that individuals purchase homes; they use the home plus their down payment as collateral for the mortgage. There is nothing inherently unusual in the structure of this contract, although those who would bar the use of high-yield bonds in takeover ventures would have us believe otherwise.

Some might argue that the risk of high-yield bonds used in takeover attempts is "too high." But high-yield bonds are by definition less risky than common stock claims on the same venture. Would these same critics argue that stock claims are too risky and thus should be barred? The risk argument makes logical sense only as an argument that the transactions costs associated with bankruptcy are too high in these ventures or that the promised yields on the bonds are too low and that investors who purchase them will not earn returns high enough to compensate for the risk they are incurring. This argument makes little sense because there is vast evidence that investors are capable of pricing risks in all sorts of other markets. It is inconceivable they are peculiarly unable to do so in the high-yield bond market.

In January 1986 the Federal Reserve Board issued a new interpretation of the margin rules that restricts the use of debt in takeovers to 50 percent or less of the purchase price. This rule reintroduces size as an effective deterrent to takeover. It was apparently motivated by the belief that the use of corporate debt had become abnormally and dangerously high and was threatening the economy.

This assessment is not consistent with the facts. Figure 2 plots three measures of debt use by nonfinancial corporations in the U.S. The debt/equity ratio is measured relative to three bases: market value of equity, estimated current asset value of equity, and accounting book value of equity measured at historical cost.

Although debt/equity ratios were higher in 1985 than in 1961, they were not at record levels. The book value debt/equity ratio reached a high of 81.4 percent in 1984, but declined to 78 percent in 1985. The fact that debt/equity ratios measured on an historical cost basis are relatively high is to be expected, given the previous decade of inflation. Maintenance of the same inflation-adjusted debt/equity ratio in times of inflation implies that the book value ratio must rise because the current value of assets in the denominator of the inflation-adjusted ratio is rising. The current value ratio, which takes account of inflation, fell from 50.7 percent in 1970 to 46.5 percent in 1985. The market-value ratio rose from 54.7 percent in 1970 to 80.5 percent in 1984 and plummeted to 60.8 percent in 1985. The 1985 market-value ratio was 45 percentage points below its 1974 peak of 105.2 percent. In short, the Federal Reserve System's own data are inconsistent with the reasons given for its restrictions on the use of debt.

High-yield bonds were first used in a takeover bid in early 1984 and have been involved in relatively few bids in total. In 1984, only about 12 percent of the $14.3 billion of new high-yield debt was associated with mergers and acquisitions. In 1985, 26 per-

*When correctly implemented they [golden parachutes] help reduce the
conflicts of interest between shareholders and managers at times of
takeover and therefore make it more likely that the productive gains
stemming from changes in control will be realized.*

cent of the $14.7 billion of new high-yield debt was
used in acquisitions.[44] Some of the acquisitions,
however, such as the Unocal and CBS offers (both
unsuccessful), have received intense attention from
the media; and this publicity has fostered the belief
that high-yield bonds are widely used in takeovers.
Nevertheless, high-yield bonds are an important innovation in the takeover field because they help
eliminate mere size as a deterrent to takeover. They
have been particularly influential in helping to bring
about reorganizations in the oil industry.

Historical default rates on high-yield bonds have
been low, but many of these bonds are so new that the
experience could prove to be different in the next
downturn. Various opponents have proposed regulations or legislation to restrict the issuance of such securities, to penalize their tax status, and to restrict
their holding by thrifts, which can now buy them as
substitutes for the issuance of nonmarketable commercial loans. These proposals are premature. Policy-
makers should be wary of responding to the clamor
for restrictions by executives who desire protection
from the discipline of the takeover market and by
members of the financial community who want to restrict competition from this new financing vehicle.

The holding of high-yield bonds by thrifts is an
interesting issue that warrants further analyis. The recent deregulation of the banking and thrift industries
presents many opportunities and challenges to the
thrifts. Elimination of restrictions on interest paid to
depositors has raised the cost of funds to these institutions. Thrifts have also received the right to engage in new activities such as commercial lending.
Survival requires these institutions to take advantage
of some of these new business opportunities.

The organizational costs of developing
commerical lending departments in the 3,500 thrifts
in the country is substantial. Thousands of new loan
officers will have to be hired and trained. The additional wage and training costs and the bad-debt
losses that will be incurred in the learning phase will
be substantial. High-yield bonds provide a promising solution to this problem. If part of the commercial lending function can be centralized in the hands
of investment bankers who provide commerical
loans in the form of marketable high-yield debt, the
thrifts can substitute the purchase of this high-yield
debt for their commercial lending and thereby avoid
the huge investment in such loan departments.

The Legitimate Concerns of Managers

Conflicts of Interest and Increased Costs to Managers

The interests of corporate managers are not the
same as the interests of corporations as organizations, and conflicts of interest can become intense
when major changes in the organization's strategy
are required. Competition causes change, and
change creates winners and losers, especially in that
branch of the managerial labor market called the
takeover market.

**Managers' private incentives sometimes
run counter to overall efficiency.** The costs of
takeovers have fallen as the legal and financial skills
of participants in the takeover market have become
more sophisticated, as the restrictions on takeovers
imposed by antitrust laws have been relaxed, and as
financing techniques have improved. Except for new
regulatory constraints on the use of debt, this means
that the largest of the Fortune 500 companies are
now potentially subject to takeover. The abolition of
mere size as a deterrent to takeover is desirable because it has made possible the realization of large
gains from reallocating larger collections of assets to
more productive uses.

This new susceptibility to takeover has created a
new contracting environment for top-level
managers. Many managers are legitimately anxious,
and it will take time for the system to work out an
appropriate set of practices and contracts reflecting
the risks and rewards of the new environment. Some
of the uncertainty of top-level managers formerly insulated from pressures from the financial markets
will fade as they learn how their policies affect the
market value of their companies.

The Desirability of Golden Parachutes

Unfortunately, a major component of the solution to the conflict of interest between shareholders
and managers has been vastly misunderstood. I am
referring to severance contracts that compensate
managers for the loss of their jobs in the event of a

44 Source: Drexel Burnham Lambert, private correspondence.

24

It makes no sense to hire a realtor to sell your house and then penalize him for doing so. Yet that is the implication of many of the emotional reactions to control-related severance contracts.

change in control—what have been popularly labeled "golden parachutes."

These contracts are clearly desirable, even when judged solely from the viewpoint of the interests of shareholders; but they are also efficient from a social viewpoint. When correctly implemented they help reduce the conflicts of interest between shareholders and managers at times of takeover and therefore make it more likely that the productive gains stemming from changes in control will be realized. The evidence indicates that stock prices of firms that adopt severance-related compensation contracts for managers on average rise about 3 percent when adoption of the contracts is announced.[45] There is no easy way to tell how much of this could be due to the market interpreting the announcement as a signal that a takeover bid is more likely and how much is due to the reduction in conflict between managers and shareholders over takeovers.

At times of takeover, shareholders are implicitly asking the top-level managers of their firm to negotiate a deal for them that frequently involves the imposition of large personal costs on the managers and their families. These involve substantial moving costs, the loss of position, power and prestige, and even the loss of their jobs. Shareholders are asking the very people who are most likely to have invested considerable time and energy (in some cases a life's work) in building a successful organization to negotiate its sale and the possible redirection of its resources.

It is important to face these conflicts and to structure contracts with managers to reduce them. It makes no sense to hire a realtor to sell your house and then penalize him for doing so. Yet that is the implication of many of the emotional reactions to control-related severance contracts. The restrictions and tax penalties imposed on these severance payments by the Deficit Reduction Act of 1984 are unwise interferences in the contracting freedoms of shareholders and managers; and they should be eliminated. Moreover, it is important to eliminate the misunderstanding about the purpose and effects of these contracts that has been fostered by past rhetoric on the topic so that boards of directors can get on with the job of structuring these contracts.

Golden parachutes can also be used to restrict takeovers and to entrench managers at the expense of shareholders. How does one tell whether a particular set of contracts crosses this line?

The key is whether the contracts help solve the conflict-of-interest problem between shareholders and managers that arises over changes in control. Solving this problem requires extending control-related severance contracts beyond the chief executive to those members of the top-level management team who must play an important role in negotiating and implementing any transfer of control. Contracts that award severance contracts to substantial number of managers beyond this group are unlikely to be in the shareholders' interests. The contracts awarded by Beneficial Corp. to 234 of its managers are unlikely to be justified as in the shareholders' interests.[46]

It is particularly important to institute severance-related compensation contracts in situations where it is optimal for managers to invest in organization-specific human capital—that is, in skills and knowledge that have little or no value in other organizations. Managers will not so invest where the likelihood is high that their investment will be eliminated by an unexpected transfer of control and the loss of their jobs. In such situations the firm will have to pay for all costs associated with the creation of such organization-specific human capital, and it will be difficult to attract and retain highly talented managers when they have better opportunities elsewhere. In addition, contracts that award excessive severance compensation to the appropriate group of managers will tend to motivate managers to sell the firm at too low a price.

No simple rules can be specified that will easily prevent the misuse of golden parachutes because the appropriate solution will depend on many factors that are specific to each situation (for example, the amount of stock held by managers, and the optimal amount of investment in organization-specific human capital). In general, contracts that award inappropriately high payments to a group that is excessively large will reduce efficiency and harm shareholders by raising the cost of acquisition and by transferring wealth from shareholders to managers. The generally appropriate solution is to make the control-related severance contracts pay off in a way that is tied to the premium earned by the stockholders. Stock op-

45. See R. Lambert and D. Larcker, "Golden Parachutes, Executive Decision-Making, and Shareholder Wealth", *Journal of Accounting and Economics*, V. 7 (April, 1985), pp. 179-204.

46. Ann Morrison, "Those Executive Bailout Deals," *Fortune*, (December 13, 1982).

Greenmail is the Trojan horse of the takeover battle in the legal and political arenas...Management can easily prohibit greenmail without legislation: it need only announce a policy that, like Ulysses tying himself to the mast, prohibits it from making such payments.

tions or restricted stock appreciation rights that pay off only in the event of a change in control are two options that have some of the appropriate properties. In general, policies that encourage increased stock ownership by managers and the board of directors will provide incentives that will tend to reduce the conflicts of interests with managers.

Targeted Repurchases

The evidence indicates takeovers generate large benefits for shareholders. Yet virtually all proposals to protect shareholders from asserted difficulties in the control market will harm them by either eliminating or reducing the probability of successful hostile tender offers. These proposals will also block the productivity increases that are the source of the gains.

Most proposals to restrict or prohibit targeted repurchases (transactions pejoratively labeled "greenmail") are nothing more than antitakeover proposals in disguise. Greenmail is an appellation that suggests blackmail; yet the only effective weapon possessed by a greenmailer is the right to offer to purchase stock from other shareholders at a substantial premium. The "damage" to shareholders caused by this action is difficult to find. Those who propose to "protect" shareholders hide this fact behind emotional language designed to mislead. Greenmail is actually a targeted repurchase, an offer by *management* to repurchase the shares of a subset of shareholders at a premium, an offer not made to other shareholders.

Greenmail is the Trojan horse of the takeover battle in the legal and political arenas. Antitakeover proposals are commonly disguised as antigreenmail provisions. Management can easily prohibit greenmail without legislation: it need only announce a policy that, like Ulysses tying himself to the mast, prohibits management or the board from making such payments.[47]

Problems in the Delaware Court

Delaware courts have created over the years a highly productive fabric of corporate law that has benefited the nation. The court is having difficulty, however, in sorting out the complex issues it faces in the takeover area. The court's problems in settling conflicts between shareholders and management over control issues reflect a fundamental weakness in its model of the corporation, a model that has heretofore worked quite well. The result has been a confusing set of decisions that, in contrast to much of the court's previous history, appears to make little economic sense.[49]

Altruism and the Business Judgment Rule

The Delaware court's model of the corporation is founded in the business judgment rule—the legal doctrine that holds that unless explicit evidence of fraud or self-dealing exists the board of directors is presumed to be acting solely in the interests of shareholders....The courts must not apply the business judgment rule to conflicts over control rights between principals and agents. If the business judgement rule is applied to such conflicts, the courts are effectively giving the *agent* (management) the right unilaterally to change the control rights. In the long run, this interpretation of the contract will destroy the possibility of such cooperative arrangements because it will leave principals (stockholders) with few effective rights.

Recently the courts have applied the business judgment rule to the conflicts over the issuance of poison pill preferred stock, poison pill rights, and discriminatory targeted repurchases, and have given managers and boards the rights to use these

47. Three excellent studies of these transactions indicate that when measured from the initial toehold purchase to the final repurchase of the shares, the stock price of target firms rises. Therefore, shareholders are benefited, not harmed, by the whole sequence of events. (See Clifford Holderness and Dennis Sheehan, "Raiders or Saviors: The Evidence on Six Controversial Investors," *Journal of Financial Economics* (December, 1985), Wayne H. Mikkelson, and Richard S. Ruback, "An Empirical Analysis of the Interfirm Equity Investment Process," *Journal of Financial Economics,* V. 14 (December, 1985), and Wayne H. Mikkelson and Richard S. Ruback, "Targeted Repurchases and Common Stock Returns", (unpublished manuscript, June, 1986).) There is some indication, however, that the stock price increases might represent the expectation of future takeover premiums in firms in which the targeted repurchase was not sufficient to prevent ultimate takeover of the firm. If so, it may well be that, much as in the final defeat of tender offers found by Bradley, Desai and Kim (Michael Bradley,

Michael, Anand Desai and E. Han Kim, "The Rationale Behind Interfirm Tender Offers: Information or Synergy?" *Journal of Financial Economics,* V. 11 (April, 1983), pp. 183-206), all premiums are lost to those shareholders in firms for which the repurchase and associated standstill agreements successfully lock up the firm. The evidence on these issues is not yet sufficient to issue a final judgement either way.

49. See, for example, Moran v. Household Intl, Inc., 490 A.2d 1059 (Del.Ch.1985) aff'd. 500 A.2d 1346 (Del.1985) (upholding poison pill rights issue), Smith v Van Gorkom, 488 A.2d 858, (holding board liable for damages in sale of firm at substantial premium over market price), Unocal v Mesa, 493 A.2d 946, 954 (Del. 1985) (allowing discriminatory targeted repurchase that confiscates wealth of largest shareholder), Revlon Inc. v MacAndrews & Forbes Holdings Inc., 506 A.2nd 173, 180 (Del. 1986), (invalidation of Revlon's lockup sale of a prime division to Forstmann Little at a below-market price).

■
26

*Rights issues like Household's and Crown Zellerbach's harm
shareholders. They will fundamentally impair the efficiency of
corporations that adopt them, and for this reason they will reduce
productivity in the economy if widely adopted.*

devices.[52] In so doing the courts are essentially giving the agents (managers and the board) the right unilaterally to change critical control aspects of the contract—in particular the right to fire the agent. This has major implications for economic activity, productivity, and the health of the corporation. If the trend goes far enough, the corporation as an organizational form will be serioiusly handicapped.

Poison Pills

Poison pill securities change fundamental aspects of the corporate rules of the game that govern the relationship between shareholders, managers, and the board of directors. They do so when a control-related event occurs, such as a takeover offer or the acquisition of a substantial block of stock or voting rights by an individual or group. The Household International version of the poison pill rights issue is particularly interesting because it was a major test case in the area.

When the Household International board of directors issued its complicated right to shareholders, it unilaterally changed the nature of the contractual relationship with Household's shareholders in a fundamental way. The right effectively restricts the alienability of the common stock by prohibiting shareholders from selling their shares, without permission of the board, into a control transaction leading to merger at a price that involves a premium over market value of less than $6 billion. Since Household had a market value of less than $2 billion at the time, this was a premium of over 300 percent—more than 6 times the average takeover premium of 50 percent common in recent times—a premium that is difficult to justify as in the shareholders' interests.

The November 1985 Delaware court decision upholding the Household International rights issue will significantly restrict hostile takeovers of firms that adopt similar provisions. Before that decision, 37 pills of various forms had been adopted. Over 150 corporations adopted pills in the seven months following that decision.[53] Unlike most other antitakeover

devices, this defense is very difficult for a prospective acquirer to overcome without meeting the board's terms (at least one who desires to complete the second-step closeout merger). An SEC study analyzed the 37 companies introducing pills between June 1983, when Lenox introduced the first one, and December 1985. Eleven of these 37 firms experienced control changes: five experienced a negotiated change in control while the pill was in effect.(Revlon, Cluett Peabody, Great Lakes, Int., Lenox, and Enstar), two were taken over by creeping acquisitions (Crown Zellerbach and William Wright), two were taken over after their pills were declared illegal (AMF and Richardson Vicks), one (Superior Oil) was acquired after the pill was withdrawn in the face of a lawsuit and proxy fight by its largest holder, and one (Amsted) has proposed a leveraged buyout. The SEC study finds that "Announcements of [twenty] poison pill plans in the midst of takeover speculations have resulted in an average 2.4 percent net of market price declines for firms adopting the plans." The effects of another twelve plans adopted by firms that were not the subject of takeover speculation were essentially nil.[53a]

Sir James Goldsmith recently gained control of Crown Zellerbach, which had implemented a rights issue similar to Household International's. Goldsmith purchased a controlling interest in the open market after Crown's board opposed his tender offer and refused to recall its rights issue. In this situation the acquirer must either tolerate the costs associated with leaving the minority interest outstanding and forsake the benefits of merging the assets of the two organizations, or incur the costs of the premium required by the rights on execution of the second-step closeout merger. The Crown case revealed a loophole in the Household/Crown version of the pill (which has been closed in newly implemented versions). Although Goldsmith could not complete a second-step merger without paying the high-premium required by the rights, he could avoid it by simply liquidating Crown.

Rights issues like Household's and Crown Zellerbach's harm shareholders. They will fundamentally impair the efficiency of corporations that adopt them, and for this reason they will reduce

52. Moran v Household Intl., and Unocal v Mesa.
53. See Office of the Chief Economist of the SEC, "The Economics of Poison Pills," (March 5, 1986), and Corporate Control Alert, (February, March and April, May and June, 1986).

53a. Ibid.

The Unocal victory over Mesa cost the Unocal shareholders $1.1 billion ($9.48 per post-offer share). This is the amount by which the $9.4 billion Mesa offer exceeded the $8.3 billion value of Unocal's "victory."

productivity in the economy if widely adopted.[53b]

A broad interpretation of the business judgment rule is important to the effectiveness of the corporation because a system that puts the courts into the business of making managerial decisions will generate great inefficiencies. The court has erred, however, in allowing the Household board, under the business judgement rule, to make the fundamental change in the structure of the organization implied by the rights issue without votes of its shareholders. It is unlikely the court would allow the board to decide unilaterally to make the organization a closed corporation by denying shareholders the right to sell their shares to anyone at a mutually agreeable price without the permission of the board. The Household International rights issue places just such a restriction on the alienability of shares, but only in the case of a subset of transactions—the control-related transactions so critical for protecting shareholders when the normal internal board-level control mechanisms break down. Several other poison pill cases have been heard by the courts with similar outcomes, but a New Jersey and two New York courts have recently ruled against poison pills that substantially interfere with the voting rights of large-block shareholders.[54] An Illinois District Court recently voided a poison pill (affirmed by the Seventh Circuit Court of Appeals) and two weeks later approved a new pill issued by the same company.[55]

The problem with these special securities and the provision they contain is not with their appropriateness (some might well be desirable), but with the manner in which they are being adopted—that is, without approval by shareholders. Boards of directors show little inclination to refer such issues to shareholders.

One solution to the problems caused by the Household decision is for shareholders to approve

amendments to the certificate of incorporation to restrict the board's power to take such actions without shareholder approval. This is not an easy task, however, given the pressure corporate managers are bringing to bear on the managers of their pension funds to vote with management.[56] Even more problematic is the provision in Delaware law that requires certificate amendments to be recommended to shareholders by the board of directors.[57]

Exclusionary Self Tenders: The Unocal v. Mesa Decision[58]

The Delaware Supreme Court surprised the legal, financial, and corporate communities in the spring of 1985 by giving Unocal the right to make a tender offer for 29 percent of its shares while excluding its largest shareholder, Mesa Partners II, from the offer. This decision enabled the Unocal management and board to avoid loss of control to Mesa. The decision imposed large costs on Unocal shareholders and, if not reversed, threatens major damage to shareholders of all Delaware corporations.

The Unocal victory over Mesa cost the Unocal shareholders $1.1 billion ($9.48 per post-offer share). This is the amount by which the $9.4 billion Mesa offer exceeded the $8.3 billion value of Unocal's "victory."[59] This loss represents 18 percent of Unocal's pre-takeover value of $6.2 billion. The $2.1 billion net increase in value to $8.3 billion resulted from Unocal's $4.2 billion debt issue which, contrary to assertions, benefits its shareholders. It does so by effectively bonding Unocal to pay out a substantial fraction of its huge cash flows to shareholders rather than to reinvest them in low-return projects, and by reducing taxes on Unocal and its shareholders.

For his services in generating this $2.1 billion gain for Unocal shareholders, T. Boone Pickens has

53b. Another study of the effects of poison pills (Paul H. Malatesta and Ralph A. Walkling, "The Impact of Poison Pill Securities on Stockholder Wealth," (unpublished, University of Washington, 1985) also indicates they have a negative effect on stock prices. On average, stock prices fell by a statistically significant 2 percent in the 2 days around the announcement in the *Wall Street Journal* of adoption of a poison pill for a sample of 14 firms that adopted these securities between December 1982 and February 1985. This price decline, however, was smaller than the average 7.5 percent increase in price that occurred in the 10 days prior to the adoption of the pill. Firms adopting pills appear to be those in which managers and directors bear a substantially smaller fraction of the wealth consequences of their actions. In all but three of the firms the percentage of common shares owned by officers and directors was substantially below the industry average ownership of shares. The average ownership of firms in the same industry was 16.5 percent and for the firms adopting pills it was 7.5 percent.

54. Ministar Acquiring Corp. v AMF Inc., 621 Fed Sup 1252. So Dis NY, 1985, Unilever Acquisition Corp. v Richardson-Vicks, Inc., 618 Fed Supp 407. So Dist. NY 1985, Asarco Inc. v M.R.H. Holmes a Court. 611 Fed Sup 468. Dist Ct of NJ.

1985, and Dynamics Corp. of America v CTS Corporation.

55. Dynamics Corp. of America v. CTS Corp., *et al.* U.S. District Court, Northern District of Illinois, Eastern Division, No. 86 C 1624, (April 17, 1986), affirmed Seventh Circuit Court of Appeals Nos. 86-16-1, 86-1608, and Dynamics Corp. of America v. CTS Corp., *et al.* (May 3, 1986).

56. See Joe, Koleman, "The Proxy Pressure on Pension Fund Managers", Institutional Investor, (July, 1985), pp. 145-147, and Investor Responsibility Research Center, Inc., Corporate Governance Service: Voting by Institutional Investors on Corporate Governance Questions, 1985 Proxy Season, pp. 19-25.

57. 8 *Del. C.* 242(c) (1).

58. This discussion is based on my article, "When Unocal Won over Pickens, Shareholders and Society Lost," *Financier*, V. IX, No. 11 (Nov., 1985), pp. 50-53.

59. The $8.3 billion value of Unocal securities held by its shareholders is calculated as $4.1 billion in stock (116 million shares at $34 7/8 on May 24, the first trading day after close of the offer), and $4.2 billion in Unocal debt trading at $73.50.

28

In addition to Mesa's losses, shareholders of all Delaware corporations lose because the court's decision gives management a weapon so powerful it essentially guarantees that no Delaware corporation that uses it will be taken over by a tender offer.

been vilified in the press, and Mesa Partners II has incurred net losses before taxes—obviously a perversion of incentives.

In addition to Mesa's losses, shareholders of all Delaware corporations lose because the court's decision gives management a weapon so powerful it essentially guarantees that no Delaware corporation that uses it will be taken over by a tender offer. A determined board could, in the extreme, pay out all the corporation's assets and leave the acquirer holding a worthless shell. Because of this new power, shareholders are denied the benefits of future actions by Pickens and others to discipline managers whose strategies are wasting resources.

Society also loses. The decision will have a chilling effect on takeovers, blocking the productivity increases that are the source of the takeover gains and thereby handicapping Delaware corporations in the competition for survival.

Unocal's self-tender for 29 percent of its shares at $72 per share ($26 over the market price) was designed to defeat Mesa's $54 per share cash offer for 50.4 percent of Unocal's shares plus $54 per share in debt securities for the remaining 49.6 percent. The Unocal offer would have paid 59 percent of Unocal's pretakeover equity to other shareholders while denying participation to the 13.6 percent minority holding of Mesa Partners II. This would transfer about $248 million from Mesa's holdings to other Unocal stockholders—a classic case of corporate raiding that contrasts with the beneficial effects of the actions of takeover specialists like Pickens, Carl Icahn and Irwin Jacobs on other shareholders.

Faced with the threat of legalized expropriation of $248 million, Mesa accepted a settlement in which Unocal backed off from the Mesa exclusion. The settlement involved repurchase of part of Mesa's shares at the terms of the tender offer, a 25-year standstill agreement, a promise to vote its shares in the same proportion as other shares are voted, and constraints on Mesa's rights to sell its remaining shares.

The essential characteristics of Unocal's exclusionary repurchase defense are now incorporated in newly popular poison pill plans called back-end plans.[60] These plans give shareholders a right to tender their shares for securities worth more than the

market value of their stock when a shareholder exceeds a certain maximum limit of stock ownership that ranges from 30 to 50 percent. As with Unocal's exclusion of Mesa, the large shareholder is denied the same right to tender his shares. This threatens a shareholder who violates the holding limit with potentially large dilution of his holdings. It thereby limits the existence of large stock holdings.

"Protection" From Two-Tier Tender Offers. The court ruled that the objective of Unocal's offer was to protect its shareholders against "a grossly inadequate and coercive two-tier, front-end-loaded tender offer" and against greenmail. This assessment of the situation was upside down. Paradoxically, the court's ruling imposed on Unocal shareholders exactly the evil it purported to prevent. Unocal defeated Mesa's $1.1 billion higher offer precisely because Mesa's offer was a level $54 offer and Unocal's offer was an extreme front-end loaded two-tier offer—$72 for 29 percent of its shares in the front-end with a back-end price of $35 for the remaining 71 percent of the shares. (The back-end price was implicit, but easy to calculate and reported in the press at the time of the offer.) The effective price of the Unocal offer was therefore only $45.73 per pre-offer share (the weighted average of the front- and back-end prices).

Comparing the Unocal offer with SEC estimates of average minimums in two-tier tender offers indicates the extreme nature of the Unocal two-tier offer. Historically the average back-end premium on outside two-tier offers is 45 percent higher than the stock price measured 20 trading days prior to the offer.[61] This contrasts sharply with the *negative* back-end premium on Unocal's self tender of -25 percent. That is, the $35 back-end price was 25 percent below the Unocal market price of $46 3/8 twenty days before the offer.

The negative back-end premium on Unocal's offer means the holders of 20 million Unocal shares who failed to tender to the first tier of the Unocal offer were particularly hurt. As of the close of the offer they suffered total losses of $382 million, $215 million from the loss of $37.12/share on 29 percent of their shares,[62] plus a loss of $167 million from being denied the $54 in debt securities they would have received in

60. See Office of the Chief Economist of the SEC, "The Economics of Poison Pills" (March 5, 1986)
61. See Comment, Robert, and Gregg A. Jarrell. "Two-Tier Tender Offers: The Imprisonment of the Free-Riding Shareholder." (unpublished manuscript, March 1, 1986); an earlier version appeared as Office of the Chief Economist,

Securities and Exchange Commission. "The Economics of Any-or-All, Partial, and Two-Tier Tender Offers." *Federal Register*, June 29, 1984, pp. 26,751-26,761.
62. Calculated as the $72 value of the Unocal debt offered in exchange for 29% of their shares less the $34.875 post-offer closing price of the shares.

*Responsible boards of directors interested in the welfare of
shareholders and the survival of the corporation as an organizational
form will implement procedures to ban all targeted repurchases that
carry premiums over market value.*

the back end of the Mesa offer.[63]

Protection From Targeted Repurchases.
The court also erred in its concern over greenmail. In
ruling to eliminate the threat of greenmail, the court
in fact authorized Unocal to make a greenmail transaction that differs from the usual variety only in that it
penalized, rather than benefited, the large-block
holder (i.e., reverse greenmail). In authorizing this
form of targeted repurchase, the court granted large
benefits to managers who desire protection from
competition but harmed shareholders.

One of the great strengths of the corporation is
the long-held principle that holders of a given class
of securities are treated identically in transactions
with the corporation. The Unocal decision threatens
to turn the corporation into a battleground where
special-interest groups of shareholders fight over
the division of the pie much as special interests in
the public sector do. The result will be a much
smaller pie.

Responsible boards of directors interested in
the welfare of shareholders and the survival of the
corporation as an organizational form will implement procedures to ban all targeted repurchases
that carry premiums over market value

Conclusion

Although economic analysis and the evidence
indicate the market for corporate control is benefit-
ing shareholders, society, and the corporation as an
organizational form, it is also making life more uncomfortable for top-level executives. This discom-
fort is creating strong pressures at both the state and
federal levels for restrictions that will seriously crip-
ple the workings of this market. In 1985 there were
21 bills on this topic in the Congressional hopper, all
of which proposed various restrictions on the market for corporate control. Some proposed major
new restrictions on share ownership and financial
instruments. Within the past several years the legislatures of numerous states have passed antitakeover
laws. This political activity is another example of special interests using the democratic political system to
change the rules of the game to benefit themselves at
the expense of society as a whole. In this case the
special interests are top-level corporate managers
and other groups who stand to lose from competition in the market for corporate control. The result
will be a significant weakening of the corporation as
an organizational form and a reduction in efficiency.

63. See Michael Bradley and Michael Rosensweig, "The Law and Economics
of Defensive Stock Repurchases and Defensive Self-Tender Offers, (Unpublished

manuscript, University of Michigan, 1985) for a thorough discussion of the issues
involved in self tender offers.

APPENDIX: Evidence From Financial Transactions in Support of the Free Cash Flow Theory of Mergers

Free cash flow theory helps explain previously
puzzling results on the effects of various financial
transactions. Smith [1986]* summarizes more than
twenty studies of stock price changes at announcements of transactions that change capital structure as
well as various other dividend transactions. These
results are summarized in Table 2.

For firms with positive free cash flow, the theory
predicts that stock prices will increase with unexpected increases in payouts to shareholders and decrease
with unexpected decreases in payouts. It also predicts
that unexpected increases in demand for funds from
shareholders via new issues will cause stock prices to
fall. In addition, the theory predicts stock prices will
increase with increasing tightness of the constraints
binding the payout of future cash flow to shareholders
and decrease with reductions in the tightness of these

constraints. These predictions do not apply, however,
to those firms with more profitable projects than free
cash flow to fund them.

The predictions of the agency cost of free cash
flow are consistent with all but three of the 32 estimated abnormal stock price changes summarized in
Table 2. Moreover, one of the inconsistencies is explainable by another phenomenon.

Panel A of Table 2 shows that stock prices rise by
a statistically significant amount with announcements of the initiation of cash dividend payments, increases in dividends, and payments of specially designated dividends; they fall by a statistically significant amount with decreases in dividend payments.
(All coefficients in the table are significantly different
from zero unless noted with an asterisk.)

Panel B of Table 2 shows that security sales and

* See Cliff Smith, "Investment Banking and the Capital Acquisition Process,"
Journal of Financial Economics 15 (1986) for references to all studies cited in

this Appendix.

30

TABLE 2
The Stock Market Response to Various Dividend and Capital Structure Transactions

Summary of two-day average abnormal stock returns associated with the announcement of various dividend and capital structure transactions.

Returns are weighted averages, by sample size, of the returns reported by the respective studies. All returns are significantly different from zero unless noted otherwise by .*

Type of Transaction	Security Issued	Security Retired
PANEL A: Dividend changes that change the cash paid to shareholders		
Dividend initiation[1]		
Dividend increase[2]		
Specially designated dividend[3]		
Dividend decrease[2]		
PANEL B: Security sales (that raise cash) and retirements (that pay out cash) and simultaneously		
Security sale (industrial)[4]	debt	none
Security sale (utility)[5]	debt	none
Security sale (industrial)[6]	preferred	none
Security sale (utility)[7]	preferred	none
Call[8]	none	debt
PANEL C: Security sales which raise cash and bond future cash flow payments only minimally		
Security sale (industrial)[4]	conv. debt.	none
Security sale (industrial)[7]	conv. preferred	none
Security sale (utility)[7]	conv. preferred	none
PANEL D: Security retirements that pay out cash to shareholders		
Self tender offer[9]	none	common
Open market purchase[10]	none	common
Targeted small holdings[11]	none	common
Targeted large block repurchase[12]	none	common
PANEL E: Security sales or calls that raise cash and do not bond future cash flow payments		
Security sale (industrial)[13]	common	none
Security sale (utility)[14]	common	none
Conversion-forcing call[20]	common	conv. preferred
Conversion-forcing call[20]	common	conv. debt
PANEL F: Exchange offers, or designated use security sales that increase the bonding of payout of		
Designated use security sale[15]	debt	common
Exchange offer[16]	debt	common
Exchange offer[16]	preferred	common
Exchange offer[16]	debt	preferred
Exchange offer[17]	income bonds	preferred
PANEL G: Transaction with no change in bonding of payout of future cash flows		
Exchange offer[18]	debt	debt
Designated use security sale[19]	debt	debt
PANEL H: Exchange offers, or designated use security sales that decrease the bonding of payout		
Security sale[18]	conv. debt	debt
Exchange offer[19]	common	preferred
Exchange offer[19]	preferred	debt
Security sale[19]	common	debt
Exchange offer[21]	common	debt

[1] Asquith and Mullins (1983).
[2] Calculated by Smith (1986, Table 1) from Charest (1978), and Aharony and Swary (1980).
[3] From Brickley (1983).
[4] Calculated by Smith (1986, Table 1) from Dann and Mikkelson (1984), Eckbo (1986), Mikkelson and Partch (1986).
[5] Eckbo (1986).
[6] Calculated by Smith (1986, Table 1) from Linn and Pinegar (1985), Mikkelson and Partch (1986).
[7] Linn and Pinegar (1985).
[8] Vu (1986).
[9] Calculated by Smith (1986, Table 1) from Dann (1981), Masulis (1980), Vermaelen (1981), Rosenfeld (1982).
[10] Dann (1980), Vermaelen (1981).
[11] Bradley and Wakeman (1983).
[12] Calculated by Smith (1986, Table 4) from Dann and DeAngelo (1983), Bradley and Wakeman (1983).
[13] Calculated by Smith (1986, Table 1) from Asquith and Mullins (1986), Kolodny and Suhler (1985), Masulis and Korwar (1986), Mikkelson and Partch (1986), Schipper and Smith (1986).

retirements that raise cash or pay out cash and simultaneously provide offsetting changes in the constraints bonding the payout of future cash flow are all associated with returns insignificantly different from zero. The insignificant return on retirement debt fits the theory because the payout of cash is offset by an equal reduction in the present value of promised future cash payouts. If the debt sales are associated with no changes in the expected investment program, the insignificant return on announcements of the sale of debt and preferred also fits the theory. The acquisition of new funds with debt or preferred

Average Sample Size	Average Abnormal Two-Day Announcement Period Return	Sign Predicted by Free Cash Flow Theory	Agreement with Free Cash Flow Theory?	Agreement with Tax Theory
160	3.7%	+	yes	no
281	0.9	+	yes	no
164	2.1	+	yes	no
48	−3.6	−	yes	no
provide off-setting changes in the constraints bonding future payment of cash flows.				
248	−0.2*	0	yes	no
140	−0.1*	0	yes	no
28	−0.1*	0	yes	yes
249	−0.1*	0	yes	yes
133	−0.1*	0	yes	no
74	−2.1	—	yes	no
54	−1.4	—	yes	no
9	−1.6	—	yes	no
147	15.2	+	yes	yes
182	3.3	+	yes	yes
15	1.1	+	yes	yes
68	−4.8	+	no**	no**
215	−3.0	—	yes	yes
405	−0.6	—	yes	yes
57	−0.4*	—	no	yes
113	−2.1	—	yes	yes
future cash flows				
45	21.9	+	yes	yes
52	14.0	+	yes	yes
9	8.3	+	yes	no
24	3.5	+	yes	yes
18	1.6	+	yes	yes
36	0.6	0	no	no
96	0.2*	0	yes	yes
of future cash flows				
15	−2.4	—	yes	yes
23	−2.6	—	yes	no
9	−7.7	—	yes	yes
12	−4.2	—	yes	yes
81	−1.1	—	yes	yes

[14]Calculated by Smith (1986, Table 1) from Asquith and Mullins (1986), Masulis and Korwar (1986), Pettway and Radcliffe (1985).
[15]Masulis (1980).
[16]Masulis (1983). These returns include announcement days of both the original offer and, for about 40 percent of the sample, a second announcement of specific terms of the exchange.
[17]McConnell and Schlarbaum (1981).
[18]Dietrich (1984).
[19]As calculated by Smith (1986, Table 3) from Eckbo (1986), Mikkelson and Partch (1986).
[20]Mikkelson (1981).
[21]Rogers and Owers (1985, Peavy and Scott 1985, Finnerty 1985).
* Not statistically different from zero.
** Explained by the fact that these transactions are frequently associated with the termination of an actual or expected control bid. The price decline appears to reflect the loss of an expected control premium.

is offset exactly by a commitment bonding the future payout of cash flows of equal present value.

Panel C shows that sales of convertible debt and convertible preferred are associated with significantly negative stock price changes. These security sales raise cash and provide little effective bonding of future cash flow payments for the following reason: when the stock into which the debt is convertible is worth more than the face value of the debt, management has incentives to call them and force conversion to common.

Panel D shows that, with one exception, security

retirements that pay out cash to shareholders increase stock prices. The price decline associated with targeted large block repurchases (often called "greenmail") is highly likely to be due to the reduced probability that a takeover premium will be realized. These transactions are often associated with standstill agreements in which the seller of the stock agrees to refrain from acquiring more stock and from making a takeover offer for some period into the future.

Panel E summarizes the effects of security sales and retirements that raise cash and do not bond future cash flow payments. Consistent with the theory, negative abnormal returns are associated with all such changes. However, the negative returns associated with the sale of common through a conversion-forcing call are statistically insignificant.

Panel F shows that all exchange offers or designated-use security sales that increase the bonding of payout of future cash flows result in significantly positive increases in common stock prices. These include stock repurchases and exchange of debt or preferred for common, debt for preferred, and income bonds for preferred. The two-day gains range from 21.9 percent (debt for common) to 2.2 percent (debt or income bonds for preferred).

Panel G of Table 2 shows that the evidence on transactions with no cash flow and no change in the bonding of payout of future cash flows is mixed. The returns associated with exchange offers of debt for debt are significantly positive, and those for designated-use security sales are insignificantly different from zero.

Panel H of Table 2 shows that all exchanges, or designated-use security sales that have no cash effects but reduce the bonding of payout of future cash flows result, on average, in significant decreases in stock prices. These transactions include the exchange of common for debt or preferred or preferred for debt, or the replacement of debt with convertible debt. The two-day losses range from −9.9% (common for debt) to −2.4% (for designated-use security sale replacing debt with convertible debt).

In summary, the results in Table 2 are remarkably consistent with free cash flow theory, which predicts that, except for firms with profitable unfunded investment projects, prices will rise with unexpected increases in payouts to shareholders (or promises to do so) and will fall with reductions in

payments or new requests for funds from shareholders (or reductions in promises to make future payments). Moreover, the size of the value changes is positively related to the change in the tightness of the commitment bonding the payment of future cash flows. For example, the effects of debt-for-preferred exchanges are smaller than the effects of debt-for-common exchanges.

Tax effects can explain some of these results, but not all—for example, the price changes associated with exchanges of preferred for common or replacements of debt with convertible debt, neither of which which have any tax effects. The last column of Table 2 denotes whether the individual coefficients are explainable by these pure corporate tax effects. The tax theory hypothesizes that all unexpected changes in capital structure which decrease corporate taxes increase stock prices and vice versa.[34] Therefore, increases in dividend and reductions of debt interest should cause stock price to fall and vice versa.[35] Thirteen of the 32 coefficients are inconsistent with the corporate tax hypothesis. Simple signaling effects, where the payout of cash signals the lack of present and future investments that promise returns in excess of the cost of capital, are also inconsistent with the results—for example, the positive stock price changes associated with dividend increases and stock repurchases.

If anything, the results in Table 2 seem too good. The returns summarized in the table do not distinguish firms that have free cash flow from those that do not have free cash flow. Yet the theory tells us the returns to firms with no free cash flow will behave differently from those which do. In addition, only unexpected changes in cash payout or the tightness of the commitments bonding the payout of future free cash flows should affect stock prices. The studies summarized in Table 2 do not, in general, control for the effects of expectations. If the free cash flow effects are large and if firms on average are in a positive free cash flow position, the predictions of the theory will hold for the simple sample averages. If the effects are this pervasive, the waste due to agency problems in the corporate sector is greater than most scholars have thought. This helps explain the high level of activity in the corporate control market over the last decade. More detailed tests of the propositions that control for growth prospects and expectations will be interesting.

[4]

Journal of Economic Perspectives— Volume 2, Number 1 — Winter 1988— Pages 49–68

The Market for Corporate Control: The Empirical Evidence Since 1980

Gregg A. Jarrell, James A. Brickley, and Jeffry M. Netter

Corporate takeovers have been very big business in the 1980s. The Office of the Chief Economist (OCE) of the Securities and Exchange Commission estimates that shareholders of target firms in successful tender offers from 1981 through 1986 received payments in excess of $54 billion over the value of their holdings before the tender offers. Almost $38 billion of the total was received after 1984. If we include the increased wealth of target firm shareholders resulting from leveraged buyouts, mergers, and corporate restructurings (prompted in large part by the threat of takeovers) these numbers are even larger. W. T. Grimm & Co. collects similar data for a larger sample of change-of-control transactions, including mergers and leveraged buyouts. They estimate that from 1981 to 1986 the total dollar value of the premiums over the pre-announcement price paid for securities involved in change-of-control transactions was $118.4 billion.[1] Corporate restructurings have created even more

---

[1] These estimates understate the total premiums (dollar value of the percentage increase in the target's stock price caused by the takeover) paid in change-of-control transactions. OCE's sample is limited to the first successful tender offer for a firm. Thus, if an "auction" for the firm develops, resulting in an even higher offer price, they do not capture that additional premium. In addition, no account is made for tender offers that do not ultimately succeed. Shareholders may sell their shares in the market at the premium induced by the offer before it is known that the offer fails. The W. T. Grimm data also understates the total profits earned by stockholders because they calculate the premium based on the market price only five days before the initial public announcement and do not capture the premium attributable to increases in share prices that occur more than five days in advance of a public announcement.

■ *Gregg A. Jarrell is Senior Vice-President, Alcar Group Inc., Skokie, Illinois; James A. Brickley is Associate Professor, William E. Simon Graduate School of Business Administration, University of Rochester, Rochester, New York; Jeffry M. Netter is Senior Financial Economist, Office of the Chief Economist, United States Securities and Exchange Commission, Washington, DC.*

wealth. For example, Jensen (1986) estimated that the restructurings of Phillips, Unocal and Arco created total gains to shareholders of $6.6 billion by reducing investment in negative net present value projects.

There are numerous factors behind the high level of takeover activity in the 1980s. For example, antitrust regulators have come to understand that in the increasingly competitive international marketplace U.S. interests are well-served by domestic mergers that could be objectionable in a more closed economy. Today's antitrust regulators almost never object to vertical combinations, and even horizontal mergers between industry leaders—completely taboo before the 1980s—are often allowed today.

Deregulation also has induced merger and acquisition activity by calling forth new skills and strategies, and new management teams to implement them. Many of the mergers, takeovers, and restructurings over the last ten years have occurred in industries that recently were deregulated such as airlines and transportation, financial services, broadcasting, and oil and gas. For example, transportation and broadcasting together accounted for 20 percent of all mergers and acquisition activity from 1981 and 1984 while oil and gas accounted for another 26.3 percent (Jensen, 1986).

Other factors motivating the high level of takeover and restructuring activity in the 1980s include innovations in takeover financing, less potent state antitakeover regulations, the retreat by the Federal courts and regulatory agencies from protecting besieged target firms, and learning about the possible returns to this type of activity. These factors are critical to understanding why firms that were considered "untouchable" not long ago have been the targets of hostile takeovers with increasing frequency. This growing list includes USX, CBS, Phillips, and TWA, to name just a few.

The Council of Economic Advisors (CEA) in the 1985 *Economic Report of the President* provides data on the extent of the takeover activity in the 1980s and the importance of large transactions in explaining this activity. The CEA states that the increase in merger and acquisition activity in the 1980s is due to a large increase in the size of the largest transactions. Their evidence indicates that in the period 1981 to 1984 the average annual reported real value of mergers and acquisitions was 48 percent greater than in any four year period from the late 1960s to the early 1970s. In addition, of the 100 largest acquisition transactions recorded through 1983, 65 occurred after 1982 and only 11 took place prior to 1979.

Returns to Bidders and Targets

Critics of takeovers question whether tender offers, mergers, and leveraged buyouts produce net gains to society. Critics argue any gains to a given party are simply redistributions resulting from losses to someone else (or more colorfully put, a pirating of assets by modern financial buccaneers). Also critics contend that battles for corporate control divert energy from more productive endeavors.[2] In this section, we find that such criticisms are ill founded, and thus conclude that battles for corporate control serve a beneficial function for the economy.✳

The market for corporate control is the market for the right to control the management of corporate resources. In a takeover, an outside party seeks to obtain control of a firm. There are several types of takeovers, including mergers, hostile and friendly tender offers, and proxy contests. In a merger the bidder negotiates an agreement with target management on the terms of the offer for the target and then submits the proposed agreement to a vote of the shareholders. In a tender offer, a bidder makes an offer directly to shareholders to buy some or all of the stock of the target firm. A "friendly" tender offer refers to offers that are supported by target management. The most controversial type of takeovers are "hostile" tender offers, which are tender offers that are opposed by target managements. In a proxy contest, a dissident group attempts through a vote of shareholders to obtain control of the board of directors. Finally, leveraged buyouts are buyouts of shareholder's equity, heavily financed with debt by a group that frequently includes incumbent management.

Many of the studies reviewed in this paper are event studies that measure the effects of certain unanticipated events (such as a takeover or other control contest) on stock prices, after correcting for overall market influence on security returns. Any finding of abnormal returns, therefore, shows how the stock market views the impact of the event on the firm's common stockholders. (See Brown and Warner, 1985, for a more thorough review of event study methods.)

Returns to Shareholders of Target Companies

Shareholders of target companies clearly benefit from takeovers. Jarrell and Poulsen (1987a) estimate the premiums paid in 663 successful tender offers from 1962 to December 1985. They find that premiums averaged 19 percent in the 1960s, 35 percent in the 1970s, and from 1980 to 1985 the average premium was 30 percent. These figures are consistent with the 13 studies of pre-1980 data contained in Jensen and Ruback (1983) which agree that targets of successful tender offers and mergers before 1980 earned positive returns ranging from 16 percent to 30 percent for tender offers.[3]

Similar results are contained in studies of leveraged buyouts and going private transactions. Lehn and Poulsen (1987) find premiums of 21 percent to shareholders in

[2] Many critics of acquisition activity (such as the Business Roundtable) are primarily concerned with alleged abuses arising from hostile takeovers. The other types of acquisition activity are approved by target firms' management who allegedly are the individuals most concerned with the welfare of the target firm and its shareholders.

[3] Jensen and Ruback (1983) review 13 studies published between 1977 and 1983—six on mergers and seven on tender offers. Their survey provides a concise summary of the pre-1980 data. But because of the lengthy review process for academic journals, the most up-to-date sample used in these studies ends in 1981, and most do not go beyond the late 1970s. This paper can be considered an update of Jensen and Ruback with a focus on recent empirical studies that cover takeovers made in the 1980s.

93 leveraged buyouts taking place from 1980 to 1984. DeAngelo, DeAngelo and Rice (1984) find an average 27 percent gain for leveraged buyouts between 1973 and 1980.

OCE (1985a) measures premiums paid by comparing the price per share offered by the bidder to the trading price of the stock one month before the offer, not adjusting for changes in the market index (also see Comment and Jarrell, forthcoming). Using a comprehensive sample of 225 successful tender offers from 1981 through 1984, including over-the-counter targets, OCE finds the average premium to shareholders to be 53.2 percent. OCE has updated these figures for 1985 and 1986 and finds a decrease over the last two years. OCE finds that the average premium is 37 percent in 1985 and 33.6 percent in 1986.[4]

While the evidence reported thus far indicates substantial gains to target shareholders, it probably understates the total gains to these shareholders. In many cases events occur before a formal takeover offer, so studies that concentrate on the stock price reactions to formal offers will understate the total gains to shareholders.

Several recent empirical studies examine the stock market reaction to events that often precede formal steps in the battle for corporate control. Mikkelson and Ruback (1985a) provide information on the stock price reaction to Schedule 13D filings. Schedule 13D must be filed with the SEC by all purchasers of 5 percent of a corporation's common stock, requiring disclosure of, among other things, the investor's identity and intent. Mikkelson and Ruback find significant price reactions around the initial announcement of the filing, and that the returns depend on the intent stated in the 13D. The highest returns, an increase of 7.74 percent, occurred when the filer in the statement of intent indicated some possibility of a control change. However, the abnormal returns were only 3.24 percent if the investor reported the purchase was for investment purposes. Holderness and Sheehan (1985) find a differential stock market effect to 13D filings depending on the identity of the filer. They show the filings of six "corporate raiders" increased target share prices by a significantly greater amount than a sample of other filers (5.9 percent to 3.4 percent).

More direct evidence that significant stock price increases occur prior to formal announcements of corporate events is contained in OCE (1987c) which finds a significant increase in the stock price of target firms in 172 successful tender offers in the period before any announcement of the offer. OCE finds a run-up in stock prices of 38.8 percent of the total control premium by the close of day *before* the offer announcement. The announcement date is, in the parlance of Wall Street, the date the target firm was put "in play" and represents some event having significant implications for corporate control. For example, the in-play date in some cases is the formal offer but in other cases is the eventual bidder's filing of a Schedule 13D with corporate control implications for the target.

---

[4]The OCE (1985a) study also explicitly tests and rejects the popular theory that two-tier tender offers disadvantage target shareholders. Some observers argue that two-tier offers—in which the bidder first makes an offer for control of the firm and then makes a "clean-up" offer for remaining shares at a lower price—coerces shareholders to tender to avoid the clean-up price. OCE finds that two-tier offers have overall premiums that are nearly identical to the average for any-or-all offers and that there is no evidence that two-tier offers "stampede" shareholders into unwise trading decisions.

Table 1

Cumulative excess returns to successful bidders for tender offers during 1960 to 1985, by decade

Trading-day Interval	Cumulative excess returns in percent			
	All	1960s	1970s	1980s
− 10 to +5	1.14	4.40	1.22	−1.10
(*t*-stat.)	(2.49)	(4.02)	(2.12)	(−1.54)
−10 to +20	2.04	4.95	2.21	−0.04
(*t*-stat.)	(3.31)	(3.52)	(2.87)	(−0.04)
Number of observations	405	106	140	159

Source: Jarrell and Poulsen (1987a)

While some commentators argue that price run-up before the formal announce-ments of tender offers indicates the presence of illegal insider trading, OCE's evidence demonstrates that the legal market for information can explain much of the run-up. OCE shows that a significant portion of the run-up can be explained by three readily identifiable influences on pre-bid trading: media speculation, the bidder's foothold acquisition in the target, and whether the bid is friendly or hostile. Systematic relations between these factors and run-up in target share prices indicate that there is an active market for information about impending takeover bids and a large portion of the run-up can be explained by factors other than illegal insider trading. OCE's results on pre-bid market activity are supported by Comment (1986).

Returns to Shareholders of Acquiring Companies

The 1980s evidence on bidders comes from Jarrell and Poulsen (1987a), with data on 663 successful tender offers covering 1962 to 1985. Table 1 summarizes the excess returns to 440 NYSE and AMEX bidders. For the entire sample period bidders on average realized small, but statistically significant, gains of about 1 to 2 percent in the immediate period around the public announcement. Most interesting is the apparent secular decline in the gains to successful bidders in tender offers. Consistent with the previous studies reviewed by Jensen and Ruback (1983), Table 1 shows positive excess returns of five percent during the 1960s, and a lower, but still significantly significant, positive average of 2.2 percent over the 1970s. However, the 159 cases from the 1980s show statistically insignificant losses to bidders.

How the Distribution of Takeover Gains Is Determined

Companies that are targets of takeovers receive the bulk of the value created by corporate combinations and these gains are not offset by losses to acquirers. As one might predict, an important factor in determining how these takeover gains are split seems to be how many bidders are trying to acquire the target company. In fact, the secular decline in the stock returns to bidders probably reflects the increased competition among bidders and the rise of auction-style contests during the 1980s.[5]

Conditions which foster an increase in multiple bidding tend to increase target premiums and reduce bidder returns. For example, Jarrell and Bradley (1980) demonstrate that Federal (Williams Act) and state regulations of tender offers have this effect because they impose disclosure and delay rules that foster multiple-bidder, auction contests and preemptive bidding.[6] In addition to greater regulation, other factors contributing to this increased competition include court rulings protecting defensive tactics, the inventions of several defenses against takeovers, and the increase in sophisticated takeover advisers to implement them.

Interesting support for this theory in the banking industry is provided by James and Wier (1987). Federal and state banking regulations effectively limit the number of eligible acquisition partners, thus affecting the number of potential substitutes for bidders or targets in particular transactions. For 39 proposed banking acquisitions, James and Wier measure a positive relation between the bidder's share of the takeover gains and the number of alternative targets, and a negative relation between the bidder's share and the number of alternative bidders.[7]

The Source of Takeover Gains

Shareholders of target companies definitely gain from mergers and tender offers. But much uneasiness has been expressed at who might be paying for those gains. In their summary several years ago, Jensen and Ruback (1983, p. 47) were forced to conclude that "knowledge of the sources of takeover gains still eludes us."[8] The studies they reviewed did not allow them to judge the many redistributive theories, which suggest that shareholder gains are offset by economic losses to others. Since then, many popular "redistributive theories" have been examined. The evidence has led many financial economists like Jensen (1986, p. 6) to attribute takeovers, leveraged buyouts, and restructurings to "productive entrepreneurial activity that improves the control and management of assets and helps move assets to more productive uses." We now turn to a review of the most important of these redistributive theories.

---

[5] Bradley, Desai, and Kim (1984) show that targets gain more in multiple bidder than single bidder contests.
[6] The Williams Act contains the Federal regulations of tender offers and was enacted in July 1968. Its main components are disclosure requirements, a regulated minimum offer period, and antifraud provisions that give target management standing to sue for injunctive relief.
[7] Other evidence supporting this point includes a recent paper by Guerin-Calvert, McGuckin, and Warren-Boulton (1986) that reexamines the effects of state and Federal regulations of tender offers. They also find the regulations increase the incidence of multiple-bidder auction takeovers among all control contests. Also consistent with this result is the evidence on the French experience presented by Eckbo and Langohr (1986). They show that the imposition of disclosure-only (not delay) rules governing tender offers in France significantly shifted the gains in French takeovers from acquirers to targets.
[8] Jensen and Ruback review the empirical work testing the market power theory of takeovers by Eckbo (1983) and Stillman (1983). This theory is that increased monopoly power in product markets explains takeover gains. Jensen and Ruback conclude the evidence rejects this theory as the source of gains from takeovers. Recent papers by Eckbo and Wier (1985) and by Eckbo (1985) provide empirical support for the conclusion that except in isolated cases, increased market power cannot explain the gains from takeovers.

Short-Term Myopia and Inefficient Takeovers. This theory is based on an allegation that market participants, and particularly institutional investors, are concerned almost exclusively with short-term earnings performance and tend to undervalue corporations engaged in long-term activity. From this viewpoint, any corporation planning for long-term development will become undervalued by the market as its resource commitments to the long-term depress its short-term earnings, and thus will become a prime takeover candidate.

Critics of this theory point out that it is blatantly inconsistent with an efficient capital market. Indeed, if the market systematically undervalues long-run planning and investment, it implies harmful economic consequences that go far beyond the costs of inefficient takeovers. Fortunately, no empirical evidence has been found to support this theory. In fact, a study of 324 high research and development firms and of all 177 takeover targets during 1981–84 by the SEC's Office of the Chief Economist (OCE, 1985b) shows evidence that (1) increased institutional stock holdings are not associated with increased takeovers of firms; (2) increased institutional holdings are not associated with decreases in research and development; (3) firms with high research and development expenditures are not more vulnerable to takeovers; and (4) stock prices respond positively to announcements of increases in research and development expenditures.

Further evidence opposing the myopia theory is provided by Hall (1987) in an NBER study and by McConnell and Muscarella (1985). Hall studies data on acquisition activity among manufacturing firms from 1977 to 1986. She presents evidence that much acquisition activity has been directed towards firms and industries which are less intensive in R & D activity. She also finds that firms involved in mergers show little difference in their pre- and postmerger R & D performance compared with industry peers. McConnell and Muscarella, in a study of 658 capital expenditure announcements, show that stock prices respond positively to announcements of increased capital expenditures, on average, except for exploration and development announcements in the oil industry.

Undervalued Target Theory. Recalcitrant target management and other opponents of takeovers often contend that because targets are "undervalued" by the market, a savvy bidder can offer substantial premiums for target firms while still paying far below the intrinsic value of the corporation. By this theory, it becomes the duty of target managements to defend vigorously against even high premium offers since remaining independent, it is argued, can offer shareholders greater rewards over the long term than are offered by opportunistic bidders seeking short-term gains.

However, the evidence shows the promised long-term gains from remaining independent do not usually materialize. When a target defeats a hostile bid, its post-defeat value reverts to approximately the (market adjusted) level obtaining before the instigation of the hostile bid (Bradley, Desai and Kim, 1983; Easterbrook and Jarrell 1984; Jarrell 1985; Ruback, 1986). Bhagat, Brickley and Lowenstein (1987) used option pricing theory to show that the announcement period returns around cash tender offers are too large to be explained by revaluations due to information about undervaluation.

This evidence indicates that the market does not, on average, learn much of anything that is new or different about target firms' intrinsic values through the tender offer process, despite the tremendous attention lavished on targets, and the huge amounts of information traded among market participants during takeover contests. If undervaluation had indeed been present, then the deluge of new information on the intrinsic value of targets should have caused fundamental price corrections even in the event of takeover defeats. But in the overwhelming majority of cases studied, prices dropped rather than increased for target firms that fought off takeovers.

Do Tax Effects Motivate Mergers and Takeovers? Tax motives have long been suspected as an important cause of merger and acquisition activity. Indeed, the Tax Reform Act of 1986 contains several provisions aimed at reducing the tax benefits available through mergers.[9] Most recent studies, however, assign tax benefits a minor role in explaining merger and takeover activity. Auerbach and Reishus (1987a) study 318 mergers and acquisitions during 1968–83 to estimate the tax benefits available in these transactions from increased use of tax losses and credits. They found that these tax benefits in general were not a significant factor in the majority of large acquisitions. In a fair number of transactions, however (potentially 20 percent of the mergers), tax factors did appear to be significant enough to affect the decision to merge.[10] Lehn and Poulsen (1987) find, in their study of leveraged buyouts from 1980–84, that the premiums paid are directly related to potential tax benefits associated with these transactions, suggesting that in part these leveraged buyouts are motivated by tax considerations.

In summary, acquiring firms' tax losses and credits, and the option to step-up the basis of targets' assets without paying corporate level capital gains, are two tax benefits that appear to have had some impact on merger activity. However, the evidence suggests that much of the takeover activity in the last twenty years was not tax motivated.

Do Bondholders Lose From Takeovers? Some critics of takeovers suggest that the premiums paid by bidders are not a result of any wealth enhancing changes, but instead represent a redistribution from the holders of the target's bonds and preferred equity. For example, the bonds of an acquiring firm can drop in value if the acquiring firm pays cash for a riskier target firm. Given that the combined value of the two firms remains unchanged, the decline in the bond value will be captured as a gain by

---

[9]A review of the effects on the takeover market of the change of the 1986 Tax Reform Act is contained in Steindel (1986). The 1986 Tax Reform Act repeals the General Utilities doctrine, which states that corporations liquidating their businesses are not subject to capital gains tax on the value of their assets. A firm using General Utilities in a liquidation (the purchaser of at least 80 percent of the stock of a corporation may treat the transaction for tax purposes as a liquidation) avoids the tax liability that comes with appreciated assets. Steindel argues that the repeal of the General Utilities doctrine combined with the changes in corporate tax rates reduces the attractiveness of many mergers and acquisitions. Other tax changes with effects on takeover activity include the increase in the personal capital gains tax and new rules on the transfer of net operating loss carryforwards.

[10]However, Auerbach and Reishus (1987b) compare actual mergers over 1968–1983 with a control group of nonmerging firms and conclude that the potential increase in interest deductions and unused tax losses and tax credits of the acquired firms have not driven acquisitions.

some other class of security holder (such as common stockholders).[11] However, the empirical evidence does not support this argument.

Denis and McConnell (1986) examine the returns on various classes of the securities of a sample of 132 mergers in the period 1962 to 1980. Denis and McConnell's results are consistent with earlier studies in that they find gains to mergers and no losses to bondholders. Their results indicate that on average holders of common stock, convertible and nonconvertible preferred stock, and convertible bonds in the acquired firm gain from a merger. Those who hold nonconvertible bonds in the acquired firm and convertible bonds, nonconvertible bonds, and nonconvertible preferred stock in the acquiring firm neither gain nor lose in a merger. Denis and McConnell also find some evidence that the acquiring firms' common shareholders do not lose and may gain from mergers, especially in the days immediately following the announcement. Lehn and Poulsen's (1987) study of 108 leveraged buyouts from 1980 to 1984 finds no support for the redistribution theory. They find no evidence that the shareholder value created by the leveraged buyouts comes at the expense of preferred shareholders or bondholders. In sum, the evidence provides no support for the hypothesis that the supposed gains from acquisitions are actually transfers from the holders of senior securities to the holders of common stock.

Do Labor's Losses Finance Takeovers? Recent takeovers in the airline industry have involved conflict between acquiring-firm management and the (usually) unionized labor of the target firm. These conflicts have contributed to the popular generalization that shareholder premiums from takeovers come largely at the expense of labor. Shleifer and Summers (1987) articulate this view more rigorously focusing on implicit long-term contracts between labor and incumbent (target) management. They argue raiders can sometimes exploit these contracts by buying a controlling share of the equity and financing the premium by using pressure tactics to force significant wage concessions. In theory, this activity can be socially inefficient by ruining the market for these implicit long-run labor contracts and forcing labor and management to use less efficient contracting devices.

This redistributive theory from labor to shareholders has not been tested widely, but a recent NBER study by Brown and Medoff (1987) presents statistical evidence based on Michigan's employment and wages that fails to support it. Although this close look at Michigan is not necessarily indicative of the U.S. experience (for example, it contains few large mergers or hostile tender offers), the results are that wages and employment rise on average for firms that are involved in acquisitions.

Summary of Source of Gains

The various redistribution theories of takeover gains have been the subject of considerable empirical work since the Jensen and Ruback (1983) review. Most convincing is the empirical rejection of the undervaluation theory: target firms cannot be depicted generally as being "undervalued" by the stock market. Also soundly

---

[11] The senior security holders of the target firm can also lose depending on the takeover's effect on the riskiness of their claims.

rejected by the data is the short-term myopia theory. The evidence gives tax-benefits theories at least a minor role in explaining merger and tender offer activity. Finally, evidence is inconsistent with the theories that the stock-price gains to shareholders come from bondholders and labor.

Although some individuals (incumbent management, for example) obviously lose in at least some takeovers, the literature, while not conclusive, offers little or no support for the notion that the redistribution theories explain a major portion of the apparent gains from takeovers. It has been impossible so far to find systematic losses which could offset the enormous gains to target and bidding firm shareholders from mergers, tender offers, and other corporate-control activities. We therefore conclude that evidence is consistent with the notion that these corporate transactions reflect economically beneficial reshufflings of productive assets.

The Effects of Defending Against Hostile Takeovers

Defensive strategies against hostile takeovers have always been controversial since they pose a conflict of interest for target management. After all, takeovers can impose significant welfare losses on managers, who may be displaced and lose their organization-specific human capital. These conflicts may tempt some managers to erect barriers to hostile takeovers, thus insulating themselves from the discipline of the outside market for control at the expense of their shareholders and the efficiency of the economy.

However, providing target management with the power to defend against hostile takeover bids might also help target shareholders during a control contest. Target management can in certain cases defeat bids that are "inadequate." Although this rationale is popular, the evidence discussed earlier shows that in very few cases do these alleged long-term gains of independence actually materialize. The other benefit of resistance comes when resistance by target management helps promote a takeover auction. Litigation and other blocking actions can provide the necessary time for the management of the target firm to "shop" the target and generate competing bids. This auction rationale for resistance is harder to reject statistically. Evidence on occasional shareholder losses after the defeat of a takeover attempt does not in itself disprove the auction theory. This negotiating leverage can be expected to fail in some cases, with the sole bidder becoming discouraged and withdrawing. It is a gamble. The hypothesis is rejected only if the harmful outcome of defeating all bids is sufficiently frequent and costly to offset the benefits of inducing higher takeover prices. One must also consider the social cost of tender offers that never occur because of the presence of defensive devices. Unfortunately, this deterrence effect is very difficult to measure and we present no direct evidence of the extent of these costs.

Evidence on the effects of defensive measures by target management is obtained mainly from two approaches, the event-type study and the outcomes-type study. The event-type study recognizes that an efficient market must judge this cost-benefit tradeoff when it adjusts the market value of a firm in response to the adoption of a charter amendment or some other kind of resistance. Alternatively, the outcomes-type study examines the actual outcomes of control contests over a significant time horizon among firms using a common kind of resistance—say all firms adopting poison pills. That is, an event study measures the stock price reaction to the introduction of defensive devices while outcomes studies follow the use of defensive devices in control contests to determine their effects on the outcomes of the contests.

Many defensive measures must be approved by a vote of the shareholders. Hence, voting has the potential to block management-sponsored proposals that harm shareholders, depending on the costs and benefits to individual shareholders from collecting relevant information and voting. In general, a shareholder with a small amount of shares will not invest heavily in the voting process since a small number of shares will not generally affect the outcome regardless of how they are voted. However, if individual voting and information costs are near zero even the share- holder with few shares can be expected to vote against management on value-decreas- ing proposals. Alternatively, large outside block holders (like institutional investors) internalize more of the benefits from participation in the voting process and can be expected to take an active interest in voting on antitakeover proposals even when the information gathering and voting costs are positive. Since voting rights can block harmful measures, we distinguish between two broad categories of defensive measures, those receiving approval by voting shareholders and those adopted unilaterally by management.

Defensive Measures Approved by Shareholders

Antitakeover amendments generally operate by imposing new conditions that must be satisfied before changing managerial control of the corporation. They are almost always proposed by management and they usually require majority voting approval by shareholders. Proposed antitakeover amendments are very rarely rejected by voting shareholders; Brickley, Lease, and Smith (forthcoming) find for a sample of 288 management-sponsored antitakeover proposals in 1984 that about 96 percent passed.

Supermajority Amendments. Most state corporation laws set the minimum approval required for mergers and other important control transactions at either one-half or two-thirds of the voting shares. Supermajority amendments require the approval by holders of at least two-thirds and sometimes as much as nine-tenths of the voting power of the outstanding common stock. These provisions can apply either to mergers and other business combinations or to changing the firm's board of directors or to both. Pure supermajority provisions are very rare today, having been replaced by similar provisions that are triggered at the discretion of the board of directors. This allows the board to waive the supermajority provisions allowing friendly mergers to proceed unimpeded.

Five years ago, Jensen and Ruback (1983) found mixed evidence on the effect of supermajority amendments passed before 1980. However, a more recent study by Jarrell and Poulsen (1987b), derived from OCE (1985c), covers 104 supermajority amendments passed since 1980 and reports significant negative stock-price effects of over 3 percent around the introduction of the proposals. They also show that firms passing supermajority amendments have relatively low institutional stockholdings (averaging 19 percent) and high insider holdings (averaging 18 percent), which they interpret as helping to explain how these amendments received voting approval despite their harmful wealth effect. That is, firms proposing these amendments have fewer blockholders with incentives to invest in the voting process. Jarrell and Poulsen further conjecture that the increased shareholder resistance to harmful supermajority amendments helps explain their declining popularity in contrast to the success of the fair price amendment which appear less likely to harm shareholders (as discussed below).

   Fair Price Amendments.   The fair price amendment is a supermajority provision that applies only to nonuniform, two-tier takeover bids that are opposed by the target's board of directors. Uniform offers that are considered "fair" circumvent the supermajority requirement, even if target management opposes them. Fairness of the offer is determined in several ways. The most common fair price is defined as the highest price paid by the bidder for any of the shares it has acquired in the target firm during a specified period of time. Jarrell and Poulsen (1987b) report that 487 firms adopted fair price charter provisions between 1979 and May 1985, with over 90 percent of these coming in the very recent period of 1983 to May 1985.

   The stock price effects reflect the low deterrence value of the fair price amendment. Jarrell and Poulsen (1987b) report an average loss of 0.73 percent around the introduction of these amendments, which is not statistically significant. They also show that firms adopting fair price amendments have roughly normal levels of insider holdings (12 percent) and of institutional holdings (30 percent). They interpret this evidence as supporting the view that shareholder voting retards adoption of harmful amendments, especially when insider holdings are low and institutional holdings are high. Further support for this view is provided by Brickley, Lease, and Smith (forthcoming) who document that "no" votes on antitakeover amendments (especially ones that harm shareholders) increase with institutional and other outside blockholdings, while "no" votes decrease with increases in managerial holdings.

   Dual-Class Recapitalizations.   These plans restructure the equity of a firm into two classes with different voting rights. Although several methods are used, the common goal is to provide management or family owners with voting power disproportionately greater than provided by their equity holdings under a "one share-one vote" rule.[12]

   Evidence before and after 1980 has confirmed that the market generally values shares with voting power more than those without. Lease, McConnell, and Mikkelson (1983) examine 30 firms having dual-class common stock and show that voting stock on average trades at a significant premium, ranging from one to seven percent. A recent paper by OCE (1987a) examines the monthly stock prices of 26 OTC and

---

[12] For over 60 years, the New York Stock Exchange did not allow any member firm to have a dual-class capitalization structure, but it has recently proposed a liberalization to allow dual-class listings in response to competitive pressures from Amex and OTC markets. Amex currently allows dual-class listings with some restrictions, and the OTC market has no restrictions beyond usual state-law requirements.

AMEX firms having dual-class common and shows an average discount of four to five percent for low-vote common, though the discount is reduced when the low-vote stock has rights to preferential dividends.

Of course, the fact that the market values voting power does not demonstrate that dual-class recapitalizations reduce the overall price of stock. DeAngelo and DeAngelo (1985) examine in detail 45 firms that had dual-voting common stock as of 1980. They find that, after restructuring, management and family insiders control a median of 57 percent of the votes and 24 percent of the common stock cash flows. This confirms that dual-class structures often confer substantial voting powers on incumbent management. However, DeAngelo and DeAngelo also suggest that the shareholders of the firms in this sample found it beneficial to contract with incumbent management to limit the competition for management of their firms. They argue that shareholders rationally accept a reduced potential for hostile takeovers in return for other benefits, such as greater incentives for incumbents to make specific long-term investments in human capital.

Two recent studies have addressed the empirical question of whether dual-voting structures are beneficial, as DeAngelo and DeAngelo suggest, or harmful to outside shareholders. Partch (1987) examines the stock-price reaction around the announcement of the proposed dual-class recapitalizations for 44 firms. She reports nonnegative share-price effects. However, for more recent recapitalizations, Jarrell and Poulsen (forthcoming, extending OCE 1987a, 1987d) find negative effects at the announcement of dual-class recapitalizations. For a sample of 89 firms delisting from 1976 through 1987, they report an average abnormal stock price effect of $-.93$ percent.

If dual-class recapitalization proposals are viewed primarily as takeover defenses, their announcement should cause negative stock price reactions, similar to those observed at the announcement of supermajority amendments. However, firms announcing dual-class recapitalizations have some unusual characteristics. Jarrell and Poulsen (forthcoming) find that the average net-of-market return to their 94 dual-class firms over the year preceding the recapitalization is over 37 percent. Jarrell and Poulsen and Partch both find that insider holdings average 44 percent before the recapitalization, and that recapitalization significantly increases insider voting control. These two characteristics suggest that the typical dual-class firm is already controlled by insiders and the recapitalization provides a means to raise needed capital for positive net present value projects without the dilution of control.

Changes in the State of Incorporation. Changing the state of incorporation can affect the contractual arrangements between management and shareholders. For example, some states such as Ohio, Indiana, and New York have elements in their corporate codes that make takeovers more difficult than in other states. Dodd and Leftwich (1980) find that firms change their state of incorporation after a period of superior performance and that the change itself is associated with small positive excess returns. More recently, Romano (1985) finds a statistically significant price increase around the reincorporation announcement in a sample of firms that reincorporate for various reasons. However, in the subsample of 43 firms who reincorporated as an antitakeover device she found a small statistically insignificant price increase at the announcement of a reincorporation. The evidence is not conclusive but it does indicate that reincorporating in a new state does not on average harm shareholders.

Reduction in Cumulative Voting Rights. Cumulative voting makes it possible for a group of minority shareholders to elect directors even if the majority of shareholders oppose their election. Dissidents in hostile takeovers and proxy contests will often attempt to elect some board members through the use of cumulative voting. Bhagat and Brickley (1984) examine the stock price reaction to 84 management sponsored charter amendments that either eliminate or reduce the effect of cumulative voting. Since these amendments decrease the power of dissident shareholders to elect directors, they increase management's ability to resist a tender offer. Bhagat and Brickley find statistically significant negative abnormal returns of about one percent at the introduction of these charter amendments.

Defensive Measures That Do Not Require Shareholder Approval

Four general kinds of defensive measures do not require voting approval by shareholders: general litigation, greenmail, poison pills, and the use of state antitakeover laws. With the exception of general litigation, these defensive actions are associated on average with negative stock-price reactions indicating that in most cases they are economically harmful to stockholders of companies whose management enacted them.

Litigation by Target Management. As described earlier, litigation can be expected to hurt shareholders of some target companies by eliminating takeovers and to help shareholders of other companies by giving their management time and weapons to cut a better deal. Jarrell (1985) examines 89 cases involving litigation against a hostile suitor based on charges of securities fraud, antitrust violations, and violations of state or Federal tender offer regulations. His results show that litigation usually delays the control contest significantly and that litigating targets are frequently the beneficiaries of auctions. The 59 auction-style takeovers produced an additional 17 percent excess return to shareholders over the original bid, while the 21 targets that remained independent lost nearly all of the original average premium of 30 percent. Overall, Jarrell concludes that this evidence cannot reject the theory that on average target litigation is consistent with shareholder wealth maximization.[13]

However, harm can result from certain types of defensive litigation. Netter (1987) finds that litigation based in part on a claim alleging the filing of a false Schedule 13D Item 4 can be detrimental to target shareholders. In an exhaustive sample of all cases where target management filed a suit alleging (among other things) that a bidder filed a false 13D Item 4, he finds that target shareholders are better off if their management loses the case than if they win. If the target firm wins the case its share price declines by a significant amount (an abnormal return of negative 3.37 percent in the two-day window around the decision) while if the bidder wins, the stock price of the target firm increases by a significant amount (positive 3.15 percent abnormal return in the two-day window.

---

[13] Jarrell also notes that while defensive litigation redistributes premiums it also, by reducing incentives to engage in takeovers and through the cost of the litigation itself, can reduce social welfare.

Targeted Block Stock Repurchases (Greenmail). Greenmail occurs when target management ends a hostile takeover threat by repurchasing at a premium the hostile suitor's block of target stock. This controversial practice has been challenged in federal courts, in congressional testimony, and in SEC hearings, and it has brought negative publicity both to payers and to receivers of greenmail. In reviewing earlier studies, Jensen and Ruback (1983) conclude that greenmail repurchases are associated with significantly negative abnormal stock returns for the shareholders of the repurchasing firms (probably because they eliminate potential takeover bids) and significantly positive abnormal stock returns for shareholders of the selling firms. These negative effects of greenmail repurchases contrast sharply with the normally positive stock-price effects associated with nontargeted offers to repurchase a company's own stock.

Since then, three new empirical studies have contributed to a more complex and less conclusive discussion of greenmail transactions. These studies indicate that it is not necessarily in the interests of shareholders to ban greenmail payments. Such a ban has the potential to discourage outside investment in the potential target's stock by investors anticipating greenmail payments and hence reduces the incentives of outsiders to monitor managers.

Mikkelson and Ruback (1985a) examine 39 cases of greenmail (based on 13Ds filed during 1978–80). They find a significant stock-price loss of 2.3 percent upon the announcement of the repurchases. However, they also report an average gain of 1.7 percent over the entire period including the original stock purchase by the hostile suitors. Holderness and Sheehan's (1985) outcome-type study includes 12 cases of greenmail, and they report a pattern of returns consistent with the evidence of Mikkelson and Ruback. Although the greenmail transaction itself harms target shareholders, the net returns to stockholders resulting from the initial purchase and related events is positive. A more comprehensive sample of targeted block stock repurchases is covered by OCE (1984). This study includes 89 cases of large repurchases (blocks greater than 3 percent of the outstanding common stock) from 1979 to 1983. The initial announcement of investor interest induces a positive return averaging 9.7 percent, while the greenmail transaction is associated with a stock price loss of 5.2 percent.

Poison Pills. Since its introduction in late 1982, the "poison pill" has become the most popular and controversial device used to defend against hostile takeover attempts. Poison pill describes a family of shareholder rights agreements that, when triggered by an event such as a tender offer for control or the accumulation of a specified percentage of target shares by an acquirer, provide target shareholders with rights to purchase additional shares or to sell shares to the target at very attractive prices. These rights, when triggered, impose significant economic penalties on a hostile acquirer.

Poison pills are considered very effective deterrents against hostile takeover attempts because of two striking features. First, pills can be cheaply and quickly altered by target management if a hostile acquirer has not pulled the trigger. This feature pressures potential acquirers to negotiate directly with the target's board. Second, if not redeemed, the pill makes hostile acquisitions exorbitantly expensive in most cases. As an obstacle to hostile takeover attempts, the poison pill is unmatched

except by dual-voting recapitalizations or direct majority share ownership by incumbent management. The concern over poison pills was heightened by the Delaware
Supreme Court's 1985 ruling in *Moran v. Household International*[14] that poison pills do
not require majority voting approval by shareholders.

The most comprehensive study of poison pills is Ryngaert (forthcoming), which is
an outgrowth of OCE (1986). The Ryngaert study features an exhaustive collection of
380 poison pills adopted from 1982 to December 25, 1986. Over 80 percent of these
were adopted after the *Household* decision. Ryngaert divides his sample into discriminatory pills (the most restrictive) and flip-over pills (the least restrictive). He also
accounts for whether firms are subject to takeover speculation and whether confounding events occur close to the announcement of the pill that contaminate the data. The
stock-price effect over the 283 cases with no confounding events is a statistically
significant − .34 percent. Focusing on 57 cases subject to takeover speculation, the
average loss is 1.51 percent, also statistically significant. These results are supported by
the findings of Malatesta and Walkling (forthcoming).

Discriminatory pills have more harmful effects on shareholder wealth than do
flip-over pills. Also, the discriminatory pills that threaten the hostile suitor with severe
dilution have become increasingly popular. Ryngaert reports that pill-adopting
managements own a surprisingly low average of around 3.0 percent of their firms'
outstanding stock. This fact, together with high institutional holdings, suggest that
many of these firms would have difficulty obtaining shareholder voting approval if it
were required.

Ryngaert also examines the stock-price effects of important court decisions
emanating from legal battles involving pill defenses during 1983–86. He shows that
15 of 18 pro-target, pro-poison pill decisions have negative effects on the target's stock
price, and 6 of 11 pro-acquirer decisions have positive effects on the target stock price.
This evidence is inconsistent with the theory that pill defenses improve shareholder
wealth by strengthening management's bargaining position in control contests.

Although these losses are not large in percentage terms, these empirical tests
suggest that poison pills are harmful to target shareholders.

State Antitakeover Amendments.   In addition to the Williams Act at the Federal
level, tender offers are regulated by many states. So-called first-generation state
antitakeover regulations are antitakeover laws that were passed by the states before
the 1982 Supreme Court decision in *Edgar v. Mite*.[15] The Jarrell and Bradley (1980)
study of state and Federal regulation of tender offers finds that first generation state
regulations significantly increase the premiums paid in tender offers. Smiley (1981)
illustrates the deterrent effects of these early state takeover regulations.

However, first generation antitakeover laws were generally extinguished in *Edgar
v. Mite* when the Supreme Court ruled the Illinois antitakeover law unconstitutional.
Justice White's opinion held the Illinois takeover statute was preempted by the
Williams Act and constituted an undue and direct burden on interstate commerce. As

[14] *Moran v. Household International*, 490 A.2d 1059 (1985).
[15] *Edgar v. Mite*, 457 U.S. 624, 102 S. Ct. 2629 (1982).

a result over 20 states passed second generation antitakeover laws to attempt to pass constitutional muster under the Supreme Court's reasoning. While some of them have also been ruled unconstitutional, the Supreme Court in 1987 (*CTS v. Dynamics Corp. of America*) ruled the Indiana antitakeover law constitutional.[16] This decision already is leading states to pass third generation antitakeover laws that would be constitutional under the CTS reasoning.

Two recent studies, Ryngaert and Netter (1987, based on OCE, 1987c) and Schumann (1987) provide more direct evidence on the wealth effects of state antitakeover regulations. Ryngaert and Netter examine the stock price effects of the passage of the Ohio antitakeover law on shareholders of firms chartered in Ohio. This act was passed during (and apparently motivated by) Sir James Goldsmith's attempted hostile takeover of Goodyear. They find that the passage of the law was accompanied by a significant stock-price loss of up to 3.24 percent to the shareholders of firms incorporated in Ohio with less than 30 percent inside ownership. This evidence on the impact of state takeover laws is supported by Schumann (1987) who finds a decline of approximately one percent to shareholders of New York firms on the announcement and passage of a New York antitakeover law. While these laws potentially could be beneficial to the individual states (if jobs are kept in the state by preventing takeovers), shareholders are harmed by state antitakeover regulations.

Summing Up Defensive Tactics

Four years ago Jensen and Ruback (1983) reviewed empirical studies of antitakeover charter amendments, shark repellents, changes of incorporation, and greenmail. They conclude (p. 47): "It is difficult to find managerial actions related to corporate control that harm stockholders; the exception are those actions that eliminate an actual or potential bidder, for example, through the use of targeted large block repurchases or standstill agreements."

Since their review, the defensive arsenal available to target management has been strengthened. These defensive tactics have been developed through a fascinating process of sequential innovations, as specific defenses arise to counter improved bidder finances and other tactics. In 1983, the now common fair-price amendment was a novel idea and the poison pill was not yet invented. Financial economists in academia and government have kept close pace with these developments, providing timely analyses of new charter amendments, poison pill defenses, greenmail transactions, and so on. While Jensen and Ruback were correct in predicting this area would be a "growth industry," we cannot reiterate their then-accurate conclusion that harmful defensive tactics are rare.

Conclusion

In the 1980s, the market for corporate control has been increasingly active, and the quantity of output of academic researchers studying corporate control questions

[16] *CTS v. Dynamics Corp. of America*, 107 S. Ct. 1637 (1987).

has mirrored the market activity. This review has confirmed the basic conclusions of
Jensen and Ruback's (1983) review article and has shed light on some questions
Jensen and Ruback were forced to leave unanswered. Financial researchers continue
to find larger premiums being paid to target shareholders for later tender offers than
for earlier tender offers. Acquirers, however, receive at best modest increases in their
stock price, and the winners of bidding contests suffer stock-price declines as often as
they do gains. This pro-target division of takeover gains appears to be partially a
result of improved defensive tactics that can effectively delay execution of the bid and
allow the target to receive improved bids from others or fashion a defensive restructuring and stock buyback. The evidence further suggests that the premiums in takeovers
represent real wealth gains and are not simply wealth redistributions.

Prominent in the 1980s are new studies of defensive measures, such as antitakeover charter amendments, targeted block stock repurchases (greenmail), dual-voting
recapitalizations, state antitakeover laws, and poison pills. The general finding,
although it is far from conclusive, is that defensive measures that require shareholder
voting approval are less likely to be harmful to shareholder wealth than are defensive
measures not subject to shareholder approval. Fair-price charter amendments and
dual-class recapitalizations that require shareholder approval are not shown to be
harmful to stock value, while poison pills and greenmail-type repurchases that do not
need shareholder approval appear on average to reduce shareholder value. However,
some proposals that require a favorable vote from shareholders to implement (e.g.,
supermajority provisions and the elimination of cumulative voting) on average appear
to reduce shareholder wealth. These findings raise serious questions about whether the
business judgment rule is operating too broadly as a shield for defensive actions by
target managements.

■ *We are especially grateful to Joseph Stiglitz, Timothy Taylor, and Annette Poulsen for their
many helpful comments and suggestions. The Securities and Exchange Commission as a matter of
policy disclaims responsibility for any private publication or statement by any of its employees. The
views expressed here are those of the authors and do not necessarily reflect the views of the
Commission or the authors' colleagues on the Staff of the Commission.*

References

Auerbach, Alan J. and David Reishus, "Taxes and the Merger Decision." In Coffee, J. and Louis Lowenstein, eds., *Takeovers and Contests for Corporate Control*, Oxford: Oxford University Press, 1987a.

Auerbach, Alan J. and David Reishus, "The Effects of Taxation on the Merger Decision," NBER Working Paper, 1987b.

Bhagat, Sanjai, and James Brickley, "The Value of Minority Shareholder Voting Rights," *Journal of Law and Economics*, 1984, *27*, 339–365.

Bhagat, Sanjai, James Brickley, and Uri Lowenstein, "The Pricing Effects of Inter-Firm Cash Tender Offers, *Journal of Finance*, 1987, *42*, 965–986.

Bradley, Michael, Amand Desai, and E. Han Kim, "Determinants of the Wealth Effects of Corporate Acquisitions," working paper, The University of Michigan, 1984.

Bradley, Michael, Amand Desai, and E. Han Kim, "The Rationale Behind Interfirm Tender Offers: Information or Synergy?" *Journal of Financial Economics*, 1983, *11*, 183–206.

Brickley, James, Ronald Lease, and Clifford Smith, "Ownership Structure and the Voting on Antitakeover Amendments," *Journal of Financial Economics*, forthcoming.

Brown, Charles and James L. Medoff, "The Impact of Firm Acquisitions on Labor," NBER Working paper, 1987.

Brown, Stephen J. and Jerold B. Warner, "Using Daily Stock Returns: The Case of Event Studies," *Journal of Financial Economics*, 1985, *14*, 3–31.

Comment, Robert, "Price and Volume Before Tender Offers: Market Anticipation Activity or Inside Trading, working paper New York University, 1986.

Comment, Robert and Gregg A. Jarrell, "Two-Tier Tender Offers: The Imprisonment of the Free Riding Shareholder," *Journal of Financial Economics*, forthcoming.

Council of Economic Advisors, "The Market for Corporate Control," *Economic Report of the President*, 1985, 187–216.

DeAngelo, Harry, and Linda DeAngelo, "Managerial Ownership of Voting Rights: A Study of Public Corporations With Dual Classes of Common Stock," *Journal of Financial Economics*, 1985, *14*, 33–69.

DeAngelo, Harry, Linda DeAngelo, and Edward M. Rice, "Going Private: Minority Freezeouts and Stockholder Wealth," *Journal of Law and Economics*, 1984, *27*, 367–402.

Denis, Debra K., and John J. McConnell, "Corporate Mergers and Security Returns," *Journal of Financial Economics*, 1986, *16*, 143–187.

Dodd, Peter, and Richard Leftwich, "The Market for Corporate Charters: 'Unhealthy Competition' Versus Federal Regulation," *Journal of Business*, 1980, *53*, 259–283.

Easterbrook, Frank H., and Gregg A. Jarrell, "Do Targets Gain From Defeating Tender Offers?" *New York University Law Review*, 1984, *59*, 277–299.

Eckbo, B. Espen, "Merger and the Market Concentration Doctrine: Evidence from the Capital Market," *Journal of Business*, 1985, *58*, 325–349.

Eckbo, B. Espen, and Herwig Langohr, "The Effect of Disclosure Regulations and the Medium of Exchange on Takeover Bids," Working paper, 1986.

Guerin-Calvert, Margaret, Robert H. McGuckin, and Frederick R. Warren-Boulton, "State and Federal Regulation in the Market for Corporate Control," U.S. Department of Justice, Economic Analysis Group Discussion Paper 86-4, 1986.

Hall, Bronwyn H., "The Effect of Takeover Activity on Corporate Research and Development," working paper, NBER, 1987.

Holderness, Clifford G. and Dennis P. Sheehan, "Raiders or Saviors? The Evidence on Six Controversial Investors," *Journal of Financial Economics*, 1985, *14*, 555–579.

James, Christopher M., and Peggy Weir, "Determinants of the Division of Gains in Corporate Acquisitions: Evidence from the Banking Industry, working paper, University of Oregon, 1987.

Jarrell, Gregg A., "The Wealth Effects of Litigation by Targets: Do Interests Diverge in a Merge?" *Journal of Law and Economics*, 1985, *28*, 151–177.

Jarrell, Gregg A., and Michael Bradley, "The Economic Effects of Federal and State Regulations of Cash Tender Offers," *Journal of Law and Economics*, 1980, *23*, 371–407.

Jarrell, Gregg A., and Annette B. Poulsen, "Bidder Returns," working paper, 1987a.

Jarrell, Gregg A., and Annette B. Poulsen, "The Effects of Recapitalization with Dual Classes of Common Stock on the Wealth of Shareholders," *Journal of Financial Economics*, forthcoming.

Jarrell, Gregg A., and Annette B. Poulsen, "Shark Repellents and Stock Prices: The Effects of Antitakeover Amendments Since 1980," *Journal of Financial Economics*, 1987b, *19*, 127–168.

Jensen, Michael C., "The Takeover Controversy: Analysis and Evidence," *Midland Corporate Finance Journal*, 1986, 6–32.

Jensen, Michael C., and Richard S. Ruback, "The Market for Corporate Control: The Scientific Evidence," *Journal of Financial Economics*, 1983, *11*, 5–50.

Lease, Ronald C., John J. McConnell, and Wayne H. Mikkelson, "The Market Value of Control in Publicly Traded Corporations," *Journal of Financial Economics*, 1983, *11*, 439–472.

Lehn, Kenneth, and Annette B. Poulsen, "Sources of Value in Leveraged Buyouts." In *Public Policy Towards Corporate Takeovers*. New Brunswick, NJ: Transaction Publishers, 1987.

Malatesta, Paul H., and Ralph A. Walkling, "Poison Pill Securities: Stockholder Wealth, Profitability, and Ownership Structure," *Journal of Financial Economics*, forthcoming.

McConnell, John J. and Chris J. Muscarella, "Capital Expenditure Decisions and Market Value of the Firm," *Journal of Financial Economics*, 1985, *14*, 399–422.

Mikkelson, Wayne H. and Richard S. Ruback, "An Empirical Analysis of the Interfirm Equity Investment Process," *Journal of Financial Economics*, 1985, *14*, 523–553.

Netter, Jeffry M. "Shareholder Wealth Effects of Litigation Based on Allegedly False Schedule 13D Item 4 Disclosure," working paper, 1987.

Office of the Chief Economist, Securities and Exchange Commission, "The Economics of Any-or-All, Partial, and Two-Tier Tender Offers," 1985a.

Office of the Chief Economist, Securities and Exchange Commission, "Update—The Effects of Dual-Class Recapitalizations on Shareholder Wealth: Including Evidence from 1986 and 1987," 1987d.

Office of the Chief Economist, Securities and Exchange Commission, "The Effects of Poison Pills on the Wealth of Target Shareholders," 1986.

Office of the Chief Economist, Securities and Exchange Commission, "The Impact of Targetted Share Repurchases (Greenmail) on Stock Prices," 1984.

Office of the Chief Economist, Securities and Exchange Commission, "Institutional Ownership, Tender Offers and Long Term Investment," 1985b.

Office of the Chief Economist, Securities and Exchange Commission, "Shareholder Wealth Effects of Ohio Legislation Affecting Takeovers," 1987b.

Office of the Chief Economist, Securities and Exchange Commission, "Shark Repellents and Stock Prices: The Effects of Antitakeover Amendments Since 1980," 1985c.

Office of the Chief Economist, Securities and Exchange Commission, "Stock Trading Before the Announcement of Tender Offers: Insider Trading or Market Anticipation?" 1987c.

Office of the Chief Economist, Securities and Exchange Commission, "The Effects of Dual-Class Recapitalizations on the Wealth Of Shareholders," 1987a.

Partch, Megan. "The Creation of A Class of Limited Voting Common Stock and Shareholders" Wealth," *Journal of Financial Economics*, 1987, *18*, 313–339.

Romano, Roberta, "Law as a Product: Some Pieces of the Incorporation Puzzle," *Journal of Law Economics and Organization*, 1985, *1*, 225–267.

Ruback, Richard S., "An Overview of Takeover Defenses," working paper #1836-86, Massachusetts Institute of Technology, 1986.

Ryngaert, Michael, "The Effect of Poison Pill Securities on Shareholder Wealth," *Journal of Financial Economics*, forthcoming.

Ryngaert, Michael, and Nettter Jeffry, "Shareholder Wealth Effects of the Ohio Antitakeover Law," working paper, 1987.

Schumann, Laurence, "State Regulation of Takeovers and Shareholder Wealth: The Effects of New York's 1985 Takeover Statutes," Bureau of Economics Staff Report to the Federal Trade Commission, March 1987.

Shleifer, Andrei and Lawrence Summers, "Hostile Takeovers as Breaches of Trust," working paper, NBER, 1987.

Smiley, Robert, "The Effect of State Securities Statutes on Tender Offer Activity," *Economic Inquiry*, 1981, *19*, 426–435.

Steindel, Charles, "Tax Reform and the Merger and Acquisition Market: The Repeal of General Utilities," *Federal Reserve Bulletin of New York*, Autumn 1986, 31–35.

[5]

Cambridge Journal of Economics 1985, 9, 43–56

A re-examination of merger studies that use the capital asset pricing model methodology

Robert L. Conn*

1. Introduction

Empirical specifications of the capital asset pricing model (CAPM), as developed by Sharpe (1963) and others, have been widely applied to testing various types of corporate behaviour. The asset pricing models have analysed such individual firm activities as earnings announcements, dividend policies, share purchases, stock splits, and mergers. In addition, the models have analysed the impact on the firm's value of external events such as changes in accounting rules and antitrust enforcement.[1] The CAPM, then, has become an important research tool with extensive applications in microfinance, accounting, and industrial organisation.[2]

This paper reviews a subset of this large body of literature, the applications of the CAPM paradigm to mergers. Mergers are examined for several reasons. First, mergers play an important role in reallocating the ownership of resources. During 1968–79 in the US, assets acquired by merger averaged between 8% and 46% of the yearly new investment in manufacturing and mining.[3] The policy issue is whether or not such merger activities should be encouraged or discouraged. Second, the implied concensus of the CAPM methodology is that the model provides a valid benchmark for evaluating the social and private justification for mergers. This benchmark, the securities market reaction as evidenced by market-adjusted share price changes, focuses on the impact of merger on the shareowners of the firm. The equating of social and private interests was recently summarised as follows: 'The aim is to determine whether the value of the merged firm exceeds the value of the constituent parts. If it does, the merger is a valid social and private justification' (Copeland and Weston, 1983, p. 625). This paper argues that such an outlook not only ignores the realities of an imperfectly structured economic system but, more importantly, has misapplied and misinterpreted its own paradigm. Finally, and most importantly, this paper reviews some of the principal shortcomings of the CAPM as applied to mergers and shows that many of the consistent findings of past

---

*Florida State University.

[1] An excellent discussion of the various empirical specifications of the CAPM, as well a review of its various applications, is found in Copeland and Weston (1983), Chapters 10, 17, and 18.

[2] For recent applications of the CAPM to antitrust enforcement see Choi and Phillippatos (1983) and Garbade, Silber and White (1982).

[3] Data on mergers prior to 1980 were published by the Federal Trade Commission annually. This source of data is no longer published and only private sources of merger data are now available. Data from private sources are not directly comparable to the FTC series owing to their inclusion of smaller mergers.

0309–166X/85/010043 + 14 $03.00/0

44   R. L. Conn

studies are due to methodological problems in applying the CAPM empirically to
mergers. Thus the results of past studies using the CAPM share common biases and
interpretation of such results must be re-examined. Section 2 of the paper reviews the
CAPM and its critical assumptions. Section 3 discusses the empirical problems of the
CAPM as applied to mergers and their effects on recent studies. Section 4 concludes
with a summary and re-interpretation of recent findings.

2. The market model and cumulative average residuals

The most commonly used empirical version of the CAPM in merger studies has been the
market model (MM),[1] which is an empirical specification of the assumed stochastic
process that generates individual security returns. The MM is specified as:

$$R_{jt} = a_j + \beta_j R_{mt} + e_{jt}$$

where

R_{jt} = expected return on security j during period t, where return reflects both
    dividends and captial gains/losses

a_j = assumed constant intercept

R_{mt} = the expected return on the market portfolio during period t, where return
    reflects both dividends and capital gains/losses

β_j = beta coefficient that measures systematic risk between security j and the general
    market

e_{jt} = residual error, or difference between actual return and predicted return on
    security j in period t.

Thus the MM argues that in efficient capital markets the return on an individual
security will be linearly related to the overall market return with the parameters of the
model, a and β, estimated using OLS regression where best linear unbiased estimators
are assumed such that $E(e)=0$, $\bar{\sigma}_e$ and $COV(R_m, e)=0$. Efficient capital markets, of
course, require that information affecting securities be fairly distributed to all investors
simultaneously and that the digestion of the new information be swift.

The parameters of the MM are generally estimated during some assumed premerger
equilibrium period, as shown in Fig. 1, where the underlying risk/return characteristics
of the firm are not undergoing systematic change. Thus, the differences between actual
returns and predicted returns are due to random processes that will even out over time.

Important firm-specific events, such as mergers, earnings announcements, or antitrust
prosecutions, will alter the set of expectations regarding the firm's future such that
temporary deviations between the new actual return and expected return will occur.

---

[1]The principal difference between the CAPM and MM is their specification of the intercept term. The
MM argues that returns on security j are linearly related to the returns on a market portfolio, such that:

$$R_{jt} = a_j + \beta_j R_{mt} + \varepsilon_{jt},$$

where a and β are assumed constant over time. The CAPM argues that the intercept term is the risk-free
rate, or the rate of return on the minimum variance zero-beta portfolio, both of which may change over time.
Thus, the CAPM is specified as:

$$R_j = R_f + \beta_j(R_m - R_f) + \varepsilon.$$

Since most merger studies have used the MM, we shall focus mostly on that, although both the CAPM and
MM related studies are reviewed herein.

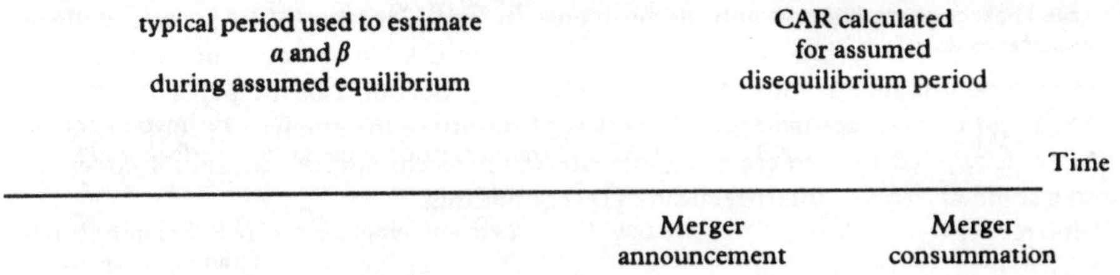

The capital asset pricing model and mergers 45

typical period used to estimate
a and β
during assumed equilibrium

CAR calculated
for assumed
disequilibrium period

Time

Merger
announcement

Merger
consummation

Fig. 1. *Schematic of time framework used by market model to estimate parameters and CAR.*

While the capital market digests this new information, cumulative residuals may be positive or negative depending on whether the market's evaluation is favourable or is unfavourable. The average of the cumulative residuals from a sample of mergers is appropriately called the cumulative average residual (CAR).[1]

The CAR is typically calculated over some assumed disequilibrium period during which the merger news is affecting security returns, as illustrated in Fig. 1. This disequilibrium period, as we shall see shortly, has varied around the dates of first public announcement to the dates of actual consumption. This, of course, can be many months.

Regardless of the vagaries of the methods used to calculate the CAR of acquiring and targeted firms, the basic interpretation of the CAR is similar. Positive CARs indicate that the market expects the merger to yield net benefits to the shareholders involved. The CAR represents the present value of the net future benefits from the merger. A positive CAR means the merger advances the financial status of the firm's owners, whereas a negative CAR implies the merger is not in the interest of the firm's owners. Similarly, if CAR is approximately zero, no gain or loss to shareholder wealth is experienced. This dual feature of the CAR—the actual short-term change in share prices adjusted for overall market influences, and also its *ex ante* valuation of longer-run merger consequences—partially accounts for its methodological popularity. The growing availability of computerised share-price data bases, an increased awareness of the problems associated with accounting-based analysis, and substantial evidence on the 'efficiency' (in the sense of Fama, 1970) of capital markets have also contributed to the acceptance of the MM methodology.

Table 1 contains a summary of eight recent studies that used the MM to estimate abnormal returns from mergers to shareholders in the US and UK. The estimated CAR of acquiring firms ranged between -0.0145 and 0.1020, with a simple average over the eight studies of 0.0474. These are, of course, relatively small changes in the wealth status for the owners of the acquiring firms. The CAR for acquired firms is, however, higher in all studies that distinguished between acquiring and acquired firms. The CAR of

---

[1]The cumulative residual (CR) for firm j is:

$$\sum_{i=1}^{N} e_{ji}$$

where the time period generally extends from a pre-announcement date to actual merger consummation or shortly thereafter. Thus, while the mergers sampled may occur at different calendar times, their residuals are calculated relative to common intervals $(t = 1, N)$. The average of the cumulative residuals of the entire sample of firms is the cumulative average residual (CAR).

46   R. L. Conn

Table 1. *Studies reporting cumulative average residuals (CAR) for acquiring and acquired firms using the market model*

Author(s)	Acquiring CAR	Acquired CAR	CAR estimation period (months prior to merger)	Estimation period for α and β
Halpern[b] (1973)	0·0997[a]	0·0997[a]	−23 to announcement	N to 7 months before announcement
Elgers and Clark (1980)	0·1020	0·4260	−24 to −1	84 to 24 months before merger
Mandelker (1974)	0·0490	0·1200	−40 to −1	60 to 1 month before merger
Dodd (1980)	0·0537	0·2342	−1 to 0	10 to 3–1/3 months before announcement
Franks[b] (1978)	0·0440	0·0810	−40 to −1	29 months before announcement and 8 months after announcement
Kummer and Hoffmeister[c] (1978)	N.A.	0·1200	−40 to announcement	60 months prior to announcement
Franks, Broyles and Hecht[b] (1977)	−0·0020	0·2060	−40 to −1	29 months before announcement and 8 months after announcement
Langetieg[b] (1978)	−0·0145	0·0143	−72 to −1	72 to 12 months before merger
Average	0·0474	0·1627		

[a]Includes acquiring and acquired firms together. Halpern also divided the sample into 'large firms' and 'small firms' and found CARs of 14·73 and 12·62, respectively. However, since not all large firms are acquirers and not all small firms are necessarily acquirees, it is inappropriate to attribute these CARs to buyers and sellers.

[b]A two-factor market model was used containing an industry return variable and a general market return variable.

[c]Kummer and Hoffmeister looked principally at targeted firms. Since their sample of bidder firms is small (only 17) it is not shown here.

acquired firms ranges from 0·0143 to 0·4260, with a simple average of 0·1627. The general conclusion emerging from these studies is that limited abnormal gains exist for acquiring firms and larger, more significant gains exist for acquired firms, with most of the gains coming in the six months or so preceding merger.

Interpretation of these findings, however, is clouded by a host of recognised institutional, theoretical, and empirical factors. For example, the relatively large abnormal returns to shareholders of acquired firms may be influenced by the tax treatment of the method of merger consideration. In the US, tax liabilities exist on capital gains on all forms of payment except voting common stock. Thus, should we discount the larger returns on the stock of the selling firms to account for capital gains taxes on mergers involving taxable exchanges of securities or cash? Similarly, the importance of the relative size of buyers and sellers in interpreting their respective CAR has been suggested by Halpern (1983, 1973) and Mandelker (1974). Since the equity base of buyers is typically several times that of sellers, it is expected that the CAR for larger buying firms would

The capital asset pricing model and mergers   47

be influenced less than for acquired firms. This does not mean that the return on the acquiring firm's investment in the smaller firm is low; rather, it means that the CAR of acquiring firms must be interpreted in the light of the size of acquired firms. While the relative sizes of acquiring and acquired firms are not provided in the eight studies noted in Table 1, other studies such as Melicher and Rush (1973), Mueller (1977) and Steiner (1975) have established that acquiring firms, on the average, are several times the size of acquired firms, depending on time periods, types of mergers, methods of payments, and other factors. Thus, the relative sizes of acquiring and acquired firms remain a recognised, although unquantified, factor influencing merger returns.

Similarly, the studies in Table 1 have used alternative specifications of the MM (single market index versus two indices, one for industry and one for general market), returns based on daily versus monthly data, as well as pre-merger data only or an average of pre-merger and post-merger data. The parameters of the MM have thus been estimated in a variety of ways with the attendant outcomes in CAR. As Table 1 shows, however, the general results (absolute and relative CAR for merging firms) appear to be reasonably robust and consistent.

3. Problems in applying the market model to mergers

The above studies, however, suffer from at least three unique empirical problems in their application of the MM to mergers: (1) the change in systematic risk of the merging firms due to merger, (2) the sample selection, and (3) the cyclical nature of aggregate merger activity. Other problems (e.g. non-stationarity of alpha and beta, measurement errors, autocorrelation, non-constant variance of the error, and non-zero covariance between R_m and e) dealing with the general applicability of the MM to measure the shock effect of such phenomena as dividend announcements, quarterly earnings announcements, changing accounting practices, and even antitrust lawsuits have been addressed previously by Brenner and Downs (1979), Francis and Fabozzi (1979), Roll (1977), and Ross (1978) and are relevant for merger analysis as well. But the three issues noted above deserve closer attention because they represent significant additional empirical difficulties for mergers.[1]

3.1 Changes in systematic risk
Perhaps the most critical problem in applying the MM to mergers is that merger may alter the operating and/or financial risks of both buyer and seller firms, whereas non-merger events, such as earnings announcements, are less likely to alter the firm's systematic risk. If merger increases a firm's beta during the disequilibrium period then that firm's CAR will indicate positive gains from merger, whereas in reality risk-adjusted returns may not have changed. Similarly, if merger decreases a firm's systematic risk then that firm's CAR will be negatively biased. Only if the parameters of the MM are constant over both the premerger equilibrium period and the merger-related disequilibrium period will the model yield unbiased results.

Studies finding beta changes. There are several studies in which the effects of merger on

---

[1]After this paper was written, two review-articles on merger studies, Halpern (1983) and Jensen and Ruback, were published containing further summaries of recent research. Unfortunately, neither of these reviews raises serious objections to the use of the MM.

48   R. L. Conn

Table 2. *Studies analysing mean betas for acquiring and acquired firms in pre-merger and post-merger periods*

	Joehnk and Nielsen (1974)			
	Conglomerate mergers (N=21)		Non-conglomerate (N=23)	
	Pre-merger[a] beta	Post-merger beta	Pre-merger beta	Post-merger beta
All acquiring firms	1·40	1·37 (t=0·19)	1·26	1·36 (t=0·24)
All acquired firms	1·06		1·08	
Sub-sample of 14 firms where beta of buyer < beta of seller				
Acquiring firms	1·13	1·40 (t=0·50)	0·74	1·13 (t=2·21)
Acquired firms	1·77		1·26	
Sub-sample of 30 firms where beta of buyer is > beta of seller				
Acquiring firms	1·46	1·40 (t=0·35)	1·66	1·43 (t=1·03)
Acquired firms	0·90		0·93	

Months prior to or after merger	Beta of acquiring firms	Beta of acquired firms
	Elgers and Clark[b] (1980)	
−24	1·003	1·057
− 3	0·986	1·026
+24	1·002	
	Mandelker (1974)	
−40	1·085	1·093
− 3	1·070	1·064
+70	0·992	

[a]Pre-merger betas based on monthly returns during the 36 months prior to the six months before merger. Post-merger betas are based on montly returns in 36 months following mergers.
[b]Beta based on a moving average of a weighted portfolio of the acquiring and acquired firms.

beta have been investigated. Table 2 highlights three recent merger studies in which betas are analysed. Joehnk and Nielsen (1974) estimated average pre-merger and post-merger betas for a sample of acquiring firms as well as pre-merger betas for the acquired firms. They further stratified their sample according to whether the merger was conglomerate or non-conglomerate and whether the acquiring firm's pre-merger beta exceeded or was less than the acquired firm's beta. While only one of the six sub-samples of acquiring firms indicated a statistically significant change between pre-merger and post-merger betas, five of the six sub-samples contained post-merger betas that were some combination of the acquiring and acquired firm's betas. They concluded that these

The capital asset pricing model and mergers   49

findings '... reveal a degree of responsiveness on the part of beta to the type of conglomeration ... [and] that changes in β are related ... to changes in a firm's operating/financial characteristics and not due solely to random factors ...' (Joehnk and Nielsen, 1974, p. 220). Similarly, Elgers and Clark (1980) found changes in betas surrounding merger, especially for acquired firms, although no statistical tests were reported.

Mandelker (1974) has provided the most complete test of the sensitivity of beta for merging firms. As Fig. 2 illustrates, Mandelker found that beta increased steadily in the pre-merger period (−100 months to −20 months) and then decreased in the next 60 months (−20 months to +40 months). In order to adjust for the change in beta,

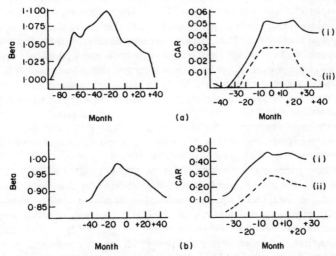

Fig. 2. *Betas and CAR for (a) Mergers (Mandelker, 1974) and (b) stock splits (Bar-Josef and Brown, 1977) using (i) past data only to estimate beta and (ii) a mixture of past and future data*

Mandelker suggested using both pre-merger data (−30 to −1) and post-merger data (+1 to +30) to estimate beta for the disequilibrium period. Using this method (i.e., equally weighted observations before and after merger) resulted in a CAR of only *half* that obtained when historical data only were used. As Fig 2 shows, the acquiring firm's CAR rose steadily in the 40 months preceding merger and then declined slightly over the next 40 months. But, most importantly, the method used to calculate beta produced significant differences in the absolute size of CAR. When only historical returns are used (−40 to −1) the CAR is much greater than when a moving average of both past and future returns is used to estimate beta. The inescapable conclusion from Mandelker's findings is that CAR is sensitive to the period chosen to estimate the parameters of the MM. This, unfortunately, creates ambiguity in interpreting the CAR.

Other studies have also indicated changing systematic risk for acquisition-prone firms, especially when capital structure changes occur. Melicher and Rush (1973), Weston and Mansinghka (1971), Kim and McConnell (1977) and others have all observed that merger-prone conglomerate firms increased their debt/capital ratios more than firms in general. Brenner and Downes (1979), in follow-up work on the sample of conglomerates used by Weston and Mansinghka, found that one-third of the conglomerates in the Weston–Mansinghka study underwent changes in systematic risk. Thus there is some evidence that changing systematic risk in merging firms is due to capital structure changes.

Studies not finding beta changes. Not all studies, however, have found significant changes in beta around merger dates. Haugen and Langetieg (1975) found that 13 out of 59 mergers sampled resulted in statistically significant changes (10% level) in betas from pre-merger to post-merger periods. However, they also found that a control group of 59 non-merging firms incurred eight significant changes in beta. Haugen and Langetieg concluded that their results indicate no clear change in risk due to merger. They also found that alpha changed significantly in 11 mergers and for nine of the non-merging firms. Two points seem important about the Haugen–Langetieg study. One, alphas and betas changed in about 20% of the mergers sampled during 1951–68. Results were not reported on the size of pre-merger and post-merger betas and alphas; only direction and significance of changes were noted. But a relatively few significant changes in alpha and beta could cause the entire sample's CAR to be distorted. Two, *none* of the reported significant changes in betas in the merger group was accompanied by equivalent changes (direction, as well as significance) in the non-merging control group.[1] Thus there is no consistent relationship between beta changes in the merger group and the control group. This seems to strengthen rather than dilute the argument that the observed changes in betas were merger-related and not due to random events.

Another recent paper using the MM is that by Dodd (1980) in which he assesses the CAR for mergers that are ultimately accepted or rejected by shareholders or management. Methodologically, Dodd's paper is interesting because it uses daily returns rather than monthly returns as did other studies. The parameters of the model '... are estimated over a maximum of 300 and a minimum of 100 days around the data of announcement, but always excluding the period for which prediction errors are calculated'. He then firmly states that '... different estimation periods were tried and in no case are the results and conclusions of this paper altered' (p. 109). Unfortunately, Dodd does not explain how he tested the sensitivity of the model's parameters.[2] Given the findings of Mandelker, however, that beta was fluctuating in the 20 months prior to merger, Dodd's findings are surprising.

Further evidence of buyer and seller betas. Finally, no effort has been made in the above studies, except by Joehnk and Nielsen (1974), to explain econometrically the changes in beta for merging firms. Joehnk and Nielsen found some evidence, as shown in Table 2, that post-merger betas are some combination of the buyer's and seller's pre-merger betas. If this finding is generally valid, then other evidence on the relative size of betas between acquiring and acquired firms becomes of interest. Mandelker (1974) and Elgers–Clark (1980), for example, found that the average beta of acquired firms exceeded

[1] See Table 1 in Haugen and Langetieg (1975).
[2] The study by Franks, Broyles and Hecht (1977) did experiment with various time periods surrounding the suspected disequilibrium period in estimating the MM. They found '... the results sensitive to the interval of time chosen ...' (p. 1515) but, like Dodd (1980), did not provide test results in their paper. While a Chow test (1960) may be assumed to have been performed in such cases, no explicit evidence is provided. Likewise, it is unclear which various time periods were analysed (e.g. pre-merger only, post-merger only, or various combinations of pre-merger and post-merger). This is, however, one of the few studies that seemed to recognise the potential problem of unstable parameters.

The capital asset pricing model and mergers 51

that of the acquiring firms. Does this mean that the pre-merger beta of the buying firm will increase in the post-merger period? The existing evidence is mixed. Joehnk and Nielsen found some indication that post-merger betas were combinations of pre-merger betas. Mandelker and Elger–Clark did not find post-merger betas to be a combination of buyer and seller pre-merger betas (see Table 2). The conflicting evidence suggests that further empirical study is needed.

Other merger-related studies, however, may shed some light on the first of the above questions: are the betas of buyers and sellers significantly different? A number of studies, such as Conn (1977), Mead (1969) and Melicher–Hempel (1971), have found that the price/earnings (PE) ratios of buyers statistically exceeds the PE ratios of sellers for conglomerate mergers. If betas are systematically related to PE ratios, such that high PE ratio firms have low betas and low PE ratio firms have high betas,[1] then we might expect that the betas of acquiring firms would be, on average, less than those of the firms they acquire. Given such relative betas, it is expected that the acquiring firms' pre-merger betas increase with merger and, as a result, post-merger CAR will be positively biased. Whether or not there are systematic differences in betas of buying and selling firms is not resolved at this time, nor is the question of direction of change of post-merger betas. But some preliminary and related data suggest that (1) buyer betas are less than seller betas, and (2) post-merger betas are a combination of the betas of acquiring and acquired firms. Given the two most commonly used methods of estimating betas in the MM (historical and moving average), this suggests an upward bias in CAR for acquiring firms and a downward bias for acquired firms.

A solution to the disequilibrium/equilibrium violation. Both of the methods used to calculate the parameters of the MM—using historical (pre-merger) returns only or a moving average of pre-merger and post-merger returns—violate the necessary conditions for application of the MM to merger. The historical approach ignores the likely change in systematic risk due to merger, and the moving average method suffers the same problem plus commingling returns from the equilibrium/disequilibrium periods. Thus not only are the necessary econometric preconditions for estimating beta violated but also the equilibrium and disequilibrium periods are overlapping. Unfortunately all the studies reviewed have used either pre-merger only data or some combination of pre-merger and post-merger returns, often including the disequilibrium period.

A solution to the dilemma is to use only post-merger, post-disequilibrium returns to estimate the parameters of the MM. This involves using data starting several months after merger announcement and extending into the future. The CAR is then based on

---

[1]The assertion that a firm's beta is inversely related to its PE ratio is based on the security market line, which posits a positive relationship between the cost of equity capital and beta, and the well-known dividend valuation model. Consider the following constant growth dividend valuation model:

$$P_0 = \sum_{t=1}^{\infty} \frac{E_0(1+g)^t}{(1+k)^t}$$

where P_0 is the price of a common share, E_0 is current earnings or dividends per share, g is the growth rate of future earnings, and k is the cost of equity capital. Dividing the above by E_0 yields,

$$P_0/E_0 = \sum_{t=1}^{\infty} (1+g)^t/(1+k)^t$$

Since $\partial(P_0/E_0)/\partial k < 0$, and from the SML we know $\partial k/\partial \text{beta} > 0$, it must follow that $\partial(P_0/E_0)/\partial \text{beta} < 0$. Empirically, the inverse relationship between PE ratios and betas has been supported in Malkiel and Cragg (1970).

backward forecasts of assumed equilibrium returns, which in turn are derived from risk-adjusted parameters in the post-merger period. The simultaneous requirements of estimating the MM in an equilibrium period and acknowledging the likely merger-induced change in systematic risk will be satisfied. This, of course, reduces the legitimate time period of CAR calculations to the disequilibrium period, which most evidence indicates is several months either side of the merger announcement date.[1] The point is that, until alternative estimation schemes for the parameters of the MM are tested, the inferences from existing studies should be interpreted with caution.

3.2   Sample selection

All the merger studies using the MM have used samples of mergers involving only major firms, where both buyer and seller are listed on national stock exchanges (New York, American or London), and only mergers involving exchanges of common stock.[2] But many acquiring firms are typically involved in other minor and major mergers, as well as in internal diversification. The FTC (1969) has reported that the most active 25 merging firms during 1961–68 acquired 695 US firms with assets of over $10 million. Teledyne had 125 mergers over the decade of the 1960s; Gulf and Western, 67 mergers; Textron, 50 mergers; and Georgia Pacific, 45 mergers. The *ceteris paribus* assumption of the MM that the acquiring firm be involved in no other mergers during the sample period would seem to be doubtful.

Mandelker (1974), Halpern (1973), Dodd (1980), and Elgers and Clark (1980) restricted their samples to mergers reported by the FTC and for which data are available on the CRSP tapes. The problems are several. One, not all mergers are reported by the FTC. Foreign mergers, until recently, and smaller acquisitions (less than $10 million) are not recorded. Two, not all of the recorded mergers are on the CRSP tape. Thus, the mergers included in the samples are inevitably selected by a filtering process which may exclude other significant mergers. Finally, no studies have attempted to adjust for major non-merger events occuring in either the merger disequilibrium period or the equilibrium period(s) of model parameter estimation. Events affecting the operating environment, such as antitrust lawsuits, resource or labour cost changes, or divestitures, could alter the firm's systematic risk. Financial events such as capital structure changes, bond refundings, or stock splits might affect beta also. To identify suitable equilibrium periods, as well as unique disequilibrium intervals, one would seem to need to consider not only other mergers but *all* other firm-related shocks. *Ceteris paribus* is a very restrictive condition and imposes more stringent conditions on research design than heretofore demonstrated.

3.3   Mergers, macro-activity, and beta

The limited studies that exist on the timing of mergers over the course of the business cycle have tentatively concluded that merger activity increases during economic expansions and slows down during contractions. Nelson's (1959) analysis of aggregate merger activity during 1895–1956, later updated to 1961, found that '... merger activity is a "leading series", especially where cyclical expansions are concerned ... [and] ... seems

---

[1]The sensitivity of beta, and hence CAR, to alternative estimation methods (historical, moving average) has also been observed in non-merger events. Bar-Josef and Brown (1977) found similar intertemporal changes in beta for firms incurring stock splits, as Mandelker found for merger. They found about one-half of the CAR in stock splits was explainable by changing beta.

[2]An exception is the Kummer–Hoffmeister (1978) study, which looked at cash tender offers, not common stock exchanges.

The capital asset pricing model and mergers 53

to be most closely related to those kinds of economic changes that reach their peaks in advance of general economic conditions' (1974, p. 54). Nelson goes on to point out that '... merger peaks tend to precede those in stock prices ...'. Steiner (1975) also produces econometric evidence that the yearly variation in aggregate merger activity is correlated positively and significantly to changes in GNP and the S&P 500 stock index. More recently, Melicher *et al.* have analysed aggregate merger activity in the US during 1947–77 and concluded that mergers '... reflect anticipation of rising stock prices and falling interest rates and thus a more receptive and possibly less costly financing environment...' (1983, p. 429). Thus, merger activity seems to be related strongly to attractive capital market conditions.

The asymmetrical incidence of mergers through time raises special problems for the MM if beta is also changing intertemporally. For example, if beta is relatively low at the beginning of an economic expansion and expands steadily throughout the expansion, then the CAR would be positively biased. Whether or not this is a significant source of bias depends on the empirical data which, to date, are relatively scarce.

The evidence on intertemporal changes in beta is developing rapidly, but econometric explanations for such changes in beta are limited. Francis and Fabozzi (1979) recently analysed the changes in the parameters of the MM over several business cycles (as defined by the National Bureau of Economic Research) and found that the parameters of the MM do show a significant tendency to change at peaks and troughs in the business cycle, and that beta is less stable than alpha. They conclude that '... the intertemporal instability of beta ... appears to result at least partially from changes which are associated with business cycle economics' (p. 358). Unfortunately, the reported results do not indicate the direction of changes in beta over the business cycle.

Beta may be increasing during merger periods for several reasons. First, higher growth expectations may result in higher beta because growth opportunities are more risky than assets in place. Second, the argument by Bar-Yosef and Brown (1977), that increased uncertainty regarding both current earnings and future dividend stability preceding stock splits may account for the temporary rise in betas for firms undergoing stock splits, may be applicable for any major policy decision by management. Merger is certainly a major policy decision that may affect business risk and/or financial risk, creating increased investor uncertainty and hence greater risk premiums. It may be that the intertemporal movements in betas shown in Fig. 2 for mergers and stock splits are associated with many other major financial decisions as well. But the potential bias in the MM from using betas calculated from past data only (e.g., −40 to −20 months), and the tendency of mergers to occur in beginning phases of economic expansion, is to overstate acquiring shareholder returns in the disequilibrium period because of the actual increase in risks. Of course, further evidence on the intertemporal behaviour of beta will shed light on this issue.

4. Summary

Some of the necessary conditions for empirical application of the market model to mergers are questionable. The strong likelihood of an unstable beta over both the assumed equilibrium period and disequilibrium period is caused by changing financial and operating risks of participants, different betas for buyers and sellers, and intertemporal changes in beta over the business cycle. Estimation methods for parameters of the market model that use pre-merger returns are thus likely to violate the econometric

54   R. L. Conn

assumptions of $E(e) = 0$ and $COV(R_m,e) = 0$. A post-merger, post-disequilibrium period is recommended for estimating the market model. In addition, the commonly used sample selection procedures have excluded other significant events (e.g., unrecorded mergers, noncommon stock exchanges, and major financial decisions) that may have an impact on the betas of acquiring and acquired firms.

There is considerable evidence that beta may be increasing (decreasing) for acquiring (acquired) firms, thus overstating (understating) the abnormal returns to shareholders, the CAR. The conventional conclusion that has emerged from existing studies is that merger is neutral or slightly beneficial for acquiring firms, but considerably more advantageous for acquired firms. Methodological problems in applying the market model to mergers have created increased uncertainty about the generality of such conclusions. A reinterpretation of existing studies suggests that merger may at best be neutral for acquiring firms but considerably more advantageous for acquired firms. These re-examined conclusions, in turn, provide support for the view that significant other motives besides maximising shareholder wealth are of considerable importance in mergers, especially for acquiring firms.

In assessing the public policy implications of the growing number of merger studies using the MM, several points must be firmly borne in mind. First, and most important, the MM's general premise, that a Pareto-optimal condition between stockholders of acquiring and acquired firms is the desired benchmark for evaluating mergers, is an extremely restrictive position from which to start. Other issues and constituencies are clearly relevant. Second, even within that limited framework, the results from the MM should be discounted for policy purposes, on the grounds that there are unresolved methodological problems. Finally, a re-examination of the MM studies even calls into question the financial status of stockholders in mergers over the last few decades.

Bibliography

Bar-Josef, S. and Brown, L. 1977. A re-examination of stock splits using moving betas, *Journal of Finance,* September

Bey, R. P. 1983. The market model as an appropriate description of the stochastic process generating security returns, *Journal of Financial Research,* May

Brenner, M. and Downes, J. D. 1979. A critical evaluation of the measurement of conglomerate performance using the capital asset pricing model, *Review of Economics and Statistics,* May

Chow, G. C. 1960. Tests of the equality between sets of coefficients in two linear regressions, *Econometrics,* vol. 28

Choi, D. and Phillippatos, G. 1983. Financial consequences of antitrust enforcement, *Review of Economics and Statistics,* August

Conn, R. L. 1973. Performance of conglomerate firms: comment, *Journal of Finance,* June

Conn, R. L. and Nielsen, J. F. 1977. An empirical test of the Larson–Gonedes exchange ratio determination model, *Journal of Finance,* September

Copeland, T. and Weston, J. F. 1983. *Financial Theory and Corporate Policy,* Reading, Massachusetts, Addison–Wesley Publishing Company

Dodd, P. 1980. Merger proposals, management discretion and stockholder wealth, *Journal of Financial Economics,* Fall

Elgers, P. T. and Clark, J. J. 1980. Merger types and shareholder returns. *Financial Management,* May

Ellert, J. C. 1976. Mergers, antitrust law enforcement and shareholder returns, *Journal of Finance,* May

Fabozzi, F. J. and Francis, J. C. 1977. Stability tests for alphas and betas over bull and bear market conditions, *Journal of Finance,* September

The capital asset pricing model and mergers 55

Fama, E. F. 1970. Efficiency of capital markets: a review of theory and empirical work, *Journal of Finance*, May

Federal Trade Commission 1969. *Economic Report of Corporate Mergers*, Washington, DC, Government Printing Office

Federal Trade Commission 1981. *Statistical Report on Mergers and Acquisitions*, Washington, DC, Government Printing Office

Firth, M. 1978. Synergism in mergers: some British results, *Journal of Finance*, May

Firth, M. 1979. The market performance of conglomerate firms in the United Kingdom, *Review of Economics and Statistics*, November

Francis, J. C. and Fabozzi, F. J. 1979. The effects of changing macro-economic conditions on the parameters of the single index market model, *Journal of Financial and Quantitative Analysis*, June

Franks, J. R. 1978. Insider information and the efficiency of the acquisitions' market, *Journal of Banking and Finance*, vol. II

Franks, J. R., Broyles, J. E. and Hecht, M. J. 1977. An industry study of the profitability of mergers in the United Kingdom, *Journal of Finance*, December

Garbade, K., Silber, W. H. and White, L. J. 1982. Market reaction to the filing of antitrust suits: an aggregate and cross-sectional analysis, *Review of Economics and Statistics*, November

Halpern, P. J. 1973. Empirical estimates of the amount and distribution of gains to companies in mergers, *Journal of Business*, October

Halpern, P. J. 1983. Corporate acquisitions: a theory of special cases? A review of event studies applied to acquisitions, *Journal of Finance*, May

Haugen, R. A. and Langetieg, T. C. 1975. An empirical test for synergism in merger, *Journal of Finance*, September

Higgins, R. C. and Schall, L. D. 1975. Corporate bankruptcy and conglomerate merger, *Journal of Finance*, March

Jensen, M. C. and Ruback, R. S. 1983. The market for corporate control: the scientific evidence, *Journal of Financial Economics*, April

Joehnk, M. D. and Nielsen, J. F. 1974. The effects of conglomerate merger activity on systematic risk, *Journal of Financial and Quantitative Analysis*, March

Kim, E. H. and McConnell, J. J. 1977. Corporate mergers and the co-insurance of corporate debt, *Journal of Finance*, May

Kummer, D. R. and Hoffmeister, J. R. 1978. Valuation consequences of cash tender offers, *Journal of Finance*, May

Langetieg, T. C. 1978. An application of a three factor performance index to measure stockholder gains from merger, *Journal of Financial Economics*, December

Lewellen, W. G. 1971. A pure financial rationale for the conglomerate merger, *Journal of Finance*, May

Lintner, J. 1971. Expectations, mergers and equilibrium in purely competitive securities markets, *American Economic Review*, May

Malkiel, B. G. and Cragg, J. G. 1970. Expectations and the structure of share price, *American Economic Review*, September

Mandelker, G. 1974. Risk and return: the case of merging firms, *Journal of Financial Economics*, December

Markowitz, H. 1959. *Portfolio Selection: Efficient Diversification of Investments*, New York, John Wiley and Sons

Mead, W. J. 1969. Instantaneous merger profit as a conglomerate merger motive, *Western Economic Journal*, December

Melicher, R. W. 1974. Evidence on the acquisition-related performance of conglomerate firms, *Journal of Finance*, March

Melicher, R. W. and Hempel, G. H. 1971. Differences in financial characteristics between conglomerate and horizontal or vertical mergers, *Nebraska Journal of Economics and Business*, Autumn

Melicher, R. W. and Rush, D. F. 1973. Performance of conglomerate firms: recent risk and return experience, *Journal of Finance*, May

Melicher, R. W., Ledolter, J. and D'Antonio, L. J. 1983. A time series analysis of aggregate merger activity, *Review of Economics and Statistics*, August

56   R. L. Conn

Mueller, D. C. 1977. The effects of conglomerate mergers, *Journal of Banking and Finance,* I

Nelson, R. L. 1959. *Merger Movements in American Industry, 1895–1956,* Princeton, N. J., Princeton University Press for the National Bureau of Economic Research

Nelson, R. L. 1974. Business cycle factors in the choice between internal and external growth, in *The Corporate Merger,* W. Alberts and J. E. Segall (eds), Chicago, University of Chicago Press

Pettit, R. R. and Westerfield, R. 1974. Using the capital asset pricing model and market model to predict security returns, *Journal of Financial and Quantitative Analysis,* September

Roll, R. 1977. A critique of the asset pricing theory's tests. Part 1: on past and potential testability of the theory, *Journal of Financial Economics,* March

Ross, S. A. 1978. The current status of the capital asset pricing model (CAPM), *Journal of Finance,* June

Scholes, M. and Williams, J. 1977. Estimating betas from non-synchronous data, *Journal of Financial Economics,* December

Sharpe, W. F. 1963. A simplified model for portfolio analysis, *Management Science,* January

Steiner, P. O. 1975. *Mergers, Motives, Effects, and Policies,* Ann Arbor, University of Michigan Press

Weston, J. F. and Mansinghka, S. K. 1971. Tests of the efficiency performance of conglomerate firms, *Journal of Finance,* September

[6]

International Journal of Industrial Organization 9 (1991) 513–532. North-Holland

The success of mergers in Germany

Rolf Bühner*

Universität Passau, D-8390 Passau, Germany

Final version received December 1990

This paper presents empirical evidence of the success of mergers in the Federal Republic of Germany. In general, the results show that the mergers are not successful. The shareholders of acquiring firms have to accept cumulative abnormal losses of −9.38 per cent. Returns on assets show also significant declines. According to the pattern of diversification it was found that product extending acquiring firms performed best. High cash flow enables to limit losses. Firms that have frequent experience of mergers tend to gain from their mergers.

1. Introduction

While the U.S. is experiencing a fourth wave of merger activity [Salter and Weinhold (1979) and Rutland and Sher (1987)], the incidence of takeovers in the Federal Republic of Germany was comparatively low up to the beginning of the 1970s. In 1989, the Federal Cartel Office (Bundeskartellamt) were notified of 1,415 takeovers, a figure double that of five years previously.[1]

In the distant future the number of takeovers might continue to rise. The institution of the Common Market, envisaged to be achieved in 1993, requires a strategic adjustment of companies so that new opportunities of products and markets will not be thrown away. Takeovers are an appropriate mean to achieve these opportunities. As a second point, the takeovers of foreign companies in the Federal Republic of Germany have risen.[2] This trend may grow stronger increasing the number of German takeovers, too.

✳ Takeovers allow management to follow a strategy of external growth. Compared to internal development, which strengthens market positions and opens up new markets by internal efforts, takeovers have a number of fundamental advantages. First, there is the advantage of time. Takeovers can

---

*Prof. Dr. Rolf Bühner, Lehrstuhl für Betriebswirtschaftslehre mit Schwerpunkt Organisation und Personalwesen, Postfach 25 40, D-8390 Passau, Germany. This paper presents parts of the results of a project financed by the German Research Foundation (Deutsche Forschungsgemeinschaft, DFG). I am grateful for its support. Special thanks are due to Dennis Mueller for his helpful comments on an earlier draft.

[1]See the data in various reports of the Federal Cartel Office (Bundeskartellamt).
[2]After 125 in 1985, 167 in 1986 and 177 in 1987 the number rose sharply up to 407 in 1988 [Wupper & Partner GmbH (1986 and following years)].

open up new lines of business quickly. The rapid technological change of the last years gave a new meaning to the advantages of time possible with takeovers. Economic opportunities diminish, the longer entry into a market lasts and the more competitors are already entrenched. Takeovers allow quick participation in new technological markets to realize potential profits.[3]

Second, the acquisition of an incumbent competitor does not introduce additional capacity or strengthen competition. Simultaneously, barriers to entry are circumvented. Not least, takeovers may be cost-saving, especially when intangible assets such as patents, goodwill, brand identities or special know-how can be acquired [Salter and Weinhold (1979)]. Moreover, there is the possibility to sell-off parts of the acquired company, thereby realizing additional profits.[4]

The purpose of the present study is to analyze the success of mergers between German companies using two different methods. First, the returns to shareholders will be studied. This method affords an ex-ante analysis, which examines the expectations of the shareholders about the future value of their investment.[5] Since the beginning of the 1970s it is commonly used to study the success of takeovers. Second, accounting numbers will be analyzed forming an ex-post analysis of the real changes of the variables taken from balance sheets and earnings statements before and after the takeover. It is the more traditional method and was already applied for consolidations of the late 1800s [see e.g. Dewing (1921)].

2. Factors affecting the success or failure of takeovers

Factors which determine takeovers and affect their success or failure can be divided into three main groups [Hughes, Mueller and Singh (1980) and Ravenscraft and Scherer (1987)]:[6] real determinants, speculative determinants and factors that rest upon management motivation.

---

[3]See Bühner (1990a) for an empirical investigation of the position of takeovers in a strategy for technological advantage.

[4]In the U.S., the number of such sell-offs after takeovers has increased [Dobrzynski (1988)]. A good example of possibilities for the realization of profits after takeovers is the tender offer for the British BAT: Valued between 6 and 7 pounds, the tender offer was at 8.50 pound. The break-up value of the highly diversified conglomerate was valued with 11 pound per share.

[5]For a comparison of methods for analysis see e.g. Halpern (1983). The results of analyses of shareholder returns are well summarized by e.g. Jensen and Ruback (1983), Jarrell, Brickley and Netter (1988). For a first analysis of mergers in the Federal Republic of Germany see Bühner (1990b).

[6]For other classifications see e.g. Halpern (1983), who, from a shareholder point of view, divides into value-maximizing and non value-maximizing determinants, Lubatkin (1983), who sees technical, pecunial and diversification effects or Weston and Chung (1983), who define four groups: effectivity, managerialism, monopoly power and taxes.

2.1. Real determinants

The most important real determinants for success are the increase of monopoly power or reductions in costs. The monopoly power of a firm can be characterized by the height of its market share and/or barriers to entry. The results of empirical studies show that there is a generally positive relationship between market share and profit performance [see e.g. Shepherd (1979)].[7] By executing a horizontal takeover, a direct competitor is bought and his market share acquired. The strengthened market position allows a rise in price. Barriers to entry may be increased, because potential entrants fear competition with a larger company.[8] Vertical takeovers, suppliers can raise barriers to entry by reducing possibilities for potential competitors to participate at one of the integrated production levels. Conglomerate takeovers can also raise monopoly power and barriers to entry [Lorie and Halpern (1970)].

Cost reductions can occur with diversification via takeovers. Horizontal takeovers with product extension[9] allow the realization of economies of scope [Teece (1980)]. These economies result out of flexible manufacturing plants, which can be applied for manufacturing several similar products. Because of their capacity to reduce market uncertainty vertical takeovers can lead to a reduction of transaction costs [Williamson (1975)]. For all forms of diversification via takeovers, there are possibilities of reducing indirect costs as overhead functions can be combined [Hughes, Mueller and Singh (1980)].

Mergers can also improve economic efficiency by improving the market for corporate control [Manne (1965)]. According to this view, takeovers shift control of the target to a better management.

Companies which are enlarged by takeovers also have the possibility to take up debt capital under more favorable conditions. This leads to additional cost reductions [Lewellen (1971)]. Furthermore, after conglomerate takeovers profits may be stabilized. So, the costs of avoiding bankruptcy are lower.

A last real determinant for carrying out takeovers is the realization of tax savings. These possibilities seem to be an important motive for takeovers in the U.S. since the mid 1970s [Hughes, Mueller and Singh (1980)]. An example illustrates the importance of tax motives in the Federal Republic of Germany: the takeover of AEG by Daimler-Benz may have led to savings of

[7]Especially empirical studies using PIMS-Data (Profit Impact of Market Strategies) resulted in high positive connections between Return on Investment and market shares, see the summary of Buzzel and Gale (1987). Schwalbach (1988) has verified for a German sample a U-shaped connection for some businesses. See also Porter (1980).

[8]However, empirical studies have found declining growth rates for the combined firm [Mueller (1980) and Mueller (1986)].

[9]Product extension takeovers are classified as horizontal by the Federal Cartel Office (Bundeskartellamt), while the American Federal Trade Commission categorizes them as conglomerate.

taxes around 1.9 billion DM. This saving was several hundred million DM above the price paid for AEG [Mundorf (1985)].

2.2. Speculative determinants

Gort (1969) explains takeovers by incorrect valuation by the market. His economic disturbance hypothesis is based on two analyses, which found high correlations between the development of share prices and takeover activity [Weston (1953) and Nelson (1959)]. If share prices rise in general, takeovers will be executed if the buyer has information about the target which leads him to a more optimistic view about it than its owners. When share prices fall and the shareholders have pessimistic expectations, they may want to sell their firm under its current market price and offer an attractive takeover target. In both cases, takeovers will take place because of different expectations. Shareholders are more pessimistic, buyers more optimistic.

According to another speculative determinant for takeovers, tender offers are based upon information about the target, which is not available to the whole capital market, and so not reflected in the market price of the target [Roll (1988)]. The results of empirical studies show that information advantages are only subjective. After cancellation of a tender offer, the share price of the target sooner or later falls to its original value [Bradley, Desai and Kim (1983)]. So, an unsuccessful tender offer does not lead to a longlasting new valuation of the target.

2.3. Factors resting upon management motivation

The separation of ownership from control [Berle and Means (1932)] allows the management of an enterprise to diverge from goals of the owners. This divergence of interests leads to takeovers initiated by the management that are often at the expense of stockholder's wealth [Lubatkin (1983)]. Factors motivating the management are the desire for power and prestige as well as the pecuniary gains from corporate growth [Marris (1966), Baumol (1967), Mueller (1969)]. Takeovers allow rapid growth [Penrose (1959)]. Consequently, some authors see a direct connection between the takeover activity of a firm and the desire for power, prestige and pecuniary gain of its management [e.g. Mueller (1977)].

The free cash flow theory developed by Jensen (1986) also bares on the agency-conflict. The managers are endeavouring to leave free cash flow in the firm and to consolidate their own influence instead of paying dividends to the shareholders. When there is a large free cash flow, there is danger that it will be used to undertake failing takeovers. According to Jensen, diversificative takeovers generally fall into this category [Jensen (1988)].

According to Roll (1986), the overestimation of the value of a target firm by the management of a bidder shifts profits from the acquiring firm to the former owners of the acquired company (Hubris-Hypothesis).

3. Data and methods

3.1. Sample

The sample was selected from the list of the 500 largest enterprises in the Federal Republic of Germany, according to their sales in 1986 [Schmacke (1976)]. Enterprises were dropped from this list if their core business was not in the manufacturing sector. Enterprises were also excluded when another company owns more than 50 per cent of their outstanding shares. For these subsidary companies it must be assumed that they do not have the right to pass their own strategic decisions.[10] The last criterion for the selection of the enterprises was the publication of a detailed earnings statement so that the variables used for the empirical analysis could be computed.

The sample of takeovers comes from the list of notifications by the 500 largest firms given the Federal Cartel Office within the time period from 1973 to 1985. Earlier takeovers could not be taken into account because the Federal Cartel Office publishes the announced takeovers with the names of the participating firms only since 1973. The end of the selection period in 1985 assures that three years after the takeover could be analyzed at a minimum. The takeovers of the selected firms were taken into the sample if the targets were consolidated. This ensures that the variables before and after the first consolidation can be compared. The last point to build the sample was the elimination of takeovers of very small firms. Because of publication restrictions, the nominal capital of the participating firms was taken as a criterion. So, only takeovers of firms with more than one per cent of the nominal capital of the acquiring firms were taken into the sample.

To calculate shareholders' returns monthly share prices must be available for a period ranging from 72 months before the announcement of the takeover to the Federal Cartel Office up to 24 months thereafter. This criterion was satisfied for 90 takeovers. The analysis of accounting numbers requires that at minimum three annual accounts before the first consolidation of the target firm and at least three annual accounts thereafter were available. All the described criteria led to a sample of 110 takeovers.

The number of stock-exchange-listed firms in the Federal Republic of Germany is generally small. Out of the target firms only nine were publicly

---

[10]The takeovers of these firms were taken into account, while they were – according to the line of proceeding of the Federal Cartel Office – imputed to the parent companies.

traded and published earnings statements. This small number prevents a detailed analysis.

3.2. Methods

The analysis of stock market reactions expresses the gains or losses of shareholders through abnormal returns. They show the takeover-induced deviation from the normal trend of returns [see Fama, Fisher, Jensen and Roll (1969)]:

$$AR_{it} = R_{it} - ER_{it}, \tag{1}$$

where AR_{it} is the abnormal return to share i in month t, R_{it} is the actual return to share i in month t, and ER_{it} is the expected return to share i in month t.

To calculate expected returns, the commonly-used market model developed by Sharpe (1963) will be employed [for a survey of methods to estimate abnormal returns see Brown and Warner (1980)]. It is based on the assumption of a linear relationship between market returns and share returns:

$$R_{it} = \alpha_i + \beta_i * R_{Mt} + \varepsilon_{it}, \tag{2}$$

where α_i and β_i are unknown parameters to be estimated, R_{Mt} is the rate of return to the market index in month t, and ε_{it} is an independent and identically distributed random disturbance term.

The parameters α and β were estimated with ordinary least squares on the basis of returns in the time period from 72 months up to 25 months before the announcement of the takeover to the Federal Cartel Office [for a comparison of different methods to estimate α and β see Brown and Warner (1985)]. Using the estimated values of α and β, predicted returns for each takeover i were generated for the investigation period. Abnormal returns for each takeover i in month t were then computed as the difference between actual and predicted returns:

$$AR_{it} = R_{it} - (\hat{\alpha}_i + \hat{\beta}_i * R_{Mt}). \tag{3}$$

To study performance effects, the abnormal returns of each takeover had to be aggregated into a portfolio. Thus an equally-weighted portfolio was constructed:

$$AR_t = \frac{1}{N} * \sum_{i=1}^{N} AR_{it}, \tag{4}$$

where AR_t is the abnormal return for the portfolio of all takeovers in month t, and N is the number of takeovers.

The total gains or losses to the shareholders during the investigation period will be obtained by cumulating the abnormal returns of the portfolio:

$$CAR_t = \sum_{t=1}^{T} AR_t, \qquad (5)$$

where CAR_t is the cumulative abnormal return in the time period up to month t, and T is the investigation period.

The accounting-based success or failure of takeovers was measured by the return on assets and the return on equity. The return on assets is calculated in the following way:

$$\begin{matrix} \text{return} \\ \text{on} \\ \text{assets} \end{matrix} \text{(ROA)} = \frac{\text{year's net earnings before taxes and interest paid}}{\text{total capitalization}}. \qquad (6)$$

The return on equity is a measure of the interests of the shareholders of the corporation. So the return on equity is important for the provision of capital and will be calculated in the following way:

$$\begin{matrix} \text{return} \\ \text{on} \\ \text{equity} \end{matrix} \text{(ROE)} = \frac{\text{year's net earnings before taxes}}{\text{total equity}}. \qquad (7)$$

The return on assets and the return on equity will be considered in the three years before and up to six years after the first consolidation of the target firms. Of course, the longer the time period of analysis chosen, the higher is the danger of influences not caused by the takeovers. On the other hand, the longer the period considered, the more likely it is that the full effect of a takeover is captured. A pairwise t-test was used to indicate the significance of the takeover-induced changes of return on equity and return on assets.

4. Results and discussion

4.1. Overall analysis

The result of the analysis of stock market reactions is given in fig. 1. It shows the development of the cumulative abnormal returns for the acquiring

520   R. Bühner, *The success of mergers in Germany*

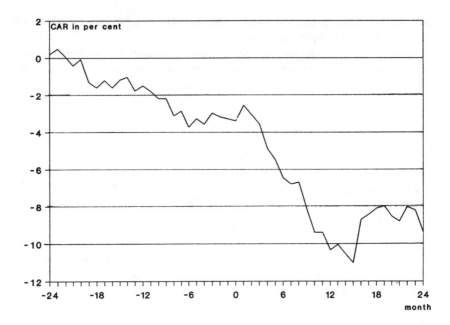

Fig. 1. Cumulative abnormal returns of acquiring firms.

firms from 24 months before to 24 months after the announcement of the takeovers to the Federal Cartel Office. The month of the announcement of the takeover to the Federal Cartel Office will be considered as month zero, the month of the takeover.

The results show declining cumulative abnormal returns even before the takeover. The highest loss is 3.72 per cent, reached 6 months before the takeover. The abnormal loss in the month of the takeover amounts to 0.12 per cent. In the month after the takeover, the acquiring firms earn abnormal gains of 0.86 per cent.

The apparently positive influence of takeovers in the month after they occurred may arise because the study is based on the notations of every fifteenth day of the month. Therefore, events which take place after the fifteenth of a month will lead to reactions in the following month.[11] Moreover, the Federal Cartel Office publishes takeovers in the month after their announcement, which may be an additional cause of a time-lag.

In the period following the takeover, the acquiring firms register high losses. Fifteen months after the takeover, the cumulative abnormal return reaches a low of −11.02 per cent. Only thereafter the wealth situation

---

[11]Even in studies based on daily returns similar problems may appear. Information may cause reactions in the stock market on one day, although they are published on the next day. Thus abnormal returns can be observed on the day before the publication, see Dodd (1980).

improves. For the 24 months period under study around the takeover, the cumulative abnormal return is −9.38 per cent.

Table 1 compares the cumulative abnormal returns for selected periods with corresponding American studies. It shows that American acquiring firms earn high cumulative abnormal returns before the takeover date, which range up to 14.5 per cent. The comparable value of the present study is −3.27 per cent.

In the month of the takeover, the American studies as well as the present one observe only slight abnormal returns. So the capital market seems to be in a wait-and-see attitude. In the year after the takeover, three of the five American studies [Asquith (1983), Langetieg (1978) and Magenheim and Mueller (1988)] found losses that are comparable with the present findings for West Germany. All these studies calculated losses of about 7 per cent.

At the point of two years after the takeover the reactions of the stock markets are considerably different. While Langetieg (1978) finds rising losses, Elgers and Clark (1980) state constant losses. Magenheim and Mueller (1988) determine declining losses in comparison to the one-year period. The sample firms used by Mandelker (1974) realize declining profits. The results of the present study show slightly declining losses and consequently seem to indicate the beginning of a consolidation phase. This may result from the solution of problems with the strategic and organizational integration of the acquired firms. Nevertheless, the long-term effects of takeovers have to be interpreted with caution. Separate strategic decisions, which are not connected with the takeovers, may be the cause of additional stock market reactions.

To summarize, the relatively high losses of the acquiring firms after their takeovers show that acquisitions did not increase shareholders' wealth. Value maximizing motives, basing on real or speculative determinants were either not realized at the expected level or the stock market did not recognize them.

The results of the accounting-based analysis are given in fig. 2. It shows the development of the returns on assets and the returns on equity within the time period ranging from three years before the first consolidation of the firm taken over up to three years after. In most of the cases, the year of the first consolidation conformed with the year of the takeover. So it will be labelled as the year of the takeover. The years before the consolidation are marked with a negative sign.

The returns on equity show an unsettled development up to the year of the merger. The highest level, reached in that year, is 18.11 per cent. In the second and third year after the merger the returns on equity declined. The t-value for the comparison of the average values before and after the merger is 0.17. The returns on assets are growing up to the year of the merger. After that, they show a sharp decline. Although, the t-value amounts to 1.37 and is not significant.

R. Bühner, The success of mergers in Germany

Table 1

Comparison of the results with corresponding American studies.

Study	Reference point of time[a]	Cumulative abnormal returns in per cent for periods (in months relative to the reference point of time)			
		(−24, −1)	0	(1, 12)	(1, 24)
Asquith (1983)	Announcement and enforcement	14.5	−0.3[b]	−7.2	−[c]
Elgers/Clark (1980)	Enforcement	10.2	0.0	−0.5	−0.5
Langetieg (1978)	Enforcement	10.88[d]	−[c]	−6.59	−12.86
Magenheim/Mueller (1988)	Announcement	9.71[e]	−0.37 / −0.70[f]	−7.47	−4.66
Mandelker (1974)	Enforcement	4.84	0.18	0.58	0.11
Present study	Enforcement	−3.27	−0.12 (0.86)[g]	−6.93	−5.98

[a]Announcement of the plan of a takeover or enforcement of the takeover.
[b]Time between the announcement of plans of a takeover and the enforcement of the takeover.
[c]Not available.
[d]Period from 18 months up to 1 month before the takeover.
[e]Ignoring different estimation periods for the sum of two values given here.
[f]Different values for different estimation periods.
[g]Month after the takeover.

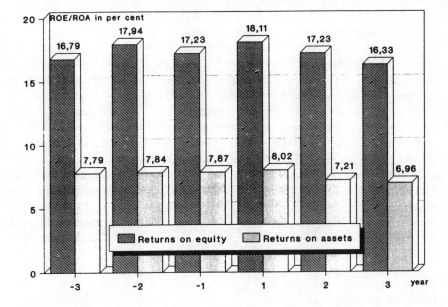

Fig. 2. Returns on equity and returns on assets of acquiring firms.

The rise in the returns on assets and – except for the year before the takeover – in the returns on equity leads to the interpretation that takeovers are carried out to support a positive development of returns. In the year of the takeover, the positive development can be maintained, but in the second and third year after the takeover there are losses.

The delayed negative effects of takeovers on returns can be delineated if the *t*-test does not contain the year of the takeover. Comparing the returns on assets for the first three years of the period under study with the two last, excepting the year of the takeover, leads to a *t*-value of 7.77 which is significant on the one-per-cent-level. For the returns on equity, the *t*-value remains not significant.

The consideration of single accounting positions may indicate the reasons for the decreasing returns after the takeover. From the year of the takeover to the third year thereafter, the year's net earnings of the firms under study increased by 19.38 per cent. The taxes show an increase of 7.82 and the interests paid of 1.51 per cent. Opposite of this, the total equity increased by 34.45 per cent and the total capitalization by 24.76 per cent. The comparison of the increases after the takeover leads to the conclusion that the enterprises were not able to realize higher profits proportional to the growth of capital. In the year of the takeover this divergence may be hidden by exhaustion of appreciation potentiality.

A second test was to see whether the falling returns on assets and returns on equity were only temporary. With a reduced sample of 94 takeovers the period under study was extended to the six years after the takeover. The results show a significant decline in the returns on assets affected by the takeover ($t=2.05$). The returns on equity show in congruence with the shorter period no significant differences ($t=0.98$).

The present results are partially supported by foreign analyses of the success of takeovers which also use return variables. Lev and Mandelker (1972) came to the result, that the returns of merged firms were below the returns of a control group. Stich (1974) investigated returns on assets and returns on equity for merged firms which were below the value for the whole industrial sector. The sample used by Meeks (1977) shows declines of returns on assets after takeovers. After takeovers using the purchase-method for accounting after takeover, Ravenscraft and Scherer (1987) ascertained losses of returns on assets of 3.84 per cent. With the pooling-of-interest-method the returns on assets increased slightly.

4.2. Analysis of diversification

To analyze the reactions of the capital market with respect to the direction of diversification, the sample was divided into the following groups:

– Horizontal mergers without product extension (38 cases);
– Horizontal mergers with product extension (23 cases);
– Vertical mergers (17 cases)
– Conglomerate mergers (12 cases.)[12]

Fig. 3 shows the cumulative abnormal returns for the four groups of takeovers. For horizontal takeovers without product extension, fig. 3 shows positive cumulative abnormal returns up to 9 months before the takeover. After that, they become negative. In the month of the takeover the returns fall to −3.94 per cent. The month after the takeover shows positive abnormal returns of 0.85 per cent. The declining trend, however, cannot be stopped. Twelve months after the takeover the losses reach their highest value. Thereafter, a slight improvement can be observed. Over the whole investigation period the cumulative abnormal returns for horizontal takeovers without product extension are −9.95 per cent.

For horizontal takeovers with product extension, the cumulative abnormal returns are negative up to seven months before the takeover. The takeover itself has positive impacts, especially in the following month, with an

[12]Remember that the German Federal Cartel Office treats product range extension takeovers as horizontal and not as conglomerate.

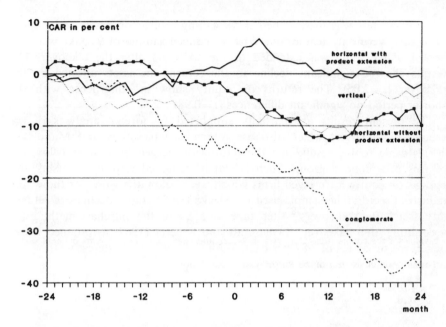

Fig. 3. Cumulative abnormal returns according to diversification.

abnormal return reaching 2.44 per cent. The highest cumulative abnormal return of 6.75 per cent appears three months after the takeover. Afterwards the returns become negative. Although the whole investigation period gives rise to losses of 1.97 per cent, horizontal takeovers with product extension achieve better results than the other categories.

Vertical takeovers show, with a few exceptions, steadily falling cumulative abnormal returns. The takeover does not stop this trend. The highest loss appears in the fifteenth month after the takeover with cumulative abnormal returns reaching −11.90 per cent.

The evaluation of conglomerate takeovers by the stock market is very negative. The cumulative abnormal returns show a sharp decline for firms diversifying into new products and markets. This trend is, moreover, only interrupted by a few months with positive returns. Even the takeover itself has a negative impact. The implementation month shows an abnormal return of −0.76, and the following month one of −0.95 per cent. The declining tendency only ceases after the seventeenth month after the takeover. For the whole investigation period, cumulative abnormal returns for this category amount to −37.31 per cent.

Table 2 shows statistical results and subsamples of the accounting-based analysis for each group of diversification. There are different levels and

Table 2

Returns on equity and returns on assets according to diversification.

Direction of diversification	Number of cases n	Returns on equity			Returns on assets		
		Before $\bar{x}$	After $\bar{x}$	t-value	Before $\bar{x}$	After $\bar{x}$	t-value
Horizontal without product extension	43	16.49	15 61	1.88**[a] (1.30)[b]	7.76	7.25	3.57** (3.28)**
Horizontal with product extension	31	16.92	16.76	0.12 (0.18)	6.84	7.00	−0.53 (0.77)
Vertical	19	13.64	15.89	−1.36 (−0.90)	7.38	7.27	0.25 (2.54)**
Conglomerate	17	24.98	24.29	0.15 (0.34)	10.61	8.77	1.59* (6.01)***

[a] t-value for the comparison of the periods before and after the merger (3 years before/3 years after);

[b] t-value without the year of the merger (first consolidation);

*** $p \leq 0.01$;

** $p \leq 0.05$;

* $p \leq 0.10$.

developments of returns on assets and returns on equity. Firms with conglomerate mergers experience significant declines in returns on assets. They are significant at the ten per cent level. Ignoring the year of the merger, the probability of error declines to less than one per cent. Horizontal mergers without product extension show decreases of returns on assets significant at the five per cent level, even when the year of the merger is not taken into consideration. This is the second-poorest result and agrees with the reactions of the capital market to these mergers. For vertical mergers only when we disregard the year of the merger do we observe a significant decline of returns to assets. Consistent with the cumulative abnormal returns on common shares, horizontal mergers with product extension show the best results. When the year of the merger was taken into consideration, there was a slight but not significant increase in returns on assets. Without the year of the merger, the mean values show a decline which is also not significant.

In connection with horizontal mergers without product extension returns on equity show a decline significant at the ten per cent level. For all other forms of diversification there are no significant changes. The extension of the period under study was not done for the diversification groups because the subsamples become too small.

4.3. Influence of free cash flow

'Free cash flow is cash flow in excess of that required to fund all projects that have positive net present values when discounted at the relevant cost of capital. ...The problem is how to motivate managers to disgorge the cash rather than investing it at below the cost of capital or wasting it on organization inefficiencies [Jensen (1986, p. 323)]. Free cash flow implies the risk to be used for acquisitions in order to enlarge the resources controlled by the management. Those acquisitions often turn out as unsuccessful.

To study the influence of cash flow on the success of takeovers, the sample was divided in two groups according to the measured cash flow (net income + depreciation on tangible and intangible fixed assets + change of accruals for pensions) of the acquiring firms. Firms with a cash flow of more (less) than 180 million DM in the year of the merger were classified as firms with high (low) cash flow.

There exists a relationship between the cash flow of firms and their merger activity. The average total number of acquisitions[13] of firms with high cash flow was 64, compared to an average of only 22 acquisitions realized by firms with low cash flow. Consequently, high cash flow probably supports acquisition activity. Fig. 4 shows the cumulative abnormal returns of the firms with high and low cash flow.

The 24 months preceding the merger as well as the first 7 months after the merger show tentatively similar results for firms with high cash flow and those with low cash flow. Afterwards, firms with low cash flow register additional losses. On average they reach − 12.02 per cent, compared to − 6.73 per cent for firms with high cash flow [see also Mueller (1969)].

This is not a test of the free cash flow theory. The results show that high cash flow − as measured − is a financial precondition allowing firms to create comparatively successful mergers. The money might help to make strategic acquisitions in the long run and allows value increasing restructurings. However, high cash flow is not a factor of merger success, it only limits failure.

The accounting-based analysis supports the results of the analysis concerning shareholder returns. Firms with high cash flow register an increase of returns on equity, significant at the level of 10 per cent. For firms with low cash flow the declines of both returns on equity ($t = 2.54$) and returns on assets ($t = 2.06$) are significant. Table 3 shows in detail the statistical results of the accounting-based analysis.

4.4. Influence of merger-activity

The success of mergers based on an external strategy was analyzed by

[13]Note that the total number of acquisitions announced to the Federal Cartel Office is not the same as the number of mergers in the sample due to the selection described in section 3.1. The total number of acquisitions covers also minority investments, acquisitions of properties and other forms of takeovers.

528   *R. Bühner, The success of mergers in Germany*

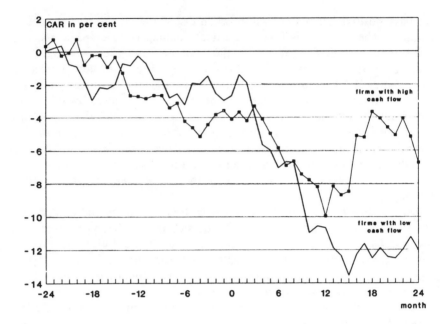

Fig. 4. Cumulative abnormal returns according to cash flow of acquiring firms.

Table 3

Returns on equity and returns on assets for mergers of firms with high cash flow and firms with low cash flow.

Acquiring firm	Number of cases n	Returns on equity			Returns on assets		
		Before $\bar{x}$	After $\bar{x}$	t-value	Before $\bar{x}$	After $\bar{x}$	t-value
High cash flow	55	15.02	17.31	-2.09**[a] (-1.53)[b]	7.62	7.61	0.04 (2.22)*
Low cash flow	55	18.88	16.52	2.54** (2.92)**	8.06	7.34	2.06* (3.25)*

[a]t-value for the comparison of the periods before and after the merger (3 years before/3 years after);
[b]t-value without the year of the merger (first consolidation);
** $p \leqq 0.05$;
* $p \leqq 0.10$.

dividing the firms of the sample into two groups. Firms were classified as merger-active (non-merger-active) when they have announced more (less) than 30 takeovers to the Federal Cartel Office between 1973 and 1985.

Fig. 5 shows the corresponding cumulative abnormal returns. Merger-active firms realized positive cumulative abnormal returns thus obtaining additional gains for their shareholders. The cumulative abnormal return for

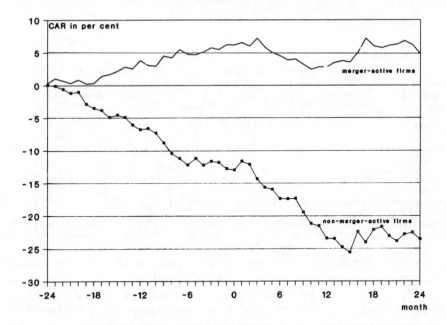

Fig. 5. Cumulative abnormal returns according to merger activity of acquiring firms.

the period under study amounts to 4.83 per cent. In contrast, non-merger-active firms register declining cumulative abnormal returns. The loss of the shareholders cumulates to 23.58 per cent.

Takeovers of merger-active firms are evaluated positively by the stock market. The main reason for this estimation might be perceived advantages in their experience to identify targets with a strategic fit and to evaluate targets and find a fair price.

Table 4 shows the results of the accounting-based analysis. The takeovers by merger-active and non-merger-active firms did not lead to significant changes in returns on equity and returns on assets. Disregarding the year of the merger, non-merger-active firms experienced a highly significant decrease in returns on assets.

5. Summary

The present study analyzes the success of takeovers in the Federal Republic of Germany. As a general conclusion, takeovers can be qualified as decisons leading to high losses for the shareholders of the acquiring firms. Within the investigation period ranging 24 months around the takeover, the cumulative abnormal return amounts to −9.38 per cent. Separating take-

530   *R. Bühner, The success of mergers in Germany*

Table 4

Returns on equity and returns on assets for mergers of merger-active and non-merger-active firms.

Acquiring firm	Number of cases *n*	Returns on equity			Returns on assets		
		Before $\bar{x}$	After $\bar{x}$	*t*-value	Before $\bar{x}$	After $\bar{x}$	*t*-value
Merger-active	55	14.28	14.43	−0.21[a] (0.14)[b]	6.89	7.15	0.77 (−0.31)
Non-merger-active	55	20.30	19.96	0.35 (0.92)	8.60	7.65	1.92* (20.28)**

[a]*t*-value for the comparison of the periods before and after the merger (3 years before/3 years after);
[b]*t*-value without the year of the merger (first consolidation);
** $p \leq 0.05$;
* $p \leq 0.10$.

overs into diversification groups the highest losses result for conglomerate takeovers. A careful diversification via horizontal takeovers with product extension leads to the best stock market reactions. High cash flow of a firm helps to limit failure of mergers. Experience advantages resulting from takeover activity seem to be a substantial factor in merger success.

The accounting-based analysis shows that mergers in general lead to significant decreases in returns on assets. Following both conglomerate or horizontal mergers without product extension, there are significant decreases in returns on assets. After conglomerate mergers the returns on assets decrease sharply. Firms with low cash flow register significant decreases of both returns on assets and returns on equity. Nor does a takeover-oriented strategy achieve significant changes in returns.

Summing up, the hypothesis of value maximizing effects for the shareholders via takeovers has to be rejected. Non-value-maximizing management motives seem to be the relevant ones for carrying out takeovers. The accounting-based analysis supports this interpretation. The relatively good evaluation of horizontal takeovers with product extension suggests that the core skills of the firm may be taken as a basis for careful diversification. Management should be restrained in its tendency to overestimate its skills to manage large-scale as well as highly diversified firms. As the results show, management can learn from past merger activity how to make acquisitions successful.

References

Asquith, Paul, 1983, Merger bids, uncertainty and stockholder returns, Journal of Financial Economics 11, 51–83.
Baumol, William J., 1967, Business behavior, value and growth, 2nd ed. (Macmillan, New York).

Berle, Adolph A. and Gardiner C. Means, 1932, The modern corporation and private property (Macmillan, New York).

Bradley, Michael, Anand Desai and E. Han Kim, 1983, The rationale behind interfirm tender offers: Information or synergy?, Journal of Financial Economics 11, 183–206.

Brown, Stephen J. and Jerold B. Warner, 1980, Measuring security price performance, Journal of Financial Economics 8, 205–258.

Brown, Stephen J. and Jerold B. Warner, 1985, Using daily stock returns: The case of event studies, Journal of Financial Economics 14, 3–31.

Bühner, Rolf, 1990a, Die Bedeutung von Unternehmenszusammenschlüssen im Rahmen einer technologieorientierten Unternehmensstrategie, Ifo-Studien 36, 17–40.

Bühner, Rolf, 1990b, Reaktionen des Aktienmarktes auf Unternehmenszusammenschlüsse: Eine empirische Untersuchung, Zeitschrift für betriebswirtschaftliche Forschung 42, 295–316.

Bundeskartellamt, several years, Bericht über seine Tätigkeit sowie über Lage und Entwicklung auf seinem Aufgabengebiet (Bonn).

Buzzel, Robert D. and Bradley T. Gale, 1987, The PIMS principles: Linking strategy to performance (The Free Press, New York).

Dewing, Arthur S., 1921, A statistical test for the success of consolidations, The Quarterly Journal of Economics 36, 84–101.

Dobrzynski, Judith H., 1988, A new strain of merger mania, Business Week, 21 March, 56–60.

Dodd, Peter, 1980, Merger proposals, management discretion and stockholder wealth, Journal of Financial Economics 8, 105–137.

Elgers, Pieter T. and John J. Clark, 1980, Merger types and shareholder returns: Additional evidence, Financial Management 9, Summer, 66–72.

Fama, Eugene F., Lawrence Fisher, Michael C. Jensen and Richard Roll, 1969, The adjustment of stock prices to new information, International Economic Review 10, 1–21.

Gort, Michael, 1969, An economic disturbance theory of mergers, Quarterly Journal of Economics 83, 624–642.

Halpern, Paul, 1983, Corporate acquisitions: A theory of special cases? A review of event studies applied to acquisitions, The Journal of Finance 38, 297–317.

Hughes, Alan, Dennis C. Mueller and Ajit Singh, 1980, Hypotheses about mergers, in: Dennis C. Mueller, ed., The determinants and effects of mergers: An international comparison (Oelgeschlager, Gunn & Hain, Cambridge, MA and Verlag Anton Hain, Königstein/Ts.) 27–66.

Jarrell, Gregg A., James A. Brickley and Jeffry M. Netter, 1988, The market for corporate control: The empirical evidence since 1980, Journal of Economic Perspectives 2, Winter, 49–68.

Jensen, Michael C., 1986, Agency costs of free cash flow, corporate finance and takeovers, The American Economic Review: Papers and Proceedings 76, 323–329.

Jensen, Michael C., 1988, The takeover controversy: Analysis and evidence, in: John C. Coffee, Jr., Louis Lowenstein and Susan Rose-Ackerman, eds., Knights, raiders and targets: The impact of the hostile takeover (Oxford University Press, New York, Oxford) 314–354.

Jensen, Michael C. and Richard S. Ruback, 1983, The market for corporate control: The scientific evidence, Journal of Financial Economics 11, 5–50.

Langetieg, Terence C., 1978, An application of a three-factor performance index to measure stockholder gains from merger, Journal of Financial Economics 6, 365–383.

Lev, Baruch and Gershon Mandelker, 1972, The microeconomic consequences of corporate mergers, Journal of Business 45, 85–104.

Lewellen, Wilbur G., 1971, A pure financial rationale for the conglomerate merger, The Journal of Finance 26, 521–537.

Lorie, James H. and Paul Halpern, 1970, Conglomerates: The rhetoric and the evidence, Journal of Law and Economics 13, 149–166.

Lubatkin, Michael, 1983, Mergers and the performance of the acquiring firm, Academy of Management Review 8, 218–225.

Magenheim, Ellen B. and Dennis C. Mueller, 1988, Are acquiring-firm shareholders better off after an acquisition?, in: John C. Coffee, Jr., Louis Lowenstein and Susan Rose-Ackerman, eds., Knights, raiders and targets: The impact of the hostile takeover (Oxford University Press, New York, Oxford) 171–193.

Mandelker, Gershon, 1974, Risk and return: The case of merging firms, Journal of Financial Economics 1, 303–335.

Manne, Henry G., 1965, Mergers and the market for corporate control, Journal of Political Economy 73, 110–120.

Marris, Robin, 1966, The economic theory of 'managerial' capitalism (Macmillan, London).

Meeks, Geoffrey, 1977, Disappointing marriage: A study of the gains from merger (Cambridge University Press, Cambridge).

Mueller, Dennis C., 1969, A theory of conglomerate mergers, Quarterly Journal of Economics 83, 643–659.

Mueller, Dennis C., 1977, The effects of conglomerate mergers: A survey of the empirical evidence, Journal of Banking and Finance 1, 315–347.

Mueller, Dennis C., 1980, The United States, 1962–1972, in: Dennis C. Mueller, ed., The determinants and effects of mergers: An international comparison (Oelgeschlager, Gunn & Hain, Cambridge, MA and Verlag Anton Hain, Königstein/Ts.) 271–298.

Mueller, Dennis C., 1986, Profits in the long run (Cambridge University Press, Cambridge).

Mundorf, Hans, 1985, Auch rote Zahlen sind interessant: Erhebliche Steuervorteile aus einer Organschaft zwischen Daimler und AEG, Handelsblatt, 22 Oct., 2.

Nelson, Ralph L., 1959, Merger movements in American industry: 1895–1956 (Princeton University Press, Princeton, NJ).

Penrose, Edith T., 1959, The theory of the growth of the firm (Basil Blackwell, Oxford).

Porter, Michael E., 1980, Competitive strategy: Techniques for analyzing industries and competitors (The Free Press, New York).

Ravenscraft, David J. and Frederick M. Scherer, 1987, Mergers, sell-offs, and economic efficiency (Brookings Institution, Washington, DC).

Roll, Richard, 1986, The hubris hypothesis of corporate takeovers, Journal of Business 59, 197–216.

Roll, Richard, 1988, Empirical evidence on takeover activity and shareholder wealth, in: John C. Coffee, Jr., Louis Lowenstein and Susan Rose-Ackerman, eds., Knights, raiders and targets: The impact of the hostile takeover (Oxford University Press, New York, Oxford) 241–252.

Rutland, John and Michael G. Sher, 1987, The fourth merger wave, Manuscript.

Salter, Malcolm S. and Wolf A. Weinhold, 1979, Diversification through acquisition: Strategies for creating economic value (The Free Press, New York).

Schmacke, Ernst, 1976, Die großen 500. Deutschlands führende Unternehmen und ihr Management. With supplement of November 1988 (Luchterhand, Neuwied).

Schwalbach, Joachim, 1988, Marktanteil und Unternehmensgewinn, Zeitschrift für Betriebswirtschaft 58, 535–549.

Sharpe, William F., 1963, A simplified model for portfolio analysis, Management Science 9, 277–293.

Shepherd, William G., 1979, The economics of industrial organization (Prentice-Hall, Englewood Cliffs, NJ).

Stich, Robert S., 1974, Have U.S. mergers been profitable?, Management International Review 14, nos. 2–3, 33–45.

Teece, David J., 1980, Economies of scope and the scope of the enterprise, Journal of Economic Behavior and Organization 1, 223–247.

Weston, J. Fred, 1953, The role of mergers in the growth of large firms (University of California Press, Berkeley, CA).

Weston, J. Fred and Kwang S. Chung, 1983, Some aspects of merger theory, Journal of the Midwest Finance Association 12, 1–33.

Williamson, Oliver E., 1975, Markets and hierarchies: Analysis and antitrust implications (The Free Press, New York).

Wupper & Partner GmbH, 1986, and following years, Wer kauft wen: Analyse des Unternehmens- und Beteiligungsmarktes (Wupper & Partner, Hamburg).

Financial Accounts and Other Studies

[7]

THE JOURNAL OF FINANCE • VOL. XLVII, NO. 3 • JULY 1992

Beatrice: A Study in the Creation and Destruction of Value

GEORGE P. BAKER*

ABSTRACT

This paper chronicles the history of the Beatrice company from its founding in 1891 as a small creamery, through its growth by acquisition into a diversified consumer and industrial products firm, and its subsequent leveraged buyout and sell-off. The paper analyzes the value consequences the firm's acquisition and divestiture policies, its organizational strategy, and its governance. The analysis sheds light on a number of issues in organization theory, strategy, and corporate finance, including the sources of value in diversifying aquisitions, the cost of over-centralization and weak corporate governance, and the mechanisms of value creation in the market for corporate control.

ON SATURDAY, AUGUST 3, 1985, James Dutt was forced to resign as Chief Executive Officer (CEO) of Beatrice Companies by the board of directors and members of his own management team. The following Monday, the firm's market value jumped by more than 6%—a single day value increase of almost $200 million. Within days, takeover rumors were surfacing. On October 17, Kohlberg, Kravis, and Roberts (KKR) announced a bid for the company that would culminate the largest leveraged buyout (LBO) in history. Less than five years after the LBO, the 100-year-old company, which had been hailed in Dunn's Review ten years earlier as one of the five best-managed companies in America, ceased to exist as an independent organization. Its pieces were sold in a dozen major divestitures ending with the sale of the leftovers to ConAgra in June of 1990.

This paper follows the 100-year history of Beatrice[1] from its founding as a local creamery, through its LBO and ultimate disassembly in the largest

*Harvard Business School. I would like to thank Alfred Chandler, David Collis, Robert Eccles, William Fruhan, Ray Goldberg, ASG, Michael Jensen, William McGuire, Cynthia Montgomery, Richard Ruback, Steven Tolliday, and Karen Wruck for help and support on this project. I would also like to thank John Collins, Neil Gazel, Walter Lovejoy, and William Karnes for being generous with their time and insights about the company for which they worked for many years. I owe great debts to Paige Manning and especially Toby Stuart, who did much of the early research for this project. This research is supported by the Division of Research, Harvard Business School.

[1] Over its 100-year history, the company has had five names. It began as Beatrice Creameries. In 1945 the company changed its name to Beatrice Foods. In 1983 the name was changed to Beatrice Companies. After the 1986 LBO, the company was named BCI Holdings, then in 1987 the name was changed to Beatrice Company. Throughout the paper, I refer to the company simply as Beatrice.

corporate sell-off in American history. The history of Beatrice is, in many ways, the history of American business during the twentieth century. Begun as a small single-business partnership in rural Nebraska, it grew by acquisition, first in its own industry, then in related industries, and then across numerous industries, into one of the largest and most diversified firms in the country. Widely admired as one of America's best run companies in the early 1970s, the firm struggled with problems of strategic direction and internal governance in the late 1970s, which resulted in tremendous value loss. In large part because of this value destruction, Beatrice was caught up in the financial restructuring mechanisms of the 1980s and was taken over in a LBO in 1986 that led to the sale of all the assets of the firm within four years. Along the way, Beatrice participated in more than 400 acquisitions and 90 divestitures, it acquired a conglomerate (Esmark), spawned a hostile take-over vehicle (E-II Holdings), and sold more than 40 units in divisional LBOs.

This paper attempts to explain the sources of value creation and reasons for value loss identified in Figure 1. The company's acquisition and divestiture activities are a large part of this value creation process. Figures 2 and 3 provide information about Beatrice's acquisitions and divestitures. Figure 2 shows the number of transactions made by Beatrice during this century, while Figure 3 gives a sense for the scale and timing of the largest of these transactions. In terms of numbers of transactions, the company was the most active acquiror in America from 1955–1979 and the most active divestor in America from 1979–1987 (Blair, Lane, and Schary (1991)). All of the companies bought between 1950 and 1979 were sold, either alone or packaged with other companies, in the 1980s. Yet Figure 1 suggests that the acquisitions of the 1950s, 1960s, and 1970s created substantial value for the shareholders of Beatrice, and that the divestitures and the LBO more than recaptured the value losses of the late 1970s and early 1980s. This raises the central puzzle in the Beatrice story: how could the acquisition of hundreds of companies create value, and then the subsequent divestitures of these same assets thirty years later also create value?

The history of Beatrice also raises a number of questions about capital markets, corporate strategy and governance, and organizational structures. How did the firm, which was operated as a highly decentralized holding company from the 1940s through the mid-1970s, add value to the firms it acquired? What brought on the decline in value between 1979 and 1981, and how did the internal and external control mechanisms respond to this value destruction? And finally, how did the LBO and the sell-off of Beatrice create so much value for both pre- and post-buyout investors?

Examination of Beatrice's history throughout the twentieth century provides insights whose relevance goes well beyond merely understanding the history of a single firm. For example, a close examination of Beatrice's transition from related to unrelated acquisitions, and the company's organizational structure and strategy for creating value through these acquisitions, sheds new light on the old controversy over the value of conglomerate-type

Beatrice: A Study in the Creation and Destruction of Value   1083

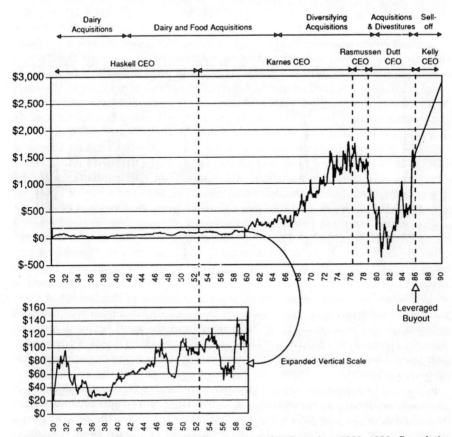

Figure 1. Cumulative abnormal dollar returns for Beatrice, 1930–1990. Cumulative abnormal dollars before the LBO are calculated by multiplying the abnormal return for a month by the market value of the firm at the end of the previous month. and then cumulating these dollar amounts. The abnormal return is calculated by subtracting the actual return from an expected return generated from CAPM. Beta's are estimated using a 60-month moving window. After the LBO, the total market adjusted value gain is calculated. and is simply plotted as a straight line increase in value. After the LBO, the asset beta from before the LBO is assumed, and is then adjusted for the declining leverage each year after the LBO.

mergers. (See Ravenscraft and Scherer (1987) for a review of this controversy.) More recently, many authors have characterized the capital markets activity of the 1980s as "deconglomeration." (See Blair, Lane, and Schary (1991), Kaplan and Weisbach (1991), and Bhagat, Shleifer, and Vishny (1990).) They argue that the wave of divestitures, spin-offs, and LBO in the 1980s represent reversals of the conglomerate mergers of the 1960s and 1970s. Once again, a close study of the history of Beatrice provides a powerful lens through which to view this phenomenon. By examining in detail the economic

1084 *The Journal of Finance*

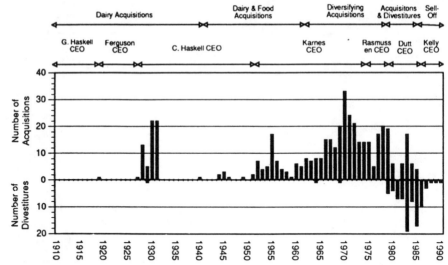

Figure 2. Number of acquisitions and divestitures by year, 1910–1990.

forces that let Beatrice be both an active acquiror in the 1950s through the 1970s, and an active divestor in the 1980s, hypotheses are generated about the process of value creation in organizations and markets that inform additional research on organizational forms, corporate governance, and capital markets.

The paper is organized chronologically, following the four major eras that punctuate the history of the company. Section I (1890–1939) discusses Beatrice's development from a local creamery to a national company and the sources of value in dairy acquisitions. Section II (1940–1976) examines Beatrice's diversification into foods and beyond and the sources of value in diversification. Section III (1977–1985) explores the changing strategic direction of the company and the destruction of value brought on by strategic muddle and the failure of governance. Section IV (1986–1990) covers the LBO and divestitures and probes the question: "value created or value recaptured?" Section V is conclusions.

I. 1890–1939: From a Local Creamery to a National Company

George Haskell founded the partnership of Haskell & Bosworth as a wholesale produce dealer in Beatrice, Nebraska in 1891. He operated as a middleman, collecting butter, eggs, and poultry from dispersed farmers and distributed the produce to retail outlets. After four years of only modest success, Haskell decided to enter the rapidly growing dairy processing industry, and leased the premises of the Beatrice Creamery Company. In 1897, Haskell & Bosworth incorporated as the Beatrice Creamery Company, with a total capitalization of $100,000 (Beatrice (1930), Gazel (1990)).

Beatrice: A Study in the Creation and Destruction of Value 1085

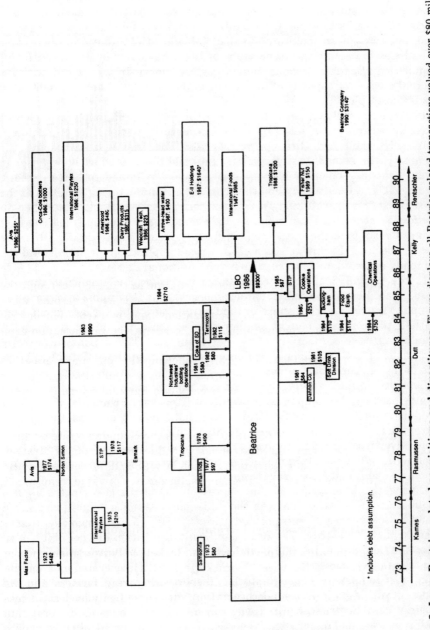

Figure 3. Large Beatrice-related acquisitions and divestitures. Figure displays all Beatrice-related transactions valued over $80 million. Placement of arrowheads marks the announcement date of the transaction. Size of the box represents the size of the transaction.

In 1905, George Haskell engineered the acquisition of Continental Creamery Company of Topeka, Kansas. At the time, this was the largest consolidation in the history of the United States dairy industry; as such, it was a
portent of events to come. Continental was one of the oldest extant dairies
and had a strong regional brand called "Meadow Gold" dairy products. This
brand was to become the cornerstone of Beatrice's dairy business. With this
acquisition, Beatrice became the largest creamery in the world with an
annual processing capacity of thirty-four million pounds of butter produced in
six different plants.

Beatrice grew slowly until 1928 when Clinton Haskell, nephew of George
Haskell, became president of Beatrice. Upon accepting the office of president,
Clinton Haskell had three primary goals. The first was to expand the
creamery, the second was to diversify into additional product lines (prior to
1928, Beatrice's business activity was principally limited to butter, cream,
and eggs), and finally to extend the company's manufacturing facilities to the
East Coast (*Fortune* (1936)). To achieve these objectives, Haskell launched an
aggressive acquisition campaign in 1928 and largely accomplished the first
two of his goals in the initial year of his presidency. On April 25, 1929, the
New York Stock Exchange accepted Beatrice's application for listing, and the
company reported plans to acquire seven additional dairies.

In the early 1930s, Beatrice continued its geographic expansion through
acquisition. Few of the individual acquisitions in a geographic area gave the
company a major market share in the territory into which it was expanding.
Rather, the company bought smaller dairies, building market share in an
area by selective acquisitions of smaller companies. This expansion program
established Beatrice, along with Borden and National Dairy (later Kraft), as
one of the big three dairy firms.

Beatrice, unlike National Dairy and Borden, generally discarded the brand
names used by the companies it acquired. It packaged the bulk of its dairy
products under the Meadow Gold brand name, which enabled Beatrice to
advertise nationally. As early as 1931 Beatrice was running national Meadow
Gold advertisements. The company regularly advertised its dairy products in
such nationally circulating magazines as the *Saturday Evening Post*, *Ladies
Home Journal*, and *Good Housekeeping*.

During the later years of the Depression, Beatrice participated in few
acquisitions. One exception was the 1931 purchase of a minority stake in
Chicago Cold Storage, a refrigerated warehousing concern, which operated as
a subsidiary of Beatrice. The next significant acquisition did not occur until
after the Depression. In 1938 Beatrice began to distribute frozen foods under
the "Bird's Eye" label.

In order to manage its geographically dispersed company, Beatrice adopted
a decentralized multidivisional corporation with a central office. Each processing plant Beatrice acquired was run as a complete operating unit that
both processed and distributed its goods. The company's central office housed
the president, vice president, treasurer, and secretary. It handled all financial and legal matters, research activities, advertisement, supervision of

Beatrice: A Study in the Creation and Destruction of Value 1087

quality control, and the formulation of general policies. Each of the field units was linked to the central office by seven district managers who monitored business at the plants. Plant managers reported directly to division managers who were located in the field. Uniform product quality was ensured by control laboratories located in each of the major processing plants. As early as 1942, Beatrice had intact eighteen committees that functioned to augment organizational cohesion and to facilitate the transfer of specific information up the organizational hierarchy.[2]

Sources of Value in Dairy Acquisitions

Beatrice grew and prospered during this period of dairy acquisitions. The company created value in several ways with its dairy acquisition program. One was the company's ability to achieve economies of scale through marketing its Meadow Gold brand in national magazines. These economies could only be captured efficiently if the company had broad geographic diversity.

There were also increasing economies of scale in production. The efficient plant size for a dairy production plant is limited by the cost of collecting the raw materials and distributing the final product. However, during this period, improved transportation and the invention of electrical refrigeration meant that the "milkshed" for a dairy plant could expand. This fact, combined with the growth of large cities and increasing mechanization of packaging, meant that the organization of the dairy industry was changing. (Mueller, Hamm, and Cook (1976)). What had once been a fundamentally fragmented industry, in which a large number of small integrated dairy companies processed and delivered milk to homes, became one in which large plants processed large volumes of dairy products and delivered them daily to local distribution centers from which home delivery trucks were dispatched. All three large dairy producers (Borden, National Dairy, and Beatrice) were making acquisition to take advantage of this change in the economics of the business (Mueller, Hamm, and Cook (1976)).

II. 1940–1976: Diversification into Foods and Beyond

The next significant step for Beatrice came on November 1, 1943, when the company acquired La Choy Food products of Archbold, Ohio. La Choy was a maker of Chinese speciality foods, and this was Beatrice's first nondairy-related acquisition. Symbolically, in the company's proxy statement filed for 1945, the board of directors recommended that the company change its name from Beatrice Creamery to Beatrice Foods Company, since "[the company] has long ceased to be just a creamery."

In the latter part of the 1940s, Beatrice continued its program of geographic expansion under the leadership of Clinton Haskell. When Haskell

---

[2] Beatrice's organizational form is described in the 1946 annual report.

died in 1952, William Karnes, a Northwestern Law School graduate and Executive Vice President for Beatrice under Haskell, became president. Karnes proved to be an even more ardent advocate of expansion through acquisitions than Clinton Haskell. In the three years following his election, Beatrice purchased twenty-six new dairy plants, including the acquisition of Creameries of America, the nation's seventh largest dairy company. This was Beatrice's largest merger to date: following this acquisition, Beatrice had book value of assets of $66.7 million and produced and sold dairy products from coast to coast. Figure 4 shows Beatrice's assets from 1911–1988.

On January 3, 1955, Beatrice entered the confectionery business with the acquisition of the D. L. Clark Co., a national manufacturer of candy bars. Two years later, Beatrice purchased the Bond Pickle Co. and established a Grocery Products division that included its nondairy food operations. Beatrice also continued to expand its dairy operations. In 1961 the company expanded overseas with the construction of a condensed milk plant in Malaysia, and in September 1962 it purchased Cie Lacsoons, S. A., a Belgian dairy with annual sales of $18 million.

Beatrice took the initial step toward unrelated diversification in 1964 when it acquired Bloomfield Industries, a maker of food service equipment for restaurants and hotels. Then, in June 1965, Karnes purchased Stahl Finish and Polyvinyl Chemicals, manufacturers of polymers, raw materials for polishes, and wood and metal coatings. These acquisitions marked Beatrice's

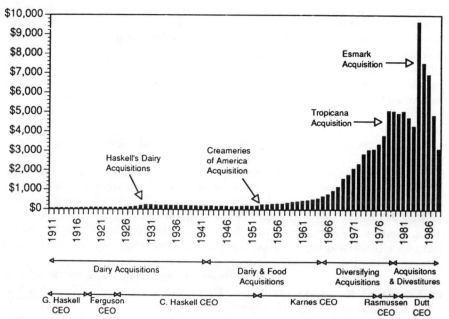

Figure 4. Book value of assets, 1911–1988. In thousands of 1982 dollars.

first move toward conglomeration; thereafter Beatrice's acquisitions were in a variety of disparate industries.

Beatrice's entry into nonfood product lines was driven in part by the actions of the Federal Trade Commission (FTC). In 1950 the government responded to the economy-wide merger and acquisitions wave with the enactment of the Celler-Kefauver Act. This act greatly strengthened Section 7 of the Clayton Act, the existing law on mergers. In 1956 the FTC issued a series of formal complaints against dairy mergers by large corporations from the period 1950–1956. One of these complaints was filed against Beatrice, challenging five of the company's more significant acquisitions from 1950 through 1955, including the Creameries of America merger. In 1964 a decision against Beatrice appeared imminent, and in April 1965 the FTC reached a verdict that required the company to divest $35 million in prior dairy acquisitions ($56.3 million in combined sales) and also placed a ten-year prohibition on future dairy mergers without FTC approval (Mueller, Hamm, and Cook (1976), FTC (1953)). After extended appeals, Beatrice and the FTC reached an agreement whereby Beatrice would divest certain plants amounting to $27 million in sales, and refrain from further acquisitions in the liquid milk and dairy industries. In any case, Beatrice had made no such acquisition since 1961. The assets selected for disposition were sold to a single purchaser in January 1969 (Gazel (1990)).

The FTC's restriction on dairy mergers had a profound impact on Beatrice's decision to participate in conglomerate-type mergers, where the FTC placed few constraints. The expansion campaign launched in 1965 was aimed at companies in a variety of industries. By 1975, only 29% of Beatrice's $1.83 billion in sales, and 21% in earnings, were attributable to the dairy industry. Twenty-eight percent of sales, and 44% of earnings were from outside the food business.

Under Karnes's direction, analysts at Beatrice studied and reported on the future of many industries to uncover areas for profitable acquisitions. For example, in 1967 Beatrice did a study of the "do-it-yourself market for home consumers" and determined it to be "a very rapid growth and potential profit industry" (FTC (1975)). Following this study, Beatrice acquired Melnor Industries in 1967, a maker of do-it-yourself gardening equipment. Between 1967 and 1969, Beatrice merged with seven additional home products companies. Beatrice followed a similar acquisitions pattern through Karnes's tenure. After analyzing an industry and orchestrating a first merger, it followed the beachhead with one or more subsequent acquisitions in the same area of business. Figure 5 shows this pattern of acquisitions. What is striking about this pattern is the extent to which Beatrice intensely acquired companies in particular industries for a limited period of time, then moved on to other industries. For example, the company acquired nine bakeries between 1963 and 1975, and nine recreational equipment companies between 1967 and 1973, but none during any other periods.

Karnes had four criteria that a potential target had to meet for takeover. First, the company had to be a viable and profitable concern in an industry

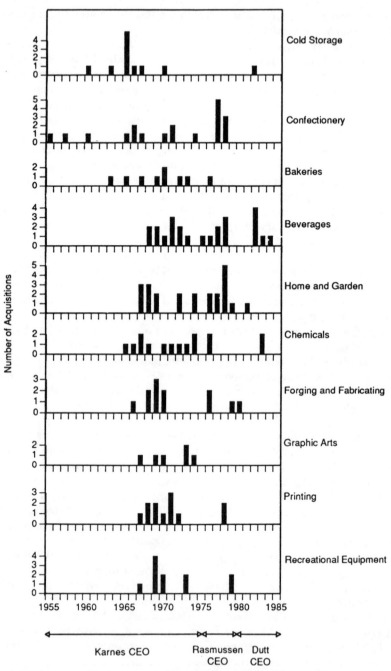

Figure 5. Patterns of industry entry for ten industries, 1955–1985.

Beatrice: A Study in the Creation and Destruction of Value   1091

growing faster than food. Second, the firm had to produce specialty products, not commodities. Third, only companies with competent managers that were willing to remain at Beatrice were acquired. Finally, Karnes preferred mergers which were small relative to the size of Beatrice. Figure 4 shows that this is true: with the single exception of Creameries of America, no acquisition before Tropicana increased the book value of assets by more than 9%. Beatrice would pinpoint the company it wished to pursue in an industry, and then carefully study the firm. The most important aspect to Beatrice was the quality of the company's incumbent managers (Gazel (1990)). The majority of the companies Beatrice purchased were family-run businesses, and Beatrice's commitment to and reputation for growing companies facilitated this type of merger. After Beatrice determined which company to pursue, Karnes would typically approach managers himself and would be personally involved in the negotiations (Gazel (1990)).

This strategy allowed Beatrice to function with the same organizational form that it had used to manage the dairy business: as a large holding company, with top executives focusing more on acquisitions than on operations as each merger brought with it a successful management team. Each Beatrice division had its own CEO. Headquarters delegated hiring, firing, and promotion decisions, determined pay scales, purchased raw materials, and advertised and promoted products to division managers. The central office, however, retained decision rights on capital expenditures and loans as well as determining inventory quotas for each subsidiary. The primary method of information flow from the divisions to the central office was monthly plant financial reports containing sales and profit data. Provided that financial results were satisfactory, headquarters did not get involved in the operations of the divisions (Gazel (1990)).

As part of this decentralized structure, Beatrice had established an incentive compensation system for division managers. Each manager received a base salary plus a bonus payment of around 2% of pretax profits. Many division managers were also given stock options; the first such program was introduced in 1957 and was then frequently expanded. The stock option plan grew to include all plant managers and, in some cases, even lower-level employees. In addition, managers were motivated by a strong internal promotion system: until 1980, every distinct and division manager in the company had been promoted from within Beatrice (Gazel (1990)).

Sources of Value in Diversification

During Karnes's tenure as president and CEO, Beatrice's sales grew from $235 million in 1952 to $5.6 billion in 1976. During this period, the total return to shareholders averaged more than 14% per year. By the time of Karnes's retirement, Beatrice was a multinational conglomerate, with divisions in 27 countries and many industrial categories.

The market reacted favorably, over several decades, to Karnes's acquisition strategy (see Figure 1). The sources of these value gains are different from those associated with Clinton Haskell's geographic diversification of the dairy business. Neil Gazel (1990) argues in his book, *Beatrice from Buildup to Breakup*, that it was Beatrice's decentralized organizational structure, and Karnes's control over the allocation of funds, that produced Beatrice's superior performance. Indeed, the degree to which Karnes abstained from getting involved in the management of divisions seems remarkable. Beatrice did not try to integrate the operations of the companies it bought into those of the parent: the word "synergy" was never used in any of Karnes's annual letters to shareholders. Divisions bought as separate companies in the 1950s and 1960s were later sold *intact* to separate buyers in the 1980s. Even a company with clear opportunities for synergistic integration, such as the Sexton food distribution business, was sold, 14 years after its acquisition, as a stand-alone company.

It is interesting to note how similar the pattern and logic of Karnes's diversification across industries was to Haskell's strategy of geographic diversification. First, the pattern of moving into an industry with an acquisition, then following with more acquisitions in the same industry is very similar to the strategy of buying a small dairy in one area, then buying more in the same area. The organizational capabilities which enabled Beatrice to expand geographically—the ability to evaluate acquisition candidates within an area or industry, the ability to evaluate management teams, and a decentralized control system—were almost as well suited to industrial diversification as they had been to geographic expansion.

In addition, this expansion strategy allowed the company to take advantage of a very valuable source of information about potential targets: the knowledge and opinions of the managers of previously acquired companies. In many instances, Karnes took advantage of the contacts with and information about other companies that his managers possessed. Subjective information about the quality of the management team, or specifics like the fact that the founder of a business wanted to retire and the children did not want to take over, gave Karnes a tremendous advantage when trying to acquire companies. In industry after industry, Beatrice used this source of information to guide his acquisitions. Karnes stated that Harry Stahl of Stahl Finish Company, Beatrice's first acquisition in the speciality chemicals industry, "lead us from one chemical company to another."[3] According to Gazel (1990), Joe Metzger, cofounder of Dannon Yogurt (an early Beatrice acquisition), was instrumental in many of Beatrice's international food acquisitions.

Another important source of value which Beatrice tapped during this period was its ability to bring capital and professional management techniques to small private firms. Almost all of the acquisitions that Beatrice made during the tenure of William Karnes were of privately held, family-run firms. Not only did these firms have poor access to sources of capital, but they were also run in a relatively unsophisticated way, with few formal management systems. In the 1960s, formal management training was almost un-

---

[3]Private telephone conversation, May 8, 1991.

Beatrice: A Study in the Creation and Destruction of Value   1093

known.[4] Beatrice, with its small staff made up predominantly of accountants, was able to provide an important service to these acquired companies by bringing modern management practices to these organizations and helping them expand and run their firms. Management education was an important component of what Beatrice provided to its company managers. Beatrice held regular meetings for the company presidents, at which management problems were discussed, and scholars from business schools lectured. The meetings would also involve smaller group sessions, in which the managers of companies in the same industry would gather to discuss common problems.[5] By bringing such management education and systems to these small firms, Beatrice was able to make these firms substantially more valuable.

In addition, Beatrice made capital available to these small private firms, allowing them to expand in the booming economy of the 1950s and 1960s.[6] The providers of capital at this time, especially commercial banks, were hesitant to lend money for expansion to small, unsophisticated management teams, especially since the banks had little expertise to allow them to realize the value of their collateral should the businesses fail.[7] Beatrice, on the other hand, could "lend" the substantial cash flow being thrown off by the dairy business to these companies and effectively monitor the performance of their loans, provide management expertise, and even provide management replacements if the need should arise. In this way, Beatrice was able to create value for these companies and itself, with little integration of the operations of these divisions into the greater company.

III. 1977–1986: A Change in Direction

When he retired in 1976, William Karnes left in place what he thought was an adequate succession plan. William Mitchell, a lawyer and former Chief Financial Officer, was named Chairman and Chief Corporate Officer, while

---

[4] In 1955–56 only 3200 Master of Business Administration degrees were granted in the United States. By 1974 this number had increased tenfold. By 1986 the number was 67,000.

[5] Private conversation and correspondence with Neil Gazel, June 6, 1990 and June 17, 1991.

[6] Beatrice acquired only five public companies during Karnes's tenure, all of which had significant family ownership.

[7] During the late 1950s and 1960s, there was a persistent concern among both economists and politicians with the financial needs of small business. In 1958, the Federal Reserve Board produced a report for the Congressional Committees on Banking and Currency and the Select Committees on Small Business entitled "Financing Small Business." This report concludes that "the core of the small business financing problem seems to be in the manufacturing area . . . . The unsatisfied demands that appear to have the greatest economic justification are mostly those of new firms or concerns with new lines or processes. Such firms also need working capital, but their greatest need is for investment funds to finance plant and major equipment installations . . . . The smaller firms . . . typically specialize in one or a few lines, because it takes capital (and a lot of other things) to diversify. Their managerial practices are frequently poor, and their internal managerial structure deficient . . . . To the potential lender or investor, this often appears to be evidence of 'no demonstrated earning potential,' 'lack of experience and spotty performance,' or the increased risks inherent in specialization" (U.S. Board of Governors of the Federal Reserve System, 1958).

Wallace Rasmussen, an operating manager who came up through the food business, was named Chief Executive Officer. Rasmussen was 62 years old and was expected to operate as a caretaker until he retired and Mitchell took over the CEO's job. Within a year, however, conflict developed between Mitchell and Rasmussen about how the company should proceed. Mitchell felt that the company should concentrate on digesting the many acquisitions made under Karnes, while Rasmussen favored a continuation of the acquisition strategy. According to the *Wall Street Journal*, Mitchell was "outflanked and outmuscled" and was forced to resign within 15 months of assuming his position (Cox and Ingrassia (1979)). Mitchell was replaced by James Dutt, a 52-year-old operating manager with a career path similar to Rasmussen's. In the following months, Rasmussen sought to purge Mitchell's and Karnes's influence from the company and fired six executives loyal to Mitchell.

Rasmussen began a series of management and strategic changes which would affect the complexion of the company dramatically over the coming ten years. One change was the creation of five executive vice presidents to "supervise specific sections of our operations permitting us to concentrate on *corporate directions and goals*" (emphasis added).[8] While Rasmussen continued to pay lip service to the company's decentralized operating strategy, he began a subtle move towards a more centralized management approach. One executive said that "people at the operating level are being told more by the people on high" (*Forbes* (1979)). Another former Beatrice executive told a story of how Rasmussen personally denied a request for a particular make of company car to the president of a recently acquired division because the car was too expensive for his rank in the company. Another change was a new emphasis on marketing. In his letter to shareholders for fiscal year 1977, Rasmussen stated:

> We have taken a number of major steps to strengthen our marketing resources. Special marketing groups now report to each of the five executive vice presidents. These groups give us the flexibility to bolster the marketing activities of individual operating units and also to seek out and capitalize on totally new opportunities.

This is the first time that marketing was ever mentioned in the president's annual letter to the shareholders. Figure 6 shows that annual expenditures on marketing increased from $54 million in 1974 to $107 million in 1977, increasing from less than 1.3% to more than 1.7% of sales.

In 1978 Rasmussen demonstrated that he rejected Karnes's strategy of acquiring small, private companies. He acquired the publicly-traded Tropicana Products Inc. for $490 million in cash and preferred stock. This price far exceeded the second highest bid, a merger proposal from Kellogg company valued at $344 million. The Tropicana acquisition was over six times the size of the largest acquisition that Beatrice made under Karnes.

---

[8] 1977 Beatrice Annual Report.

Beatrice: A Study in the Creation and Destruction of Value 1095

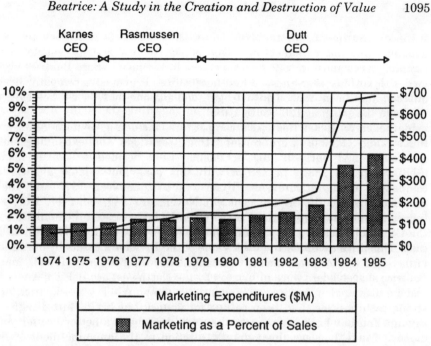

Figure 6. Marketing expenditures, 1974-1985.

In July of 1979 Rasmussen reached mandatory retirement age, and in March of that year, the board elected James Dutt to succeed him. Dutt's election was highly controversial. Beatrice's outside directors purportedly favored Richard Voell, deputy chairman, to succeed Rasmussen. However, Rasmussen persuaded all of the inside directors and two outside directors to vote for Dutt, creating an acrimonious rift between board members. Two outside directors as well as Voell resigned because of this incident (Colvin (1982)). It also prompted a lawsuit from King Shwayder, a Beatrice stockholder, alleging that Rasmussen had gone back on a promise to appoint a majority of outsiders to the board, and warning against insider domination of the Beatrice board. The suit came to nought, and a slate of directors favoring Dutt's appointment was voted in by the stockholders in June of 1979. By this time, Beatrice was a diversified consumer and industrial products company, with sales of over $8 billion and 80,000 employees in nearly 90 countries.

In Dutt's first annual letter to shareholders, he committed to maintaining the three steadfast principles behind Beatrice's historical growth: diversification, decentralization, and balance.[9] In the annual report he filed for fiscal year 1981, Dutt added that in the 1980s a commitment to growth necessitated an emphasis on brand marketing, asserting that "if you want to run

---

[9] Balance was interpreted to mean that Beatrice maintained both food and nonfood business and domestic and international operations.

successful businesses in the 80s, it will be absolutely necessary to have dynamic, innovative marketing." One of Dutt's first actions was to move company headquarters to 2 North LaSalle in Chicago, where Beatrice occupied a luxurious four-and-one-half-floor office. Previously, company headquarters had been housed in a frugal, one-and-one-half floor office several blocks to the south at 120 South LaSalle.

In the early 1980s Beatrice's competitors, including General Mills and Procter and Gamble, were consolidating operations and expanding their marketing, and early in his presidency Dutt decided to do the same (Shellenbarger (1983)). In accord with this goal, Dutt slated about fifty companies for divestiture. As Figure 2 shows, between 1979 and 1981, Beatrice divested fifteen divisions. In November 1981, however, Dutt returned to the historic growth strategy when he orchestrated the aquisition of the Coca Cola Bottling Division of Northwest Industries for $580 million in cash. This price exceeded the book value of the Division's assets by over $450 million and was 22 times current earnings. According to Colvin (1982), many Beatrice shareholders were infuriated by the Northwest acquisition. Analysts and institutional investors, looking at the company's low stock price and strong cash position, had been calling for a stock buy-back. Dutt disagreed, saying "You buy back your stock when you don't have a better use for your money." Table 1 shows the market's reaction to the announcement of the Northwest acquisition, as well as to Dutt's other acquisitions and divestitures. In the three-day interval around the announcement of the Northwest acquisition, Beatrice's stock price fell by a market-adjusted 7.1%, equal to $136 million in equity value.

In 1982 Dutt announced the first of what were to be a continuing set of reorganizations of the company's businesses. He streamlined the firm's reported business segments, moving from ten segments to five, in order to "more accurately reflect our internal organization." This realignment of the firm's businesses was to become almost an annual event: the businesses were realigned again in 1984, then again in 1985.

At the 1983 annual meeting, Dutt announced a radical break with the past, abandoning the decentralized management philosophy that had served the company for ninety years. He stated,

> In the past, our system of a number of small, regional profit centers worked well. But to be competitive and to grow in the future, we need broader product lines, with national marketing and advertising and with national distribution systems.... The result will be a much smaller number of free-standing and self-supporting businesses operating in the company's principal marketing areas. These new "businesses of Beatrice" will be larger, cohesive business units" (Gazel (1990)).

In addition, Dutt announced that Beatrice had embarked upon a new strategic direction centered around a "total commitment to marketing." According to the new plan, a program of internal growth was to surpass

Beatrice: A Study in the Creation and Destruction of Value 1097

acquisitions in its contribution to overall development. Dutt reorganized the company into six groups, which he argued would allow Beatrice to "achieve synergies among the operations, make quicker decisions, and build effective marketing strategies. At the same time, he launched the "We're Beatrice" ad campaign designed to connect the Beatrice name with its many regional and national brands and thereby dramatically increase the company's public exposure.[10] Symbolically, the company once again proposed a name change, this time from Beatrice Foods to Beatrice Companies, to "recognize a clear departure from the past."

As part of the 1983 reorganization, Dutt created several new corporate offices, including a corporate marketing department under senior vice president John McRobbie, and a corporate strategic planning vice president, William Reidy, brought in from Dart & Kraft. The marketing group was to focus on the corporate image campaign and on expanding regional brands to national distribution. Beatrice, like Nabisco and General Mills, would include its name and new logo on all consumer products. This move was designed to help boost the sales of less successful brands by associating them with Beatrice's more well-known products. Reidy was to oversee the consolidation of the hundreds of Beatrice profit centers into 27 divisions, combining many small related units into larger ones. For instance, eight confectionery units were consolidated into a single profit center, two Mexican food companies were combined under the Rosarita brand, as were several of the cheese lines under the County Line brand (*Advertising Age* (1983), Collis (1991)). The number of advertising agencies that the firm used dropped from 100 to just seven.

The strategic and organizational changes which Dutt initiated were accompanied by poor financial performance. For thirty consecutive years, Beatrice had reported record sales and earnings for each quarter when compared to the same quarter of the previous year. This record was maintained until the first quarter of fiscal 1983, when the company reported a 34% plummet in net earnings and a 36% drop in earnings per share on annual sales of $9.2 billion.

In May 1984 Dutt announced that he had orchestrated a $2.7 billion takeover of Chicago-based Esmark, with 1983 sales of $4.1 billion. Esmark, created in 1973 as a holding company intended to restructure Swift & Co., was headed by Donald Kelly. Esmark was formed to hold Swift's four major lines of business: food, chemicals, energy, and financial services. Kelly became financial vice president of Esmark when it was organized in April 1977. In September 1973 he was made president and chief operating officer, and CEO in 1977. Kelly reshaped the company, operating it as an investment portfolio. He spun off Swift's fresh meat packing business, and then began making conglomerate-type acquisitions and divestitures. Esmark bought and sold more than sixty companies before it was acquired by Beatrice

---

[10] The most notable use of this ad campaign was during the 1984 Olympics, when Beatrice spent $30 million for commercials on ABC (Louis (1985)).

in 1984. Included among these were International Playtex, purchased for $210 million in 1975, and Norton Simon, itself a conglomerate consisting of Avis and Hunt-Wesson foods, acquired for $990 million in September 1983. As president of Esmark, Kelly gained a reputation on Wall Street as an expert dealmaker, able to negotiate premium prices on sales and bargains on acquisitions. He also was known for his ability to trim excess expenses and close down unprofitable operations. He was the "hatchet man" for the closing of 300 Swift facilities before spinning the unit off. As Frederick Rentschler, head of Beatrice's Hunt-Wesson business, said of him "Don . . . tries not to fall in love with any asset, because he must do what is necessary to protect investor interests" (Hodge (1988)). According to Diana Temple, a Solomon Brothers analyst, "There was no noted restructuring artist in the consumer field at that time. Kelly was among the first to take a coldhearted view of asset values" (Ipsen (1988)).

Three months prior to Beatrice's acquisition, Esmark had purchased 1.4 million Beatrice shares, equal to about 1.5% of the total shares outstanding. Around this time, rumors began about Beatrice as a potential takeover candidate. Beatrice later repurchased these shares at a premium.

Shortly after Esmark purchased the Beatrice shares, Kohlberg, Kravis & Roberts Company (KKR) organized a $55-a-share (worth $2.4 billion) LBO of Esmark, which Kelly and Esmark managers had accepted. Table I gives the history of interaction between KKR and Donald Kelly, which involves three separate LBO proposals and two instances of competitive bidding involving KKR and Kelly. Under the KKR-Esmark LBO, Kelly would remain Esmark's chairman and would institute the divestiture of numerous operations to meet the largest debt burden incurred in the transaction. However, Dutt topped the KKR bid with a $56-a-share offer; after persuasion from Kelly, he

Table I
The Courtship of Donald Kelly and KKR

June 1983	KKR proposes a leveraged buyout of Norton Simon for $925 million, or $33 per share.
August 1983	Esmark chairman Donald Kelly overbids KKR, and acquires Norton Simon for $990 million.
February 1984	Rumors surface that Esmark is buying shares of Beatrice in anticipation of a possible takeover.
May 1984	KKR and Donald Kelly propose a $55 per share leveraged buyout of Esmark. The proposal is approved by the Esmark board.
May 1984	Beatrice overbids KKR, acquiring Esmark for $2.7 billion, or $60 per share. Kelly and vice chairman Roger Briggs quit Esmark to form Kelly, Briggs & Associates. Frederick Rentschler and Joel Smilow, both top executives at Esmark, also leave shortly after the acquisition in policy disputes with Beatrice CEO James Dutt.
August 1985	Dutt is fired as CEO of Beatrice.
October 1985	KKR and Donald Kelly along with Briggs, Rentschler, and Smilow propose $45 per sshare leveraged buyout for Beatrice

Beatrice: A Study in the Creation and Destruction of Value 1099

trumped his own proposal by sweetening the offer to $60-a-share, or $2.7 billion. Beatrice borrowed all of the $2.7 billion purchase price of Esmark. According to Dutt, the largest benefit of the acquisition to Beatrice was Esmark's Swift/Hunt-Wesson grocery distribution/marketing operation, which included a staff of 500 salespeople. Ideally, Beatrice would integrate its regional brands into this network and distribute them nationally. Dutt declared that the Esmark acquisition was essential to make Beatrice "the world's premier marketer." Kelly received roughly $2.7 million in a golden parachute from the Esmark acquisition, and netted about $12 million on the sale of his Esmark stock (Esmark Proxy (1984)).

The financial press reported, however, that Dutt's Esmark acquisition was as much a retaliatory gesture as a business move. Dutt was purportedly galled by Kelly's purchase of Beatrice shares, and became determined to acquired Esmark at any the cost (Rublin (1985)). When asked what he would do if KKR tried to outbid him for Esmark, Dutt indicated that he would "go to the mat" to prevail "I don't lose," he said (Morris and Shellenbarger (1984)).

Following the merger, Kelly and Roger Briggs, vice chairmen, left Esmark to form Kelly, Briggs & Associates, an investment partnership intended to make large, highly leveraged acquisitions. Frederick Rentschler, head of Esmark's Swift/Hunt-Wesson food business, moved to Beatrice but was soon fired as a result of personality and management conflicts with Dutt. Similarly, Joel Smilow, head of Playtex International, came to Beatrice but resigned shortly thereafter. For fiscal 1985, Beatrice's earnings excluding realignment activity dropped 22% from fiscal 1984.

On Saturday August 3, 1985 Dutt resigned as Chairman and CEO of Beatrice; his early retirement was forced by the board of directors and members of his management team. Wall Street had become increasingly skeptical of Dutt's leadership, and Beatrice management was in revolt. Indeed, the final push that led the board to fire Dutt was an ultimatum from the five top operating officers of the company that either Dutt be fired or they would quit (Gazel (1990)). A number of factors were cited in Dutt's termination. The prudence of the Esmark acquisition was incessantly questioned, and Dutt was frequently accused of abusing the power of his office. One frequently mentioned abuse involved Beatrice's sponsorship of two auto racing teams, which necessitated in excess of $70 million in corporate expenditures over several years. A racing enthusiast and collector of automobiles, Dutt outbid Anheuser Busch to sponsor the teams, in spite of the fact that Beatrice's only connection to auto racing was its STP Corporation subsidiary, that had sales of $97 million and was already slated to be sold to Union Carbide.

Press accounts also suggested that the expansion of the company's marketing image smacked of self-aggrandizement: "Particularly perplexing to . . . analysts was the ['We're Beatrice'] corporate advertising campaign. . . . Analysts suggested that the company was getting little benefit from the costly advertising program, which they said seemed more to glorify Dutt and the company" (Potts (1985)). Such a conclusion is consistent with Horsky's

The Journal of Finance

and Swyngedouw's 1987 analysis. They find that marketing expenditures which affect *corporate* image are wasteful in consumer goods companies, where individual brand identity matters more than corporate identity. Finally, Beatrice had experienced an unremitting exodus of executives since Dutt became chairman. From 1980 to July 1985, thirty-nine of fifty-eight executives had left the company.

Dutt resigned on August 3, 1985: Beatrice's three-day cumulative abnormal return around this date was 10.6%, implying a market adjusted value increased of $301 million (see Table II). William Granger, a 66-year-old retired Beatrice vice president, was elected to replace Dutt, and William Karnes was brought back on the board as chairman of the executive committee. Both men were selected in part because of their conciliatory nature which, the board hoped, would stymie the flight of managers from Beatrice.

Destruction of Value: Strategic Muddle and the Failure of Governance

During the tenures of CEOs Rasmussen and Dutt, almost $2 billion in market value was destroyed. As is clear from Figure 1, most of the decline in value occurred in 1979–1981, years before the Esmark acquisition or the allegations of Dutt's abuse of power. Indeed, it appears that the market had begun to lose confidence in Beatrice's strategy of growth by acquisition by the time Dutt became CEO. As Table II shows, every acquisition in excess of $30

Table II
Market Reactions to Announcements of Acquisitions and Divestitures, by CEO, 1965–1984

Company	Type of Transaction	Announce-ment Date	Announce-ment Price ($m)	Trans-action Price[a] ($m)	Price ÷ Market Value[b] (%)	Three Day CAR	Market Value Change ($m)
Karnes (Transactions more than $10 million)							
Stahl Finish/Polyvinyl	A	01–20–65	17	—	1.12	0.006	10
Inland Underground	A	04–12–65	11	—	0.75	0.000	0
Colorado By-Products	A	10–15–65	11	—	0.79	−0.006	8
Melnor Industries	A	11–03–66	11	—	0.99	0.015	18
Air Stream	A	05–10–67	15	156	1.24	−0.008	−10
John Sexton	A	07–18–68	35	38	1.99	0.038[2]	72
Hart Ski	A	09–17–68	—	14	0.64	0.011	24
E.R. Moore	A	03–17–69	11	—	0.58	−0.026[1]	−49
Eckrich	A	01–10–72	64	—	2.19	0.030[1]	86
Southwestern Investments	A	11–30–72	62	54	2.07	−0.013	−42
Brookside Enterprises	A	01–10–73	—	16	0.39	0.006	24
Samsonite	A	04–12–73	100	80	3.13	−0.013	−42
Martha White Foods	A	08–01–75	—	25	0.83	0.021	60
Rasmussen (Transactions more than $30 million)							
Harman International Industries	A	01–11–77	103	97	3.91	0.010	27
Culligan	A	01–12–78	54	51	1.83	−0.049[2]	−146
Tropicana	A	03–06–78	590	—	16.28	−0.001	−3

Beatrice: A Study in the Creation and Destruction of Value   1101

Table II—*Continued*

Company	Type of Transaction	Announce- ment Date	Announce- ment Price ($m)	Trans- action Price[a] ($m)	Price ÷ Market Value[b] (%)	Three Day CAR	Market Value Change ($m)
Dutt (Transactions more than $30 million)							
Fiberite	A	10–19–79	60	—	2.41	−0.027[1]	−67
Bob Evans Farms	A	09–08–80	200	—	8.78	−0.027[1]	−61
Bob Evans Farms[c]		12–30–80				0.057[2]	124
Dannon[d]	D	06–24–81	84	—	3.71	0.020	44
Northwest Industries	A	11–09–81	600	580	31.61	−0.071[2]	−136
LouverDrape	A	11–20–81	—	50	2.63	−0.041[1]	−79
Soft Drink Division	D	12–16–81	105	—	5.61	0.027[1]	50
Coca-Cola of S.D.	A	02–26–82	80	—	4.45	−0.021	−38
Termicold	A	12–15–82	—	115	4.94	−0.043[2]	−100
John Sexton	D	09–28–83	—	70	2.43	0.004	11
Esmark[e, f]	A	05–22–84	2500	2800	106.11	−0.065	−153
J. Dutt Resigns		08–06–85				0.106[2]	301

Transactions shown in bold are divestitures, or announcements of the cancellation of an acquisition.

[a] Transactions price represents the value of the deal at the time of the final transaction. It is reported if terms were undisclosed at announcement or if the price changed between the announcement of the transaction and the final deal.

[b] Price ÷ Market Value = value of the transactions divided by the total market value of Beatrice at the time of the exchange.

[c] Beatrice announced that it dropped its pursuit of Bob Evans Farms on 12–30–80. The deal was never finalized.

[d] This divestiture was of symbolic importance because it was the first Dutt's promised larger asset sales.

[e] Beatrice's cumulative abnormal returns from 5–22–84 to 6–26–84, the period beginning with the rumors of the Esmark takeover and ending when Dutt became chairman and CEO of Esmark, was −0.118 for a total loss in market value of $263 million.

[f] After the Esmark merger, the market response to Beatrice transactions was highly confused by speculation regarding management changes and takeover rumors.

[1] *t*-statistic greater than 1.

[2] *t*-statistic greater than 2.

million during Dutt's early tenure is met with a reduction in market value, and every divestiture or announcement of a withdrawal of an acquisition offer is met with an increase in market value. The Esmark acquisition appears to be merely the final act in a long series of ill-conceived and poorly received purchases by Dutt.

The decline in the market value of the firm arises in part from the reduced profitability of the company. Panel A of Figure 7 shows that the reported return on assets became much more volatile after 1980. Panel B shows that the trend of earnings net of realignment activities was largely downward from the time of Karnes's retirement. The company had also become very centralized. In 1976, the headquarters staff had numbered 161 people; by 1985 that number had risen to 750 (Gazel (1990)). Dutt was criticized by

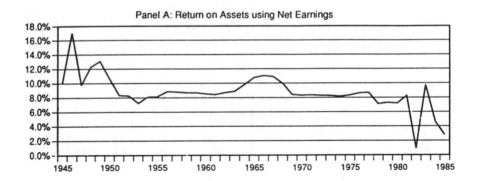

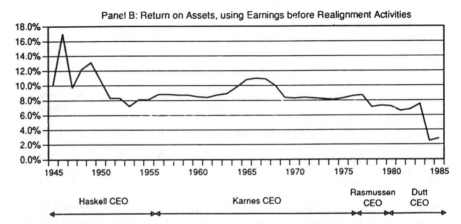

Figure 7. Return on assets, 1940–1985. Panel A shows net earnings divided by total assets. Panel B shows earnings before realignment activities divided by total assets.

many of the departing managers for his autocratic manner and his tendency, especially in the food business, to "get involved in the nittiest and grittiest of details, initiating management changes at practically every level and steeping himself in the minutiae of day-to-day operations" (Louis (1985)).

However, the decline in value is also not adequately explained by poor operating performance. Figure 8 shows that the company's price-earnings ratio also fell during this period to below the level of the S & P 400: Beatrice's P-E had matched or exceeded the S & P since 1974. The loss of value during the period 1979–1981 seems to have resulted from a loss of confidence in the company and its strategy on the part of investors. The evidence suggests two reasons for this change in investor confidence: a skepticism about management's ability to implement the new strategic vision, and concern that the company's governing body (the board of directors) would be unable to rectify the problems.

Beatrice: A Study in the Creation and Destruction of Value 1103

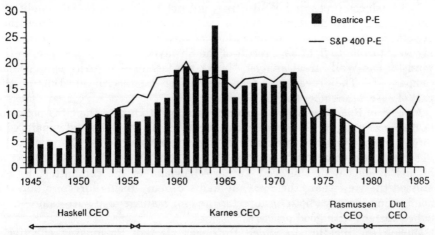

Figure 8. Beatrice-price earnings multiples and S & P 400 price-earnings multiples, 1945–1985. Price earnings multiples for Beatrice are calculated using year-end stock price and earnings before special actions. S & P 400 multiples are the average of the high and low P-E's for the year, as reported in Standard and Poor's *Analysts' Handbook*, 1987.

As early as 1978, the business press was taking note of the changing nature of Beatrice's strategy under Rasmussen. The Tropicana acquisition was seen as an important departure from the past, as this quote from *Business Week* suggests:

> The Tropicana acquisition...represents a break with the traditional growth strategy at Beatrice. In the past, the $6.2 billion company has steered clear of commodity-type businesses.... And despite its hundreds of acquisitions, it has rarely entered a business that competes directly with one of the nation's premier marketing companies. This too has changed because of Tropicana.
>
> With Tropicana, Beatrice...faces the brutal prospect of going head-on with Coca-Cola. That will be a challenge, notes one food company executive.
>
> Though Beatrice leads the industry in sales and profits, it trails such companies as General Foods, Pillsbury, and General Mills in terms of marketing savvy.
>
> For the most part, Beatrice sells food and nonfood products that, by dint of either a quality image or an established position, have carved secure niches in national markets or dominate regional ones. Its Dannon yogurt, Louis Sherry ice cream, Peter Eckrich sausages, JBL stereo equipment, and Samsonite luggages are all examples.
>
> Thus the Tropicana move seems to reflect a new emphasis at Beatrice on marketing and a willingness to take on the leading practitioners of that art (*Business Week* (1978)).

The business press and Wall Street did not begin to seriously doubt the value of this new strategy, however, until after the boardroom brawl that brought Dutt to power. The revelations of serious disagreement and infighting which came to light as a result of the Shwayder lawsuit served to, in the words of one Wall Street analyst, "break the facade of Beatrice as a 'golden company.'"[11] They revealed a deep mistrust of Rasmussen and Dutt on the part of several members of the board.

As part of Rasmussen's maneuvering to appoint Dutt to the CEO position, he demonstrated his ability to control the board. In 1978, he had appointed a three-person committee of outside directors to recommended changes in the Beatrice board composition and to choose a successor to himself. As part of his discussions with Durwood Varner, chairman of the committee, he expressed the view that "the company had too many inside directors and the nominating process—both for directors and for management succession—was not consistent with good practice...."[12]

During the meeting in which Dutt was elected, Rasmussen effectively ignored the recommendations of the committee to change the composition of the board, and retained a board which would vote with him. At this same meeting, Varner, along with Voell and another member of the outside committee, resigned. Varner delivered a speech to the board at this meeting, the transcript of which was later made public in a court filing, in which he said:

> the action being taken today...will serve as evidence that some major corporations are indeed controlled by employee directors. It will heighten the anxiety existing in many quarters that self-interest is a factor in vital decisions in corporate affairs. It will serve as a clear warning that outside directors must beware—that unpopular positions may well result in punitive action.... I am astounded by the actions taken here today.

Coming shortly after a major change in strategy, it is hardly surprising that this level of discord on the board would lead to a lack of investor confidence. Doubt about Rasmussen's and Dutt's abilities to implement the new centralized strategy, which would require shrinking the company and exploiting marketing capabilities that the company had never demonstrated, seems to be the reason that Beatrice investors earned a total return of negative 4.2% between January 1979 and January 1982, while the market returned 57.0%.[13] In retrospect, it is clear that these doubts were well-founded; Beatrice's operations never again achieved the level of profitability that they had attained in 1975.

[11] Telephone conversation with William McGuire of Merrill Lynch, April 29, 1991.

[12] From the complaint of King Shwayder v. Beatrice in The United States District Court for Northern Illinois, 1979. Exhibit C, p. 3.

[13] Value-weighted market returns, including dividends, from the CRSP database.

Beatrice: A Study in the Creation and Destruction of Value 1105

IV. 1986–1990: Leveraged Buyout and Divestiture

Within two months of Dutt's resignation in early August, rumors of a LBO by Kohlberg, Kravis & Roberts surfaced. On October 14, 1985, KKR and a management team headed by Donald Kelly offered $45 per share for Beatrice. After several weeks of negotiations and a last-minute bid from Dart Group, KKR and Kelly offered $50 per share, and the board approved the sale of the company in the then-largest LBO in history. The price represented a premium of 53% over the price the day after Dutt's resignation, resulting in a dollar gain to Beatrice shareholders of $1 billion. As Figure 1 shows, the KKR bid for Beatrice resulted in the "recapture" of virtually all of the value lost during the Rasmussen-Dutt period.

KKR brought in four former Esmark executives to manage Beatrice. Donald Kelly was made chairman and CEO, Roger Briggs (previously vice chairman and CFO of Esmark) was made chief financial officer, Frederick Rentschler (who came to Esmark through Norton Simon) was to head the food division, and Joel Smilow (formerly of Playtex) was to head the consumer products group. These four were each given a seat on the board of directors, with KKR controlling the remaining six seats. The sources of the funds for the purchase, and the ownership fractions which resulted are shown in Table III.

Managers purchased 1% of the shares and were given options for an additional 11.5% of the stock outstanding on a fully diluted basis. Donald Kelly's advisory firm received a payment of $6.75 million for helping to

Table III
Capital Structure of the Beatrice LBO, with Equity Ownership

	$ Millions	% of Total Liabilities	% of Fully Diluted Equity
Debt			
Bank Debt	3,300		
Subordinated Debt	2,500		
Assumed Debt	1,050		
Total Debt	6,850	84.1	
Redeemable Preferred Stock			
Total Preferred[a]	880	10.8	
Common Stock			
KKR Stock	400		57.5
Management Stock	7		1.0
Management Options	0		11.5
Warrants	10		30.0
Total Common	417	5.1	100.0
Total Funding	8,147	100.0	

[a] Redeemable preferred was valued at the time of the LBO at $880 million. It was exchanged for $1,200 million of exchange debentures four months later.

arrange the Beatrice LBO: Kelly's investment in stock cost him $5.2 million. KKR bought 80 million shares at $5 apiece. Warrants with an exercise price of $5 were also issued. In the LBO prospectus, KKR estimated that $1.5 billion of asset dispositions would be required to meet the first two interest payments in nine and eighteen months; after this, cash flow from operations would be sufficient to meet the interest obligation on all outstanding indebtedness.

Almost immediately after stockholders approved the LBO proposal, Kelly began large-scale divestitures at Beatrice, spinning off the bulk of its businesses in nine major asset sales engineered during a two-year period. Figure 3 shows all of Beatrice's post-LBO divestitures. The divestitures began on April 30, 1986 when Beatrice sold its Avis car-rental division in a LBO to Wesray Capital for $255 million. In the same year, Kelly orchestrated the sale of Beatrice's Coca Cola Bottling Division, International Playtex, Americold cold storage warehouses, the Dairy Products division, and Webcraft Technologies, a speciality printing business. Of the six sales made by Kelly in 1986, four were LBO sales to the managers of the units.

By 1987 the Beatrice LBO demonstrated a degree of success even greater than KKR's initial predictions. Divestitures in 1986 generated $3.5 billion in proceeds, allowing Beatrice to pay down virtually all of the bank debt in the first year. The asset sales were facilitated by the bull market, which resulted in higher asset prices than had been predicted at the time of the LBO. Kelly had also eliminated $100 million in annual administrative expenses through staff cuts and the elimination of the "We're Beatrice" ad campaign. Ads that promoted individual brands were retained.[14]

Beatrice's next move was to spin-off E-II Holdings in May 1987. E-II was a conglomerate containing a melange of fifteen Beatrice divisions. It consisted of all the remaining nonfood businesses, including Samsonite luggage and Stiffel lamps, plus a number of specialty food concerns. It is interesting to note that the operating strategy of E-II was very similar to that of Beatrice under Karnes, and of Esmark prior to its purchase by Beatrice. The E-II prospectus explains the company's management philosophy:

> Management believes that a substantially decentralized approach to managing operating companies is the best way to maximize a holding company's returns from such companies. Under the company's decentralized system, management of each individual operating company is responsible for attaining financial and other goals established jointly with them and then monitored by the holding company and segment managements.

---

[14] Indeed, in an interview in 1990, after the purchase of Beatrice by ConAgra, the Chief Operating Officer of ConAgra stated that Beatrice was spending more on advertising individual brands than the market average in virtually every product line (Liesse (1990)).

Beatrice: A Study in the Creation and Destruction of Value   1107

The E-II prospectus also quoted the following passage from a 1983 letter from Donald Kelly to the shareholders of Esmark.

"Constantly reviewing areas of opportunity in keeping with the realities of everchanging markets is considered an ongoing management responsibility. At Esmark there will continue to be changes as management and the Board strive to improve the overall value of your investment. Changes are not made for the sake of change, but rather as an extension of management's philosophy that a holding company must constantly review its investment mix. As a consequence, no serious proposal for possible acquisitions, dispositions, joint venture, etc., regardless of size, will be passed without full and careful consideration."
The company intends to follow this philosophy.[15]

Donald Kelly became chairman and CEO of E-II and remained chairman of Beatrice, retaining responsibility for selling the remaining businesses. E-II gave Beatrice $800 million in debt for the assets included in E-II and distributed 41.1 million shares (initially estimated to be worth $616 million) of E-II equity to the investors in the Beatrice LBO. At the time of the E-II spin-off, Beatrice also paid out an $800 million special dividend to holders of common stock, warrants, and options. In May 1987, E-II filed to offer 28.7 million shares to the public, as well as $750 million of senior subordinated notes and senior subordinated debentures. The stock offering and debt issues were expected to generate $1.2 billion in cash, which Kelly purportedly referred to as his "acquisition war chest" (Johnson (1987a)). 7.3 million of the shares (worth $109.5 million) were distributed to Beatrice investors and were sold in the E-II public offering. Management retained a 6.4% stake in E-II.

E-II's first serious takeover target was American Brands. In December 1987 E-II disclosed that it had acquired a 4.6% equity stake in American Brands, with an estimated market value of $5–6 billion (Johnson (1987b)). The following January, American Brands initiated a "Pac Man" antitakeover defense, launching a hostile $13-a-share tender offer for E-II. After a short negotiation period, American Brands sweetened its bid for E-II to $17.05-a-share or $1.1 billion, and Kelly accepted the offer. The financial press reported that Kelly's hand was forced because of the October market crash: E-II lost about $147 million on its stock portfolio (in part consisting of losses from its American Brands equity holdings), and finding junk-bond financing for large LBOs became appreciably less likely. E-II public investors made a pretax return of 14% on their equity during a seven-month period. Beatrice investors received an additional $650 million as a result of their E-II equity stake, with the result that they had already more than doubled their initial

---

[15] Even the company's name, "E-II," was derived from Esmark: the newly-formed conglomerate was to be a reincarnation of Kelly's former company.

investment in the Beatrice LBO. American Brands ultimately sold most of the assets of E-II to the closely held Riklis Family Corporation in 1988. Donald personally made more than $55 million on the E-II deal.

In addition to E-II, Beatrice sold its Bottled Water Division and its International Food Division in 1987. Figure 9 shows the initial capitalization of Beatrice after the LBO and the proceeds from the sell-off. By the end of the year, Beatrice had divested assets worth a total of about $6.55 billion, and all that remained of the company was its domestic food group, consisting of Beatrice/Hunt-Wesson foods, Tropicana Products, Swift-Eckrich meats, and Beatrice Cheese. In 1987, these businesses had earnings of $494 million on sales of $7.5 billion. At this time, the Beatrice LBO appeared as if it would become the most profitable LBO ever. The *Wall Street Journal* reported that Kelly hoped to sell the remaining Beatrice assets for $6 billion (Johnson and Smith (1987)). With such a sale, investors would earn a pretax profit of more than $2 billion.

However, the deal did not continue as intended. During 1988, more than 100 companies reportedly examined the remaining Beatrice divisions, including every major food company, and all refused to buy the major business segments (Burrough and Johnson (1988)). KKR first hired Drexel, then First Boston, and finally Saloman Brothers to sell the remaining divisions, all to no avail.

Around this time, frictions between KKR and Kelly became severe. Henry Kravis insisted on maintaining final control over all major decisions affecting Beatrice, and Kelly resented the limitation. When the remaining businesses failed to sell, Kelly proposed to engineer an "E-III" transaction, under which Kelly would purchase or take public Swift-Eckrich as an investment vehicle for future LBOs. KKR rejected this proposition, probably to prevent being associated with future corporate raids. In September 1988, Donald Kelly resigned as chairman of Beatrice (Burrough and Johnson (1988)).

One more divestiture, that of Fisher Nut in 1989, was forced on the company by KKR's LBO of RJR Nabisco. The FTC insisted that KKR sell either RJR's Planters Nut operations or Beatrice's Fisher Nut. Planters was a much larger company, and Fisher was sold for $150 million to Proctor and Gamble. Finally, in June of 1990, Beatrice Company was sold by KKR to ConAgra for $1.34 billion, plus the assumption of roughly $1.8 billion in debt and other liabilities. The price, widely reported to be below what KKR had hoped to receive, still represented a premium over book value (which had been generously restated only four years earlier in the LBO). It resulted in an annual compounded return on the equity investment in the Beatrice LBO (including warrants and management options) of 83%, and an annual return to the nonmanagement investors of 78%. The value of the Beatrice post-LBO equity increased by about $1.8 billion, equal to about $1.2 billion in market-adjusted value. The pre-LBO equity holders made approximately $1 billion as a result of the LBO. Thus the total market-adjusted value increase for all equity investors in Beatrice was $2.2 billion. Donald Kelly is estimated to have made over $135 million from the E-II and Beatrice transactions.

Beatrice: A Study in the Creation and Destruction of Value   1109

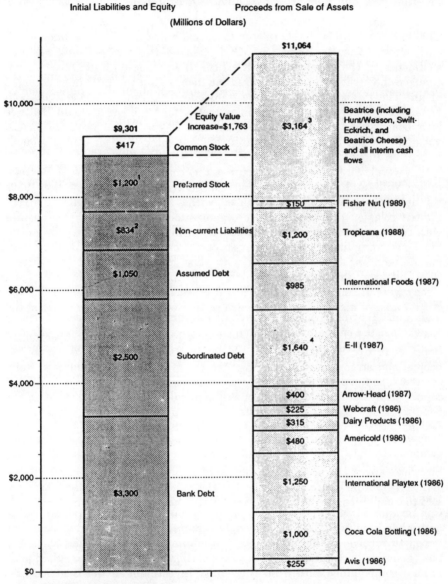

Initial Liabilities and Equity   Proceeds from Sale of Assets
(Millions of Dollars)

Figure 9. Beatrice liabilities and equity at the time of the LBO, and proceeds from sales of units.

1. Preferred Stock was valued at $880 million when issued, but was redeemed for $1,200 million in exchangable debentures four months after the deal.
2. Includes mostly contingent tax liabilities resulting from previous M&A activity. The magnitude of these liabilities was roughly comparable when ConAgra acquired Beatrice.
3. Includes $1,340 million pay-out directly to Beatrice shareholders, plus about $1.8 billion in deferred taxes and other non-current liabilities , most of which represent contingent tax liabilities.
4. Includes $840 million pay-out directly to Beatrice shareholders, plus the assumption of $800 million in debt.

1110 *The Journal of Finance*

Leveraged Buyout: Value Created or Value Recaptured?

Any explanation of the value increase which occurred during the Beatrice LBO and break-up is closely related to the causes of the value declined in the early 1980s. Clearly Kelly and KKR changed the strategy and restored confidence in the governance of the firm. If Rasmussen and Dutt had not changed the strategy and centralized the firm, would the LBO have occurred at all? The 1980s were marked by tremendous capital market activity both among conglomerates and companies in the food industry; would Beatrice have been caught up in this activity anyway? Of course, such counter-factual questions cannot be answered definitively, but some analysis can be brought to bear on them.

In several ways, Kelly restructured the company to resemble Beatrice under William Karnes. Recall that the successful company of the 1950s through 1976 was highly decentralized, with a small central staff and a very limited role for the headquarters organization. Karnes bought companies with competent management, and left them in place to run their organizations, providing little more than easy access to capital and training in modern management practice. Beginning with Rasmussen, and then intensifying with Dutt, the company became highly centralized. More and more decision rights were taken back by the central office in Chicago, especially in the crucial area of marketing. This centralization was arguably one cause of the decline in value of Beatrice in the early 1980s.[16]

After the LBO, Kelly restored Beatrice's highly decentralized organizational structure. He reduced the headquarters staff by 70%, down to 120 people, and streamlined operations. According to Beatrice executives, Kelly cut red tape for divisions dealing with headquarters and generously funded capital requests. Donald Rosuck of Culligan said "Under Kelly, you'd do the paperwork and pass it up the system, and in a couple of days, you'd have a decision." (Ipsen (1988)). Malcolm Candlish of Samsonite noted, "I never had Kelly turn down a single [capital] request" (Ipsen (1988)). Indeed, Kelly was at times criticized by his managers for his "hands-off" attitude toward Beatrice's operating units while they were owned by Beatrice (Burrough and Johnson (1988)). The fact that many of the assets of post-LBO Beatrice were sold to companies owned in large part by the managers of the units indicates that whatever value Beatrice once brought to those companies, the managers felt that they could operate more efficiently without a corporate parent.

Another cause for the decline of value during the Rasmussen and Dutt tenures relates to the problem of strategic muddle. During Karnes's tenure,

[16]Alfred Chandler (1990) argues that "Such... diversification created another new phenomenon in the evolution of the managerial industrial enterprise: it often led to a... breakdown of communications between top management at the corporate office—the executive responsible for coordinating, managing, and planning and allocating resources for the enterprise as a whole —and the middle managers who were responsible for maintaining the competitive capabilities of the operating divisions.... [T]op managers often had little specific knowledge of and experience with the technological processes and markets of many of the divisions or subsidiaries they had acquired."

Beatrice: A Study in the Creation and Destruction of Value 1111

Beatrice was an almost archetypal example of Rumelt's (1974) acquisitive conglomerate, buying unrelated or loosely related companies, and managing them in a highly decentralized way. Following the leads of his competitors, Dutt tried to move Beatrice towards a more focused, less diversified strategy. This involved divestiture of the unrelated divisions and a more centralized organizational structure that would allow the firm to capitalize on its distinctive core competence in foods and beverages. However, it was never clear whether the firm had or could develop any such core competence. The success of Beatrice's brands was based on their regional appeal or their niche approach, and the firm lagged behind its national rivals in terms of marketing and advertising expenditures. Even after Dutt's 1983 consolidation of product lines and increased emphasis on marketing, Beatrice's (now national) County Line cheese brand spent only $2 million on advertising, compared with Kraft's $2.8 million on its Cracker Barrel line, and $68 million on all of its cheese products. Similarly, Coca Cola's Minute Maid orange juice brand outspent Tropicana by 33%.

Once again, after the LBO Kelly reversed Dutt's changes and returned the firm closer to Rumelt's model of a decentralized, diversified company. Kelly decentralized marketing decisions, spending these resources at the brand rather than the corporate level, and in certain instances actually tried to reduce synergies between groups. Erik Ipsen describes how Kelly stopped a project to integrate Tropicana and Beatrice's cheese operations. Dutt had tried to centralize Beatrice's fresh food operations in order to integrate sales, marketing, research, and distribution. Kelly, who saw that such an integration would hamper his efforts to sell off pieces of the company, killed the integration attempt (Ipsen (1988)).

That Kelly was recasting Beatrice's organization back to the pre-1976 structure does not explain the value that was created during Kelly's tenure. Karnes had created value by *acquiring* firms, but Kelly was creating value by *divesting* them. How could 25 years of the acquisition of the assets of small private firms have created value and then several more years of divestiture of these same assets have added more value?

One possible explanation of these facts is that the market value increases that accompanied the acquisitions of the 1960s and early 1970s were the result of the capital market's misunderstanding of the effects of conglomeration. Such a hypothesis supposes that during the 1960s and 1970s investors were fooled into accepting the arguments of managers (and many management theorists) that centralized decision-making and capital allocation would lead to synergies which would make the whole worth more than the sum of the parts. It was largely these synergies on which James Dutt justified his centralization of Beatrice. What these management theories failed to account for was the importance of a detailed understanding of the operations of the businesses, and thus these theories did not predict that such organizations were doomed to fail when the centralized (and uninformed) bureaucracy acquired too many decision rights, and made decisions which destroyed value in the businesses. This hypothesis continues that around 1979 the market recognized the weaknesses of the conglomerate strategy, and so discounted Beatrice's stock heavily. This discount is what explains the tremendous loss of value in 1979–1981, and also explains why the market bid the stock back up when the firm changed direction in the 1980s.

This hypothesis can be tested by looking at the stock market performance of a portfolio of conglomerates. If the decline in Beatrice value was the result of a generalized realization that the conglomerate strategy was flawed, then all conglomerates should have suffered a similar loss in value during the same period. To test this hypothesis, I constructed a portfolio of conglomerates and examined their market-adjusted performance over the period 1940–1986. This analysis, shown in Figure 10, demonstrates that the decline in Beatrice market value was not a result of a generalized loss of confidence in conglomerates. Indeed, during the period in which Beatrice lost much of its market value, the market adjusted returns to the portfolio of conglomerates were high. Thus, the loss and recapture of value cannot be explained by appealing to the market's changing views on conglomerates.

A second hypothesis about the apparent value increases from acquisition, and the additional value increase from divestiture, argues that both sets of transactions created real economic value. Data from several empirical studies of acquisitions and divestitures are consistent with this hypothesis.

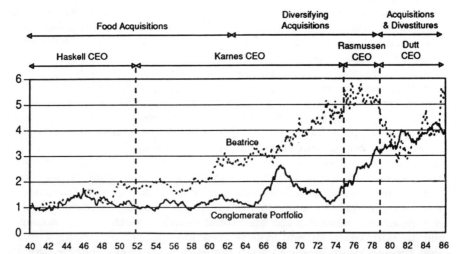

Figure 10. Stock market performance of Beatrice and a portfolio of conglomerates, 1940–1986. Conglomerate portfolio is made up of companies in *Business Week*'s list of conglomerates for three out of four years 1972, 1975, 1980, 1985. The companies are Avco, Colt Industries, Household International, IC Industries, Kidde, LTV, Martin Marietta, Gulf & Western, Signal, Teledyne, Textron, and Whittaker. The performance index is calculated as follows: expected returns for Beatrice are generated using the Capital Asset Pricing Model, with betas estimated using a 60-month moving window. The performance index is the ratio of Beatrice's cumulative (multiplicative) actual return dividend by Beatrice's cumulative expected return. The performance index for the conglomerate portfolio is calculated in the same manner.

Beatrice: A Study in the Creation and Destruction of Value 1113

Matsusaka (1990) found that, for acquisitions in 1968, 1971, and 1974, acquiring companies that diversified had positive abnormal returns around the time of the acquisition announcements and that this result was strongest when the target was a strong performer in its industry and when target management was retained. Schipper and Thompson (1983) found significant positive stock returns to firms announcing acquisition programs in the 1950s and 1960s. Kaplan and Weisbach (1990) studied divestitures in the 1980s of units acquired in the 1970s. Using a sample of 271 large acquisitions, 44% of which were subsequently divested, they found that most of these divested acquisitions were not disasters. Thirty-four to 50% of these subsequently divested acquisitions were classified as failures, and 55% showed a market adjusted gain on sale when comparing the sale price to the preannouncement value of the target.

Hite, Owers, and Rogers (1987) studied the market's reaction to divestiture announcements. They found that in their sample, drawn mostly from the late 1970s and early 1980s, divesting firms show a positive stock price effect on the announcement of divestitures, while Hite and Vetsuypens (1989) found small but positive stock price effects upon the announcement of divisional leveraged buyouts in a sample of divestitures from 1973–1985.

One way that a set of transactions (acquisitions in the 1960s and 1970s) can be value increasing and a reversing set of transactions (divestitures of these same assets in the 1980s) can also be value increasing, is if there is some change in the economic environment which alters the constraints or opportunity sets for firms in these periods. Two important environmental changes, which allowed both the efficient build-up of companies like Beatrice, and their efficient dismantling, were the development of a high-yield bond market in the mid-1970s and the increased supply of well-trained professional managers in the American economy.

As argued above, Beatrice bought small private companies, often managed by the founders or their families that had very limited access to capital markets or bank financing. In this environment, companies like Beatrice could add substantial value by providing an internal capital market and providing training and know-how to these managers. Such a strategy was not without costs: The acquisition did eliminate the equity stake in the businesses which the former owners had, and thus reduced the incentives which unit managers had to run the business like their own. However, this cost was more than outweighed by the fact that the firms now had access to capital and the skills which allowed them to grow and prosper.

By the mid-1970s, however, two things had begun to change. One was the availability of high-yield bonds, which essentially securitized commercial lending and which provided access to growth capital for many small firms. Figure 11 gives the dollar amount of original issue high yield bonds issued from 1976–1986 and shows that by 1984, over $25 billion in so-called "junk bonds" had been issued, little of which was for mergers and acquisitions activities. Another important change was the tremendous influx of professionally trained managers into the ranks of American management. Figure

12 shows the number of Masters of Business Administration degrees granted
in the United States from 1956–1986. The point of this is not so much that
these degree holders per se were in top management positions by this time,
but that the diffusion of modern management practices was much greater by
the 1980s than it had been in the 1950s and 1960s. Both of these changes had
the effect of decreasing the advantages which a company like Beatrice had in
owning and managing divisions. The benefits which the company headquarters had provided (access to capital and sophisticated management) were
more readily available, while the disadvantage of corporate ownership (the
weakened incentives due to the lack of an equity stake for the unit managers)
was still present. In this new environment, companies like Beatrice should
have been able to move assets to higher valued use, and thus create value by

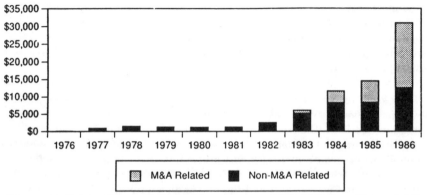

Figure 11. Original issue high-yield bond issues, 1976–1986. In millions of dollars.
Source for totals: Asquith, Mullins, and Wolff (1989). Source for M&A related: Wigmore (1990).

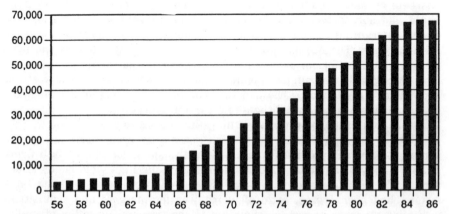

Figure 12. Number of MBA degrees granted, 1956–1986. Source: U.S. Department of
Education.

selling the divisions either back to their managers or to related companies whose headquarters organizations could provide more valuable operating or marketing synergies.

Such a hypothesis is consistent with the findings of Bhagat, Shleifer, and Vishny (1990) in their study of hostile takeovers, including LBOs. They find that the majority (70%) of the assets sold off after a hostile takeover are sold to companies in their same industry, and 16% are sold to management in divisional LBOs. Beatrice's divestitures are consistent with the findings of Bhagat, Shleifer, and Vishny, but in Beatrice's case the incidence of asset sales to managers is substantially greater. Table IV shows all divestitures of Beatrice valued at more than $80 million; these transactions represent over 90% of the value of all Beatrice divestitures. Of these assets sold, 42% were to companies with substantial management ownership, 47% were to public companies, and 11% were to foreign companies. A close examination of the ownership of the units divested before Beatrice bought them reveals a very interesting pattern: in almost every case, companies bought as small private firms were sold to investor groups with significant management ownership, while companies bought as public companies were sold back to public companies. The two significant exceptions, the sale of the dairy business, and the sale of Beatrice to ConAgra, bear closer scrutiny.

The assets of the dairy products division, sold to Borden, were bought by Beatrice before the diversifying acquisitions of the 1960s and 1970s. As argued in Section I, the basis for these acquisitions was increasing economies of scale in dairy production, not access to capital or management expertise. When Beatrice acquired these firms originally, the value of capturing these economies by buying the smaller firms outweighed the cost of weakened management incentives, and nothing had changed in the intervening years to alter this economic calculus.

The sale of Beatrice itself to ConAgra is confounded by tax issues. There was persistent speculation in the press that Beatrice was considering a recapitalization in an effort to stay private. However, there were compelling tax reasons to sell Beatrice to a public company. KKR wanted a transaction that would give Beatrice investors a choice either of liquidity or a tax deferred capital gain on the sale. If the company had recapitalized and paid a substantial dividend, or sold to another private company, the cash pay-out would have been immediately taxable. However, if KKR could sell the company for 50% stock, the stock portion of the proceeds would not be taxed until the stock in the acquiror was sold. By selling Beatrice to a publicly traded company, KKR provided liquidity to those investors who wanted it and allowed others to defer taxes on the gain indefinitely. Thus, while remaining private or selling to another private company might have been more efficient absent tax considerations, the end result was the sale to ConAgra.

Table IV demonstrates that most of the previously private companies bought by Karnes during the period of diversifying acquisitions were ultimately sold back to their managers by Kelly. The fact that Kelly had a strong incentive to sell these companies to the highest bidder suggests that manage-

Table IV

Major Divestitures of Beatrice

Year Sold	Unit Sold	Status when Acquired by Beatrice	Mgt/LBO	Public Company	Foreign Company	Buyer
				Nature of Buyer and Price		
1981	Dannon	Private company			84,300	BSN-Gervais-Danone
1981	Soft Drink Division	Private companies	105,000			Forstman Little
1984	Buckingham	Part of Northwest Industries			110,000	Whitebreat & Co. PLC.
1984	Food-service equip.	Private companies	116,000			Gibbons, Green, van Amerongen
1984	Chemical operations	Private Companies			750,000	Imperial Chemical Industries
1985	Cookie Operations	Private Companies	253,000			Prospect Group
1985	STP	Part of Esmark		87,000		Union Carbide
1986	Avis	Part of Esmark	255,000			Wesray Capital
1986	Coca Cola bottling	Part of Northwest Industries		1,100,000		Coca Cola Company
1986	International Playtex	Part of Esmark	1,250,000			Playtex Holdings
1986	Americold cold storage	Private companies	480,000			Kelso Americold
1986	Dairy products	Private companies		315,000		Borden
1986	Webcraft Technologies	Private companies	225,000			Riordan Freeman & Spogli
1987	Bottled Water Division	Private companies			400,000	Source Perrier SA
1987	E-II Holdings	Private companies	1,640,000			E-II Holdings
1987	International foods	Private companies	985,000			TLC Group
1988	Tropicana	Public company		1,200,000		Seagrams
1989	Fisher Nut	Private company		150,000		Procter & Gamble
1990	Beatrice	Private companies and parts of Esmark		3,140,000		ConAgra
	Total Value		5,309,000	5,992,000	1,344,400	
	Percent of Total		42.0%	47.4%	10.6%	

Beatrice: A Study in the Creation and Destruction of Value   1117

ment ownership was once again the most efficient organizational form for these companies. The LBO in 1986 created an organizational form that was destined to break-up. Indeed, the financial structure of the Beatrice LBO demanded that substantial asset sales take place and provided rich rewards to Donald Kelly and his management team if they could successfully sell off the diverse businesses of Beatrice. The value increased which accrued to the owners of Beatrice before and after the LBO can be attributed to the movement of the assets of the company into more appropriate organizational forms, which, because of a changing economic environment, often resembled the forms from which Beatrice had bought the assets years earlier.

V. Conclusions

The history of Beatrice reflects the history of American business from the turn of the century to the 1990s. Begun as a small single-business firm, it grew by acquisition into a large, diversified company. The path that Beatrice took from a local creamery to an international consumer and industrial products firm had few sharp turns: the company's early acquisitions in the dairy industry were a response to a changing environment that made consolidation an economically efficient strategy. When further expansion in the dairy business was precluded, William Karnes leveraged his organization's capabilities to evaluate companies and managers, and his own organizational philosophy and systems, and bought companies outside the dairy industry, first in foods and then in a wide array of industries. This strategy proved very successful and provided Beatrice investors with superior returns over a twenty-five year period.

The success of the firm's diversification strategy appears due, in large part, to the organizational structure and systems set up by William Karnes. Karnes insisted that the company be run in a decentralized way, with minimal interference from headquarters. The subsequent decline in value suffered by the company in the late 1970s and early 1980s seems attributable to a flawed strategic vision that demanded organizational capabilities that the company did not possess, and to the break-down of the internal control system which might have prevented this strategic muddle. Rasmussen and Dutt centralized control of the firm in the CEO's office, stripping decision rights from the division managers and from the members of the board of directors. Once this centralization of control had occurred, and the firm's value had fallen, it was the capital market, in the form of hostile corporate control activity, that ultimately directed the firm's fate. When the dust had settled, control of the assets of what had been Beatrice had passed, in many cases, back into the decentralized hands of the managers of the assets themselves.

Several hypotheses and conclusions can be drawn from this analysis of the history of Beatrice. First, this analysis provides an organization-level explanation for the findings that the diversifying mergers of the 1950s–1970s created value. To the extent that the acquirors of this period were buying smaller companies that valued the financial and managerial resources that these acquiring firms could offer, these transactions generated real economic value. Furthermore, the fact that many of these transactions were later reversed in the 1980s is not necessarily evidence of either the foolishness or the failure of these acquisitions; changes in financing technology and managerial sophistication available to small and large firms can explain these reversals. Finally, the history of Beatrice demonstrates the importance of organizational structure and governance in the creation of economic value. It was largely internal policies and organizational structure that created the value in Beatrice, and it was largely the failure of these policies and structures that lead to its destruction.

REFERENCES

Advertising Age, 1983, Beatrice revamp has marketing look, February 21, 54, 72.

Asquith, Paul, David Mullins, and Eric Wolff, 1989. Original issue high yield bonds: Aging, analysis of defaults, exchanges, and calls, *Journal of Finance*, 44, 923–952.

Beatrice Annual Reports, February 28, 1911–1986.

Bhagat, Sanjai, Andrei Shleifer, and Robert Vishny, 1990, The aftermath of hostile takeovers, *Brookings Papers on Economic Activity: Microeconomics* (The Brookings Institution, Washington D.C.). 1–64.

Blair, Margaret, Sarah Lane, and Martha Schary, 1991, Patterns of corporate restructuring, 1955–1987, Brookings Discussion Paper.

Burrough, Bryan and Robert Johnson, 1988, Tarnished trophy: Beatrice, once hailed deal of the century, proves disappointing, *Wall Street Journal*, November 21, A1.

Business Week, 1978, Beatrice Foods: Adding Tropicana for a broader nationwide network, May 15, 114.

Chandler, Alfred, 1990, *Scale and Scope: The Dynamics of Industrial Capitalism* (Harvard University Press, Cambridge, MA).

Collis, David, 1991, Beatrice Companies—1985, Harvard Business School Case N9-391-191, 1991.

Colvin, Geoffrey, 1982, The bigness cult's grip on Beatrice Foods, *Fortune*, September 20, 106, 122–129.

Cox, Meg and Paul Ingrassia, 1979, Discord at the top: Beatrice Foods' board, officers split bitterly in a battle for control, *Wall Street Journal*, May 21, 1.

Esmark Proxy Statement, 1984, January 27.

Federal Trade Commission, FTC Decisions, Decision on Beatrice Foods, Docket 6653, April 26 1953.

Federal Trade Commission, FTC Decisions, Decision on Beatrice Foods, Docket 8864, July 1975.

Forbes, 1979, The man who came to dinner, February 19, 123, 86–88.

Fortune, 1936, Beatrice, 13, 83–132.

Gazel, Neil R., 1990, *Beatrice From Buildup Through Breakup* (University of Illinois Press, Chicago, IL).

Hite, Gailen, James Owers, and Ronald Rogers, 1987, The market for interfirm asset sales: Partial sell-offs and total liquidations, *Journal of Financial Economics*, 18, 229–252.

——— and Michael Vetsuypens, Management buyouts of divisions and shareholder wealth, *Journal of Finance*, 44, 953–970.

Hodge, Sally S., 1988, Chicago's unabashed centimillionaire, *Forbes*, May 30, 141, 252–260.

Horsky, Dan and Patrick Swyngedouw, 1987, Does it pay to change your company's name? A stock market perspective, *Marketing Science*, 6, 320–335.

Ipsen, Erik, 1988, The master of junkyard capitalism, *Institutional Investor*, 22, 132–137.

Beatrice: A Study in the Creation and Destruction of Value   1119

Johnson, Robert, 1987a, Beatrice's Kelly is back in the hunt, *Wall Street Journal*, May 22, 23.
————, 1987b, American Brands plans stock buy-back, says E-II holdings owns stake of 4.6%, *Wall Street Journal*, December 7, 8.
———— and Timothy Smith, 1987, Beatrice decides to put itself on block and expects offers to top $6 billion, *Wall Street Journal*, September 3, 2.
Kaplan, Steven and Michael Weisbach, 1990, The success of acquisitions: Evidence from divestitures, Unpublished manuscript.
Liesse, Julie, 1990, ConAgra: Not a secret anymore, *Advertising Age*, November 26, 61, 18.
Louis, Arthur M., 1985, The controversial boss of Beatrice, *Fortune*, July 22, 112, 110–115.
Matsusaka, John, 1990, Takeover motives during the conglomerate merger wave, Working paper, University of Chicago.
Morris, Betsy and Sue Shellenenbarger, 1984, Beatrice begins offer for Esmark today in an attempt to build marketing muscle, *Wall Street Journal*, May 23, 10.
Moskal, Brian S., 1985, Dutt's done: What now? *Industry Week*, August 19, 18.
Mueller, Willard, Larry Hamm, and Hugh Cook, 1976, *Public Policy Toward Mergers*, Research Division, University of Wisconsin, Madison, Wisconsin.
Potts, Mark, 1985, Chairman of Beatrice ousted, *Washington Post*, August 6, 1.
Ravenscraft, David and F. Scherer, 1987, *Mergers, Sell-Offs, and Economic Efficiency* (The Brookings Institution, Washington D.C.).
Rublin, Lauren, 1985, No piece of cake: Beatrice bought both Esmark and trouble, *Barrons*, May 27, 16.
Rumelt, Richard, 1974, *Strategy, Structure, and Economic Performance* (Harvard Business School Press, Boston).
Schipper, Katherine and Rex Thompson, 1983, Evidence on the capitalized value of merger activity for acquiring firms, *Journal of Financial Economics*, 11, 85–119.
Shellenbarger, Sue, 1983, Slimming down: Beatrice Foods moves to centralize business to reverse its decline, *Wall Street Journal*, September 27, 1.
U.S. Board of Governors of the Federal Reserve System, 1958, Financing small business, April 11.
Wigmore, Barrie, 1990, The decline in credit quality of new-issue junk bonds, *Financial Analysts Journal*, 46, 53–62.

[8]

International Journal of Industrial Organization 7 (1989) 101–116. North-Holland

THE PROFITABILITY OF MERGERS*

David J. RAVENSCRAFT

University of North Carolina, Chapel Hill, NC 27154, USA

F.M. SCHERER

Swarthmore College, Swarthmore, PA 19081, USA

Final version received March 1988

Using data on 2,732 lines of business operated by U.S. manufacturing corporations, this paper analyzes the pre-merger profitability of acquisition targets and post-merger operating results for the years 1957–77. Acquired companies are found to be extraordinarily profitable pre-merger, the more so, the smaller their size. Following merger, the profitability of acquired entities declined except among pooling-of-interests merger partners of roughly equal pre-merger size. The decline was larger than expected under Galtonian regression. This and the high divestiture rate for acquired entities point toward control loss as an explanation of the profit drop.

1. Introduction

Corporate mergers can occur for many reasons: to displace inefficient managers; to achieve economies of scale and scope in production, distribution, and financing; to enhance monopoly or monopsony power; to exploit tax reduction opportunities; to take advantage of 'bargains' on the stock market or in the private 'company for sale' market; and/or to build managerial empires.[1] By analyzing the actual outcomes of mergers in the United States, this paper investigates the statistical support for the first two motivations. Two main hypotheses are tested. First, if mergers displace managers who have performed poorly at the task of profit maximization, acquired companies should have lower average pre-merger profitability than their home industry peers. Second, if mergers lead to economies of scale or scope, post-merger profits should rise relative to pre-merger profits and/or peer industry averages, other relevant variables held equal.

*Scherer's work was supported under National Science Foundation grant SES-8209766, two Swarthmore College faculty research grants, and a Brookings Institution visiting fellowship. Use is made of Line of Business data collected by the Federal Trade Commission. A review by FTC staff has determined that individual company data are not disclosed. The conclusions are the authors' and not necessarily those of the FTC.

[1] For surveys, see Steiner (1975), Mueller (1980), and Keenan and White (1982).

Our main performance data come from the U.S. Federal Trade Commission's Line of Business surveys for the years 1975–77, to which corresponding pre-merger profitability and merger history data have been linked.[2] Under the Line of Business program, between 459 and 471 U.S. corporations reported income statement and balance sheet data finely disaggregated into standardized manufacturing industry categories defined at the three- or four-digit S.I.C. level. The sample companies accounted for three-fourths of manufacturing and minerals industry acquisitions, measured by the value of acquired company assets reported in the FTC's 'large merger' series,[3] between the years 1950 and 1976. The Line of Business data set is peculiarly well-suited for investigating the profit consequences of mergers, since the typical acquired company is quite small relative to the overall size of the acquiring corporation, but large relative to the individual reporting lines of business (LBs) into which it is fitted. On average, acquired assets valued at the time of acquisition accounted for 20 percent of total 1977 assets for acquisition-making LBs that were already part of the parent's operations in 1950 and 48 percent of 1977 assets for acquisition-making LBs that joined the parent after 1950. Thus, disaggregation increases the mean and variance of merger intensity variables and permits the performance of merger-intensive units to be compared against that of narrowly-targeted industry control groups.

In evaluating post-merger profit performance, it is also important to recognize that U.S. corporations have used, with roughly equal historical frequency, two quite different methods of accounting for the assets subsumed into their financial statements through merger.[4] Under *pooling of interests* accounting, the assets of the acquired firm are recorded at their book value when the acquisition is consummated. If the acquirer pays more (less) for the assets than their book value, the difference is debited (credited) to the acquirer's stockholders' equity account. In contrast, under *purchase* accounting, the acquired assets are entered at the effective price paid for them. If a premium is paid over the acquired entity's book value, the acquired assets are 'stepped up' relative to their pre-merger book values, and/or an addition may be made to the acquirer's good will (asset) account. Plant and equipment value increases following from purchase accounting mergers are always depreciated in subsequent years. Amortization of good will increments has been required on acquisitions made since 1970. When positive premiums are paid, as has been true on average, post-merger profitability of purchase accounting acquisitions will be systematically lower than that of pooling acquisitions, all else equal. The numerator of the post-merger profit

---

[2] For details of the linking procedure, see Ravenscraft and Scherer (1987, Chapter 4).
[3] See U.S. Federal Trade Commission (1980).
[4] For elaboration, see Steiner (1975, Chapter 5). On the methods used in the U.K., see Meeks (1977, Appendix A).

ratio for the average purchase accounting acquisition will be smaller owing to increased depreciation, and the denominator of any profit/assets ratio will be larger. Indeed, if markets for acquisitions are competitive, the profit/assets ratio on purchase accounting acquisitions should on average approximate a competitive return. To control for these effects, an extensive effort was exerted to ascertain the accounting method used on the nearly 6,000 acquisitions linked to Line of Business sample company manufacturing LBs. For the approximately 13 percent of acquired assets on which accounting choice information could not be obtained, a logit model was used to predict (with an 84 percent success rate on known choices) the accounting method employed.[5]

2. Pre-merger profitability

Several previous studies have examined the pre-merger profitability of acquired U.S. companies.[6] All were limited to acquired companies with publicly-traded securities – an attribute correlated with size. Because most of the acquisitions made in the 1950–76 period by Line of Business sample members were of 'private' companies, a broader data source was tapped. The 'listing applications' filed when New York Stock Exchange companies issue securities to make acquisitions include pre-merger financial statements (usually for only one year) for both private and public acquired companies. A sample was drawn of 392 manufacturing company acquisitions made by Line of Business panel companies during 1968, 1971, and 1974 and covered by NYSE listing applications.[7] Of these, 251 were linked to LBs filing 1975–77 Line of Business financial reports in non-miscellaneous manufacturing categories. The 251 linked acquirees, with median pre-merger assets of $4.81 million, were significantly larger than the 141 acquired companies on which no link was achieved, with median assets of $0.99 million.[8] The most probable reasons for non-linking were subsequent divestiture,[9] assignment

---

[5]See Ravenscraft and Scherer (1987, Appendix A).

[6]For surveys, see Steiner (1975, pp. 185–188), Harris et al. (1982), and Mueller (1980).

[7]The sample covered all such acquisitions made in 1968 and 1974, years of peak and low merger activity respectively, and that part of 1971 for which financial reports were centered on the recession year 1970. Also sampled, but excluded from the analysis here, were 242 manufacturing acquisitions made in the same years by non-Line of Business survey companies.

[8]There was no significant difference in pre-merger profitability between linked and unlinked companies, nor were companies acquired by LB sample non-members different. For the ratio of operating income to assets, unadjusted unweighted averages were 21.3 percent for the 251 linked companies, 19.9 percent for the 141 LB company non-links, and 19.3 percent for the acquisitions of non-LB sample companies. The F-ratio in a test of equality of means (2 and 631 degrees of freedom) is 0.71.

[9]In Ravenscraft and Scherer (1987, pp. 162–166), we estimate that one-third of acquisitions are subsequently sold off. However, the divestiture of mergers made in the late 1960s and early 1970s had not yet run its full course by 1975–77 – the years for which our Line of Business sample is drawn.

Table 1

Average linked company supra-normal pre-merger returns, by year of
acquisition and merger accounting method.[a]

	1968	1971	1974	All years
All acquisitions	$7.74\%_{143}$	$13.57\%_{45}$	$9.73\%_{63}$	$9.29\%_{251}$
Poolings	8.71_{122}	15.47_{39}	12.81_{48}	10.91_{209}
Purchases	2.41_{21}	1.18_{6}	-0.15_{15}	1.19_{42}

[a]The subscripted variables give the number of acquired companies in
each cell.

to a miscellaneous (code 99.99) catch-all reporting category excluded from
our analysis, and acquired company size too small to leave traces on the
basis of which coding to particular LBs was possible.

Consistent with the post-merger analysis to follow, pre-merger profitability
of the linked companies was measured as operating income (before interest
charges, extraordinary charges or credits, and income taxes) as a percentage
of end-of-period assets. To control for industry differences, we subtracted
from each such percentage the corresponding percentage for the acquired
company's principal two-digit industry group in the most nearly comparable
accounting period.[10] The resulting index SUPRA is in effect a measure of
returns above home industry norms.

Table 1 presents the unweighted average SUPRA values by year and
merger accounting method. (Unweighted averages are appropriate because
we will subsequently analyze similarly unweighted Line of Business values,
and the typical LB had only one or two acquisitions.) The average SUPRA
value for all years and accounting types is significantly above zero; $t = 9.23$.
The SUPRA values of linked acquired companies exceeded home industry
operating income/asset ratios (averaging 11.99 percent) by 77 percent. The
SUPRA differences across years are not statistically significant
$[F(2,248) = 2.33$, with the 5 percent point being 3.89]. The SUPRA differences
between accounting types, controlling also for year, are highly significant
$[F(3,245) = 5.20]$. Pooling accounting was favored following the acquisition
of highly profitable companies, apparently to avoid asset stepups that would
depress later reported returns on assets. Purchase accounting, on the other
hand, was preferred for acquisitions of only normal profitability.

The SUPRA values also differed systematically with acquired company
size, as shown in the following regression, where PDUM is a purchase
accounting dummy variable, LOGAST is the logarithm (to base 10) of

---

[10]The universe data were drawn from U.S. Federal Trade Commission, *Quarterly Financial
Reports*, various years. Until Line of Business reporting commenced for 1974, two-digit
breakdowns were the finest for which profitability benchmarks were available, and even they
suffer from much misallocation of secondary activity into a firm's primary industry category.

Table 2

Acquired company supra-normal pre-merger returns, by type of acquisition.

	Number	Average SUPRA
HORIZ	93	11.8%
VERT	6	−7.0
RELAT	39	5.4
CONGLOM	82	9.9
Mixed HORIZ and other	31	8.2
All types	251	9.3%

acquired company assets, measured in thousands of dollars, and the *t*-ratios are given in subscripted parentheses:

$$SUPRA = 27.76 - 9.57 \text{ PDUM} - 4.47 \text{ LOGAST}, \qquad (1)$$
$$(5.41) \ (3.70) (3.35)$$

$$N = 251, \ R^2 = 0.093.$$

Evidently, a selection bias was at work. The smaller the acquisition, the more acquirers favored (within the large population of candidates) firms of superior profitability.[11] This selection bias was not identified in previous pre-merger profitability studies limited to larger, publicly-traded, targets. Even the largest acquirees, however, exhibited at least 'normal' profitability. In analogues of regression (1) computed separately for pooling and purchase acquisitions, SUPRA goes to zero at acquired company asset values of $464 to 524 million − sizes exceeded by only three of the 251 pre-merger sample companies. Thus, there is no broad-gauged support for the 'inefficient management displacement' hypothesis that acquired companies were sub-normal performers.

Table 2 prepares the way for our analysis of post-merger performance by classifying the 251 linked acquisitions into four commonly-used categories, as follows:

HORIZ   Acquiring company had at least five years experience in the same FTC four-digit category before acquisition.

---

[11] It is possible, but unlikely, that this selection bias was linked to pre-merger accounting differences. Stigler (1963, pp. 125–127) found that the owners of small corporations over-paid themselves in the form of salaries and perquisites, thus reducing reported profits and tax liabilities. This is the opposite of what would be needed to impart a bias toward profitability decreasing with size. Nor do more recent *Quarterly Financial Report* size breakdowns for the late 1960s and early 1970s reveal a general tendency for smaller corporations to be more profitable.

VERT   Acquired company B made at least 5 percent of its sales to, or purchases from, another unit operated by the parent company for at least five years before acquisition.

RELAT   Acquiring company had at least five years experience in the same two-digit industry group before acquisition, but no horizontal or vertical connection.

CONGLOM None of the above criteria satisfied.

The 'horizontal' acquisitions had the best pre-merger performance on average, the verticals (with very few observations) the worst, with 'pure conglomerates' and 'related business' acquisitions in between. The F-ratio in a test of differences among the five classes of table 2 is 2.82, which is significant at the 5 percent level.

NYSE listing applications normally provide profit and loss data for only the last accounting year prior to merger. To test whether merger selection biases favor acquisition candidates with unsustainably high peak profitability, manufacturing companies covered by the COMPUSTAT research files for at least five years before their acquisition by Line of Business sample members were identified. To approximate the NYSE results as closely as possible, entities with final-year assets exceeding $50 million and final year operating income less than 15 percent of assets were excluded. The 33 companies that remained had final year operating income/asset ratios, adjusted for business cycle influences,[12] of 25.2 percent – a reasonable approximation to the comparably-adjusted 23.2 percent return (before deduction of industry norms) of the 251 NYSE listing application sample. There was evidence that when one selects on a high final-year profitability criterion (and also, but more weakly, without such a bias[13]), profitability in earlier years was lower, but not significantly so [with $F(160,5)=1.24$]. With T as the year of merger, the pre-merger profit pattern was 25.2 percent in T-1, 20.8 percent in T-2, 16.9 percent in T-3, 18.6 percent in T-4, and 21.1 percent in T-5. Although the final pre-merger year was the peak, profits in earlier years were above all-manufacturing averages, and the acquired companies appear to have had the staying power to recover from a profit slump three to four years before merger.

[12]To correct for cyclical movements and a slow drift toward rising reported profit rates, positive profit ratios were divided (and the few negative values multiplied by) the correction factor:

$$MACRO = \frac{\text{Quarterly Financial Report Manufacturing Universe Operating Income/Assets for the Pre-Merger Year}}{\text{QFR Manufacturing Universe Average Annual Operating Income/Assets Ratios over the Years 1974–77}}$$

[13]For 61 companies chosen subject to no minimum profitability constraint but with assets less than or equal to $50 million, operating income in the last pre-merger year was 16.5 percent of assets, with earlier but insignificant ($F=0.42$) declines to a trough three years before merger.

3. Line of business cross-sectional analysis

In our investigation of post-merger performance, we use three profitability variables, each the unweighted average of the individual lines' values for 1975, 1976, and 1977:

PROF:A   Operating income/end-of-year assets.
PROF:S   Operating income/sales.
FLOW:S   Cash flow (operating income plus depreciation)/sales.

All are measured in percentage terms. Comparison of the three is informative, since the choice of a merger accounting method can affect both the numerator and denominator of PROF:A, the numerator only of PROF:S, and neither numerator nor denominator of FLOW:S. The sample includes 2,732 lines of business (LBs) on which profit data for all three years were available and for which merger histories of adequate quality could be compiled.[14]

3.1. The explanatory variables

The extent of merger activity in a line is measured by the variable MERGSHR, which is the average value across the three years of assets acquired at the time of acquisition (with an exception to be noted in the next paragraph), divided by 1975, 1976, or 1977 LB assets. Approximately nine percent of the MERGSHR observations had values exceeding unity (implying more than 100 percent origination of assets through merger). These were truncated at 1.0.[15] From MERGSHR come two related variables, POOL, which is MERGSHR times the fraction of acquired assets in an LB accounted for under pooling of interests rules, and PURCH, which is MERGSHR times the fraction of acquired assets in an LB subjected to purchase accounting. MERGSHR is also subdivided into the variables HORIZ, VERT, RELAT, and CONGLOM, measuring the fraction of 1975–77 assets originating through horizontal, vertical, 'related business', and pure conglomerate mergers as defined in section 2.

[14]The maximum possible number of observations, for 1977 profits alone, would have been 3,674. The three-year averaging criterion eliminated inter alia lines that were divested in 1976 or 1977. Such lines tended to be merger-intensive and to have unusually low profits. Also excluded were lines with substantial new acquisitions, since mergers and divestitures within the measurement period impart systematic profit biases. See Meeks and Meeks (1981). To avoid 'outlier' problems, 58 lines with PROF:A or PROF:S values exceeding +100 percent or −100 percent in any one of the years 1975–77 were excluded. Sensitivity tests using 1977 samples including the extreme-value cases and the LBs with low-quality merger histories showed that the results were not materially affected. See Ravenscraft and Scherer (1987, p. 107).
[15]Sensitivity tests reported in Ravenscraft and Scherer (1987, pp. 106–107), showed the results to be little affected when MERGSHR had values exceeding unity, when an alternative MERGSHR formulation let acquired assets be 'grown' to 1977 at an industry-wide asset growth rate, and when merger activity was measured through categorical rather than continuously scaled variables.

108   *D.J. Ravenscraft and F.M. Scherer, The profitability of mergers*

In certain cases, it was difficult to tell which corporation acquired the other. Sixty-nine pooling of interests mergers between companies that differed in size at the time of merger by no more than a factor of two were treated as 'mergers of equals.' The 251 lines of business operated by the partners at the time of their merger of equals are distinguished by the unit-valued dummy variable EQUALS. The assets of EQUALS mergers were not counted in measuring MERGSHR and related merger intensity variables.

Another dummy variable, NEW, has unit value for 258 LBs in which the parent corporation did not operate in 1950, and for which no acquisitions were recorded. These represent cases of growth by internal development.

Prior research at the line of business level has shown profitability to be higher, the larger the line's market share. See Scherer et al. (1987, pp. 207–209). We introduce this influence with the variable SHR, which measures (in ratio form) the market share of an LB in its nationally-defined four-digit industry category.

3.2. Model structure

We use a 'fixed effects' regression model to investigate how profitability varies with merger intensity and accounting method, holding other relevant variables constant.[16] Differences in profitability associated with industry-specific conditions are controlled by letting each of 257 four-digit industry categories with reporting LBs have its own intercept value. LBs with high merger activity are compared to lines of comparable industry membership and market share that existed in 1950 and that had little or no merger activity. Because there are conflicting a priori hypotheses, tests on the merger variable (and NEW) are two-tailed. For SHR, with a positive predicted effect, a one-tailed test is used. No significant relationship was found between regression residuals and the merger variables POOL and PURCH, and so the regression technique is ordinary least squares without correction for heteroskedasticity.

3.3. Results

Table 3 reports the results for the 1975–77 cross-sectional analysis of 2,732 LBs. *T*-ratios are given in subscripted parentheses.

Regression (3a) is most like previously published merger profitability analyses, with no control for merger accounting methods.[17] It implies a significantly negative impact of merger on profitability.

In the more complex regressions (3b) and (3c), the picture changes.

---

[16] For earlier applications to Line of Business data, see Schmalensee (1985) and Scott and Pascoe (1986).

[17] The only prior study controlling for merger accounting adjustments was Meeks (1977).

D.J. Ravenscraft and F.M. Scherer, The profitability of mergers   109

Table 3

Line of business cross-section regressions, $N = 2,732$.[a]

Dependent variable	(3a) PROF:A	(3b) PROF:A	(3c) PROF:A	(3d) PROF:S	(3e) FLOW:S	(3f) PROF:A
Mean	13.34%	13.34%	13.34%	7.54%	10.12%	13.34%
Intercept			[257 values]			
MERGSHR	−2.75 (3.19)	−	−	−	−	−
POOL		−0.69 (0.61)	+0.36 (0.32)	+0.38 (0.57)	+0.38 (0.57)	−
PURCH		−5.06 (4.34)	−3.84 (3.26)	−1.18 (1.67)	−1.23 (1.75)	−3.84 (3.25)
EQUALS		1.06 (1.10)	1.37 (1.43)	0.83 (1.45)	0.71 (1.23)	1.38 (1.43)
NEW		−0.25 (0.24)	+0.77 (0.77)	−0.10 (0.16)	+0.14 (0.24)	+0.78 (0.77)
SHR			30.16 (5.67)	21.90 (6.87)	23.11 (7.29)	30.18 (5.67)
HORIZ:POOL						+0.69 (0.32)
VERT:POOL						−1.00 (0.28)
RELAT:POOL						+1.02 (0.56)
CONGLOM:POOL						0.00 (0.00)
R^2	0.1662	0.1697	0.1804	0.2121	0.2387	0.1805

[a]T-ratios are given in subscripted parentheses.

Purchase acquisitions have a strongly negative profit effect, but more so with no control for LB market share than with such a control. For pooling mergers (and also for NEW LBs), the coefficient changes from weakly negative to weakly positive when SHR is added.[18] This SHR impact stems from the fact that LBs entering their parents' operations after 1950, with or without mergers, had much lower market shares (averaging 2.1 percent) than 1950 lines *with* mergers (whose average SHR value was 5.6 percent), while 1950 lines *without* mergers (comprising 14 percent of the sample) had average shares of 7.6 percent. Thus, including SHR controls for an influence that otherwise depressed the profits of small-share, acquisition-prone post-1950 lines.

Whether the SHR effect is independent of merger history and hence exogenous is arguable. Dennis Mueller (1985) found that the inherited or

---

[18] In individual year operating income/assets regressions with SHR included, the POOL coefficient was positive and insignificant in 1975, negative and insignificant in 1976, and significantly positive (with a value of 3.36) in 1977. All three years' PURCH coefficients were significantly negative. See Ravenscraft and Scherer (1987, p. 86).

combined market shares of lines subjected to both horizontal and conglomerate mergers declined over time more rapidly than the market shares of a control group without mergers. His conclusion (p. 267) that acquirers were relatively unsuccessful in their ability to gain and retain customers implies that but for merger, the market shares of at least conglomerate mergers (for which merger was not intrinsically share-increasing) would have been greater than the values we actually observe for 1975–77. LBs whose acquisitions were of a related business or purely conglomerate character comprised roughly half of all sample LBs and two-thirds of all LBs with acquisitions. Had larger (but unknown and hence unmeasured) pre-merger values of SHR been introduced into regression (3c), intercept values of the regression for merger-intensive LBs would be shifted downward. Thus, inclusion of the atrophied rather than the pre-merger SHR values biases POOL and PURCH upward.[19] Given the important impact of SHR on profitability, it appears preferable to include SHR with the caveat that its dependence upon prior merger history may bias the merger effect coefficients upward. To omit it, when profitability clearly depends upon it, would impart to the POOL and PURCH coefficients a demonstrated downward bias.

Regressions (3d) and (3e) test alternate versions of the profit measure. For pooling mergers, which experienced no merger-related accounting adjustments, there is little change. For purchase mergers, PURCH becomes less negative, revealing that some of the negative effect observed in regression (3c) came from asset denominator stepups attributable to the payment of typically positive acquisition premiums. However, even after all such accounting adjustments are purged by analyzing the ratio of cash flow to sales, as in regression (3e), the PURCH coefficient remains negative and significant at the 0.10 level. This, combined with the evidence that pre-merger profit returns for purchase accounting mergers were insignificantly different from industry norms, is inconsistent with the hypothesis that merger *raised* the average profitability of purchase accounting acquisitions. For pooling of interests acquisitions, the evidence goes even more strongly against the hypothesis of merger-induced profitability gains. Our 1968–74 pre-merger analysis shows that the operating income/assets percentages of pooling merger targets exceeded industry norms by 10.9 points on average. In 1975–

---

[19]In a Monte Carlo analysis, profitability was assumed to conform to the equation: $PROF:A_i = 9.61 + 0.4\ SHR_i + e_i$. The error distribution was assumed to be normal, with standard deviation of 12. To simulate observed skewness tendencies, SHR values, with mean of 9.7 percent, were taken from 1982 *Census of Manufactures* four-seller concentration ratios divided by four. A merger dummy variable was assigned randomly to half of the 448 observations. For merged lines, the pre-merger market share SHR* was assumed to be non-stochastically $1.25 \times SHR$ – i.e., with at most half as much attenuation as the 40 to 70 percent declines found by Mueller (1985) over the 1950–72 period. When the merger variable was added to the profits regression, its coefficients averaged 0.65 points higher in regressions with SHR as compared to those with SHR*.

77, post-merger returns differ insignificantly from no-merger values in any of regressions (3b) through (3e). On average, then, returns must have fallen, not risen.

Mergers of equals are a possible exception. In all of the table 3 regressions, the EQUALS coefficients are positive, although none quite approaches statistical significance by conventional standards. An analysis reported in Ravenscraft and Scherer (1987, pp. 71–72) found that pre-merger, the mergers of equals partners had operating income/assets ratios slightly, but insignificantly, below contemporary manufacturing universe values. Thus, there is weak evidence that for the EQUALS mergers, performance improved.

For companies seeking to expand and diversify, growth by internal development is an alternative to growth by merger. Such internal development LBs, identified by the NEW dummy variable, had to pay prevailing post-1950 market prices for their plant and equipment, and in this respect they are comparable to the PURCH acquisitions. Yet the PURCH coefficients are consistently more negative than the NEW coefficients, suggesting that on average, holding industry locus constant, growth by purchase acquisition was less profitable than growth by internal development.

Regression (3f) of table 3 subdivides the POOL variable into four merger type categories. 'Related business' acquisitions fared best relative to non-merged units of similar industry membership and market share; vertical acquisitions (with the fewest observations) fared least well. The differences are not statistically significant, however, and the increase in R^2 is minute.[20] It would appear that horizontal, related business, and pure conglomerate acquisitions all experienced profitability declines from the high pre-merger levels indicated in table 2.

4. A matched pre- vs. post-merger analysis

The apparent decrease in profitability following mergers, which was stronger for the more profitable pooling of interests acquisitions, could have several explanations. It may reflect the tendency (first identified by Francis Galton, and explored concerning profits by Mueller (1986)) for abnormal returns, negative or positive, to regress over time toward 'normal' levels. Second, and more squarely at odds with scale or scope economies hypotheses, acquiring corporations may have experienced what Williamson (1970, pp. 160–161) calls 'control loss' in managing their acquisitions. Third, parents may have treated many of their acquisitions as 'cash cows,' charging high prices and inducing profit-eroding entry or electing not to reinvest earnings in modernization and expansion. Fourth, and in conflict with the cash cow

[20] The differences for PURCH acquisitions (not separately broken out in table 3) were even smaller.

112   *D.J. Ravenscraft and F.M. Scherer, The profitability of mergers*

hypothesis, the supra-normal pre-merger profitability of companies acquired in pooling mergers may have been caused by the (typically private) firms' inability to finance all attractive investments. By breaking capital rationing constraints, merger may have permitted expansion down the marginal efficiency of investment schedule until marginal capital costs and returns were equalized.

To help discriminate among these alternatives, a matched pre- vs. post-merger analysis was undertaken. It was limited to Line of Business sample LBs satisfying several criteria:

(1) The line was new to the parent company, originating from a single conglomerate acquisition not augmented by further acquisitions.
(2) Pre-merger financial data were available (usually from NYSE listing applications) on the acquired company.
(3) Post-merger Line of Business data were available for all the years 1974–77; and
(4) The acquisition was accounted for as a pooling of interests, so that no asset revaluation occurred.

These stringent criteria were satisfied for 67 company acquisitions made between 1965 and 1974. The sample is probably biased on the side of more successful acquisitions, since the resulting lines survived several years of high sell-off activity and since parent corporations were not required under Line of Business rules to disaggregate their financial reports for lines with sales below a $10 million threshold. The reporting threshold together with the single acquisition criterion imply not only survival fitness, but also a bias toward larger pre-merger size. Median pre-merger assets were $12.0 million, compared to $4.8 million for the less constrained sample of tables 1 and 2.

Like the table 1 sample, the matched sample firms enjoyed returns well above all-manufacturing averages in the year before their acquisition. Their simple average operating income was 21.0 percent of assets unadjusted, or 25.2 percent when the profitability ratios were divided by the MACRO adjustment variable described in footnote 12. The matched lines' average 1974–77 (post-merger) operating income was 12.24 percent of assets – a decline of more than half from the MACRO-adjusted pre-merger values over the average of seven years from the time of their last pre-merger earnings report to the midpoint of the 1974–77 period. Despite the passage of time and an average GNP deflator increase of 62 percent, only 57 percent of the matched lines experienced an absolute (i.e., not asset-deflated) current-dollar operating income increase between the pre- and post-merger periods.

Although there was little rise in profits and a sharp decline in profit rates, considerable asset growth occurred. Fifty-two percent of the lines experienced nominal asset growth rates greater than those of the four-digit industry category to which they belonged. The mean asset growth rate was 8.93

percent per annum, compared to a mean of 7.68 percent over matched time periods for the counterpart four-digit industries. Thus, there is no evidence that the acquired and surviving (i.e., not sold off) lines were on average treated as cash cows or otherwise deprived of investible funds. A few lines grew extraordinarily rapidly – e.g., nine at 20 percent or more per year.

To probe further, a transformed 1974–77 operating income/assets percentage POSTPI was regressed on two variables: the comparable ratio PREPI for the last pre-merger year, and the average annual percentage growth rate of acquired unit assets GROW. To capture the spirit of the Galtonian regression-toward-normal hypothesis, 12.5 percent, the average operating income/assets value for all manufacturing corporations over 1974–77, was subtracted from each profit observation, pre- and post-merger. Before this normalization, pre-merger profit rates were also made comparable over time through adjustment with the 1974–77 benchmark variable MACRO.[21] The resulting regression was

$$POSTPI = -2.84 + 0.10 \ PREPI + 0.15 \ GROW, \qquad (2)$$
$$(1.31) \ (0.81) \qquad\quad (0.81)$$

$$R^2 = 0.034, \ N = 67.$$

The coefficient on PREPI would have a value of 1.0 if there were no regression toward 'normal' and zero if there were complete regression.[22] It is not significantly different from zero, but differs from 1.0 with high significance ($t = 7.18$).

There remains the counter-factual question of whether profits would have declined as much had merger not occurred. Like all counter-factuals, it can have no certain answer. However, to test it a special control sample was drawn. The sample consisted of all primarily-manufacturing corporations listed on the COMPUSTAT data tape from 1965 through 1980, whose 1965 assets were $50 million or less, and whose 1965 operating income was 15 percent or more of assets. The median 1965 assets of the 261 'independent survivors' meeting these criteria was $13.8 million, closely approximating the 67 matched merger company pre-merger value of $12.0 million. The survivors' 1965 average operating income/assets ratio, adjusted by MACRO, was 24.1 percent, again approximating the matched merger company value of 25.2 percent. Thus, the two samples were as alike as possible in key respects, except that one group remained independent and the other did not.

[21] As explained in footnote 12, positive values were divided by MACRO and negative values multiplied by it.

[22] If 12.50 is not the correct norm toward which Galtonian regression occurs, the intercept term will be biased away from what otherwise should be a zero value – negatively if the norm is set too high, as appears to be the case in our regressions. Thus, from regression (2), it appears that the norm should have been approximately 9.5 percent.

The 67 matched merger companies and the 261 independent survivor firms were analyzed in a combined sample. Letting DM be a dummy variable identifying the 67 matched merger lines, the regression analogous to Eq. (2) was[23]

$$\text{POSTPI} = -4.55 + 0.32\ \text{PREPI} - 0.19\ \text{DM} \times \text{PREPI} \tag{3}$$
$$(4.68) + (5.76) \qquad\qquad (2.78)$$

$$+ 0.24\ \text{GROW},\ R^2 = 0.157,\ N = 328.$$
$$(3.48)$$

The 0.32 coefficient on PREPI again implies considerable regression toward the 'norm.' However, the negative and significant coefficient on DM × PREPI reveals that the profits of matched merger lines regressed (mostly, fell) more rapidly than those of the independent survivor companies, even though, with an average pre-merger reporting date of 1968, the merged firms had less time to change than the independent survivors (with data uniformly for 1965).

By selecting the control group with a relatively high 15 percent floor on 1965 operating income/assets, a variable subject to random variation over time, we have virtually guaranteed a Galtonian regression effect on the PREPI coefficient. However, case study interviews [see Ravenscraft and Scherer (1987, pp. 127–132)] revealed that acquiring companies tried to find candidates with sustainable profitability, not one-year flashes in the pan. The multi-year pre-merger analysis of section 2 also suggests sustainability. Therefore, the independent survivor group was culled to eliminate companies whose 1966 or 1967 operating income/assets ratio was less than 70 percent of the 1965 value. Pooling the 179 companies that survived this screen with the 67 matched merger companies, we obtain

$$\text{POSTPI} = -3.59 + 0.40\ \text{PREPI} - 0.29\ \text{DM} \times \text{PREPI} \tag{4}$$
$$(3.13)\ (5.06) \qquad\qquad (3.54)$$

$$+ 0.19\ \text{GROW},\ R^2 = 0.160,\ N = 246.$$
$$(2.36)$$

The larger PREPI value here implies a smaller regression-to-the-mean effect, as expected, while the matched merger offset coefficient DM × PREPI increases commensurately. In each of eqs. (2) through (4), the matched merger group lines retained only 10 to 13 percent of their pre-merger supra-normal profits, while the control group retained 32 to 40 percent.

The positive and significant coefficients on GROW in eqs. (3) and (4)

---

[23] The methodology here follows Mueller (1985).

suggest that rapid asset growth is associated with higher end-of-period profitability. It is of interest too that the average ($N = 261$) independent survivors' asset growth rate was 13.1 percent per year, compared to 8.9 percent for the matched merger group – a difference that is highly significant. Evidently, the small, profitable companies that chose to remain independent were not deprived of growth capital relative to the acquired lines. Had the mostly private, highly profitable acquired firms chosen to remain independent but 'go public', their growth in the no-merger counter-factual might not have been stunted. However, this counter-factual inference is necessarily speculative.

4. Conclusion

In this paper we have tested two main hypotheses: that acquired companies are profit under-performers, and that merger improves profitability on average. Although individual exceptions certainly exist, no broad statistical support was found for the first hypothesis, and the second was supported only for the special 'mergers of equals' case. On average, U.S. acquisitions of the late 1960s and early 1970s exhibited a selection bias toward extraordinarily profitable companies, the more so, the smaller the target was. Prior studies of pre-merger performance failed to detect this phenomenon because they were limited to companies with publicly-traded securities. On the second hypothesis, earlier research has for the most part shown no significant increase in post-merger profitability. The results here allow more detailed insights and better control for industry and accounting effects. Seven or eight years on average following merger, acquired units' profitability had declined sharply relative to pre-merger levels. For companies acquired under purchase accounting, the decline is attributable in part to asset stepups reflecting the payment of acquisition premiums above book value, although evidence of a modest decline remains even after accounting effects are purged. For pooling-of-interest acquisitions, a part of the decline is attributable to Galtonian regression from unsustainably high pre-merger profit levels. For a small subset of the poolings, the breaking of capital constraints to support higher investment may also have reduced post-merger profitability but improved resource allocation. However, similarly profitable small companies that remained independent managed to sustain even more rapid growth. The profits of those non-merged control group companies regressed to normal significantly more slowly than those of the acquisition targets. The residual explanation for acquired units' sharp profit decline must be control loss owing to more complex organizational structures and lessened managerial competence and/or motivation. This control loss explanation is consistent with the high incidence of divestiture following acquisition and the tendency for sold-off units to have *negative* operating income in the year before their

116   *D.J. Ravenscraft and F.M. Scherer, The profitability of mergers*

divestiture. See Ravenscraft and Scherer (1987, Chapter 6). It is also consistent with Mueller's findings (1985) that market shares declined following both horizontal and conglomerate mergers. Although the counter-factual question of what would have happened but for merger cannot be answered confidently, the evidence mandates considerable skepticism toward the claim that mergers are on average efficiency-enhancing.

References

Harris, Robert S., J.F. Stewart and W.T. Carleton, 1982, Financial characteristics of acquired firms, in: Michael Keenan et al., Mergers and acquisitions: Current problems in perspective (Heath-Lexington, Lexington, MA) 223–241.

Keenan, Michael and Lawrence J. White, ed., 1982, Mergers and acquisitions: Current problems in perspective (Heath-Lexington, Lexington, MA).

Meeks, Geoffrey, 1977, Disappointing marriage: A study of the gains from merger (Cambridge University Press, Cambridge).

Meeks, Geoffrey and J.G. Meeks, 1981, Profitability measures as indicators of post-merger efficiency, Journal of Industrial Economics 29, 335–344.

Mueller, Dennis C., ed., 1980, The determinants and effects of mergers (Oelgeschlager, Gunn & Hain, Cambridge, MA).

Mueller, Dennis C., 1985, Mergers and market share, Review of Economics and Statistics 67, 259–267.

Mueller, Dennis C., 1986, Profits in the long run (Cambridge University Press, Cambridge).

Ravenscraft, David J. and F.M. Scherer, 1987, Mergers, sell-offs, and economic efficiency (Brookings Institution, Washington).

Scherer, F.M. et al., 1987, The validity of studies with Line of Business data, American Economic Review 77, 205–217.

Schmalensee, Richard, 1985, Do markets differ much? American Economic Review 75, 341–351.

Scott, John T. and George Pascoe, 1986, Beyond firm and industry effects on profitability in imperfect markets, Review of Economics and Statistics 68, 284–292.

Steiner, Peter O., 1975, Mergers: Motives, effects, policies (University of Michigan Press, Ann Arbor).

Stigler, George J., 1963, Capital and rates of return in manufacturing industries (Princeton University Press, Princeton, NJ).

U.S. Federal Trade Commission, Quarterly financial report for manufacturing corporations (serially).

U.S. Federal Trade Commission, 1980, Statistical report on mergers and acquisitions: 1978 (Washington).

Williamson, Oliver, 1970, Corporate control and business behavior (Prentice-Hall, Englewood Cliffs, NJ).

[9]

Journal of Financial Economics 31 (1992) 135–175. North-Holland

Does corporate performance improve after mergers?*

Paul M. Healy

Massachusetts Institute of Technology, Cambridge, MA 02139, USA

Krishna G. Palepu and Richard S. Ruback

Harvard Business School, Cambridge, MA 02163, USA

Received April 1990, final version received January 1992

We examine post-acquisition performance for the 50 largest U.S. mergers between 1979 and mid-1984. Merged firms show significant improvements in asset productivity relative to their industries, leading to higher operating cash flow returns. This performance improvement is particularly strong for firms with highly overlapping businesses. Mergers do not lead to cuts in long-term capital and R&D investments. There is a strong positive relation between postmerger increases in operating cash flows and abnormal stock returns at merger announcements, indicating that expectations of economic improvements underlie the equity revaluations of the merging firms.

1. Introduction

This study examines the postmerger cash flow performance of acquiring and target firms, and explores the sources of merger-induced changes in cash flow performance. Our research is motivated by the inability of stock price

*We acknowledge the helpful comments of the referee, Michael Jensen (the editor), Robin Cooper, George Foster, Robert Kaplan, Richard Leftwich, Mark Wolfson, Karen Wruck, and seminar participants at Baruch College, Carnegie Mellon University, Columbia University, Dartmouth College, Duke University, the Federal Reserve Bank (Washington, DC), Harvard University, the London School of Economics, the University of Michigan, Massachusetts Institute of Technology, New York University, Northwestern University, the University of Minnesota, the University of Rochester, Stanford University, the University of Southern California, the University of Alberta, and the U.S. Department of Justice. We are thankful to Chris Fox and Ken Hao, who provided research assistance, and the International Financial Services Center at MIT and the Division of Research at the Harvard Business School for financial support.

performance studies to determine whether takeovers create real economic gains and to identify the sources of such gains.

There is near-unanimous agreement that target stockholders benefit from mergers, as evidenced by the premium they receive for selling their shares. The stock price studies of takeovers also indicate that bidders generally breakeven, and that the combined equity value of the bidding and target firms increases as a result of takeovers. These increases in equity values are typically attributed to some unmeasured source of real economic gains, such as synergy. But researchers have had little success in relating the equity value gains to improvements in subsequent corporate performance.[1] Therefore, the equity value gains could also be due to capital market inefficiencies, arising simply from the creation of an overvalued security.

To determine whether the equity value increases in takeovers are from real economic gains or capital market inefficiencies, stock price studies have analyzed unsuccessful takeovers.[2] But these studies, too, are unable to distinguish between the real economic gains and the market inefficiency explanations. That the stock prices of unsuccessful merger targets return to their preoffer level is consistent with the loss of an anticipated premium – whatever its source. From the stock price perspective, the antici-pation of real economic gains is observationally equivalent to market mispric-ing. It is therefore difficult to conceive of a pure stock price study that could resolve the ambiguity in the interpretation of the evidence.

Stock price studies are also unable to provide evidence on the sources of any merger-related gains. Yet differences of opinion about the source of the gains in takeovers underlie much of the public policy debate on their desirability. Gains from mergers could arise from a variety of sources, such as operating synergies, tax savings, transfers from employees or other stakehold-ers, or increased monopoly rents. Equity gains from only some of these sources are unequivocally beneficial at the social level.

Our approach is to use postmerger accounting data to test directly for changes in operating performance that result from mergers.[3] Our tests use accounting data collected from company annual reports, merger prospec-tuses, proxy statements, and analysts' reports for 50 large mergers between U.S. public industrial firms completed between 1979 and mid-1984. We recognize that accounting data are imperfect measures of economic perfor-

---

[1]See Caves (1989) for a review of the studies that examine the *ex post* performance of merged firms.

[2]Dodd (1980), Asquith (1983), Dodd and Ruback (1977), Bradley, Desai, and Kim (1983), and Ruback (1988).

[3]Three recent studies have examined earnings performance following management buyouts of corporations [Bull (1988). Kaplan (1990), and Smith (1990)]. Our paper focuses on acquisitions of one public company by another in either a merger or a tender offer. rather than on management buyouts.

mance and that they can be affected by managerial decisions. As we explain in section 2, we use cash flow measures of economic performance to mitigate the impact of the financing of the acquisition and the method of accounting for the transaction. We also recognize that our cash flow variables measure period-by-period performance, which is affected by firm-specific and industry factors. We therefore use industry performance as a benchmark to evaluate postmerger performance.

Results reported in section 3 show that the merged firms have increases in postmerger operating cash flow returns in comparison with their industries. These increases arise from postmerger improvements in asset productivity. We find no evidence that the improvement in postmerger cash flows is achieved at the expense of the merged firms' long-term viability, since the sample firms maintain their capital expenditure and R & D rates in relation to their industries. Our results differ from the findings reported by Ravenscraft and Scherer (1987) and Herman and Lowenstein (1988), who examine earnings performance after takeovers and conclude that merged firms have no operating improvements.

In section 4 we examine the relation between our cash flow measures of postmerger performance and stock market measures used in earlier studies. Postmerger improvements in operating cash flow returns explain a significant portion of the increase in equity values of the merging firms at the announcement of the merger. This suggests that the stock price reaction to mergers is driven by anticipated economic gains after the merger.

Section 5 discusses the implications of our primary findings and explores some popular hypotheses on factors that influence postmerger performance. There is little evidence that transaction characteristics such as the method of financing, whether the merger is hostile or friendly, or the size of the target firm explain cross-sectional variation in postmerger performance. We find some support, however, for the view that mergers between firms in overlapping businesses lead to better performance than other mergers.

2. Experimental design

2.1. Sample

The analysis in this study is based on the largest 50 acquisitions during the period January 1979 to June 1984. We limit the number of acquisitions studied to make the hand data collection tasks manageable. The largest acquisitions have several important advantages over a similarly sized random sample. First, although the sample consists of a small fraction of the total acquisitions in the sample period, the total dollar value of the 50 firms selected accounts for a significant portion of the dollar value of domestic merger activity.[4] Second, if there are economic gains from a takeover, they are most likely to be detected when the target firm is large. Third, it is less likely that the acquirers in the sample undertake equally large acquisitions before or after the events we study, reducing the probability of confounding events. Finally, public concern about the consequences of takeovers is typically triggered by the largest transactions, making them interesting in their own right.

The sample period is selected to focus on recent mergers and also to have sufficient postmerger performance data.[5] To select the acquisition sample, we identify the 382 merger-related delistings on the Center for Research in Security Prices (*CRSP*) database in the sample period. The names of the acquirers are identified from the *Wall Street Journal Index*. The sample comprises acquisitions involving the 50 largest targets that satisfy the following two criteria: the acquirer is a U.S. company listed on the New York Stock Exchange (NYSE) or the American Stock Exchange (Amex), and the target and acquirer are not financial or regulated companies. Target-firm size is computed from *Compustat* as the market value of common stock plus the book values of net debt and preferred stock at the beginning of the year before the acquisition. Acquisitions are deleted from the sample if the acquirers are non-U.S. or private companies, since post-acquisition financial information is not available for these mergers. Regulated (railroads and utilities) and financial firms are deleted because they are subject to special accounting and regulatory requirements, making them difficult to compare with other firms.

A summary of the sample is provided in the appendix. The information provided includes target and acquiring firms' names, a description of their businesses and industries from *Value Line* reports, target equity value before the merger, the target's assets as a percentage of the acquirer's assets, and the merger completion date. The sample targets and acquirers represent a wide cross-section of *Value Line* industries. The target firms belong to 27 industries; the acquiring firms come from 33 industries.

The transactions are approximately evenly distributed over the sample years: eight acquisitions in the sample were completed in 1979, seven in 1980, twelve in 1981. eleven in 1983, and two in 1984. Since we focus on mergers completed in only a few years, however, the sample firms' postmerger performance is likely to be influenced by economywide changes. Our tests, therefore, control for these factors by comparing sample firms' performance with their corresponding industries'.

---

[4]The aggregate market value of equity of the 50 target firms in our sample one year before the acquisition is $43 billion.

[5]The sample period ends in June 1984 to ensure that when the study was initiated, at least five years of postmerger data were available on *Compustat* for the sample firms. *Compustat* files end in June each year.

The sample acquisitions are significant economic events for purchasing firms. On average, target firms are 42% of the assets of acquirers, where assets are measured by the book value of net debt (long-term debt, plus short-term debt, less cash and marketable securities) plus the market value of equity one year prior to the merger.

2.2. Performance measurement

We use pretax operating cash flow returns on assets to measure improvements in operating performance. Conceptually, we focus on cash flows because they represent the actual economic benefits generated by the assets. Since the level of economic benefits is affected by the assets employed, we scale the cash flows by the assets employed to form a return measure that can be compared across time and across firms. We measure assets employed using market values, which represent the opportunity cost of the assets. In our opinion, market-based measures of asset values dominate accounting and other historical estimates in this context because they simplify intertemporal and cross-sectional comparisons. Our market-based measure has a potential limitation, however, because unexpected cash flow realizations can change expectations about future cash flows, and hence market values. The sensitivity tests in section 3.2 show no evidence of such a feedback effect for our sample of mergers.

We define operating cash flows as sales, minus cost of goods sold and selling and administrative expenses, plus depreciation and goodwill expenses. This measure is deflated by the market value of assets (market value of equity plus book value of net debt) to provide a return metric that is comparable across firms. Unlike accounting return on book assets, our return measure excludes the effect of depreciation, goodwill. interest expense and income, and taxes. It is therefore unaffected by the method of accounting for the merger (purchase or pooling accounting) and the method of financing (cash, debt, or equity). As discussed below, these factors make it difficult to compare traditional accounting returns of the merged firm over time and cross-sectionally.

2.2.1. Effects of purchase and pooling accounting

In our sample, 38 mergers (76%) use the purchase method and the remaining 12 use the pooling of interests method. The purchase method restates the assets and liabilities of target firms at their current market values. No such revaluation is permitted under the pooling method. Further, under the purchase method the acquirer records any difference between the acquisition price and the market value of identifiable assets and liabilities of the target company as goodwill, and amortizes it. No goodwill is recorded under the pooling-of-interests method. Finally, for the first year of the merger, the purchase method consolidates results of the target with those of the acquirer from the date the merger took place; the pooling method consolidates results for the two firms from the beginning of the year regardless of when the merger took place.

The same transaction typically results in lower postmerger earnings under purchase accounting than under pooling. The purchase method increases depreciation, cost of goods sold, and goodwill expenses after the takeover. Also, in the year of the merger, earnings are usually lower under purchase accounting because the target's and acquirer's earnings are consolidated for a shorter period than under pooling. The lower earnings reported under the purchase method are due to differences in the method of accounting for the merger and not to differences in economic performance. Further, postmerger book assets under the purchase method will be larger than those under pooling because of the asset write-up under the purchase method. It is therefore misleading to compare post- and premerger accounting rates of return for firms that use purchase accounting to infer whether there are economic gains from mergers.

Our operating cash flow performance measure – unlike earnings-based performance measures – is unaffected by depreciation and goodwill. It is comparable cross-sectionally and on a time-series basis when firms use different methods of accounting for the merger. We exclude the first year of the merger in our analysis because of the differences between the purchase and pooling methods in timing the consolidation of the target with the acquirer. Excluding the first year also mitigates the effect of inventory write-ups under the purchase method, since this inventory is usually included in cost of sales in the merger year.[6] Because the asset base in our return metric is the market value of assets, rather than book value, it is also unaffected by the accounting method used to record the merger.

2.2.2. Effects of method of financing mergers

The method used to finance the sample transactions varies considerably. Thirty percent of the sample mergers are stock transactions, 26% are financed by cash, and the remaining 14% are financed by combinations of cash, stock, and other securities. It is important to control for these financing differences in measuring postmerger performance. If an acquisition is financed by debt or cash, its post-acquisition profits will be lower than if the

---

[6]Firms using the LIFO inventory valuation method expense the written-up inventory as inventory layers are depleted, making it difficult to determine when to adjust earnings for the effect of the write-up. We therefore do not make any adjustments for these firms. This lack of adjustment will not lead to a serious downward bias in our earnings measure, however, since LIFO inventory liquidations are relatively infrequent.

same transaction is financed by stock, because income is computed after deducting interest expenses (the cost of debt), but before allowing for any cost of equity. Since the differences in earnings reflect the financing choice and not differences in economic performance, it is misleading to compare reported accounting earnings, which are computed after interest income and expense, for firms that use different methods of merger financing. We use operating cash flows before interest expense and income from short-term investments deflated by the market value of assets (net of short-term investments) to measure performance. This cash flow return is unaffected by the choice of financing.

2.3. Performance benchmark

We aggregate performance data of the target and bidding firms before the merger to obtain the pro forma premerger performance of the combined firms. Comparing the postmerger performance with this premerger benchmark provides a measure of the change in performance. But some of the difference between premerger and postmerger performance could be also due to economywide and industry factors, or to a continuation of firm-specific performance before the merger. Hence, we use abnormal industry-adjusted performance of the target and bidding firms as our primary benchmark to evaluate postmerger performance.

Abnormal industry-adjusted performance is measured as the intercept of a cross-sectional regression of postmerger industry-adjusted cash flow returns on the corresponding premerger returns. For each year and firm, industry-adjusted performance measures are calculated by subtracting the industry median from the sample firm value. The data for sample firms are excluded when calculating the industry median. *Value Line* industry definitions immediately before the merger are used for the target and acquirer in both the premerger and the postmerger analysis. Industry data are collected from *Compustat Industrial and Research* files.

2.4. Comparison with prior research

Earlier studies of postmerger performance have a number of methodological problems, making their findings difficult to interpret. Ravenscraft and Scherer (1987) examine the performance in 1974 to 1977 for firms acquired between 1950 and 1977. Since the postmerger years examined are not aligned with the merger, it is hard to know what to make of the performance comparisons.

Ravenscraft and Scherer focus exclusively on acquired firms' lines of business. It is not obvious why gains from mergers would be reflected only in the acquired segments; synergies are just as likely to improve the performance of the other lines of business of the acquiring firms. The authors also use FTC line-of-business data, which have several potential problems. Definitions of business segments may change systematically after mergers if acquirers restructure their operations. Results of tests using segment data reported to the FTC are also likely to be difficult to interpret, since reporting firms have incentives to use accounting discretion to mask superior performance, thereby reducing the likelihood of antitrust suits by the FTC [see Watts and Zimmerman (1986)].

Herman and Lowenstein (1988) examine postmerger performance using a sample of hostile acquisitions between 1975 and 1983. Complete postmerger data are unavailable for transactions after 1979, however, which limits the analysis to a small number of postmerger years for many sample firms. Further, the return on equity measure, which is used to judge postmerger performance, does not control for differences in pooling and purchase accounting, methods of merger financing, or the effect of common industry shocks. These limitations make it difficult to interpret the study's findings.

3. Cash flow return performance

3.1. Operating cash flow returns

As described in section 2, we aggregate pretax operating cash flows for the target and acquiring firms to determine pro forma cash flows for the combined firms in each of the five years before the merger (years -5 to -1). Postmerger operating cash flows are the actual values reported by the merged firm in years 1 to 5. We deflate the operating cash flows by the market value of assets. Operating cash flow returns are the ratio of operating cash flows during a given year to the market value of assets at the beginning of that year. The market value of assets is recomputed at the beginning of each year to control for changes in the size of the firm over time. For premerger years the market value of assets is the sum of the values for the target and acquiring firms. The market value of assets of the combined firm is used in the postmerger years.

We exclude the change in equity values of the target and acquiring firms at the merger announcement from the asset base in the postmerger years. For the target the change in equity value is measured from five days before the first offer is announced (not necessarily by the ultimate acquirer) to the date the target is delisted from trading on public exchanges. For the acquirer the change in equity value is measured from five days before its first offer is announced to the date the target is delisted from trading on public exchanges. In an efficient stock market these revaluations represent the capitalized value of any expected postmerger performance improvements. If merger announcement equity revaluations are included in the asset base, measured cash flow returns will not show any abnormal increase, even though the merger results in an increase in operating cash flows.

For example, consider an acquiring firm (company A) and a target (company T) with annual operating cash flows of $20 and $10 forever. Both firms have the same cost of capital (10%), implying that their market values are $200 and $100. Therefore, a portfolio comprising of A and T has a market value of $300 and cash flows of $30, producing an annual return of 10%. Suppose that when A acquires T combined cash flows increase to $35 per year. An efficient market capitalizes this $5 improvement at $50. If postmerger cash flow returns are computed as the ratio of postmerger cash flows ($35) and postmerger assets including the premium ($350), measured performance will be identical to the premerger operating return for the portfolio of A and T (10%). There is no improvement in the measured cash flow return even though cash flows per year have increased by $5. Our measure of performance is computed as the ratio of postmerger cash flows ($35) and postmerger assets excluding the asset revaluation ($350 − $50). This return measure (11.7%) correctly reflects the improvement in operating performance after the merger.

We also adjust the merging firms' performance for the impact of contemporaneous unrelated events by measuring industry cash flow returns during the same ten-year period. We use *Value Line* industry definitions, and exclude the target and acquiring firms' returns from the industry computations. Before the merger, industry values for the sample firms are constructed by weighting median performance measures for the target and acquiring firms' industries by the relative asset sizes of the two firms at the beginning of each year. In all of the postmerger years target and acquirer industry cash flow returns are weighted by the relative asset sizes of the two firms one year before the merger.

We focus our analysis on years −5 to −1 and 1 to 5. Year 0, the year of the merger, is excluded from the analysis for two reasons. First, many of the acquiring firms use the purchase accounting method, implying that in the year of the merger the two firms are consolidated for financial reporting purposes only from the date of the merger. Results for this year are therefore not comparable across firms or for industry comparisons. Second, year 0 figures are affected by one-time merger costs incurred during that year, making it difficult to compare them with results for other years.

3.1.1. Changes in cash flows and assets

Table 1 reports the changes in cash flows and assets in years 1 to 5 relative to the year before the merger. The merged firms have a median increase in cash flows of 14% in year 1, 17% in year 2, 16% in years 3 and 4, and 9% in year 5. This cash flow growth does not indicate that the merged firms

Table 1

Postmerger firm and industry growth in operating cash flows and market value of assets for 50 combined target and acquirer firms in mergers completed in the period 1979 to mid-1984.[a]

Growth period in relation to merger	Firm cash flow growth rate	Firm asset growth rate	Industry cash flow growth rate	Industry asset growth rate
Year −1 to 1	14%	15%	10%	20%
Year −1 to 2	17	20	11	33
Year −1 to 3	16	28	14	40
Year −1 to 4	16	23	22	43
Year −i to 5	9	18	24	56

[a]Operating cash flows are sales less cost of goods sold, less selling and administrative expenses, plus depreciation. The market value of assets, measured at the beginning of the year, is the market value of equity plus the book values of preferred stock and net debt. Year −1 cash flow and asset values for the combined firm are weighted averages of target and acquirer values, with the weights being the relative asset values of the two firms. Postmerger values use data for the merged firms. Industry-adjusted cash flow and asset growth rates are computed for each firm and year as the difference between the sample-firm growth rate in that year and growth rates for aggregated cash flows and assets of other firms in the same industry (as defined by *Value Line* in year −1). Target and acquirer industry growth rates are weighted by the relative asset values of the acquirer and target firms in year −1.
[b]Significantly different from zero at the 1% level, using a two-tailed test.
[c]Significantly different from zero at the 5% level, using a two-tailed test.

performed better in the postmerger period, however, because assets also increased during this period. Asset values increase by 15% in year 1, 20% in year 2, 28% in year 3, 23% in year 4, and 18% in year 5. Also, the sample firms' industries experience growth in cash flows and assets in the postmerger period. The cash flow return measures we use to gauge performance adjust for changes in the size of the sample firms and their corresponding industries that are evident in table 1.

3.1.2. Raw cash flow returns

Panel A of table 2 reports median pretax unadjusted operating cash flow returns for the merged firms (column 2) in years −5 to −1 and 1 to 5. The median pretax operating returns range from 24.5% to 26.8% in the five years before the merger, with a median annual value of 25.3%.[7] After the merger, the median pretax operating returns are lower, ranging from 18.4% to 22.9% with a median annual value of 20.5% for the whole period. As indicated in table 1, this decline arises because cash flows grow more slowly than assets in

---

[7]To calculate the sample median pretax operating cash flow return for years −5 to −1, we first compute the median return in these years for each sample firm. The reported sample median is the median of these values. Sample median returns in the postmerger period are calculated the same way.

the postmerger period. These changes cannot be attributed to the merger, however, if there is a contemporaneous downward trend in industry cash flow returns. Industry-adjusted returns, which are differences between values for the merged firms and their weighted-average industry median estimates, correct for this problem.

3.1.3. Industry-adjusted cash flow returns

Columns 3 and 4 in panel A, table 2 show median industry-adjusted cash flow returns and the percentage of sample firms with positive industry-adjusted returns. Merged firms have higher operating cash flow returns on assets than their industries' in the postmerger period. Median industry-adjusted operating returns for the merged firms are 3.0% in year 1, 5.3% in year 2, 3.2% in year 3, and 3.0% in year 4, all significantly different from zero.[8] Year 5 also shows better performance than the industry, but is not statistically significant. The percentage of positive industry-adjusted returns is 67% in year 1, 79% in year 2, 70% in year 3, and 68% in year 4, all well above the value expected by chance alone (50%). Overall, the annual median return for the sample firms in the five postmerger years is 2.8%, about 16% larger than their industries' returns.[9]

The benchmark for the significant postmerger industry-adjusted returns depends on the relation between industry-adjusted returns before and after the merger. If there is no relation between pre- and postmerger industry-adjusted returns, the appropriate benchmark for the postmerger industry-adjusted returns is zero. Alternatively, the appropriate benchmark is the premerger industry-adjusted return if firms that perform above or below their industries before the merger are likely to realize the same performance after the merger.

For our sample, there is no evidence of superior industry-adjusted pretax operating cash flow returns in the premerger period. Median returns are not significantly different from zero in four of the five years. The percentage of positive industry-adjusted returns is not significantly different from the value expected by chance in four of the five years before the merger. The overall median annual return in the premerger period is only 0.3%. which is statistically insignificant. This suggests that, on average, the postmerger performance is not due to a continuation of superior premerger industry performance. In the next section we use a cross-sectional regression approach to compare performance before and after the merger.

[8]Throughout the paper we use a two-tailed test and a 10% or lower cutoff significance level. This is equivalent to a 5% cutoff one-tailed test for the many cases where the hypotheses examined are directional.

[9]We calculate the percentage increase relative to the industry as $2.8/(20.5 - 2.8)$.

Table 2

Median operating cash flow return on actual market value of assets for 50 combined target and acquirer firms in years surrounding mergers completed in the period 1979 to mid-1984.[a]

Panel A: Pre- and postmerger operating cash flow returns

Year relative to merger	Firm median	Industry-adjusted		Number of observations
		Median	% positive	
−5	24.5%	0.4%	50%	48
−4	26.2	0.1	51	49
−3	26.8	2.1[d]	63[c]	49
−2	26.4	0.0	49	49
−1	25.4	1.2	54	46
Median annual performance for years −5 to −1	25.3%	0.3%	52%	50
1	21.5%	3.0%[b]	67%[c]	48
2	22.9	5.3[b]	79[b]	47
3	20.6	3.2[c]	70[b]	46
4	18.4	3.0[d]	68[b]	44
5	18.5	2.5	60	40
Median annual performance for years 1 to 5	20.5%	2.8%[b]	73%[b]	48

Panel B: Abnormal industry-adjusted postmerger operating cash flow returns (t-values in parentheses)

$$IACR_{post,i} = 2.8\% + 0.37\ IACR_{pre,i}, \quad R^2 = 0.10, \quad F\text{-statistic} = 5.3^c \quad N = 47$$
$$\quad\quad\quad\quad (2.4)^c \quad\ (2.3)^c$$

[a]Operating cash flow return on assets is sales less cost of goods sold, less selling and administrative expenses, plus depreciation, divided by the market value of assets at the beginning of the year. Change in equity values of the target and acquiring firms at the merger announcement are excluded from the market values of assets in the postmerger years. Industry-adjusted cash flow returns are computed for each firm and year as the difference between the sample firm value in that year and median values for other firms in the same industry (as defined by *Value Line* in year −1). Premerger returns for the combined firm are weighted averages of target and acquirer returns, with the weights being the relative asset values of the two firms. Postmerger returns use data for the merged firms. Premerger industry returns are weighted averages of target and acquirer industry median returns, with the weights being the relative asset values of the acquirer and target firms each year. In the postmerger period the weights used to compute industry returns are the relative asset values of the acquirer and target firms in year −1. $IACR_{post,i}$ and $IACR_{pre,i}$ are the median annual industry-adjusted operating cash flow returns in the post- and premerger periods for firm i.
[b]Significantly different from zero at the 1% level, using a two-tailed test.
[c]Significantly different from zero at the 5% level, using a two-tailed test.
[d]Significantly different from zero at the 10% level, using a two-tailed test.

3.1.4. Abnormal industry-adjusted cash flows returns

Our measure of abnormal industry-adjusted returns extends the industry-adjusted return measure to incorporate the relation between pre- and post-merger industry-adjusted returns. Abnormal industry-adjusted cash flow returns are estimated using the following cross-sectional regression:

$$IACR_{post,i} = \alpha + \beta\, IACR_{pre,i} + \varepsilon_i, \tag{1}$$

where $IACR_{post,i}$ is the median annual industry-adjusted cash flow return for company i from the postmerger years and $IACR_{pre,i}$ is the premerger median for the same company. Our measure of the abnormal industry-adjusted return is the intercept α from (1). The slope coefficient β captures any correlation in cash flow returns between the pre- and postmerger years so that $\beta\, IACR_{pre,i}$ measures the effect of the premerger performance on postmerger returns. The intercept α is therefore independent of premerger returns.

As shown in panel B of table 2, for our sample, the estimate of β is 0.37, indicating that industry-adjusted cash flow returns tend to persist over time. The estimate of α shows that there is a 2.8% per-year increase in postmerger cash flow returns after premerger performance is controlled for. This evidence indicates that there is a significant improvement in the merged firms' cash flow returns in the post-merger period.[10]

3.2. Sensitivity analysis

3.2.1. Use of Value Line industry definitions

The industry-adjusted results are strikingly different from the operating cash flow returns before industry adjustment. The industry-adjusted results show a significant *increase* in postmerger performance and the unadjusted returns show a *decrease*. We think that industry-adjusted returns are a more reliable measure of performance, since they control for industry events unrelated to the merger. But, they are also sensitive to the definitions of industries used in the analysis. To test whether the industry-adjusted results are sensitive to the particular industry definitions employed by *Value Line*, we use a market performance benchmark. We estimate the market index each year as the median operating cash flow return for all firms on the *Compustat Industrial and Research* tapes. Median market-adjusted cash flow returns for the sample firms are 1.3% (statistically insignificant) in the

---

[10]These results remain unchanged when we reestimate the model excluding outlier observations identified using Belsley, Kuh, and Welsch (1980) influence diagnostics. We also conduct specification tests for regression equation (1) to assess whether the residuals are homoskedastic [see White (1980)] and normally distributed. We cannot reject the hypotheses that the residuals are homoskedastic and normally distributed at the 5% level.

premerger period and 4.3% (statistically significant) in the postmerger years, confirming improvements in industry-adjusted performance. A reestimation of (1) using market-adjusted cash flow returns indicates that, on average, returns increase by 5.4% per year in the postmerger period after premerger performance is controlled for.

3.2.2. Change in market value of assets

Our measure of industry-adjusted returns can increase in the postmerger period if investors lower their assessment of merged firms' prospects in relation to their industries. Since we use the market value of equity in our computation of asset values. a postmerger decline in equity value will reduce our measure of asset values. If cash flows are held constant, such a decline in asset values would lead to an increase in cash flow returns, making the postmerger improvements documented in the previous section spurious. To examine this possibility, we compute the difference between annual stock returns for the sample firms and their industries in years surrounding the merger.

Summary statistics on equity returns in years surrounding the merger are reported in table 3. We compute both raw equity returns and industry-adjusted returns for years -5 to -1 and 1 to 5 using *Compustat* data. These same data are used to estimate the market value of assets to compute cash flow returns. Because daily data are not available on *Compustat*, we use *CRSP* returns to compute raw and industry-adjusted equity returns for three subperiods in year 0: the premerger period, the period from the merger announcement to completion, and the postmerger period.

Consistent with the evidence reported in the literature, the median returns in the preannouncement and announcement periods in year 0 are -3.0% and 7.7%, which are statistically significant. There is no evidence that the market value of equity for the sample firms declines in comparison with their industries in the postmerger period. Median industry-adjusted returns are insignificant in the postmerger period in years 0 to 4, and are significantly positive in year 5. Mean industry-adjusted returns, which are not reported here, are comparable to the sample medians. Therefore, the postmerger cash flow return improvements do not appear to be driven by a postmerger decline in equity value, which is used in the denominator of our return measure.

3.2.3. Use of market value of assets to compute returns

We also evaluate the sensitivity of the results to the use of the market value of equity in computing asset values by replicating the cash flow returns using an alternative asset measure. Market equity values incorporate investor's revaluations of firms' growth opportunities, as well as existing assets. We construct an alternative measure of equity values that excludes the effect of revisions in growth opportunities after the merger announcement.

Table 3

Median industry-adjusted and raw stock returns for combined target and acquirer companies in the five years before the merger, and for the merged firm for five years after the merger, for mergers completed in the period 1979 to mid-1984.[a]

Year relative to merger		Industry-adjusted returns	Raw returns	Number of observations
−5		2.8%	17.9%	48
−4		5.3[c]	22.6	49
−3		0.9	19.2	49
−2		−0.1	10.9	49
−1		−2.6	10.9	45
	Premerger	−3.0[c]	4.9	42
Year 0	Merger	7.7[b]	12.0	50
	Postmerger	−3.8	4.7	46
1		0.1	10.0	48
2		0.8	18.5	48
3		0.8	10.0	46
4		−2.5	9.8	41
5		7.1[c]	14.4	40

[a]Returns in years −5 to −1 and 1 to 5 are taken from *Compustat*, consistent with the equity values reported in table 1. Returns in year 0 are from *CRSP*. For target firms, the merger announcement period is the date from the first announcement of a takeover offer for the target to the date a merger is completed. For acquirers, the merger announcement period is the date from the first announcement of a takeover offer by the acquirer to the date a merger is completed. Premerger returns for the combined firm are weighted averages of target and acquirer values, with the weights being the relative equity values of the two firms. Postmerger performance measures use data for the merged firms. Industry-adjusted returns are computed for each firm and year as the difference between the sample-firm value in that year and median values for other firms in the same industry (as defined by *Value Line* in year −1). Premerger industry returns are weighted averages of target and acquirer industry median returns, with the weights being the relative equity values of the acquirer and target firms each year. In the postmerger period the weights used to compute industry returns are the relative equity values of the acquirer and target firms in year −1.
[b]Significantly different from zero at the 1% level, using a two-tailed test.
[c]Significantly different from zero at the 10% level, using a two-tailed test.

To compute the value of equity for the combined firm at the beginning of year 1, we start with the total market equity value for the target and acquirer at the beginning of year −1. We then add year −1 and year 0 values of the merged firm's after tax cash from operations (net of interest expense, nonoperating income, and cash taxes) and cash from new share issues, and subtract cash dividends to common and preferred stockholders and cash used to acquire treasury stock.[11] In each of years 2 through 5, we repeat this procedure using the estimated equity at the beginning of the prior year, and

[11]For firms that use purchase accounting, new debt or equity issued at the merger includes the merger premium for the target, whereas for firms that use the pooling method it does not. To make the measure comparable across firms, we deduct the target premium for the purchase accounting firms in computing the quasi-market values of equity.

adding changes in equity cash flows for the merged firm during the prior year. The resulting quasi-market equity measure captures changes in equity available for reinvestment, but does not reflect revaluations of growth opportunities after the merger announcement.

To provide a benchmark for evaluating the postmerger returns, we also compute comparable equity values at the beginning of years -5 to -1. For year -1 we use the actual market value of assets at the beginning of the year. To compute the pro forma equity value for the combined firm at the beginning of year -2, we start with the total market value of equity for the target and acquirer at the beginning of year -1. We then subtract year -2 values of the target's and acquirer's after-tax cash from operations (net of interest expense, nonoperating income, and cash taxes) and cash from new share issues, and add cash dividends to common and preferred stockholders and cash used to acquire treasury stock. This procedure is repeated for years -3 to -5.

We estimate the quasi-market value of assets in each of the years -5 to $+5$ as the sum of the quasi-market value of equity estimated as above and the book value of net debt. We then compute the ratio of operating cash flow to the estimated quasi-market value of assets in each year to provide an alternative return measure.

The main advantage of the cash flow return on the quasi-market value of assets is that it excludes postmerger equity market revaluations from the asset base. The measure preserves some important features of the original measure: it is unaffected by the method of merger financing or asset write-ups, and reflects funds invested in the firm in each year. But, it is not without limitations. The measure does not take into account reductions in asset values from economic depreciation. This can lead to a significant overstatement of asset values in the postmerger period, leading in turn to an understatement of measured postmerger performance. Also, for firms that use purchase accounting, cash from operations for the target in year 0 is reflected in the acquirers' records only from the date the merger is consummated. This leads to a small understatement of the postmerger asset values. Both these limitations are avoided by the market value of assets used in our original cash flow return measure.

Cash flow returns computed using the alternative measure of asset values are reported in table 4. The results are generally consistent with the findings reported in table 2. The merged firms continue to show higher cash flow returns on assets than their industries in the postmerger period. Median industry-adjusted pretax operating returns for the merged firms are 2.8% in year 1, 2.6% in year 2, and 2.1% in year 3, all significantly different from zero. The percentage of industry-adjusted returns that are positive is 67% in year 1, 62% in year 2, and 65% in year 3, all above the value expected by chance alone (50%). Overall, the annual median pretax return in the five postmerger years is 3.2%.

P. Healy et al., Performance improvements after mergers   151

Table 4

Median operating cash flow return on quasi-market value of assets for 50 combined target and acquirer firms in years surrounding mergers completed in the period 1979 to mid-1984.[a]

Year relative to merger	Firm median	Industry-adjusted		Number of observations
		Median	% positive	
−5	31.7%	−2.5%	47%	43
−4	31.1	0.3	51	45
−3	32.5	2.7	59	46
−2	26.8	2.0	54	46
−1	25.4	1.2	54	46
Median annual performance for years −5 to −1	31.3%	2.1%	56%	49
1	23.9%	3.8%[b]	67%[c]	48
2	20.3	3.0[c]	62[c]	47
3	18.7	2.1[d]	65[c]	46
4	15.6	0.8	56	43
5	18.2	0.5	53	39
Median annual performance for years 1 to 5	17.9%	3.2%[c]	66%[c]	48

Panel A: Pre- and postmerger operating cash flow returns

Panel B: Abnormal industry-adjusted postmerger operating cash flow returns
(t-values in parentheses)

$$IACR_{post,i} = 2.7\% + 0.18 \ IACR_{pre,i}, \qquad R^2 = 0.05, \quad F\text{-statistic} = 2.3, \quad N = 46$$
$$(2.0)^c \qquad (1.5)$$

[a] Pretax operating cash flow return on assets is sales less cost of goods sold, less selling and administrative expenses, plus depreciation, divided by quasi-market value of assets at the beginning of the year. The computation of quasi-market value of assets begins with market values in year −1 and adjusts for changes in capital available for reinvestment in other years. Premerger returns for the combined firm are weighted averages of target and acquirer values, with the weights being the relative asset values of the two firms. Postmerger returns are for the merged firm. Industry-adjusted cash flow returns are computed for each firm and year as the difference between the sample-firm value in that year and median values for other firms in the same industry (as defined by *Value Line* in year −1). Premerger industry returns are weighted averages of target and acquirer industry median returns, with the weights being the relative asset values of the acquirer and target firms each year. In the postmerger period the weights used to compute industry returns are the relative asset values of the acquirer and target firms in year −1. $IACR_{post,i}$ and $IACR_{pre,i}$ are the median annual industry-adjusted pretax operating cash flow returns in the post- and premerger periods for firm i.
[b] Significantly different from zero at the 1% level, using a two-tailed test.
[c] Significantly different from zero at the 5% level, using a two-tailed test.
[d] Significantly different from zero at the 10% level, using a two-tailed test.

In contrast to the postmerger performance, there is no strong evidence of superior industry-adjusted pretax operating cash flow returns in the premerger period. Median returns are not significantly different from zero in each of the five years. Also, the percentage of positive industry-adjusted returns is not significantly different from the value expected by chance in any of the five years before the merger. The overall median annual industry-adjusted return in the premerger period is 2.1%, which is statistically insignificant.

To examine whether there are abnormal postmerger industry-adjusted cash flow returns, we again estimate (1) using return on assets based on quasi-market equity values. The slope coefficient, which captures any persistence of performance between the pre- and postmerger years, is 0.18 and insignificant. The intercept, which captures postmerger performance controlling for premerger returns, is 2.7% and is statistically reliable. These results remain unchanged when we reestimate the model excluding outliers identified using Belsley, Kuh, and Welsch (1980) influence diagnostics.[12]

In summary, the evidence presented in this section indicates that the postmerger performance improvements are not driven by the use of market equity values in computing assets.

3.3. Components of industry-adjusted cash flow returns

The improvements in cash flow returns in the postmerger period can arise from a variety of sources. These include improvements in operating margins, greater asset productivity, or lower labor costs. Alternatively, they may be achieved by focusing on short-term performance improvements at the expense of the long-term viability of the firm. In this section we provide evidence on which of these sources contribute to the sample firms' postmerger cash flow return increases. The specific variables analyzed are italicized in the text and defined in table 5. The results are reported in table 6.

3.3.1. Operating performance changes

The operating cash flow return on assets can be decomposed into *cash flow margin on sales* and *asset turnover*. Cash flow margin on sales measures the pretax operating cash flows generated per sales dollar. Asset turnover measures the sales dollars generated from each dollar of investment in assets. The variables are defined so that their product equals the operating cash flow return on assets.

---

[12] We again conduct specification tests for (1) to assess whether the residuals are homoskedastic [see White (1980)] and normally distributed. We cannot reject the hypotheses that the residuals are homoskedastic and normally distributed at the 5% level.

Table 5

Definitions of variables used to analyze actual performance of 50 targets and 50 acquirers in years surrounding mergers.

Variable	Definition
(A) *Operating characteristics*	
Cash flow margin on sales	Earnings before depreciation, interest, and taxes as a percentage of sales
Asset turnover	Sales divided by market value of assets at the beginning of the year (the market value of common equity plus the book values of debt and preferred stock)
Employee growth rate	Change in number of employees as a percentage of number of employees in the previous year
Pension expense/employee	Pension expense per employee
(B) *Investment characteristics*	
Capital expenditure rate	Capital expenditures as a percentage of the market value of assets at the beginning of the year
Asset sale rate – Cash value	Cash receipts from asset sales as a percentage of the market value of assets at the beginning of the year
Asset sale rate – Book value	Book value of asset sales as a percentage of the market value of assets at the beginning of the year
R & D rate	Research and development expenditures as a percentage of the market value of assets at the beginning of the year

The results in table 6 suggest that the increase in industry-adjusted operating returns is attributable to an increase in asset turnover, rather than an increase in operating margins. In years −5 to −1 the merged firms have industry-adjusted median asset turnover of −0.2, implying that they generated 20 cents *less* in sales than their competitors for each dollar of assets. In years 1 to 5 they close this gap as they achieve asset turnovers comparable to their industries'. The intercept in the cross-sectional regression of postmerger industry-adjusted asset turnover on premerger turnover is 0.2 and is statistically significant. The evidence thus indicates that there is a significant improvement in sample firms' asset turnover in the postmerger period.

The merged firms also have higher pretax operating margins on sales than their industries in the postmerger years. But these cannot be attributed to the merger itself, because they are also higher in the premerger period. Before the merger, the higher operating margins are primarily due to higher industry-adjusted margins for acquirers. Targets do not show higher operating

Table 6

Firm and industry-adjusted operating performance and investment policy measures for 50 combined target and acquirer firms in years surrounding mergers completed in the period 1979 to mid-1984.[a]

Variable	Firm medians		Industry-adjusted medians		Abnormal industry-adjusted postmerger performance[b]	Number of observations
	Premerger	Postmerger	Premerger	Postmerger		
Operating characteristics						
Cash flow margin on sales	14.3%	13.3%	1.4%[c]	1.1%[d]	0.2%	46
Asset turnover	1.9x	1.9x	-0.2x	0.0x	0.2x[c]	48
Employee growth rate	3.0%	-3.0%	0.4%	-2.5%[d]	-2.3%[d]	44
Pension expense per employee	$796.3	$840.7	$101.1[c]	-$60.4	-$119.5	40
Investment characteristics						
Capital expenditure rate	14.4%	10.6%	1.0%	-0.1%	0.5%	47
Asset sale rate – Cash value	0.6	0.6	0.0	0.1	0.3	45
Asset sale rate – Book value	0.9	1.3	0.1[d]	0.6[c]	0.9[d]	42
R&D rate	2.0	2.1	0.1	0.0	0.1	33

[a] Operating performance and investment policy measures are defined in table 5. Industry-adjusted values of these variables are computed for each firm and year as the difference between the firm value in that year and the median value for other firms in the same industry (as defined by *Value Line* in year −1). Before the merger, performance measures for the merged firm are weighted averages of target and acquirer values, with the weights being the relative sizes of the two firms. Performance measures for the merged firm's industry in the premerger period are weighted averages of target industry and acquirer industry medians, with the weights being the relative sizes of the two test firms. Medians in the premerger (postmerger) period are the median values of the variables in years −5 to −1 (1 to 5).

[b] Postmerger industry-adjusted performance measures controlling for premerger performance are the estimated intercepts from regressing postmerger industry-adjusted performance on premerger values.

[c] Significantly different from zero at the 1% level, using a two-tailed test.
[d] Significantly different from zero at the 5% level, using a two-tailed test.
[e] Significantly different from zero at the 10% level, using a two-tailed test.

margins than their industries in these years. When we control for premerger operating margins, there is no evidence of a significant change in margins after the merger. Rather, merged firms seem to use their assets more productively.

Mergers also give the acquirer an opportunity to renegotiate explicit and implicit labor contracts to lower labor costs and achieve a more efficient mix of capital and labor [see Shleifer and Summers (1988)]. Because we are unable to obtain sufficient data on wages directly, we examine *employee growth rates* and *pension expense per employee* to analyze changes in labor costs in years surrounding the mergers.

The median number of employees declines in each of the postmerger years. Overall, the industry-adjusted employee growth rate is negative after we control for the growth rate in the premerger period. There is also evidence of a decline in pension expense per employee after the merger. Before the merger the sample firms have a significantly higher pension expense per employee than their industries. After the merger the pension expense of the merged firms is reduced to the industry level. There are two ways to view these findings. One interpretation is that mergers are followed by improvements in operating efficiency achieved through reduced labor costs. Alternatively, mergers lead to a wealth redistribution between employees and stockholders through renegotiations of explicit and implicit employment contracts. Whatever the explanation, the labor cost reductions in the postmerger period do not appear to be large, since they do not lead to significant changes in postmerger operating margins.[13]

3.3.2. Investment policy changes

Since our analysis is limited to five years after the merger, we cannot provide direct evidence on cash flows beyond this period. To assess whether the merged firms focus on short-term performance improvements at the expense of long-term investments, we examine their *capital outlays* and *research and development* (R&D) expense. These expenditure patterns are reported in table 6. The median capital expenditures as a percentage of assets is 14.4% in the premerger period and 10.6% in the postmerger years. The median R&D expense is 2% of assets in years −5 to −1 and 2.1% in years 1 to 5. The capital expenditures and R&D of the sample firms are not significantly different from those of their industry counterparts in either the pre- or the postmerger period.

---

[13]Pontiff, Shleifer, and Weisbach (1990) report that 11% of takeovers involve pension fund reversions, accounting for 10–13% of takeover premiums in these transactions. Thus for their sample as a whole pension fund reversions account for an average 1–2% of the takeover premium. Similarly, Rosett (1990) reports that labor union wealth changes in the six years following takeovers account for 1–2% of the premiums. Our conclusions are consistent with the results of both these studies.

Asset sales also reflect changes in merged firms' investment policies. It is possible that postmerger improvements in asset turnover arise from the sale of assets with low turnover. We therefore examine cash proceeds from asset sales and their book values in the pre- and postmerger years. Statistics on asset sales as a percentage of the market value of assets are reported in table 6. The median cash proceeds from asset sales for the merged firms is 0.6% of assets in both the pre- and postmerger periods, not significantly different from their industry level in either period. The book values of asset disposals before and after the merger are 0.9% and 1.3% of assets. Both of these rates are significantly higher than the rates for their industry counterparts. Further, controlling for the level of premerger book values of asset sales, there is an increase in asset sales in the postmerger period.

There are two potential explanations for the increase in book value of asset sales, but not in cash proceeds from disposals. First, the merged firms sell poorly performing assets after the merger. This could in part explain the improved asset productivity and the decline in employee growth rates.[14] Second, the assets sold are written up at the merger to a value higher than their true market value. Managers have considerable discretion in allocating merger premiums to assets and goodwill, and have incentives to write up assets as high as possible to increase depreciation tax shields. If these assets are subsequently sold, cash proceeds from the sale are likely to be below the written-up book values. Whatever the explanation, the effect of asset sales on postmerger performance is unlikely to be significant, because disposals in all years are very small in relation to capital expenditures or the market value of total assets. This is confirmed by the insignificant correlation between asset sales and postmerger cash flow return improvements.[15]

In summary, we find that improvements in cash flow operating returns in the five years following mergers arise from increased asset productivity. There is no evidence of decreased capital expenditures or R&D following mergers, indicating that the cash flow improvements do not come from policies that impede the long-term viability of the merged firms.

4. Relation between cash flow and stock price performance

Our postmerger data on cash flow performance are consistent with the hypothesis that the stock market revaluation of merging firms at merger announcements reflects expected future improvements in operations. A more powerful test of this hypothesis is to correlate the merger-related stock

[14] Kaplan and Weisbach (1992) find that acquirers of firms in unrelated businesses are more likely to later divest their targets than acquirers of related businesses. They find no evidence, however, that divested businesses are systematically poor performers.

[15] We reestimate (1) after including asset sales in the pre- and postmerger periods. The coefficients on both these variables are insignificant, and the intercept remains positive and significant.

Table 7

Unexpected equity and asset returns at merger announcements for target, acquirer, and combined firms, and tests of the relation between unexpected asset returns and ex post cash flow returns for 50 target and acquiring firms merging in the period 1979 to mid-1984.[a]

Panel A: Distribution of unexpected equity returns at merger announcement

	Target	Acquirer	Combined
Mean	45.6%[b]	−2.2%	9.1%[b]
First quartile	21.2%	−16.6%	−2.9%
Median	41.8%[b]	−3.6%	6.6%[b]
Third quartile	64.1%	3.4%	16.7%

Panel B: Distribution of unexpected asset returns at merger announcement

	Target	Acquirer	Combined
Mean	40.6%[b]	0.6%	8.8%[b]
First quartile	19.0%	−9.3%	−2.3%
Median	32.5%[b]	−2.2%	5.2%[b]
Third quartile	55.0%	6.1%	15.1%

Panel C: Relation between median postmerger industry-adjusted cash flow returns and unexpected asset returns at merger announcement (t-values in parentheses)

$$IACR_{post,i} = \underset{(1.6)}{1.9\%} + \underset{(1.7)^c}{0.26\ IACR_{pre,i}} + \underset{(3.4)^b}{0.24\ (\Delta V/V^i)}$$

$$R^2 = 0.30, \quad F\text{-statistic} = 8.5,^b \quad N = 42$$

[a]Unexpected merger announcement equity returns are the sum of market-adjusted changes in equity values for the target and acquirer firms in the merger announcement period as a percentage of the sum of the premerger equity values for the two firms. Unexpected merger announcement asset returns ($\Delta V/V$) are unlevered market-adjusted equity returns. $IACR_{post}$ and $IACR_{pre}$ are median industry-adjusted cash flow returns for each firm in the five years after and the five years before the merger.
[b]Significantly different from zero at the 1% level, using a two-tailed test.
[c]Significantly different from zero at the 10% level, using a two-tailed test.

market performance and the postmerger cash flow performance. If the stock market capitalizes expected improvements, there should be a significant positive correlation between the stock market revaluation of merging firms and the actual postmerger cash flow improvements.

4.1. Stock returns at merger announcements

Market-adjusted stock returns for the target and acquirer at the announcement of the merger are reported in panel A of table 7.[16] Returns for the target are measured from five days before the first offer is announced (not

[16]Risk-adjusted returns, computed using premerger market model estimates, are similar to the market-adjusted returns reported in the paper.

necessarily by the ultimate acquirer) to the date the target is delisted from trading on public exchanges. Returns for the acquirer are measured from five days before its first offer is announced to the date the target is delisted from trading on public exchanges. Much as earlier studies have found, target shareholders earn large positive returns from mergers (mean 45.6% and median 41.8%), and acquiring stockholders earn insignificant returns.

We also compute the aggregate market-adjusted return for the two firms in the merger announcement period. This return is the weighted average of the market-adjusted returns for the target and acquirer, where the weights are the relative market values of equity of the two firms before the merger announcement period. The mean aggregate return, reported in panel A of table 7, is 9.1%, and the median is 6.6%. Both these values are significantly different from zero. These findings are consistent with those of Bradley, Desai, and Kim (1988).

4.2. Asset returns at merger announcements

Our tests examine whether the change in equity values at merger announcements can be explained by cash flow return improvements in the postmerger period. In section 3 we measured postmerger performance using cash flow return on *assets*, whereas the merger announcement returns computed above are returns on *equity*. Therefore, before we correlate merger announcement returns and postmerger cash flow improvements, we compute *asset* returns at merger announcements from equity returns to ensure that the *anticipated* gains from mergers and the measured gains are comparable.

Asset returns at the merger announcement $\Delta V/V$ are weighted averages of returns to equity $\Delta E/E$ and debt $\Delta D/D$:

$$\frac{\Delta V}{V} = \frac{\Delta E}{E}\frac{E}{V} + \frac{\Delta D}{D}\frac{D}{V}. \tag{2}$$

Assuming that the value of debt does not change at takeover announcements, asset returns equal the equity announcement returns multiplied by the equity-to-assets ratio E/V.[17] We use leverage at the beginning of the year of the takeover announcement to compute the equity-to-assets ratio. We use the book value of debt and the market value of equity to measure leverage.

Summary statistics on the estimated asset returns at the announcement of the merger for the target firms, acquiring firms, and combined firms are reported in panel B of table 7. The mean and median asset returns for the

---

[17]A number of studies, including Asquith and Kim (1982), report evidence consistent with this assumption.

targets are 40.6% and 32.5% and for the combined firms 8.8% and 5.2%. The asset returns for the bidding firm are insignificant.

4.3. Relation between announcement returns and postmerger cash flow improvements

The hypothesis that merger-induced abnormal returns reflect the capitalized value of future cash flow improvements implies:

$$\Delta V = \frac{\Delta CF}{\Theta}, \tag{3}$$

where ΔV is the change in the market value of assets at the merger announcement, $1/\Theta$ is the present value operator, and ΔCF is the vector of cash flow improvements. Transposing (3) and dividing both sides by V, to express both sides as returns:

$$\frac{\Delta CF}{V} = \Theta \frac{\Delta V}{V}. \tag{4}$$

We measure $\Delta CF/V$ as abnormal industry-adjusted cash flow returns [(1) in section 3]:

$$\frac{\Delta CF}{V} = \alpha = IACR_{post,i} - \beta \, IACR_{pre,i} - \varepsilon_i, \tag{5}$$

where $IACR_{post,i}$ and $IACR_{pre,i}$ are the median annual industry-adjusted operating cash flow returns in the post- and premerger periods for firm i. We measure asset returns, $\Delta V/V$, as unlevered market-adjusted stock returns for the combined target and acquirer firms at the merger announcement, discussed in section 4.2. Substituting these two measures for variables in (4) and rearranging yields:

$$IACR_{post,i} = \beta \, IACR_{pre,i} + \Theta \frac{\Delta V}{V^i} + \varepsilon_i. \tag{6}$$

Eq. (6) forms the basis for our tests of the relationship between ex post cash flow improvements and the *anticipated* gains represented by merger announcement returns. Since $\Delta V/V$ is the *capitalized* value of future cash flow return improvements and $IACR_{post}$ is the pretax cash flow return improvement *per year*, the coefficient Θ in (6) equals the pretax capitalization rate. For example, if the cash flow return improvements are permanent and the pretax capitalization rate is 20%, the coefficient Θ would be 0.20.

Although (6) does not have a constant, we estimate a regression equation with an intercept and test whether it is zero.

The regression results are shown in panel C of table 7. The estimated model has an R^2 of 30%. The estimated slope coefficient on asset returns at the merger announcement is 0.24 and is statistically reliable, implying that if cash flow return improvements are permanent, the pretax discount rate for the sample firms is 24%. This estimated discount rate is economically plausible, although it exceeds the pretax cost of capital for our sample firms assuming a 10% pretax risk-free rate and an 8% risk premium. Consistent with findings reported earlier, the estimated coefficient on premerger performance is positive and statistically significant. Finally, as predicted by (6), the intercept is insignificant.[18]

As an alternative specification, we estimate a regression equation with merger announcement returns, $\Delta V/V$, as the dependent variable and abnormal industry-adjusted cash flow returns from (1), $\Delta CF/V$. as the independent variable. The estimated coefficient for the abnormal industry-adjusted cash flow returns is 1.01 and is statistically significant with a t-statistic of 3.2. The implied capitalization rate from this specification is 100%. Since this specification, as well as the specification in (6), suffers from potential errors-in-variables problems, the actual rate at which the market capitalizes postmerger cash flow improvements is likely to be between 24% and 100%.

There are two interpretations of the statistically and economically significant relation between our measure of postmerger performance improvements and the market's revaluation of the merged firms' equity at the merger announcement. First, if equity markets are efficient, the findings indicate that our estimates of postmerger performance are reasonable. Alternatively, the findings can be viewed as evidence that the stock price gains at the merger announcement are related to expectations of subsequent cash flow improvements.

5. Discussion

Our finding that there are postmerger cash flow increases advances the debate on mergers from *whether* there are cash flow changes after these transactions to *why* these cash flow improvements occur. The improvements in sample firms' cash flow returns are primarily a result of increased asset

---

[18]Specification tests are conducted for (6) to assess whether the residuals are homoskedastic [see White (1980)] and normally distributed. We cannot reject the hypotheses that the residuals are homoskedastic and normally distributed at the 5% level. We also reestimated the regression excluding observations more than two standard deviations from the mean for each variable. The results are very similar to those reported. Finally, we estimate Spearman rank correlation coefficients between the median annual postmerger industry-adjusted cash flow return and unexpected asset returns at the merger announcement. The correlation is 0.41 and is significant at the 1% level.

productivity. The reported postmerger gains cannot be attributed to tax benefits, since the cash flow returns are pretax. Although there is some evidence that gains come at the expense of labor, reduced labor costs do not significantly increase sample firms' cash flows. Finally, there is no decrease in capital outlays and R&D expenditures after the merger, indicating that merged firms do not reduce their long-term investments.

Our findings raise two interesting questions. First, are the increases in cash flow returns and asset productivity caused by the merger, or would they have occurred without it? Mergers can lead to increased asset productivity if suboptimal policies pursued by the target or the acquirer before the merger are eliminated, or if they provide new opportunities to use existing resources of the merging firms. In contrast, if mergers arise from undervaluation of the target firms by the stock market, cash flow returns will improve whether or not there is a merger. Managers who anticipate the cash flow improvements will pay a premium to acquire the targets.

Our findings also raise another question: what economic factors explain the cross-sectional variation in postmerger cash flow changes? Although cash flow performance improves on average, a quarter of the sample firms have negative postmerger cash flow changes. These firms may have performed poorly because of bad luck. Alternatively, systematic business and managerial reasons may have led to these outcomes.

These questions, which have important managerial and public policy implications, can be answered only through development of structural models of how mergers improve cash flows. We do not attempt to undertake such an ambitious exercise in this paper, but, we do provide some preliminary evidence and suggest directions for future research.

5.1. Business overlap of merging firms and postmerger performance

One popular hypothesis on how mergers improve cash flows is that they provide opportunities for economies of scale and scope, synergy, or product market power. This implies that mergers by firms that have overlapping businesses will show greater cash flow improvements than mergers between firms with no overlap. We examine this proposition by classifying our sample mergers as those with high, medium, and low business overlap between the target and acquiring firms. This classification is made by reading the line of business discussion in the merging firms' annual reports, merger prospectuses, *Value Line* reports, and *Moody's Industrial Manuals*.

The following cases illustrate our classifications. The combination of Best Products and Modern Merchandising, both of which are catalog showroom retailers, is classified as a high overlap transaction. The merger between Holiday Inns and Harrahs is treated as a transaction with medium overlap because Holiday Inns operates a hotel chain and Harrahs operates casinos and associated hotels. Exxon Corp's acquisition of Reliance Electric is an unrelated transaction: Exxon is an oil company and Reliance Electric is a producer of industrial equipment. Classification of the degree of business overlap of each of the sample transactions is reported in the appendix, where we describe our sample mergers in detail.

To evaluate whether postmerger performance improvements differ by the degree of business overlap, we estimate the following regression:

$$IACR_{post,i} = \alpha + \beta \ IACR_{pre,i} + \theta \ MEDIUM_i + \psi \ HIGH_i + \varepsilon_i, \qquad (7)$$

where $IACR_{post,i}$ and $IACR_{pre,i}$ are the median annual industry-adjusted cash flow returns in the post- and premerger periods for firm i, $HIGH$ is a dummy variable that is one if the target and acquirers are in highly overlapping businesses and zero otherwise, and $MEDIUM$ is a dummy variable that is one if there is a medium overlap between the target and acquiring firms' businesses and zero otherwise. The intercept coefficient (α) represents the postmerger abnormal cash flow returns for firms in nonoverlapping businesses, whereas the coefficients θ and ψ show the differential postmerger returns of firms in medium and high overlapping businesses. As in (1), the variable $IACR_{pre}$ is included in the model to control for premerger performance.

The results are reported in panel A of table 8. The estimated coefficient on $IACR_{pre}$ is positive and significant, similar to that reported in earlier regressions. The estimated intercept and coefficients on $MEDIUM$ and $HIGH$ are not significant, indicating that the degree of business overlap has no impact on postmerger performance improvements. These results, however, are sensitive to two extreme observations identified using Belsley, Kuh, and Welsh (1980) outlier diagnostics. We reestimate the model excluding these observations and report the results in panel B of table 8. The intercept and the coefficient of $MEDIUM$ remain insignificant, indicating that there is no performance improvement associated with mergers between firms with little or medium business overlap. Transactions with a high business overlap, however, have 5.1% improvements in postmerger performance. Mergers with a high business overlap, therefore, show significant postmerger improvement, whereas other types of mergers do not.

The two outliers in the above analysis are the LTV–Republic Steel merger and Penn Central's acquisition of G.K. Technologies. LTV and Republic Steel have highly overlapping businesses, yet the combination performed very poorly. In contrast, there is little overlap between the businesses of Penn Central and G.K. Technologies, yet the merger was followed by excellent performance. These two observations are obviously exceptions to the conclusion above, indicating that the relation between the merging firms' businesses is not the sole determinant of postmerger performance.

Table 8

Comparison of postmerger performance for mergers between firms whose industries have high, medium, and low overlap for 50 target and acquiring firms merging in the period 1979 to mid-1984.[a]

Panel A: Full sample
(t-values in parentheses)

$$IACFR_{post,i} = 0.018 + 0.005\ MEDIUM_i + 0.033\ HIGH_i + 0.35\ IACR_{pre,i}$$
$$(0.9)\quad (0.2)\qquad\qquad (1.3)\qquad\qquad (2.2)^c$$

$$R^2 = 0.13,\quad F\text{-statistic} = 2.2,^d\quad N = 47$$

Panel B: Sample excluding outliers[b]
(t-values in parentheses)

$$IACFR_{post,i} = 0.006 + 0.016\ MEDIUM_i + 0.051\ HIGH_i + 0.33\ IACR_{pre,i}$$
$$(0.3)\quad (0.6)\qquad\qquad (1.8)^d\qquad\qquad (2.1)^c$$

$$R^2 = 0.17\quad F\text{-statistic} = 2.9^c\quad N = 45$$

---

[a] $IACR_{post}$ and $IACR_{pre}$ are median industry-adjusted cash flow returns for each firm in the five years after and the five years before the merger. *MEDIUM* and *HIGH* are dummy variables that take the value one if the merger is between two firms whose product markets have medium and high overlap.

[b] This sample excludes two observations identified as influential outliers using Belsey, Kuh, and Welsch (1980) diagnostics. These transactions are the LTV–Republic Steel and the Penn Central–GK Technologies mergers.

[c] Significantly different from zero at the 5% level, using a two-tailed test.

[d] Significantly different from zero at the 10% level, using a two-tailed test.

5.2. Transaction characteristics of merging firms and postmerger performance

Transaction characteristics, such as the form of financing, whether the transaction is hostile or friendly, and the size of the target firm, are frequently cited as important to the ultimate success of mergers. We use postmerger cash flow returns for different types of transactions to examine each of the hypotheses associated with these characteristics. We estimate a cross-sectional regression similar to (7) with dummy variables representing the form of financing and find no significant postmerger performance differences between transactions financed with equity, cash, or a mixture of securities. We also do not find any relation between the merger-related abnormal stock returns for the combined firm and the form of financing.[19]

A similar approach is used to test whether postmerger performance differs for hostile and friendly transactions. Using the information from *Wall Street Journal* articles that discuss the initial offer, we classify transactions as hostile, friendly, white knight, and indeterminate. We do not find any

---

[19] Previous studies examine the relation between stock returns and the form of financing for acquiring and target firms separately. See Huang and Walkling (1987) and Asquith, Bruner, and Mullins (1990).

evidence of postmerger cash flow performance or merger-related abnormal stock return differences among any of these transaction types.

Finally, we examine whether size of the acquisition influences postmerger performance. Two variables are used in this analysis: the log of target assets and the ratio of target assets to acquirer's assets, both one year prior to the acquisition. Neither variable explains cross-sectional variation in postmerger performance.

In summary, while there is some evidence that the degree of business overlap between merging firms influences postmerger performance, there is little evidence that transaction characteristics have a significant impact.[20] We view our analysis on the determinants of postmerger performance as preliminary, however, since our study is designed to examine whether performance improves after a merger.

Given the complexity and heterogeneity of reasons for mergers, we believe that large-sample studies will provide limited new insights into factors that influence the outcomes of mergers. A promising approach is to examine a smaller number of mergers in greater detail. These clinical studies can provide valuable evidence on the mechanisms through which mergers increase cash flows, and are likely to be fruitful avenues for future research.[21]

6. Summary

This paper examines the post-acquisition operating performance of merged firms using a sample of the 50 largest mergers between U.S. public industrial firms completed in the period 1979 to mid-1984. We develop a methodology to deal with a number of measurement issues that arise in studying the consequences of takeovers. Further, we integrate accounting and stock return data in a consistent fashion to permit richer tests of corporate control theories. This general approach has been adopted by several recent studies to examine mergers and acquisitions – Tehranian and Cornett (1991) and Linder and Crane (1991) analyze performance in bank mergers, and Jarrell (1991) investigates postmerger performance using analysts' forecasts of sales margins.

Our findings indicate that merged firms have significant improvements in operating cash flow returns after the merger, resulting from increases in asset productivity relative to their industries. These improvements are particularly strong for transactions involving firms in overlapping businesses. Postmerger cash flow improvements do not come at the expense of long-term perfor-

---

[20]The findings on the relation between transaction characteristics and postmerger performance are not sensitive to outliers.

[21]Recent examples of clinical studies on corporate control issues include Baker and Wruck (1989), Kaplan (1989), and Donaldson (1990).

mance, since sample firms maintain their capital expenditure and R&D rates relative to their industries after the merger. Finally, there is a strong positive relation between postmerger increases in operating cash flows and abnormal stock returns at merger announcements, indicating that expectations of economic improvements explain a significant portion of the equity revaluations of the merging firms.

Appendix

Acquiring / target firms and their industries

This appendix provides a detailed description of the sample used in the analysis. The business descriptions and industry classifications of acquirer and target firms are based on *Value Line* reports before the merger. The relation between the firms is a subjective classification by the authors of the degree of overlap between the target's and acquirer's businesses. Relative size of the target is the ratio of the target's assets to acquirer's assets one year before the merger. Assets are measured as the market value of common equity plus the book values of preferred stock and net debt. Acquisition date is the date the merger was completed and the target was delisted from the public exchange. Target equity values are the market value of common equity one year before the merger. Acquirer stock return is the market-adjusted stock return from five days before the acquirer's offer announcement to the merger completion. Target stock return is the market-adjusted stock return from five days before the first offer announcement (not necessarily by the ultimate acquirer) to the merger completion.

1. American Medical International / Lifemark (Acquirer / Target)
American Medical owns and operates proprietary hospitals and other health-care businesses (94% of revenue in 1982) and offers medical–technical support. Lifemark owns and manages general hospitals (90% of 1982 revenues) and provides cardiopulmonary, physical therapy, pharmacy, and clinical laboratory services.

Acquirer industry:	Medical services	Target industry:	Medical services
Acquisition date:	Jan. 20 1984	Relation between firms:	High overlap
Target equity value:	$808.0 million	Relative size of target:	34%
Acquirer stock return:	− 16.0%	Target stock return:	55.1%

2. Anheuser-Busch Companies / Campbell Taggart Inc.
Anheuser-Busch is the world's largest brewer of beer. Campbell Taggart's business is baking and distributing bread, rolls, crackers, cake and other sweet products, and food products.

Acquirer industry:	Brewing	Target industry:	Food processing
Acquisition date:	Nov. 2 1982	Relation between firms:	Low overlap
Target equity value:	$536.3 million	Relative size of target:	15.8%
Acquirer stock return:	− 3.0%	Target stock return:	− 4.8%

166   *P. Healy et al., Performance improvements after mergers*

3. Associated Dry Goods / Caldor Inc.

Associated Dry Goods operates general department stores in 25 states. Caldor operates 65 promotional discount department stores in five states.

Acquirer industry:	Retail stores	Target industry:	Retail stores
Acquisition date:	May 27 1981	Relation between firms:	High overlap
Target equity value:	$309.5 million	Relative size of target:	47.5%
Acquirer stock return:	9.3%	Target stock return:	36.7%

4. Avon Products Inc. / Mallinckrodt

Avon is the world's largest manufacturer of cosmetics and toiletries, and also sells costume jewelry and ceramics. Mallinckrodt develops and manufactures fine chemicals. drugs and other health care products, and chemicals for the food, cosmetics, laboratory, petrochemical, and printing industries.

Acquirer industry:	Toiletries/cosmetics	Target industry:	Speciality chemical
Acquisition date:	March 8 1982	Relation between firms:	Low overlap
Target equity value:	$574.6 million	Relative size of target:	31.2%
Acquirer stock return:	−5.9%	Target stock return:	18.3%

5. Best Products / Modern Merchandising Inc.

Best Products and Modern Merchandising sell general merchandise through catalog showrooms.

Acquirer industry:	Retail–special lines	Target industry:	Retail–special lines
Acquisition date:	Sept. 15 1982	Relation between firms:	High overlap
Target equity value:	$114.3 million	Relative size of target:	55.6%
Acquirer stock return:	−16.7%	Target stock return:	15.7%

6. Brown-Forman Distillers / Lenox Inc.

Brown-Forman manufactures a wide variety of alcoholic beverages. Lenox produces home furnishings (including china and crystal) and personal-use products (including jewelry and luggage).

Acquirer industry:	Distilling and tobacco	Target industry:	Household products
Acquisition date:	July 21 1983	Relation between firms:	Low overlap
Target equity value:	$407.0 million	Relative size of target:	19.1%
Acquirer stock return:	−7.7%	Target stock return:	55.7%

7. Burroughs Corp. / Memorex Corp.

Burroughs is a major participant in the data processing and business computer equipment industry. Memorex develops, manufactures, markets, and services a wide range of computer peripheral equipment systems, and products employed in the recording, retrieval, communication, and storage of information.

Acquirer industry:	Computer/data processing products	Target industry:	Computer/data processing products
Acquisition date:	Dec. 3 1981	Relation between firms:	High overlap
Target equity value:	$98.8 million	Relative size of target:	10.4%
Acquirer stock return:	−2.7%	Target stock return:	52.9%

8. Coca Cola Co. / Columbia Pictures Industries Inc.

Coca Cola is the largest manufacturer and distributor of soft drink concentrates and syrups in the world. The company also manufactures citrus, coffee. tea, wine, and plastic products. Columbia Pictures produces and distributes theatrical motion pictures. television series and features. amusement games, and commercials.

Acquirer industry:	Soft drinks	Target industry:	Recreation
Acquisition date:	June 21 1982	Relation between firms:	Low overlap
Target equity value:	$704.3 million	Relative size of target:	11.4%
Acquirer stock return:	2.2%	Target stock return:	78.2%

9. Con Agra Inc. / Peavey Co.

Con Agra is a diversified food processor engaged in agriculture (agricultural chemicals, formula feed. and fertilizers), grain (flour, by-products, and grain and feed merchandising), and food (frozen foods, broiler chicken, eggs, seafood, and pet products) industries. Peavey is also a diversified food processor and retailer engaged in grain merchandising, food processing (flour, bakery mixes, and jams), and the operation of specialty retail stores.

Acquirer industry:	Food processing	Target industry:	Food processing
Acquisition date:	July 20 1982	Relation between firms:	High overlap
Target equity value:	$186.5 million	Relative size of target:	71.9%
Acquirer stock return:	2.7%	Target stock return:	58.1%

10. Cooper Industries / Gardner-Denver
Cooper is a diversified, international corporation that produces consumer and industrial tools, aircraft services, mining and construction, and energy services. Gardner-Denver makes portable and stationary air compressors, drilling equipment for above- and underground, and air-operated tools. Drilling equipment for mining, petroleum, and construction industries makes up 67% of sales.

Acquirer industry:	Machinery	Target industry:	Construction and mining machinery
Acquisition date:	April 30 1979	Relation between firms:	Medium overlap
Target equity value:	$605.5 million	Relative size of target:	66.7%
Acquirer stock return:	−5.2%	Target stock return:	49.7%

11. Dart Industries / Kraft Inc.
Dart is a diversified company that manufactures and markets consumer products (including Tupperware containers, Duracell batteries, and West Bend appliances), chemicals, plastics, and packaging products. Kraft manufactures food products and markets them to retail, industrial, and food service customers.

Acquirer industry:	Household products	Target industry:	Food processing
Acquisition date:	Sept. 25 1980	Relation between firms:	Low overlap
Target equity value:	$1,099.4 million	Relative size of target:	78.7%
Acquirer stock return:	−17.0%	Target stock return:	−6.6%

12. Diamond Shamrock / Natomas Co.
Diamond Shamrock is a domestic integrated oil and gas company with interests in coal and chemicals. Natomas is principally engaged in petroleum exploration and production. Its operations also include ocean shipping, coal, real estate, and geothermal energy.

Acquirer industry:	Integr. petroleum	Target industry:	Integr. petroleum
Acquisition date:	Aug. 31 1983	Relation between firms:	High overlap
Target equity value:	$1,610.0 million	Relative size of target:	86.2%
Acquirer stock return:	−1.6%	Target stock return:	66.7%

13. E. I. Du Pont de Nemours / Conoco Inc.
Du Pont manufactures diversified lines of chemicals, plastics, specialty products, and fibers. Conoco is engaged in the exploration, production, and transportation of crude oil, coal, and natural gas; petroleum refining; and the production, processing, and transportation of chemicals.

Acquirer industry:	Basic chemicals	Target industry:	Integr. petroleum
Acquisition date:	Sept. 30 1981	Relation between firms:	Low overlap
Target equity value:	$5,524.9 million	Relative size of target:	82.7%
Acquirer stock return:	−16.5%	Target stock return:	33.1%

14. Eaton Corp. / Cutler-Hammer Inc.
Eaton is engaged in areas of transportation, materials handling, industrial automation, security, construction, agriculture, and consumer durables. Cutler-Hammer designs and manufactures electronic and electrical components and systems for industrial, aerospace, air traffic control, semiconductor, housing, and consumer markets.

Acquirer industry:	Replacement auto parts	Target industry:	Electrical equipment
Acquisition date:	Jan. 2 1979	Relation between firms:	Low overlap
Target equity value:	$382.7 million	Relative size of target:	19.7%
Acquirer stock return:	−8.4%	Target stock return:	60.7%

15. Exxon Corp./Reliance Electric Co.
Exxon is engaged in the exploration, production, and transportation of crude oil and natural gas, and in the production and transportation of petroleum and chemicals. Reliance develops, manufactures, and services a broad line of industrial equipment, including electric motors and drives, mechanical power transmission components, industrial and retail scales and weighting systems, and telecommunications equipment.

Acquirer industry:	Integr. petroleum	Target industry:	Electrical equipment
Acquisition date:	Dec. 27 1979	Relation between firms:	Low overlap
Target equity value:	$1,133.2 million	Relative size of target:	2.5%
Acquirer stock return:	1.2%	Target stock return:	97.9%

16. Fairchild Industries/VSI Corp.
Fairchild produces military aircraft and parts, commercial aircraft and parts, spacecraft and parts, and domestic communications systems. VSI is a diversified manufacturer of a wide range of precision metal products, including fastening systems for aircraft and missiles, steel mold bases for the plastics industry, door knobs, stainless steel cabinets, and building hardware.

Acquirer industry.	Diversified aerospace	Target industry:	Machinery
Acquisition date:	Nov. 7 1980	Relation between firms:	Medium overlap
Target equity value:	$279.1 million	Relative size of target:	87.3%
Acquirer stock return:	19.1%	Target stock return:	71.2%

17. Fluor Corp./St. Joe Minerals Corp.
Fluor designs, engineers, procures, and constructs complex manufacturing plants, processing plants, and related facilities for energy, natural resources, and industrial clients. St. Joe is a diversified producer of natural resources (principally lead, gold, zinc, silver, coal, oil and gas, and iron ore).

Acquirer industry:	Building	Target industry:	Lead, zinc & minor metals
Acquisition date:	Aug. 3 1981	Relation between firms:	Low overlap
Target equity value:	$2,011.7 million	Relative size of target:	86.0%
Acquirer stock return:	−19.3%	Target stock return:	60.9%

18. Fort Howard Paper Co./Maryland Cup Corp.
Fort Howard manufactures a broad line of disposable sanitary paper products, principally table napkins, paper towels, toilet tissue, industrial and automotive wipes, and boxed facial tissues. Maryland Cup manufactures a variety of single-use paper and plastic products for food and beverage service, including plates, cups, bowls, cutlery, drinking straws, and toothpicks. Maryland Cup markets its products to major fast-food chains, restaurants, vending operators, soft drink bottlers, contract feeders, and dairy and other food packagers.

Acquirer industry:	Paper and forest products	Target industry:	Packaging and container
Acquisition date:	Aug. 31 1983	Relation between firms:	Medium overlap
Target equity value:	$554.8 million	Relative size of target:	25.9%
Acquirer stock return:	−9.5%	Target stock return:	30.4%

19. Freeport Minerals Co./McMoran Oil & Gas Co.
Freeport Minerals is a diversified company engaged in exploration and development of natural resources, including agricultural minerals, uranium, oxide and kaolin, and oil and gas. (Oil and gas account for 3% of Freeport's sales.) McMoran is engaged in the acquisition, exploration, and development of oil and gas properties, and the production and sale of oil and natural gas.

Acquirer industry:	Metals and mining	Target industry:	Oil and gas
Acquisition date:	April 7 1981	Relation between firms:	Medium overlap
Target equity value:	$455.1 million	Relative size of target:	22.5%
Acquirer stock return:	14.7%	Target stock return:	27.4%

20. Gannett Co. Inc./Combined Communications Corp.
Gannett and its subsidiaries publish daily newspapers. Combined Communications Corporation is engaged in outdoor advertising (45% of revenues), television and radio broadcasting (30% of revenues), and newspaper publishing (25% of revenues).

Acquirer industry:	Newspaper	Target industry:	Broadcasting
Acquisition date:	June 7 1979	Relation between firms:	Medium overlap
Target equity value:	$309.6 million	Relative size of target:	30.8%
Acquirer stock return:	−1.4%	Target stock return:	−5.0%

21. General Foods Corp./Oscar Mayer & Co. Inc.
General Foods is a leading processor of packaged grocery products. Oscar Mayer operates in the meat packing and processing industry.

Acquirer industry:	Food processing	Target industry:	Food processing
Acquisition date:	May 5 1981	Relation between firms:	High overlap
Target equity value:	$460.8 million	Relative size of target:	16.7%
Acquirer stock return:	5.6%	Target stock return:	66.2%

22. Genstar Ltd./Flintkote Co.
Genstar manufactures building materials and cement (31% of revenues), and is engaged in housing and land development (36% of sales), construction (10% of sales), marine transportation, financial services, and venture capital investment. Flintkote is engaged in mining, and manufactures various building and construction materials, including gypsum wallboard, floor tile, sand and gravel products, concrete, cement, and various lime products.

Acquirer industry:	Building	Target industry:	Building
Acquisition date:	Jan. 3 1980	Relation between firms:	High overlap
Target equity value:	$400.1 million	Relative size of target:	38.7%
Acquirer stock return:	−23.8%	Target stock return:	47.6%

23. Gulf & Western Industries/Simmons Co.
Gulf & Western is a conglomerate with interests in the manufacture of automotive and air-conditioning components, paper products, leisure, financial services, automotive replacement parts, consumer products, sugar growing and processing, citrus farming, natural resources, and apparel. Simmons produces furnishings for home, commercial, and institutional customers.

Acquirer industry:	Conglomerate	Target industry:	Building
Acquisition date:	Jan. 5 1979	Relation between firms:	Low overlap
Target equity value:	$134.3 million	Relative size of target:	9.0%
Acquirer stock return:	−2.5%	Target stock return:	38.6%

24. Harris Corp./Lanier Business Products Inc.
Harris designs and produces voice and video communication, and information processing systems, equipment, and components. Lanier develops, manufactures, and services a broad line of dictating equipment, several models of video-display text-editing typewriters, and small-business computers.

Acquirer industry:	Electronics	Target industry:	Office equipment
Acquisition date:	Oct. 28 1983	Relation between firms:	Medium overlap
Target equity value:	$275.3 million	Relative size of target:	22.5%
Acquirer stock return:	0.4%	Target stock return:	30.4%

25. Holiday Inns Inc./Harrahs
Holiday Inns owns and operates hotels throughout the world. Harrahs operates two luxury casinos.

Acquirer industry:	Travel services	Target industry:	Recreation
Acquisition date:	Feb. 28 1980	Relation between firms:	Medium overlap
Target equity value:	$315.1 million	Relative size of target:	25.6%
Acquirer stock return:	−14.3%	Target stock return:	67.8%

26. Internorth Inc./Belco Petroleum Corp.
Internorth owns and operates natural gas businesses; produces, transports, and markets liquid fuels and petrochemicals; and is involved in the exploration and production of oil and gas. Belco

is engaged in the exploration and production of crude oil and natural gas and in the production of coal.

Acquirer industry:	Natural gas	Target industry:	Integr. petroleum
Acquisition date:	July 29 1983	Relation between firms:	High overlap
Target equity value:	$803.2 million	Relative size of target:	30.0%
Acquirer stock return:	50.4%	Target stock return:	17.1%

27. Kroger Inc./Dillon Companies Inc.
Kroger operates the country's second largest supermarket chain, manufactures and processes food for sale by these supermarkets, and operates one of the country's largest drugstore chains. Dillon distributes retail food through supermarkets and convenience stores.

Acquirer industry:	Grocery store	Target industry:	Grocery store
Acquisition date:	Jan. 25 1983	Relation between firms:	High overlap
Target equity value:	$593.9 million	Relative size of target:	42.6%
Acquirer stock return:	−17.3%	Target stock return:	21.4%

28. Litton Industries/Itek Corp.
Litton industries is a conglomerate. Its businesses include production of office equipment, material handling equipment, machine tools, microwave cookers. medical equipment, and oil drilling equipment. Litton is also engaged in geophysical exploration, ship building, and production of advanced electronics products for defense, industrial automation, and geophysical markets. Itek develops and manufactures a variety of aerial reconnaissance and surveillance products based on optical and electronic technologies.

Acquirer industry:	Conglomerate	Target industry:	Precision instruments
Acquisition date:	Feb. 15 1983	Relation between firms:	Medium overlap
Target equity value:	$196.2 million	Relative size of target:	14.0%
Acquirer stock return:	8.5%	Target stock return:	40.9%

29. LTV Group/Republic Steel
LTV is the nation's third largest steel producer. In addition, the company manufactures oil field equipment and commercial aerospace and defense products. Republic Steel is the nation's seventh largest steel producer. Republic Steel also produces coal that is used in its steel operations.

Acquirer industry:	Integrated steel	Target industry:	Integrated steel
Acquisition date:	June 29 1984	Relation between firms:	High overlap
Target equity value:	$408.7 million	Relative size of target:	58.4%
Acquirer stock return:	−23.5%	Target stock return:	−3.9%

30. Mapco Inc./Earth Resources Company
Mapco is a diversified energy company principally engaged in the exploration and production of coal, oil, natural gas. and natural gas liquids; pipeline transportation of natural gas liquids and anhydrous ammonia; and marketing of natural gas liquids, refined petroleum products, domestic and foreign crude oil, and liquid fertilizers. Earth Resources is a diversified energy and resources development company engaged primarily in refining, transporting, and marketing petroleum products.

Acquirer industry:	Coal/uranium/ geothermal	Target industry:	Integr. petroleum
Acquisition date:	Feb. 9 1981	Relation between firms:	Medium overlap
Target equity value:	$369.7 million	Relative size of target:	24.6%
Acquirer stock return:	−4.1%	Target stock return:	35.3%

31. McGraw-Edison Co./Studebaker Worthington Inc.
McGraw-Edison manufactures and distributes electrical appliances, tools. and other products for the consumer market; power-system and related equipment for electrical utilities and industry; and a wide range of services and equipment for industrial and commercial uses. Studebaker

Worthington has diversified business operations that deal with the manufacture of process equipment and industrial products.

Acquirer industry:	Home appliance	Target industry:	Diversified manufg.
Acquisition date:	Oct. 23 1979	Relation between firms:	Medium overlap
Target equity value:	$712.9 million	Relative size of target:	82.4%
Acquirer stock return:	2.9%	Target stock return:	92.1%

32. Motorola Inc./Four-Phase Systems Inc.

Motorola produces data communication equipment and systems, semiconductors, and other high-technology electronic equipment. Four-Phase produces clustered video display computer systems for distributed data processing applications.

Acquirer industry:	Electronics	Target industry:	Computer/data processing
Acquisition date:	March 2 1982	Relation between firms:	Medium overlap
Target equity value:	$234.7 million	Relative size of target:	6.8%
Acquirer stock return:	−6.2%	Target stock return:	42.7%

33. Morton-Norwich Products/Thiokol Corporation

Morton-Norwich produces ethical and proprietary drugs, salt for domestic and industrial uses, household cleaning and laundry products, and specialty chemicals. Thiokol manufactures specialty chemical products (44% of revenues), and propulsion and ordnance products and services for the government.

Acquirer industry:	Proprietary drug	Target industry:	Aerospace/diversified
Acquisition date:	Sept. 24 1982	Relation between firms:	Low overlap
Target equity value:	$564.4 million	Relative size of target:	69.3%
Acquirer stock return:	1.3%	Target stock return:	33.5%

34. Occidental Petroleum/Cities Service Company

Occidental produces and markets crude oil and coal, and manufactures industrial chemicals and plastics, metal finishes, agricultural chemicals, and fertilizers. Oil and gas business accounts for 70% of the company's sales. Cities Service is an integrated oil company.

Acquirer industry:	Integr. petroleum	Target industry:	Integr. petroleum
Acquisition date:	Dec. 2 1982	Relation between firms:	High overlap
Target equity value:	3,792.5 million	Relative size of target:	130.1%
Acquirer stock return:	−24.3%	Target stock return:	12.9%

35. Pan Am Corp./National Airlines Inc.

Pan Am is primarily an international commercial air carrier providing services to 73 cities in 43 foreign countries. National Airlines is a domestic air carrier with routes extending from its hub in Miami to New York, San Francisco, and Los Angeles. Although the company also has transatlantic service to London, Paris, Frankfurt, and Amsterdam, 96% of its revenues are derived from domestic routes.

Acquirer industry:	Air transportation	Target industry:	Air transportation
Acquisition date:	Jan. 7 1980	Relation between firms:	Medium overlap
Target equity value:	$426.0 million	Relative size of target:	29.8%
Acquirer stock return:	−27.8%	Target stock return:	158.4%

36. Penn Central Corp./GK Technologies Inc.

Penn Central is a diversified company whose primary businesses include oil refining, the transportation and marketing of refined petroleum products and crude, real estate development, operation of amusement parks, and production of offshore drilling rigs. GK Technologies produces wire and cable, primarily for the telecommunications industry, and electronic components, and provides engineering services for weapons systems and environmental products.

Acquirer industry:	Conglomerate	Target industry:	Electronics
Acquisition date:	May 14 1981	Relation between firms:	Low overlap
Target equity value:	$636.5 million	Relative size of target:	27.5%
Acquirer stock return:	96.3%	Target stock return:	73.7%

172   *P. Healy et al., Performance improvements after mergers*

37. Phillips Petroleum / General American Oil of Texas

Phillips Petroleum is a fully integrated oil company engaged in petroleum exploration, production, and refining. General American is primarily engaged in oil and gas production and exploration.

Acquirer industry:	Integr. petroleum	Target industry:	Petroleum production
Acquisition date:	March 8 1983	Relation between firms:	High overlap
Target equity value:	$572.0 million	Relative size of target:	14.0%
Acquirer stock return:	−8.1%	Target stock return:	20.1%

38. Raytheon Corp. / Beech Aircraft Corp.

Raytheon develops and manufactures electronic systems for government and commercial use. Raytheon also supplies energy services, manufactures major home appliances, designs and manufactures heavy construction equipment, and publishes textbooks. Beech Aircraft designs, manufactures, and sells airplanes for the general aviation market. Beech is also a substantial aerospace contractor producing a variety of military aircraft, missile targets, and cryogenics systems for aerospace vehicles.

Acquirer industry:	Electrical equipment	Target industry:	Aerospace / diversified
Acquisition date:	Feb. 8 1980	Relation between firms:	Medium overlap
Target equity value:	$740.7 million	Relative size of target:	42.1%
Acquirer stock return:	22.5%	Target stock return:	110.4%

39. Revlon Inc. / Technicon Corp.

Revlon is in the beauty products (65% of revenues) and health products and service business (35% of revenues). Technicon designs and produces automated testing systems for blood and other biological fluids, chemical reagents and consumables, industrial analytical instruments, and medical information systems.

Acquirer industry:	Toiletries / cosmetics	Target industry:	Health care / hospital supplies
Acquisition date:	May 2 1980	Relation between firms:	Medium overlap
Target equity value:	$392.7 million	Relative size of target:	19.8%
Acquirer stock return:	−10.2%	Target stock return:	34.9%

40. R.J. Reynolds Corp. / Del Monte Corp.

R.J. Reynold's lines of business are the domestic and international manufacture and sale of tobacco products (64% of revenues), transportation (14% of revenues), energy (15% of revenues), food and beverage products (5% of revenues), and aluminum products and packaging (2% of revenues). Del Monte's principal business is in food products (primarily processed foods and fresh fruit) and related services (including transportation and institutional services).

Acquirer industry:	Tobacco	Target industry:	Food processing
Acquisition date:	Feb. 2 1979	Relation between firms:	Low overlap
Target equity value:	$583.0 million	Relative size of target:	13.5%
Acquirer stock return:	4.2%	Target stock return:	63.3%

41. Signal Companies / Wheelabrator Frye Inc.

Signal is a diversified, technology-based company that manufactures aerospace equipment, professional audio-video systems, and heavy trucks. Wheelabrator Frye's products and services include environmental, energy, and engineered products and services, and chemical and specialty products.

Acquirer industry:	Auto and trucks	Target industry:	Machinery
Acquisition date:	Feb. 1 1983	Relation between firms:	Low overlap
Target equity value:	$904.7 million	Relative size of target:	36.3%
Acquirer stock return:	8.5%	Target stock return:	15.6%

42. SmithKline Corp. / Beckman Instruments Inc.

SmithKline researches, develops, manufactures, and markets ethical drugs, proprietary medicines, animal health products, ethical and proprietary eye care products, and ultrasonic and electronic instruments. Beckman is an international manufacturer of laboratory analytical instruments and related chemical products that are used widely in medicine and science and in a broad range of industrial applications.

Acquirer industry:	Ethical drugs	Target industry:	Precision instruments
Acquisition date:	March 4 1982	Relation between firms:	Medium overlap
Target equity value:	$1,000.8 million	Relative size of target:	15.5%
Acquirer stock return:	3.1%	Target stock return:	85.4%

43. Sohio / Kennecott Corp.

Sohio is an integrated petroleum company engaged in all phases of the petroleum business. Kennecott produces copper, gold, silver, molybdenum, and lead; manufactures industrial abrasive and resistant materials; manufactures and markets industrial engineered systems; and owns two-thirds of a Canadian producer of titanium dioxide slag, high-purity iron, and iron powders.

Acquirer industry:	Integr. petroleum	Target industry:	General metals and mining
Acquisition date:	June 3 1981	Relation between firms:	Low overlap
Target equity value:	$1,760.4 million	Relative size of target:	11.6%
Acquirer stock return:	−21.4%	Target stock return:	140.3%

44. Standard Brands / Nabisco Inc.

Standard Brands is a manufacturer, processor, and distributor of food and related products. Nabisco is a manufacturer and marketer of food products (specializing in cookies and crackers, which account for 60% of total sales), toiletries, pharmaceuticals, and household accessories.

Acquirer industry:	Food processing	Target industry:	Food processing
Acquisition date:	July 2 1981	Relation between firms:	High overlap
Target equity value:	$929.0 million	Relative size of target:	81.4%
Acquirer stock return:	1.0%	Target stock return:	−5.7%

45. Tenneco / Houston Oil & Minerals Corp.

Tenneco is a diversified company. Its major businesses include natural gas, petrochemicals, construction and farm equipment, automotive components, shipbuilding, chemicals, packaging, agriculture and land management, and life insurance. The recent business emphasis of Houston Oil & Minerals has been on exploration for oil and natural gas on undeveloped properties, and the development of production upon discovery. In 1980. the breakdown of revenues was oil 21%, gas 61%, and pipeline and other 21%.

Acquirer industry:	Natural gas	Target industry:	Petroleum producing industry
Acquisition date:	April 23 1981	Relation between firms:	Medium overlap
Target equity value:	$1,447.0 million	Relative size of target:	13.9%
Acquirer stock return:	−21.4%	Target stock return:	−3.4%

46. Tosco Corp. / AZL Resources Inc.

Tosco owns and operates petroleum refineries and related wholesale distribution facilities. Prior to the merger AZL had been in the process of changing its focus from agricultural-based businesses to oil and gas exploration and production.

Acquirer industry:	Integr. petroleum	Target industry:	Agricultural products
Acquisition date:	Dec. 31 1982	Relation between firms:	Low overlap
Target equity value:	$77.9 million	Relative size of target:	42.8%
Acquirer stock return:	−29.0%	Target stock return:	30.8%

47. U.S. Steel / Marathon Oil Co.

U.S. Steel's principal businesses include steel, chemicals, resource development, fabricating and engineering. and transportation. Marathon is an integrated petroleum company engaged in the production. refining, and transportation of crude oil, natural gas, and petroleum products.

Acquirer industry:	Integr. steel	Target industry:	Integr. petroleum
Acquisition date:	March 11 1982	Relation between firms:	Low overlap
Target equity value:	$4,438.3 million	Relative size of target:	145.0%
Acquirer stock return:	21.4%	Target stock return:	29.0%

48. United Technologies / Carrier Corp.
United Technologies designs and produces high-technology power systems, flight systems, and industrial products and services. Carrier's principal business is the manufacture and sale of air conditioning equipment.

Acquirer industry:	Aerospace/ diversified	Target industry:	Building
Acquisition date:	July 6 1979	Relation between firms:	Low overlap
Target equity value:	$757.1 million	Relative size of target:	42.8%
Acquirer stock return:	−21.3%	Target stock return:	44.7%

49. Westinghouse Electric / Teleprompter Corp.
Westinghouse Electric is a diversified corporation primarily engaged in the manufacture and sale of electrical equipment. Westinghouse's wholly owned subsidiary WBC operates six TV stations, 12 radio stations, and cable television systems. Teleprompter is the nation's largest cable television company and owns MUZAC, the leading supplier of music to offices and other commercial establishments.

Acquirer industry:	Electrical equipment	Target industry:	Broadcasting
Acquisition date:	Aug. 18 1981	Relation between firms:	Medium overlap
Target equity value:	$642.7 million	Relative size of target:	41.8%
Acquirer stock return:	4.8%	Target stock return:	44.5%

50. Williams Companies / Northwest Energy Company
Williams is primarily engaged in the chemical fertilizer (49% of revenues), natural gas (27% of sales), and metals (24% of sales) businesses. Northwest is primarily engaged in interstate natural gas transmission, oil and gas exploration, and the marketing of natural gas liquids.

Acquirer industry:	Chemical/ diversified	Target industry:	Natural gas
Acquisition date:	Nov. 30, 1983	Relation between firms:	Medium overlap
Target equity value:	$721.2 million	Relative size of target:	61.1%
Acquirer stock return:	−5.6%	Target stock return:	42.6%

References

Asquith, Paul, 1983, Merger bids, uncertainty, and stockholder returns, Journal of Financial Economics 11, 51–84.

Asquith, Paul and E. Han Kim, 1982, The impact of merger bids on participating firms' security holders, Journal of Finance 37, 1209–1228.

Asquith, Paul, Robert Bruner, and David Mullins, 1988, Merger returns and the form of financing, Working paper (MIT Sloan School, Cambridge, MA).

Baker, George and Karen Wruck, Organizational changes and value creation in leveraged buyouts: The case of The O.M. Scott & Sons Company, Journal of Financial Economics 25, 163–190.

Belsley, David, Edwin Kuh, and Roy Welsch, 1980, Regression diagnostics (Wiley, New York, NY).

Bradley, Michael, Anand Desai, and E. Han Kim, 1983, The rationale behind interfirm tender offers: Information or synergy?, Journal of Financial Economics 11, 183–206.

Bradley, Michael, Anand Desai, and E. Han Kim, 1988, Synergistic gains from corporate acquisitions and their division between the stockholders of target and acquiring firms, Journal of Financial Economics 21, 3–40.

Bull, Ivan, 1988, Management performance and leveraged buyouts: An empirical analysis, Unpublished paper (University of Illinois at Urbana-Champaign, IL).

Caves, Richard, 1989, Takeovers and economic efficiency: Foresight vs. hindsight, International Journal of Industrial Organization 7, 151–174.

Dodd, Peter, 1980, Merger proposals, management discretion and stockholder wealth, Journal of Financial Economics 8, 105–138.

Dodd, Peter and Richard Ruback, 1977, Tender offers and stockholder returns: An empirical analysis, Journal of Financial Economics 5, 351–374.

Donaldson, Gordon, Voluntary restructuring: The case of General Mills, Journal of Financial Economics 27, 117–142.

Herman, Edwin and Louis Lowenstein, 1988, The efficiency effects of hostile takeovers, in: John Coffee Jr., Louis Lowenstein, and Susan Rose-Ackerman, eds., Knights, raiders and targets: The impact of the hostile takeover (Oxford University Press, New York, NY).

Huang, Yen-Shong and Ralph Walkling, 1987, Target abnormal returns associated with acquisition announcements: Payment, acquisition form, and managerial resistance, Journal of Financial Economics 19, 329–349.

Jarrell, Sherry, 1991, Do takeovers generate value? Evidence on the capital market's ability to assess takeovers, Working paper (Southern Methodist University, Dallas. TX).

Kaplan, Steven, 1989a, The effects of management buyouts on operating performance and value, Journal of Financial Economics 24, 581–618.

Kaplan, Steven, 1989b, Campeau's acquisition of Federated: Value destroyed or value added?, Journal of Financial Economics 25, 191–212.

Kaplan, Steven and Michael Weisbach, 1992, Acquisitions and diversification: What is divested and how much does the market anticipate?, Journal of Finance, forthcoming.

Linder, Jane and Dwight Crane, 1991, Bank mergers: Integration and profitability, Working paper (Harvard Business School, Boston, MA).

Pontiff, Jeffrey, Andre Shleifer, and Michael Weisbach, 1990, Reversion of excess pension assets after takeovers, Rand Journal of Economics 21, 600–613.

Ravenscraft, David and Frederick M. Scherer, 1987, Mergers, selloffs, and economic efficiency (Brookings Institution, Washington, DC).

Rosett, Joshua, 1990, Do union wealth concessions explain takeover premiums? The evidence of contract wages, Journal of Financial Economics 27, 263–282.

Ruback, Richard, 1988, Do target shareholders lose in unsuccessful control contests?, in: Corporate takeovers: Causes and consequences (National Bureau of Economic Research. Cambridge, MA).

Shleifer, Andre and Larry Summers, 1988, Breach of trust in hostile takeovers, in: A. Auerbach, ed., Corporate takeovers: Causes and consequences (University of Chicago Press, Chicago, IL).

Smith, Abbie, 1990, Corporate ownership structure and performance: The case of management buyouts, Journal of Financial Economics 27, 143–164.

Tehranian, Hassan and Marcia Cornett, 1991, An investigation of the change in corporate performance associated with bank acquisitions, Journal of Financial Economics, forthcoming.

Watts, Ross and Jerold Zimmerman, Positive accounting theory (Prentice-Hall, Englewood Cliffs, NJ).

White, Halbert, 1980, A heteroskedasticity-consistent covariance covariance matrix estimator and a direct test for heteroskedasticity, Econometrica 48, 817–838.

[10]

THE JOURNAL OF INDUSTRIAL ECONOMICS   0022-1821 $2.00

Volume XXXVI   December 1987   No. 2

LIFE AFTER TAKEOVER

DAVID J. RAVENSCRAFT AND F. M. SCHERER*

Economic consequences of takeovers are investigated by analyzing profitability of enterprises acquired as a direct or indirect ("white knight") result of tender offers. Target companies' pre-tender profitability averaged 0.97 percentage points below peer industry norms. Nine years after takeover, acquired lines of business had operating income/assets percentages 3.10 points below those of non-tender lines with similar industry bases, market shares, and merger accounting methods. Most of the targets' post-takeover profit decline stemmed from asset value writeups. There is no indication that on average the acquirers raised their targets' operating profitability, net of merger-related accounting adjustments.

FOR THE fourth time in this century, the United States has experienced merger mania. A distinguishing characteristic of the 1980's merger wave has been the high incidence of tender offer takeovers—that is, mergers effected following an offer from a would-be acquirer directly to target company share-holders, bypassing management.

There is a substantial literature in economics, corporate finance, and law arguing that such tender offer takeovers play an important role in purging inefficient managers and forcing incumbents to hew to the profit maximization line or face displacement.[1] This implies two testable hypotheses. First, to the extent that a sizable fraction of takeovers are directed toward displacing inefficient managers, the pre-takeover profitability of targets should be lower than that of non-target peer firms, other things (such as industry business conditions) being held equal. Second, both the logic of inefficient management displacement and the possibility of gaining post-takeover "synergies" imply an improvement in post-takeover profitability relative to the pre-takeover situation. These are hypotheses that should be tested directly and not merely

* Federal Trade Commission Bureau of Economics and Swarthmore College respectively. Scherer's work was supported under National Science Foundation grant SES-8209766 and a Brookings Institution visiting fellowship. The authors are indebted to Nathaniel Levy for research assistance and to Larry White and Willard Carleton for helpful comments.

Use is made of Line of Business data collected by the Federal Trade Commission. A review by FTC staff has determined that individual company data are not disclosed. The conclusions are the authors' and not necessarily those of the FTC.

[1] See e.g. Marris [1963], Manne [1965], Easterbrook and Fischel [1981], Jensen and Ruback [1983], Yarrow [1985, p. 3], and US Council of Economic Advisers [1985, Chapter 6]. In his pioneering article on the subject, Marris [1963, pp. 189–190] proposed two further behavioral hypotheses we do not test here: that firms will retain too high a share of their earnings, and that they will maintain excessive liquidity.

148   DAVID J. RAVENSCRAFT AND F. M. SCHERER

offered as one of many possible explanations for the movement of stock prices
at the time of a takeover "event".[2]

I. THE LINE OF BUSINESS DATA

An obstacle to evaluating post-merger performance is that the acquired entity
normally ceases to publish income statement and balance sheet information
once it is absorbed. To continue tracking the target's history, one needs
financial performance data disaggregated to the level of individual operating
units. Such data were systematically gathered under the Federal Trade
Commission's (now discontinued) Line of Business program. For the years
1975–77, a panel of more than 450 large corporations broke down their
domestic financial reports by individual "LBs" defined to conform with
261 possible manufacturing and 14 (broader) nonmanufacturing industry
categories. The average sample member reported in 1977 on eight manufacturing LBs, with a range of one to approximately 53. The Line of Business
companies were responsible for three-fourths of all manufacturing and
minerals industry mergers, measured by volume of assets acquired, on the
Federal Trade Commission's lists [1978] of acquisitions of companies with
$10 million assets or more over the years 1950–76. The Line of Business data
share the well-known limitations of accounting-based performance information and carry the added burdens associated with segmental reporting.
However, diverse studies have shown that the data reflect underlying supply
and demand conditions and have considerable power in explaining such
phenomena as exit from an industry. (See Scherer *et al.* [1987].)

In addition to consummating approximately 6000 "normal" (i.e., bilaterally
negotiated) mergers, the Line of Business respondents were involved in at
least 96 manufacturing company tender offer acquisitions, according to lists
compiled by Douglas V. Austin and Anand Desai.[3] Most were not opposed
overtly by the target firms' managements, but in 25 cases, a "hostile" tender
offer went through despite incumbent management opposition, and in 20
other cases the acquirer was a "white knight" favoured by target management
over a "hostile" tender offer from some other company. The median time of
consummation was 1968, if all of the acquisitions are included, or 1967, if a
1974 terminal date is imposed, as we shall do in most of what follows.

[2] See Jensen and Ruback [1983], and the studies surveyed therein.
[3] The Austin lists are published in Austin [1969, 1973, 1975, 1980]. The "Desai" list also
includes data collected by Michael Bradley, Peter Dodd, and Richard Ruback. It was brought to
our attention by Ellen Magenheim only after Scherer [1986] summarized results of an analysis
using the Austin lists only. Twenty-two relevant tender offers were on the Desai list but not on
the Austin lists; 15 verified tender offers were on the Austin lists but not on the Desai list.
Cross-checking also permitted the elimination of certain borderline tender offers that were
"arranged" by key controlling "inside" stockholders or that involved "mopping up" share
purchases following a negotiated merger.

LIFE AFTER TAKEOVER   149

II. PRE-OFFER PERFORMANCE

For 95 of the 96 targets, it was possible to obtain information on profitability for two years prior to (or in some cases partially overlapping) the precipitating tender offer announcement. Consistent with the post-tender analysis that follows in section III, the profitability statistic used, OPINC: A, is the ratio of operating income (before deduction of interest charges, extraordinary items, and income taxes) to end-of-fiscal year assets. To control for industry membership and business cycle effects, each individual company's pre-tender operating income/assets percentage was "normalized" by subtracting the comparable percentage for the most closely corresponding industry covered by the FTC's *Quarterly Financial Report* series for the most closely coinciding fiscal year.[4] Before normalization, the simple average operating income/assets percentage was 11.15% in the last year before (or overlapping) takeover initiation and 11.01% in the preceding year. The inter-year differences between both non-normalized and normalized profit figures were minute and statistically insignificant ($F < 0.05$), and so the two years' data are pooled.

Over the two pre-tender offer years, the average normalized profitability percentages for the 95 targets and subsets thereof were as follows, with standard errors given in subscripted parentheses:

All 95 tender offer targets	−0.973%
	(0.513)
25 companies taken over by acquirers incumbent management opposed	−2.281% (0.839)
20 companies acquired by "white knights"	−0.558% (0.718)
50 companies acquired in other tender offers uncontested by management	−0.486% (0.829)

For all target companies together, pre-tender profitability was below industry norms by 0.97 points on average—a difference statistically significant at the 0.05 level in a one-tail test. If operating income/assets ratios for all manufacturing companies, rather than the targets' principal two-digit industries, are used as the standard, the average deviation is −0.403, which is not statistically significant. Thus the home base industries of the tender offer targets had profit returns 0.57 percentage points on average above the all-manufacturing norm (the mean of which was 11.49%). Although the companies taken over in "hostile" bids exhibited lower average returns than

---

[4] For 12 relatively diversified targets, two or more *QFR* industry category norms were averaged, and for two highly diversified targets, the all-manufacturing benchmarks were used. Even so, the "fit" between company activities and the (typically two-digit) *QFR* industry categories was sometimes imperfect—e.g., when a paint maker had to be compared to the entire chemicals industry, or a sporting goods producer to lumber, furniture, and miscellaneous durable goods.

150   DAVID J. RAVENSCRAFT AND F. M. SCHERER

other targets, the differences among the three classes are not statistically significant $[F(2,187) = 1.16]$.

III. POST-TAKEOVER PERFORMANCE

Our post-takeover analysis covers a much broader sample encompassing 2732 manufacturing lines of business (LBs) for which data quality control criteria over all three years 1975–77 were satisfied. Among those lines, 153 had a tender offer acquisition history, including 46 LBs affected by "hostile" tenders unsuccessfully opposed by incumbent management and 44 LBs acquired by "white knights". The remaining 2579 non-tender lines serve as a control group. The 153 tender offer lines belonged to 62 target companies. Thirty-three tender offer acquisition companies for which pre-merger profitability data were available (plus one without pre-merger data) were excluded from the main analysis because the acquired lines were divested before 1975; because the tender offer acquisitions occurred only in 1975 or 1976, too late for the three-year sample analysis; or because other sample inclusion criteria were not satisfied.[5] The two-year average pre-acquisition normalized profit performance of the included and excluded company cohorts was as follows:

	Normalized Operating Income / Assets
62 companies included in the three-year analysis	−1.57%
11 companies acquired in 1975 or 1976	−1.93%
4 companies whose lines were sold off before 1975	−0.49%
18 companies failing to meet other sample inclusion criteria	+1.57%

The profitability differences among groups are not statistically significant; $F(3,186) = 2.02$, with the 5% point being 2.65. Nevertheless, the negative 1.57% average for the three-year analysis companies, which is significantly different from zero (t = 2.35), cautions that the tender offer companies began life after takeover with modestly sub-par performance records.

The principal dependent variable OPINC:A used in our analysis of post-acquisition performance is the operating income/assets percentage for an individual line of business (LB), averaged over the three reporting years 1975–77. Inter-industry differences are taken into account by means of a "fixed effects" regression analysis. That is, each of the 257 four-digit manu-

---

[5] All but four of the 18 "other" excluded companies' LBs had extensive acquisition or sell-off activity in one or more of the years 1975–77. The data for such years often contain significant biases, and must therefore be excluded. See Meeks and Meeks [1981]. In the other four cases, company merger histories were incomplete, precluding an accurate assignment of non-tender mergers to LBs. A sensitivity analysis adding those cases to the sample produced no noteworthy changes in results.

facturing industry categories with LB observations was allowed to have its own profitability regression intercept term. Also controlled for are the following variables, each measured at the individual LB level:

SHR   Market share of LB in its four-digit industry category (scaled in ratio form).

POOL   Fraction of end-of-period assets traced to acquisitions treated under pooling-of-interests accounting.

PURCH   Fraction of end-of-period assets traced to acquisitions treated under purchase accounting.

EQUALS   Dummy variable with value of 1 if the LB had a "merger of equals", defined as a pooling merger among firms whose pre-merger size differed by no more than a factor of two.

NEW   Dummy variable with value of 1 if the line entered the parent's operations after 1950 and experienced no acquisitions.

The POOL and PURCH variables take into account not only the fraction of assets acquired, but also the type of accounting used in transferring acquired assets to the acquirer's books. Under pooling of interests accounting, assets are recorded at their pre-merger book value. Under purchase accounting, assets are recorded in effect at the price actually paid, which usually exceeded pre-merger book values because prevailing replacement costs and/or stock market values were above accounting values and because tender offers are almost always consummated at a stock price premium. Details on these measurements and other methodological matters are presented in Ravenscraft and Scherer [1987].

If we hold those other variables constant, the influence of a tender offer history is ascertained by means of a dummy variable TENDER, with unit value if the line was acquired in whole or in part as the consequence of a tender offer and zero otherwise. Alternatively, a more detailed breakdown is achieved by forming three distinct tender offer dummies:

HOSTILE Acquisition actively opposed by target management.

WHITE   Acquirer was a white knight.

OTHER   Tender offer acquisition meeting neither of the above conditions.

Averaging the data for all lines meeting quality control criteria for the years 1975–77, the following regressions, with t-ratios in subscripted brackets, resulted:

(1)   OPINC: A = [257 constants] − 3.10 TENDER + 30.18 SHR

                           [2.41]   [5.68]

          + 0.66 POOL − 2.81 PURCH + 0.83 NEW + 1.43 EQUALS;

          [0.58]   [2.24]   [0.82]   [1.48]

          $R^2 = 0.1823$, $N = 2732$; mean OPINC: A = 13.34.

152   DAVID J. RAVENSCRAFT AND F. M. SCHERER

(2) $OPINC: A = [257 \text{ constants}] - 3.65 \text{ } HOSTILE - 3.77 \text{ } WHITE$
                                      $[1.65]$ $[1.69]$

           $-2.23 \text{ } OTHER + 30.15 \text{ } SHR + 0.68 \text{ } POOL - 2.82 \text{ } PURCH$
             $[1.18]$ '$[5.67]$ $[0.60]$ $[2.24]$

           $+0.84 \text{ } NEW + 1.46 \text{ } EQUALS; R^2 = 0.1824, N = 2732.$
             $[0.83]$ $[1.51]$

With all tender offer types combined in regression (1), the coefficient on
TENDER is negative and significant at the 0.02 level in a two-tail test.
Breaking the tender offer set into three subsets, as in regression (2), contributes
insignificant variance reduction $[F(2,2467) = 0.20]$.

The TENDER coefficient value of regression (1) indicates that lines with a
tender offer history were 3.10 percentage points less profitable on average
than lines without such a history, but with similar industry membership,
market shares, merger accounting methods, and levels of (non-tender)
acquired assets.[6] Relative to the all-sample operating income/assets average
of 13.34 percent, this is a substantial difference. In conjunction with our
earlier finding that the 62 tender offer targets included in the three-year
analysis had average pre-merger profitability 1.57 percentage points lower
than that of their two-digit industry peers, the -3.10 TENDER coefficient is
inconsistent with the hypothesis that post-tender acquisition profitability
improved, all else equal. Indeed, the implication is in one sense more severe.
Roughly two-thirds of the tender offer acquisitions were treated under
purchase accounting or "dirty pooling" (a blend of purchase and pooling
accounting). To find the full impact on reported profitability of an acquisition
that stemmed from tender offer *and* that contributed 100 percent of a line's
assets under purchase accounting ($PURCH = 1.0$), one must add the -3.10
TENDER coefficient and the -2.81 PURCH coefficient. Together, the
coefficients imply a 5.91 percent degradation of returns relative to control
values. For a line with an average market share in an industry of average
profitability, this means an average return on assets of approximately 7.43
percent.[7] This is well below the median 12 percent after-tax "hurdle rate"
applied by US corporations during the late 1960s in judging new capital
investment proposals. See Williams [1970, p. 21].

---

[6] Other coefficients in regression (1) are interpreted as follows. Moving from having an
infinitesimal market share to controlling the whole market ($SHR = 1$) raises the operating
income/assets percentage by an impressive 30.2 points. Lines originating under pooling of
interests mergers were slightly, but insignificantly, more profitable than their no-merger
counterparts. Mergers of equals were 1.43 percentage points more profitable on average; new
internal growth lines 0.83 points more profitable.

[7] The mean 1975–77 operating income/assets value for the 153 tender offer lines was 10.09
percent, which is well below the all-sample average of 13.34%. This average differs from the value
predicted by regression analysis because only the latter controls for industry, market share, and
accounting choice influences.

LIFE AFTER TAKEOVER 153

A major reason for the depressed post-acquisition returns of tender offer mergers must be the premiums paid to reflect prevailing stock market values and to induce target firm shareholder and/or management acquiescence. Under the purchase accounting adopted following most tender offer takeovers, acquired assets were written up to reflect the value of premiums paid over pre-acquisition book entries. Such writeups increase the denominator of *OPINC: A* and hence reduce the ratio. They may also affect the numerator by raising depreciation charges, but this is less certain, since asset writeups charged to a goodwill account were seldom amortized before 1970 and were subjected to long (e.g., 40 year) amortization periods thereafter.

To test for the role of asset writeups, equation (1) is re-estimated with a dependent variable measured as the ratio of operating income to sales. The result is:

(3) $OPINC: s = [257 \text{ constants}] - 1.20 \text{ } TENDER + 21.91 \text{ } SHR$
$$[1.56] \qquad [6.88]$$

$$+ 0.50 \text{ } POOL - 0.78 \text{ } PURCH - 0.07 \text{ } NEW + 0.86 \text{ } EQUALS;$$
$$[0.73] \qquad [1.03] \qquad [0.12] \qquad [1.49]$$

$R^2 = 0.2128, N = 2732$, mean $OPINC: s = 7.54$.

Here the tender offer effect is significant only at the 0.12 level. It indicates an average deviation in proportion to all-sample operating income/sales ratios of only 15.9 percent, compared to the 23.2 percent deviation in assets-denominated regression (1). Evidently, a substantial component of the post-takeover depression of tender offer LB profitability came from the asset writeups resulting from the premiums over book value paid in effectuating the takeovers.

To purge the effect of such writeups from the numerator of profitability measures, a third variable, the ratio of cash flow (i.e., operating income before deduction of depreciation) to sales, was computed. With it as dependent variable, the result is:

(4) $CASHFLO: s = [257 \text{ constants}] - 1.09 \text{ } TENDER + 23.12 \text{ } SHR$
$$[1.43] \qquad [7.29]$$

$$+ 0.49 \text{ } POOL - 0.87 \text{ } PURCH + 0.16 \text{ } NEW + 0.73 \text{ } EQUALS;$$
$$[0.72] \qquad [1.16] \qquad [0.27] \qquad [1.26]$$

$R^2 = 0.2393, N = 2732$; mean $CASHFLO: s = 10.12$.

The tender offer coefficient and its t-ratio fade a bit more, suggesting the presence of a modest depreciation effect in regression (3). At 10.8 percent of the all-sample cash flow/sales ratio, the negative tender offer coefficient approximates the 12.9 percent *pre-merger* operating income/assets deficit relative to industry norms recorded for the three-year sample tender offer targets. The closeness of the two deviations, one pre-merger and the other

154   DAVID J. RAVENSCRAFT AND F. M. SCHERER

post-merger, compels an agnostic inference that takeover neither improved
nor degraded the basic operating performance of target firms.[8]

It is widely believed that the Williams Act increased takeover premiums. If
so, we might expect the negative effect of TENDER on OPINC:A to be
greater for post-1968 takeovers than for those carried out before the Act took
force. Eighty-nine of the 153 tender offer LBs came from acquisitions
commenced (at least by the successful bidder) after most Williams Act
provisions became effective July 29, 1968. When TENDER is multiplied by a
dummy variable with a value of 1 for post-Williams Act cases, the resulting
regression is:

(5)   OPINC:A = [257 constants] − 3.72 TENDER + 1.09 WILLIAMS
                                          [1.99]   [0.46]

                   + 30.13 SHR + 0.67 POOL − 2.83 PURCH + 0.83 NEW
                     [5.67]   [0.59]   [2.26]   [0.82]

                   + 1.43 EQUALS; $R^2 = 0.1823$, $N = 2732$.
                     [1.49]

There is a hint of less, not more, negative profitability for post-Williams Act
acquisitions, but the WILLIAMS coefficient is not statistically significant,
there are signs of multi-collinearity, and there is no increase in R^2 relative to
equation (1).[9]

                            IV. CONCLUSION

Tender offer targets of the 1960s and early 1970s entered their acquirers'
organizations with a profit record slightly inferior to that of their two-digit
industry peers. Nine years later on average, they performed appreciably less
well. An important reason for their deteriorated post-takeover returns was
the writeup of asset values stemming from the payment of acquisition
premiums. But those premiums were supposedly paid in anticipation of
enhanced profitability, which is not evident in our post-takeover operating

---

[8] That the pre-merger deviation is statistically significant while the post-merger coefficient is
not does not vitiate the conclusion that the two differ trivially. The significance difference stems
from the fact that Line of Business profit data are more variable, with a standard deviation nearly
three times that of comparably-defined company-level data.

[9] Two additional analyses were suggested by referees. A linear time-weighted version of
TENDER implied that the significantly negative profits were *most* negative for the most recent
tender offers. However, the regression had explanatory power inferior to that of equation (1).
Relating operating income to mid-period assets rather than end-of-year assets moved the
TENDER coefficient in the analogue of equation (1) to −3.31, with $t = 2.53$.

A further check added a dummy variable when a Line of Business company had been acquired
in a tender offer made by a foreign company, and when the US corporate shell was retained after
the acquisition. Asset revaluations are less likely in such cases. The dummy variable was positive
but statistically insignificant ($t = 0.58$) in the operating income/assets regression, while the
TENDER coefficient became slightly more negative. The foreign parent dummy was negative
but statistically insignificant ($t = 0.18$) in the operating income/sales regression.

LIFE AFTER TAKEOVER 155

income and cash flow regressions. This is an anomaly for the theory of takeovers as an efficiency-increasing mechanism. If improvements did occur, their impact must have been concentrated not in operating returns, but below the "bottom line" of our operating income measures—e.g., in income taxes or interest costs. Tax savings are a zero-sum game against the Treasury. Since there are clear and persistent economies of scale in financing,[10] capital cost savings may have been overlooked by our analysis. Yet they could scarcely have been large enough to justify the low average pre-interest returns on assets revealed by regressions (1) and (2), nor was tender offer takeover the only way to secure them.

At the very least, these results suggest a need for direct and affirmative evidence on whence the purported economic benefits of takeovers originate and whether tenderers have in fact succeeded in managing their acquisitions better than the displaced managers. Absent such evidence, the hypothesis that tender offer takeovers are on average efficiency-increasing warrants much more skepticism than it has received thus far in the literatures of economics, corporate finance, and securities law.

DAVID J. RAVENSCRAFT,   ACCEPTED DECEMBER 1986
School of Business Administration,
University of North Carolina,
Chapel Hill, NC 27514,
USA.

F. M. SCHERER,
Department of Economics,
Swarthmore College,
Swarthmore, Pennsylvania 19081,
USA.

REFERENCES

AUSTIN, DOUGLAS V. and FISHMAN, JAY A., 1969, 'The Tender Takeover', *Mergers & Acquisitions*, 4 (May–June), pp. 4–23.
AUSTIN, DOUGLAS, V., 1973, 'Tender Offers Revisited: 1968–72', *Mergers & Acquisitions*, 8 (Fall), pp. 16–29.
AUSTIN, DOUGLAS V., 1975, 'Tender Offer Statistics: New Strategies Are Paying Off', *Mergers & Acquisitions*, 10 (Fall), pp. 9–18.
AUSTIN, DOUGLAS V., 1980, 'Tender Offer Update: 1978–1979', *Mergers & Acquisitions*, 15 (Summer), pp. 13–32.
EASTERBROOK, FRANK H. and FISCHEL, DANIEL R., 1981, 'The Proper Role of a Target's Management in Responding to a Tender Offer', *Harvard Law Review*, 94 (April), pp. 1161–1204.
JENSEN, MICHAEL C. and RUBACK, RICHARD S., 1983, 'The Market for Corporate Control', *Journal of Financial Economics*, 11 (No. 1), pp. 5–50.

[10] See Scherer *et al.* [1975, pp. 284–288], where a tenfold increase in company size was found to reduce interest rates paid by 0.46 percentage points during the mid-1960s.

156   DAVID J. RAVENSCRAFT AND F. M. SCHERER

MANNE, HENRY G., 1965, 'Mergers and the Market for Corporate Control', *Journal of Political Economy*, 73 (April), pp. 110–120.

MARRIS, ROBIN, 1963, 'A Model of the "Managerial" Enterprise', *Quarterly Journal of Economics*, 77 (May), pp. 185–209.

MEEKS, G. and MEEKS, J. G., 1981, 'Profitability Measures as Indicators of Post-Merger Efficiency', *The Journal of Industrial Economics*, 29 (June), pp. 335–344.

RAVENSCRAFT, DAVID J. and SCHERER, F. M., 1987, *Mergers, Sell-Offs, and Economic Efficiency* (Brookings: Washington).

SCHERER, F. M., BECKENSTEIN, ALAN, KAUFER, ERICH, and MURPHY, R. D., 1975, *The Economics of Multi-Plant Operation: An International Comparisons Study* (Harvard University Press, Cambridge, MA).

SCHERER, F. M., 1986, 'Takeovers: Present and Future Dangers', *The Brookings Review*, 4 (Winter/Spring), pp. 15–20.

SCHERER, F. M., LONG, W. F., MARTIN, STEPHEN, MUELLER, DENNIS C., PASCOE, GEORGE, RAVENSCRAFT, D. J., SCOTT, JOHN T. and WEISS, LEONARD W., 1987, 'The Validity of Studies with Line of Business Data: Comment', *American Economic Review*, 77 (March), pp. 205–217.

US COUNCIL OF ECONOMIC ADVISERS, 1985, *Annual Report*, in *Economic Report of the President* (Washington, DC).

US FEDERAL TRADE COMMISSION, *Quarterly Financial Report for Manufacturing and Mining Corporations* (various dates, Washington, DC).

US FEDERAL TRADE COMMISSION, 1978, *Statistical Report on Mergers and Acquisitions* (December, Washington, DC).

WILLIAMS, JR., R. B., 1970, 'Industry Practice in Allocating Capital Resources', *Managerial Planning*, 19 (May/June), pp. 15–22.

YARROW, G. K., 1985, 'Shareholder Protection, Compulsory Acquisition and the Efficiency of the Takeover Process', *The Journal of Industrial Economics*, 34 (September), pp. 3–16.

[11]

Chapter 8

The Causes and Effects of Takeovers in the United Kingdom: An Empirical Investigation for the Late 1960s at the Microeconomic Level

Andrew Cosh, Alan Hughes, and Ajit Singh

INTRODUCTION

A number of factors distinguish in general terms the nature of merger activity in the United Kingdom from that in other countries. First, although in common with many of the latter, the United Kingdom has experienced an intense and historically unprecedented wave of mergers during the last two decades, the merger wave appears to have started a few years earlier in the United Kingdom than elsewhere. Second, inter-company stock market transactions have played a far more important role in merger activity in the United Kingdom than in other countries, with the possible exception of the United States. This is because, for institutional and historical reasons, the United Kingdom and the United States have the most developed and sophisticated stock markets. In both countries, the number of quoted companies is very much greater than elsewhere. Third, unlike the United States, but more in common with the continental countries, the government in the United Kingdom has followed a benign policy toward mergers, if not positively encouraged them. Thus, there have been few antitrust and other restrictions on the market for corporate control in the United Kingdom. This country therefore provides a unique opportunity to study the nature and efficiency of such a market—(such studies as those by Singh 1971, 1975; and Kuehn 1975).

228 / The Determinants and Effects of Mergers

It is also important to mention a further factor that distinguishes the empirical analysis rather than the institutional framework of merger activity in the United Kingdom. United Kingdom merger statistics, particularly for companies quoted on the stock market, are more reliable and complete than for any of the other industrial countries. The reasons for this are both the statutory requirements of the companies acts and the immense amount of work done by the government departments and the research institutions in the country in producing comparable standardized accounting information on an individual company basis. (These data are described in Singh and Whittington 1968; Singh 1971; Whittington 1971; and Hughes 1977.)

The analysis here concentrates upon the microeconomic aspects of takeovers and considers their impact on the individual company.[1] In particular this chapter analyzes those takeovers that took place in the three years 1967–1969 among those large public companies quoted on the United Kingdom stock exchanges that operated mainly in the United Kingdom and in the manufacturing and distributive industries. An attempt is made however to place these takeovers in a broader historical and institutional perspective so that conclusions based upon their analysis can be more properly assessed.

The chapter is organized as follows: In the following section we consider the definition of takeover used in this study and the institutional forms that takeover has taken in our period of analysis and in earlier takeover movements in the United Kingdom. In the second section we examine those aspects of industrial and competition policy that have formed the immediate backdrop to takeovers in this country in the 1960s. The third section discusses the dimensions of the takeover movement in the United Kingdom in the postwar period and in particular the degree of takeover activity among our population of companies in the years 1967–1969. Section four introduces the approach and terminology adopted in carrying out the specific tests on the determinants and effects of mergers described in Chapter 2. Section five presents a comparison of the premerger characteristics of acquiring, acquired, and other (control group) companies. The results of the tests on the determinants of mergers are given in section six and those of their effects in section seven. The final section draws together our conclusions and suggests possible future directions for research in this field.

DEFINITION OF TAKEOVER

The accounting data for companies quoted on the United Kingdom stock markets—which are the basic source of information for the present study—distinguish between two kinds of merger. First, there are those that involve the acquisition of 50 percent or more of the shares of one company (*A*) by another (*B*). The second category consists of those in which two companies A and B amalgamate to form a new legal entity C. This distinction is purely legal, and the choice between these two forms of merger is affected by financial and administrative considerations rather than by broader economic reasons (Moon 1968; Singh 1971). The most thorough examination of the quoted manufacturing sector in the United Kingdom available so far shows that of the 1599 companies disappearing through merger in the period 1948–1972, only 77 fell in the second category—namely, disappeared through what may be termed amalgamation (Hughes 1977). In this chapter we have excluded amalgamations from the analysis and use the term merger to describe only acquisition or takeover.[2]

There are a number of ways in which acquisition of a controlling share may be affected. The required block of shares in a company may be purchased privately from their owners by a deal between the boards of directors of the companies involved, or a "scheme of arrangement" may be agreed whereby the share capital of one company is canceled and replaced by new shares issued by the other (Davies 1976). Where shares are publicly quoted on the stock exchange they may also be purchased in a piecemeal covert fashion without any prior consultation between the directors or shareholders of the companies involved.

Although such a process is subject to legal restriction requiring disclosure of any significant holdings accumulated,[3] during most of the postwar period the restriction was easy to circumvent by having apparently independent buyers act in concert to accumulate small holdings, all ultimately held on behalf of the would-be acquirer of a controlling interest (Spiegelberg 1973). Nevertheless, such transactions are usually only a preparatory stage to the public announcement of a takeover bid,[4] which appears to be overwhelmingly the most popular method of effecting changes of control on the United Kingdom Stock Exchange. There are no precise figures on acquisition alone available, but of 898 changes of control (including amalgamations) on the stock exchange noted by the City Panel on Takeovers and Mergers in the years 1969–1972, 841 involved the use of the bid technique (Davies 1976).

This prevalence of the bid may be contrasted with its virtual absence from the scene in earlier United Kingdom merger waves at the turn of the century and in the interwar years (Hannah 1974a). In the earlier of these two waves, multifirm amalgamations associated with the flotation of new companies were the predominant form of merger (Macrosty 1907; Payne 1967; Hannah 1974b). In the interwar period, on the other hand, although multifirm combination largely disappeared, most mergers took the form of agreed transactions between boards of directors without resort to open or direct bidding to the shareholders of the companies acquired, even where the companies involved were quoted.

This reflects a number of factors differentiating the postwar and interwar years. In the first place there was a much wider dispersion of share

230   /   The Determinants and Effects of Mergers

ownership by the 1950s than had existed in the interwar period. In 1936 the average proportion of total votes held by the top twenty shareholders in large quoted companies in the United Kingdom was 30 percent; by 1951 it was 19 percent. At the same time the proportion of shares held by directors declined, as did the number of directors among the largest shareholders, while the number of directors listed as holding no more than their minimum qualifying shares grew (Sargent 1961; Hannah 1976b). Second, the amount and quality of information available to investors grew with the stock market itself and with the increasingly stringent legal requirements relating to the provision of accounting information contained in successive companies acts. These factors tended to reduce the importance of obtaining prior directorial acceptance of takeover proposals, as well as reducing directors' control over information pertaining to their companies. Direct appeals to shareholders became, therefore, more attractive propositions for would-be acquirers.

Third, the economic environment for takeover on the stock exchange in the immediate postwar years was particularly suitable for the development of the bid techniques by astute entrepreneurs (Wright 1962). This was in part due to government exhortation and fiscal discrimination in favor of retained profits (as well as other factors), which depressed share prices because of the associated poor dividend prospects. The result was a discrepancy between market values and the underlying productive value of the assets.[5] Further, many managements with freehold properties in their books from the prewar years had not adjusted their book value in line with general price rises. These companies were excellent targets for astute bidders because of the opportunity afforded once control was gained to sell such properties to institutions looking for safe investments while renting them back for continued use in the business. This situation was particularly notable in retailing where a leaseback arrangement was an attractive proposition, as it realized large surplus cash proceeds for use both for further bids and for internal investment at a time of restrictions on bank lending and control of capital issues by the Capital Issues Committee.

It should be emphasized, however, that although the aggressive takeover bids bred by these factors established the framework for further merger activity in the United Kingdom, they were concentrated in a narrow range of industry and had ceased to be the main force behind it by the late 1950s. The reduction of controls affecting the company sector and the stock market, along with the activities of the bidders themselves, reduced the opportunities for this kind of takeover. The method pioneered by the early tycoons instead became the general weapon of the professional managers who came to dominate merger activity in the United Kingdom after the 1950s in a much wider range of industries (Bull and Vice 1961; Brooks and Smith 1963; Mennel 1962).

However, it is doubtful whether aggressive, free-raiding, takeover bidding can genuinely be said to have survived as a dominant force behind the merger wave. This is especially so if we look not just at the quoted sector but at companies in general, among which it is apparent that the vast majority of mergers are either deals between directors or uncontested bids (Newbould 1970). This is not to deny that very large, very fiercely contested takeover bids have occurred, but in terms of frequency they are a small, though well publicized, proportion of total activity. Just as an "uncontested bid" or an "agreed deal" does not necessarily mean that the merger is a voluntary undertaking by both companies, similarly, the predominant role of the bid technique should not be assumed to show that the merger by agreement practices of the 1920s and 1930s have been entirely replaced by ruthless mergers forced on unwilling victims by aggressive raiders. It is interesting in this respect to note that victim and bidder may come together at the request of the former or because of long-standing mutual interests and contacts between the firms concerned (Newbould 1970).

GOVERNMENT POLICY AND MERGER ACTIVITY

The legislation governing competition policy relating to mergers is mainly contained in Part V of the Fair Trading Act of 1973, which incorporates the provisions in respect of mergers first laid down in the Monopolies and Mergers Act of 1965 (Davies 1976; H.M.G. 1969) and which was in force for the period of our analysis. Broadly speaking, the legislation empowered the secretary of state at the then Department of Prices and Consumer Protection to adopt a pragmatic, case-by-case approach in deciding whether to refer to the Monopolies and Mergers Commission, for investigation, those mergers that met certain qualifying conditions. In particular, those mergers qualified that either would create or intensify a situation in which more than one-quarter of a defined United Kingdom national or regional market was supplied by a single producer[6] or that involved the acquisition of book value of assets of more than £5m. In addition all newspaper mergers over a certain size had to be referred for investigation. Thus in effect the legislation provided for the surveillance of all significant horizontal and large mergers.

Although many mergers met the qualifying conditions of the 1965 legislation, few have been referred for investigation to assess their impact on the "public interest" that the legislation seeks to protect. From 1965 to 1974 it has been estimated that 1038 mergers in the United Kingdom met these conditions, but only 35 were referred to the Monopolies and Mergers Commission (including 6 automatic newspaper references). Of these referrals, only eight were held to be against the public interest, and a further ten were abandoned upon referral (Davies 1976; Gribbin 1974). It is difficult to interpret these figures as suggesting that mergers in the United Kingdom have been subjected to a restrictive competition policy. On the contrary, a number of commentators have concluded that the legislation and its enforcement should be considerably strengthened (Sutherland 1969, 1970; Utton 1974a; Meeks 1977).

In addition to the indirect influence of competition policy, the central authorities have also influenced the level of merger activity by including direct intervention in their industrial policy. In the period of our analysis (1967–1969), the most significant form that direct intervention took was the Industrial Reorganization Corporation (IRC), created by the Labour government in the late 1960s (Young and Lowe 1974). This body, in addition to carrying out investigations of the structure and performance of particular sectors of industry and providing loans and other financing for investment, also acted directly in the financing and promotion of mergers. During its period of active operation between January 1967 and December 1970 (prior to its abolition by the incoming Conservative administration), the IRC was directly involved in a financial, promotional, or advisory capacity in twenty-two mergers of larger quoted companies, involving the acquisition of around £1 billion of net assets by the acquiring companies concerned.[7] These mergers included the largest to occur in the postwar period as a whole, including the acquisition of English Electric and AEI by the GEC, the formation of British Leyland and Rowntree Mackintosh, the acquisition of IPC by Reed, and the formation of Ransome Hoffman Pollard in the roller bearing industry.

It seems fair to conclude that on balance, pragmatism in the practice of competition and industrial policy led to a generally permissive attitude toward merger in the United Kingdom in the postwar period as a whole, including our period of analysis. Privately inspired mergers were rarely referred for investigation, and direct intervention was responsible in part for the many massive mergers that transformed large sectors of manufacturing industry.[8]

THE DIMENSIONS OF MERGER ACTIVITY IN THE UNITED KINGDOM IN THE POSTWAR PERIOD

The United Kingdom has experienced a merger wave of major proportions in the postwar years. As Figure 8–1 illustrates, this wave reached its peak in the late 1960s and early 1970s, when annual expenditure on acquiring controlling interests in companies of all kinds accounted for up to 28 percent of all uses of funds by quoted manufacturing and distributive companies. Until the late 1950s, acquisition expenditure did not rise above 10 percent of total uses; after 1960, it rarely fell below this level. As Figure 8–1 also shows, the pattern of acquisition expenditure over time was roughly similar in both manufacturing and distribution. Within the quoted sector itself, merger activity on this scale has had a

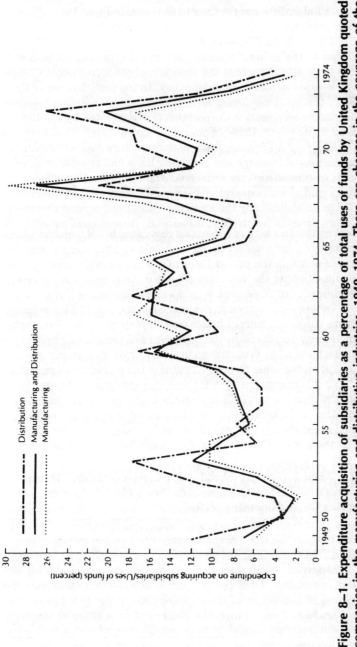

Figure 8–1. Expenditure acquisition of subsidiaries as a percentage of total uses of funds by United Kingdom quoted companies in the manufacturing and distributive industries, 1949–1974. There are changes in the coverage of the underlying population of companies in 1960, 1964, and 1969. For this and other reasons connected with changes in the definitions of expenditure used in the collection and analysis of the data, figures are only roughly comparable over time. (*Sources: Income and Finance of Public Quoted Companies 1949–60* (1962); *Business Monitors* M3 and M7 (various issues); *Statistics on Incomes Prices, Employment and Production* (various issues).)

234 / The Determinants and Effects of Mergers

Table 8–1. Vital Statistics of the Quoted Manufacturing Sector, 1948–1972

		Number	Percent of Row 5
1	Companies in 1948	1919	60.9
2	Continuing companies	598	19.0
3	Births	1233	39.1
4	Deaths	1845	58.5
	(a) of which acquisition and amalgamation	1597	50.7
5	Total number of companies	3152	100.0
6	Double counting (i.e., born and died 1948–1972)	524	16.6
7	Companies in 1972	1307	41.5
8	Percent change in number of companies 1948–1972	−31.9%	

Source: Hughes (1977).

major effect on the numbers of companies remaining in independent existence. An analysis for manufacturing alone shows that merger was the major form of death in the period 1948–1972 and was responsible for the death rate outstripping the birth rate of quoted companies. The net result was the decline of over 30 percent in independent companies that is shown in row 8 of Table 8–1.[9] Row 4a shows that over one-half of all companies existing were subject to merger in this period. Moreover, as the intensity of merger activity increased in the later years of the period, so did the extent to which the large firms were acquired (Singh 1975; Hughes 1976).

Table 8–2 provides some recent estimates of the annual average probability of "dying" through merger for five size quintiles and three subperiods in the years 1948–1972 that confirm this point. In the earlier subperiods the table shows that the largest 20 percent of companies experienced substantially lower death rates by merger than the other 80 percent. In the period 1966–1972, although the largest companies were

Table 8–2. Annual Average Probability of a Company "Dying" Through Merger for Each of Five Size Quintiles in the Years 1949–1972 in the Manufacturing Quoted Company Sector[a]

	Probability of Merger Death		
Size Category	1949–1958	1959–1965	1966–1972
Largest	0.6	2.7	4.1
2	1.5	3.5	5.4
3	1.3	3.8	5.7
4	1.6	4.3	4.5
Smallest	1.7	3.4	4.8
All	1.3	3.6	4.9

Source: Hughes (1977).
[a] It should be noted that this table includes both acquisition and amalgamation deaths.

still somewhat more secure than the rest (with the firms in the top quintile having a 20 percent lower chance of being acquired), their position had deteriorated noticeably.[10] Since 1959, the death rate from merger alone for all groups outstripped previous estimates of the death rate from all causes taken together on the United Kingdom Stock Exchange since the 1880s.[11]

Clearly the causes and economic consequences of activity of this scope and magnitude are of major importance. In this study we focus our attention on the peak merger years of 1967–1969 (see Figure 8–1) and upon those mergers, in those years, that involved the disappearance of larger quoted companies in the manufacturing and distributive industries. Although quoted company mergers are a small proportion of the total number of mergers occurring, they dominate in terms of size and account for the bulk of acquisition expenditure (Hughes 1976).

The number and industrial distribution of the mergers studied here are shown in Table 8–3. There are two points to note about these mergers. First, the companies analyzed constitute the total population takeover deaths in those industries shown in the table where the companies involved were quoted and had net assets of over £500,000, or gross income of over £50,000 in 1964. In all there were 290 takeover deaths involving 233 acquirers. Second, the percentage of takeovers in which both companies involved were classified within the same two-digit industry group, which we term horizontal mergers, was 54 percent within manufacturing industries but below 50 percent in the distributive industries. This implies that in the peak merger years examined in this study horizontal merger was somewhat less predominant than in the merger wave as a whole. Even quite disaggregated studies for the postwar years have suggested that horizontal mergers accounted for 70 percent of the total number of takeovers occurring (Gribbin 1974; Hughes 1976; Newbould 1970). It is apparent, however, that the importance of horizontal takeover has declined as the merger wave has proceeded, and our sample of years represents a culmination of a trend that has seen the proportion of horizontal acquisitions within the United Kingdom quoted manufacturing and distributive sector fall from 68 percent in the period 1950–1956 to 63 percent in the period 1957–1963 to 48 percent in the period 1964–1970 (authors' own estimates based on the DI company accounts data bank).

In view of the almost equal numerical importance of horizontal and other mergers, the following analysis examines the sample as a whole and as two separate categories. horizontal and other.

MICROECONOMIC ANALYSIS OF UNITED KINGDOM TAKEOVERS, 1967–1969

Before presenting the results of the specific tests of the determinants and effects of mergers described in Chapter 2, it will be useful to

Table 8–3. The Number of Companies Acquired, 1967–1969, and Their Industrial Classification by Acquiring and Acquired Company

Industry of Acquired Company	Industry of Acquiring Company																					Acquired Companies	
	21	23	26	31	33	36	37	38	39	41	43	44	46	47	48	49	50	70	81	82	88	Total	of which horizontal
Food 21	6		3																			12	6
Drink 23	1	10	1																			12	10
Chemicals 26	1	1	7													1						12	7
Metal manufacturing 31			4	2	1					1			1									9	2
Nonelectrical engineering 33			3	5	21	3	1	1	1	1			1									47	21
Electrical engineering 36			3	3	3	14		1	4	1						2	3				1	20	14
Marine engineering 37							1															1	1
Vehicles 38						1				1			1									2	0
Other metal 39			1	1	2	1	1		2	1			1					1				11	2
Textiles 41			1	1	1	1			1	24	1		1							1		30	24
Leather, etc. 43									1	1	1		1							1		2	0
Clothing and footwear 44										9											1	11	0
Bricks, etc. 46	1					1							13	1		1				1		15	13
Timber, etc. 47													1	2	1	1	3					9	2
Paper, etc. 48										1	1		3	1	8	2						10	8
Other manufacturing 49					1								1		2	2						7 (210)[b]	2 (113)
Construction 50			2		1	1	1			1	1					4	1					13	4
Transport, etc. 70			1			3	1															4	0
Wholesale 81			1		2			1	1	6			3		1		1	1	9	3		30	9
Retail 82	2		1						1	2						1	3	3	2	6	3	17	6
Other services 88						4														3	5	16 (80)	5 (24)
Total acquired companies by industry of acquiring company	9	14	23	10	31	27	3	3	10	47	3	0	25	3	10	6	12	10	16	15	13	290	137
Total acquiring companies[a]	9	10	18	8	30	21	3	3	10	26	3	0	20	3	8	6	11	6	14	13	11	233	

[a] Some companies acquired more than one company; therefore they are fewer in number than the acquired companies.
[b] Figures in parentheses are column totals up to that point.

compare the characteristics of the acquired, acquiring, and other (control group) firms in the population. Such a comparison, apart from being necessary for a fuller understanding of the subsequent test results, is as explained in Chapter 2 of interest in its own right. It bears directly on a range of economic issues, which are important from the point of view of both economic theory and policy (for a full discussion of these issues, see Singh, 1971, 1975). For example, a major question of current theoretical interest is the nature of the selection mechanism generated by the normal workings of real world markets and its implications for the behavior of economic agents (Hahn 1973, Johnson 1968). (For an account of the various theories concerning the nature of the selection mechanism which is presumed to exist, see Singh 1971; Winter 1971.)

In view of the institutional background to the takeover movement in the United Kingdom described earlier, an examination of these questions is particularly pertinent for this country. For not only has the magnitude of the takeover phenomenon been very significant in the period considered in this study, but, as noted, mergers in the United Kingdom have been less subject to government regulations and restrictions than in countries such as the United States. Furthermore, as we are confining ourselves to mergers of companies quoted on the stock market, and as London possesses one of the most well organized and sophisticated of such markets, it should be possible to observe the kind of selection process produced by the relatively free play of forces in effectively functioning markets.

Variables and Time Periods Used

The comparison of the average characteristics of the acquired, acquiring, and other firms is made in terms of the following variables—size, profitability, profits variability, growth, leverage, price-earnings ratio, and stockholder return.[12] Most of these variables are approximated by a number of different indicators based on the accounting data of individual firms.

Size has been measured in terms of the following indicators: (1) the balance sheet or book value of the net assets of the firm; (2) its total assets; and (3) sales. Net assets are defined as total fixed assets plus current assets net of current liabilities; assets are valued, as is the usual practice in balance sheets, at historic cost net of depreciation. Total assets include both current and fixed assets and are net of depreciation. In relation to sales, it is important to remember that disclosure of these data became obligatory only with the 1967 Companies Act. As a consequence there are many firms, particularly smaller ones, for which such data are not available for the years before 1967.

The profitability performance of companies is indicated by the following variables: (1) profit margin, which is represented by gross trading profits as a percentage of sales; (2) pretax profitability on net assets, where, in line

238 / The Determinants and Effects of Mergers

with the definition of net assets given above, pretax profits include investment and other income of the firm and are net of depreciation and any
charge for current liabilities (e.g., bank interest), but are taken before the
deduction of taxation and long-term interest payments; and (3) posttax
profitability on equity assets, where posttax profits comprise retained
earnings plus dividends after tax and equity assets represent the book
value of assets owned by ordinary shareholders of the firm.

Profits variability is measured by the coefficient of variation of a firm's
profits over the last five accounting years. All three indicators of profits
—gross trading profits, pretax profits, and posttax profits—are used for
this purpose. Growth is measured by two separate indicators—growth of
net assets (i.e., the long-term financial capital employed in the firm) and
growth of physical assets. Again, two different variables are used to
measure leverage: first, a stock measure, which expresses the book value
of long-term liabilities plus preference capital as a percentage of the book
value of total capital and reserves plus long-term liabilities; and second, a
flow measure, which shows the percentage of a firm's posttax income that
is allocated to fixed interest and dividend payments. The price-earnings
ratio is measured by the ratio of the company's share price to its posttax
earnings per share.[13]

The stockholder return for a company is measured by the compound
percentage return per annum on holding that company's ordinary shares.
The return includes the capital gain and dividend income, including income
derived from reinvesting dividend income at a market rate of return.[14]
Since considerable work was involved in the collection of data for calculation of the stockholder return, the tests involving this measure were
confined to a sample of the group of mergers studied in the other tests.

As noted above, the study examines mergers that occurred in the three
years 1967–1969. The analysis for each of these years was carried out separately, but to save space this chapter reports results for all three years together. Most of the variables are measured over the five-year period prior
to merger and over three and five years after merger. The price-earnings
ratio is measured over the three years prior to merger; however, the size
variable is always measured at the last accounting date before takeover.

Definition of the Groups of Firms

The findings reported in the following sections concern the univariate comparisons of the mean values of the above variables for various groups of
firms:

1. AG—the group of quoted firms that acquired other quoted firms in
   the population in the years 1967–1969;[15]
2. AD—the group of companies that were acquired;

3. C—the control group companies, which neither were acquired nor carried out any significant acquisition over the period from five years before the year of merger considered to five years after.
4. MAG—the sample of companies, drawn from the control group, that matched the acquiring companies by industry and, as far as possible, by size of each acquiring company.[16]
5. MAD—the sample of companies, drawn from the control group, that matched the acquired companies by industry and by size for each acquired company.

Further, in every case the analysis was carried out separately for (1) all mergers (A), (2) horizontal mergers (H), and (3) nonhorizontal mergers (NH).[17] With nearly 300 quoted firms in manufacturing and distribution being acquired during the period 1967–1969, there were enough observations for each of the two types of mergers. However, this also unfortunately means a vast array of results including a separate analysis for each industry,[18] of which only a small selection is presented in the tables in the following sections.

COMPARISON OF PREMERGER CHARACTERISTICS OF ACQUIRING, ACQUIRED, AND CONTROL GROUP COMPANIES

The Acquiring and Acquired Companies

Table 8–4 reports results comparing the characteristics of the group of acquiring firms with those of the group of firms they acquired, on a univariate basis. For each main variable results are presented only for a single indicator in each case, since those for the other indicators were broadly similar. However, the table gives figures for each of the two merger types—horizontal (H) and nonhorizontal (NH)—and for all mergers (A). The results for individual industries are not shown, since that would have required a separate table of this kind for each of the fourteen industries (where there were sufficient observations for individual industry analysis; those results are available on request from the authors). Instead we report here only figures for all industries together, as well as summary results pertaining to individual industries (based on the binomial probability test).[19]

The nature of the information contained in the table is best explained by considering the figures in a particular row (e.g., row 4). These figures show that for all mergers, the average pretax profitability on net assets of the group of all quoted acquiring firms (i.e., firms that undertook acquisitions

240 / The Determinants and Effects of Mergers

Table 8–4.   Comparison of Premerger Characteristics of Acquiring and Acquired Companies

Variable	Merger Type	Group 1	Number of Companies N_1	Mean Value $\bar{X}_1$	Group 2	Number of Companies N_2	Mean Value $\bar{X}_2$
						All Industries Results	
Size							
In net assets	A	AG	290	10.05	AD	290	7.91
	H	AG	137	9.85	AD	137	8.04
	NH	AG	153	10.22	AD	153	7.79
Profitability							
Pretax return on	A	AG	226	15.39	AD	226	13.90
net assets	H	AG	113	14.43	AD	113	13.32
	NH	AG	113	16.34	AD	113	14.48
Profits Variability							
Coefficient of varia-	A	AG	240	0.32	AD	240	0.50
tion of net income	H	AG	117	0.42	AD	117	0.37
	NH	AG	123	0.23	AD	123	0.63
Growth							
Growth of net assets	A	AG	241	11.99	AD	241	6.08
	H	AG	117	10.17	AD	117	6.55
	NH	AG	124	13.72	AD	124	5.63
Leverage							
Stock measure	A	AG	240	18.53	AD	240	15.73
	H	AG	117	18.04	AD	117	16.47
	NH	AG	123	18.99	AD	123	15.04

Notes: Period of comparison is five years prior to merger except for size, which is measured in the year prior to merger.
   AG—acquiring companies.
   AD—acquired companies.
   C—control group companies.
   MAG—control group companies matched with acquiring companies.
   MAD—control group companies matched with acquired companies.

during the period 1967–1969 was 15.4 percent; the corresponding average profitability of the firms they acquired was 13.9 percent. The observed difference of 1.5 percent was statisticlly significant at the 5 percent level (as indicated by the *t*-value of 2.28). This result, however, pertains to all industries together and, for reasons explained earlier, may therefore be subject to aggregation bias.

This fear is to a certain extent borne out by the figures given in the next three columns. They show that in only nine of the fourteen individual industries was the average profitability of acquiring firms greater than that of the firms they acquired (i.e., in five industries, the acquired firms

Takeovers in the United Kingdom / 241

		Summary of Individual Industry Results		
Difference in Mean Values $\bar{X}_1 - \bar{X}_2$	Statistical Significance t-Value	Number of Industries with Positive $\bar{X}_1 - \bar{X}_2$	Total Number of Industries	Proportion Positive and its Significance
2.14**	17.38	14	14	1.00**
1.81**	10.07	14	14	1.00**
2.43**	14.53	14	14	1.00**
1.49*	2.28	9	14	0.64
1.11	1.37	9	14	0.64
1.87	1.84	9	14	0.64
−0.18	−1.63	5	14	0.36
0.06	0.45	5	14	0.36
−0.40*	−2.26	3	14	0.21*
5.91**	5.90	14	14	1.00**
3.61**	2.91	11	14	0.79*
8.08**	5.23	14	14	1.00**
2.79*	2.43	11	14	0.79*
1.57	0.99	10	14	0.71
3.95*	2.40	11	14	0.79*

A—all mergers.
H—horizontal mergers.
NH—nonhorizontal mergers.
** Indicates (two-tail) significance at the 10 percent level or better.
 * Indicates (two-tail significance at the 5 percent level (5.732 percent level in the case of the binomial probability test) or better.
In indicates the natural logarithm.

were more profitable than the acquiring). If there was no difference between the average profitability of the two groups of firms, one would expect that in about half the industries, the acquiring firms would be more profitable than the acquired, and in the other half, the acquired would be relatively more profitable. The last column shows that this null hypothesis is not rejected by the data at the 5 percent level of significance.

Therefore, to the extent that the concept of industry is economically and statistically meaningful, as there is every reason to believe it is (despite the coarseness of the two-digit industrial categories used in this study), one cannot conclude that the observed differences in the average profita-

242   /   The Determinants and Effects of Mergers

bility of the two groups of firms are statistically significant at the 5 percent level, notwithstanding the result for all industries together. Considered in economic terms, the observed differences are of very little quantitative significance in view of the very large degree of variability in the profitability of firms in each group: the typical standard deviation of profitability in an industry is of the order of 12 percent.

Continuing with the discussion of the profitability variable, the next two rows show that the differences in the average profitability of the two groups of firms are relatively larger in the case of nonhorizontal mergers than in the case of horizontal mergers (the figure for all mergers in row 4 shows the combined result for the two categories). However, these differences are not large enough to alter the above conclusion with respect to the economic and statistical significance of profitability as a discriminator between the two groups of firms (even if only nonhorizontal mergers are considered).

The interpretation of the other results in Table 8–4 is quite straightforward. For the size variable, for each of the two merger types and for both merger types together, the mean differences between the groups are both economically and statistically significant (the latter at the 1 percent level). Further, with respect to statistical significance, both the binomial probability test and the *t*-test for aggregate data for all firms yield a similar result. The acquiring companies are on average several times larger than the companies that they acquire. The results for the growth variable are similar to those for size: the acquiring companies grow on average nearly twice as fast as the companies they acquire, and the observed differences are statistically highly significant in both tests. It is worth noting that acquirers involved in nonhorizontal merger activity are, on average, faster growing (13.7 percent as against 10.2 percent) than other acquirers.

The stock measure of the leverage variable also yields unambiguous results for all mergers and for nonhorizontal mergers. Taken together these results suggest that acquiring companies are appreciably more highly levered, on average, than acquired companies.

The results of the profits variability test are somewhat more complex. They show that in the case of horizontal mergers, there is little difference in the volatility of the profits of the average acquiring company, compared with the average acquired company. However in the case of nonhorizontal mergers, the acquiring firms have on average a significantly more stable profits record (at the 5 percent level) than the firms they acquire.

To sum up, we find that acquiring companies are very much larger and have higher leverage ratios and a much faster growth rate, on average, than the acquired companies. There is, however, little difference in the average profitability of the two groups of firms. Finally, there is some evidence that for the category of nonhorizontal mergers, the firms acquired have a more volatile profits record.[20] These results are somewhat different from those obtained by Singh (1971) for acquisitions of United Kingdom quoted companies during the period 1955–1960. For this earlier period also, the acquiring companies were on the whole much bigger and had a much faster growth rate than the acquired; however, they were then appreciably more profitable on average than the companies they acquired.

Comparison of Acquiring and Control Group Companies

The nature of the differences between the premerger characteristics of the acquiring companies and the control group companies is revealed by the figures in Table 8–5. In Table 8–5 (and in Table 8–6, which compares the acquired with the control group companies), we do not give separate figures for each merger type, as this yielded similar conclusions; instead, we show additionally the results obtained for different measures of each variable. In Table 8–5 the acquiring companies are usually compared with the control group of all nonacquiring and nonacquired quoted companies in the population (indicated by letter C). However, there is evidence that firm size is correlated in an important way with some of the indicators,[21] which significantly affects the conclusions with respect to these variables. We have therefore (in both tables) also reported figures obtained by comparing the acquiring (acquired) firms with the alternative control group of matched nonacquiring-nonacquired firms (indicated as MAG or MAD). Since matching is done by size of firm within the same industry year, such a comparison should totally eliminate the influence of size (if the matching were perfect; but as noted earlier, it is not).

The most important conclusions which emerge from Table 8–5 are that the acquiring firms are much larger than the control group firms and have higher leverage ratios and a much faster growth rate. The differences between the groups are both statistically significant and quantitatively important and are larger when nonhorizontal acquirers are considered separately.

However, the results with respect to differences in profitability are apparently ambiguous. For example, we find that on each of the two statistical tests, there are highly significant differences between the two groups with respect to pretax profitability when acquiring companies are compared with the control group of all nonacquiring firms. Such differences, however, appear to arise from the fact that size and pretax profitability are negatively related, so that when the acquiring companies are compared with the control group of matched nonacquiring firms we find little difference in the average profitability of the two groups. Finally, as far as profits variability is concerned, there seems to be little difference between the groups, although the results are somewhat mixed.

Table 8–5. Comparison of Premerger Characteristics of Acquiring and Nonacquiring Companies

					All Industries Results		
Variable	Merger Type	Group 1	Number of Companies N_1	Mean Value $\bar{X}_1$	Group 2	Number of Companies N_2	Mean Value $\bar{X}_2$
Size							
In sales (t)	A	AG	208	10.47	C	858	8.61
In total assets	A	AG	230	10.13	C	1186	8.25
In net assets	A	AG	236	9.70	C	1186	7.85
Profitability							
Trading profits– sales (t)	A	AG	208	10.96	C	858	11.10
Net income–net assets	A	AG	217	15.16	C	1186	17.42
Posttax income– equity assets	A	AG	217	8.79	C	1186	9.40
Net income–net	A	AG	256	15.55	MAG	256	15.68
assets	H	AG	122	14.80	MAG	122	15.48
	NH	AG	134	16.23	MAG	134	15.87
Profits variability							
Trading profits	A	AG	217	0.42	C	1186	0.23
Net income	A	AG	217	0.34	C	1186	0.55
Net income	A	AG	268	0.31	MAG	268	0.22
	H	AG	126	0.41	MAG	126	0.25
	NH	AG	142	0.23	MAG	142	0.19
Growth							
Physical assets	A	AG	217	12.85	C	1186	9.13
Net assets	A	AG	217	12.50	C	1186	7.02
Net assets	A	AG	269	12.66	MAG	269	5.84
	H	AG	126	10.74	MAG	126	5.35
	NH	AG	143	14.34	MAG	143	6.27
Leverage							
Stock measure	A	AG	217	17.83	C	1186	12.73
Flow measure	A	AG	214	10.64	C	1166	8.50
Stock measure	A	AG	269	18.97	MAG	269	12.20
	H	AG	126	18.26	MAG	126	11.90
	NH	AG	143	19.60	MAG	143	12.47

Notes: See Table 8–4.

Comparison of Acquired and Control Group Companies

Table 8–6 shows that acquired companies on average are significantly larger (at the 5 percent level) than the control group firms when size is measured in terms of log sales. Moreover, this result holds not only for the

Takeovers in the United Kingdom / 245

		Summary of Individual Industry Results		
Difference in Mean Values $\bar{X}_1 - \bar{X}_2$	Statistical Significance t-Value	Number of Industries with Positive $\bar{X}_1 - \bar{X}_2$	Total Number of Industries	Proportion Positive and its Significance
1.86 **	17.38	14	14	1.00 **
1.86 **	17.94	14	14	1.00 **
1.85 **	16.81	14	14	1.00 **
−0.14	−0.29	4	14	0.29
−2.27 **	−4.56	2	14	0.14 *
−0.62 *	−2.23	5	14	0.36
−0.13	−0.24	8	14	0.57
−0.68	−0.85	9	14	0.64
0.36	0.50	9	14	0.64
0.19	1.31	8	14	0.57
−0.21	−1.30	6	14	0.43
0.09	1.70	10	14	0.71
0.16	1.38	8	14	0.57
0.04	1.87	9	14	0.64
3.72 **	4.08	11	14	0.79 *
5.48 **	5.77	11	14	0.79 *
6.82 **	7.61	12	14	0.86 *
5.39 **	5.00	13	14	0.93 **
8.07 **	5.86	11	14	0.79 *
5.10 **	5.47	12	14	0.86 *
2.14 *	1.66	11	14	0.79 *
6.77 **	6.67	11	14	0.79 *
6.36 **	4.35	11	14	0.79 *
7.12 **	5.06	10	14	0.71

aggregate of all firms, but also for the binominal probability test based on data for individual industries. However, in view of the fact that tests on alternative measures of size (log net assets and log total assets) do not produce statistically significant results and that the information on sales was not available for a considerable proportion of companies (44 percent of taken over and 28 percent of control group firms), this conclusion must be regarded as rather tentative at this stage of investigation. More impor-

246 / The Determinants and Effects of Mergers

Table 8–6.   Comparison of Premerger Characteristics of Acquired and Nonacquired Companies

					All Industries Results		
Variable	Merger Type	Group 1	Number of Companies N_1	Mean Value $\bar{X}_1$	Group 2	Number of Companies N_2	Mean Value $\bar{X}_2$
Size							
In sales *(t)*	A	AD	160	8.85	C	856	8.61
In total assets	A	AD	290	8.33	C	1186	8.25
In net assets	A	AD	290	7.92	C	1186	7.85
Profitability							
Trading profits– sales *(t)*	A	AD	160	9.31	C	856	11.10
Net income–net assets	A	AD	262	13.51	C	1186	17.42
Posttax income– equity assets	A	AD	262	7.82	C	1186	9.40
Net income–net	A	AD	238	13.90	MAD	238	17.80
assets	H	AD	121	13.51	MAD	121	16.98
	NH	AD	117	14.30	MAD	117	18.65
Profits Variability							
Trading profits	A	AD	262	0.51	C	1186	0.23
Net income	A	AD	262	0.49	C	1186	0.55
Net income	A	AD	257	0.50	MAD	257	0.31
	H	AD	127	0.38	MAD	127	0.38
	NH	AD	130	0.61	MAD	130	0.25
Growth							
Physical assets	A	AD	262	8.15	C	1186	9.13
Net assets	A	AD	262	5.96	C	1186	7.02
Net assets	A	AD	258	5.98	MAD	258	6.70
	H	AD	127	6.42	MAD	127	6.50
	NH	AD	131	5.55	MAD	131	6.89
Leverage							
Stock measure	A	AD	262	15.84	C	1186	12.73
Flow measure	A	AD	251	10.51	C	1166	8.50
Stock measure	A	AD	257	15.87	MAD	257	11.05
	H	AD	127	16.65	MAD	127	12.55
	NH	AD	130	15.10	MAD	130	9.61

Notes: See Table 8–4.

tantly, it should be noted that the control group does not simply consist of nonacquired firms; it also excludes all acquiring firms, which as Tables 8–4 and 8–5 have shown tend to be relatively big.

On the other hand, the figures point to an unambiguous conclusion with respect to profitability. Whichever measure of profitability is used, and on either of the two tests, it appears that the acquired firms are on average significantly less profitable (at the 1 percent level) than the control group

		Summary of Individual Industry Results		
Difference in Mean Values $\bar{X}_1 - \bar{X}_2$	Statistical Significance t-Value	Number of Industries with Positive $\bar{X}_1 - \bar{X}_2$	Total Number of Industries	Proportion Positive and its Significance
0.24*	2.47	11	14	0.79*
0.08	1.12	9	14	0.64
0.06	0.85	8	14	0.57
−1.80**	−3.35	2	14	0.14*
−3.91**	−8.55	2	14	0.14*
−1.58**	−5.31	2	14	0.14*
−3.90**	−5.74	2	14	0.14*
−3.47**	−4.29	3	14	0.21*
−4.35**	−3.96	2	14	0.14*
0.23	1.42	8	14	0.57
−0.06	−0.35	8	14	0.57
0.18	1.95	10	14	0.71
0.00	0.04	8	14	0.57
0.36*	2.12	10	14	0.71
−0.98	−1.77	6	14	0.43
−1.06	−1.90	5	14	0.36
−0.72	−1.11	4	14	0.29
−0.07	−0.08	4	14	0.29
−1.34	1.46	4	14	0.29
3.11**	3.62	12	14	0.85*
2.02	1.66	11	14	0.79*
4.80**	4.41	11	14	0.79*
4.10*	2.49	10	14	0.71
5.49*	3.86	10	14	0.71

firms. However, it is important to emphasize, in view of the wide variability in profitability of firms in a typical industry, that there is likely to be a large degree of overlap in the profitability figures for the two groups of firms. Thus, although profitability may be a statistically significant discriminator between the living and the dead, it may not be a very good one (this point is discussed more fully in Singh 1971).

Table 8–6 also shows that acquired firms are on average more volatile in

248 / *The Determinants and Effects of Mergers*

their profits records than control group firms. Further, the data reveal the acquired firms to be somewhat slower growers than control group firms. The average differences between the groups in relation to these two characteristics are, however, quite small and in most cases statistically insignificant. On the other hand, the results for leverage suggest that acquired firms are significantly more highly geared than control group firms.

Summary of Comparative Characteristics of Acquiring, Acquired, and Control Group Companies

The results of the univariate comparisons of the average characteristics of the acquired, acquiring, and control group companies in the period immediately prior to merger may be summarized as follows:

Size	AG > AD ≥ Others
Profitability	Others > AD; Others ≥ AG; AG ≥ AD
Profits Variability	AD > Others; AD ≥ AG
Growth	AG > AD; AG > Others ≥ AD
Leverage	AG > AD > Others

In the above summary, > indicates a statistically significant and quantitatively relatively important difference between the group; similarly, ≥ connotes either a statistically insignificant (at the 5 percent level) or a quantitatively small difference.

With respect to the economic issues of the stock market selection process and its implications for firm motivation, evidence of the above results can only be regarded as a preliminary step. This is mainly because we have up to now attempted only a limited statistical analysis of the characteristics of the various groups of firms. Specifically, the analysis has been done only on a

Table 8–7. Determinants: Size Comparisons

					All Industries Results		
Variable	Merger Type	Group 1	Number of Companies N_1	Mean Value $\bar{X}_1$	Group 2	Number of Companies N_2	Mean Value $\bar{X}_2$
In sales	H	AGAD	76	9.69	C	858	8.61
In total assets	H	AGAD	137	9.08	C	1186	8.25
In net assets	H	AGAD	137	8.95	C	1186	7.85

Notes: Period of comparison—year prior to merger. For key to terminology adopted, see notes to Table 8–4.

univariate basis. Because of the intercorrelation between variables, it is not possible to obtain a proper profile of firms selected by the market for survival (and hence of the nature of the selection mechanism) without a multivariate analysis. Further, even the univariate investigations that have been carried out so far have been of a rather limited variety. The analysis presented here has been confined to examining the differences between the average characteristics of various groups of firms. A more refined analysis of the degrees of overlap between the groups with respect to these characteristics is also required. These investigations, which are currently being carried out, are the subject of a further paper.

TEST RESULTS ON THE DETERMINANTS OF MERGERS

Having considered the nature of the differences between the characteristics of the acquired, acquiring, and nonmerging firms, we now proceed to present results on the specific tests on the determinants of mergers given in Chapter 2. The results for each test are presented successively in Tables 8–7 through 8–9.

Table 8–7 gives results for the size test. It shows quite unambiguously that the merging firms are on average much larger than the nonmerging ones. This conclusion holds for all industries together, as well as in thirteen of the fourteen individual industries, and is statistically highly significant on both the statistical tests used.

However, it must be stressed that this does not imply that mergers do not take place for reasons of economies of scale. All that it suggests is that the latter is unlikely to be the overriding or the single dominant motive for mergers, unless all firms in most industries are in any case below their efficient size or unless the smaller suboptimal firms that wish to merge are

		Summary of Individual Industry Results		
Difference in Mean Values $\bar{X}_1 - \bar{X}_2$	Statistical Significance t-Value	Number of Industries with Positive $\bar{X}_1 - \bar{X}_2$	Total Number of Industries	Proportion Positive and its Significance
1.08**	8.53	13	14	0.93**
0.83**	8.24	13	14	0.93**
1.10**	0.27	13	14	0.93**

250 / *The Determinants and Effects of Mergers*

Table 8–8.   Determinants: High-Low Ratio of Coefficients of Variation of Profits Prior to Merger

						All Industries Results	
Variable	*Merger Type*	*Group 1*	*Number of Companies N_1*	*Mean Value $\bar{X}_1$*	*Group 2*	*Number of Companies N_2*	*Mean Value $\bar{X}_2$*
Trading profits	A	AGAD	240	4.20	MAGMAD	240	2.59
	H	AGAD	116	5.30	MAGMAD	116	2.81
	NH	AGAD	124	3.17	MAGMAD	124	2.37
Net income	A	AGAD	240	3.59	MAGMAD	240	3.08
	H	AGAD	116	2.64	MAGMAD	116	3.48
	NH	AGAD	124	4.49	MAGMAD	124	2.71
Posttax income	A	AGAD	240	6.39	MAGMAD	240	3.20
	H	AGAD	116	9.22	MAGMAD	116	3.87
	NH	AGAD	124	3.74	MAGMAD	124	2.58

Notes: Period of comparison—five years prior to merger. For key to terminology adopted, see notes to Table 8–4.

prevented from doing so for a variety of institutional reasons. There is, however, little direct evidence to support either of these suppositions.

Next, Table 8–8 gives results that bear on the hypothesis concerning risk spreading as a motive for mergers. Here we recall that although acquiring firms experience the same kind of profits variability as matched control group firms, they are somewhat more stable performers than acquired firms. The information given in Table 8–8 shows that there is a tendency for the average value of the high/low ratio of the coefficients of variation of profits for merging firms to be greater than the ratio for nonmerging firms

Table 8–9.   Determinants: Absolute Differences in Premerger Leverage Ratios

						All Industries Results	
Variable	*Merger Type*	*Group 1*	*Number of Companies N_1*	*Mean Value $\bar{X}_1$*	*Group 2*	*Number of Companies N_2*	*Mean Value $\bar{X}_2$*
Leverage (net flow	A	AGAD	253	17.64	MAGMAD	253	10.57
measure)	H	AGAD	117	18.09	MAGMAD	117	9.76
	NH	AGAD	136	17.26	MAGMAD	136	11.27

Notes: Period of comparison—year prior to merger. For key to terminology, see notes to Table 8–4.

Takeovers in the United Kingdom   /   *251*

Difference in Mean Values $\bar{X}_1 - \bar{X}_2$	Statistical Significance t-Value	Summary of Individual Industry Results		
		Number of Industries with Positive $\bar{X}_1 - \bar{X}_2$	Total Number of Industries	Proportion Positive and its Significance
1.62	1.30	9	14	0.64
2.49	1.02	7	14	0.50
0.80	1.18	11	14	0.79*
0.51	0.79	10	14	0.71
−0.84	−1.54	7	14	0.50
1.78	1.43	11	14	0.79*
3.18	1.00	11	14	0.79*
5.35	0.83	6	14	0.43
1.16	0.79	11	14	0.79*

when considering nonhorizontal mergers. For each measure of profits used in calculating the ratio, the binomial probability test is significant at the 5 percent level (the average value of the ratio is greater for the nonhorizontal merging firms in eleven of the fourteen industries).

✓ Thus, there is some evidence to indicate that risk spreading may be a motive for mergers. However, this conclusion, even in its present form, is subject to some serious qualifications. First, the test described above only shows greater relative profits variability between merging firms than between their matched control group firms and not that acquiring firms are

Difference in Mean Values $\bar{X}_1 - \bar{X}_2$	Statistical Significance t-Value	Summary of Individual Industry Results		
		Number of Industries with Positive $\bar{X}_1 - \bar{X}_2$	Total Number of Industries	Proportion Positive and its Significance
7.07**	2.75	10	14	0.71
8.33*	2.42	11	14	0.79*
5.99	1.60	8	14	0.57

252 / *The Determinants and Effects of Mergers*

Table 8–10. Determinants: Comparison of Variance of Premerger Leverage Ratios of Merging Firms with That of Control Group

Merger Type	Group 1	Number of Companies	Sample Variance	Group 2	Number of Companies	Sample Variance	Calcu- lated F-ratio	Critical F-value at 5% Level
A	AG	253	119.9	MAG	253	141.9	1.18	1.20
H	AG	117	129.1	MAG	117	121.1	1.07	1.36
NH	AG	136	112.8	MAG	136	160.6	1.42*	1.34
A	AD	253	1658.0	MAD	253	148.0	11.20*	1.20
H	AD	117	1439.4	MAD	117	129.9	11.08*	1.36
NH	AD	136	1853.6	MAD	136	163.7	11.32*	1.34

Notes: Net flow measure of the leverage ratio is used here.
Period of comparison—year prior to merger.
For key to terminology adopted, see notes to Table 8–4.

more volatile than the nonacquiring firms. Second, the evidence given earlier suggests, if anything, that acquirers are seeking out more volatile victims, so that if risk spreading were a motive, it would be for the acquired rather than the acquiring firms. Third, we should note that at a more theoretical level, risk spreading in any case is not necessarily best achieved by a more stable firm merging with a more variable one; the best strategy would also depend on the degree of correlation between the profits streams of the acquirer and its potential victims.

Nevertheless, the results of Table 8–8 could be regarded as being consistent with a risk-spreading hypothesis since important differences in profits variability ratios between pairs of merging and nonmerging firms are found only in the case of nonhorizontal mergers, where it might reasonably be argued that the risk-spreading gains from uncorrelated profit streams were more likely to occur.[22]

With respect to the leverage ratio there is also some evidence to suggest that firms may be seeking merger partners with dissimilar leverage ratios to their own. Thus as Table 8–9 shows, the average absolute difference in the leverage ratios of merging firms is significantly greater (at the 5 percent level) than for the corresponding nonmerging firms. The differences are also economically important, being on average over 7 percent when a comparison is made between all merging firms and the control group. Table 8–10 shows that as a group, acquired companies tend to have relatively extreme values of the leverage ratio compared to either acquiring companies or the nonacquired companies, which is also consistent with the view that acquirers seek out either very highly or very lowly levered companies. Moreover, as Table 8–11 shows, the potential impact upon

Table 8–11. Determinants: Contribution of Victim to Merged Company's Leverage Ratio

	All Mergers			Horizontal			Other		
	N	$\bar{x}_t$	t-ratio	N	$\bar{x}_t$	t-ratio	N	$\bar{x}_t$	t-ratio
Food	8	0.72*	6.08	6	0.82*	9.00	2	0.40	1.60
Drink	14	1.28*	5.17	10	0.94*	3.73	4	2.13*	6.18
Chemicals	22	3.16*	2.84	7	5.43*	1.94	15	2.10*	2.20
Metal manufacture	10	1.88*	2.86	2	2.85	1.18	8	1.64*	2.46
Nonelectrical engineering	28	2.91*	3.61	18	2.35*	3.15	10	3.93*	2.14
Electrical engineering	23	1.31*	3.41	12	2.01*	3.05	11	0.54*	2.60
Metal goods	9	1.53*	2.45	2	2.35	1.24	7	1.29*	1.91
Textiles	42	1.82*	2.09	21	2.66	1.57	21	0.97*	2.36
Building materials	24	2.75*	2.39	13	4.37*	2.15	11	0.83*	2.90
Paper, printing	9	4.43	1.77	7	5.60	1.80	2	0.32	1.11
Construction	10	1.82	1.74	4	0.73	1.99	6	2.55	1.49
Wholesale distribution	15	3.04*	4.66	8	3.15*	3.03	7	2.91*	3.57
Retail distribution	13	1.34	1.76	6	0.69	1.91	7	1.90	1.36
Other services	13	1.83*	3.76	5	2.90*	3.54	8	1.16*	2.64
All industries	264	2.14*	8.57	124	2.71*	5.95	140	1.63*	6.98

Notes: Net flow measure of the leverage ratio used here.

Period of comparison—year prior to merger.

x_t = absolute difference between the acquiring company's leverage ratio and the weighted average leverage ratio of the acquiring and acquired companies, in the year prior to merger.

$\bar{x}_t$ = mean value of x_t for all the mergers in the sample. This is tested against the null hypothesis that $x_t = 0$ using a one-tail t-test at the 5 percent level of significance.

For key to terminology adopted, see notes to Table 8–4.

leverage of combining the merging partners' capital structures is statistically and economically significant.

As in the case of profits variability, there are difficulties in making a straightforward interpretation of the leverage results. Earlier in the chapter, we found that acquiring firms have significantly greater premerger leverage ratios than those of the acquired firms, while the latter, in turn, were found to be more highly levered than the nonacquired and nonacquiring control group. Thus, if on average, the acquiring firms had been seeking to reduce their leverage, their most obvious partners are to be found in the control group and not in the group of companies they actually acquired. Second, it is of course the case that the impact upon leverage of an acquisition will depend upon the method of payment used to effect it.

Table 8–12. Gort's Economic Disturbance and Bargain Tests

					All Industries Results		
Variable	*Merger Type*	*Group 1*	*Number of Com-panies N_1*	*Mean Value $\bar{X}_1$*	*Group 2*	*Number of Com-panies N_2*	*Mean Value $\bar{X}_2$*
Ratio of highest price-earnings ratio to lowest price-earnings ratio							
One year prior to merger	H	AD	28	2.3	MAD	28	2.0
Two years prior to merger	H	AD	27	2.8	MAD	27	2.5
Three years prior to merger	H	AD	27	3.2	MAD	27	2.7
Mean value of highest and lowest price-earnings ratios							
One year prior to merger	H	AD	28	20.4	MAD	28	17.4
Two years prior to merger	H	AD	27	17.8	MAD	27	16.0
Three years prior to merger	H	AD	27	17.1	MAD	27	15.7

Notes: For key to terminology adopted, see notes to Table 8–4.

Table 8–13. Comparison of Three Years Postmerger Profitability of Merging Companies with Control Group Companies

					All Industries Results		
Variable	*Merger Type*	*Group 1*	*Number of Com-panies N_1*	*Mean Value $\bar{X}_1$*	*Group 2*	*Number of Com-panies N_2*	*Mean Value $\bar{X}_2$*
Trading profits–sales	A	AG	111	10.32	C	858	10.03
	A	AG	111	10.32	MAGMAD	111	9.73
	H	AG	52	10.35	MAGMAD	52	9.54
	NH	AG	59	10.30	MAGMAD	59	9.89
Net income–net assets	A	AG	225	13.78	C	1186	16.29
	A	AG	225	13.78	MAGMAD	225	13.39
	H	AG	109	12.68	MAGMAD	109	13.25
	NH	AG	116	14.81	MAGMAD	116	13.52
Posttax income–equity assets	A	AG	221	7.32	C	1180	7.62
	A	AG	221	7.32	MAGMAD	221	6.37
	H	AG	107	6.27	MAGMAD	107	5.97
	NH	AG	114	8.30	MAGMAD	114	6.73

Notes: See notes to Table 8–4.

Difference in Mean Values $\bar{X}_1 - \bar{X}_2$	Statistical Significance t-Value	Summary of Nonparametric Test Results		
		Number of Observations with Positive $X_1 - X_2$	Total Number of Observations	Proportion Positive and its Significance
0.3	0.94	15	28	0.54
0.3	0.64	14	27	0.52
0.5	1.19	14	27	0.52
3.0	1.88*	15	28	0.54
1.8	1.09	14	27	0.52
1.4	0.87	14	27	0.52

Difference in Mean Values $\bar{X}_1 - \bar{X}_2$	Statistical Significance t-Value	Summary of Individual Industry Results		
		Number of Industries with Positive $\bar{X}_1 - \bar{X}_2$	Total Number of Industries	Proportion Positive and its Significance
0.29	0.53	4	14	0.29
0.60	0.88	7	14	0.50
0.81	0.81	7	14	0.50
0.41	0.45	8	14	0.57
−2.51**	−4.98	2	14	0.14*
0.39	0.64	7	14	0.50
−0.57	−0.68	7	14	0.50
1.29	1.46	9	14	0.64
−0.30	−0.81	6	14	0.43
0.95*	2.52	8	14	0.57
0.30	0.56	8	14	0.57
1.57**	3.09	10	14	0.71

Table 8–14.   Comparison of Five Years Postmerger Profitability of Merging Companies with Control Group Companies

						All Industries Results	
Variable	Merger Type	Group 1	Number of Companies N_1	Mean Value $\bar{x}_1$	Group 2	Number of Companies N_2	Mean Value $\bar{x}_2$
Trading profits–sales	A	AG	106	10.50	C	858	10.21
	A	AG	106	10.50	MAGMAD	106	10.16
	H	AG	47	10.57	MAGMAD	47	9.81
	NH	AG	59	10.45	MAGMAD	59	10.43
Net income–net assets	A	AG	211	14.65	C	1185	16.68
	A	AG	211	14.65	MAGMAD	211	14.88
	H	AG	98	13.74	MAGMAD	98	14.93
	NH	AG	113	15.43	MAGMAD	113	14.84
Posttax income–	A	AG	208	8.94	C	1177	8.87
equity assets	A	AG	208	8.94	MAGMAD	208	8.04
	H	AG	96	7.98	MAGMAD	96	7.91
	NH	AG	112	9.77	MAGMAD	112	8.15

Notes: See notes to Table 8–4.

Before it can be concluded that the highly levered acquiring firms sought on average to reduce their leverage, we must also look at what actually happened to their leverage ratios as a result of merger. As we shall see below, the effect on average was if anything to increase rather than reduce leverage.

Finally, Table 8-12 presents some results on Gort's disturbance theory. The information given pertains to a small sample of only twenty-eight acquired firms and a corresponding number of matched nonacquired firms. The results show little difference between either the variability or the average price-earnings ratios of acquired and nonacquired companies.[23]

TEST RESULTS ON EFFECTS OF MERGERS

Profitability

Tables 8–13 through 8–16 report the postmerger profitability of the merged firms relative to that of the control group firms. The findings

Takeovers in the United Kingdom   /   257

Difference in Mean Values $\bar{X}_1 - \bar{X}_2$	Statistical Significance t-Value	Summary of Individual Industry Results		
		Number of Industries with Positive $\bar{X}_1 - \bar{X}_2$	Total Number of Industries	Proportion Positive and its Significance
0.29	0.50	6	14	0.43
0.35	0.51	5	14	0.36
0.76	0.74	7	14	0.50
0.02	0.02	7	14	0.50
−2.03**	−3.83	6	14	0.43
−0.24	−0.38	8	14	0.57
−1.19	−1.28	10	14	0.71
0.59	0.71	7	14	0.50
0.07	0.17	8	14	0.57
0.91	1.94	11	14	0.79*
0.07	0.10	11	14	0.79*
1.62*	2.57	10	14	0.71

in Tables 8–13 and 8–14 indicate little difference between the two groups when the control group firms are matched by industry, year, and size, except in the case of posttax profitability on equity assets.[24] In the case of this measure there is weak evidence that merging firms are more profitable in the postmerger period than the matched control group companies.

However, the most interesting point to emerge from these results is that the postmerger profitability of merging firms is not lower than that of control group firms. Earlier in the chapter it was found that although the premerger profitability of acquiring firms was about the same as that of the matched control group firms, the profitability record of acquired firms before acquisition was distinctly less favorable than that of their matched control group, which suggests that the postmerger performance of merging firms may have improved somewhat relative to that of control group firms.

This hypothesis is to some extent borne out by the results presented in Tables 8–15 and 8–16, which compare the postmerger changes in profitability for the merging companies with those for the control group.[25] For example, in relation to net income on net assets, Table 8–15 shows that there was a small decline (on average of 0.25 percentage points) in the

258 / The Determinants and Effects of Mergers

Table 8–15. Effects: Difference Between Post- and Premerger Profitability

						All Industries Results	
Variable	Merger Type	Group 1	Number of Companies N_1	Mean Value $\bar{X}_1$	Group 2	Number of Companies N_2	Mean Value $\bar{X}_2$
Trading profits–sales	A	AGAD	111	−0.87	C	858	−1.08
	A	AGAD	111	−0.87	MAGMAD	111	−1.44
	H	AGAD	52	−1.08	MAGMAD	52	−1.53
	NH	AGAD	59	−0.68	MAGMAD	59	−1.37
Net income–net assets	A	AGAD	225	−0.26	C	1186	−1.13
	A	AGAD	225	−0.26	MAGMAD	225	−1.78
	H	AGAD	109	−0.71	MAGMAD	109	−1.89
	NH	AGAD	116	0.16	MAGMAD	116	−1.67
Posttax income–equity assets	A	AGAD	221	−0.90	C	1180	−1.77
	A	AGAD	221	−0.90	MAGMAD	221	−1.82
	H	AGAD	107	−1.47	MAGMAD	107	−2.22
	NH	AGAD	114	−0.36	MAGMAD	114	−1.45

Notes: Period of comparison—difference in average profitability in three years after merger compared with that five years before merger. For key to terminology adopted, see notes to Table 8–4.

Table 8–16. Effects: Difference Between Post- and Premerger Profitability

						All Industries Results	
Variable	Merger Type	Group 1	Number of Companies N_1	Mean Value $\bar{X}_1$	Group 2	Number of Companies N_2	Mean Value $\bar{X}_2$
Trading profits–sales	A	AGAD	106	−0.57	C	858	−0.89
	A	AGAD	106	−0.57	MAGMAD	106	−0.80
	H	AGAD	47	−0.62	MAGMAD	47	−0.76
	NH	AGAD	59	−0.54	MAGMAD	59	−0.83
Net income–net assets	A	AGAD	211	0.63	C	1185	−0.74
	A	AGAD	211	0.63	MAGMAD	211	−0.24
	H	AGAD	98	0.47	MAGMAD	98	0.15
	NH	AGAD	113	0.78	MAGMAD	113	−0.58
Posttax income–equity assets	A	AGAD	208	0.73	C	1177	−0.54
	A	AGAD	208	0.73	MAGMAD	208	−0.06
	H	AGAD	96	0.27	MAGMAD	96	−0.06
	NH	AGAD	112	1.13	MAGMAD	112	−0.06

Notes: Period of comparison—average profitability in five years after compared with five years before merger. For key to terminology adopted, see notes to Table 8–4.

		Summary of Individual Industry Results		
Difference in Mean Values $\bar{X}_1 - \bar{X}_2$	Statistical Significance t-Value	Number of Industries with Positive $\bar{X}_1 - \bar{X}_2$	Total Number of Industries	Proportion Positive and its Significance
0.21	0.80	7	14	0.50
0.57	1.88	7	14	0.50
0.45	1.81	9	14	0.64
0.69	1.60	8	14	0.57
0.87*	2.36	8	14	0.57
1.52**	3.52	9	14	0.64
1.18	1.77	9	14	0.64
1.83**	3.36	8	14	0.57
0.87**	2.86	8	14	0.57
0.92**	2.87	8	14	0.57
0.75	1.48	9	14	0.64
1.09**	2.78	9	14	0.64

		Summary of Individual Industry Results		
Difference in Mean Values $\bar{X}_1 - \bar{X}_2$	Statistical Significance t-Value	Number of Industries with Positive $\bar{X}_1 - \bar{X}_2$	Total Number of Industries	Proportion Positive and its Significance
0.32	0.93	8	14	0.57
0.23	0.62	6	14	0.43
0.14	0.32	8	14	0.57
0.29	0.54	8	14	0.57
1.38*	3.47	10	14	0.71
0.87	1.91	7	14	0.50
0.32	0.43	7	14	0.50
1.35*	2.41	9	14	0.61
1.27**	3.61	10	14	0.71
0.79*	2.00	8	14	0.57
0.33	0.54	10	14	0.71
1.18**	3.03	8	14	0.57

Table 8–17.   Comparison of Three Years Postmerger Growth of Merging Companies with Control Group Companies

						All Industries Results	
Variable	Merger Type	Group 1	Number of Companies N_1	Mean Value $\bar{X}_1$	Group 2	Number of Companies N_2	Mean Value $\bar{X}_2$
Growth of net assets	A	AGAD	225	10.62	C	1186	5.21
	A	AGAD	225	10.62	MAGMAD	225	5.04
	H	AGAD	109	8.94	MAGMAD	109	3.99
	NH	AGAD	116	12.20	MAGMAD	116	6.03
Growth of physical assets	A	AGAD	225	11.85	C	1186	8.30
	A	AGAD	225	11.85	MAGMAD	225	6.13
	H	AGAD	109	10.10	MAGMAD	109	6.47
	NH	AGAD	116	13.49	MAGMAD	116	5.80

Notes: See notes to Table 8–4.

postmerger profitability of the merging firms three years after merger compared with their profitability in the five years before merger. However, the corresponding decline in the profitability of the matched control group firms was larger (an average of 1.78 percentage points). Statistically significant relative improvements in profitability are found (at the 5 percent level) for all mergers and for nonhorizontal mergers for two measures

Table 8–18.   Comparison of Five Years Postmerger Growth of Merging Companies with Control Group Companies

						All Industries Results	
Variable	Merger Type	Group 1	Number of Companies N_1	Mean Value $\bar{X}_1$	Group 2	Number of Companies N_2	Mean Value $\bar{X}_2$
Growth of net assets	A	AGAD	210	12.24	C	1181	7.65
	A	AGAD	210	12.24	MAGMAD	210	7.60
	H	AGAD	98	10.24	MAGMAD	98	7.14
	NH	AGAD	112	13.99	MAGMAD	112	8.00
Growth of physical assets	A	AGAD	211	12.24	C	1184	9.14
	A	AGAD	211	12.24	MAGMAD	211	7.88
	H	AGAD	98	10.04	MAGMAD	98	7.08
	NH	AGAD	113	14.16	MAGMAD	113	8.57

Notes: See notes to Table 8–4.

		Summary of Individual Industry Results		
Difference in Mean Values $\bar{X}_1 - \bar{X}_2$	Statistical Significance t-Value	Number of Industries with Positive $\bar{X}_1 - \bar{X}_2$	Total Number of Industries	Proportion Positive and its Significance
5.41**	5.09	12	14	0.86*
5.58**	5.00	11	14	0.79*
4.95**	3.26	11	14	0.79*
6.17**	3.86	12	14	0.86*
3.55**	3.01	11	14	0.79*
5.72**	4.59	13	14	0.93**
3.63*	2.29	11	14	0.79*
7.69**	4.09	13	14	0.93**

of profitability. On the other hand, it must be noted that the results on the binomial probability test are not statistically significant.

The combined results on profitability thus provide some evidence (admittedly rather weak) that the relative profitability of merging firms improved slightly after merger; it certainly did not decline, as other investigators have concluded (Meeks 1977; Utton 1974a). Further work is being carried out to discover the reason for this difference from the results of other studies, particularly that of Meeks, who carried out a comprehensive study of mergers over roughly the same time period as we have used.

		Summary of Individual Industry Results		
Difference in Mean Values $\bar{X}_1 - \bar{X}_2$	Statistical Significance t-Value	Number of Industries with Positive $\bar{X}_1 - \bar{X}_2$	Total Number of Industries	Proportion Positive and its Significance
4.59*	4.59	12	14	0.86*
4.64**	5.27	13	14	0.93**
3.09**	2.88	11	14	0.79*
5.99**	4.51	11	14	0.79*
3.10**	3.70	11	14	0.79*
4.36**	4.76	12	14	0.86*
2.96**	2.71	11	14	0.79*
4.59**	3.30	10	14	0.71

Table 8–19.   Effects: Differences in Post- and Premerger Growth Rate

Variable	Merger Type	Group 1	Number of Companies N_1	Mean Value $\bar{X}_1$	Group 2	Number of Companies N_2	Mean Value $\bar{X}_2$
							All Industries Results
Growth of net assets	A	AGAD	210	1.77	C	1181	0.59
	A	AGAD	210	1.77	MAGMAD	210	1.74
	H	AGAD	98	0.60	MAGMAD	98	1.70
	NH	AGAD	112	2.79	MAGMAD	112	1.78
Growth of physical assets	A	AGAD	211	0.49	C	1184	−0.01
	A	AGAD	211	0.49	MAGMAD	211	0.33
	H	AGAD	98	−0.54	MAGMAD	98	−0.41
	NH	AGAD	113	1.38	MAGMAD	113	0.97

Notes: Period of comparison—difference in growth rate in the five years after merger compared with the growth rate in the five years prior to merger. For key to terminology adopted, see notes to Table 8–4.

Growth

Tables 8–17 through 8–22 report corresponding results for the growth variables. A comparison of the postmerger growth performance in the three and five years after merger (Tables 8–17 and 8–18) provides strong evidence that acquiring companies continue to grow faster than control group companies after merger.

Table 8–20.   Effects: Differences in Post- and Premerger Growth Rate

Variable	Merger Type	Group 1	Number of Companies N_1	Mean Value $\bar{X}_1$	Group 2	Number of Companies N_2	Mean Value $\bar{X}_2$
							All Industries Results
Growth of net assets	A	AGAD	225	0.24	C	1186	−1.82
	A	AGAD	225	0.24	MAGMAD	225	−0.76
	H	AGAD	109	−0.63	MAGMAD	109	−1.43
	NH	AGAD	116	1.06	MAGMAD	116	−0.12
Growth of physical assets	A	AGAD	225	0.16	C	1186	−0.83
	A	AGAD	225	0.16	MAGMAD	225	−1.42
	H	AGAD	109	−0.55	MAGMAD	109	−1.20
	NH	AGAD	116	0.82	MAGMAD	116	−1.64

Notes: Period of comparison—difference in growth rate in the three years after merger compared with the growth rate in the five years prior to merger. For key to terminology adopted, see notes to Table 8–4.

| | | Summary of Individual Industry Results | | |
Difference in Mean Values $\bar{X}_1 - \bar{X}_2$	Statistical Significance t-Value	Number of Industries with Positive $\bar{X}_1 - \bar{X}_2$	Total Number of Industries	Proportion Positive and its Significance
1.18	1.08	6	14	0.43
0.03	0.02	5	14	0.36
−1.10	−0.72	6	14	0.43
1.01	0.62	6	14	0.43
0.50	0.47	8	14	0.57
0.16	0.14	8	14	0.57
−0.13	−0.08	7	14	0.50
0.41	0.24	7	14	0.50

Turning, however, to the more interesting comparison of changes in growth rates of merging and control group firms, the results shown in Table 8–19 for five years after merger and in Table 8–20 for three years indicate little difference between the two groups. As with profitability, this conclusion is important from an economic point of view in that it shows that the postmerger performance of merging firms did not deteriorate or improve relative to other firms.[26]

| | | Summary of Individual Industry Results | | |
Difference in Mean Values $\bar{X}_1 - \bar{X}_2$	Statistical Significance t-Value	Number of Industries with Positive $\bar{X}_1 - \bar{X}_2$	Total Number of Industries	Proportion Positive and its Significance
2.06	1.60	9	14	0.64
1.00	0.74	5	14	0.36
0.80	0.44	6	14	0.43
1.18	0.61	7	14	0.50
0.99	0.71	8	14	0.57
1.58	1.07	8	14	0.57
0.65	0.34	7	14	0.50
2.46	1.10	7	14	0.50

264 / The Determinants and Effects of Mergers

Table 8–21. Comparison of Postmerger Leverage Ratios of Merging Companies with Control Group Companies

Variable	Merger Type	Group 1	Number of Companies N_1	Mean Value $\bar{X}_1$	Group 2	Number of Companies N_2	Mean Value $\bar{X}_2$
All Industries Results							
Three years after merger							
Net flow leverage	A	AGAD	173	17.32	C	1127	12.30
ratio	A	AGAD	173	17.32	MAGMAD	173	8.69
	H	AGAD	81	20.15	MAGMAD	81	9.21
	NH	AGAD	92	14.83	MAGMAD	92	8.23
Five years after merger							
Net flow leverage	A	AGAD	143	16.68	C	1120	12.40
ratio	A	AGAD	143	16.68	MAGMAD	143	7.48
	H	AGAD	64	19.65	MAGMAD	64	7.59
	NH	AGAD	79	14.27	MAGMAD	79	7.39
Book value leverage	A	AGAD	208	24.61	C	1177	11.31
ratio (stock	A	AGAD	208	24.61	MAGMAD	208	12.08
measure)	H	AGAD	96	24.93	MAGMAD	96	11.74
	NH	AGAD	112	24.33	MAGMAD	112	12.37

Notes: See notes to Table 8–4.

Table 8–22. Effects: Difference Between Post- and Premerger Leverage Ratios

Variable	Merger Type	Group 1	Number of Companies N_1	Mean Value $\bar{X}_1$	Group 2	Number of Companies N_2	Mean Value $\bar{X}_2$
All Industries Results							
Three years after merger							
Net flow leverage	A	AGAD	173	1.54	C	1127	4.58
rate	A	AGAD	173	1.54	MAGMAD	173	2.11
	H	AGAD	81	3.64	MAGMAD	81	2.38
	NH	AGAD	92	−0.31	MAGMAD	92	1.92
Five years after merger							
Net flow leverage	A	AGAD	143	0.13	C	1120	4.67
ratio	A	AGAD	143	0.13	MAGMAD	143	0.59
	H	AGAD	64	1.35	MAGMAD	64	0.02
	NH	AGAD	79	−0.87	MAGMAD	79	1.05
Book value leverage	A	AGAD	208	5.63	C	1177	−1.33
ratio (stock	A	AGAD	208	5.63	MAGMAD	208	−0.51
measure)	H	AGAD	96	6.29	MAGMAD	96	−1.26
	NH	AGAD	112	5.07	MAGMAD	112	0.14

Notes: Period of comparison—difference in leverage ratio in three and five years after merger compared with five years prior to merger. For key to terminology adopted, see notes to Table 8–4.

Difference in Mean Values $\bar{X}_1 - \bar{X}_2$	Statistical Significance t-Value	Summary of Individual Industry Results		
		Number of Industries with Positive $\bar{X}_1 - \bar{X}_2$	Total Number of Industries	Proportion Positive and its Significance
5.02*	2.26	10	14	0.71
8.64**	7.32	11	14	0.79*
10.94**	5.85	13	14	0.93**
6.60**	4.60	11	14	0.79*
4.28	0.99	11	14	0.79*
9.20**	6.79	11	14	0.79*
12.07**	5.84	13	14	0.93**
6.88**	3.93	11	14	0.79*
13.30**	14.62	13	14	0.93**
12.52**	11.41	12	14	0.86*
13.19**	7.83	13	14	0.93**
11.96**	8.36	13	14	0.93**

Difference in Mean Values $\bar{X}_1 - \bar{X}_2$	Statistical Significance t-Value	Summary of Individual Industry Results		
		Number of Industries with Positive $\bar{X}_1 - \bar{X}_2$	Total Number of Industries	Proportion Positive and its Significance
−3.04	−1.26	4	14	0.29
−0.60	−0.43	7	14	0.50
1.26	0.58	7	14	0.50
−2.24	−1.22	5	14	0.36
−4.55	−1.01	5	14	0.36
−0.46	−0.27	7	14	0.50
1.34	0.49	7	14	0.50
−1.92	−0.90	4	14	0.29
6.97**	9.98	14	14	1.00**
6.14**	7.78	13	14	0.93**
7.55**	6.88	12	14	0.86*
4.93**	4.43	12	14	0.86*

Leverage

Tables 8–21 and 8–22 present the results for the leverage ratio variables. Table 8–21 shows that the merging firms had, on average, higher leverage ratios than control group firms in the three and five years following merger. This is not surprising given the finding, discussed earlier, that the premerger leverage ratios of both acquiring and acquired firms tended to be higher than amongst the control group firms.

The findings for changes in the leverage ratio in postmerger periods relative to the premerger period, shown in Table 8–22 are rather mixed. The results for the net flow measure of leverage suggest that there is no significant difference between merging and control group firms in the average change in the leverage ratio. On the other hand, the results for the stock measure of leverage provide strong evidence that merger increases leverage. While the leverage ratio of merging firms has, on average, risen

Table 8–23. Stockholder Returns for Acquiring and Matched Nonacquiring Companies, Pre- and Postmerger

Measure	Merger Type	Number of Companies	AG	MAG	Difference AG − MAG	t-ratio
1. Stockholder return for five years preceding merger (percent per annum)	A	63	13.3	6.4	6.9*	3.97
2. Stockholder return for one year after merger (percent per annum)	A	63	51.8	33.1	18.7*	3.10
3. Stockholder return for two years after merger (percent per annum)	A	63	20.8	14.1	6.7*	2.21
4. Stockholder return for three years after merger (percent per annum)	A	63	7.6	6.4	1.2	0.55
5. Stockholders return for four years after merger (percent per annum)	A	63	11.8	10.0	1.8	0.80
6. Stockholder return for five years after merger (percent per annum)	A	63	17.9	16.4	1.5	0.77
7. 2 − 1	A	63	38.5	26.6	11.9	1.99
8. 3 − 1	A	63	7.5	7.6	−0.2	−0.05
9. 4 − 1	A	63	−5.7	−0.1	−5.6*	−2.00
10. 5 − 1	A	63	−1.5	3.6	−5.0	1.78
11. 6 − 1	A	63	4.6	9.9	−5.3*	−2.00

Mean Values span AG and MAG columns.

Notes: See notes to Table 8–4.

by about six percentage points in the five years after merger (compared with the five years prior to merger), the leverage ratio of the control group firms has, on average, slightly declined.

Stockholder Return

Table 8–23 examines the impact of mergers on the financial returns to stockholders. For this, stockholder returns[27] were calculated for a sample of sixty-three acquiring companies and their matched control group companies in the five years prior to merger and for one, two, three, four, and five years after merger.[28] The results (rows 1 to 6) show that the stockholder return is consistently higher on average, in all periods, for acquiring companies than for matched control group companies. However, the difference in stockholder return between these groups becomes less, on average, in the postmerger period. This implies that the change in stockholder return following merger is worse for acquiring firms than for control group firms. This implication is supported by the results shown in rows 7 to 11. Apart from the comparison of premerger stockholder return (five years) with stockholder return in the year after merger, the results show on average a decline in the stockholder return of acquiring companies relative to their matched control group firms. Nevertheless, it remains true that the shareholders of acquiring firms over the period as a whole were better off in terms of the return on their shares than those of the nonacquiring companies.[29]

CONCLUSION

In this chapter, we have outlined the differences in the institutional environment that has characterized the merger movement of the last two decades in the United Kingdom, as compared both with the previous merger movements in this country and with contemporary merger waves in other countries. The detailed microeconomic analysis for the peak merger years 1967–1969 has shown that there were some important differences in the average premerger characteristics of the acquired-acquiring and nonacquired-nonacquiring companies. In general, it was found easier to discriminate between the acquiring companies and the rest than between those acquired and the others. The most important distinguishing features of the acquirers, on a univariate basis, were their higher average growth, greater average leverage ratio, and bigger average size.

The test results on determinants of mergers did not yield evidence in support of there being any one single dominant motive for mergers (of those considered). This is not surprising, since there are many different reasons why firms merge. As for the effects of mergers, the United Kingdom evidence shows that the growth and profitability performance of

268 / The Determinants and Effects of Mergers

merging companies did not deteriorate after merger. Other things being equal, this evidence is compatible with the view that although the takeover mechanism may not be particularly beneficial in terms of its effects on resource allocation, it is at least not perverse.

However, the fundamental issues involved in defining and measuring efficiency are complex in an economy that can be regarded as being in long-term disequilibrium (see Singh 1977b) and where, therefore, the ceteris paribus assumption of the conventional welfare analysis is particularly inappropriate. This and other aspects of the overall economic efficiency of mergers are discussed in Chapter 11.

NOTES

1. More specifically, the issues of industrial concentration and macroeconomic efficiency are not examined in this study. These will be discussed in forthcoming papers.
2. It should be noted that although small in number, many amalgamations are very large in size. None of the results reported in this chapter include amalgamations, but tests suggested that their exclusion did not invalidate conclusions drawn from the analysis.
3. Section 33 of the Companies Act 1967 required anyone becoming beneficially interested in one-tenth or more of the nominal value of voting equity to disclose his interest within fourteen days to the company concerned, which had to make it public in its share register within a further three days. In 1976 the law was made even more restrictive in these respects.
4. The takeover bid normally consists of a company making a bid for the shares of another company at a given price, subject to a predetermined proportion of shareholders accepting the bid by a given date. The proportion chosen has varied with the prevailing legal and stock exchange protection afforded to minority shareholders (see Weinberg 1971).
5. Singh and Whittington (1968) found that in 1954, for more than 60 percent of the firms in the four industries studied by them, the valuation ratio (i.e., the ratio of stock market valuation of a firm's ordinary shares to the book value of its assets) was less than 1; the mean valuation ratio was 0.94. However by 1960, as a result of the share price boom of 1959–1960, the mean valuation ratio had increased to 1.26, although 40 percent of the firms still had a valuation ratio below unity.
6. From 1965 to 1973 the definition was one-third of a national market. The 1973 legislation therefore tightened the net in this respect.
7. Calculated by listing the merger investments of the IRC, shown in Young & Lowe (1974: Appendix) and calculating the net assets of the seventeen companies disappearing as a result of merger, which could be identified in the databank of merger activity compiled by A. Hughes at the Department of Applied Economics, Cambridge University. Where an amalgamation was involved, the net assets of the firm ending up with the smaller share of equity in the new concern was taken as the disappearance.
8. We have not in this section considered the ways in which the stock market itself has sought to influence merger activity. While this might seem an important omission, it can be argued that for our purposes it is not. The major institution involved here is the City Panel on Take Overs and Mergers, first constituted in 1968 for surveillance on merger practices on the exchange. Its main concern, however, is with shareholder protection in bid situations rather than the extent or direction of merger activity itself. In general the evidence suggests that its impact in controlling abuses has been restricted. See further Spiegelberg (1973) and Davies (1976).

9. No comparable series is available for the distributive industries, but it seems clear that this trend was more widespread than manufacturing alone. See, for instance, the decline in all industrial and commercial quoted companies shown in Prais (1976: 91, table 5.2).

10. No straightforward inferences can be drawn from Table 8–2 due to possible aggregation errors (see below). However, nothwithstanding the aggregation problem, the hypothesis of no difference in the probabilities of acquisition in the various size quintiles is rejected at the 2 percent level. As the table suggests, there is a nonlinear relationship between size and probability of acquisition (See Singh 1975; Kuehn 1975; and Singh 1976a).

11. The highest death rate recorded in earlier periods was 2.3 percent in the years 1885–1896 during the first United Kingdom merger wave (Hart and Prais 1956).

12. These variables were dictated by the requirements of the statistical tests described in Chapters 1 and 2, rather than by the nature of the issues discussed above. Nevertheless, they do bear directly on these issues. For a discussion of these variables in connection with questions of market selection processes and market discipline, see Singh (1971).

13. The price-earnings ratio is linked to Marris's (1964) valuation ratio by the following identity:

Valuation ratio = P/E multiplied by the posttax rate of return on equity assets.

14. The market rate of return was taken to be the return on the Fortune 500 industrial ordinary shares.

15. Firms making more than one acquisition are counted as separate acquirers for each of the acquisitions they make.

16. The condition of noninvolvement in takeover activity over a ten-year time span used in forming the control group was dictated by the requirements of the statistical tests of Chapter 2. It is, however, important to note that, given the very high incidence of takeover activity during the decade of the 1960s, the number of companies in the control group was relatively small. This results in the matching for size being rather inadequate, particularly in the upper size ranges.

17. Horizontal mergers were taken to be those mergers between two companies within the same two-digit industry.

18. The individual industry analysis is, in all cases, carried out for fourteen industries. Industries 37, 38, 43, 47, 49 and 70 were excluded from the individual industry analysis due to the small number of takeovers in these industries. It is worth noting at this stage why the number of observations vary in the results presented in the tables, and why the number of observations may fall short of the maximum of 290: (a) some acquiring and acquired companies did not exist throughout the period of five years prior to merger; (b) some acquiring companies did not continue to exist three (or five) years after merger; (c) "rate of return on assets" measures require balance sheet figures for six years prior to merger and so have less observations than for the other measures because companies not existing six years prior to merger are excluded in this case; (d) sales figures were universally available only after 1967; (e) coefficients of variation of profits were not calculated for those companies with zero average profit over the period; (f) leverage ratios calculated on the net flow basis were removed when negative values were obtained; (g) in tests involving ratios of post- to premerger performance. observations were removed when nonpositive values occurred.

19. This test considers whether the proportion of industries in which the difference in group means is positive is significantly different from the null hypothesis of 0.5. It would have been statistically more appropriate to analyze differences in group medians (nonparametric measure of location), but the enormous task of calculation precluded this approach being adopted.

20. There is evidence that the profits variability indicator used here is negatively related to size. Since the acquired companies are on the whole much smaller than the acquiring ones, this may explain the relatively greater variability of their profits record.

21. This conclusion is rather different from that of Singh and Whittington (1968) for the period 1954–1960. They found that size was uncorrelated with any of fourteen main

270 / The Determinants and Effects of Mergers

indicators, including profitability, growth, leverage, liquidity ratio, valuation ratio, and so forth, that they were investigating.

22. The available evidence is of course perfectly compatible with an alternative hypothesis that it is not the more volatile acquired firms that are seeking to reduce profits variability by merging with the more stable acquiring firms, but that the latter take over the former simply because the acquired firms are relatively cheaper to buy owing to their more variable profits record.

23. The *t*-test shows that the average price-earnings ratio of acquired firms (a year before merger) was significantly greater than that of nonacquired firms at the 10 percent level. However, this conclusion is not supported by the distribution-free binomial probability test, which shows that thirteen out of twenty-eight acquired firms had a lower than average price-earnings ratio.

24. The differences between the results for pretax profitability on net assets and posttax profitability on equity assets arise from the differences in the gearing ratios of the two groups of firms.

25. In this chapter all the change tests are carried out in terms of arithmetic differences in performance, but they were also done in terms of performance ratios (i.e., after/before). Since the results were essentially the same, it was decided to save space by excluding the ratio tests from our presentation.

26. It could be argued that the postmerger growth performance of merging firms is overstated to the extent that while the control group companies by definition did not grow by acquisition, the merging firms could and may have done so. However, Meeks (1977) has shown that the superior growth performance of merging firms is due as much to internal as to acquisition growth.

27. The stockholder return for a company is measured by calculating the capital gain and dividend income (including income from reinvesting dividend income in the FT 500 share index) on £100 of investment in that company's ordinary stock.

28. The analysis was also carried out for horizontal and nonhorizontal mergers separately. The results obtained were similar to those reported in Table 8–23.

29. There is considerable evidence that the shareholders of the acquired companies invariably gain from merger (because of the premium that they are paid to persuade them to accept the takeover bid: Firth 1979; Newbould 1970). This may in part explain the decline in stockholder return of the acquiring companies. It should be noted that the discussion in the text does not take into account the risk associated with the mean returns reported. Sharp and Treynor tests required for this purpose could not unfortunately be carried out in this study because of the difficulties involved in obtaining data of the necessary quality.

Part V
Managers and Shareholders
in the Takeover Process

Managers and Shareholders:
Acquirers and Targets

[12]

Richard Roll
University of California, Los Angeles

The Hubris Hypothesis of Corporate Takeovers*

Finally, knowledge of the source of takeover gains still eludes us. [Jensen and Ruback 1983, p. 47]

I. Introduction

Despite many excellent research papers, we still do not fully understand the motives behind mergers and tender offers or whether they bring an increase in aggregate market value. In their comprehensive review article (from which the above quote is taken), Jensen and Ruback (1983) summarize the empirical work presented in over 40

The hubris hypothesis is advanced as an explanation of corporate takeovers. Hubris on the part of individual decision makers in bidding firms can explain why bids are made even when a valuation above the current market price represents a positive valuation error. Bidding firms infected by hubris simply pay too much for their targets. The empirical evidence in mergers and tender offers is reconsidered in the hubris context. It is argued that the evidence supports the hubris hypothesis as much as it supports other explanations such as taxes, synergy, and inefficient target management.

* The earlier drafts of this paper elicited many comments. It is a pleasure to acknowledge the benefits derived from the generosity of so many colleagues. They corrected several conceptual and substantive errors in the previous draft, directed my attention to other results, and suggested other interpretations of the empirical phenomena. In general, they provided me with an invaluable tutorial on the subject of corporate takeovers. The present draft undoubtedly still contains errors and omissions, but this is due mainly to my inability to distill and convey the collective knowledge of the profession. Among those who helped were C. R. Alexander, Peter Bernstein, Thomas Copeland, Harry DeAngelo, Eugene Fama, Karen Farkas, Michael Firth, Mark Grinblatt, Gregg Jarrell, Bruce Lehmann, Paul Malatesta, Ronald Masulis, David Mayers, John McConnell, Merton Miller, Stephen Ross, Richard Ruback, Sheridan Titman, and, especially, Michael Jensen, Katherine Schipper, Walter A. Smith, Jr., and J. Fred Weston. I also benefited from the comments of the finance workshop participants at the University of Chicago, the University of Michigan, and Dartmouth College, and of the referees.

(*Journal of Business*, 1986, vol. 59, no. 2, pt. 1)

papers. There are many important details in these papers, but Jensen and Ruback interpret them to show overall "that corporate takeovers generate positive gains, that target firm shareholders benefit, and that bidding firm shareholders do not lose" (p. 47).

My purpose here is to suggest a different and less conciusive interpretation of the empirical results. This interpretation may not turn out to be valid, but I hope to show that it has enough plausibility to be at least considered in further investigations. It will be argued here that takeover gains may have been overestimated if they exist at all. If there really are no aggregate gains associated with takeovers, or if they are small, it is not hard to understand why their sources are "elusive."

The mechanism by which takeover attempts are initiated and consummated suggests that at least part of the large price increases observed in target firm shares might represent a simple transfer from the bidding firm, that is, that the observed takeover premium (tender offer or merger price less preannouncement market price of the target firm) overstates the increase in economic value of the corporate combination. To see why this could be the case, let us follow the steps undertaken in a takeover.

First, the bidding firm identifies a potential target firm.

Second, a "valuation" of the equity of the target is undertaken. In some cases this may include nonpublic information. The valuation definitely would include, of course, any estimated economies due to synergy and any assessments of weak management et cetera that might have caused a discount in the target's current market price.

Third, the "value" is compared to the current market price. If value is below price, the bid is abandoned. If value exceeds price, a bid is made and becomes part of the public record. The bid would not generally be the previously determined "value" since it should include provision for rival bids, for future bargaining with the target, and for valuation errors inter alia.

The key element in this series of events is the valuation of an asset (the stock) that already has an observable market price. The preexistence of an active market in the identical item being valued distinguishes takeover attempts from other types of bids, such as for oil-drilling rights and paintings. These other assets trade infrequently and no two of them are identical. This means that the seller must make his own independent valuation. There is a symmetry between the bidder and the seller in the necessity for valuation.

In takeover attempts, the target firm shareholder may still conduct a valuation, but it has a lower bound, the current market price. The bidder knows for certain that the shareholder will not sell below that; thus when the valuation turns out to be below the market price, no offer is made.

Consider what might happen if there are no potential synergies or other sources of takeover gains but when, nevertheless, some bidding firms believe that such gains exist. The valuation itself can then be considered a random variable whose mean is the target firm's current market price. When the random variable exceeds its mean, an offer is made; otherwise there is no offer. Offers are observed only when the valuation is too high; outcomes in the left tail of the distribution of valuations are never observed. The takeover premium in such a case is simply a random error, a mistake made by the bidding firm. Most important, the observed error is always in the same direction. Corresponding errors in the opposite direction are made in the valuation process, but they do not enter our empirical samples because they are not made public.

If there were no value at all in takeovers, why would firms make bids in the first place? They should realize that any bid above the market price represents an error. This latter logic is alluring because market prices do seem to reflect rational behavior. But we must keep in mind that prices are averages. There is no evidence to indicate that every individual behaves as if he were the rational economic human being whose behavior seems revealed by the behavior or market prices. We may argue that markets behave as if they were populated by rational beings. But a market actually populated by rational beings is observationally equivalent to a market characterized by grossly irrational individual behavior that cancels out in the aggregate, leaving the trace of the only systematic behavioral component, the small thread of rationality that all individuals have in common. Indeed, one possible definition of irrational or aberrant behavior is independence across individuals (and thus disappearance from view under aggregation).

Psychologists are constantly bombarding economists with empirical evidence that individuals do not always make rational decisions under uncertainty. For example, see Oskamp (1965), Tversky and Kahneman (1981), and Kahneman, Slovic, and Tversky (1982). Among psychologists, economists have a reputation for arrogance mainly because this evidence is ignored; but psychologists seem not to appreciate that economists disregard the evidence on individual decision making because it usually has little predictive content for market behavior. Corporate takeovers are, I believe, one area of research in which this usually valid reaction of economists should be abandoned; takeovers reflect individual decisions.

There is little reason to expect that a particular individual bidder will refrain from bidding because he has learned from his own past errors. Although some firms engage in many acquisitions, the average individual bidder/manager has the opportunity to make only a few takeover offers during his career. He may convince himself that the valuation is right and that the market does not reflect the full economic value of the

200   **Journal of Business**

combined firm. For this reason, the hypothesis being offered in this paper to explain the takeover phenomenon can be termed the "hubris hypothesis." If there actually are no aggregate gains in takeover, the phenomenon depends on the overbearing presumption of bidders that their valuations are correct.

Even if gains do exist for some corporate combinations, at least part of the average observed takeover premium could still be caused by valuation error and hubris. The left tail of the distribution of valuations is truncated by the current market price. To the extent that there are errors in valuation, fewer negative errors will be observed other than positive errors. When gains exist, a smaller fraction of the distribution will be truncated than when there are no gains at all. Nonetheless, truncation will occur in every situation in which the gain is small enough to allow the distribution of valuations to have positive probability below the market price.

Rational bidders will realize that valuations are subject to error and that negative errors are truncated in repeated bids. They will take this into account when making a bid. Takeover attempts are thus analogous to the auctions discussed in bidding theory wherein the competing bidders make public offers. In the takeover situation, the initial bidder is the market, and the initial public offer is the current price. The second bidder is the acquiring firm who, conscious of the "winner's curse," biases his bid downward from his estimate of value. In fact, he frequently abandons the auction altogether, allowing the first bidder to win.

In a standard auction, we would observe all cases, including those in which the initial bid was victorious. Theory predicts that the winning bid is an accurate assessment of value. In takeovers, however, if the initial bid (by the market) wins the auction, we throw away the observation. If all bidders accounted properly for the "winner's curse," there would be no particular bias associated with discarding bids won by the market; but if bidders are infected by hubris, the standard bidding theory conclusion would not be valid. Empirical evidence from repeated sealed bid auctions (Capen, Clapp, and Campbell 1971; and Dougherty and Lohrenz 1976), indicates that bidders do not fully incorporate the winner's curse. Unless there is something curative about the public nature of corporate takeover auctions, we should at least consider the possibility that the same phenomenon exists in them.

The hubris hypothesis is consistent with strong-form market efficiency. Financial markets are assumed to be efficient in that asset prices reflect all information about individual firms. Product and labor markets are assumed efficient in the sense that (*a*) no industrial reorganization can bring gains in an aggregate output at the same cost or reductions in aggregate costs with the same output and (*b*) management talent is employed in its best alternative use.

Most other explanations of the takeover phenomenon rely on strong-form market inefficiency of at least a temporary duration. Either financial markets are ignorant of relevant information possessed by bidding firms, or product markets are inefficiently organized so that potential synergies, monopolies, or tax savings are being ineffectively exploited (at least temporarily), or labor markets are inefficient because gains could be obtained by replacement of inferior managers. Although perfect strong-form efficiency is unlikely, the concept should serve as a frictionless ideal, the benchmark of comparison by which other degrees of efficiency are measured. This is, I claim, the proper role for the hubris hypothesis of takeovers; it is the null against which other hypotheses of corporate takeovers should be compared.

Section II presents the principal empirical predictions of the hubris hypothesis and discusses supportive and disconfirming empirical results. Section III concludes the paper by summarizing the results and by discussing various objections to the hypothesis.

II. Evidence for and against the Hubris Hypothesis

If there are absolutely no gains available to corporate takeovers, the hubris hypothesis implies that the average increase in the target firm's market value should then be more than offset by the average decrease in the value of the bidding firm. Takeover expenses would constitute the aggregate net loss. The market price of a target firm should increase when a previously unanticipated bid is announced, and it should decline to the original level or below if the first bid is unsuccessful and if no further bids are received.

Implications for the market price reaction of a bidding firm are somewhat less clear. If we could be sure that (*a*) the bid was unanticipated and (*b*) the bid conveys no information about the bidder other than that it is seeking a combination with a particular target, then the hubris hypothesis would predict the following market price movements in bidding firms:

1. a price decline on announcement of a bid;
2. a price increase on abandoning a bid or on losing a bid; and
3. a price decline on actually winning a bid.

It has been pointed out by several authors, most forcefully by Schipper and Thompson (1983), that condition *a* above is by no means assured in all cases. Bids are not always surprises. As Jensen and Ruback (1983, pp. 18–20) observe, this alone complicates the measurement of bidder firm returns.

The possibility that a bid conveys information about the bidding firm's own operations, that is, violation of condition *b*, is an equally serious problem (cf. Jensen and Ruback 1983, p. 19 and n. 14). For example, the market might well interpret a bid as signaling that the bidding firm's immediate past or expected future cash flows are higher than previously estimated, that this has actually prompted the bid, and that, although the takeover itself has a negative value, the combination of takeover and new information is on balance positive.

Similarly, abandoning a previous bid could convey negative information about the bidding firm's ability to pay for the proposed acquisition, perhaps because of negative events in its own operations. Losing a bid to rivals could signal limited resources. These problems of contaminating information make it difficult to interpret bidding firm price movements and to interpret the combined price movements of bidder and target.

A.   *The Evidence about Target Firms*

Let us first examine, therefore, the more straightforward implications of the hubris hypothesis for target firms. Bradley, Desai, and Kim (1983*b*) present results for target firms in tender offers that are consistent with the implications. Target firms display increases in value on the announcement of a tender offer, and they fall back to about the original level if no combination occurs then or later.

A similar pattern is observed in Asquith's (1983) sample of target firms in unsuccessful mergers. These firms were targets in one or more merger bids that were later abandoned and for whom no additional merger bids occurred during the year after the last original bid was withdrawn. The original merger bid announcement was accompanied by a 7.0% average increase in target firm value that appears to be almost entirely reversed within 60 days (fig. 1, p. 62). By the date when the last bid is abandoned, the target's price decline amounts to 8.1% (table 9, p. 81), slightly more than offsetting the original increase.

The result may be partially compromised by the following problem. The "outcome date" of an unsuccessful bid is the withdrawal date of the final offer following which no additional bid is received for 1 year. Thus as of the outcome date the market could not have known for certain that other bids would not arrive. However, if the market had known that no other bids would arrive, the price decline would likely have been ever larger, so perhaps this partial use of hindsight was not material. In summary, target firm share behavior, as presented in Bradley et al. (1983*b*) for tender offers and in Asquith (1983) for mergers, is consistent with the hubris hypothesis.

B.   *The Evidence about Total Gains*

The central prediction of the hubris hypothesis is that the total combined takeover gain to target and bidding firm shareholders is nonpositive. None of the evidence using returns can unambiguously test this prediction for the simple reason that average returns of individual firms do not measure average dollar gains, especially in the typical takeover situation in which the bidding firm is much larger (cf. Jensen and Ruback 1983, p. 22). In some cases, the observed price increase in the target would correspond to such a trivial loss to the bidder that the loss is bound to be hidden in the bid/ask spread and in the noise of daily return volatility.

In an attempt to circumvent the problem that returns cannot measure takeover gains when bidder and target have different sizes, Asquith, Bruner, and Mullins (1983) take the unique approach of regressing the bidder announcement period return on the relative size of target to bidder. They reason that, if acquisitions benefit bidder firms, large acquisitions should show up as having larger return effects on bidder firm returns. They do find this positive relation for bidding firms. The same relation is not significant for target firms, although, as usual, target firms have much larger average returns. The positive relation for bidding firms is consistent with more than one explanation. It is consistent with the bidding firm losing on average, but losing less the larger the target. Perhaps a more accurate valuation is conducted when the stakes are large and this results in a smaller percentage loss to the bidder. Perhaps large targets are less closely held so that the takeover premium can be smaller relative to the preoffer price and still convince shareholders to deliver their shares. Perhaps bidders for larger targets have fewer rivals and can thus get away with a bidder-perceived "bargain."

The absence of any relation for target firms is puzzling under every hypothesis unless the entire gain accrues to the target firm shareholders (and Asquith et al. [1983] interpret their results to indicate that takeover gains are shared). If synergy is the source of gains, for example, target shareholder's returns would increase with the relative size of its bidder-partner.

Several studies have attempted to measure aggregate dollar gains directly. Halpern (1973) finds average market adjusted gains of $27.35 million in a sample of mergers between New York Stock Exchange–listed firms (p. 569); the gain was calculated over a period 7 months prior to the first public announcement of the merger through the merger consummation month. The standard error of this average gain, assuming cross-sectional independence, was $19.7 ($173.2/$\sqrt{77}$ [see table 3, p. 569]). In 53 cases out of 77, there was a dollar gain.

Bradley, Desai, and Kim (1982) present dollar returns for a sample of 162 successful tender offers from 20 days before the announcement until 5 days after completion. The average combined dollar increase in value of bidder plus target was $17 million, but this was not statistically significant. The $17 million gain was divided between a $34 million average gain by targets and a $17 million average loss to bidders. The authors note that the equally weighted average rate of return to bidders is positive, though the dollar change is a loss; they argue that this can be explained by skewness in the distribution of dollar changes.

In a revision of their 1982 paper, Bradley, Desai, and Kim (1983*a*) present slightly different results. The sample is expanded from 162 and 183 tender offer events, although the underlying data base appears to be the same (698 tender offers from October 1958 to December 1980). The only stated difference in the selection of samples is that the earlier paper excludes offers that are not "control oriented" (cf. Bradley et al. 1982, p. 13; and Bradley et al. 1983*a*, pp. 35–36). This sample change resulted in an average gain to targets of $28.1 million and to bidders to +$5.8 million (table 9). The authors say, however, that "the distributional properties of our dollar gain measures preclude any meaningful inferences about their significance" (p. 58).

Malatesta (1983) examines the combined change in target and bidder firms before, during, and after a merger. Jensen and Ruback summarize Malatesta's results as follows: "Malatesta examines a matched sample of targets and their bidders in 30 successful mergers and finds a significant average increase of $32.4 million ($t = 2.07$) in their combined equity value in the month before and the month of outcome announcement. . . . This evidence indicates that changes in corporate control increase the combined market value" (1983, p. 22).

Malatesta (1983) himself does not reach so definite a conclusion. In fact, his overall interpretation of the evidence is that "the immediate impact of merger per se is positive and highly significant for acquired firms but *larger in absolute value and negative* for acquiring firms" (p. 155; emphasis added). Jensen and Ruback were referring to smaller samples of matching pairs. Even for this sample, Malatesta says, the results "provide *weak* evidence that successful resolution of these mergers had a positive impact on combined shareholder wealth" (p. 170; emphasis added). In 2 months culminating in board approval of the merger, the combined gain was positive, but "over the entire interval −60 to 0 [months], the cumulative dollar return is a trivial 0.29 million dollars" (p. 171). Of course, this could be due to selection bias; bidding or acquired firms or both may tend to be involved in mergers after a period of poor performance. According to Asquith's (1983) results, however, this is true only for targets. The opposite is true for bidders; they tend to display superior performance prior to the merger bid announcement. During the culminating merger months, the acquiring firms' gains in Malatesta's sample were not statistically significant (although the acquired firms' were).

Malatesta's month zero is when the board announced merger approval, not when the merger proposal first reached the public. Even if the merger per se has no aggregate value, the price reaction on approval could be positive because it signals that court battles, further bids to overcome rivals, and other costly events associated with hostile mergers will not take place in this case, although their possibility was signaled originally by the merger proposal. Malatesta does not present evidence about the dollar reactions of the combined firm on the first announcement of the merger proposal.

Firth (1980) presents the results of a study of takeovers in the United Kingdom. In his sample, target firms gain, and bidding firms lose, both statistically significantly. The average total change in market value of the two firms in a successful combination, from a month prior to the takeover bid through the month of acceptance of the offer, is £ − 36.6 million. No t-statistic is given for this number, but we can obtain a rough measure of significance by using the fact that 224 of 434 cases displayed aggregate losses. If these cases were independent, the t-statistic that the true proportion of losing takeovers is greater than 50% is about .67.

The relative division of losses was examined by Firth (1980) in an ingenious calculation that strongly suggests the presence of bidding errors. The premium paid to the target firm (in £) as a fraction of the size of the bidding firm was cross-sectionally related to the percentage loss in the bidding firm's shares around the takeover period. The regression coefficient was − .89 ($t = -5.94$). Firth concludes (p. 254), "This supports the view that the stock market expects zero benefits from a takeover, that the gains to the acquired firm represent an 'over-payment' and that the acquiring company's shareholders suffer corresponding losses."

Using dollar-based matched pairs of firms, Varaiya (1985) finds that the aggregate abnormal dollar gain of targets is $189.4 million while the average abnormal dollar loss of bidders is $128.7 million for 121 days around the takeover announcement. The aggregate gain of $60.7 ($189.4 − 128.7) is not statistically significant, on the basis of a parametric test, though a nonparametric test does indicate significance. Varaiya also reports a cross-sectional regression that indicates that, the larger the target's dollar gain, the larger the bidder's dollar loss. The regression coefficient was − .81 ($t = -2.81$).

To summarize, the evidence about total gains in takeovers must be judged inconclusive. Results based on returns are unreliable. Malatesta's dollar-based results show a small aggregate gain in the months just around merger approval in a small matched sample and an aggregate loss in a larger unmatched sample. The interpretation of Malatesta's results is rendered difficult by the possibility of losses or gains in prior months, after announcement of a merger possibility but before final approval is a certainty. Dollar-based results presented by Bradley et al. (1982, 1983a) show a small and insignificant aggregate gain. Firth's (1980) British results show an insignificant aggregate loss. Both Firth (1980) and Varaiya (1985) present persuasive evidence for the existence of overbidding. But, on balance, the existence of either gains or losses to the combined firms involved in corporate combinations remains in doubt.

This mixed and insignificant evidence is made even less conclusive (if that is possible) by potential measurement biases. There is a potential upward bias in the measured price reaction of bidding firms (and thus of the aggregate) caused by contaminating information. There is a potential downward bias due to prior anticipation of the takeover event, as explained by Schipper and Thompson (1983), and another potential downward bias in some studies due to an improper computation of abnormal returns (Chung and Weston 1985). These biases will be discussed in detail next, in connection with the empirical findings for bidding firms.

C. Evidence about Bidding Firms: The Announcement Effect

The hubris hypothesis predicts a decrease in the value of the bidding firm. As pointed out previously, this decrease may not be completely reflected in a market price decline because of contaminating information in a bid, because the bid has been (partly) anticipated, or simply because the economic loss is too small to be reliably reflected in prices.

The data contain several interesting patterns. Asquith (1983) finds that bidding firm shares show "no consistent pattern" around the announcement date, but, "in summary, bidding firms appear to have small but insignificant positive excess returns at the press day" (p. 66). Some of Asquith's other results are understandable under the hubris hypothesis. Before the first merger bid, for instance, firms who become successful bidders have much larger price increases than firms whose bids are unsuccessful. One would expect a higher level of hubris and thus more aggressive pursuit of a target in firms that had experienced recent good times.

Asquith's results are in conflict with those of Dodd (1980), who finds statistically significant negative returns at the bid announcement. Jensen and Ruback (1983) noted the difference in results, and they asked Dodd to check his data and computer program, which they report (Jensen and Ruback 1983, p. 17, n. 12) he did without finding an error.[1]

Negative bidder returns were also found by Eger (1983) in her study of pure exchange (noncash) mergers. Bidding firm stock prices de-

---

1. Recently, Chung and Weston (1985) suggested that part of the difference in results could be explained by an improper calculation of "abnormal" returns around the merger announcement. Chung and Weston point out that the premerger period generally displays statistically significant positive returns for bidding firms. If data from this period are used to estimate abnormal returns at merger announcement, the measured announcement effect will be biased downward. The reported diffrence between, say, Dodd (1980) and Asquith (1983) would be reduced by a recalculation by Dodd excluding the preannouncement period. However, it probably would not be entirely eliminated; the bias appears to be only a small fraction of Dodd's observed announcement effect.

clined, on average by about 4%, from 5 days prior to merger bid announcement to 10 days afterward (Eger 1983, table 4, p. 563). The decline was statistically significant. Eger suggests that the difference between her results and Asquith's (1983) might be attributable to a difference between mergers involving cash and pure stock exchange mergers; and she notes that tender offers, which often involve cash, seem to display more positive bidder stock price reactions (see below).

In his study of United Kingdom takeovers, Firth (1980) reports statistically significant negative bidding firm returns in the month of the takeover announcement. Eighty percent of the bidders had negative abnormal returns during that month, and the t-statistic for the average return was about -5.0 (cf. Firth 1980, table 5, p. 248).

Varaiya (1985) also finds statistically significant negative returns for bidding firms on the announcement day. He reports also that the bidder's loss is significantly larger when there are rival bidders.

A recent paper by Ruback and Mikkelson (1984) documents announcement effects of corporate purchases of another corporation's shares according to the stated purpose of the acquisition (filed on form 13-D with the Securities and Exchange Commission). The 2-day announcement effect for acquiring firms was positive and statistically significant for the 370 firms whose stated purpose was not a takeover. In contrast, for 134 acquiring firms indicating an intention to effect a takeover, the announcement effect was negative and significant (table 4, p. 17).

Studies of individual cases have been mixed. For example, Ruback (1982) argues that DuPont's large stock price decline in announcing a bid to take over Conoco could be an indication that managers (of DuPont) "had an objective function different from that of shareholder wealth maximization" (p. 24). However, he rejects this explanation because of "the magnitude of Conoco's revaluation and the lack of evidence that DuPont's management benefitted from the acquisition" (p. 24). He also rejects every other explanation except inside information possessed by DuPont and not yet appreciated by the market; but even this hypothesis "cannot be confirmed since the nature of the information is unknown" (p. 25).

One interesting aspect of the DuPont/Conoco case is that DuPont's decline was more than offset by Conoco's gain; that is, the total gain was positive (although the bidding firm lost). This suggests that nonhubris factors were indeed present, bringing a total gain to the corporate combination, but that overbidding was present too, resulting in a loss to DuPont shareholders.

The other case study by Ruback (1983) finds only a small negative effect for Occidental Petroleum in its bid for Cities Service. Cities Service's stock price increased by a relatively small amount for a target firm, and the total effect was positive. Apparently, there was little

208   **Journal of Business**

significant hubris evidenced by Occidental (who offered only a small premium). An interesting sidelight was the performance of Gulf Oil, a rival bidder who withdrew. It suffered a loss far in excess of Cities Service's gain.

Schipper and Thompson (1983) find a positive price reaction around the announcement that a firm is embarking on a program of conglomerate acquisitions. Also they observe negative price reactions of such firms to antimerger regulatory events. The two findings are interpreted as at least consistent with the proposition that acquisitions are positive net present value projects for the bidding firm. However, the authors emphasize the tentative nature of their conclusion (pp. 109–11). For example, they note that the announcement of an acquisition program is sometimes accompanied by "announcements of related policy decisions, such as de-emphasis of old lines of business, changes in management, changes in capital structure or specific merger proposals" (p. 89). Even without such explicit contaminating information, announcement of the program could be interpreted as good news about the future profitability of the bidder's current assets rather than about the prospect of an undisclosed future target firm to be obtained at a bargain price.

The possibility of contaminating information is a central problem in interpreting the price movement of a bidding firm on the announcement date of an intended acquisition. Bidders are activists in the takeover situation, and their announcements may convey as much information about their own prospects as about the takeover. To mention one example of the measurement problem, mergers are usually leverage-increasing events. It is well documented from studies of other leverage-increasing events, such as exchange offers (Masulis 1980) and share repurchases (Vermaelen 1981), that positive price movements are to be expected. Thus to measure properly that part of the gain of a bidding firm in a merger that is attributable to the merger per se and not to an increase in leverage, we ought to deduct the price increase that would have been obtained by the same firm through independently increasing its leverage by the same amount.[2]

The measurement problem induced by the disparate sizes of target and bidder is the subject of a paper by Jarrell (1983). Jarrell argues that, when a bidder is several times larger than a target, a gain to the bidder equal in size to the gain observed in the target can be hidden in the noise of the bidder's return variability; that is, the t-statistic for the bidder's effect is likely to be much smaller than for the target's effect. Jarrell suggests solving this problem by adjusting the bidder's t-statistic upward by a factor proportional to the relative sizes of bidder and target. When he makes the adjustment in his sample, bidding firms

---

2. I am grateful to Sheridan Titman for pointing out this possibility.

display significantly positive price movements from 30 days prior to 10 days after the takeover announcement. The mean abnormal return prior to adjustment is 2.3%; after adjustment it is 9.2%. Similarly, the combined bidder and target returns become more statistically significant.

The problem with the Jarrell adjustment is that it can be applied to any sample in order to render a sample mean of either sign statistically significant. For example, if Firth (1980) had adjusted his bidding firm returns downward according to the relative sizes of bidder and target, he could have concluded that British takeovers had significant aggregate negative effects on shareholders. This does not imply that Jarrell's conclusions are incorrect, but we are certainly entitled to remain skeptical. Several studies have reported positive bidder gains, and several others have reported losses. Applying the Jarrell technique indiscriminately to all of them could make the gains or losses more "significant," but this would simply create more confusion since the now "significant" results would disagree across studies.

D. Evidence about Bidding Firms: Resolution of Doubtful Success

There is some evidence available to help isolate the reevaluation of a bidding firm's own assets induced by the bid but not caused by the proposed corporate combination itself. Asquith's (1983) sample of bidding firms in mergers is separated into successful and unsuccessful bidders, and both samples are examined prior to bid announcement, between announcement and merger outcome, and after outcome. For the successful group, merger outcome is the actual date when the target firm is delisted; this is presumably the effective date of the merger. At the original bid announcement, the market cannot know for sure whether such firms actually will consummate the merger, that is, be in the "successful" group. There is only a probability of success. Between the bid announcement and the final outcome this probability goes to 1.0 for firms in the successful group. Thus if the combination itself has value for the bidder, these bidding firms should increase in value over this interim period. They do not. On average, successful bidding firms decline in value by .5% over the interim period (see Asquith 1983, fig. 4, p. 71; table 9, p. 81). The decrease in value is small and statistically insignificant, but the result has economic significance because the opposite sign must be observed if the corporate combination per se has value. If the combination has substantial value, one might have expected to observe a statistically significant upward price movement between bid announcement and outcome, provided, of course, that the upward revision in probability of success is large enough to show up.

Firms in Asquith's successful bidder group have very large prebid returns; abnormal returns average 14.3% over a 460-day period ending

20 days before the bid announcement. They have small positive returns (.2%) on the announcement date. The entire sequence of returns for successful bidding firms is consistent with the hubris hypothesis. In the prebid period, excellent performance endows management with both hubris and cash. A target is selected. The bid itself signals a small upward revision in the market's estimate of the bidding firm's current assets that is not completely offset by the prospect of paying too much for the target. Then there is a small downward revision in bidder firm value as it becomes more probable and then certain that the target will be acquired (at too high a price).

Eckbo (1983) reports a small and insignificant decline during the 3 days subsequent to the initial merger bid. But Eckbo's "successful" bidder is defined as one who is unchallenged on antitrust grounds; this may be a less relevant representation of actual success for our purposes here.

Eger (1983, p. 563) finds significant negative bidder firm returns averaging −3.1% in the 20 days after the original announcement of a merger that is ultimately successful. Most of this decline occurs in the first 10 days after the merger announcement. The bonds of these firms also decline slightly in price over the same period. This is consistent with a price decline in the total value of the bidding firm as it becomes more certain that the merger will succeed.

The most significant price decline between merger proposal and outcome is reported by Dodd (1980). Successful bidding firms decline in value by 7.22% from 10 days before the bid is announced until 10 days after the merger outcome, where outcome is defined as target stockholder approval of merger bid. The price decline is statistically significant. In the 20 days prior to the outcome date, successful bidder firms in Dodd's sample fall in price by about 2% (p. 124).

Evidence from papers using monthly data is more difficult to interpret, but the patterns do seem consistent with a negative price movement between merger announcement and successful outcome. For example, Langetieg's (1978, p. 377) bidding firms show a significant price decline continuing in the combined firm after the merger outcome. Similarly, Chung and Weston (1982, p. 334) report price declines between merger announcement month and merger completion in pure conglomerate mergers. However, the decline is not statistically significant.

Similar evidence is given in Malatesta (1983, table 4, p. 172). Acquiring firms in this sample have significant negative price performance in the period after the first announcement of a merger proposal. Since the data are monthly, the merger outcome date could be included somewhere in the sample period. This means that part of the puzzling post-outcome negative performance detected by Langetieg (1978) and Asquith (1983) might be included in Malatesta's table 4 results. In tables 5 and 6 Malatesta presents performance results for acquiring firms after the "first announcement of board/management approval of the merger" (p. 170). The returns are strongly negative in this period. This might not be such a puzzle if "board/management approval" still leaves open the possibility of withdrawal, for then the absolute certainty of merger (and the concomitant price drop expected under the hubris hypothesis) would occur sometime after this particular event date.

In summary, during the interim period between initial bid and successful outcome, the average price movement of successful merger bids is small, so it is not possible to draw strong implications. However, the pattern is generally consistent with the hubris hypothesis, which predicts the observed loss in value of bidding firm's shares. The loss is statistically insignificant in Asquith's sample but is significant in the samples of Dodd (1980) and Eger (1983) and in the monthly data samples of Langetieg (1978) and Malatesta (1983).

Evidence about the interim period from tender offer studies is mixed. One study seems to be clearly inconsistent with hubris alone; Bradley's (1980) sample of 88 successful bidding firms shows a price rise after the announcement data and before the execution date. The number is not given, but the plot of the mean abnormal price index (p. 366) indicates that the gain is approximately 2%–3%.

The interim price movement of the successful acquiring firm is reported by Ruback and Mikkelson (1984) as -1.07% with a t-statistic of -2.34 (table 6). Their sample is not dichotomized by merger versus tender offers, however, and it probably contains some of both types of takeovers.

The results given by Kummer and Hoffmeister (1978) for a 17-firm matched sample of tender offers are more difficult to interpret because the data are monthly and, apparently because of the small size of the cross-sectional sample, the time series of prices relative to the event data appears to be more variable. Abnormal returns are positive and largest in the announcement month but are also positive in months $+1$ and $+2$. If the tender offer is revolved sometime during these 2 months, the results are basically the same as Bradley's (1980). Months $+3$ to $+12$ witness a decline of about 4%. If the success of the tender offer is not known until sometime during this period, an interpretation could be made similar to the one discussed above concerning Asquith's and Dodd's samples of successful merger bids.

An identical set of nonconclusive inferences can be drawn from the monthly data of Dodd and Ruback (1977). There appears to be a positive price movement by successful bidders just after the announcement month followed by a price decline later. The decline over the 12 months after a bid amounts to -1.32%, but it is not statistically significant.

Bradley's daily results probably represent the best available evidence against the hubris hypothesis. The detected movement is small, but, unlike the case of merger's, the bidding firm's price does increase on average in Bradley's sample. This is consistent with the proposition that tender offers increase aggregate value and that some of the increase accrues to tender offer bidders. Whether the evidence is sufficiently compelling, particularly when balanced against evidence of an opposite character, is up to further investigation to decide definitely.

One other piece of evidence from the interim period between announcement and outcome is worthy of comtemplation. This is the price behavior of the first bidder's stock on the announcement of a rival bid. In their study of unsuccessful tender offers, Bradley et al. (1983*b*) report a significant price drop in the first bidder's stock. In contrast, Ruback and Mikkelson (1984) report a significant price increase (table 5); however, the latter sample consists not only of ultimately unsuccessful bidders in tender offers but of all corporate investors in other stock (including many who are not contemplating a takeover).

A price drop in the first takeover bidder's stock on the announcement of a rival bid is explainable by hubris. The rival bid may set off a bidding war that the market expects to result in a large loss for the winner. It would be extremely informative to observe the price reaction of the first bidder when it becomes evident that the rival bidder has won.

Finally, it should be noted that the price change after the resolution of a successful bid (either merger or tender offer) is almost uniformly negative (cf. Jensen and Ruback 1983, table 4, p. 21) and is relatively large in magnitude. This is a result that casts doubt on all estimates of bidding firm returns because it suggests the presence of substantial measurement problems.

III. Summary and Discussion

The purpose of this paper is to bring attention to a possible explanation of the takeover phenomenon of mergers and tender offers. This explanation, the hubris hypothesis, is very simple: decision makers in acquiring firms pay too much for their targets on average in the samples we observe. The samples, however, are not random. Potential bids are abandoned whenever the acquiring firm's valuation of the target turns up with a figure below the current market price. Bids are rendered when the valuation exceeds the price. If there really are no gains in takeovers, hubris is necessary to explain why managers do not abandon these bids also since reflection would suggest that such bids are likely to represent positive errors in valuation.

The hubris hypothesis can serve as the null hypothesis of corporate takeovers because it asserts that all markets are strong-form efficient.

Financial markets are aware of all information. Product markets are efficiently organized. Labor markets are characterized by managers being employed in their best operational positions.

Hubris predicts that, around a takeover, (*a*) the combined value of the target and bidder firms should fall slightly, (*b*) the value of the bidding firm should decrease, and (*c*) the value of the target should increase. The available empirical results indicate that the measured combined value has increased in some studies and decreased in others. It has been statistically significant in none. Measured changes in the prices of bidding firms have been mixed in sign across studies and mostly of a very small order of magnitude. Several studies have reported them to be significantly negative, and other studies have reported the opposite. Target firm prices consistently display large increases, but only if the initial bid or a later bid is successful. There is no permanent increase in value for target firms that do not eventually enter a corporate combination.

The interpretation of bidding firm returns is complicated by several potential measurement problems. The bid can convey contaminating information, that is, information about the bidder rather than about the takeover itself. The bid can be partially anticipated and thus result in an announcement effect smaller in absolute value than the true economic effect. Since bidders are usually much larger than targets, the effect of the bid can be buried in the noise of the bidder's return volatility. There is weak evidence from the interim period between the announcement of a merger and the merger outcome that the merger itself results in a loss to the bidding firm's shareholders; but the interim period in tender offers shows some results that favor the opposite view. Both findings have minimal statistical reliability.

The final impression one is obliged to draw from the currently available results is that they provide no really convincing evidence against even the extreme (hubris) hypothesis that all markets are operating perfectly efficiently and that individual bidders occasionally make mistakes. Bidders may indicate by their actions a belief in the existence of takeover gains, but systematic studies have provided little to show that such beliefs are well founded.

Finally, I should mention several issues that have arisen as objections by others to the hubris idea. First, the hubris hypothesis might seem to imply that managers act consciously against shareholder interests. Several recent papers that have examined nontakeover corporate control devices have concluded that the evidence is consistent with conscious management actions against the best interests of shareholders.[3] But the hubris hypothesis does not rely on this result. It is

---

3. See Bradley and Wakeman (1983), Dann and DeAngelo (1983), and DeAngelo and Rice (1983). Linn and McConnell (1983) disagree with the last paper. The possibility that managers do not act in the interest of stockholders has frequently been associated with the takeover phenomenon. For example, in a recent review, Lev (1983, p. 15) concludes

214 **Journal of Business**

sufficient that managers act, de facto, against shareholder interests by issuing bids founded on mistaken estimates of target firm value. Management intentions may be fully consistent with honorable stewardship of corporate assets, but actions need not always turn out to be right.

Second, it might seem that the hubris hypothesis implies systematic biases in market prices. One correspondent argued that stock prices would be systematically too high for reasons similar to those advanced in E. M. Miller's (1977) paper. This implication is not correct, however, for the simple reason that firms can be either targets or bidders. If bidders offer too much, their stock price will fall ex post while their target's price will rise. On average over all stocks, this cancels. Unless one can predict which firms will be targets and which will be bidders, there is no bias in any individual firm, and there is certainly no bias on average over all firms.

Third, an argument can be advanced that the hubris hypothesis implies an inefficiency in the market for corporate control. If all takeovers were prompted by hubris, shareholders could stop the practice by forbidding managers ever to make any bid. Since such prohibitions are not observed, hubris alone cannot explain the takeover phenomenon.

The validity of this argument depends on the size of deadweight takeover costs. If such costs are relatively small, stockholders would be indifferent to hubris-inspired bids because target firm shareholders would gain what bidding firm shareholders lose. A well-diversified shareholder would receive the aggregate gain, which is close to zero.

Fourth, and finally, a frequent objection is that hubris itself is based on a market inefficiency defined in a particular way; in the words of one writer, "It seems to me that your hypothesis does not rest on strong form efficiency, because it presumes that one set of market bidders is systematically irrational" (private correspondence). This argument contends that a market is inefficient if some market participants make systematic mistakes. Perhaps one of the long-term benefits of studying takeovers is to clarify the notion of market efficiency. Does efficiency mean that every individual behaves like the rational, maximizing ideal? Or does it mean instead that market interactions generate prices and allocations indistinguishable from those that would have been generated by rational individuals?

References

Asquith, P. 1983. Merger bids, uncertainty, and stockholder returns. *Journal of Financial Economics* 11 (April): 51–83.

---

by saying. I think we are justified in doubting . . . the argument that mergers are done to maximize stockholder wealth." Foster (1983) seems to share this view or at least the view that bidders make big mistakes. Larcker (1983) presents interesting results that managers in large takeovers are more likely to have short-term, accounting-based compensation contracts. He finds that, the more accounting-based the compensation, the more negative is the market price reaction to a bid. Larcker also suggests that managers who own less stock in their own company are more likely to make bids.

Asquith, P.; Bruner, R. F.; and Mullins, D. W., Jr. 1983. The gains to bidding firms from merger. *Journal of Financial Economics* 11 (April): 121–39.

Bradley, M. 1980. Interfirm tender offers and the market for corporate control. *Journal of Business* 53 (October): 345–76.

Bradley, M.; Desai, A.; and Kim, E. H. 1982. Specialized resources and competition in the market for corporate control. Typescript. Ann Arbor: University of Michigan, Graduate School of Business.

Bradley, M.; Desai, A.; and Kim, E. H. 1983a. Determinants of the wealth effects of corporate acquisition via tender offers: Theory and evidence. Typescript. Ann Arbor: University of Michigan, Graduate School of Business.

Bradley, M.; Desai, A.; and Kim, E. H. 1983b. The rationale behind interfirm tenders offers: Information or synergy? *Journal of Financial Economics* 11 (April): 183–206.

Bradley, M., and Wakeman, L. Mac. 1983. The wealth effects of targeted share repurchases. *Journal of Financial Economics* 11 (April): 301–28.

Capan, E. C.; Clapp, R. V.; and Campbell, W. M. 1971. Competitive bidding in high risk situations. *Journal of Petroleum Technology* (June), pp. 641–53.

Chung, K. S., and Weston, J. F. 1982. Diversification and mergers in a strategic long-range planning framework. In M. Keenan and L. I. White (eds.), *Mergers and Acquisitions*. Lexington, Mass.: D. C. Heath.

Chung, K. S., and Weston, J. F. 1985. Model-created bias in residual analysis of mergers. Working paper. Los Angeles: University of California, Los Angeles, Graduate School of Management.

Dann, L. Y., and DeAngelo, H. 1983. Standstill agreements, privately negotiated stock repurchases, and the market for corporate control. *Journal of Financial Economics* 11 (April): 275–300.

DeAngelo, H., and Rice, E. M. 1983. Antitakeover charter amendments and stockholder wealth. *Journal of Financial Economics* 11 (April): 329–60.

Dodd, P. 1980. Merger proposals, managerial discretion and stockholder wealth. *Journal of Financial Economics* 8 (June): 105–38.

Dodd, P., and Ruback, R. 1977. Tender offers and stockholder returns: An empirical analysis. *Journal of Financial Economics* 5 (December): 351–74.

Dougherty, F. L., and Lohrenz, J. 1976. Statistical analysis of bids for Federal offshore leases. *Journal of Petroleum Technology* (November), pp. 1377–90.

Eckbo, B. E. 1983. Horizontal mergers, collusion and stockholder wealth. *Journal of Financial Economics* 11 (April): 241–73.

Eger, C. E. 1983. An empirical test of the redistribution effect in pure exchange mergers. *Journal of Financial and Quantitative Analysis* 18 (December): 547–72.

Firth, M. 1980. Takeovers, shareholder returns and the theory of the firm. *Quarterly Journal of Economics* (March): 235–60.

Foster, G. 1983. Comments on M & A analysis and the role of investment bankers. *Midland Corporate Finance Journal* 1 (Winter): 36–38.

Halpern, P. J. 1973. Empirical estimates of the amount and distribution of gains to companies in mergers. *Journal of Business* 46 (October): 554–75.

Jarrell, G. A. 1983. Do acquirers benefit from corporate acquisition? Typescript. Chicago: University of Chicago, Center for the Study of the Economy and the State.

Jensen, M. C., and Ruback, R. S. 1983. The market for corporate control. *Journal of Financial Economics* 11 (April): 5–50.

Kahneman, D.; Slovic, P.; and Tversky, A. 1982. *Judgment under Uncertainty: Heuristics and Biases*. New York: Cambridge University Press.

Kummer, D. R., and Hoffmeister, J. R. 1978. Valuation consequences of cash tender offers. *Journal of Finance* 33 (May): 505–16.

Langetieg, T. C. 1978. An application of a three-factor performance index to measure stockholder gains from merger. *Journal of Financial Economics* 6 (December): 365–83.

Larcker, D. 1983. Managerial incentives in mergers and their effect on shareholder wealth. *Midland Corporate Finance Journal* 1 (Winter): 29–35.

Lev, B. 1983. Observations on the merger phenomenon and review of the evidence. *Midland Corporate Finance Journal* 1 (Winter): 6–16.

Linn, S. C., and McConnell, J. J. 1983. An empirical investigation of the impact of "antitakeover" amendments on common stock prices. *Journal of Financial Economics* 11 (April): 361–99.

Malatesta, P. H. 1983. The wealth effect of merger activity and the objective functions of merging firms. *Journal of Financial Economics* 11 (April): 155–81.

Masulis, R. W. 1980. The effects of capital structure change on security prices: A study of exchange offers. *Journal of Financial Economics* 8 (June): 139–77.

Miller, E. M. 1977. Risk, uncertainty and the divergence of opinion. *Journal of Finance* 32 (September): 1151–68.

Oskamp, S. 1965. Overconfidence in case study judgments. *Journal of Consulting Psychology* 29 (June): 261–65.

Ruback, R. S. 1982. The Conoco takeover and stockholder returns. *Sloan Management Review* 14 (Winter): 13–33.

Ruback, R. S. 1983. The Cities Service takeover: A case study. *Journal of Finance* 38 (May): 319–30.

Ruback, R. S., and Mikkelson, W. H. 1984. Corporate investments in common stock. Working paper. Cambridge: Massachusetts Institute of Technology, Sloan School of Business.

Schipper, K., and Thompson, R. 1983. Evidence on the capitalized value of merger activity for acquiring firms. *Journal of Financial Economics* 11 (April): 85–119.

Tversky, A., and Kahneman, D. 1981. The framing of decisions and the psychology of choice. *Science* 211 (January 30): 453–58. Reprinted in Peter Diamond and Michael Rothschild. 1978. *Uncertainty in Economics.* New York: Academic Press.

Varaiya, N. 1985. A test of Roll's Hubris Hypothesis of corporate takeovers. Working paper. Dallas, Tex.: Southern Methodist University, School of Business.

Vermaelen, T. 1981. Common stock repurchase and marketing signalling: An empirical study. *Journal of Financial Economics* 9 (June): 139–84.

[13]

THE JOURNAL OF FINANCE • VOL. XLVII, NO. 4 • SEPTEMBER 1992

The Post-Merger Performance of Acquiring Firms: A Re-examination of an Anomaly

ANUP AGRAWAL, JEFFREY F. JAFFE, AND GERSHON N. MANDELKER

ABSTRACT

The existing literature on the post-merger performance of acquiring firms is divided. We re-examine this issue, using a nearly exhaustive sample of mergers between NYSE acquirers and NYSE/AMEX targets. We find that stockholders of acquiring firms suffer a statistically significant loss of about 10% over the five-year post-merger period, a result robust to various specifications. Our evidence suggests that neither the firm size effect nor beta estimation problems are the cause of the negative post-merger returns. We examine whether this result is caused by a slow adjustment of the market to the merger event. Our results do not seem consistent with this hypothesis.

MERGERS ARE ONE OF the most researched areas in finance, yet some basic issues still remain unresolved. While most empirical research on mergers focuses on daily stock returns surrounding announcement dates, a few studies also look, in passing, at the long-run performance of acquiring firms after mergers. Some conclude that these firms experience significantly negative abnormal returns over one to three years after the merger (for example, Langetieg (1978), Asquith (1983), and Magenheim and Mueller (1988)). These findings led Jensen and Ruback (1983, p. 20) to remark: "These post-outcome negative abnormal returns are unsettling because they are inconsistent with market efficiency and suggest that changes in stock prices during takeovers overestimate the future efficiency gains from mergers." Ruback (1988, p. 262) later writes: "Reluctantly, I think we have to accept this result—significant negative returns over the two years following a merger—as a fact."

However, a conclusion of underperformance is not clearly warranted based on prior research. First, the results are not all one-sided. Langetieg (1978) finds that post-merger abnormal performance is not significantly different

* From the North Carolina State University, University of Pennsylvania, and University of Pittsburgh, respectively. This paper has benefitted from comments from Mustafa Gultekin, Craig MacKinlay, Robert Stambaugh, René Stulz, two anonymous referees, and participants at the Friday lunch microfinance seminar of the Finance Department, Wharton School, University of Pennsylvania. We gratefully acknowledge financial support from a faculty research grant at North Carolina State University and a grant from the Geewax-Terker Corporation and the Rodney L. White Center, Wharton School, University of Pennsylvania.

from that of a control firm in the same industry. He appears to place more weight on this finding than on the one mentioned above. Neither Mandelker (1974) nor Malatesta (1983) find significant underperformance after the aquisition. In addition, using Magenheim and Mueller's sample but employing a different methodology, Bradley and Jarrell (1988) do not find significant underperformance in the three years following acquisitions. Recently, using a multifactor benchmark, Franks, Harris, and Titman (1991) also do not find significant underperformance over three years after the acquisition.

Furthermore, recent studies typically examined post-merger returns as part of a larger study focusing on announcement period returns. Hence, they generally do not provide thorough analyses of the long-run performance of acquirers. In particular, one problem with prior studies is that they do not properly adjust for the firm size effect.[1] Evidence in Dimson and Marsh (1986) suggests that an adjustment for firm size is important in studies of long-run performance. This adjustment is likely to be particularly important in a study of mergers since acquirers are usually large firms. In addition, none of the previous studies allows for month-to-month shifts in beta. The resulting bias can be significant when abnormal returns are cumulated over a long period.

A finding of underperformance has three important implications. First, the concept of efficient capital markets is a major paradigm in finance. Systematically poor performance after mergers is, of course, inconsistent with this paradigm. Second, much research on mergers examines returns surrounding announcement dates in order to infer the wealth effects of mergers. This approach implicitly assumes that markets are efficient, since returns following the announcement are ignored. Thus, a finding of market inefficiency for returns following mergers calls into question a large body of research in this area. Third, a finding of underperformance may also buttress certain studies (e.g., Ravenscraft and Scherer (1987) and Herman and Lowenstein (1988)) showing poor accounting performance after takeovers. However, the evidence is not one-sided here (see, e.g., Healy, Palepu, and Ruback (1992)).

The purpose of this paper is to provide a thorough analysis of the post-merger performance of acquiring firms. We present evidence on two issues. First, after adjusting for the firm size effect as well as beta risk, our results indicate that stockholders of acquiring firms experience a statistically significant wealth loss of about 10% over five years after the merger completion date. This finding is based on a nearly exhaustive sample of mergers over 1955 to 1987 between NYSE acquirers and NYSE/AMEX targets. The result is robust to a variety of specifications and does not seem to be caused by changes in beta. Second, we test whether the market is slow to adjust to the merger event. Under this hypothesis, the long-run performance would reflect

---

[1] To our knowledge, only Franks, Harris, and Titman (1991) adjust for firm size. However, we later point out that their results are specific to their sample period (1975–1984). In addition, while prior studies find negative performance after mergers but not after tender-offers, Franks, Harris, and Titman mix the two samples.

Post-Merger Performance of Acquiring Firms: An Anomaly 1607

that part of the net present value of the merger to the acquirer that is not captured by the announcement period return. Our results are not consistent with this hypothesis.

The structure of the paper is as follows. The data are discussed in Section I. Our methodology is described in Section II. The results are presented in Section III and our conclusions appear in Section IV.

I. Data

Our database of mergers and tender offers was obtained by a two-step process.[2] First, a list of all the firms that disappeared from the files of the Center for Research in Security Prices (CRSP) over the interval from January 1955 to December 1987 was prepared. Second, the *Wall Street Journal Index* was consulted to determine which of these firms disappeared due to tender offers or mergers. An event was classified as a tender offer if the acquiring firm purchased at least 60 percent of the target firm's shares by tender offer and later bought the remaining shares through a clean-up merger. The sample consists of 937 mergers and 227 tender offers.[3] This represents nearly the entire population of acquisitions of NYSE and AMEX firms by NYSE firms over the period 1955 to 1987.[4]

Our study focuses on two dates, the date when the *Wall Street Journal* first mentions a bid involving the acquiring firm and the date when the acquired firm is delisted. These dates are referred to as the announcement date and the completion date, respectively.

II. Methodology

Beginning with Fama, Fisher, Jensen, and Roll (1969), event studies in finance measure stock performance after substracting a benchmark return based on beta risk. This adjustment seems to be sufficient in most of the studies, which examine short-run returns over several *days* surrounding an event. However, when investigating long-run returns over several *years*, Dimson and Marsh (1986, especially Fig. 1) present persuasive evidence that measured performance can be significantly affected by the firm size effect.

The size bias in long-term returns is especially important if the sample is clustered in a certain size category. Over 60% of our sample of acquiring firms is clustered in the top 3 deciles of the population of firms on the NYSE,[5]

[2] The sample was kindly supplied by Robert Harris.
[3] The sample sizes in some of our tables are somewhat lower since data for firm size, beta estimation, etc., are not available for all firms.
[4] The data set does not include acquisitions where the acquirer is on the AMEX. However, this restriction represents a loss in the sample size of less than 6%.
[5] About 30% of the sample falls in the top decile, 15% in decile 9, and 16% in decile 8.

based on the market value of their equity at the end of the year of completion of the merger. Given such a strong clustering, an explicit adjustment for firm size seems to be important.[6]

We employ two alternative methodologies, each of which adjusts for both beta risk and market capitalization. For both methods, we form the following set of size control groups. At the end of each calendar year, all stocks on the NYSE are ranked according to their market capitalization and allocated to 10 decile portfolios.[7] For each month over the following year, the return on each decile portfolio is computed as the equally weighted average return across all securities in the portfolio.[8]

A. Method #1

We first use the methodology of both Dimson and Marsh (1986) and Lakonishok and Vermaelen (1990). These two studies measure a stock's abnormal performance, ϵ_{it}, as:

$$\epsilon_{it} = R_{it} - R_{st} - (\beta_i - \beta_s)(R_{mt} - R_{ft}),^9 \qquad (1)$$

where R_{it} = the return on security i over month t.

R_{st} = the equally weighted average return during month t on the control portfolio of all firms in the same size decile as firm i, based on the market value of equity at the end of the previous year.[10]

---

[6] Following Rozeff and Zaman (1988), we also considered an adjustment for the price-earnings (p-e) ratio effect. However, our sample is almost uniformly distributed over the 10 p-e deciles of all firms on the NYSE. This implies that the empirical regularity concerning p-e ratios is unlikely to explain the post-acquisition performance. Hence, we do not pursue it further.

[7] If the total number of securities at the end of any year is not divisible by 10, the portfolios of the largest and smallest size securities are allocated extra securities.

[8] As securities drop out from one month to the next, the equally weighted average return is calculated using the remaining securities.

[9] Equation (1) follows from the return-generating process:

$$R_{it} - R_{ft} = \alpha_i + \beta_i(R_{mt} - R_{ft}) + \epsilon_{it}, \qquad (A)$$

where α_i is a function only of firm size. This is a plausible process since the extensive literature on the size effect suggests that excess returns from the CAPM are strongly related to firm size.

One way of explaining the size effect is to postulate that small firms are more responsive to some priced size factor than are large firms. This is reflected in the following model:

$$R_{it} - R_{ft} = \beta_{im}(R_{mt} - R_{ft}) + \beta_{is}(R_t^s - R_{ft}) + \epsilon_{it}, \qquad (B)$$

where R_t^s is the return on some unspecified size factor. (Alternatively, there could be many size factors in (B).) Assuming that β_{is} is a function only of firm size leads to equation (1) as well. Although equation (B) has not been studied in depth, the work of Chan, Chen, and Hsieh (1985) suggests that betas on a variety of factors are negatively related to firm size. At any rate, equation (B) is a sufficient, but not necessary, condition for equations (A) and (1).

[10] We also perform all subsequent tests by redefining R_{st} as the value-weighted average return during month t on the control portfolio. The results are almost identical.

Post-Merger Performance of Acquiring Firms: An Anomaly 1609

β_i = the beta of security i. We estimate β_i using monthly data over the period from month $+1$ to month $+60$ after the merger completion.[11, 12]

β_s = the beta of the control group. We estimate β_s over months $+1$ to $+60$ relative to the completion month.

R_{mt} = the return on the market index. We report results using the NYSE value-weighted index. Results are similar with the NYSE equally weighted index.

R_{ft} = the risk-free rate in month t, as measured by the yield on a one-month Treasury bill.

The average abnormal return (AAR) over all stocks in month t is:

$$\text{AAR}_t = \frac{1}{N_t} \sum_{i=1}^{N_t} \epsilon_{it},$$

where N_t is the number of securities in the sample with a return in event month t. The cumulative average abnormal return (CAAR) from event month t_1 to t_2 is:

$$\text{CAAR}_{t_1}^{t_2} = \sum_{t=t_1}^{t_2} \text{AAR}_t$$

Test statistics for abnormal returns between t_1 and t_2 follow the crude dependence adjustment method of Brown and Warner (1980, pp. 251–252, especially equations A.5 and A.6). In addition, test statistics using the portfolio approach of Jaffe (1974) and Mandelker (1974) are computed as well. These results are generally quite similar to those using the Brown and Warner technique. To conserve space, only the latter are reported.

B. Method #2

Our second approach combines the Returns Across Time and Securities (RATS) methodology of Ibbotson (1975) with an adjustment for firm size. For each month t relative to the month of completion, we estimate the following cross-sectional regression:

$$R_{it} - R_{st} = \alpha_t + \beta_t (R_{mt} - R_{ft}) + \cap_{it},^{13} \tag{2}$$

[11] We also estimate β_{it} for month t after ignoring the observation in month t. The results are similar.

[12] Our results are presented for the case in which a company must have at least 20 months of post-acquisition data. A hindsight bias could arise here since firms may drop out before registering 20 observations. Therefore, we re-estimate beta using shortened post-merger intervals, so that virtually no firm drops out. In addition, we used pre-merger data for estimating beta as well. Since the results are virtually identical, we do not present them. Furthermore, we also use the Ibbotson RATS procedure which eliminates the possibility of a hindsight bias, since no data requirements are imposed for including a firm in the sample. Again, the results are similar.

[13] When more than one firm makes an acquisition in the same calendar month, the dependent variable becomes an equally weighted portfolio of all firms whose completion dates are in the same calendar month.

1610   *The Journal of Finance*

where R_{it}, R_{ft}, R_{st}, and R_{mt} are as defined earlier. The constant α_t measures the average abnormal return across all firms in event month t.

The first approach (equation (1)) calculates a different beta for each security, implicitly assuming that each beta is constant over the entire post-completion period. The second approach (equation (2)) calculates a different beta for each month relative to the event, implicitly assuming that this beta is identical for all acquiring firms.

III. Post-Merger Performance of Acquiring Firms

A. *Results on Performance for the Entire Sample*

We first measured post-merger abnormal performance using formula (1) above. Results for our entire sample using the value-weighted market index are shown in Table I. The CAARs are significantly negative for holding periods of two, three, four, and five years. For the five-year period the CAAR

Table I
Post-Merger Performance of Acquiring Firms After Adjustment for Firm Size and Beta Risk

The abnormal return for firm i in month t is computed as in (1):

$$\epsilon_{it} = R_{it} - R_{st} - (\beta_i - \beta_s)(R_{mt} - R_{ft}),$$

where R_{it} and R_{st} are the stock returns on firm i and its size control portfolio s, respectively, in month t; β_i and β_s are their betas measured over 60 months after the merger; and R_{ft} and R_{mt} are the returns in month t on one-month Treasury bills and the NYSE value-weighted market index, respectively. The sample consists of 765 mergers between NYSE acquirers and NYSE/AMEX targets over 1955–87. The t-statistics for AAR and CAAR, shown in parentheses, are computed according to the crude dependence adjustment method of Brown and Warner (1980, pp. 250–252). The results are similar using the calendar portfolio approach of Jaffe (1974) and Mandelker (1974). The statistical significance of the difference of the percentage of positive residuals from 50% is tested using the z-statistic, shown in parentheses.

Months After Merger Completion	Average Abnormal Return (AAR)	Cumulative Average Abnormal Return (CAAR)	Percent of Positive CARs (%)
1–12	−1.53% (−0.98)	−1.53% (−0.98)	46.56% (−1.90)
13–24	−3.41 (−2.00)[b]	−4.94 (−2.10)[b]	47.67 (−1.26)
25–36	−2.44 (−1.73)	−7.38 (−2.72)[a]	46.39 (−1.91)
37–48	−1.29 (−0.54)	−8.67 (−2.62)[a]	44.98 (−2.61)[a]
49–60	−1.59 (−0.07)	−10.26 (−2.37)[b]	43.97 (−3.03)[a]

[a,b] Statistical significance in 2-tailed tests at the 1% and 5% levels, respectively.

Post-Merger Performance of Acquiring Firms: An Anomaly 1611

is -10.26% ($t = -2.37$). These results are not driven by merely a few outliers. The percentage of positive abnormal returns over the five-year period is 43.97, which is significantly lower than 50 ($z = -3.03$). The median abnormal return over the five-year time period is -7.50%.

Results (not shown in the table) with the equally weighted market index are similar, with a CAAR over five years of -11.2%. We also find similar results (unreported) when the RATS method of formula (2) is used to calculate the abnormal returns.[14] The CAAR for the five-year period is -10.7% with the value-weighted index and -12.8% with the equally weighted index.

Our results are also robust to (a) changes in the time period used for estimating β (see footnote 12), (b) changes in the time period used for estimating the residual standard error for computing t-statistics, and (c) adjustment for firm size based on equity value of the acquirer at the end of the year of the completion of the acquisition rather than the end of the previous year. In addition, results not reported using up to 10 years of post-merger data indicate that the abnormal returns level off after the fifth year. This finding reduces the possibility that the model is mis-specified.

Since acquiring firms generally outperform the market prior to the merger, the underperformance subsequent to the merger may merely be an artifact of the mean-reversion in long horizon returns on individual stocks observed by DeBondt and Thaler (1985, 1987). However, Ball and Kothari (1989) and Chan (1988) find that mean-reversion all but disappears when β is allowed to vary over time. Since we use the Ibbotson RATS approach (equation (2)), which explicitly adjusts for shifts in beta over time, the work of Ball and Kothari (1989) and Chan (1988) suggests that the negative post-merger performance that we observe is not due to the mean-reversion. A recent paper by Chopra, Lakonishok, and Ritter (1992) disputes the results of Ball and Kothari and those of Chan. We leave the resolution of this dispute to future research.

B. Tender Offers

Prior research finds that acquirers underperform over the long-run after mergers, but not after tender offers. Therefore, this paper focuses on mergers. Nevertheless, for the sake of completeness, we next examine tender offers.

We measure performance using both equations (1) and (2) and using both a value-weighted and an equally-weighted market index. For all four methods, the CAARs (unreported) are small and insignificantly different from zero. Thus, we find no evidence of unusual performance for tender offers. This result is similar to previous findings that announcement period returns are

---

[14] As discussed above. the RATS method allows β to change every month. While we find considerable variation in measured β from month to month, the average annual beta (i.e., the average of 12 successive monthly betas) remains a constant (to the first decimal place) 1.2 over the seven-year period from two years before to five years after the merger completion. Given this finding, it is not surprising that the results using this method are similar to those from equation (1).

higher for acquirers in tender offers than in mergers (see Jensen and Ruback (1983), especially Table 3).

Some authors (e.g., Hansen (1987)) have suggested that the form of financing serves as a signal that can explain the difference between tender offers and mergers in announcement period returns. Cash financing, which is typical in tender offers, is likely to occur when the acquirer is undervalued. Conversely, equity financing, which is typical of mergers, is likely to occur when the acquirer is overvalued.

Consistent with this signalling interpretation, we find (but do not report) that the long-run post-acquisition performance is worse for tender offers financed by equity rather than cash. However, only 18 tender offers are equity-financed, so firmer statistical inferences cannot be reached. Similarly, post-acquisition performance is worse for mergers financed by equity rather than cash. While these results are intriguing, a signalling explanation is not fully satisfying. In an efficient market, stock prices should adjust to corporate signals immediately, not slowly over a period of years. We leave a full treatment of this issue to further research.

C. Analysis of Subsamples

The above results indicate that the stocks of acquiring firms perform poorly after mergers. It can be instructive to examine whether this anomaly pervades our entire sample or is confined to certain subsamples. Accordingly, we next subdivide our results by time periods and by conglomerate vs. non-conglomerate acquisitions.

C.1. Subperiods

We first examine whether the underperformance is limited to acquisitions over certain time periods. We subdivide the sample into five subperiods: (1) the fifties, (2) the sixties, (3) the seventies, (4) the eighties,[15] and (5) the 1975–1984 sample period of Franks, Harris, and Titman (1991). The results[16] are shown in Table II. There is a distinct difference betweeen the performance in the decade of the seventies and the other decades. In the fifties, the sixties, and the eighties, the CAARs are significantly negative. During these decades, the average investor lost about 15 to 23% of their investment over the five years after the merger. However, in the seventies, the CAARs are insignificant.

One might have conjectured that underperformance would have occurred only in earlier time periods, since the capital markets as a whole have

---

[15] Because we follow acquirers for five years after the merger and use the 1988 CRSP files, we are limited by the number of years we can include in the eighties. The last year of merger for which we can calculate five years of post-acquisition performance is 1983. For mergers that occurred up to 1984, we can calculate four years of post-acquisition performance, etc.

[16] Throughout the rest of the paper, only results from formula (1) are presented, since results from formula (2) are similar.

Table II

Post-Merger Performance of Acquiring Firms Over Different Decades

The abnormal return for firm i in month t is computed as in (1):

$$\epsilon_{it} = R_{it} - R_{st} - (\beta_i - \beta_s)(R_{mt} - R_{ft}),$$

where R_{it} and R_{st} are the stock returns on firm i and its size control portfolio s, respectively, in month t; β_i and β_s are their betas measured over 60 months after the merger; and R_{ft} and R_{mt} are the returns in month t on one-month Treasury bills and the NYSE value-weighted market index, respectively. The sample consists of 765 mergers between NYSE acquirers and NYSE/AMEX targets over 1955-87. The t-statistics for AAR and CAAR, shown in parentheses, are computed according to the crude dependence adjustment method of Brown and Warner (1980, pp. 250-252). The results are similar using the calendar portfolio approach of Jaffe (1974) and Mandelker (1974).

Months After Merger Completion	Mergers Completed During									
	1955–59 (N = 51)		1960–69 (N = 299)		1970–79 (N = 247)		1980–87 (N = 168)		1975–84 (N = 290)	
	AAR	CAAR	AAR	CAAR	AAR	CAAR	AAR	CAAR	AAR	CAAR
1–12	-2.4% (-0.86)	-2.4% (-0.86)	-1.8% (-0.56)	-1.8% (-0.56)	0.0% (-0.42)	0.0% (-0.42)	-2.8% (-0.73)	-2.8% (-0.73)	-0.9% (-0.30)	-0.9% (-0.30)
13–24	-4.0 (-1.06)	-6.4 (-1.36)	-4.1 (-1.14)	-5.9 (-1.21)	0.7 (0.55)	0.7 (0.09)	-7.6 (-3.53)[a]	-10.4 (-3.02)[a]	-3.4 (-1.50)	-4.2 (-1.27)
25–36	-5.0 (-2.09)[b]	-11.4 (-2.32)[b]	-4.4 (-1.79)	-10.3 (-2.02)[b]	0.1 (0.07)	0.8 (0.11)	-2.0 (-1.12)	-12.4 (-3.11)[c]	0.3 (-0.07)	-4.0 (-1.07)
37–48	-7.3 (-2.66)[a]	-18.7 (-3.34)[a]	-2.0 (-1.07)	-12.3 (-2.28)[b]	0.8 (0.91)	1.6 (0.55)	-1.4 (0.36)	-13.8 (-2.51)[b]	1.0 (1.66)	-3.0 (-0.10)
49–60	-4.5 (-0.94)	-23.2 (-3.41)[a]	-2.8 (-1.07)	-15.1 (-2.52)[b]	2.5 (2.03)[b]	4.1 (1.40)	-5.6 (-1.17)	-19.4 (-2.77)[a]	0.2 (1.50)	-2.8 (-0.58)

[a],[b] Statistical significance in 2-tailed tests at the 1% and 5% levels, respectively.

probably become more efficient over time. However, since Table II shows that the underperformance in the 1980s is about as severe as the underperformance in the 1950s and 1960s, we cannot conclude that the anomaly has diminished in recent years.

The last two columns of Table II show the post-merger performance over the 1975–1984 time period of the recent paper by Franks, Harris, and Titman (1991). We find no abnormal performance during this time period, a result consistent with that of Franks, Harris, and Titman.[17] A breakdown (not reported) of our 33-year sample period into five-year subperiods (1955 to 1959, 1960 to 1964, etc.) shows that 1975 to 1979 is the only five-year period when the post-merger performance is significantly positive.[18] This period constitutes one half of Franks, Harris, and Titman's sample. Over the remainder of their sample period, 1980 to 1984, the post-merger performance is significantly negative. Thus, the performance over the combined period, 1975 to 1984, is insignificant. We conclude that Franks, Harris, and Titman's results are specific to their sample period.

C.2. Conglomerate vs. Non-Conglomerate Mergers

It is often claimed that conglomerate mergers are less likely to succeed, because managers of acquiring firms are not familiar with the target industry or they waste free cash flow on bad acquisitions (see Jensen (1986)). Since conglomerate mergers were quite frequent in the 1960s, our findings of significant negative returns for this period may merely reflect the performance of conglomerate mergers.

To examine this issue, we subdivide our sample into conglomerate and non-conglomerate mergers. A merger is defined as non-conglomerate if an acquirer and its target are in the same industry, as measured by their four-digit Standardized Industrial Classification (SIC) codes.[19] All other mergers are classified as conglomerate. In Table III we report the CAARs calculated after adjusting for both firm size and beta, as in equation (1). The CAARs for both groups of acquirers show negative performance over the five-year post-merger period. In contrast with popular belief, the underperformance of acquirers is worse in non-conglomerate mergers than in conglomer-

---

[17] The closeness between our results and those of Franks, Harris, and Titman (1991) is not surprising since our methodologies are similar; both approaches adjust for size, though Franks, Harris, and Titman do not adjust for beta. Franks, Harris, and Titman adjust for dividend yield and past returns as well, though prior research indicates that these factors have lower explanatory power than do size and beta (see, e.g., Miller and Scholes (1982), Chan (1988), and Ball and Kothari (1989)).

[18] An examination of the 1975 to 1979 subperiod does not provide us with any explanation for its positive performance. For example, the percentage of conglomerate vs. non-conglomerate mergers, the relative size of the acquired vs. the acquiring firm, and the frequency of mergers were not unusual during this period. Furthermore, we did not find any news events (e.g., passage of takeover-related laws) during this period that could explain the unusual performance. Thus, the results of this subperiod may be just random variation.

[19] We repeat this analysis using the three-digit SIC code. The results are similar.

Post-Merger Performance of Acquiring Firms: An Anomaly 1615

Table III
Post-Merger Performance of Acquiring Firms in Conglomerate and Non-Conglomerate Mergers

The abnormal return for firm i in month t is computed as in (1):

$$\epsilon_{it} = R_{it} - R_{st} - (\beta_i - \beta_s)(R_{mt} - R_{ft}),$$

where R_{it} and R_{st} are the stock returns on firm i and its size control portfolio s, respectively, in month t; β_i and β_s are their betas measured over 60 months after the merger; and R_{ft} and R_{mt} are the returns in month t on one-month Treasury bills and the NYSE value-weighted market index, respectively. The sample consists of 765 mergers between NYSE acquirers and NYSE/AMEX targets over 1955–87. The t-statistics for AAR and CAAR, shown in parentheses, are computed according to the crude dependence adjustment methods of Brown and Warner (1980, pp. 250–252). The results are similar using the calendar portfolio approach of Jaffe (1974) and Mandelker (1974).

Months After Merger Completion	Conglomerates ($N = 686$)		Non-Conglomerates ($N = 79$)	
	AAR	CAAR	AAR	CAAR
1–12	−1.5%	−1.5%	−1.5%	−1.5%
	(−0.92)	(−0.92)	(−0.42)	(−0.42)
13–24	−2.9	−4.4	−8.0	−9.5
	(−1.63)	(−1.80)	(−2.01)[b]	(−1.71)
25–36	−1.9	−6.3	−7.7	−17.2
	(−1.21)	(−2.17)[b]	(−2.91)[a]	(−3.08)[a]
37–48	−1.3	−7.6	−1.2	−18.4
	(−0.52)	(−2.13)[b]	(−0.17)	(−2.75)[a]
49–60	−1.0	−8.6	−7.1	−25.5
	(−0.20)	(−1.82)	(−1.51)	(−3.14)[a]

[a, b] Statistical significance in 2-tailed tests at the 1% and 5% levels, respectively.

ate mergers. The t-statistics are actually higher in magnitude for non-conglomerate mergers, even though they occur with lower frequency than conglomerate mergers in our sample.

In addition, we examine (but do not report in the table) the performance of both conglomerate and non-conglomerate mergers for each of the four decades in our sample. For each of the decades except the seventies, the five-year performance is significantly negative for both types of mergers. In the 1970s, the results are insignificant for both types of mergers. These findings are consistent with those of the overall sample. In each decade, the five-year post-merger performance in the non-conglomerate sample is below that of the conglomerate sample. Consequently, the finding of negative post-merger returns is unlikely to be explained by the inferior performance of conglomerate mergers.

Finally, we consider the possibility that non-conglomerate mergers were concentrated in industries that underperformed over several years after the

1616 *The Journal of Finance*

merger. There are 79 non-conglomerate mergers in our sample. Of these, 23 mergers from 14 different industries took place in the sixties. Similarly, 24 mergers spanning 19 industries took place in the seventies, and 32 mergers in 18 industries took place in the eighties. Where multiple mergers do take place in a given industry in the same decade, they are often several years apart. Thus, it seems unlikely that concentration in poorly performing industries can explain the poor post-merger performance of acquirers in non-conglomerate mergers.

D. Underperformance and the Speed of Stock Price Adjustment to Merger News

Our finding of significant post-merger underperformance is consistent with two alternative hypotheses. The first hypothesis is that the market adjusts fully to merger news at the time of its announcement, and the subsequent underperformance occurs because of unrelated causes. The second hypothesis is that the market is slow to adjust to the merger announcement. In the latter case, the long-run post-merger performance would reflect that part of the net present value of the merger to the acquirer not captured by the announcement period return. Support for the latter hypothesis would be inconsistent with market efficiency and would also call into question much of the previous research on mergers based on announcement period returns. We investigate these two hypotheses below.

D.1. The Relation Between Announcement Period Returns and Post-Merger Returns

If the market adjusts slowly to information concerning the merger, we might expect the acquirer's announcement period return to be related to its post-merger return. Conversely, if the post-merger performance is unrelated to the impact of the merger, the acquirer's return after the merger completion should be unrelated to the return during the announcement period.

To investigate this issue, we examine the following relation:

$$\text{CAR}_{Ci} = b_0 + b_1 \text{CAR}_{Ai} + e_i,$$

where CAR_{Ci} is the cumulative abnormal return over the post-acquisition period for firm i. The period always begins with the month after the merger completion and, depending on the regression, ends from one to five years after the merger completion. CAR_{Ai} is the cumulative abnormal return for firm i over the announcement period, defined in one of two ways:

(1) The three-month period ending with the announcement month, which we designate as (A-2, A).
(2) The period from two months before the announcement month to the merger completion month, designated as (A-2, C).

Post-Merger Performance of Acquiring Firms: An Anomaly   1617

Table IV shows the estimates of the coefficients b_0 and b_1 for these two sets of regressions. The estimates of b_1 are negative in most of the regressions and their absolute values generally increase with the length of the post-completion period. Both estimates of b_1 are strongly significant when the post-completion period is the full five years. In addition, the coefficients border on significance in three of the eight regressions covering the first four years. The evidence seems to indicate a negative relation between the market reaction to the announcement and the subsequent performance of the firm. However, when we examine these regressions by subperiods, we find that the coefficient b_1 is negative for the decades of the 1960s, 1970s, and 1980s but is statistically significant only for the 1960s. Thus, we cannot conclude that the negative relationship is pervasive over our entire sample period.

Table IV

Regression of the Performance of Acquiring Firms After Mergers on Their Announcement Period Performance

The table shows the estimated coefficients from the following regression:

$$\text{CAR}_{Ci} = b_0 + b_1 \, \text{CAR}_{Ai} + \epsilon_i,$$

where CAR_{Ci} and CAR_{Ai} are the cumulative abnormal returns of firm i measured over the post-merger and announcement periods, respectively. A and C denote the periods of announcement and completion, respectively, of the merger. The t-values are in parentheses. The abnormal return for firm i in month t is computed as in (1):

$$\epsilon_{it} = R_{it} - R_{st} - (\beta_i - \beta_s)(R_{mt} - R_{ft}),$$

where R_{it} and R_{st} are the stock returns on firm i and its size control portfolio s, respectively, in month t; β_i and β_s are their betas measured over 60 months after the merger; and R_{ft} and R_{mt} are the returns in month t on one-month Treasury bills and the NYSE value-weighted market index, respectively. The sample consists of mergers between NYSE acquirers and NYSE/AMEX targets over 1955–87.

CAR_{Ci} Measured Over Post-Merger Months	CAR_A Measured Over Months (A-2, C)		CAR_A Measured Over Months (A-2, A)	
	b_0	b_1	b_0	b_1
(1, 12)	−0.02	0.05	−0.02	0.01
	(−1.61)	(1.18)	(−1.65)	(0.07)
(1, 24)	−0.05	0.05	−0.04	−0.21
	(−3.27)[a]	(0.76)	(−3.00)[a]	(−1.88)
(1, 36)	−0.07	−0.03	−0.07	−0.16
	(−4.19)[a]	(−0.36)	(−4.06)[a]	(−1.17)
(1, 48)	−0.09	−0.19	−0.09	−0.29
	(−4.29)[a]	(−1.81)	(−4.23)[a]	(−1.78)
(1, 60)	−0.10	−0.32	−0.10	−0.44
	(−4.18)[a]	(−2.84)[a]	(−4.13)[a]	(−2.43)[b]

[a, b] Statistical significance in 2-tailed tests at the 1% and 5% levels, respectively.

D.2. Relative Size of the Acquisition

The acquisition of a relatively large target is likely to be a more important economic event for the acquirer than is the acquisition of a relatively small target. Thus, if the post-merger underperformance reflects the impact of the merger, underperformance should be greater when the target is relatively large. In Table V we examine the effect of relative size on the post-merger performance of acquirers. We calculate the relative size of the acquisition as S_t/S_a, where S_t and S_a are the market values of equity of the target and acquirer, respectively, measured six months before the first public announcement about an acquisition involving the target firm. We then rank all the mergers by relative size and form quintile portfolios, where portfolio 1 consists of the mergers of the smallest relative size.

Portfolios 4 and 5 exhibit large underperformance, particularly over four to five years after the acquisition. However, the relationship is not monotonic, since large underperformance occurs for portfolio 2 as well. Furthermore, very few of the post-merger time periods in any of the five portfolios exhibit significant returns. Thus, the evidence here does not suggest that the acquirer's post-merger return is a function of the relative size of the acquisition.

This subsection and the previous one examine the hypothesis that the market is slow to adjust to the merger event. Taken together, our results do not support this hypothesis. This subsection finds no relation between post-merger abnormal returns and the acquisition's relative size, a result not consistent with slow adjustment to the merger event. The results of the previous subsection support a slow adjustment only for the decade of the 1960s.

IV. Conclusions

A number of studies report that acquirers exhibit significant underperformance after a merger. However, the issue has by no means been resolved, because of both methodological problems and conflicting results of prior studies. Using a nearly exhaustive sample of mergers over 1955 to 1987 between NYSE acquirers and NYSE/AMEX targets, this paper measures post-acquisition performance after adjusting for the firm size effect as well as beta risk. We use (1) the methodology of both Dimson and Marsh (1986) and Lakonishok and Vermaelen (1990) and (2) the Ibbotson (1975) RATS model with an adjustment for firm size. We find that stockholders of the acquiring firms suffer a statistically significant wealth loss of about 10% over the five years following the merger completion. This finding is robust to a variety of specifications and does not seem to be caused by changes in beta following the merger. Therefore, we conclude that the efficient-market anomaly of negative post-merger performance highlighted in Jensen and Ruback (1983) is not resolved. This conclusion runs contrary to Franks, Harris, and Titman's (1991) results which, as we show, are specific to their sample time period and are also due to their mixing of tender offers with mergers.

Table V

Post-Merger Performance of Acquiring Firms by the Relative Size of Their Acquisitions

The abnormal return for firm i in month t is computed as in (1):

$$\epsilon_{it} = R_{it} - R_{st} - (\beta_i - \beta_s)(R_{mt} - R_{ft}).$$

where R_{it} and R_{st} are the stock returns on firm i and its size control portfolio s, respectively, in month t; β_i and β_s are their betas measured over 60 months after the merger; and R_{ft} and R_{mt} are the returns in month t on one-month Treasury bills and the NYSE value-weighted market index, respectively. The sample consists of mergers between NYSE acquirers and NYSE/AMEX targets over 1955–87. The t-statistics for AAR and CAAR shown in parentheses are computed according to the crude dependence adjustment method of Brown and Warner (1980, pp. 250–252). The results are similar using the calendar portfolio approach of Jaffe (1974) and Mandelker (1974). Relative size of the acquisition is the ratio of the market value of equity of the target firm to that of the acquiring firm, as of six months before the first public announcement of an acquisition bid for the target.

Months After Merger Completion	Relative-Size Quintile Portfolios									
	Quintile 1 (Smallest)		Quintile 2		Quintile 3		Quintile 4		Quintile 5 (Largest)	
	AAR	CAAR	AAR	CAAR	AAR	CAAR	AAR	CAAR	AAR	CAAR
1–12	2.4%	2.4%	−5.4%	−5.4%	−0.9%	−0.9%	−1.7%	−1.7%	−5.9%	−5.9%
	(1.51)	(1.51)	(−2.93)[a]	(−2.93)[a]	(−0.30)	(−0.30)	(−0.23)	(−0.23)	(−1.38)	(−1.38)
13–24	−1.1	1.3	−3.7	−9.1	−1.7	−2.6	−6.5	−8.1	0.6	−5.2
	(−0.32)	(0.84)	(−1.55)	(−3.17)[a]	(−0.49)	(−0.56)	(−2.48)[b]	(−1.91)	(0.26)	(−0.79)
25–36	−1.5	−0.2	−0.4	−9.5	−2.3	−4.9	−3.5	−11.7	−4.0	−9.3
	(−0.23)	(0.55)	(−0.12)	(−2.66)[a]	(−0.95)	(−1.00)	(−1.95)	(−2.69)[a]	(−1.87)	(−1.73)
37–48	−1.3	−1.5	−1.9	−11.4	2.9	−2.0	1.8	−9.9	−1.0	−10.3
	(−0.26)	(0.35)	(−0.41)	(−2.51)[b]	(1.74)	(0.00)	(0.42)	(−2.12)[b]	(0.22)	(−1.38)
49–60	−2.0	−3.4	2.3	−9.1	−0.3	−2.3	−0.1	−10.0	−6.0	−16.3
	(−1.00)	(−0.14)	(1.51)	(−1.57)	(1.09)	(0.49)	(0.57)	(−1.64)	(−1.63)	(−1.97)[b]

[a,b] Statistical significance in 2-tailed tests at the 1% and 5% levels, respectively.

1620 *The Journal of Finance*

The anomaly holds for the 1950s, 1960s, and 1980s but does not hold for the 1970s. Since the underperformance in the 1980s is as severe as the underperformance in the 1950s and the 1960s, the market does not appear to become more efficient over time. At this point, we do not know what causes the large negative returns after the merger. One possibility is that the market is slow to adjust to the merger event. If so, the long-run performance reflects that part of the NPV of the merger to the acquirer which is not captured by the announcement period return. However, our results do not seem to be consistent with this hypothesis. The resolution of this anomaly remains a challenge to the profession.

REFERENCES

Asquith, Paul, 1983, Merger bids, uncertainty and stockholder returns, *Journal of Financial Economics* 11, 51–83.

Ball, Ray and S. P. Kothari, 1989, Nonstationary expected returns: Implications for tests of market efficiency and serial correlations in returns, *Journal of Financial Economics* 25, 51–74.

Bradley, Michael and Gregg Jarrell, 1988, Comment, in John Coffee Jr., Louis Lowenstein, and Susan Rose-Ackerman, eds.: *Knights, Raiders and Targets* (Oxford University Press, Oxford, England), 252–259.

Brown, Steve and Jerold B. Warner, 1980, Measuring security price performance, *Journal of Financial Economics* 8, 205–258.

Chan, K. C., 1988, On the contrarian investment strategy, *Journal of Business* 61, 147–163.

———, Nai-Fu Chen, and David Hsieh, 1985, An exploratory investigation of the firm size effect, *Journal of Financial Economics* 14, 451–471.

Chopra, Navin, Joseph Lakonishok, and Jay R. Ritter, 1992, Measuring abnormal performance: Do stocks overreact? *Journal of Financial Economics* 31, 235–268.

DeBondt, Werner F. M. and Richard Thaler, 1985, Does the stock market overreact? *Journal of Finance* 40, 793–805.

———, 1987, Further evidence of investor overreaction and stock market seasonality, *Journal of Finance* 42, 557–581.

Dimson, Elroy and Paul Marsh, 1986, Event study methodologies and the size effect: The case of UK Press recommendations, *Journal of Financial Economics* 17, 113–142.

Fama, Eugene F., Lawrence Fisher, Michael C. Jensen, and Richard Roll, 1969, The adjustment of stock prices to new information, *International Economic Review* 10, 1–21.

Franks, Julian R., Robert S. Harris, and Sheridan Titman, 1991, The post-merger shareprice performance of acquiring firms, *Journal of Financial Economics* 29, 81–96.

Hansen, Robert G., 1987, A theory for the choice of exchange medium in the market for corporate control, *Journal of Business* 60, 75–95.

Healy, Paul M., Krishna G. Palepu, and Richard S. Ruback, 1992, Does corporate performance improve after mergers? *Journal of Financial Economics* 31, 135–175.

Herman, Edward and Louis Lowenstein, 1988, The efficiency effects of hostile takeovers, in John Coffee, Jr., Louis Lowenstein, and Susan Rose-Ackerman, eds.: *Knights, Raiders and Targets* (Oxford University Press, Oxford, England), 211–240.

Ibbotson, Roger G., 1975, Price performance of common stock new issues, *Journal of Financial Economics* 3, 235–272.

Jaffe, Jeffrey F., 1974, Special information and insider trading, *Journal of Business* 47, 410–428.

Jensen, Michael C., 1986, Agency costs of free cash flow, corporate finance and takeovers, *American Economic Review* 76, 323–329.

——— and Richard S. Ruback, 1983, The market for corporate control: The scientific evidence, *Journal of Financial Economics* 11, 5–50.

Post-Merger Performance of Acquiring Firms: An Anomaly   1621

Lakonishok, Josef and Theo Vermaelen, 1990, Anomalous price behavior around repurchase tender offers, *Journal of Finance* 45, 455–477.

Langetieg, Terence C., 1978, An application of a three-factor performance index to measure stockholder gains from merger, *Journal of Financial Economics* 6, 365–383.

Magenheim, Ellen B. and Dennis C. Mueller, 1988, Are acquiring firm shareholders better off after an acquisition? in John Coffee, Jr., Louis Lowenstein, and Susan Rose-Ackerman, eds.: *Knights, Raiders and Targets* (Oxford University Press, Oxford, England), 171–193.

Mandelker, Gershon, 1974, Risk and return: The case of merging firms, *Journal of Financial Economics* 1, 303–335.

Malatesta, Paul H., 1983, The wealth effect of merger activity and the objective function of merging firms, *Journal of Financial Economics* 11, 155–181.

Miller, Merton H. and Myron Scholes, 1932, Dividends and taxes: Some empirical evidence, *Journal of Political Economy* 90, 1118–1141.

Ravenscraft, D. and F. M. Scherer, 1987, *Mergers, Selloffs and Economic Efficiency* (The Brookings Institution, Washington, DC).

Rozeff, Michael S. and Mir A. Zaman, 1988, Market efficiency and insider trading: New evidence, *Journal of Business* 6, 25–44.

Ruback, Richard J., 1988, Comment, in Alan J. Auerbach, ed.: *Corporate Takeovers: Courses and Consequences* (University of Chicago Press, Chicago).

[14]

THE JOURNAL OF FINANCE • VOL. XLV, NO. 3 • JULY 1990

The Distribution of Target Ownership and the Division of Gains in Successful Takeovers

RENÉ M. STULZ, RALPH A. WALKLING, and MOON H. SONG*

ABSTRACT

This paper presents evidence that the distribution of target ownership is related to the division of the takeover gain between the target and the bidder for a sample of successful tender offers. In the whole sample, the target's gain is negatively related to bidder and institutional ownership. In the sample of multiple-bidder contests, the target's gain increases with managerial ownership and falls with institutional ownership.

RECENT PAPERS EMPHASIZE THE importance of the distribution of target share ownership in takeover contests.[1] Although these papers differ in the issues they address, they share the common idea that large blockholders use their voting rights to further their own interests by influencing the likelihood and outcomes of takeover attempts. This literature suggests that management and non-management blockholders have different incentives in the presence of a takeover attempt. On one hand, managers who value incumbency can use their voting rights to decrease the likelihood of a takeover and increase its cost for the bidder. On the other hand, non-management blockholders are likely to use their voting rights to facilitate takeovers that, if successful, increase the value of their holdings. Blockholders who use their stake to increase the bidder's cost increase the target's share of the takeover gain if the takeover succeeds, whereas those who use their stake to decrease the bidder's cost decrease the target's share. In this paper, we present evidence that the distribution of target ownership is related to the division of the takeover gain (defined as the increase in the combined value of the target and the bidder) for a sample of successful tender bids.

The value of managerial incumbency varies widely across firms. Consequently, so does target management's incentive to use its ownership position to resist acquisition attempts. Unopposed offers often occur because management believes the offer to be in the shareholders' best interests or because of retirement plans. Management may also choose not to resist because it has conceded defeat or

* Riklis Chair in Business and Associate Professor of Finance, The Ohio State University, and Assistant Professor of Finance, San Diego State University, respectively. We are grateful to Anup Agrawal, Warren Bailey, John Byrd, K. C. Chan, Larry Dann, Harry DeAngelo, Mike Fishman, Gerald Garvey, Rob Heinkel, Mike Jensen, Gregg Jarrell, Jon Karpoff, Mike Long, Francis Longstaff, Wayne Marr, David Mayers, Wayne Mikkelson, Patricia Reagan, Richard Ruback, Andrei Shleifer, Bill Schwert, Rex Thompson, and Mark Wolfson for useful discussions and comments, to participants at sessions at the American Finance Association and the Western Finance Association, and to the seminar participants at Harvard University, Indiana University, the Ohio State University, Southern Methodist University, the University of Rochester, and the Washington State University for helpful comments.

[1] See Jensen and Warner (1988) for a review of these papers.

because it has been assured of the continuation of most of its perquisites. In other cases, managers' perquisites are threatened and they use their ownership stake to increase the bidder's acquisition cost and/or to generate additional bids.

To segregate firms where the value of managerial incumbency is high, we follow Morck, Shleifer, and Vishny (1988) and consider separately single- and multiple-bidder takeovers.[2] Multiple-bidder contests, where several bidders expect to benefit from the acquisition, are more likely to be disciplinary takeovers of firms where target management derives rents from incumbency. We find that the effect of target managerial ownership on the sharing of gains in successful bids is associated with multiple-bidder contests. We show no significant empirical relation between the target's share of the takeover gain and target managerial ownership for single-bidder takeovers.

After discussing the theoretical determinants of the division of gains in takeovers, we present our data in Section II. In Section III, we show how the target's gain depends on the distribution of ownership of the target. Concluding remarks are provided in Section IV.

I. The Distribution of Target Ownership and the Market for Corporate Control

Early research on the market for corporate control assumed target shareholders to be atomistic. Such shareholders have no incentive to consider the impact of their tendering decision on the probability of tender offer success. More recently, researchers have emphasized the incentives of large shareholders to act strategically. These researchers have focused mainly on managerial and bidder holdings of target shares.[3] There has also, however, been some analysis of the effect of target ownership by institutional shareholders.[4] In this section, we motivate hypotheses about the effect of managerial, bidder, and institutional ownership of the division of gains in successful takeovers. Other shareholders are assumed to be atomistic, and we discuss their role first.

A. Atomistic Shareholders

An atomistic shareholder tenders if the expected value of tendering exceeds the expected value of not tendering. If the bid fails and no shares are bought, the atomistic shareholder's wealth is the same whether he or she tendered or not. Consequently, the shareholders' decision to tender is made by comparing the payoffs of tendering with those of not tendering assuming that the offer succeeds. Some shareholders may avoid tendering because it forces the realization of

---

[2] As discussed in Section III, we also investigated offers opposed by management.

[3] See, for instance, Harris and Raviv (1988) and Stulz (1988) for managerial holdings and Shleifer and Vishny (1986a) for bidder holdings. In an earlier version of this paper we considered the role of large shareholders not related to target management and not related to the bidder. However, relatively few firms in our sample had such shareholders prior to the first bid. We do not consider the role of arbitrageurs in this paper since they mostly acquire significant stakes after the stare of takeover activity and hence do not affect the division of target ownership observed by the bidder before making a bid.

[4] See, for instance, Brickley, Lease, and Smith (1988).

Target Ownership Distribution and Takeover Gains 819

taxable capital gains. Further, shareholders are likely to have different beliefs about the value of shares not tendered if the offer succeeds. As a result of heterogeneity in beliefs and differences in tax status, the supply curve of shares tendered is an increasing function of the price per share offered by the bidder. This supply curve is represented in Figure 1. We assume that the supply curve for atomistic investors is the same irrespective of the fraction of target shares they hold as a group. Since a shareholder can always sell shares at the market price, this supply curve must intersect the vertical axis at or above the market price. Assuming that the bidder can capture most of the takeover gains not paid

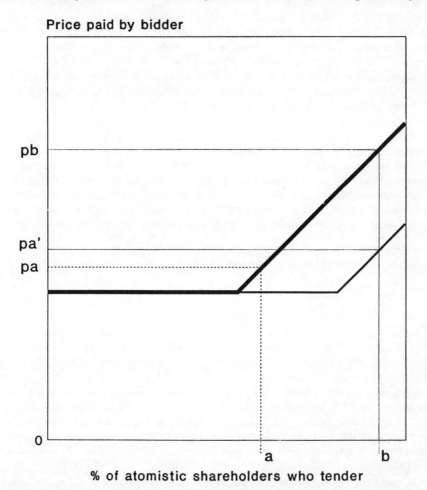

Figure 1. The supply curve of shares as a function of the price paid by the bidder. An increase in managerial ownership increases the required fraction of shares to be tendered by atomistic shareholders from *a* to *b* for the bidder to succeed. It therefore forces the bidder to increase the price paid from *pa* to *pb*. An increase in ownership by shareholders that do not pay taxes shifts the supply curve to the right, so that, for high institutional ownerships, a fraction *b* of the shares can be acquired for a price *pa'* instead of *pa*.

out to tendering shareholders, there are shareholders who pay no taxes and are willing to tender for a small premium.[5] An increase in the fraction of shares held by such shareholders pushes the supply curve of shares to the right, as shown in Figure 1.

B. The Bidder

The bidder offers target shareholders a package that consists of a premium for the shares tendered and rights to a fraction of the cash flow resulting from the combination of the bidder and the target for shares not tendered. The bidder chooses this package to maximize the net present value of acquiring a given number of target shares. Since the true supply curve of shares is not known, the bidder chooses a premium based on its knowledge of the distribution of the true supply curve. For a given premium, the bid may fail because the supply of shares tendered turns out to be lower than the minimum number of shares tendered required by the bidder. The opportunity cost of losing the bid increases with the bidder's estimate of the total takeover gain. Hence, we assume that the bidder is willing to pay more as the expected total takeover gain increases.[6]

Bidders often own a fraction of the target's shares prior to an offer. Large bidder holdings of target shares mean that fewer shares must be tendered for the bidder to succeed. In Figure 1, this means that the pivotal shareholder, i.e., the marginal shareholder who must tender for the offer to succeed, is lower on the supply curve. Hence, the premium offered to target shareholders falls with the fraction of shares owned by the bidder, and the bidder gets to keep a larger fraction of the total takeover gain. This suggests the following hypothesis:

H1: For a given total takeover gain, the target's gain is a decreasing function of the fraction of target shares held by the bidder prior to the offer.

C. Target Management

At the time the bid is made, target management holdings of target shares are fixed. Target management has to decide the price at which it is willing to tender. If management's holdings are not trivial, its tendering decision will affect the probability of bid success. If management tenders, the bidder has to acquire fewer shares from atomistic shareholders and hence offers a smaller premium. By not tendering or by tendering only for a high premium, management forces the bidder to pay to target shareholders a larger fraction of the takeover gain. In Figure 1, larger ownership by non-tendering managers means that the pivotal shareholder is higher on the supply curve. However, by tendering only for high premia, management risks not receiving any takeover premium. That is, the bid may succeed without its shares or not succeed at all.

If management earns rents in its position, it is likely to lose them if the bid

---

[5] If the bidder cannot capture most of the gains not paid out to tendering shareholders, shareholders may refrain from tendering since their shares will appreciate as part of the takeover gain accrues to them. See Grossman and Hart (1980).

[6] See Stulz (1988) for assumptions that lead to this result.

succeeds. Consequently, we would expect management to tender for a given premium only if the present value of the benefits from remaining the incumbent are less than the takeover premium management would receive. Clearly, management's reluctance to tender is a mixed blessing for target shareholders. On one hand, this reluctance increases the premium offered, but, on the other hand, it makes it less likely that the offer will succeed and hence that a premium will be paid. Alternatively, if incumbent management wants to sell out, there may be cases where management does not act strategically to increase the target's gain but instead uses its holdings to facilitate the takeover. This leads to our second hypothesis:

> H2: When the value of incumbency is high, the target's gain conditional on the total takeover gains is an increasing function of target management's stake.[7]

To the extent that multiple-bidder offers are disciplinary offers, one would expect the value of incumbency to be high for firms that attract multiple offers. This is because the takeover gains in such cases partly result from eliminating the rents that accrue to incumbents. Alternatively, one could view offers opposed by management to be cases where incumbency has value. Although in this paper we generally assume that firms that receive multiple offers are those where the value of incumbency is high, we also consider the case of offers opposed by management in our analysis.

D. Institutional Investors

Investors with low marginal capital gains tax rates are more likely to tender for a given premium. Consequently, the larger the fraction of low-tax shareholders, the lower the premium offered by the bidder and the smaller the target's share of the takeover gain for a given total takeover gain. While no data are directly available on the shape and location of the supply curve of shares, data are available on the fraction of shares held by institutional investors. The number of different institutional investors is also available for each firm, and generally this number is large. It seems reasonable to assume that the typical institutional investor ignores the effect of tendering on the probability of bid success and can therefore be treated as an atomistic investor. Since institutional investors are generally in low tax brackets, the target's share of the takeover gain should be inversely related to the fraction of target equity held by institutions. This assumes, however, that institutional investors cannot collude. On Figure 1, this means that the pivotal investor is lower on the supply curve if the fraction of shares held by institutional shareholders is large. This leads us to our third and last hypothesis:

> H3: For a given total takeover gain, the target's gain is a decreasing function of the fraction of target shares held by institutional investors.

---

[7] See also Stulz (1988).

The Journal of Finance

II. Data Sources

A. *Estimates of the Target, Bidder and Total Gains*

The initial sample of tender offers comes from two sources: (a) the Rochester Merc Data Base on tender offers for the period from October 1968 through September 1980 and (b) the Austin Database on tender offers for the period from September 1980 through 1986.[8] To belong to our sample, tender offers must meet the following criteria:

1. Both the target and bidding firms are on the CRSP daily returns tape for 300 days before the first takeover announcement.
2. The bidder acquires some shares in the offer.
3. The tender offer occurs after October 1968.

Two hundred nine tender offers satisfy these criteria (125 from the Rochester list and 84 from the Austin list). As in Bradley, Desai, and Kim (1988), an offer where the bidder acquired some shares is defined to be successful. We focus on successful offers to insure that our estimates of the target and bidder gains are not biased downward because of the attenuation effect resulting from a probability of success that is less than one. This bias could lead us to believe that higher managerial ownership decreases the target's gain if, as argued in Stulz (1988), the probability of success of a bid falls with target managerial ownership.

To conduct our study, we need data on ownership. Consequently, we retain only those firms for which we have ownership data. This restricts the usable sample to 104 takeovers.[9] These takeovers are classified as single-bidder takeovers and multiple-bidder takeovers. There are 40 multiple-bidder takeovers in the sample.

The estimation of the target and bidder gains follows closely the method developed by Bradley, Desai, and Kim (1988). We refer the interested reader to their extensive discussion of their method. Market model parameters are estimated on a period from 300 to 60 days before the first announcement of takeover activity for the target firm. For single-bidder unrevised offers, these market model parameters are used to estimate the cumulative abnormal return for a period of 11 days centered on the first announcement date of takeover activity by the bidder. For multiple-bidder and revised offers, the cumulative abnormal return is estimated from 5 days before the first takeover announcement to 5 days after the last revision in terms by the successful bidder.

Table I reports summary statistics on bidder and target cumulative abnormal returns. The statistics for the complete sample are similar to those of Bradley, Desai, and Kim (1988), although our estimate for target cumulative returns (39%) is somewhat higher than theirs. In their sample, the target abnormal return from

---

[8] See Tenderbase, Version 1.03, Douglas Austin & Associates, Inc., 1987. The Tenderbase provides machine readable information on all tender offers registered with the SEC.

[9] As explained later, our managerial ownership data are obtained from *Value Line*. *Value Line* started to report ownership in 1968, so that our use of *Value Line* precludes consideration of offers made before 1968. Of the 125 firms obtained from the Rochester data base. 40 were not in *Value Line* and 20 other firms had missing data on one or more independent variables. For the 84 firms obtained from the Austin list, 31 were not in *Value Line* and 14 had data missing on some independent variable.

Table I

Abnormal Returns and Significance Tests for Data for Targets and Bidders

The sample comprises 104 successful takeovers from 1968 to 1986. The abnormal returns are estimated using the market model. The parameters of the market model are estimated on a period from 300 to 60 days prior to the first announcement of takeover activity. The cumulative abnormal returns are estimated on a period that starts 5 days before the first announcement by a bidder to 5 days after the final revision in terms by the successful bidder. The value-weighted portfolio of the bidder and the target uses as the value of the target the value of the shares not held by the bidder to avoid double-counting of these shares.

(Number of Offers)	All (104)	Single Bidder (64)	Multiple Bidders (40)
Panel A: Target Abnormal Returns			
Average abnormal return	0.3934	0.3545	0.4558
t-Statistic (H0: mean equal to zero)[a]	18.73***	13.26***	14.27***
t-Statistic (H0: means of subgroups are equal)[b]		-2.40**	
Median abnormal return	0.3793	0.3250	0.4594
Standard deviation of the abnormal return	0.2142	0.2139	0.2020
Panel B: Bidder Abnormal Returns			
Average abnormal return	-0.0083	0.0129	-0.0421
t-Statistic (H0: mean equal to zero)	-0.49	0.94	-1.11
t-Statistic (H0: means of subgroups are equal)		1.59	
Median abnormal return	-0.0026	-0.0043	0.0040
Standard deviation of the abnormal return	0.1726	0.1094	0.2396
Panel C: Value-Weighted Portfolio Abnormal Returns			
Average abnormal return	0.1091	0.0966	0.1290
t-Statistic (H0: mean equal to zero)	6.89**	5.55**	4.26***
t-Statistic (H0: means of subgroups are equal)		-0.93	
Median abnormal return	0.0941	0.0732	0.1470
Standard deviation of the abnormal return	0.1614	0.1393	0.1917

[a] * denotes significance at the 0.10 level, ** at the 0.05 level, and *** at the 0.01 level.
[b] The t-statistics assume equal variances for the two subgroups.

1968 to 1984 is slightly more than 35%. The difference seems to be explained by the period from 1968 to 1980. For that period, the average target abnormal return in their study is equal to 35.29% while here it is 41.2%.[10] It is possible that this difference is caused by the firms that are in the Bradley, Desai, and Kim (1988) sample but are eliminated from this one because we do not have ownership data for them.[11] Finally, the average cumulative abnormal return is significantly lower for single-bidder takeovers than for multiple-bidder takeovers.

The mean cumulative abnormal return for bidders is negative for the whole sample but not significantly different from zero. The average bidder return is negative for multiple-bidder contests and positive otherwise. The difference of about 5.5 percentage points between bidder abnormal returns for multiple- and single-bidder contests has a t-statistic of 1.59. The high standard deviation of bidder returns for multiple-bidder takeovers shows that there is substantial variation in the bidder gain in such contests and explains why such a large return difference is not significant at the 0.10 level.

Finally, Panel C of Table I reports statistics on the abnormal return for a value-weighted portfolio of the target and the bidder.[12] To compute the portfolio weights, the market value of target equity is defined as the closing market price for the month end prior to the initial acquisition announcement times the number of shares outstanding not held by the bidder. Double-counting of the gains that accrue to the bidder through its holdings of target shares is avoided by using the number of target shares not held by the bidder. All of the bidder's shares are used to compute its market value of equity. In most cases, these data are obtained from the CRSP tapes. Where necessary, we supplement the CRSP data with figures from the *Standard and Poor's Stock Guide*. Although the point estimate of the gain to the value-weighted portfolio is larger in the case of multiple-bidder takeovers, the difference from the single-bidder case is not statistically significant.

B. Ownership Variables

The cross-sectional regressions reported in this study use *Value Line* ownership data from the appropriate issue immediately preceding the initial takeover announcement. *Value Line* reports ownership of officers, directors, and other insiders.[13] In this study, the fraction of target shares held by officers, directors,

---

[10] This implies that in our sample the target returns are lower in the 1980's than in the 1970's. Jarrell and Poulsen (1987) also find lower target returns in the 1980's.

[11] An alternative explanation for this difference is the choice of announcement dates. We define the first announcement to be any acquisition-related news concerning the target preceding the tender offer such that there is no other acquisition-related news for the previous three-month period. Examples include the announcement that a firm is a possible target, that a large block of shares has been acquired, or that an actual bid has been made. Thus, we are more likely to include anticipatory price increases than Bradley, Desai, and Kim (1988).

[12] The portfolio gain is larger than the one reported by Bradley, Desai, and Kim (1988). This is likely to be due to different criteria for sample selection.

[13] *Value Line* obtains its ownership data from proxy statements, corporate news releases, and Forms 3 and 4 filed with the SEC. Form 3 is an initial ownership statement filed by officers, directors, and 10% principal stockholders. The statement must be filed within 10 days after acquiring the security. Form 4 records any changes in ownership. It must be filed within 10 days after the end of

and other insiders is defined as "managerial ownership."[14] Shares held by the bidder obtained from the Rochester and the Austin databases constitute our measure denoted "bidder ownership." Our measure "institutional ownership" is obtained from the *S&P Stock Guide* and corresponds to the fraction of target shares held by institutional investors at the end of the month preceding the initial takeover announcement.[15]

Table II describes our ownership data. Although managerial ownership is lower on average for multiple-bidder takeovers than for single-bidder offers, the difference is not significant. The level of institutional ownership is about the same for multiple-bidder and single-bidder takeovers. The fact that bidder ownership is significantly higher for single- than for multiple-bidder offers suggests that in the case of single-bidder offers the bidder already has a strong position when the first takeover rumor occurs and that this position may deter further bidders. As evidence of the relative bargaining power of management in single- versus multiple-bidder offers, it is useful to note that in single-bidder offers the successful bidder typically has a larger pre-offer stake in the target than management. In multiple-bidder offers, both the first bidder and the successful bidder have a smaller pre-offer stake in the target than management. The difference in the size of bidder ownership relative to managerial ownership in multiple- and single-bidder contests suggests that multiple-bidder contests are more likely to occur when the first bidder has a weak position relative to target management.

III. The Relation Between the Target's Share and Ownership Measures

A. The Regression Model

Section I develops hypotheses that relate the target's gain to ownership variables. To summarize the hypotheses of Section I, let t_i and g_i be, respectively, the target and the total takeover dollar gains. It follows from Section I that we

---

the month in which the change occurred. *Value Line* treats as insiders those shareholders related to management or board members. Malatesta and Walkling (1988) also use *Value Line* ownership data and discuss some of its properties.

[14] Alternative measures of managerial ownership are available. On a subset of our sample, we used the Spectrum 6 report. This report constructs a measure of managerial ownership using the information published in SEC Forms 3 and 4. We also had proxy statements available for some firms in the sample. The correlation coefficient between the *Value Line* ownership measure and the proxy statement measure is about 0.85. Although the three ownership measures are not perfectly correlated, they yield similar results. In particular, we estimated our cross-sectional regressions on a subsample that uses the Spectrum 6 measure and the proxy measure. This subsample contains 95 successful takeovers, of which 67 are unopposed. These regressions, which led to results similar to those reported in this paper, suggest that the results of this paper are robust to changes in data sources for managerial ownership.

[15] The *S&P Stock Guide* measures institutional holdings as the sum of shares held by investment companies, banks, insurance companies, college endowments, and other 13f institutions and money managers. The 13f filings are required by the SEC since December 31, 1978. All institutions with equity assets exceeding $100 million are required to file on a quarterly basis. *Value Line* also reports institutional holdings but does not do so continuously throughout our sample period.

Table II
Target Ownership Measures

The ownership measures are for a sample of 104 successful takeovers bids from 1968 to 1986. Managerial ownership is the sum of the target stock ownership of officers, directors, and other insiders reported by *Value Line* in the appropriate issue immediately preceding the initial announcement of takeover activity expressed as a fraction of total stock outstanding. Institutional ownership is the fraction of shares held by institutional investors as reported by the *Standard and Poors Stock Guide* for the end of the month preceding the initial announcement of takeover activity. Bidder ownership data are obtained from the Rochester Merc Database and the Austin Database and confirmed through the *Wall Street Journal*.

(Number of Offers)	All (104)	Single Bidder (64)		Multiple Bidders (40)
Panel A: Managerial Ownership				
Average	0.0937	0.1044		0.0767
t-Statistic (H0: mean equal to zero)[a]	7.87**	6.42**		4.60**
t-Statistic (H0: means of subgroups are equal)[b]			1.13	
Median	0.0400	0.0500		0.0250
Standard deviation	0.1215	0.1302		0.1055
Panel B: Institutional Ownership				
Average	0.1906	0.1842		0.2007
t-Statistic (H0: mean equal to zero)	11.52**	8.46**		7.88***
t-Statistic (H0: means of subgroups are equal)			−0.48	
Median	0.1390	0.1218		0.1716
Standard deviation	0.1687	0.1741		0.2007
Panel C: Bidder Ownership				
Average	0.1024	0.1380		0.0454
t-Statistic (H0: mean equal to zero)	6.64**	6.16**		3.23***
t-Statistic (H0: means of subgroups are equal)			3.04***	
Median	0.0235	0.0475		0.0000
Standard deviation	0.1572	0.1772		0.0891

** denotes significance at the 0.10 level, ** at the 0.05 level, and *** at the 0.01 level.
[b] The t-statistics assume that the variances of the two subgroups do not differ.

Target Ownership Distribution and Takeover Gains 827

can write

$$t_i = f(\underline{x}_i, \underline{y}_i, g_i), \tag{1}$$

where $\underline{x}$ is a 3×1 vector of ownership variables and $\underline{y}_i$ is an $n \times 1$ vector of variables that affect the target's share of the total takeover gain. The hypotheses of Section I are that $f(\underline{x}_i, \underline{y}_i, g_i)$ is an increasing function of managerial ownership and a decreasing function of institutional and bidder ownership.

Assuming that the target gain depends linearly on the explanatory variables, we can estimate (1) by regressing the target's gain on the constant, the ownership variables, the total gain, and the other explanatory variables. The gain variables are normalized by the size of target equity to avoid heteroscedasticity. (Heteroscedasticity is implied by the positive relation between the variance of the estimation error in the target dollar gain and the size of the target dollar gain.) The normalized target gain is simply the target's abnormal return associated with the takeover. The normalized total gain is in the same units as the normalized target gain, so that, if the target shareholders got all of the total gain irrespective of the other explanatory variables, the regression coefficient on the normalized total gain would be one. We allow for a different effect of positive and negative total gains on the target's abnormal return. The target gain does not have to be positively related to the takeover gain when the total gain is negative. Using circumflexes to denote the estimates of the normalized variables, we therefore estimate the following equation:

$$\hat{t}_i = c + \underline{a}'\underline{x}_i + \underline{b}'\underline{y}_i + d^+\hat{g}_i^+ + d^-\hat{g}_i^- + u_i, \tag{2}$$

where $\hat{g}_i^+$ ($\hat{g}_i^-$) is the normalized total gain if positive (negative). The estimates of the regression coefficients on the ownership variables can be interpreted as the effect of these variables on the target's abnormal return conditional on the total takeover gain. Note, however, that, if the probability of a firm being a target were negatively related to managerial ownership, a firm with high managerial ownership would have a small probability of being a target.[16] Hence, if an offer is made, the firm's value might increase more than if it had low managerial ownership because the element of surprise in the offer is greater. This relation between the probability of being a target and managerial ownership could lead to a positive relation between the target's gain and managerial ownership.[17] By the same argument, one can derive a negative relation between the probability of being taken over and bidder and institutional ownership that could lead to a negative relation between the target's gain. We will discuss later why this issue is not of great concern given our empirical estimates. However, if our results could be partly attributed to the relation between the probability of a takeover and the ownership variables, this would still be supporting evidence for the role

---

[16] See Stulz (1988). Mikkelson and Partch (1989) provide evidence that lower managerial ownership is associated with higher frequency of control events.

[17] See Lanen and Thompson (1988) for a discussion of how the interaction between the cash flow implications of an event and the probability of the event taking place affect the stock price reaction to an event.

of the distribution of ownership in takeovers, since it would indicate that the distribution of ownership affects the probability that a firm will be a target.

The variables affecting bidder and target gains in takeovers are not well understood. However, to estimate (2) we do not need to know every variable which could affect the target's gain. We want, however, to make sure that we control for those variables that are correlated with ownership variables to insure that the regression coefficients on the ownership variables are not biased. From Demsetz and Lehn (1985), we know that target size is likely to be correlated with managerial ownership and, possibly, with institutional ownership.[18] It also seems plausible that bidder size might be correlated with bidder ownership. Finally, Section I implies that the target's share of the gains should increase with the fraction of the shares acquired by the bidder; bidder ownership and the fraction of target shares the bidder acquires through the tender offer are likely to be negatively correlated. In our regressions, we therefore control for target size, bidder size, and the fraction of target shares acquired by the bidder.

We expect the impact of ownership on the target's gain to be nonlinear; for example, an increase in managerial ownership from 30 to 35% would have a smaller effect than an increase from 0 to 5%. With holdings of, say, 30%, management may be able to block any takeover attempt. Increasing its holdings further would have no effect on takeover contests. The same argument can be made for bidder and institutional ownership. To account for this nonlinear effect, we estimated the ownership effects using both levels and square roots of the ownership measures. Regressions that use square roots of ownership measures have greater explanatory power than regressions that use the levels of ownership measures, but none of the qualitative conclusions of the paper depend on whether regressions are estimated using levels or square roots of ownership measures.[19] In regressions that use both levels and square roots of ownership measures, multicollinearity leads to less significant coefficients for the ownership measures. However, in these regressions, the coefficients of the square root ownership measures are more significant than the coefficients of the level ownership measures.

B. Estimates of the Regression Model

Table III provides estimates of the regression model given by equation (2). The results in Table III show that the target managerial holdings have a significant positive effect on target abnormal returns for the sample of multiple-bidder takeovers. For this sample and the whole sample, institutional holdings have a significant negative effect. Somewhat surprisingly, bidder holdings of the target have a significant negative effect only for the whole sample. The coefficient on bidder holdings has a p-value of 0.16 in the single-bidder sample and 0.24 in the

---

[18] See Demsetz and Lehn (1985).

[19] Since one might argue that the effects of bidder and institutional ownership do not decrease as bidder and institutional ownership increases, we also estimated regressions where the square root of managerial ownership and the levels of the other ownership measures are the dependent variables. Such regressions have slightly less explanatory power than the regressions reported here but lead to the same qualitative conclusions.

Target Ownership Distribution and Takeover Gains   829

Table III

Cross-Sectional Regressions Using the Target Abnormal Return as the Dependent Variable

The sample contains 104 successful takeovers from 1968 to 1986. To estimate the target and bidder dollar gains, we use market model residuals. The cumulative abnormal returns are estimated on a period that starts 5 days before the first announcement by a bidder to 5 days after the last revision in terms by the successful bidder. The market value of target and bidder equity is obtained by multiplying the number of shares outstanding times the closing market price for the month end prior to the initial acquisition announcement. (The market value is expressed in billions of dollars in the regression.) The bidder acquiring percentage is the percentage acquired by the bidder through the tender offer and is obtained from the Rochester Merc Database or the Austin Tenderbase. The ownership measures are expressed as a fraction of the shares outstanding. The sources for managerial, institutional, and bidder ownership of the target are, respectively, *Value Line*, the *Standard and Poor's Stock Guide*, and the Merc and Austin databases. The total takeover gain is the sum of the target dollar gain and of the bidder dollar gain normalized by the value of target equity. The target dollar gain is computed using the shares not held by the bidder.

Type of Contests (Number of Tender Offers)	All (104)	Single Bidder (64)	Multiple Bidders (40)
Regression coefficient			
Intercept	0.34571	0.28737	0.41695
Market value of target equity	0.0965	0.00687	0.1531
t-Statistic	(1.79)	(0.07)	(2.42)
Market value of bidder equity	0.0096	0.0122	−0.03372
t-Statistic	(0.99)	(1.54)	(−1.39)
Bidder acquiring percentage	0.1068	0.1675	0.0022
t-Statistic	(1.49)	(1.80)	(0.02)
Square root of management ownership	0.1376	0.0176	0.4140
t-Statistic	(1.30)	(0.13)	(2.34)
Square root of institutional ownership	−0.2693	−0.1975	−0.3620
t-Statistic	(−2.37)	(−1.27)	(−2.12)
Square root of bidder ownership	−0.2256	−0.1604	−0.2092
t-Statistic	(−2.57)	(−1.43)	(−1.19)
Total gain if negative	−0.0296	−0.0398	−0.0596
t-Statistic	(−0.91)	(−0.73)	(−0.98)
Total gain if positive	0.1192	0.1132	0.1658
t-Statistic	(3.60)	(2.54)	(2.85)
R-squared	0.2749	0.2734	0.4083

multiple bidder sample. The bidder acquiring percentage, defined as the fraction of target shares acquired by the bidder through the tender offer, has a significant positive coefficient in the single-bidder sample but not in the multiple-bidder sample. The total takeover gain has a significant positive effect on the target's gain for the whole sample and the subsamples if it is positive, but it has no effect if it is negative. Finally, the market value of target equity is significantly positively related to the target's gain for both the whole sample and the multiple-bidder sample.

The coefficients on the ownership measures always have the sign predicted by our hypotheses, but the level of significance on the coefficients varies dramatically across subsamples. The coefficient on managerial ownership is positive for the whole sample and both subsamples; however, the coefficient is only significantly different from zero in the multiple-bidder sample. For the whole sample, we can reject (at the 0.10 level) the hypothesis that the coefficient is negative. For institutional ownership, the coefficient is negative for the whole sample and all subsamples, but it is insignificantly different from zero in the single-bidder subsample. Finally, the coefficient on bidder ownership is always negative, but it is significant only for the whole sample. From Table II, we know that bidder ownership is small for the multiple-bidder contests and larger for the single-bidder contests. The negative effect of bidder ownership in the whole sample may therefore be caused by the difference in bidder ownership across subsamples, since the single-bidder contests have a lower average target gain than the multiple-bidder contests. Targets with small bidder ownership and large managerial ownership are the most likely to have multiple bidders. There seems, therefore, to exist a relation between the distribution of target ownership and the number of bidders.

The hypotheses tested in this paper are conditional on a successful offer. Rather than performing the difficult task of estimating the target and bidder gains conditional on success, we focus on successful offers. In our sample of successful offers, successful resistance to an offer by target management leads to a multiple-bidder contest since all targets are eventually acquired. Thus, our sample does not contain cases where high managerial ownership prevents a successful takeover and target management retains control of the target. The multiple-bidder contests we consider differ from simple auctions, in the sense that they often take place as a result of managerial resistance to the first bidder.[20] This resistance is made effective by management's strategic use of its holdings of target shares. When we divide the sample further according to target management attitude toward the bid, the size of the subsamples becomes small.[21] Nevertheless, we find that the effect of managerial ownership is strongest for the multiple-bidder contests where target management opposes a bidder.

The use of the total gain as a regressor in Table III could be a cause for concern since it includes a transformation of the dependent variable. However, sensitivity tests using alternate specifications produce similar results. In particular, we estimated the regressions in Table III both excluding the normalized total gain as a dependent variable and using the normalized bidder gain (i.e., the bidder dollar gain divided by the market value of the target) instead of the normalized total gain. These regressions led to similar coefficient estimates for the ownership measures. We also estimated regressions that used the target's share, i.e., the target dollar gain divided by the total takeover gain, as the dependent variable.

[20] Baron (1983), Giammarino and Heinkel (1986), Shleifer and Vishny (1986b), and Fishman (1988) all discuss the role of target management in facilitating the entry of additional bidders.

[21] We define resistance as the case where target management opposition to a bidder is explicitly noted in the *Wall Street Journal*. Resistance ranges from verbal opposition to lawsuits and defensive restructurings.

Target Ownership Distribution and Takeover Gains   831

Table IV

Cross-Sectional Regressions Using the Abnormal Return of a Value-Weighted Portfolio of the Bidder and the Target as the Dependent Variable

The sample contains 104 successful takeovers from 1968 to 1986. To estimate the target and bidder dollar gains, we use market model residuals. The cumulative abnormal returns are estimated on a period that starts 5 days before the first announcement by a bidder to 5 days after the last revision in terms by the successful bidder. The market value of target and bidder equity is obtained by multiplying the number of shares outstanding times the closing market price for the month end prior to the initial acquisition announcement. (The market value is expressed in billions of dollars in the regression.) The bidder acquiring percentage is the percentage acquired by the bidder through the tender offer and is obtained from the Rochester Merc Database or the Austin Tenderbase. The ownership measures are expressed as a fraction of the shares outstanding. The sources for managerial, institutional, and bidder ownership of the target are, respectively, *Value Line*, the *Standard and Poor's Stock Guide*, and the Merc and Austin databases. The total takeover gain is the sum of the target dollar gain and of the bidder dollar gain normalized by the value of target equity. The target dollar gain is computed using the shares not held by the bidder.

Type of Contests (Number of Tender Offers)	All (104)	Single Bidder (64)	Multiple Bidders (40)
Regression coefficient			
Intercept	0.06344	0.02124	0.15204
Market value of target equity	0.1057	0.05885	0.1161
t-Statistic	(2.39)	(0.87)	(1.68)
Market value of bidder equity	−0.0130	−0.0114	−0.28531
t-Statistic	(−2.26)	(−2.18)	(−1.19)
Bidder acquiring percentage	0.0837	0.1605	−0.0455
t-Statistic	(1.43)	(2.54)	(−0.37)
Square root of management ownership	−0.0637	−0.0999	−0.0459
t-Statistic	(−0.74)	(−1.09)	(−0.24)
Square root of institutional ownership	−0.0246	−0.0316	0.0278
t-Statistic	(−0.27)	(−0.31)	(0.15)
Square root of bidder ownership	0.0327	0.0823	−0.0569
t-Statistic	(0.46)	(1.10)	(−0.37)
R-squared	0.1187	0.1651	0.1385

While statistical inference for such regressions is difficult, the OLS estimates support the conclusions reached using the regressions in Table III.

Table IV provides another check on our results. It shows estimates of regressions using the return to a value-weighted portfolio of the bidder and the target as the dependent variable. If the ownership variables are significant in such a regression, it implies that they affect the size of the total gain. In this case, our previous results could be affected by the potential effect of the ownership variables on the total takeover gain or on the probability of a bid being made. The evidence in Table IV does not support this hypothesis, since it shows that the total takeover gain is not related to the ownership variables. This makes it more likely that our results can be attributed to the effect of target ownership on the division of gains.[22]

IV. Conclusion

This paper documents that, for a sample of successful tender offers, the target's share of the total takeover gain depends on the distribution of target ownership. We show this with estimates of a regression of target abnormal returns on ownership and other explanatory variables. We demonstrate that, for multiple-bidder offers, the target's gain increases with target managerial ownership and decreases with institutional ownership. Further, bidder and institutional ownership of the target decreases the target's gain for the whole sample. For multiple-bidder contests, bidder ownership seems to be less important. In general, multiple-bidder contests take place when the bidder has a weak ownership position in the target and target management has a strong ownership position. This paper also shows that the gain to a value-weighted portfolio of the bidder and the target does not depend on the distribution of target ownership.

One would expect managerial ownership to matter more when management has strong incentives to use its holdings to increase the bidder's acquisition price. We assumed that these incentives would be strong for multiple-bidder takeovers. The importance of managerial ownership in multiple-bidder contests suggests that it is erroneous to view such contests as simple auctions. If multiple-bidder contests were simple auctions, managerial ownership would have less importance in such contests than in single-bidder contests because competition among bidders drives up the target's gain in such contests. Our results suggest that target management with a large stake is better able to transform a single-bidder contest into a multiple-bidder contest.

[22] Note that a regression that uses the bidder's gain as a dependent variable would not provide useful additional evidence. An ownership variable that increases the target's dollar gain should decrease the bidder's dollar gain. When measured in percentage terms, however, the gains and losses will not be offsetting unless both the bidder and the target dollar gains are expressed in percentage of the target value. Using as the dependent variable the bidder dollar gain divided by the target market value yields regression estimates that contain no new information relative to the regression estimates given in Table III. The sum of regressions that use, respectively, the bidder dollar gain and the target dollar gain divided by the target market value as the dependent variables yields the identity that the total normalized takeover gain equals itself. Consequently, we cannot study the determinants of the bidder's gain to evaluate the robustness of our results.

REFERENCES

Baron, D. P., 1983, Tender offers and management resistance, *Journal of Finance* 38, 331–342.

Bradley, M., A. Desai, and E. H. Kim, 1988, Synergistic gains from corporate acquisitions and their division between the stockholders of target and acquiring firms, *Journal of Financial Economics* 21, 3–40.

Brickley, J. A., R. C. Lease, and C. W. Smith, Jr., 1988, Ownership structure and voting on antitakeover amendments. *Journal of Financial Economics* 21, 267–292.

Demsetz, H. and K. Lehn, 1985, The structure of corporate ownership: Causes and consequences. *Journal of Political Economy* 93, 1155–1177.

Target Ownership Distribution and Takeover Gains 833

Fishman, M. J., 1988, A theory of preemptive takeover bidding, *The Rand Journal of Economics* 19, 88–101.

Giammarino, R. M. and R. L. Heinkel, 1986, A model of dynamic takeover behavior, *Journal of Finance* 41, 465–480.

Grossman, S. and O. Hart, 1980, Takeover bids, the free-rider problem and the theory of the corporation, *The Bell Journal of Economics* 11, 42–64.

Harris, M. and A. Raviv, 1988, Corporate control contests and capital structure, *Journal of Financial Economics* 20, 55–86.

Jarrell, G. A. and A. B. Poulsen, 1987, Shark repellants and stock prices, *Journal of Financial Economics* 19, 127–168.

Jensen, M. and J. S. Warner, 1988, The distribution of power among corporate managers, shareholders, and directors, *Journal of Financial Economics* 20, 3–24.

Lanen, W. N. and R. Thompson, 1988, Stock price reactions as surrogates for the net cash flow effects of corporate policy decisions, *Journal of Accounting and Economics* 10, 311–334.

Malatesta, P. and R. A. Walkling, 1988, Poison pill securities: Stockholder wealth, profitability, and ownership structure, *Journal of Financial Economics* 20, 347–376.

Mikkelson, W. H. and M. M. Partch, 1989, Managers' voting rights and corporate control, Unpublished working paper, University of Oregon.

Morck, R., A. Shleifer, and R. W. Vishny, 1988, Characteristics of targets of hostile and friendly takeovers, in A. J. Auerbach, ed.: *Corporate Takeovers: Causes and Consequences* (University of Chicago Press, Chicago, IL).

Shleifer, A. and R. Vishny, 1986a, Large shareholders and corporate control, *Journal of Political Economy* 94, 461–488.

——— and R. Vishny, 1986b, Greenmail, white knights, and shareholders' interest, *Rand Journal of Economics* 17, 293–309.

Stulz, R., 1988, Managerial control of voting rights: Financing policies and the market for corporate control, *Journal of Financial Economics* 20, 25–54.

[15]

J ECO BUSN
1987; 39:251-266

Merger Proposals, Managerial Discretion, and Magnitude of Shareholders' Wealth Gains

Gili Yen

Recently, the market for corporate control has attracted much attention. Scholars have attempted to ascertain whether managerial resistance is in the interests of shareholders. This study compares the average actual changes in wealth of accepted merger proposals with those of rejected merger proposals. It also compares the realized changes in shareholder wealth of the rejected proposals with the realizable shareholder wealth changes. In either case, managerial resistance leads to smaller gains in wealth. Based on these results, we cannot reject the view that managerial resistance is detrimental to the interests of shareholders.

I. Introduction

A. Issue and Objective

The market for corporate control has attracted much attention. In particular, is managerial resistance in the interest of shareholders?[1] Walkling and Long (1984) summarize the two opposing views, the shareholder welfare hypothesis and the managerial welfare hypothesis. According to the shareholder welfare hypothesis, "Target managements that oppose tender bids frequently defend their actions by claiming that the bid price is inadequate." In contrast,

---

Gili Yen is from the Graduate Institute of Industrial Economics, National Central University, Republic of China.

Address reprint requests to Dr. Gili Yen, Graduate Institute of Industrial Economics, National Central University, Chung-li, Taiwan, Republic of China.

This research was supported by a dissertation fellowship from Center for the Study of American Business at Washington University in St. Louis. I would like to acknowledge the guidance of my dissertation committee: Barry Weingast, Bill Marshall, James Little, Seth Norton, and especially Lee Benham (chairman). Besides, I am indebted to Gregg Jarrell, Alan K. Severn, an anonymous referee, Harold Demsetz, Ken Lehn, and Ron Smith for their helpful comments on earlier drafts.

[1] The shareholder welfare and managerial welfare hypotheses are not mutually exclusive. Generally speaking, conflicts between shareholders and top managers can be partially resolved by the use of incentive schemes such as stock option or firm value-based pay. However, in the case of a merger, arrangements of this kind are not easy. In one guise or another, long-term contracts are a principal device for coping with opportunistic behavior since they provide the opportunity for settling up. Agents can be paid by principals ex post on the basis of performance. In the last period, however, opportunistic behavior is less constrained. This issue is raised in our study since we are concerned with opportunistic behavior among directors during what may be their last period of employment.

0148-6195/87/$03.50

under the managerial welfare hypothesis, "Target managements will base their response to a tender offer on the bid-induced changes in their own utility." (Walkling and Long (1984, p. 55)).

Unfortunately, the evidence is contradictory. On the one hand, Smiley (1976) and Kummer and Hoffmeister (1978) found that managers who perform poorly, realizing the consequences of renegotiating (and/or seeking employment elsewhere), are more likely to resist takeover attempts. Similarly, Walkling and Long (p. 62) found that "Managers with smaller personal wealth changes tend to oppose offers, while those with larger personal gains do not."[2] These findings support the managerial welfare hypothesis. In contrast, Dodd (1980) and Bradley (1980) conclude that target managements do not act to the detriment of shareholders' best interests when they reject an outstanding merger bid.

Before trying to reconcile these contradictory studies, we need to discuss both Dodd's and Bradley's research. They examine the impact of managerial resistance on shareholder wealth, and ask whether managerial resistance is in the best interests of shareholders. Walkling and Long (and others), on the other hand, examine the endogeneity of managerial decisions. They ask whether managerial decisions are tied more closely to managerial utility than to shareholder wealth. From this perspective, these two types of studies are complementary. The present paper examines whether Dodd and Bradley's conclusion holds when the realized changes in shareholder wealth are compared with the realizable shareholders wealth changes.

B. A Brief Review of the Studies by Dodd and Bradley

Dodd (1980) proposed that rejected merger proposals can be used to test whether or not managerial resistance is in the best interests of shareholders. He claimed (p. 125) that managerial resistance can be viewed as maximizing shareholder wealth if cancelled merger proposals—vetoed by management—attract a more favorable market response than cancelled merger proposals that were not vetoed by management.[3] Dodd stated (p. 137):

> ...when the sample of cancelled merger proposals is classified on the basis of whether or not the target firm's management terminate the negotiations, the market reaction is different. Where the merger proposal is vetoed by incumbent management, target stockholders earn, on average, 10.95% over the duration of the proposal and this represents a permanent revaluation of the targeted shares. In the remaining cancelled proposals it is not clear from the termination announcement that the incumbent managements have used their veto power—either bidder firm managements retract their offers or no reason for the terminations are given. Stockholders of target firms in these cases earn only 0.18% over the duration of the proposal...

Bradley argued that managerial resistance is consistent with maximization of shareholders' wealth if the shareholders' gain in wealth associated with rejection of tender offers is greater than the premium offered by the bidding firm. In his examination, Bradley (1980) found:

> In a sample of 97 unsuccessful tender offers, target stockholders realized an average capital gain

---

[2] Nevertheless, note that the contradictory evidence we observed may be caused by the differences in methodology in the previous studies.

[3] Putting aside the issues of the inclusion of inappropriate merger proposals and heterogeneity in vetoed vs. non-vetoed merger proposals, Dodd's test is akin to our intergroup comparison. His results show that shareholder wealth gain associated with the non-vetoed merger proposals exceeds its counterpart associated with the vetoed merger proposals. Accordingly, his results indicate that managerial opposition harms shareholders.

of 45%. This average post-offer return exceeds the average premium of these rejected offers, which is 29%. (In other words, stockholders were 16% better off in these rejected cases.)

He concluded:

> This finding lends support to an implication of the theory that target managers may be acting in their stockholders' interests by opposing an outstanding offer.

There are two problems in Dodd's comparison of cancelled merger proposals according to whether they are vetoed by the target firm's management. First, his treatment of non-vetoed cancelled merger proposals is improper for several reasons. On the one hand, non-vetoed cancelled merger proposals should be grouped with vetoed cancelled merger proposals if they are caused by managerial resistance in the targeted firm. (Under such circumstances, the targeted management resist both vetoed and non-vetoed cancelled merger proposals.) On the other hand, non-vetoed cancelled merger proposals should be excluded from his sample if they are terminated by the raiding firm or enjoined from completion by the court, because the targeted management does not cause the termination. But more importantly, the observed positive CAR (Cumulative Average Residuals) of vetoed merger proposals indicates only that shareholders gain from such proposals. The sign of the CAR cannot tell us whether top managers are maximizing shareholder wealth unless we also know the magnitude of the would-be wealth gain, had the vetoed proposals been accepted.

These two criticisms do not apply to Bradley's study. To judge whether or not managerial resistance is in the interest of shareholders, Bradley compared the average market returns of the rejected tender offers with the average premium offered by the raiding firm. Nevertheless, the Bradley's sample is a source of concern. First, offers withdrawn because of target management opposition are omitted from his data (Bradley (1980, p. 349)). Second, since shareholders make the final decision to accept or reject tender offers, Bradley's results may be attributed to the shareholders' decision (Dodd (1980, p. 106, fn 5)).

C. Scope and Structure of this Study

To correct these limitations, our research has the following three features. First, we follow Dodd and use merger proposals instead of interfirm tender offers, because targeted managers can more directly exert their discretion there. Second, we classify merger proposals on the basis of managerial decisions (acceptance or rejection) after removing cases which were terminated by the raiding firm or enjoined from completion by the court.[4] Finally, we compare the average actual wealth gain associated with the rejected merger proposals with the would-be average wealth gain (as Bradley did) to see whether the realizable wealth gain would be greater, had the rejected merger proposals been accepted.

Thus, the current study examines whether a refined test provides evidence inconsistent with the postulate of shareholder wealth maximization. Given the assumption of maximization of shareholders' wealth, Section II derives testable implications from two perspectives. We compare the average actual wealth change of accepted merger proposals with that of rejected merger proposals. For rejected merger proposals, we compare the actual wealth change under

---

[4] There are only two cases in this category. In one case, the raiding firm (TWR) withdrew its merger proposal after the proposal had been approved by directors and shareholders in the target (General Battery). In the other, Amax and Copper Range were enjoined from completion by the court.

managerial resistance with the would-be wealth change that would have occurred in the absence of managerial resistance. Section III discusses the collection and classification of data, describes event days, and provides empirical evidence. Section IV contains the conclusion.

II. Testable Implications

There are two reasons why managers may be acting in the interest of shareholders when they reject merger proposals. First, in the absence of new merger bids, the targeted management should reject a merger proposal if rejection will increase its stock price by more than the premium offered by the raiding firm. Second, they may reject a merger proposal in order to strike a better deal.[5]

Accordingly, managerial resistance is consistent with the postulate of shareholder wealth maximization if the rejected cases fare as well as, or better than, accepted cases; or, alternatively, if the actual wealth gain of the rejected cases is greater than its matching would-be wealth gain, had the rejected cases been accepted.[6]

A. The One-Factor Market Model

Our "event" model follows Dodd's application of Fama, Fisher, Jensen, and Roll (1969) (FFJR).

This methodology uses an equation to determine the equilibrium return, and attributes deviation from this equilibrium return to some specific event. The FFJR model posits that the underlying return is generated as

$$Y_{jt} = \alpha_j + \beta_j Y_{mt} + \epsilon_{jt},$$

where

Y_{jt} = continuous rate of return for firm j over day t,

Y_{mt} = continuous rate of return on a value weighted market portfolio over day t,

α_j = $E(Y_{jt}) - \beta_j E(Y_{mt})$,

β_j = cov(Y_{jt}, Y_{mt})/var(Y_{mt}), and

ϵ_{jt} = residual return of firm j over day t reflecting firm-specific or industry-specific events or random price fluctuation; by assumption, $E(\epsilon_{jt}) = 0$, var(ϵ_{jt}) = σ_ϵ^2, and cov(ϵ_{jt}, Y_{mt}) = 0.

---

[5] Managerial resistance takes various forms including (1) the sale of valuable assets or a subsidiary, (2) a "lock-up"—in a lockup, the target agrees to sell either stock or an attractive part of the company to an acquirer of its choice, and (3) by adopting supplement stock plans (Source: *Newsweek*, May 11, 1981). In the present study, managerial resistance is defined operationally to occur where the board of directors of the targeted company rejects the merger proposal at the time of the first bid. Moreover, it is hypothesized that a shareholder-wealth-maximizing resistance can be carried out in two ways. The targeted management can induce the original bidder to agree to more favorable terms by successful negotiation with the bidder. Alternatively, the targeted management can send out the valuable information that the target is worth more than it currently quoted in the corporate control market to other potential, more generous, bidders. A referee noted that David P. Baron (1983, p. 322) discussed optimal resistance strategy for a target whose management has a preference for control and hence has interests that diverge from those of target shareholders.

[6] Theoretically, there is a third possibility. We can compare the would-be wealth change, had the accepted cases been rejected, with the actual wealth change associated with such accepted cases. However, I have failed to figure out way(s) to measure the would-be wealth changes. Hence, I will limit my comparisons to the two tests stated in the text.

Magnitude of Shareholders' Wealth Gains **255**

The measure of abnormal performance for N securities over E event period days is the cumulative average excess returns, CAR_{NE}, which can be calculated as

$$CAR_{NE} = \frac{1}{N} \sum_{\tau=\tau 1}^{\tau 2} \sum_{j=1}^{N} R_{j\tau},$$

where

$R_{j\tau} = Y_{j\tau} - (\alpha_j + \beta_j Y_{m\tau})$, excess return,

$E = \tau 2 - \tau 1 + 1$, number of trading days.

List of Variables.

n: number of interested merger proposals;

n_A: number of merger proposals accepted at first bid;

n_R: number of merger proposals rejected at first bid;

n_R^s: number of target firms which reject the first bid and accept a later bid within the next 12 months;[7]

n_R^s: number of target firms which reject the first bid and do not accept a successive bid in the next 12 months;

p^f: bidding price contained in the first merger proposal;

p^l: bidding price contained in the last accepted revised or new merger offer;

p^o: base price, the arithmetic mean of stock prices before the arrival of the original merger proposal.

B. Test I, Relative Market Performance: An Intergroup Comparison of Rejected and Accepted Merger Proposals

The cumulative average excess returns of the rejected group is

$$CAR_{n_R E} = \frac{1}{n_R} \sum_{\tau=\tau 1}^{\tau 2} \sum_{\substack{j=1 \\ j \in R}}^{n_R} R_{j\tau}.$$

The cumulative average excess returns of the accepted group is

$$CAR_{n_A E} = \frac{1}{n_A} \sum_{\tau=\tau 1}^{\tau 2} \sum_{\substack{j=1 \\ j \in A}}^{n_A} R_{j\tau}.$$

The null hypothesis is that the CAR of the rejected group is no less than the CAR of the accepted group. The alternative hypothesis drawn from the managerial utility maximization can be stated as follows: the CAR of the accepted group is greater than the CAR of the rejected group.

---

[7] Asquith (1980) arbitrarily chose one calendar year as the critical period to make such judgment.

C. Test II, Actual Wealth Change versus Would-be Wealth Change: An Intragroup Comparison in the Rejected Group

The would-be average excess return without managerial resistance is

$$AR_w(R) = \frac{1}{n_R} \sum_{j \in R} \frac{p_j f - p_j o}{p_j o} \ .$$

The actual average excess return with managerial resistance is

$$AR_a(R) = \frac{1}{n_R} \left[\sum_{j \in R^s} \frac{p_j l - p_j o}{p_j o} + \sum_{j \in R^s} \sum_{\tau = \tau 1}^{\tau 2} R_{j\tau} \right] \ .$$

The null hypothesis is that the actual average excess return is no less than the would-be average excess return. The alternative hypothesis drawn from the managerial utility maximization is: the average would-be excess return is greater than the average actual excess return.

III. Empirical Analysis

A. Collection and Classification of the Merger Proposals

The *Wall Street Journal Index*, the source of the merger data, is composed of two parts— *General News Index* and *Corporate News Index*. The sample of merger proposals include all those appearing under the heading *Mergers and Acquisitions* in the *General News Index*, in which the date of announcement falls within the period starting January 1, 1971, and ending December 31, 1980. Seven screening rules exclude irrelevant cases or cases with inadequate data. [8]

After these screens, 303 cases remained. Applying the screening rules once again to *Corporate News Index* and/or microfilms of the *Wall Street Journal*, a preliminary sample 60 cases was obtained. [9] (See Appendix A for a breakdown of the unusable cases.) After

----

[8] Specifically, we exclude: i) cases in which the means of acquisition is a tender offer; ii) cases in which the merging units are non-business concerns, e.g., unions; iii) cases in which the merging firms are privately held firms, or those which include a privately held or foreign-owned targeted firm; iv) cases in which the merging firms form a new corporation by eliminating both existing firms; v) cases in which the merging firms belonging to the following three regulated industries—(a) airlines, (b) railroads, and (c) financial institutions; vi) cases in which the target is the raiding firm's own subsidiary; vii) cases in which the merger proposal was withdrawn by the bidding firm or was enjoined from completion by the court. (See Appendix A.)

[9] Although I follow the criteria and procedure adopted in Dodd and Asquith, additional criteria are inevitable since additional information is needed concerning managerial decisions toward merger bids, outcomes of managerial resistance, and would-be wealth changes.

Asquith (1980) applied screens to decide which merger proposals are to be included. He has written, "first, the target firm must be independent of the bidding firm, i.e., merger bids for partially owned subsidiaries were not included; second, the target firm must be listed on the NYSE for the seven preceding years; and third, the merger must not have to undergo a lengthy approval process by a regulatory agency." (pp. 6–7) His first and third criteria are observed. Instead of requiring that the targeted firm be listed on the NYSE, the targeted firm must not be privately held. In the later estimation, I follow the common practice to require that the targeted firm be listed on the CRSP (Center for Research in Security Prices) tape.

Although I follow Dodd, footnote 5, by not including "defensive merger" where a targeted firm finds a merger partner in response to a tender offer by a third firm, my sample differs from his in three aspects. First, my sample includes merger proposals that were preceded by a tender offer, since we see in some cases that the targeted management can successfully resist a merger proposal of this nature (for instance, Marcor (1976) and Amax (1978)). Second, I arbitrarily choose not to include a consolidation where two or more firms combine via the merger to form a new firm because of the difficulty of ascertaining who is taking over whom. Third, my sample does not include cases in which the merger proposal is withdrawn by the bidding firm or is enjoined by a court. See Appendix A.

elimination of cases in which stock prices and/or event days are not available, the final sample contained 16 accepted cases and 14 rejected cases. Four out of the 14 rejected cases were defined to be "retargeted" since they received either a bid revision or a new offer. Among these four retargeted cases, managerial resistance generated improved bids in three cases. (See Appendix B for a classification of the merger proposals.)

B. Event Dates

Among accepted merger proposals, there are at least two event days—the date of announcement and the date of shareholders' approval. There are also two event days for the rejected merger proposals: the date of announcement and the date of termination. All event dates are the dates reported in the *Wall Street Journal*.

The date of announcement is the date that a merger proposal (or a letter of intent) has been made to the target. [10] Unfortunately, for some cases, the date of shareholders' approval cannot be located. As a starting point, we checked whether or not these mergers have been completed. If completed, shareholders' approval must have been obtained. Consequently, the prearranged date for shareholders' voting is the date of "shareholders' approval." For other

Table 1. Cumulative Residuals for Accepted Merger Proposals ($N = 16$)

Target	Period of Duration of Merger Proposal	Cumulative Residuals	Year of Proposal
Parke, Davis & Co.	81	0.59259	1970
Pyle–National Co.	80	0.314935	1970
Granite City Steel Co.	92	0.246008	1971
Standard Kollsman Industries Inc.	139	0.03914	1972
Southwestern Investment Co.	158	0.790988	1972
Kelsey–Hayes Co.	45	0.319304	1973
Utah International Inc.	267	0.324952	1975
Reed Tool Co.	30	0.200262	1975
Airpax Electronics Inc.	89	0.456145	1976
Otis Elevator Co.	80	0.146313	1976
Copper Range Co.	142	0.149375	1976
Kewanee Industries Inc.	76	0.04463	1977
Lykes Corp.	285	1.64889	1977
Hycel Inc.	127	0.283017	1978
Skil Corp.	42	0.658329	1979
C.I.T. Financial Corp.	126	0.012579	1979

Summary statistics: Mean = 0.389216
Standard deviation = 0.403993
Median = 0.298976
Minimum value = 0.012579
Maximum value = 1.64889

[10] Alternatively, the date of announcement is the date that a tentative agreement has been reached by the involved parties resulting from the merger discussions. Agreement of this sort is evidenced by the use of modifiers such as "agreed in principle," "reached an agreement (in principle)," "agreed to acquire," "agreed to its acquisition by," or "set an accord."

cases, the date of board approval, the date of completed agreement, or the date that the acquiring firm indicates that it has enough votes.

C. An Intergroup Comparison of Rejected and Accepted Cases

Estimation of excess returns in the FFJR model is a two-step procedure. First, return data from 260 days through 11 days prior to announcement of the merger proposal are used to estimate α_j, β_j. Then, cumulative excess returns are computed for each accepted or rejected case over the duration of the merger proposal. Following Dodd, the duration of a merger proposal is defined as 10 days before the announcement, through 10 days after approval by target shareholders or termination of the last merger bids (proposal or tender offer). If the targeted share was delisted from the CRSP tape within 10 days after approval by target shareholders or since termination of the last proposal, then the delisting date is the ending date. Tables 1 and 2, respectively, show excess returns for accepted and rejected merger proposals. In these tables, note that the sample mean of the CAR for the accepted group, 0.3892, is greater than its counterpart for the rejected group, 0.1134. The median, which is less susceptible to extreme values, shows a similar pattern. Every targeted firm in the accepted group had a positive wealth gain. For the rejected group, the mean wealth gain is 11.3%, but some firms suffer a substantial wealth loss. In addition, the largest wealth gainer is in the accepted group. Thus, the accepted group apparently attracted a more favorable market reaction than did the rejected group. The probability that this difference occurred by chance is smaller than 0.05. ($t = 1.98$).[11]

These results should be interpreted with caution. The observed differences can be attributed

---

[11] For computational convenience, we instead test against $\text{CAR}_{n_R} = \text{CAR}_{n_A}$. Given that $\text{CAR}_{N_A E} > \text{CAR}_{N_R E}$, the rejection of $\text{CAR}_{n_R} = \text{CAR}_{n_A}$ guarantees the rejection of $\text{CAR}_{n_R} > \text{CAR}_{n_A}$. The test statistic, t

$$= \frac{\text{CAR}_{N_A E} - \text{CAR}_{N_R E}}{\sqrt{\dfrac{\sum\limits_{i=1, i \in A}^{N_A} (\text{CR}_{iE} - \text{CAR}_{N_A E})^2 + \sum\limits_{j=1, j \in R}^{N_R} (\text{CR}_{jE} - \text{CAR}_{N_R E})^2}{N_A + N_R - 2}} \sqrt{\dfrac{1}{N_A} + \dfrac{1}{N_R}}}$$

$$= 1.98$$

where

CR_{iE} : cumulative excess returns for security i, i belongs to the accepted group, over the duration, E, of the merger proposal,

CR_{jE} : cumulative excess returns for security j, j belongs to the rejected group, over the duration, E, of the merger proposal,

$\text{CAR}_{N_A E}$: cumlative average excess returns for the accepted group,

$\text{CAR}_{N_R E}$: cumulative average excess returns for the rejected group,

E : the period of duration of the merger proposal,

N_A : number of the accepted cases; $N_A = 16$,

N_R : number of the rejected cases; $N_R = 14$,

$d.f.$: degree of freedom, $N_A + N_R - 2$, $\Pr(t > 1.701) = 0.05$.

Magnitude of Shareholders' Wealth Gains   **259**

Table 2. Cumulative Residuals for Rejected Merger Proposals ($N = 14$)

Target	Period of Duration of Merger Proposal	Cumulative Residuals	Year of Merger Proposal	Final Outcome of Follow-Up Offer
* Kayser-Roth Corp.	30	0.105197	1971	n.a.
** CNA Financial Corp.	315	-0.01335	1973	accepted, tender offer
* Occidental Petroleum Corp.	63	-0.054383	1974	n.a.
* Staley (A.E.) Co.	23	-0.029957	1975	n.a.
Falcon Seaboard Inc.	65	0.15150	1975	n.a.
Anaconda Co.	250	0.743493	1976	accepted, m.p.
* Shenandoah Oil Corp.	127	-0.49006	1976	n.a.
** Marcor Inc.	88	0.149005	1976	accepted, revised m.p. from the original bidder
* Ex-Cell-O Corp.	51	0.020057	1976	n.a.
* Koehring Co.	49	-0.17531	1977	n.a.
** Tropicana Products Inc.	270	0.588014	1977	accepted, m.p.
* Marshall Field & Co.	23	0.414131	1977	n.a.
* Amax Inc.	21	0.216495	1978	n.a.
* McGraw-Hill Inc.	23	0.265173	1979	n.a.

* Did not receive a new bid in one year.
** Received a new bid in one year.
Summary statistics:
Mean = 0.113357
Standard deviation = 0.320922
Median = 0.062627
Minimum value = -0.49006
Maximum value = 0.743493

to the decisions of board members if the average quality (wealth-enhancing ability) of merger proposals is identical across groups, see Asquith (1980, p. 34).

To get around this quality issue, we limit ourselves to the rejected merger proposals when we try to gauge the wealth consequences of various managerial decisions.

D. An Intragroup Comparison within the Rejected Group

The would-be change in wealth is defined as the percentage change of return per targeted share, had the merger proposal been accepted. Two pieces of information are needed for its computation: the market value per targeted share embedded in the merger proposal. and some base price index (after adjusting for stock splits and stock dividends of the targeted share) upon which the wealth gain can be computed.

We use one of four mutually exclusive methods to estimate the realizable market value of the targeted share, depending on how the merger proposal is financed.

1. In a cash offer, the offer price is the realizable market value per targeted share, had the rejected offer been accepted;
2. If the target shareholders have a cash option, the price per share stated in that option is the realizable market value per targeted share, had the rejected offer been accepted;
3. If the proposed offer is financed through exchange of securities, the computation of the market value is in two steps. First, the value of the common stock of the acquiring firm is approximated by its average closing price. The general rule is to use the arithmetic mean of closing prices over the period starting from the date of the announcement (included) up to 10 days after the merger proposal. [12] Then the estimated value of the acquiring firm's share is multiplied by the proposed exchange ratio to approximate the market value per targeted share;
4. In some cases, common stocks and/or preferred stocks yet to be issued are involved in the proposed transaction. If this happens, the estimate reported in the *Wall Street Journal* is used. Market values are summarized in column 2, Table 3.

Base prices are summarized in column 3, Table 3. "Base price" is the arithmetic mean of stock prices within the period starting m.p.-70, and ending m.p.-11, where m.p. is the date of announcement of a merger proposal.

In percentage points, the would-be wealth change per targeted share is the difference between the value per targeted share embedded in the merger proposal and, the base price per targeted share divided by the base price as shown in column 2, Table 4.

When managerial resistance did not generate improved merger bids, the actual wealth changes are computed with reference to the CRSP tape over the period of duration of the merger proposals. However, to be consistent with the period used to estimate base price, a 60-day period (m.p.-70~m.p.-11) is used instead of the original 250-day period (m.p.-260 ~m.p.-11) to reestimate α_j, β_j. [13] Therefore, the excess returns reported in Table 4 are slightly different from those appearing in Table 2.

---

[12] In some cases, the interval between the date of announcement and date of termination is shorter than 10 days. In such cases, the arithmetic mean is computed over the period starting from the date of announcement up to one day earlier than termination.

[13] I have also used 30 trading days to estimate the base prices; however, the estimates are not reported here because they are similar. There were no stock splits or stock dividends for our targeted firms that occurred during the 60-day estimation period. Hence, no adjustments are necessary.

Magnitude of Shareholders' Wealth Gains **261**

Table 3. Base Price and Realizable Market Value per Targeted Share ($N = 13$)

Target	Base Price	Realizable Market Value (Computation Method in Parentheses)
Kayser–Roth Corp.	21.40	33.87 (exchange offer)
Occidental Petroleum Corp.	9.04	17 (cash offer)
Staley (A.E.) Co.	36.50	50.06 (exchange offer)
Falcon Seaboard Inc.	28.81	53.33 (exchange offer)
Anaconda Co.	16.81	23.15 (*WSJ* estimate)
Shenandoah Oil Corp.	21.97	29.57 (exchange offer)
Marcor Inc.	29.35	54 (*WSJ* estimate)
Ex-Cell-O Corp.	21.22	30 (cash option)
Koehring Co.	15.69	20.15 (exchange offer)
Tropicana Products Inc.	27.49	38.12 (exchange offer)
Marshall Field & Co.	19.95	36 (cash option)
Amax Inc.	36.23	57 (cash offer)
McGraw-Hill Inc.	23.03	34 (cash offer)

Sources: Standard and Poor's Daily Stock Price Record, 1969–1981, Wall Street Journal Index, 1969–1981, and Wall Street Journal, 1969–1981.

Table 4. Would-be and Actual Excess Returns per Targeted Share ($N = 13$)

Target	Would-be Excess Returns	Actual Excess Returns
Kayser–Roth Corp.	0.582609	0.072827
Occidental Petroleum Corp.	0.880531	−0.22074
Staley (A.E.) Co.	0.371452[a]	0.075732
Falcon Seaboard Inc.	0.851356	0.076653
Anaconda Co.	0.377156	0.852945[b,c]
Shenandoah Oil Corp.	0.346033	−0.64069
Marcor Inc.	0.201404	0.332561[b]
Ex-Cell-O Corp.	0.414094	0.104884
Koehring Co.	0.284257	−0.33880
Tropicana Products Inc.	0.386650	0.891597[b]
Marshall Field & Co.	0.804150	0.369150
Amax Inc.	0.573325	0.180226
McGraw-Hill Inc.	0.476271	0.269986
Summary Statistics:		
Mean	0.503791	0.155872
Standard deviation	0.220717	0.424339
Median	0.414094	0.104884
Minimum value	0.201414	−0.64069
Maximum value	0.880531	0.891597

[a] In *Standard and Poor's Daily Price Record*, information concerning stock dividends or stock splits is also reported. Since the offer price is referred to the post-split Staley stock, the average price of its common stock on "when-issued" basis, between the split and one day earlier than the proposal, is used as the approximate of the base price.

[b] These estimates are based on terms embedded in the new or revised merger proposal. If CAR's are instead used, the estimate would be 0.305218 (Anaconda), 0.2571576 (Marcor), and 0.765407 (Tropicana), respectively.

[c] Adjusted for an Arco's two for one stock split.

Where managerial resistance generated an improved bid, the actual wealth change is the value per targeted share embedded in the new or revised offer minus the base price, divided by the base price (column 3, Table 4).

The sample mean of the would-be excess returns, 0.5038, is greater than its counterpart for the actual excess returns, 0.1559. The median shows a similar pattern, 0.4141 versus 0.1049. Furthermore, actual excess returns for three cases turn out to be negative. Also, despite the wealth gains shown in Table 4, the three improved bids—Anaconda, Marcor, and Tropicana—fail to change this conclusion.[14] Overall, the average would-be excess return is about 3.23 times as great as the average actual excess return.

The comparisons suggest that shareholders would realize a larger wealth gain had the rejected merger proposals been accepted. The results suggest that top managers are engaged in wealth-reducing resistance. The question is, what is the probability that these results arise by chance?

Again, we test against the null hypothesis that there is no difference in the average actual wealth gain and the average would-be wealth gain within the rejected group. With a t value of 2.52, the null hypothesis can be rejected at 0.05 significance level.[15]

E. A Note on the Intragroup Comparison

In the within-group comparison, we may overestimate the would-be excess returns for cases in which the proposed merger is financed by an exchange of securities. For instance, the price per share of the acquiring firm may decline if the actual synergistic gain turns out to be smaller than that claimed by the raiding firm. If so, the realizable market value of the targeted share will be overestimated, since the higher closing price on the date of announcement (rather than the price of the raiding firm, on the later date of settlement), is used in the estimation.

To investigate this potential problem, we examined the differences between the average

---

[14] Only four out of the 14 rejected cases have accepted a new or revised offer. Of these four cases, 'Marcor received an improved bid from the original bidder, Mobil.' Moreover, at least one case (in which CNA is the target) can be classified as "unsuccessful resistance" since the observed CR (cumulative residuals) is −0.01. Therefore, unless the associated would-be change is lower than 0.34, including this case would increase the original means difference, which is 0.35. Incidentally, this is the case that will be excluded in the significance test because the stock of the Canadian subsidiary of the raiding firm, Gulf Oil, is involved in the proposed transaction.

[15] The test statistic, t

$$= \frac{AR_w - AR_a}{\sqrt{\dfrac{\sum\limits_{i=1, i \in R}^{N_R} (R_{wi} - AR_w)^2 + \sum\limits_{i=1, i \in R}^{N_R} (R_{ai} - AR_a)^2}{2(N_R - 1)}} \; \sqrt{\dfrac{2}{N_R}}}$$

$$= 2.52$$

where

AR_w : average would-be excess return,

AR_a : average actual excess return,

$d.f.$: degree of freedom, in our sample, $d.f. = 24$, $Pr(t > 1.711) = 0.05$.

would-be and average actual excess returns by using only cash merger proposals and merger proposals which contained a cash option. The sample consists of five firms: 1) Occidental Oil, 2) Ex-Cell-O, 3) Marshall Field, 4) Amax, and 5) McGraw-Hill.

The average would-be excess return is 62.79%, while the average actual excess return is 14.07%. Moreover, the null hypothesis that there are no differences between the average would-be and actual excess returns can be rejected, with a *t* statistic of 3.2 (significant at the 1% level).

F. Interpretation of the Empirical Results

Here we compare the value of the proposal versus the value of the target stock immediately after the proposal is rejected. This comparison could be misleading in two ways. First, other (independent) bad news could be released just after the proposal is rejected. In this case management could have rationally expected the ex post price to be above the price we observe. If their expectation was above the offer value, the managers were actually acting in the stockholders' best interest. The size of the price differences involved makes this explanation unlikely. Alternatively, the managers may believe that the firm is undervalued. Again, the size of the premiums makes this unlikely. Moreover, if the market is rational, this argument cannot be repeatedly correct or the stock prices will be revised upward (above the offer value) when a proposal is rejected.

Given conventional event methodology, our results from both intragroup and intergroup test are inconsistent with the hypothesis of shareholder wealth maximization. While our procedures are similar to those of previous studies, the possibility of an improper selection of the beginning event date or an unrepresentative sample still remains.

In addition, there are limitations on the extent to which these results should be generalized to the overall performance of the market for corporate control and the contractual efficiency arising from the principal–agent relationship.

Concerning the effectiveness of the market for corporate control, we cannot rule out the possibility that the best way to avoid a hostile merger bid is to run a firm efficiently. If the real discipline that the market for corporate control imposes on top managers is the potential takeover threat, the observed sample—be it in the form of merger talks, proxy fights or formal merger bids—can never substantiate the existence of such forces.

The current study also ignores the global efficiency of employment contracts. In a world where many contingencies are possible, not all contingencies will be dealt with optimally. Consequently, locally-observed inefficient non-shareholder wealth maximizing behavior such as opportunistic anti-takeover behavior does not necessarily imply that separation of ownership and control results in organizational inefficiency. As long as productivity gains arising from the principal–agent relationship dominate the agency costs thereby created, both shareholders and managers may benefit.

IV. Conclusion

This study examines the relationship between shareholder wealth gains and managerial strategies in merger proposals. Given some limitations of previous studies, we conducted an intergroup and an intragroup comparison to test whether the hypothesis of shareholder wealth maximization survives the refined experiment.

The findings indicate that the average wealth gain of the accepted group (38.92%) exceeds the average wealth gain of the rejected group (11.34%). Second, within the rejected group, the average would-be wealth gain (50.38%) is about 3.23 times as large as the average actual wealth gain (15.59%). The test indicates that the probability of a chance inconsistency in either the intergroup or the intragroup comparison is less than 0.05.

Our findings are in line with Walkling and Long's. We conclude therefore that managerial resistance may not be in the best interests of shareholders.

Appendix A: Composition of 243 Unusable Cases

Rejecting Reasons	Number of Cases	Supplementary Remarks
Tender offer	52	
Consolidation	16	
Firms in highly regulated industries	21	Railroad
	27	Airline
	8	Financial Institutions[a]
Mergers/acquisitions prior to 1970	20	
Legal issues	3	Lawsuit
	12	Divesture
	6	Legal ruling, or regulatory agency's approval
	8	Antitrust
Acquisitions	3	Acquiring offices
	7	Buying assets
	9	Buying units, fields, and subsidiaries of other concerns
	1	Joint operation
Targeted firms are acquiring firms' own subsidiaries[b]	4	(Name of the target; % of shares owned by the bidding firm)
		Sharon Steel Corp. (86%) (1974)
		Northeastern Insurance (60.9%) (1977)
		Hawkeye-Security Insurance (80.5%) (1978)
		New Jersey Life Co.[c] (1978)
Targeted firms are foreign owned	2	(Name of the target) Granby Mining Co. (1972) Granisle (1972)
Merger talks[d]	5	
Change in stock holdings; proxy fights	8	
Termination of the merger proposal has nothing to do with the attitude of management	2	(Name of the target) General Battery Corp.[e] (1971) Copper Range[f] (1974)
Miscellaneous	19	Licensing, debenture, editorial comment, etc.

Sources: Wall Street Journal Index, 1969–1981.

Magnitude of Shareholders' Wealth Gains **265**

ᵃ This sample, however, does include insurance companies.

ᵇ The target is regarded as the raiding firm's subsidiary if it is so reported in the *Wall Street Journal*. They are not included in my sample since managerial discretion under such circumstances is substantially impaired, if not totally lost.

ᶜ In this case, the acquiring firm New Jersey Life is a newly formed company owned by Paul R. Cory, President of New Jersey Life. (*WSJ*, 78/12/4-31:3)

ᵈ The term "merger talks" refers to cases in which the involved parties began to explore the possibility of a business combination. These cases are excluded because the attitude of the targeted management is nebulous at this stage. Besides, the terms of the merger in most cases were not revealed in the wake of "merger talks" which make the estimation of the would-be change in wealth impossible.

ᵉ In this case, the merger proposal is unilaterally withdrawn by the acquiring firm, TRW Inc., after it has already been approved by both directors and shareholders of General Battery Corp. (*WSJ*, 71/7/1-24:4) According to newspaper clippings I kept on file, General Battery Corp. told TRW Inc. to complete the merger now, and oppose FTC or else the plan would be off. (*Wall Street Journal*, June 30, 1971) We can, therefore, infer that TRW withdrew its merger bid for fear of pending FTC action.

ᶠ In this case, the merger proposal which was agreed upon by both firms is enjoined from completion by the court.

Appendix B: Classification of the Merger Proposals

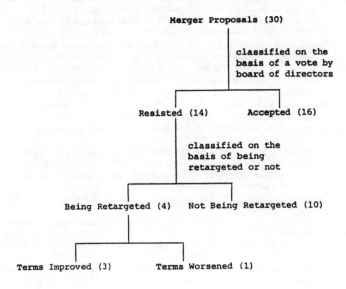

References

Asquith, P. May 1980. A two-event study of merger bids, market uncertainty, and stockholder returns. Unpublished draft.

Baron, D. P. May 1983. Tender offers and management resistance. *Journal of Finance* 38(2):331–347.

Bradley, M. Oct. 1980. Interfirm tender offers and the market for corporate control. *Journal of Business* 54(4):345–376.

Copeland, T. E., and Weston, J. F. 1979. *Financial Theory and Corporate Policy*. Massachusetts: Addison-Wesley.

Dodd, P. June 1980. Merger proposals, management discretion and stockholder wealth. *Journal of Financial Economics* 8(2):105–137.

Dodd, P., and Ruback, R. Dec. 1977. Tender offers and stockholder returns: An empirical analysis. *Journal of Financial Economics* 5(3):351–373.

266   Gili Yen

Easterbrook, F. H., and Fischel, D. R. April 1981. The proper role of a target's management in responding to a tender offer. *Harvard Law Review* 94(6):1161–1204.

Eckbo, B. E. Jan. 1981. Assessing the anticompetitive significance of large mergers. Unpublished draft.

Ellert, J. C. May 1976. Mergers, antitrust law enforcement, and stockholder returns. *Journal of Finance* 31(2):715–732.

Fama, E. F. 1976. *Foundations of Finance*. New York: Basic Books.

Fama, E. F. April 1980. Agency problems and the theory of the firm. *Journal of Political Economy* 88(2):288–307.

Fama, E. F., Fisher, L., Jensen, M., and Roll, R. Feb. 1969. The adjustment of stock prices to new information. *International Economic Review* 10(1):1–21.

Firth, M. A. March 1980. Takeovers, shareholder returns, and the theory of the firm. *Quarterly Journal of Economics* 94(2):235–260.

Franks, J. R., Broyles, J. E., and Hecht, M. J. Dec. 1977. An industry study of the profitability of mergers in the United Kingdom. *Journal of Finance* 32(5):1513–1525.

Furubotn, E., and Pejovich, S. Dec. 1972. Property rights and economic theory: A survey of recent literature. *Journal of Economic Literature* 10(4):1137–1162.

Haugen, R. A., and Udell, J. G. Jan. 1972. Rates of return to stockholders of acquired companies. *Journal of Financial and Quantitative Analysis* 7(1):1387–1398.

Hindley, B. Nov. 1969. Capitalism and the corporation. *Economica* 36(144):426–438.

Jarrell, G. A., and Bradley, M. Oct. 1980. The economic effects of federal and state regulations of cash tender offers. *Journal of Law and Economics* 23(2):371–408.

Jensen, M., and Meckling, W. Oct. 1976. Theory of the firm: Managerial behavior, agency costs, and ownership structure. *Journal of Financial Economics* 3(4):305–360.

Kummer, D. R., and Hoffmeister, J. R. May 1978. Valuation consequences of cash tender offers. *Journal of Finance* 33(2):505–516.

Langetieg, T. C. Dec. 1978. An application of the three-factor performance index to measure stockholder gains from merger. *Journal of Financial Economics* 6(4):365–383.

Levy, H., and Sarnat, M. Oct. 1977. A pedagogic note on alternative formulations of the goal of the firm. *Journal of Business* 50(4):526–528.

Mandelker, G. Dec. 1974. Risk and return: The case of merging firms. *Journal of Political Economy* 1(4):303–335.

Manne, H. G. April 1965. Mergers and the market for corporate control. *Journal of Financial Economics* 73(2):110–120.

Smiley, R. Feb. 1976. Tender offers, transaction costs and the theory of the firm. *Review of Economics and Statistics* 58(1):22–32.

Standard and Poor's Daily Stock Price Record. 1969–1981. New York: Standard and Poor's.

Stevens, D. L. March 1973. Financial characteristics of merged firms: A multivariate analysis. *Journal of Financial and Quantitative Analysis* 8(2):149–165.

Walkling, R. A., and Long, M. S. Spring 1984. Agency theory, managerial welfare, and takeover bid resistance. *The Rand Journal of Economics* 15(1):54–68.

Wall Street Journal. 1969–1981. Princeton, New Jersey: Dow Jones Books.

Wall Street Journal Index. 1969–1981. Princeton, New Jersey: Dow Jones Books.

Williamson, O. E. 1964. *The Economics of Discretionary Behavior: Management Objectives in a Theory of the Firm*. Englewood Cliffs, New Jersey: Prentice-Hall.

Yen, G. L. May 1983. Managerial descretion, antitakeover activities and shareholder wealth. Unpublished Ph.D. Dissertation.

[16]

THE JOURNAL OF FINANCE • VOL. XLV, NO. 1 • MARCH 1990

Do Managerial Objectives Drive Bad Acquisitions?

RANDALL MORCK, ANDREI SHLEIFER, and ROBERT W. VISHNY*

ABSTRACT

In a sample of 326 US acquisitions between 1975 and 1987, three types of acquisitions have systematically lower and predominantly negative announcement period returns to bidding firms. The returns to bidding shareholders are lower when their firm diversifies, when it buys a rapidly growing target, and when its managers performed poorly before the acquisition. These results suggest that managerial objectives may drive acquisitions that reduce bidding firms' values.

THERE IS NOW CONSIDERABLE evidence that making acquisitions is a mixed blessing for shareholders of acquiring companies. Average returns to bidding shareholders from making acquisitions are at best slightly positive, and significantly negative in some studies (Bradley, Desai and Kim 1988, Roll 1986). Some have suggested that negative bidder returns are purely a consequence of stock financing of acquisitions that leads to a release of adverse information about acquiring firms (Asquith, Bruner, and Mullins 1987). In this case, negative bidder returns are not evidence of a bad investment. An alternative interpretation of poor bidder performance is that bidding firms overpay for the targets they acquire. In this paper, we present evidence that some types of bidders *systematically* overpay.

There are at least two reasons why bidding firms' managers might overpay in acquisitions, thereby truly reducing the wealth of their shareholders as opposed to just revealing bad news about their firm. According to Roll (1986), managers of bidding firms are infected by hubris, and so overpay for targets because they overestimate their own ability to run them. Another view of overpayment is that managers of bidding firms pursue personal objectives other than maximization of shareholder value. To the extent that acquisitions serve these objectives, managers of bidding firms are willing to pay more for targets than they are worth to bidding firms' shareholders.

Our view is that when a firm makes an acquisition or any other investment, its manager considers both his personal benefits from the investment and the consequences for the market value of the firm. Some investments are particularly attractive from the former perspective: they contribute to long term growth of the firm, enable the manager to diversify the risk on his human capital, or

* University of Alberta, University of Chicago, and University of Chicago, respectively. We are indebted for comments to Steve Kaplan, Wayne Marr, Wayne Mikkelson, Sam Peltzman, Rene Stulz and an anonymous referee and for financial support to the Russell Sage Foundation, the Center for the Study of the Economy and the State, the National Center for Management Research and Development, the William S. Fishman and the Dimensional Fund Advisers Faculty Research Funds at the Graduate School of Business, University of Chicago.

32   *The Journal of Finance*

improve his job security (Shleifer and Vishny, 1990). When an investment provides a manager with particularly large personal benefits, he is willing to sacrifice the market value of the firm to pursue that investment. Other things equal, the net present value of an acquisition with high private benefits should be lower than that of an acquisition with no such benefits. Put differently, managers will overpay for targets with high private benefits.

If shareholders could perfectly monitor and control the investment decisions of managers, acquisitions that reduce shareholder wealth because they deliver managerial benefits would not be allowed (or would be allowed on a small scale only when they are an efficient form of compensation (Shleifer and Vishny, 1988)). However, managers of large public corporations are typically subject to only loose scrutiny. Boards of directors give managers considerable leeway in choosing investment projects, and do not use negative stock market reactions to investment or acquisition announcements as the definitive indicator of long-run value consequences. There is some ex post settling up in that firms pursuing value-decreasing acquisitions are taken over with a higher frequency themselves (Mitchell and Lehn, 1990), but these takeovers are too expensive and infrequently used to provide the necessary deterrence. Management ownership of shares may be the most effective deterrent to investments that dissipate market value,[1] but in most large corporations top managers own only a small stake. In sum, while it is incorrect to say that managers make investment decisions without regard for market value consequences, it is also incorrect to say that existing monitoring and control devices keep managers from pursuing personal non-value-maximizing objectives. We therefore expect some observed investments to reflect pursuit of these objectives. Our methodology is designed to uncover the hypothesized negative relation between the managerial benefits of an acquisition and its consequences for the market value of the acquiring firm.

Specifically, we try to find out which acquisitions are bad investments for bidding shareholders and determine whether those acquisitions appear to provide private benefits to bidding managers. We focus on two aspects of acquisition strategies that can be readily understood in terms of managerial objectives: buying growth and diversification. We also look at the relationship between bidders' past performance and their returns from acquisitions. This relationship sheds light on the bidding managers' motives for acquiring. Before presenting the evidence, we briefly summarize the literature on managerial objectives to justify looking at relatedness, target growth and past performance of the bidder to uncover managerial objectives in making acquisitions.

Relatedness

Several models predict that managers would pursue unrelated diversification even when it hurts shareholders. First, if managers themselves are not properly diversified, they would diversify the holdings of the firm to reduce the risk to their human capital even when diversification offers few if any benefits to shareholders (Amihud and Lev 1981). Second, to assure the survival and conti-

---

[1] Lewellyn, Loderer and Rosenfeld (1985) find that returns to acquiring firms are positively correlated with the equity stake of the acquirer's top management.

Do Managerial Objectives Drive Bad Acquisitions?   33

nuity of the firm even when shareholder wealth maximization dictates shrinkage or liquidation, managers would try to enter new lines of business (Donaldson and Lorsch, 1983). Third, when poor performance of the firm threatens a manager's job, he has an incentive to enter new businesses at which he might be better (Shleifer and Vishny, 1990). In all these cases, managers might be willing to overpay for targets outside the bidding firm's industry, reducing the wealth of their shareholders.

Buying Growth

Many authors argue that managers want their firms to grow even at a cost to market value. Baumol (1959) simply assumes that growth of sales is part of the manager's utility function. Donaldson (1984) suggests that growth of the firm creates attractive promotion opportunities for its junior managers, enabling the firm to attract young managers concerned with upward mobility. By buying a growing firm, a mature firm ensures that its younger managers do not have to compete for only a few top positions. Growth of this sort can be value maximizing if it serves to attract and retain required managerial talent. It can also be wasteful if managers overpay for growing targets just to promote their proteges. Finally, pursuit of growth can be part of a strategy of ensuring long run survival of the corporation as an independent entity (Donaldson and Lorsch 1983), a goal likely to be more important to managers than to shareholders.

On these views, managers maximize growth, and not just pure size, to create attractive opportunities for the insiders and to assure the survival of the firm. Managers spend corporate resources to buy rapidly growing firms, even if such investments have a negative present value.

Past Performance of Acquirer Management

Bad managers might make bad acquisitions simply because they are bad managers. Alternatively, bad managers have more incentive to acquire to assure the survival of the firm or to find new businesses they might be good at. The prediction is that acquisitions by bad managers are particularly disastrous. In contrast, a plausible version of Roll's hubris hypothesis predicts that the worst acquisitions are made by well performing firms, since their managers are most likely to be infected by hubris.

The evidence presented below evaluates the importance of diversification, buying growth, and past bidder performance for bidder returns in acquisitions. We also evaluate and control for alternative explanations of negative bidder returns. In particular, we control for the form of payment in the acquisition since the announcement of stock financing may release information, as well as be correlated with our variables. In addition, we test a particular version of Roll's hubris hypothesis, according to which managers of bidding firms are infected by hubris and so overpay for targets because they overestimate their own ability at running them. A plausible version of this hypothesis predicts that the worst acquisitions are made by well-performing firms, since their managers are the most likely ones to be infected by hubris. Our prediction is the opposite.

Our evidence suggests that bad acquisitions are driven by managerial objectives;

34   *The Journal of Finance*

they are not just cases of information release via stock financing or of hubris of successful managers. We find that unrelated diversification and buying growth reduce the returns to making an acquisition. We also find that bad managers are also bad acquirers, consistent with the notion that poor performance drives managers to try something new. Finally, we find that the market penalizes unrelated diversification much more heavily in the 1980's than in the 1970's, coincident with the rise of hostile bust-up takeovers.

These results fit well with some recent findings of others. Lang, Stulz and Walkling (1989) find that having a low Tobin's Q, which might stand for poor quality of the bidding firm's management, reduces the bidder's return in a takeover. They also find that a low Tobin's Q of the target, which is likely to be correlated with low sales growth, is associated with a higher bidder return. The latter finding is also obtained by Servaes (1988). Lewellen, Loderer and Rosenfeld (1985) and You, Caves, Henry and Smith (1986) show that low management ownership in the bidding firm is associated with lower returns from making acquisitions. This result suggests that managers who have little incentive to maximize market value make bad acquisitions. Mitchell and Lehn (1990) find that firms making acquisitions that reduce their market value are subsequently more likely to be acquired than firms not making bad acquisitions. Although neither these papers nor our own work identify managerial objectives precisely, the importance of these objectives in determining acquisition choices seems well supported.

Section I of the paper describes the data we use in the analysis. Sections II and III present our empirical results. Section IV concludes.

I. The Sample and Construction of Variables

The Sample

Our data set is obtained by combining Bronwyn Hall's (1988) sample of mergers based on deletions of firms from Compustat with Jarrell and Poulsen's (1988) sample of acquisitions. We only consider acquisitions in which the bidder has actually obtained control. Table I presents the details of sample construction. The main reasons we lose observations include unavailability of stock price data on CRSP, absence of data in COMPUSTAT needed to construct our bidder performance variables, and missing data in the *Dun and Bradstreet Million Dollar Directory* (MDD) on the lines of business in which each firm operates. We use these lines of business to construct our diversification measures. We also omit 63 observations because the equity value of the target is less than 5% of the equity value of the bidder. These observations would only add noise to the results. Finally, we omit one outlier firm whose market value dropped more than 150% of the price it paid for the acquisition. Table I shows that our full sample consists of 326 acquisitions.

Return Variable

The traditional measure of the bidder's payoff from making an acquisition is the percentage change in the bidder's equity value at or around the time the

Do Managerial Objectives Drive Bad Acquisitions? 35

Table I

Construction of the 1975–1987 Sample of Acquisitions

Panel A: Construction of the Basic Full Sample

Bronwyn Hall Sample

1095	Partial list of firms that disappeared from Compustat
−322	Name changes/bankruptcies/LBOs/foreign bidder/reorganizations/ consolidations/disappearance before 1975
−296	Bidder or target not in CRSP, or bidder not in Compustat
−2	No *Wall Street Journal* event date
−79	No listing of bidder or target in Million Dollar Directory
396	Usable mergers from Bronwyn Hall's sample

Jarrell-Poulsen Sample

657	Bids
−584	Toeholds but not takeovers/bidder or target not in CRSP/bidder not in Compustat/disappearance before 1975 or duplicate entry with Bronwyn Hall sample
−17	No listing of bidder or target in Million Dollar Directory
56	
+396	From Bronwyn Hall sample
452	Total from Bronwyn Hall and Jarrell-Poulsen samples
−44	Bidder or target data missing from CRSP on the event date
−18	Date of first bid is 1974, even though firm disappeared from Compustat in 1975 or later
−63	Target < 5% of the equity value of the bidder
−1	Outlier: bidder price declined over 150% of the purchase price of the target around announcement
326	Basic full sample

Panel B: Construction of More Restricted Sample for Empirical Work

1. Quality of Bidder Management Measured by Relative Income Growth

326	Basic full sample
−26	Bidder income missing in 1 of the 2 years needed to construct bidder income growth variable
−1	Outlier: 250% income growth due to end of lawsuit writeoffs
299	Sample for income growth means in Table II
−33	Target sales missing in 1 of the 2 years needed to construct target sales growth
266	Sample for relative income growth regressions

2. Quality of Bidder Management Measured by Relative Equity Return

326	Basic full sample
−37	Bidder returns missing in more than 33 of 36 months needed to construct bidder equity return
289	Sample for relative equity return means in Table II
−35	Target sales missing in 1 of the 2 years needed to construct target sales growth
254	Sample for relative equity return regressions.

3. Target Sales Growth Analysis

326	Basic full sample
−39	Target sales missing in 1 of the 2 years needed to construct target sales growth
287	Sample for target sales means in Table II

acquisition is announced. This measure is somewhat unsatisfactory because it makes equally good acquisitions differentially good to firms of different sizes. When a firm with an equity value of $1000 buys another firm for $200 and as a result loses $50 in equity value, its return is −5%. But when a firm with an equity value of $500 makes the very same acquisition for $200 and loses $50 in equity value, its return is −10%. In this calculation, the same bad investment is evaluated differently depending on the initial equity value of the bidding firm. A good return measure should make the quality of the investment independent of the equity value or other characteristics of the bidding firm.

A measure not suffering from this problem is the ratio of the change in the market value of the bidder to the acquisition price of the target. This variable is equal to the ratio of the acquisition's net present value to its price. This measure is obviously −25% in both cases mentioned above. Using the price paid for the target as the normalizing factor seems more natural than using the initial market value of the bidder.

We use the date on which the acquirer's first bid is announced in the *Wall Street Journal* as our event date. We then compute the change in the bidder's equity value from two trading days before to one trading day after the event date.[2] We get a proxy for the acquisition price by looking at the equity value of the target on the first trading day following the last bid mentioned in the *Wall Street Journal*. Our return variable is then the ratio of the change in the bidder equity value to the acquisition price.[3]

While we prefer this approach to the traditional approach of just looking at the percentage change in the bidder's share price upon announcement of the acquisition as a means of evaluating the acquisition decision, the traditional approach is not completely without merit. In particular, it may be that acquiring managers are primarily concerned with the impact of an acquisition on their share price and not so much with the market's view of the wisdom of the acquisition itself. In that case, when a large corporation grossly overpays for a small target, the traditional measure's treatment of this action is not that worrisome for management may not be far off base. Accordingly, we have done our analysis using the traditional return measure for the bidder as well as the measure discussed above. The results for the two measures are quite similar. Results for the traditional measure are available from the authors upon request.[4]

Another measure of the value consequences of the acquisition would be the

---

[2] We have repeated the analysis using various event windows other than −2 to +1 and have found similar results. In particular, we have looked at (−1,+1), (−2,+2), (−3,+3) and (−4,+4).

[3] The target's value after the bid is announced is only a proxy for the acquisition price since that value may reflect only probabilistic success of the bid as well as the possibility of future higher bids. In addition, not all bids are for 100% of the target's stock (although experience suggests that second tier "cleanup offers" at prices in the range of the initial bid are the rule rather than the exception). Deflating by the target's post-bid value is just intended to give a better normalization factor by which to gauge the change in the bidder's market value.

[4] In the regressions using the traditional measure of the bidder's stock return as the dependent variable, a variable corresponding to the ratio of the market values of the target and the bidder prior to any bidding for the target is also included as a regressor. This relative size variable enters positively in the regression using the traditional bidder return measure and is statistically significant. On the other hand, this variable neither enters significantly nor changes the results for any of the other variables using our bidder return measure.

Do Managerial Objectives Drive Bad Acquisitions?   37

sum of the market value changes of the target and the bidder surrounding the takeover contest. A decline in the combined value of the two firms as the market learns about the acquisition would be evidence of diseconomies or a bad expected match between the target and the bidding management team, as when a conglomerate becomes so diversified that top management's expertise gets spread too thinly. This is not the focus of our study. Even when the combined value of the two firms rises because of the existence of a synergy, we are still interested in the regularity with which the bidder's value actually declines and in relating those declines to the managerial benefits flowing to bidding management. Hence, when we talk about overpayment we are referring to the negative reaction of the bidder's share price only. It is interesting, however, that our estimate of the change in combined value for the target and bidder is negative in roughly 25% of the cases.[5] This suggests that many of these acquisitions are not only ill-advised from the standpoint of bidding shareholders but also that there may be negative synergies associated with these combinations.

Relatedness Measures

One of the main issues addressed in this paper is the relative attractiveness of related and unrelated acquisitions. We construct two measures of relatedness. The first measures whether the target has any lines of business in common with the bidder. For each target and bidder in the sample, we use the *Dun and Bradstreet Million Dollar Directory* (MDD) to obtain the 4-digit SIC codes of the three main lines of business (by sales) that the firm operates in.[6] If the firm operates in fewer than three 4-digit industries, we use all its industries. All the data are for the year prior to the acquisition. If the bidder and the target have a 4-digit industry in common among the top three they operate in, we call the acquisition related. Otherwise we call the acquisition unrelated. This procedure leaves us reasonably confident that a related acquisition really falls in the firm's field of expertise.[7]

The second measure of relatedness is the correlation coefficient of monthly stock returns between the target and the bidder over the three years prior to the acquisition. The data are taken from both the NYSE/AMEX and the OTC files of CRSP. Although this variable is highly correlated with the previous measure, it is perhaps better for asking whether managers make acquisitions to diversify either their personal risk or the firm's risk.

Target Growth Measure

To evaluate the value consequences of buying growing firms, we must measure the growth rate of the target. We use the total growth rate of sales between 5

---

[5] Our estimate of the sum of the two value changes is obtained as follows. The change in target value is calculated as the difference between its market value two days before any bid for the target and one day after the successful bidder's first bid. The successful bidder's market value change is the same as the numerator of our bidder return measure. It is the change from 2 days before that bidder's first bid to 1 day after that bid. These two market value changes are then added to get the net value consequences of the acquisition.

[6] SIC code 6711, used for holding companies, is not treated as a separate line of business.

[7] We have also conducted the analysis using 2-digit SIC codes to measure relatedness. Not surprisingly, the difference between related and unrelated acquisitions is much smaller in this case.

38   *The Journal of Finance*

years before the acquisition and the year before, defined as $\log(S(t\text{-}1)) - \log(S(t\text{-}6))$, where t is the year of the acquisition, and $S(x)$ is constant dollar sales in year x from COMPUSTAT using the CPI as the deflator.

Measures of Past Performance of the Bidder

We use two measures of the past performance of the bidding firm: one based on stock returns (including dividends) and one based on growth of income. We use the firm's performance relative to its industry because the industry component of performance is presumably not under the management's control. Use of industry-adjusted performance to measure the quality of management is supported by the finding that firms underperforming their industries have more internally-precipitated management turnover (Morck, Shleifer and Vishny 1989).

Our measure of the bidding firm's industry-adjusted stock return is the difference between the cum dividend stock return of the bidder (from CRSP) and that of its "industry" over the three-year period ending in December of the year before the acquisition. To define the average stock return of the bidder's industry, we use the top three 4-digit SIC codes that the bidder operates in, discussed above. For each code, we take up to 10 other firms operating in the same 4-digit SIC code, making sure that for each of these firms this SIC code is one of its two most important in terms of sales. We take 10 firms in alphabetical order from the list of firms operating in each 4-digit SIC code that the MDD provides. When there are fewer than 10 firms, we take all the ones the MDD offers. When a firm does not have return data going four years back, we take a substitute that does. Using this procedure, we can construct an equally weighted average stock return for each 4-digit industry in which each bidder operates. Last, we take the simple arithmetic average of the industry stock returns for the top three 4-digit industries that each bidder operates in to arrive at the equity return of the bidder's "industry."

A similar procedure gives us 3-year bidder income growth relative to industry. Three-year income growth is defined as $\log(I(t-1)) - \log(I(t-4))$, where t is the year of the acquisition and I is defined as the sum of net income, interest and deferred taxes taken from COMPUSTAT.[8]

Other Variables Used in the Analysis

We use three other variables in the analysis. First, we use a dummy variable equal to 1 when multiple bidders are involved in the contest, since it has been documented that bidders do worse when they are involved in an open contest for

---

[8] An alternative earnings based measure of past performance is the level of earnings (normalized by value of assets) relative to industry rather than recent growth in earnings relative to industry. We tried this measure at the suggestion of the referee, with mixed results. We think there are two reasons for this. First, the level of earnings relative to asset value is a noisier measure of how the current management team is doing than is the recent change in earnings. This is true because the level of earnings is probably more a result of decisions made by previous managements than are recent changes in earnings and also because extra noise is introduced by the need to normalize by some measure of assets-in place. Second, the level of earnings may proxy for the amount of free cash flow available to management. According to Jensen's free cash flow theory, all other things equal, one would expect more negative returns on the investments of firms in which management had access to more free cash flow.

the target (Bradley, Desai and Kim 1988). Second, we examine whether the returns to bidders in related and unrelated acquisitions have changed in the 1980s. At least two changes have occurred under the Reagan administration. First, the antitrust policy has become laxer, presumably raising the returns to related diversification by allowing some extremely profitable matches to occur. Second, investors have apparently become disillusioned with unrelated diversification, which has led to the advent of hostile bustup takeovers. Finally, we include a dummy variable for whether the bidder's offer included any stock. In light of Asquith, Bruner and Mullins (1987) we want to be sure that the acquisition announcement effects that we observe are not explained by information conveyed through the choice of whether or not to issue stock to finance an acquisition. Table II contains summary statistics for all of the variables that we use in our analysis.

II. Preliminary Evidence

In this section, we present some simple statistics on bidder returns in acquisitions. In the next section, we present the regressions.

Recall that we define the bidder return as the ratio of the 3-day change in the bidding firm's equity value around the announcement date to the price of the target's equity. The mean value of bidder return in the 326 acquisitions is $-.70\%$, with a standard error of 1.22%; and 41.4% of the returns are positive. Hereafter we use the notation $-.70\%$ (1.22, .414 > 0). Although we define the bidder return variable differently from previous studies, the common finding that the average bidder return is not significantly different from zero obtains in our data set as well. The question is: which properties of the match make this return (more) negative? The three properties we look at are the growth rate of the target, the past performance of the bidding firm, and relatedness of the acquisition. Table III presents mean bidder returns for various categories of firms, as well as t-tests of the difference in means across categories and chi-squared tests of the difference in percent positive.

As a preliminary look at the effects of the growth rate of target's sales, we divide the sample into faster than the median and slower than the median growing targets. For fast growing targets, the mean bidder return is -2.43% (2.35, .389 > 0). For slow growing targets, the mean bidder return in 2.15% (1.91, .448 > 0). Buying a fast growing company is unattractive relative to buying a slow growing one. However, neither mean is significantly different from 0, and their difference, equal to 4.58%, is not quite significant at conventional levels (t = 1.51). The more precise regression tests of the effect on the bidder's return from buying growth do reject the null hypothesis of no effect (see Section III).

Recall that we measure the quality of bidding firm's management in two distinct ways: 3-year income growth relative to industry and 3-year cum dividend equity returns relative to industry. For both income and equity value, we split the sample into firms that do better than their industry and firms that do worse than their industry. Bidders with fast relative income growth earn an average return of 3.02% (2.24, .473 > 0). Bidders with slow relative income growth earn an average return of -5.02% (1.80, .338 > 0). According to this measure, bad

Table II

Summary Statistics for the Variables Used in the Analysis

Sample of 326 acquisitions between 1975 and 1987. The variables are defined in the text.

	Median	Mean	Standard Deviation	Minimum	Maximum	Sample Size
Bidder's Return on Acquisition of Target	-.0156	-.0070	.252	-.866	1.22	326
Dummy = 1 if Acquisition Is at Least Partly Equity-Financed	0	.485	.501	0	1	326
5-Year Target Real Sales Growth	.143	.179	.482	-1.37	2.74	287
Bidder 3-Year Income Growth Relative to Industry	.0608	.0969	.627	-2.78	3.00	299
Bidder 3-Year (cum dividend) Stock Return Relative to Industry	.0522	.165	1.35	-4.80	7.81	289
Dummy = 1 if Deal Is in 1980–1987	1	.528	.500	0	1	326
Dummy = 1 if Bidder and Target Share a 4-Digit SIC Industry	0	.279	.449	0	1	326
Correlation Coefficient of Bidder and Target Stock Returns over 3 Years Prior to Takeover	.365	.343	.206	-.706	.878	326
Dummy = 1 if Deal Is in 1980–1987 *and* Bidder/Target Share 4-Digit SIC Industry	0	.175	.380	0	1	326
Dummy = 1 if Deal Is in 1980–1987 Times Correlation Coefficient of Target and Bidder Returns	0	.164	.211	-.184	.878	326
Dummy = 1 if there Are Multiple Bidders	0	.239	.427	0	1	326

Do Managerial Objectives Drive Bad Acquisitions? 41

Table III

A Comparison of Mean Bidder Return on Acquisition by Characteristics of the Match

Characteristics of the match covered include target sales growth prior to the acquisition, bidder's income growth prior to the acquisition, bidder's stock return prior to the acquisition, measures of relatedness of the target and the bidder, and the time period during which the acquisition occurred. Sample of 326 acquisitions between 1975 and 1987.

	5-Year Target Sales Growth			3-Year Bidder Income Growth			3-Year Bidder Stock Return		
	Faster Than Sample Median	Slower Than Sample Median	Tests of Difference in Means & in % > 0	Faster Than Industry Average	Slower Than Industry Average	Tests of Difference in Means & in % > 0	Higher Than Industry Average	Lower Than Industry Average	Tests of Difference in Means & in % > 0
Mean Bidder Return	-2.43	2.15	$t = 1.51$	3.02	-5.02	$t = 2.67$	2.12	-2.12	$t = 1.39$
(Standard Error)	(2.35)	(1.91)	($p = .132$)	(2.24)	(1.80)	($p = .0078$)	(2.25)	(2.02)	($p = .167$)
Number of Observations	144	143	$\chi^2 = 1.01$	169	130	$\chi^2 = 5.47$	153	136	$\chi^2 = .20$
Percent Positive	38.9	44.8	($p = .314$)	47.3	33.8	($p = .0194$)	43.8	41.2	($p = .654$)

	Bidder and Target Share 4-Digit SIC Industry			3-Year Bidder and Target Correlation of Stock Returns			Year of the Acquisition		
	Yes	No	Tests of Difference in Means & in % > 0	Below Sample Median	Above Sample Median	Tests of Difference in Means & in % > 0	1975–1979	1980–1987	Tests of Difference in Means & in % > 0
Mean Bidder Return	2.38	-1.89	$t = 1.37$	.983	-2.37	$t = 1.20$	.517	-1.78	$t = .821$
(Standard Error)	(2.41)	(1.70)	($p = .171$)	(2.21)	(1.70)	($p = .230$)	(1.86)	(2.06)	($p = .412$)
Number of Observations	91	235	$\chi^2 = .69$	163	163	$\chi^2 = .62$	154	172	$\chi^2 = 3.42$
Percent Positive	45.1	40.0	($p = .406$)	43.6	39.3	($p = .431$)	46.8	36.6	($p = .064$)

42   *The Journal of Finance*

managers earn significantly negative returns from making acquisitions. More-over, they earn significantly less than do good managers. The return difference of 8.04% has a t-statistic of 2.67.

A similar result obtains using the bidder's past equity returns relative to industry, except now we cannot as reliably conclude that firms underperforming their industries lose from making acquisitions. The difference between returns to good and bad managers from making an acquisition, at 4.24%, is different from 0 with a p-value of .167.

Our first measure of relatedness is defined above through commonality of 4-digit SIC industries that the target and the bidder operate in. The evidence in Table III shows that the average bidder return in a related acquisition is 2.38% (2.41, .451 > 0), and in an unrelated acquisition it is −1.89% (1.70, .400 > 0). Although the two mean returns are of opposite signs and differ by 4.2%, they are not statistically significantly different from 0 or from each other. A similar picture emerges when we measure relatedness by correlation of bidder and target returns. The average bidder return in the subsample with above median correlation of bidder/target stock returns is .938% (2.21, .436 > 0) and that in the subsample with below median correlation is −2.37% (1.70, .393 > 0). The two mean returns are not significantly different from 0 or from each other.

The results become sharper when we distinguish between the 1970s and the 1980s, as is done in Table IV. Table IV shows that the difference between returns to related and unrelated acquisitions is both statistically and substantively more pronounced in the 1980s than in the 1970s. In Panel A of Table IV we call an acquisition related if the target and the bidder operate in the same 4-digit SIC industry. The panel shows that the returns to both related and unrelated acquisitions have changed from the 1970s to the 1980s. The mean return to related acquisitions has risen (insignificantly) by 1.3% in the 1980s, while the mean return to unrelated acquisitions has declined (also insignificantly) by 4.3%. Note that the sharp decrease over time in the fraction of returns that are positive in unrelated acquisitions is statistically significant. This evidence indicates that unrelated diversification became unattractive in the 1980s.

We can also see this point by comparing related to unrelated acquisitions in the two subperiods separately. Mean returns in related vs unrelated acquisitions are not statistically or substantively different in the 1970s, but are different in the 1980s. In the 1980s, the difference in mean returns in related and unrelated acquisitions is 6.97%, with a t-statistic of 1.60 (p = .11). During this period, in 45.6% of related acquisitions bidder returns are positive, but in only 32.2% of unrelated acquisitions are bidder returns positive (p = .09). Not surprisingly, the rise in the relative attractiveness of related acquisitions has led to an increase in the fraction of acquisitions that are related, from 22% in the 1970s to 33% in the 1980s.

These results are qualitatively confirmed using correlation of stock returns as a measure of relatedness, although the evidence is much weaker. One reason the results are weaker is that we split the sample at the median, and call acquisitions with above median stock return correlation related, even though according to our previous measure of relatedness over two thirds of the acquisitions are unrelated. The finding that the consequences of diversification are different in the two

Table IV

A Comparison of Mean Bidder Returns in Related and Unrelated Acousitions in the 1970s and 1980s

Each panel consists of 3 main rows corresponding to related acquisitions, unrelated acquisitions, and tests of equality of bidder returns between these two types of acquisitions. Within each row, there is a column of four numbers. They correspond to the mean bidder return on acquisition for that cell, the standard error of that mean return, the number of observations in the cell, and the percentage of observations in that cell for which the bidder's return on acquisition is positive (as in Table III). Sample of 326 acquisitions between 1975 and 1987.

Panel A: Diversification Measured Using 4-Digit SIC Industries in Which Bidder and Target Operate

	1975–1979	1980–1987	Tests of Equality of Means & of % > 0 in Two Periods
Bidder and Target Share a 4-Digit SIC Industry	1.54 (3.82) 34 44.1	2.88 (3.12) 57 45.6	$t = .268$ $(p = .7897)$ $\chi^2 = .02$ $(p = .8896)$
Bidder and Target Do Not Share a 4-Digit SIC Industry	.227 (2.13) 120 47.5	−4.09 (2.65) 115 32.2	$t = 1.27$ $(p = .2037)$ $\chi^2 = 5.69$ $(p = .0171)$
Tests of Equality of Means & of % > 0 between Related and Unrelated	$t = .293$ $(p = .770)$ $\chi^2 = .12$ $(p = .728)$	$t = 1.60$ $(p = .112)$ $\chi^2 = 2.94$ $(p = .0865)$	

Panel B: Diversification Measured Using Correlation Coefficient of Bidder and Target Monthly Stock Returns over 3 Years Prior to the Year of the Bid

	1975–1979	1980–1987	Tests of Equality of Means & of % > 0 in Two Periods
Correlation of Bidder and Target Stock Returns above Sample Median	.770 (2.62) 93 46.2	1.27 (3.83) 70 40.0	$t = .111$ $(p = .9120)$ $\chi^2 = .63$ $(p = .4270)$
Correlation of Bidder and Target Stock Returns below Sample Median	.132 (2.47) 61 47.5	−3.87 (2.28) 102 34.3	$t = 1.14$ $(p = .2558)$ $\chi^2 = 2.78$ $(p = .0955)$
Tests of Equality of Means & of % > 0 between Related and Unrelated	$t = .168$ $(p = .8672)$ $\chi^2 = .03$ $(p = .8739)$	$t = 1.23$ $(p = .2220)$ $\chi^2 = .58$ $(p = .4474)$	

periods guides our regression analysis, in that we distinguish between the 1970s and the 1980s in measuring the effect of diversification on returns to the bidding firms.

III. Regressions

Table V presents the regressions of bidder returns (change in value of bidder divided by target value) on the characteristics of the match. The left panel of Table V uses 3-year income growth relative to industry as a measure of the quality of bidder management, and the right panel uses 3-year stock returns relative to industry. The three regressions on each side use commonality of 4-digit industries between the bidder and the target, correlation coefficient of bidder and target returns, and both of them at the same time as measures of relatedness. In all regressions, we use both a time dummy for the 1980s and an

Table V

Regressions of Bidder's Return on Acquisition on Characteristics of the Match

These regressions for our 1975–1987 sample of acquisitions estimate the effect of target sales growth, bidder's prior performance, and relatedness of the bidder and target on the acquisition return to the bidder. The regression allows for the 1970s and 1980s to have a separate intercept and separate relatedness effects. The use of equity as a method of payment and the presence of competing bidders are also included as control variables. Numbers in brackets are standard errors. White (1980) adjustments are used in regressions where a χ^2 test indicates significant heteroskedasticity.

Variable Name	Quality of Bidder Management Measured by 3-Year Income Growth Relative to Industry			Quality of Bidder Management Measured by 3-Year Equity Return Relative to Industry		
	I	II	III	I	II	III
Intercept	.0769[b]	.0871[c]	.0878[c]	.0871[b]	.0887[c]	.0928[c]
	(.0340)	(.0456)	(.0451)	(.0352)	(.0487)	(.0478)
Dummy = 1 if Acquisition Is at	−.0340	−.0424	−.0376	−.0314	−.0407	−.0354
Least Partly Equity-Financed	(.0336)	(.0324)	(.0326)	(.0345)	(.0338)	(.0336)
5-Year Target Sales Growth	−.101[a]	−.0947[b]	−.102[a]	−.0953[a]	−.0900[b]	−.0996[b]
	(.0348)	(.0392)	(.0394)	(.0345)	(.0396)	(.0399)
Quality of Bidder Management	.0519[b]	.0530[b]	.0511[b]	.0230[c]	.0268[c]	.0231
	(.0257)	(.0233)	(.0220)	(.0128)	(.0164)	(.0153)
Dummy = 1 if Deal Is in 1980–	−.0813[b]	−.126[b]	−.143[b]	−.0762[c]	−.104[c]	−.127[b]
87	(.0376)	(.0548)	(.0562)	(.0392)	(.0601)	(.0624)
Dummy = 1 if Bidder and Target Share a 4-Digit SIC Industry	−.0163 (.0531)		−.0145 (.0470)	−.0254 (.0544)		−.0248 (.0484)
Dummy = 1 if Deal Is in 1980– 87 *and* Target and Bidder Share a 4-Digit SIC Industry	.127[c] (.0737)		.113 (.0731)	.122[c] (.0743)		.115[c] (.0696)
Correlation Coefficient of Bidder and Target Monthly Stock Returns over 3 Years Prior to Takeover		−.0278 (.0930)	−.0196 (.100)		−.0140 (.103)	−.0047 (.107)
Dummy = 1 if Deal Is in 1980– 87 Times Correlation Coefficient of Bidder and Target Stock Returns		.250[b] (.126)	.203 (.132)		.190 (.130)	.157 (.135)
Dummy = 1 if there Are Multiple Bidders	−.0988[b]	−.0970[a]	−.104[a]	−.0918[b]	−.0850[a]	−.0944[a]
	(.0389)	(.0259)	(.0265)	(.0395)	(.0264)	(.0267)
Number of Observations	266	266	266	254	254	254
R^2	.09	.08	.10	.08	.07	.08

[a] Significant at 1%.
[b] Significant at 5%.
[c] Significant at 10%.

Do Managerial Objectives Drive Bad Acquisitions?   45

interaction of that dummy with the relatedness measure to allow for different returns to diversification in the 1970s and the 1980s.

In all regressions, the coefficient on the dummy equal to 1 when there are multiple bidders is highly significant and is equal to about −0.1. This means that entry by additional bidders reduces the winning bidder's market value by 10 cents on each dollar paid for the target. The second control variable, the dummy equal to 1 if the acquisition is at least partly equity financed, is not statistically significant in any of the regressions.

Depending on the specification, estimated bidder return falls between 9.0% and 10.2% as the target's change in log sales over the five years prior to the year of the acquisition goes from 0 to 1. In all specifications, this estimate of the cost of buying growth is highly statistically significant. To interpret the magnitude of this effect better, note that the value of 0 for the 5-year change in log sales represents 35th percentile sales growth performance, while the value of 1 represents 95th percentile performance. In our data, buying rapidly growing firms is extremely costly to the bidders.

Whether we measure past performance of the bidder by income growth relative to industry or by stock returns relative to industry, its effect is significant. When the industry-adjusted 3-year change in the log of bidder income goes from 0 to 1, the average return from making an acquisition rises by somewhere between 5.1% and 5.3% depending on the specification. An industry-adjusted change in the log of income of 0 represents median relative income growth, while a value of 1 represents growth at the 95th percentile.

Similarly, when the industry adjusted 3-year bidder's stock return goes from 0 to 100%, the average return from making an acquisition rises by somewhere between 2.3% and 2.7%, depending on the specification. An industry-adjusted 3-year stock return of 0 is about median, and a return of 100% is at about the 85th percentile.

As do the findings of Lang, Stulz and Walkling (1989), these results show that firms with better managers are also better acquirers. These results are inconsistent with a particular version of Roll's hubris hypothesis, in which managers of better performing firms are more arrogant and therefore overestimate the target's value under their control by more.

Comparing the effect of diversification on bidding firm's returns in the 1970s and the 1980s requires looking at three variables: the measure of relatedness, the time period dummy, and the interaction of the two. We do not discuss the regressions with both measures of relatedness included at the same time, since the strong correlation between the two measures makes the results insignificant and difficult to interpret. We also focus, for concreteness, on the left panel, where past bidder performance is measured by 3-year relative income growth. The results for the right panel are very similar. Note finally that the correlation coefficient of stock returns can be interpreted similarly to the shared 4-digit SIC codes dummy. We can think of unrelated acquisitions as those for which the value of the correlation of stock returns is 0, and of related acquisitions as those for which this correlation is 1.

When the relatedness measure, the time period dummy, and the interaction are all equal to 0, we are in the benchmark case of unrelated acquisitions in the

46   *The Journal of Finance*

1970s. The coefficient on the 1980s dummy therefore captures the difference in returns on *unrelated* acquisitions between the 1980s and the 1970s. In regression I, the return on unrelated acquisitions was 8.1% lower in the 1980s than in the 1970s (t = 2.16). In regression II, the return from aquiring a target whose stock returns are uncorrelated with the bidder's was 12.6% lower in the 1980s than in the 1970s (t = 2.30). Using the zero correlation of stock returns to define unrelatedness yields bigger magnitudes simply because this is a more extreme form of unrelatedness than non-sharing of a 4-digit SIC industry. The results confirm our earlier finding that returns to unrelated acquisitions have declined substantially in the 1980s.

To see what happened to returns in *related acquisitions* between the 1970s and the 1980s, we add the coefficient on the relatedness measure to the coefficient on the interaction between the relatedness measure and the 1980s dummy. In regression I, the return on related acquisitions is 12.7% − 8.1% = 4.6% higher in the 1980s than in the 1970s (t = .78). In regression II, the return from acquiring a firm with a perfectly correlated stock return is 25.0% − 12.6% = 12.4% higher in the 1980s than in the 1970s (t = 1.34). In contrast to the statistically significant decline in returns to *unrelated* acquisitions over this period, the returns to *related* acquisitions have risen, but not significantly. The apparent overall decline of returns to acquisitions from the 1970s to the 1980s documented in Table III is completely a consequence of the large decline in returns to unrelated diversification.

The coefficient on the interaction of the 1980s dummy and the relatedness measure describes the change from the 1970s to the 1980s of the returns difference in related and unrelated acquisitions. In regression I, the return from doing a related as opposed to an unrelated deal has gone up by 12.7% from the 1970s to the 1980s (t = 1.72, p-value = .085). In regression II, the return from buying a target whose stock returns are perfectly correlated with the bidder's rather than a target with uncorrelated stock returns has gone up by 25.0% (t = 1.98, p-value = .048) from the 1970s to the 1980s. In the 1980s, the penalty for diversification relative to making a related acquisition has gone way up.

Similar results obtain when we use industry-adjusted stock returns to measure past performance of the bidding firm. In the 1980s, returns to related acquisitions have gone (insignificantly) up, returns to diversification have gone (significantly) down, and the cost of diversifying relative to buying related has risen significantly. The overall verdict on diversification is clear: it is a bad idea in the 1980s.

The results in Table V support the proposition that managerial objectives drive acquisitions. For example, they show that buying growth is a bad idea from the point of view of bidding firm's shareholders. Of course, growth is one of the much discussed managerial objectives, pursued either for its own sake or for the sake of assuring the survival of the bidding firm and the continuity of its top management.

The results in Table V also suggest that unrelated diversification is a bad idea from the point of view of the bidding firm's shareholders in the 1980s. Like pursuit of growth, diversification can be understood as serving the objectives of managers.

Perhaps surprisingly, we do not find that diversification reduces bidding firms'

Do Managerial Objectives Drive Bad Acquisitions? 47

shareholder wealth in the 1970s. We take this to mean one of two things. First, there might have been some efficiency reasons for diversification in the earlier period, such as imperfect capital markets, foreclosure of related acquisitions due to antitrust policy, or the attractiveness of conglomerate control. Second, the market might have favored diversification during this period given the information it had, even though ex post diversification proved unattractive and by the 1980s the market caught on.

Finally, the results in Table V demonstrate that firms with bad managers (identified by poor firm performance relative to its industry) do much worse in making acquisitions than firms with good managers. The negative return to acquisitions by poorly performing acquirers is evidence that bad acquisitions are a manifestation of agency problems in the firm.

IV. Implications

Although this paper has focused on managerial objectives in making mostly friendly acquisitions, the results may also shed light on the source of gains in hostile bust-up takeovers, leveraged buyouts, and defensive recapitalizations involving large scale divestitures. Our finding that in the 1980s the stock market punishes unrelated diversification is consistent with the view that the source of bust-up gains in the 1980s is the reversal of the unrelated diversification of the 1960s and the 1970s. Hostile bust-up takeovers simply undo past conglomeration.

At the same time, our finding that managerial objectives drive bad acquisitions suggests a different interpretation of the gains from bustup takeovers. Raiders in these deals facilitate the sale of each piece of the target to the highest bidder. Part of the gain from this activity is doubtless the improvement in the operations of particular divisions under a more talented or a better motivated management team. But part of the gain from bustups may come from the willingness of other non-value-maximizing managers to buy the pieces of the target for their own empires. By allowing each buyer to overpay only for the piece of the target he really wants, the raider can collect more than any single bidder would pay for the whole target. This suggests that takeover premia may overestimate the efficiency gains from hostile bustup takeovers.

REFERENCES

Amihud, Yakov and Baruch Lev, 1981, Risk reduction as a managerial motive for conglomerate mergers, *Bell Journal of Economics* 12, 605–617.
Asquith, Paul R., R. F. Bruner, and David W. Mullins, Jr., 1987, Merger returns and the form of financing, Working paper, Harvard Business School.
Baumol, William J., 1959, *Business Behavior, Value and Growth* (Macmillan, New York).
Bradley, Michael, A. Desai, and E. Han Kim, 1988, Synergistic gains from corporate acquisitions and their division between the stockholders of target and acquiring firms, *Journal of Financial Economics* 21, 3–40.
Donaldson, Gordon, 1984, *Managing Corporate Wealth* (Praeger, New York).
—— and Jay Lorsch, 1983. *Decision Making at the Top* (Basic Books, New York).
Dun and Bradstreet, 1974–1987, *Million Dollar Directory* (Dun and Bradstreet, New York).
Hall, Bronwyn H., 1988, The effect of takeover activity on corporate research and development, in

48   *The Journal of Finance*

Alan J. Auerbach, ed.: *Corporate Takeovers: Causes and Consequences* (University of Chicago Press, Chicago, IL).

Jarrell, Gregg and Anette Poulsen, 1988. The returns to acquiring firms: Evidence from three decades, Working paper, University of Rochester.

Jensen, Michael C., 1986, Agency cost of free cash flow, corporate finance, and takeovers, *American Economic Review* 76, 323–329.

Lang, Larry, René M. Stulz, and Ralph A. Walkling, 1989, Tobin's q and the gains from successful tender offers, *Journal of Financial Economics* 24, 137–154.

Lewellen, Wilbur, Claudio Loderer, and Ahron Rosenfeld, 1985, Merger decisions and executive stock ownership in acquiring firms, *Journal of Accounting and Economics* 7, 209–231.

Mitchell, Mark L. and Kenneth Lehn, 1990, Do bad bidders become good targets?, *Journal of Political Economy*, Forthcoming.

Morck, Randall, Andrei Shleifer, and Robert W. Vishny, 1989, Alternative mechanisms for corporate control, *American Economic Review* 79, 342–852.

Roll, Richard, 1986, The hubris hypothesis of corporate takeovers, *Journal of Business* 59, 197–216.

Servaes, Henri, 1988, Tobin's Q, agency costs and corporate control, Working paper, University of Chicago.

Shleifer, Andrei and Robert W. Vishny, 1988, Value maximization and the acquisition process, *Journal of Economic Perspectives* 2, 7–20.

———— and Robert W. Vishny, 1990, Managerial entrenchment: The case of manager-specific investments, *Journal of Financial Economics*, Forthcoming.

You, Victor L., Richard E. Caves, James S. Henry, and Michael M. Smith, 1986, Mergers and bidders' wealth: Managerial and strategic factors, in L. G. Thomas, ed.: *The Economics of Strategic Planning* (Lexington Books, Boston, MA).

[17]

THE JOURNAL OF INDUSTRIAL ECONOMICS
Volume XXXIX   March 1991

0022-1821 $2.00
No. 3

SYNERGY, AGENCY, AND THE DETERMINANTS
OF PREMIA PAID IN MERGERS*

ALEXANDER R. SLUSKY and RICHARD E. CAVES

Hypotheses about the creation of value by mergers are tested on premia
paid in a sample of 100 recent acquisitions. The premia increase with
financial although not with real synergies and with the scope for
"managerial" behavior in the target firms. The acquirers' willingness to
pay also increases with their scope for managerial behavior. The presence
of either actual and potential rival bidders has a powerful effect, and we
ascertain that market gains (losses) to acquirers' shareholders do not
distort the associations between acquisition premia and sources of value.

IN MERGER transactions among large US corporations, shareholders of target
firms receive large premia over market value for yielding control to the
acquiring firm. Because on average the acquirer's shareholders break even,
targets' gains represent most of the value that the market assigns to these
transactions. Some observers ascribe this value to synergies in the
coordination of business assets. Others attribute it to gains from shifting
control of assets into the hands of more effective managers.

Each hypothesis claims some support. The stock market assigns more
value to mergers between firms that exhibit some potential for relatedness, as
identified in the theory of corporate diversification (Singh and Montgomery
[1987]; Shelton [1988]). Potential target firms following poorly selected
policies are more likely to be acquired (Palepu [1986]). However, there has
been little use of multivariate analysis to impute the variance among premia
paid for targets to these and other sources of gain (cf. Jahera, Hand, and
Lloyd [1985]; Walkling and Edminster [1985]). That is our goal.

The first section provides a conceptual framework and presents the main
hypotheses, and the second gives them quantitative forms. The third describes
the sample and reports the results.

I. ANALYTICAL FRAMEWORK

The premium paid in a completed merger transaction, PR, can be related to
the market value of the target as an independent firm (MV) by this expression:

$$(1) \qquad PR = (BRES[X_i]/MV)B(Z_i)$$

* We are grateful to Denise Neumann and Kenneth C. Griffin for assistance and to Cynthia
Montgomery for suggestions. Research support was provided by the Division of Research,
Harvard Business School.

278   ALEXANDER R. SLUSKY AND RICHARD E. CAVES

where *BRES* is the reservation price of the successful acquirer, net of the buyer's transaction costs. It depends on factors (X_i) that predict the increase in cash flows due to combining the two firms' assets or changing the policies of the target's management, but also any factors that represent the acquiring management's willingness to pay for those cash flows. The X_i could include any propensity of the target's management to elevate the transaction costs incurred by the acquirer, and thus to lower *BRES*, in order to preserve its independence. $B(*)$ is a bargaining function that determines where the actual price falls between the reservation prices of the would-be acquirer (*BRES*) and current owners (*MV*), and the Z_i are determinants such as the presence of competing bidders.

We derive the X_i and Z_i variables by considering the two main hypotheses about the sources of value in mergers—labelled synergy and managerial effectiveness—as well as factors determining the acquirer's bargaining situation.

Synergistic gains

A coherent account of synergistic gains comes from the theory of corporate diversification. This theory rests on the assumption that the large business enterprise can be regarded as a coalition of heterogeneous, "lumpy" assets subject to administrative coordination. Some assets have multiple uses, entering into the production functions of several activities or generating externalities between activities that can be internalized by the firm. The lumpiness of such an asset induces the owning firm to deploy it in several activities rather than use its full capacity to produce one output that faces a downward-sloping demand.[1]

This model of diversification explains mergers as firms' responses to growing markets and changing conditions. At any time some firms find themselves either needing the services of such a lumpy asset or possessing one with excess capacity. Mergers provide a common solution, although the arm's-length rental of the services of such assets is an alternative. This explanation of mergers has several implications for their empirical analysis. It warrants expressing the dollar premium paid for the target as a ratio to its value as a free-standing firm, because the acquirer's reservation premium should rest on the target's value as a source of or site for the use of such assets. However, the scales of some of the acquirer's assets may also affect the potential value of the merger. If the target's assets generate an externality, such as a technical skill, for the acquirer's activity, then the gain is related to the scale of the acquirer's assets.

---

[1] This approach has evolved from Penrose [1959] and numerous other contributors. For a recent application see Montgomery and Hariharan (forthcoming).

Managerial effectiveness

Mergers are also believed to create value by shifting business assets into the hands of managers who can generate more value from them, thanks to greater ability or stronger incentive to maximize value. The evidence supporting this gain from mergers is thin. Acquired firms' book profits are not subnormal for their industries (Ravenscraft and Scherer [1987, ch. 3]). Mergers pick off firms with low ratios of market to book value (Hindley [1970]), but the synergy hypothesis suffices to explain that regularity.[2] Some evidence indicates improvement in three aspects of management of the target firms' resources: (1) ending suboptimal use of debt (papers cited in Caves [1989]); (2) eliminating mismatches between their market opportunities and policies (Palepu [1986]); and (3) making profitable asset switches and sales that the target's managers had not chosen to make (Bhagat, Shleifer, and Vishny [1990]). Relevant if indirect is the finding of Lang, Stultz, and Walkling [1988] that the largest increases in the combined values (abnormal returns) of acquirer and target occur when firms with high values of Tobin's q acquire targets with low values of q.

The value potentially created by a merger and thus the maximum premium paid ($BRES/MV$) should increase with the target management's underperformance. To test that hypothesis requires either an independent measure of the target management's performance or a hypothesis about the source of its shortfall. We shall focus on the incentives provided by compensation and governance arrangements identified by the theory of principal–agent relationships. High levels of managerial shareholding (or compensation strongly tied to share value) encourage managers to select policies aligned with the interest of shareholders in maximum value, reducing the value that a managerial change could create.

However, this familiar hypothesis about incentives runs counter to another based on entrenchment: managers with substantial shareholdings can more easily resist a hostile tender offer and thus can entrench themselves and defend any preference for other objectives over maximum income from their shareholdings (Stulz [1988]). The entrenchment hypothesis also applies to managers who are short of competence rather than motivation. Underperforming managers should lose more utility following a change in control because their compensation exceeds their productivity.[3] Therefore they gain more from using the firm's resources to create transaction costs for the

---

[2] The fact that shares of acquired firms tend to yield negative abnormal returns in months or years previously has been ascribed to inferior managerial performance; however, a sufficient explanation (tested below) is that acquiring firms pick up what they see as bargains in the market for corporate control (Scherer [1988]).

[3] Replacing a less accomplished management with a better but costlier one does not obviously create value, which is why overcompensation is up to a point the core issue (a poor manager could of course depress the firm's value by more than his total compensation).

280   ALEXANDER R. SLUSKY AND RICHARD E. CAVES

acquirer and deter an acquisition that will terminate their rent streams. The entrenchment effect makes it uncertain how levels of underperformance and resistance to takeovers vary with managerial shareholding. Walkling and Long [1984] found that resistance to takeover bids is more likely, the smaller are the shareholdings of the target's managers and directors. They also found some evidence associating resistance with the size of estimated rent components in the salaries of targets' executives. However, large managerial shareholdings sometimes help to install value-impairing antitakeover provisions (Brickley, Lease, and Smith [1988]),[4] and managerial shareholdings beyond a threshold seem to decrease the firm's value of Tobin's q (Morck, Shleifer, and Vishny [1988]).

Entrenchment complicates determining which managements are likely to be underperforming and thus the premia earned for displacing them. The incentive-alignment hypothesis proposes that the premium will decrease with some measure of alignment such as the fraction of the target's shares held by insiders ($TINS$). In equation (1) we defined the bidder's premium $PR = BRES/MV$, which can be expanded to $PR = BRES'/MV - T/MV$, where $BRES'$ is the acquirer's gross reservation price and T the transaction cost of making the acquisition. The incentive-alignment effect holds simply that $\partial PR/\partial TINS < 0$ because $\partial(BRES'/MV)/\partial TINS < 0$ and $\partial(T/MV)/\partial TINS = 0$. If managers with low shareholdings place more obstacles before would-be acquirers,[5] entrenchment implies that $\partial(T/MV)/\partial TINS < 0$ and possibly $\partial PR/\partial TINS > 0$. If high-shareholding managements value their independence, the effective reservation price for the firm is raised, although not the MV that we observe. Some takeovers are precluded; in those that occur entrenchment acts like a Z_i variable in $B(*)$ to press the purchase price up toward $BRES$. With $\partial B/\partial TINS > 0$ (and possibly $\partial(BRES'/MV)/\partial TINS > 0$ as well), $\partial PR/\partial TINS > 0$. Thus the effect of managers' shareholdings on PR is of indeterminate sign, negative on the incentive-alignment hypothesis, positive from the entrenchment effect in either of its forms.

Although discussion of managerial behavior in merger transactions has focused mostly on target firms, acquirers have also come into the spotlight. Jensen's [1986] "free cash flow" hypothesis holds that managers assign low opportunity costs to internally generated funds not needed for reinvestment in their base activities and squander these on low-yield acquisitions. Mergers can provide utility to the acquirer's managers by reducing risk to the viability

---

[4] Debate persists over whether these provisions are hostile to shareholders' welfare, but a negative effect is clearly possible. See Dann and DeAngelo [1988], Malatesta and Walkling [1988], and the survey by Jensen and Warner [1988].

[5] Golden parachutes, poison pills, and the like. Some of these devices can in principle be used to assist management to extract maximum value from an acquirer for the target's shareholders (Knoeber [1986]), but their negative effect on the firm's value in the face of a takeover attempt is clear (Dann and DeAngelo [1988]).

of the enterprise (Amit and Livnat [1988]) or conveying advantages associated with increased size, such as higher compensation (Firth [1980]) and decreased vulnerability to takeovers. You, Caves, Smith, and Henry [1986] demonstrated empirically that excess returns to acquiring firms' shareholders are smaller (more likely to be negative), the smaller is the fraction of shares held by managers and directors and the larger is the proportion of insider members of the board of directors. Thus the agency situation of the acquiring firm also affects the premium paid for the target,[6] because a managerial bidding firm's reservation price can exceed a value maximizer's.

Bargains in market for corporate control

Unless stock-market efficiency is believed to hold in the short run, mergers can occur because the market undervalues the income stream expected to flow from the target's assets (Scherer [1988]). The financial investor cannot readily arbitrage between the markets for physical capital assets and for financial claims on the income streams of those assets, but some acquiring firms can. The prices of financial claims are typically more volatile than the prices of capital goods—certainly during the years 1986–1988, covered in our empirical investigation. If stock prices were also more volatile than the cash flows expected by business investors, then their reservation premia for acquisitions should move inversely with the general level of securities prices relative to the prices of real capital goods.

Bargaining considerations

The bargaining function $B(Z_i)$ determines where the premium falls between the buyer's reservation price and the target's market value. It should depend on the number of actual and potential competitors for each target. Within the limits set by competing bidders it should depend on tactical bargaining skills and objectives (assumed as unobservable in practice).[7] That leaves the Z_i with the role of representing the density of the upper tail of potential bidders' reservation prices. The synergy and agency hypotheses offer different implications about these densities. The synergy hypothesis implies that going concerns represent different bundles of assets that are heterogeneous in attributes and qualities, and therefore have diverse reservation prices for a given target firm. The managerial-efficiency hypothesis can be read narrowly

---

[6] This proposition implies that excess returns to the shareholders of acquiring and target firms in a merger should be negatively correlated, which was confirmed by You *et al.* [1986] and Bradley, Desai, and Kim [1988].

[7] It is not obvious, for example, that a target management pursuing objectives other than maximum value in managing the firm would choose to forego extracting the maximum price from the successful acquirer.

282   ALEXANDER R. SLUSKY AND RICHARD E. CAVES

to predict the contrary: all efficient, value-maximizing managements can wring the same value from a given asset bundle and will have the same reservation prices.

The densities of reservation-price distributions could be pursued along this and other lines, but with little practical value. We control for the presence of active competing bidders, a factor that has repeatedly been found to increase merger premia. Although the closeness of potential competition for acquirers may defy direct measurement, it can perhaps be inferred indirectly from the structure that the successful bidder chooses for its transaction.

The position of the acquisition premium within the bargaining range can be approached indirectly, because any surplus expected to accrue to the acquiring firm should generate excess returns to the acquirer's shareholders at the time the acquisition is announced. We shall indeed use acquirers' excess returns to assure that findings about the determinants of the premium are not distorted by systematic relationships between the hypothesized determinants of the premium and the estimated gains (losses) to the acquirer's shareholders.[8]

II. EMPIRICAL SPECIFICATION OF THE MODEL

We now propose variables to embody these hypotheses about takeover premia and test them on a sample of large merger transactions among US nonfinancial companies during 1986–1988.

Synergistic gains

The synergistic potential implied by the theory of lumpy, multi-use assets can be measured in various ways. The relatedness of the businesses of a diversified firm can be calculated by observing the policies used to integrate its assorted businesses (or from the lack of such policies) (Rumelt [1974]), but it raises questions of objectivity and replicability when applied to mergers. The standard industrial classification (SIC) has served to measure relatedness objectively because of its construction based on similarities of technologies and principal inputs (e.g. Caves [1975]). The potential synergy resulting from a merger can be measured similarly from the closeness of the activities of the acquiring and acquired enterprises.

We employ a variant of the approach developed by Shelton [1985, 1988] to measure a merger's potential for relatedness. She obtained the distribution of sales among SIC industries for each acquirer and target firm shortly before the time of the acquisition. She then determined judgmentally (on stated criteria)

---

[8] The potential importance of controlling for the change in the acquiring firm's value is shown by the finding of You *et al.* [1986] that the estimated *total* values of 24 of their 133 mergers were negative, despite pervasive gains to the target's shareholders.

SYNERGY, AGENCY AND PREMIA PAID IN MERGERS   283

TABLE I
SUMMARY OF VARIABLE DEFINITIONS AND DATA BASE

Symbol	Definition	Mean	Std. dev.
PR	Transaction price % prior market value	50.5%	41.4%
FIT	Extent of relatedness of companies' assets	0.52	0.42
H	Horizontal merger dummy	0.31	0.46
V	Vertical merger dummy	0.09	0.29
R	Related merger dummy	0.45	0.50
SIZE	Sales of acquirer/sales of target	31.6	61.5
TDEBTEQ	Target long-term debt/equity	10.4%	24.4%
ADEBTEQ	Acquirer long-term debt/equity	22.9%	38.0%
DEDIF	TDEBTEQ − ADEBTEQ	−12.5%	45.8%
TINS	Target shares of managers, directors	19.1%	19.3%
TFIVE	Target shares in blocks > 5%	12.0%	11.7%
TBOARD	Target officers % board of directors	36.3%	17.1%
AINS	Acquirer shares of managers, directors	8.5%	12.2%
AFIVE	Acquirer shares in blocks > 5%	6.5%	10.2%
ABOARD	Acquirer officers % board of directors	34.9%	18.5%
S&PCLOSE	S&P index, closing day of transaction	265	27.8
ALLCASH	Dummy for all-cash transactions	0.72	0.45
RIVAL	Dummy for presence of rival bidder	0.25	0.44

Sources: Transactions were identified and dated from ADP Network Services, which also supplied information on PR, SIZE, ALLCASH, and RIVAL. Standard and Poor's Compustat provided information used to calculate FIT, H, V, R, and DEBTEQ; INS, FIVE, and BOARD were obtained from Moody's Corporate Reports, Value Line Reports, and corporate annual proxy statements. The history of each transaction was traced through stories published in the *Wall Street Journal* and retrieved through its index; S&PCLOSE was also obtained from the *Journal.*

whether each pair of activities of the two firms held synergistic potential. For each pair deemed to fit she calculated the product of the activities' shares of acquirer's and target's sales, then summed the resulting products. Specifically, this procedure yields the measure:

$$FIT = \sum_{1}^{AT} \delta_{at}s_a s_t$$

where s_a is the share of activity a in the acquirer's total sales $(a = 1,...,A)$, s_t is the share of activity t in the target's total sales $(t = 1,..., T)$, and δ_{at} equals one if activity pair at is deemed to possess synergistic potential, zero if they do not. We set $\delta_{at} = 1$ when the two activities serve a common set of customers, pass through similar distribution channels, employ related technologies of production, or utilize important inputs in common.[9] Of course, all these commonalities will be present when the combined firms operate in the same market, and combinations of vertically related activities have their own familiar set of bases for creating value, so horizontally and vertically related

[9] These criteria flow from Rumelt [1974] and subsequent research and were strongly supported in the statistical study of diversification by Lemelin [1982].

284   ALEXANDER R. SLUSKY AND RICHARD E. CAVES

activities will be assumed to achieve a synergistic fit.[10] *FIT* ranges between zero (when no pair of acquirer and target activities is deemed related) and one (when every pair shows relatedness). The premium paid in a merger should increase with *FIT.* Table I lists all regressors used in the analysis, gives their sources, and reports means and standard deviations for the sample.

We also assigned each transaction a zero/one dummy variable to indicate whether the synergistic element arose chiefly from a horizontal (*H*), vertical (*V*), or related (*R*) pair of activities.[11] These types of relation need not generate systematically differing surpluses, but it is interesting to check the possibility.

FIT does miss one dimension of synergy that arises if the target's assets yield positive externalities for the acquirer's business units, once integrated into the acquirer's organization. The relative sizes of the two firms then matter, and the gain in productivity of the target's assets (expressed as a proportion of their free-standing market value) should increase with:

> *SIZE* = total sales of acquiring firm divided by total sales
> of the target.

On the hypothesis stated, the effect of *SIZE* should be interactive with *FIT,* or *SIZE* should be measured from individual fitting pairs of businesses.

A discrepancy between the two firms' levels of financial stringency can also make a merger valuable. If parties' opportunity costs of internal funds differ, and obtaining funds externally entails significant transaction costs, a merger could create value to the extent of the avoided costs of securing external funds *net* of the transaction costs of the merger itself. Bruner [1988] found evidence that acquirers had significantly greater financial slack in the two years prior to the merger and targets displayed significantly higher leverage than their acquirers; nonetheless his data rejected the hypothesis that the market value of the merger depends on the extent of this financial synergy.

We obtained the variable:

> *TDEBTEQ* = ratio of long-term debt to the sum of debt, common
> equity (market value), and preferred stock, target
> firm, year prior to merger.

ADEBTEQ is its counterpart for the acquiring firm. What should matter is the relation between *TDEBTEQ* and *ADEBTEQ.* Either the absolute or the algebraic value of their difference might be appropriate: in principle a merger could absorb the financial slack of either partner, although Bruner's [1988] results suggest the primacy of the acquirer's slack. Rhoades [1987] found that premia paid for acquired banks increase with a measure analogous to their

---

[10] Horizontal and vertical mergers can of course also generate monopoly rents. In this paper we simply neglect any discrepancies between private and social gains.

[11] Because most target firms in the sample were not large enough to operate diversified lines of business, determining the principal mode of fit was uncomplicated.

leverage (i.e. decrease with the ratio of equity and subordinated notes to assets).

Agency situations of target and acquirer

Value could arise either because value-maximizing managers differ in effectiveness or because some managers are more strongly motivated than others to maximize value. The former source is impossible to test except on *ex post* evidence, which allows that hypothesis to be put aside without deep concern for omitted-variable bias; see Ravenscraft and Scherer [1987] and other evidence surveyed by Caves [1989].

That leaves the state of the principal–agent relation between owners and managers of both target and acquiring firms as a basis for predicting differences in managerial performance. We expect the alignment of the objectives of managers to shareholders' interest in maximized present value to depend on the effectiveness of external monitoring of the managers and the structure of their compensation. The following variables are used:

$TINS$ = fraction of shares held by corporate officers and members of the board of directors;

$TFIVE$ = fraction of shares not held by officers and directors that are in the hands of individual shareholders owning five per cent or more of the firm's outstanding equity shares;

$TBOARD$ = fraction of members of the board of directors who are officers of the company.

$TFIVE$ embodies the hypothesis that substantial (minority) shareholding blocks emerge where the payout of intensive monitoring is high (Demsetz and Lehn [1985]) and serve as a base for potential takeovers (Shleifer and Vishny [1986]). The premium should therefore decrease with $TFIVE$. Similarly, directors who are outsiders monitor managers more efficiently (Weisbach [1988]), so that the premium should increase with $TBOARD$.[12] The effect of $TINS$ is ambiguous, however, for the reason developed above—its incentive and entrenchment effects run in opposite directions.

If changes in the policies of a managerial target firm yield increased value, we also expect that managerial firms will pursue acquisitions more actively than value-maximizing managers, and variables $AINS$, $AFIVE$, and $ABOARD$ were developed for each acquirer exactly parallel to those for the target. Managers who gain utility from mergers can imprint their preferences

---

[12] If entrenched managers can choose their boards of directors freely. and substantial outside holders can demand representation. $TBOARD$ becomes an endogenous variable partially explained by $TINS$ and $TFIVE$. Hermalin and Weisbach [1988] did establish some endogeneity in $TBOARD$, but also observed a fairly high long-run stability in firms' values of $TBOARD$.

286   ALEXANDER R. SLUSKY AND RICHARD E. CAVES

on merger transactions in two ways. They can simply overpay, causing premia to increase with *AINS* and *ABOARD* and decrease with *AFIVE*. Also they can undertake mergers with value-creating potential less than the owner's reservation price for yielding control. In that case *AINS* and *ABOARD* would be negatively correlated with *FIT* (*AFIVE* would be positively correlated), but the acquirer variables would not necessarily be associated with *PR* once we control for *FIT* and the variables that measure the managerial situation of the target. You *et al.* [1986] concluded that utility-maximizing managers of acquiring firms tend to undertake mergers that diminish the wealth of their shareholders; the acquiring firm's owners fare worse, the lower is *AINS*[13] and the higher is *ABOARD*. Such managers also undertake mergers that create less value for target and acquiring shareholders taken together.

Other regressors

Several variables remain to be defined. The first of them tests the hypothesis that merger premia decrease with the costliness of acquiring financial claims on productive assets rather than the assets themselves. The variable used is:

> *S&PCLOSE* = value of the S&P 500 index at the end of the
> closing day of the transaction, normalized by the
> GNP deflator for capital expenditures in the year
> of the transaction.

The variable is crude because it neglects the fact that the relations between prices of financial and real assets for individual sectors diverge substantially from the economy-wide average represented by *S&PCLOSE*. The premium should decrease with *S&PCLOSE*.

One regressor picks up an effect on the premium of the form of the nominal payment offered by the acquirer. Payments may be in cash or packages of various securities with or without a cash component:

> *ALLCASH* = 1 if the payment of the takeover price is made
> entirely in cash, zero otherwise.

Target shareholders may discount noncash payments due to uncertainty about their value or transaction costs of redeeming them. On the other hand, cash payments force the target shareholders to pay capital-gain taxes that could under some other payment arrangements be deferred until the swapped securities are sold. Thus no sign can be predicted for *ALLCASH*; Huang and Walkling [1987] reported a positive coefficient, implying that the tax effect dominates. Another significance was recently proposed for the means of

---

[13] The same ambiguity may apply to *AINS* as to *TINS*, insofar as acquisitions increase the utility of an entrenched management, and large shareholdings assure entrenchment. The results of You *et al.* [1986] imply that convergence of interests dominates.

payment. One reason for an acquirer to employ an all-cash offer is to complete the transaction quickly, without regulatory and other delays that occur when issues of securities are involved, before potential rival bidders can spring into action. Formally, *ALLCASH* can register the acquirer's signal of a high valuation and intent to pre-empt potential rivals (Fishman [1989]).

Actual competition for the acquirer is measured by:

$RIVAL = 1$ if some other entity submitted a rival bid for the
target, zero otherwise.

RIVAL and *ALLCASH* are the only variables entering the $B(Z_i)$ function. Other influences on the bargain that must go into the error term include the availability of other target firms that might similarly satisfy the acquirers' objectives, as well as tactical skills, temporal urgency, and competing but qualitatively different transaction opportunities that may have been available to the two firms.

Dependent variable

The exact construction of the dependent variable remains to be specified. The denominator of *PR* is the target's stock price one month (twenty trading days) before the offer's announcement. The announcement date is the day on which the target received its first official bid. The first bid need not come from the eventual acquirer, but it must be the obvious first link in a chain of events leading to the acquisition. The final price per share (numerator) is the one at which the deal is consummated, and the premium is adjusted for the movement of the stock market (S&P 500 Index) between the base date and the date of closing the transaction.

It is important to determine the premium for the full transaction period, not just for the value offered at the announcement date. The acquirer who negotiates a deal at a given price for later completion obtains the equivalent of a free "call" on the entire target company. If the equities market is rising, some of the premium can be expected to be absorbed by the general price increase. The acquirer, however, bears little downside risk. It can usually back out if a fall of the equities market should make the transaction no longer attractive, and indeed most of the deals agreed to but not completed before the crash of October 1987 were later renegotiated at lower prices. We assume that the target held out for a price at the date of announcement that compensated target shareholders for this risk.

III. SAMPLE AND STATISTICAL RESULTS

Sample of mergers

Because patterns of merger activity and abnormal returns associated with them have changed over time (Jarrell, Brickley, and Netter [1988]), we chose

288   ALEXANDER R. SLUSKY AND RICHARD E. CAVES

to analyze a sample of mergers that were completed within a short period, the years 1986–1988. A list of merger transactions was obtained from the Merger and Acquisitions Database collected by ADP Network Services. It includes all corporate acquisitions that were completed during the stated period and brought independent publicly held corporations under the control of other publicly held corporations. The acquisition mechanism could not be a two-tier tender offer. The consideration paid for the target had to exceed $50 million. The target's main line of business had to lie outside of the banking and savings and loan sectors, and it could not possess two or more substantially different classes of common stock. Both the target and acquiring companies had to be incorporated and based in the United States, and the acquiring corporation could not own more than 25 percent of the target's stock before the acquisition announcement was made.

The 100 observations that remained after this screening yielded an average premium over the market price one month earlier of 50.5 percent. The distribution is substantially skewed, and the standard deviation is 41.4 percent.[14] Only 15 mergers showed no evident relatedness between the companies' activities, with related (45) and horizontal (31) mergers prevalent.[15] The mean value of FIT is fairly high. The targets were on average only 3.2 percent as large as their acquirers. Neither group was highly leveraged on average, but the targets less so. Nearly one-fifth of the targets' shares (nearly one-tenth of acquirers' shares) were held by managers and directors, but the concentration of outside shareholdings was fairly low for both groups. About two-thirds of board members were outsiders. About three-fourths of the transactions were paid entirely in cash and involved no evident competing acquirers.

Final model

To summarize the model, the acquirer's normalized reservation price should increase with *FIT* (interacting positively with *SIZE*) and *DEDIF* (the difference between the target's and the acquirer's leverage) and decrease with *S&PCLOSE*. The consideration of incentive alignment indicates that the reservation price should decrease with *TINS*, *TFIVE*, *AINS*, and *AFIVE*, and increase with *TBOARD* and *ABOARD*; due to the entrenchment effect the signs of *TINS* and *AINS* are ambiguous. Premia could either increase or decrease with *ALLCASH*. The outcome within the bargaining range should increase with *RIVAL*, and a positive sign for *ALLCASH* could indicate the

---

[14] The premium was also obtained on the price one week before announcement, yielding a mean premium of 44.7 percent (standard deviation 38.4 percent). The reduction in the mean premium can be read as a measure of the average effect of anticipations and insider trading.

[15] The criterion for a horizontal merger was that the companies operate in the same four-digit industry in the Standard Industrial Classification, which may mean potential rather than actual direct competition. The targets were smaller (*SIZE* = 44.5) in horizontal than in other mergers.

SYNERGY, AGENCY AND PREMIA PAID IN MERGERS 289

effect of potential competition. The absolute values of the slope coefficients of the reservation-price variables should be greater where a rival is present,[16] with the exception of *ALLCASH* and perhaps the variables related to the acquirer's agency situation.

We report one modification that was made to the model prior to estimation. In this sample the proportions of shares held by managers and directors and the insider proportions of boards of directors are highly correlated, 0.43 for targets and 0.30 for acquirers. When regression models include both *TINS* (*AINS*) and *TBOARD* (*ABOARD*) the board-composition variable is always insignificant and usually takes the wrong sign. Because managerial shareholding seems more likely to influence board composition than to be determined by it, we put the board-composition variables aside.

With that decision taken, equation 1 in Table II represents an initial naive version of the model that treats *RIVAL* only as an additive influence and omits the interactive effects of the presence of rival bidders. Equation 2 continues in this fashion to test for a positive interaction between *FIT* and *SIZE*. Equation 3 adopts the interactive specification of the model to let slope coefficients differ when rival bidders are present. Notice that equation 3 possesses considerably greater explanatory power than equations 1 and 2.

Results: real and financial synergies

The first result of the analysis is a surprising negative one—the absence of any favourable effect of fit between acquirer and target on the premium received by the target, despite the use of a more sophisticated measure of fit than in most previous studies. The weak negative relation between premium and fit is present in the zero-order relationships and the mean values of the premia for mergers with various types of fit.[17] Equation 2 tests the hypothesis that the target's assets have positive externalities for the value generated by the acquirer's assets; the coefficient of *FIT*SIZE* is positive as expected but not significant. Allowing the slope coefficient of *FIT* to differ between mergers with and without rival bidders clears up some of the mystery. When rivals are absent, *FIT*'s coefficient is positive though still insignificant, while in the presence of a rival bidder it is negative and highly significant. Could it be that rivalry unleashes competitive instincts that promote overbidding, and that bids grow more inflated the less synergistic basis exists for establishing a "hard" reservation price? *RIVAL* certainly exerts a large and highly

---

[16] This would be the case if the price falls in the middle of the bargaining range in the absence of rivalry (a Nash solution)—see Rubinstein [1982]—but the presence of a rival results in a Bertrand auction that extracts all but epsilon of the acquirer's expected surplus.

[17] The average premium for mergers classed as horizontal or vertical was about 46 percent, that for related or unrelated mergers about 53 percent. The zero-order correlation between *PR* and *FIT* is −0.06.

290   ALEXANDER R. SLUSKY AND RICHARD E. CAVES

significant influence on the premium, with its regression coefficient in equations 1 and 2 not much smaller than the mean difference of 36.5 percent found in the data set.[18]

In the reported models $TDEBTEQ$ and $ADEBTEQ$ are entered as the difference $DEDIF = TDEBTEQ - ADEBTEQ$. Its highly significant positive coefficient implies that the opportunity to infuse capital to a heavily leveraged or capital-constrained target may be a more important basis for gains from mergers than operating synergies.[19] When $DEDIF$ is factored into its components, the (absolute) value of $ADEBTEQ$'s coefficient is somewhat but not significantly larger than $TDEBTEQ$'s; the disaggregation does not improve the model's overall fit. $DEDIF$'s coefficient differs as expected between mergers with and without rivals present (equation 3).

Results: managerial effectiveness

Of the agency-related variables, the concentration of external shareholding in the target firm ($TFIVE$) exerts its expected negative influence on the acquisition premium and is statistically significant. The coefficient of $TINS$ is negative, its significance short of 10 percent in a two-tail test. A negative effect is predicted by incentive-alignment considerations and contradicts the entrenchment hypothesis. When transactions with rival acquirers are distinguished (equation 3), the expected effect on $TFIVE$'s coefficient is strongly evident—indeed, $TFIVE$'s effect is negative only when rivals are present to affect the premium. That pattern is not evident for $TINS$, however.[20]

The agency situation of the acquiring firm also affects the merger premium. Managements that hold larger proportions of their firms' shares offer smaller premia (significant at 5 percent in a one-tail test); the effect of the concentration of outside shareholding ($AFIVE$) is also negative but not

---

[18] Jahera, Hand, and Lloyd [1985] reported 14 percent, Walkling and Edminster [1985] 33 percent, Bradley, Desai, and Kim [1988] 20 percent. We checked for major differences in other regressors between transactions with and without rival bidders. Surprisingly, the target is relatively smaller in cases where rivals are present ($SIZE = 54.0$) than when absent (24.1). FIT does not differ significantly. More rivalrous transactions are all-cash deals (88 percent vs. 67 percent), probably because cash transactions can be executed more quickly. Insider holdings of the target's shares are much higher when rivalry is absent (22.4 vs. 9.3 percent), suggesting that these deals may commonly be negotiated with entrenched managements.

[19] Recall the finding of Ravenscraft and Scherer [1987] that small target firms have typically been abnormally profitable before their acquisition, consistent with a high marginal return to additional capital. You et al. [1986] did not find a significant influence of leverage differences, but the target firms were on average much larger in that study than in the present one.

[20] Because the target firms are rather small, one might expect that their shareholdings are concentrated and that $TFIVE$ and $TINS$ would be negatively correlated, decreasing the chances that both variables will reveal significant negative effects on premia. The correlation is in fact -0.24. For the larger acquiring firms it is positive, 0.12. Walkling and Edminster [1985] did not test directly for agency effects, but they did conclude that premia decrease with the target's ratio of market to book value.

significant. When *AINS*'s coefficient differs between transactions with and without rival bidders, the deterrent effect of managerial shareholding is found to operate only when rivals are absent; it does not seem to curb the competitive-spirits effect of rivalry on merger bids noted above.

Results: other variables

The effect of *S&PCLOSE* is negative as expected but significant only when rival bidders are present. The weakness of this support for the hypothesis of arbitrage between real and financial assets is consistent with the insignificance of *FIT*; the acquisition of "bargain" assets should yield little net payoff unless the buyer has some specific use for or competence in their management.

Finally, the coefficient of *ALLCASH* is positive and significant at 5 percent (two-tail). The size of its coefficient, similar (and comparable) to that of *RIVAL* in equations (1) and (2), exceeds any reasonable estimate of the tax effect and must reflect the role of potential competition. *RIVAL* and *ALLCASH* together indicate that competition in the market for corporate control exerts a powerful influence on merger premia.

Changes in acquiring firms' values

We have taken the premium paid for control by the acquirer to measure the buyer's expected gain. However, the acquirer's shareholders register their own view of their net gain or loss from the transaction in the abnormal returns to acquirer's stock. Acquiring firms' stockholders about break even on average, but behind this mean lurks a substantial variance. If their net gains should be systematically related to any of the hypothesized determinants of premia, the coefficients reported in Table II would be biased estimators of effects on total benefits. One result of You *et al.* [1986] illustrates the hazard: their measure of operating synergy was found to increase the excess return to the acquiring firm's shareholders but not the sum of gains to acquirer and target shareholders together.

We were reluctant to use the standard measure of returns to the acquirer's shareholders — the cumulative abnormal return at the announcement date — because it does not correspond to *PR*, the premium paid adjusted for the market return from before the announcement to the completion of the transaction. If the acquisition price should reflect the call option on the target, the gain to the acquirer's shareholders should be measured over the same interval by the change in the value of the acquirer's shares (adjusted for the change in the market index) between one month prior to the announcement and the date of closing.[21] To make it commensurable with *PR* the market-

---

[21] The objections to this measure are its failure to take account of the acquirer's beta and its inclusion of noise from new information other than the announcement of transaction itself.

TABLE II
REGRESSION RESULTS, DETERMINANTS OF MERGER PREMIA

Independent variable	Equation 1	Equation 2	Equation 3	
			RIVAL = 1	RIVAL = 0
FIT	−1.836	−3.866	−53.851	10.205
	(0.20)	(0.38)	(2.93)	(1.12)
DEDIF	0.211	0.207	0.547	0.132
	(2.40)	(2.34)	(3.30)	(1.39)
TINS	−0.342	−0.323	0.249	−0.168
	(1.62)	(1.50)	(0.43)	(0.87)
TFIVE	−0.702	−0.686	−3.663	0.229
	(2.04)	(1.98)	(5.74)	(0.68)
AINS	−0.574	−0.609	−0.341	−0.621
	(1.84)	(1.91)	(0.39)	(2.07)
AFIVE	−0.385	−0.430	−0.609	−0.214
	(1.00)	(1.09)	(1.04)	(0.49)
S&PCLOSE	−0.158	−0.149	−0.849	−0.119
	(1.11)	(1.04)	(2.20)	(0.95)
ALLCASH	22.823	23.326	18.800	
	(2.53)	(2.57)	(2.37)	
RIVAL	26.234	25.246	301.585	
	(2.79)	(2.64)	(2.74)	
FIT*SIZE		0.069		
		(0.57)		
Constant	95.260	92.752	64.582	
	(2.30)	(2.22)	(1.77)	
R^2	0.224	0.218	0.449	

adjusted change in the acquirer's value is divided by the pre-merger market value of the target firm (not the acquirer). It is designated *APR*.

To determine whether hypothesized influences on *PR* were partly or wholly captured by *APR*, we simply substitute *APR* for *PR* in the models reported in Table II. For equation 1 of Table II the result is:

$$APR = -2000 - 666FIT - 0.216DEDIF + 6.455TINS$$
$$(0.91) \quad (1.34) \quad (0.05) \quad (0.58)$$
$$+ 10.42TFIVE + 14.03AINS + 80.80AFIVE$$
$$(0.57) \quad (0.85) \quad (3.97)$$
$$+ 7.462S\&PCLOSE - 616ALLCASH + 336RIVAL$$
$$(0.99) \quad (1.29) \quad (0.68)$$
$$\bar{R}^2 = 0.120$$

The negative result supports Table II's findings. *APR* is significantly related only to *AFIVE*, confirming that mergers provide more benefit to acquirers' shareholders when the managers are closely monitored. The coefficient of *AINS* is positive although not statistically significant (as it was for You *et al.*).[22] When equation 3 of Table II is reestimated with *APR* as the dependent variable, *RIVAL* takes a significant negative coefficient, and the positive effect of *AFIVE* is found entirely in transactions where no rivals are present. This result is consistent with the "competitive spirits" hypothesis offered for the perversely signed and significant coefficient of *FIT* in Table II, equation 3, for transactions with rivals present.[23]

IV. CONCLUSIONS

This paper brings together in a single analysis the various factors that have been hypothesized (and in some cases found) to affect the value created by mergers—real and financial synergies, behavior of managers in both the target and acquiring firms, and arbitrage between real and financial assets. We obtained no evidence of real synergies, some evidence of arbitrage, and clearly significant effects of both agency and financial synergy. We can quantify these differing effects on merger premia roughly by determining how much their explained variance is reduced by removing the variable or variables that embody each factor. With nearly half of the (uncorrected) variance unexplained in equation 3, this exercise faces the uncertainty that important components or dimensions of each causal factor may have been omitted. With that caveat noted we find the following proportional reductions in the variance explained when the variable(s) embodying the indicated factor are deleted from equation 3: real synergies, 10.6 percent; arbitrage between real and financial assets, 5.9 percent; financial synergy, 13.5 percent; agency factors, 46.0 percent; rivalry, 20.8 percent.[24] Interestingly, real and financial synergy together evidently contribute less to explaining the variance of premia than do agency factors.

We close with brief comments on the study's normative implications. The negative findings on real synergies are a surprise, and we do not stress them because of their disagreement with both other studies of mergers and analyses of corporate diversification (Lemelin [1982]; Wernerfelt and Montgomery [1988]). Our findings about agency factors agree with other evidence of the salutary effect of the market for corporate control on managers of potential targets. However, they qualify that benign effect sharply in showing that weakly monitored managers of acquiring firms overpay (and presumably undertake too many mergers). Also, the dramatic effects on premia of actual

---

[22] *APR* has a very large variance and outlying values, both positive and negative. That pattern results when plausibly distributed percentage returns on the market values of the acquirers are re-expressed as returns on the market values of targets on average only 3 percent as large. It accounts for the extreme coefficient values in the equation.

[23] Equation 3 with *APR* as dependent variable is unsatisfactory in ways suggested by note 22, however, so this conclusion does not deserve much weight.

[24] The incremental effect of *RIVAL* was inferred from the effect of deleting that variable from equation 1.

294   ALEXANDER R. SLUSKY AND RICHARD E. CAVES

and potential competing acquirers qualify the precision of acquiring managers' judgments. Agency and managerial factors are strongly bound up with corporate mergers, and we cannot say whether too many or too few mergers take place.

ALEXANDER R. SLUSKY AND   ACCEPTED MAY 1990
RICHARD E. CAVES,
Department of Economics,
Harvard University,
Cambridge, MA 02138,
USA.

REFERENCES

AMIT, R. and LIVNAT, J., 1988, 'Diversification Strategies, Business Cycles, and Economic Performance', *Strategic Management Journal*, 9, pp. 99–110.

BHAGAT, S., SHLEIFER, A. and VISHNY, R. W., 1990, 'The Aftermath of Hostile Takeovers', *Brookings Papers on Economic Activity*, Microeconomics, pp. 1–72.

BRADLEY, M., DESAI, A. and KIM, E. H., 1988, 'Synergistic Gains from Corporate Acquisitions and Their Distribution between the Stockholders of Target and Acquiring Firms', *Journal of Financial Economics*, 21, pp. 3–40.

BRICKLEY, J. A., LEASE, R. C. and SMITH, C. W. JR., 1988, 'Ownership Structure and Voting on Antitakeover Amendments', *Journal of Financial Economics*, 20, pp. 267–291.

BRUNER, R. F., 1988, 'The Use of Excess Cash and Debt Capacity as a Motive for Merger', *Journal of Financial and Quantitative Analysis*, 23, pp. 199–217.

CAVES, R. E., 1975, *Diversification, Foreign Investment, and Scale in North American Manufacturing Industries* (Economic Council of Canada, Ottawa).

CAVES, R. E., 1989, 'Mergers, Takeovers, and Economic Efficiency: Foresight vs. Hindsight', *International Journal of Industrial Organization*, 7, pp. 151–174.

DANN, L. Y. and DEANGELO, H., 1988, 'Corporate Financial Policy and Corporate Control: A Study of Defensive Adjustments in Asset and Ownership Structure', *Journal of Financial Economics*, 20, pp. 87–127.

DEMSETZ, H. and LEHN, K., 1985, 'The Structure of Corporate Ownership: Causes and Consequences', *Journal of Political Economy*, 93, pp. 1155–1177.

FIRTH, M., 1980, 'Takeovers, Shareholder Returns, and the Theory of the Firm', *Quarterly Journal of Economics*, 94, pp. 235–260.

FISHMAN, M. J., 1989, 'Preemptive Bidding and the Role of the Medium of Exchange in Acquisitions', *Journal of Finance*, 44, pp. 41–57.

HERMALIN, B. E. and WEISBACH, M. S., 1988, 'The Determinants of Board Composition', *Rand Journal of Economics*, 19, pp. 589–606.

HUANG, Y.-S. and WALKLING, R. A., 1987, 'Target Abnormal Returns Associated with Acquisition Announcements: Payment, Acquisition Form, and Managerial Resistance', *Journal of Financial Economics*, 19, pp. 329–349.

JAHERA, J. S., JR., HAND, J. and LLOYD, W. P., 1985, 'An Empirical Inquiry into the Premiums for Controlling Interests', *Quarterly Review of Business and Economics*, 24, pp. 67–77.

JARRELL, G. A., BRICKLEY, J. A. and NETTER, J. M., 1988, 'The Market for Corporate Control: The Empirical Evidence since 1980', *Journal of Economic Perspectives*, 2, pp. 49–68.

JENSEN, M. C., 1986, 'Agency Costs of Free Cash Flow, Corporate Finance, and Takeovers', *American Economic Review: Papers and Proceedings*, 76, pp. 323–329.

JENSEN, M. C., 1988, 'Takeovers: Their Causes and Consequences', *Journal of Economic Perspectives*, 2, pp. 21–48.

JENSEN, M. C. and WARNER, J. B., 1988, 'The Distribution of Power among Corporate Managers, Shareholders, and Directors', *Journal of Financial Economics*, 20, pp. 3–24.

KNOEBER, C. R., 1986, 'Golden Parachutes, Shark Repellants, and Hostile Tender Offers', *American Economic Review*, 76, pp. 155–167.

LANG, L., STULZ, R. M. and WALKLING, R. A., 1988, 'Tobin's Q and the Gains from Successful Tender Offers', Working paper WPS 88-72, Ohio State University.

LEMELIN, A., 1982, 'Relatedness in the Patterns of Interindustry Diversification', *Review of Economics and Statistics*, 64, pp. 646–657.

MALATESTA, P. H. and WALKLING, R. A., 1988, 'Poison Pill Securities: Stockholder Wealth, Profitability, and Ownership Structure', *Journal of Financial Economics*, 20, pp. 347–376.

MONTGOMERY, C. A. and HARIHARAN, S., forthcoming, 'Diversified Expansion by Large Established Firms', *Journal of Economic Behavior and Organization*.

MORCK, R., SHLEIFER, A. and VISHNY, R. W., 1988, 'Management Ownership and Market Valuation: An Empirical Analysis', *Journal of Financial Economics*, 20, pp. 293–315.

PALEPU, K. G., 1986, 'Predicting Takeover Targets: A Methodological and Empirical Analysis', *Journal of Accounting and Economics*, 8, pp. 3–35

PENROSE, E. T., 1959, *The Theory of the Growth of the Firm* (Basil Blackwell, London).

RAVENSCRAFT, D. J. and SCHERER, F. M., 1987, *Mergers. Sell-offs, and Economic Efficiency* (Brookings Institution, Washington).

RHOADES, S. A., 1987, 'Determinants of Premiums Paid in Bank Acquisitions', *Atlantic Economic Journal*, 20, pp. 20–30.

RUBINSTEIN, A., 1982, 'Perfect Equilibrium in a Bargaining Model', *Econometrica*, 50, pp. 97–110.

RUMELT, R. P., 1974, *Strategy, Structure, and Economic Performance* (Division of Research, Graduate School of Business Administration, Harvard University, Boston).

SCHERER, F. M., 1988, 'Corporate Takeovers: The Efficiency Arguments', *Journal of Economic Perspectives*, 2, pp. 69–82.

SHELTON, L. M., 1985, 'The Role of Strategic Business Fits in Creating Gains in Acquisition', Ph.D. dissertation, Harvard University, 1985.

SHELTON, L. M., 1988, 'Strategic Business Fits and Corporate Acquisition: Empirical Evidence', *Strategic Management Journal*, 9, pp. 279–287.

SHLEIFER, A. and VISHNY, R. W., 1986, 'Large Shareholders and Corporate Control', *Journal of Political Economy*, 94, pp. 461–488.

SINGH, H. and MONTGOMERY, C., 1987, 'Corporate Acquisition Strategies and Economic Performance', *Strategic Management Journal*, 8, pp. 377–386.

STULZ, R. M., 1988, 'Managerial Control of Voting Rights: Financing Policies and the Market for Corporate Control', *Journal of Financial Economics*, 20, pp. 25–54.

WALKLING, R. A. and EDMINSTER, R. O., 1985, 'Determinants of Tender Offer Premiums', *Financial Analysts Journal*, 41, pp. 27–37.

WALKLING, R. A. and LONG, M. S., 1984, 'Agency Theory, Managerial Welfare, and Takeover Bid Resistance', *Rand Journal of Economics*, 15. pp. 54–68.

WEISBACH, M. S., 1988, 'Outside Directors and CEO Turnover', *Journal of Financial Economics*, 20, pp. 431–460.

WERNERFELT, B. and MONTGOMERY, C. A., 1988, 'Tobin's q and the Importance of

Focus in Firm Performance', *American Economic Review*, 78, pp. 246–250.

YOU, V., CAVES, R., SMITH, M. and HENRY, J., 1986, 'Mergers and Bidders' Wealth: Managerial and Strategic Factors', in L. G. THOMAS (ed.), *The Economics of Strategic Planning: Essays in Honor of Joel Dean* (Lexington Books, Lexington, MA), pp. 201–221.

[18]

MANAGERIAL AND DECISION ECONOMICS, VOL. 12, 421–428 (1991)

Corporate Takeovers, Stockholder Returns and Executive Rewards

Michael Firth

University of Colorado, USA

Various motives for making corporate acquisitions have been forwarded in the managerial economics literature. Two that have received a lot of attention are the maximization of stockholder wealth and the maximization of senior management's utility. These two alternative views can lead to different acquisition decisions. The paper examines the returns to senior management and the returns to stockholders following corporate takeovers in the United Kingdom. The evidence suggests that if shareholders profit from takeovers then so do the senior management. Of more interest, however, is the finding that if acquisitions result in a reduction in stock market value for the acquiring firm, their senior management appear to gain. In particular, senior management remuneration increases substantially after an acquisition. This evidence is consistent with the maximization of senior management's utility being an important motive in many corporate-acquisition decisions.

The rationale for corporate takeovers is traditionally couched in terms of maximizing stockholder wealth and that firms will make acquisitions only if they believe it will enhance stock prices. While acquisition decisions are made by the senior executives and directors of the company, and not by stockholders themselves, it is argued that the market for managerial labour will discipline the executives into making acquisition decisions that are in the best interests of stockholders (Manne, 1965; Fama, 1980). The early empirical evidence from the USA suggested that takeovers resulted in stock market gains for acquiring companies (Mandelker, 1974; Shick and Jen, 1974), and this research is consistent with the traditional view that acquisitions are beneficial to stockholders of the bidding firms.

An alternative motive for making acquisitions has been forwarded, and this rationale is not directly related to maximizing stock market value. The motive notes that it is senior management who make acquisition decisions, and these managers will be influenced by their own self-interest. This rationale also argues that stockholder discipline of managers is weak enough so that managers can pursue, to some extent, their own goals. Remuneration, power, prestige, and safety of tenure are likely to be major desires of management, and maximizing firm size may be an objective that enables these goals to be attained (Baumol, 1959; Marris, 1964; Mueller,

1969; Williamson, 1964). Amihud and Lev (1981) argue that diversification is a method by which managers can reduce their employment risk, and this may act as a prime motive in explaining some takeovers and especially conglomerate mergers. Perhaps the quickest way for a company to increase its size or diversify into unrelated activities is to make major corporate acquisitions, and it is contended that some managements pursue takeover and merger activity even if stockholders suffer reduced returns (Reich, 1983). Because of the very competitive market for takeovers in countries such as the USA and the UK it should not be too surprising that acquiring-firm management may pay too much for some acquisitions in their haste for maximizing size or diversification.

Research in the UK has found that acquiring firms suffered reduced accounting-based profitability subsequent to the takeover (Meeks, 1977; Utton, 1974), and Firth (1976, 1979, 1980), in contrast to the early US studies, concluded that, on average, bidding-company investors fared poorly. In particular, the stock prices of acquiring firms fell when the takeover was announced and this loss was not recovered in the months afterwards. Similar results have been reported in Australia (Dodd, 1976). This evidence is consistent with the scenario of management maximizing size even at the expense of their company's stock price. It is also consistent with Roll's (1986) hubris hypothesis, which argues that

0143–6570/91/060421–08$05.00

managements' overpay for targets because they overestimate their own ability to run them.

Recent empirical research based on US data has also cast doubts on the supposed profitability of takeovers for acquiring company stockholders (Dodd, 1980; Malatesta, 1983). These studies indicated some acquirors experienced stock price increases upon the takeover announcement while others suffered declines. Research by Lang *et al.* (1989) and Morck *et al.* (1990) has explored factors that might help explain why the stock market perceives some takeovers as being good for the acquiring-firm stockholders and other takeovers as being poor. Lang *et al.* concluded that poorly managed acquiring firms (as evidenced by low Tobin's q-ratios) suffered price declines, presumably because the stock market expects the poor management to be extended to the acquired firm. In contrast, they found that well-managed bidding companies who were taking over poorly managed firms had a good reception in the stock market, with their stock prices rising.[1] Morck *et al.* similarly report that poorly managed acquirors suffer negative stock returns when a takeover announcement is made; their measurement of poorly managed is based on past stock price performance rather than Tobin's q. They also found that returns to bidding firms were lower when the acquisition is in an unrelated field (i.e. diversification) and when the target firm has experienced rapid growth. Morck *et al.* conclude that managerial objectives may depart from maximization of stockholder utility, and this has resulted in negative returns in some takeovers.

Firth (1980) has argued that one reason why shareholders may be tolerant of reduced stock market values of the acquiring company is that investors are well diversified, and they are therefore likely to be invested in the acquired company (whose stock price increases) as well as the acquiring firm. His research showed that the losses in market value of the acquiring firm were offset by gains in the acquired company and thus a well-diversified investor would be no worse off from the takeover. Shleifer and Vishny (1988) have also provided some suggestions as to why poorly performing managers have often been able to retain tenure, although they do not explicitly discuss poor performance generated by an ill-conceived and expensive acquisition.

The potentially conflicting self-interests of management and stockholders can be ameliorated if the managers are themselves substantial investors in the company; that is, managers are motivated by their stockholder role. Prior research in the UK (Firth, 1980) has intimated that the negative stock market reaction borne by the acquiring firm was mitigated somewhat for those companies where the senior management had a relatively large investment stake in their own concern. This is consistent with the view that management may scrutinize the profitability of takeovers more earnestly when they have a substantial equity ownership stake at risk. Similar findings are reported by Amihud *et al.* (1990) in their study of US acquisitions in the period 1981–3. They concluded that bidders who experienced negative stock returns were characterized by having low managerial ownership. Additionally, the study by Lewellen *et al.* (1985) found that managers whose equity ownership in their firms was low relative to the value of their remuneration are associated with making acquisitions that produce negative returns for stockholders. In a more general context, Shleifer and Vishny (1986) discuss the role of large shareholders (who are not involved in the day-to-day management of the firm's operations) and the discipline they can bring to bear on the company's managers. They demonstrate that a large shareholder can have a significant influence on the performance of managers, sometimes by threatening or initiating a takeover bid.

The traditional view that takeover decisions are motivated by concerns of maximizing stock prices and the counterview of acquisitions being motivated more by maximizing management utility may lead to differing outcomes. While maximizing stock price returns is likely, *ceteris paribus*, to lead to higher management remuneration (and possibly greater job security and prestige), other actions (such as increasing firm size) may have an even greater influence on executive compensation (job security and prestige), and these actions could reduce stock returns. Although prestige, power, and job security are difficult (and in some cases impossible) to measure, managerial remuneration and managerial wealth tied up in company stockholdings (monetary rewards) can be ascertained.

The purpose of this paper is to examine the impact of UK corporate takeovers on the remuneration and stockholding wealth of the top management of the acquiring company and to see whether the results are consistent with either of the two motivations for takeovers. The findings will add to the growing literature in this area, much of which is based on US data. Publicly available data allow us to examine the remuneration of the highest-paid director and the chairperson of the acquiring company; compensation data of other senior management are not available. Partitioning the remuneration data on the basis of abnormal returns accompanying the takeover by partitioning and the director's equity investments in their company on the basis of abnormal returns allows some insight into the alternative motives behind takeover activity.

DATA AND METHODOLOGY

Data

The data used in the study consisted of takeover bids for stock exchange listed firms (the offeree) made by stock exchange listed firms (the offeror) in the period 1974–80. Takeover bids where the offeror already held a 20% stake (or more) in the offeree six months prior to the bid announcement were omitted from the sample. This condition was adopted because the stock market is likely anticipating a full bid, and the share price will reflect this. Firms that made more than one successfully completed takeover of another listed company within any three-year period in 1972–82 were excluded from the sample. If a company did make more than one successful acquisition in this period then this will confound the remuneration tests, which examine compensation in the two financial years subsequent to the takeover.

A total of 215 offerees were identified in this period and 254 offerors were involved in making the bids; some takeovers were contested, with several companies bidding for the same offeree. A total of 171 bids were successfully completed and 83 of the offerors were unsuccessful in their acquisition attempt. The 171 successful offerors and the 83 unsuccessful bidders make up the sample data used in the study. For the successful offerors the average of the total assets of the acquired firm to the total assets of the acquiror was 0.23.

Remuneration

The UK Companies Acts of 1948 and 1967 require certain public disclosures of remuneration paid to directors and senior management. In particular, the 1967 Act calls for disclosure of the annual remuner-

ation paid to the highest-paid director and to the chairperson of the company, and that these disclosures be contained in the Annual Report and Accounts sent to shareholders. This information provides the data used in the tests of changes in remuneration. Although the name of the highest-paid director is not stated, it is assumed to be the person designated as the Managing Director in the firm's Annual Report and Accounts, except in those cases where the chairperson appears to be the highest-paid director.

In order to examine the impact of the takeover on the remuneration of the acquiring company's executives, some measure is needed of what the remuneration would have been without the takeover. A review of the literature (Cosh, 1975; Meeks and Whittington, 1975; McGuire *et al.*, 1962; Roberts, 1956; Lewellen and Huntsman, 1970) suggested that firm size, growth in size, and corporate profitability are all candidates as explanators of executive pay. Therefore, measures of size, growth, and profitability were used to model expected remuneration absent a takeover. The procedure involved regressing, for an individual firm, the highest-paid director's salary against firm size, growth in size, and profitability (measured as the ratio of net income to book value of shareholders' equity), using ten years of annual financial statement data prior to the takeover. A similar approach was used to model the chairperson's remuneration. All data (remuneration, size, net income, and stockholders' equity) were restated in 1980 £s using the Consumer Price Index (CPI) as the adjustment for inflation. Two measures of firm size were used: one was the natural logarithm of sales revenue and the other was the natural logarithm of total assets. While these are simple models of executive compensation they nevertheless provide reasonable explanators of remuneration, with coefficients of determination ranging from 0.42 to 0.81 (across the 254 companies in the sample). Inspection of the individual regressions revealed that company size was by far the most important variable in the model, with growth in size and profitability being invariably non-significant ($p > 0.10$).[2] In general, the model using total assets as the measure of size gave higher R^2s than those utilizing sales revenue. The above findings resulted in developing, for each company, a model of remuneration based on firm size (using either ln (total assets) or ln (sales revenue), the choice depending on maximizing R^2).

Profitability and growth in size were omitted.[3]

The model is

$$ACTREM_i = \alpha_i + \beta_i \ln SIZE$$

$$\text{(total assets or sales)} \quad (1)$$

where $ACTREM_i$ = actual remuneration of managing director (chairperson) for firm i. Estimates of α_i and β_i ($\hat{\alpha}_i, \hat{\beta}_i$) were derived as the coefficients from a regression model of Eqn (1) using ten years of data. The coefficients of determination ranged from 0.38 to 0.80.

The model is used to predict remuneration in the financial year following the takeover and the year thereafter. Thus

$$PREREM_{i,t+1} = \hat{\alpha}_i + \hat{\beta}_i \ln SIZE^*_{i,t+1}$$

$$PREREM_{i,t+2} = \hat{\alpha}_i + \hat{\beta}_i \ln SIZE^*_{1,t+2}$$

where $PREREM_i$ = prediction of remuneration for the highest-paid director for firm i; similarly, when chairperson is substituted for the highest-paid director. $SIZE^*$ is the estimate of size had no takeover occurred.

Two measures of $SIZE^*_i$ were calculated. One consisted of adjusting the size in year $t+1$ to 'reflect' assets (sales) relating to the acquiror and assets (sales) relating to the acquired. For example, if the acquiring company contributed 75% of the combined assets (sales) of the two firms (acquiring and acquired) prior to the takeover then $SIZE^*_{t+1} = 0.75 (SIZE)_{t+1}$. This is admittedly a crude estimate of what $SIZE^*$ should be. For example, a takeover may lead to increased sales because of marketing synergies, and hence our estimate of $SIZE^*$ may be too high. Similarly, there may be significant sales of assets in the year after acquisition, and this may lead to our estimate of $SIZE^*$ being too low. The second measure of $SIZE^*$ requires extrapolating size (assets or sales) via a time-series analysis. A simple time-trend analysis was used to calculate what size would be. Ten years of inflation-adjusted data prior to the takeover were used to compute an average rate of change in assets (sales). This rate was then used to predict size in year $t+1$. The two estimates of $SIZE^*_i$ gave similar numbers, and in the results that follow the $SIZE^*$ variable was defined as the time-trend version. The results using the first measure were essentially the same as with using the time-trend computation of size.

The predicted remuneration, based on assuming that the takeover had not been made, was then compared against the actual remuneration. Thus

$$\Delta REM_{i,t+1} = ACTREM_{i,t+1} - PREREM_{i,t+1}$$

$$\Delta REM_{i,t+2} = ACTREM_{i,t+2} - PREREM_{i,t+2}$$

$\Delta REM_{i,t}$ was not calculated as year t, the year of the acquisition, may have been substantially completed by the time the takeover was finalized, and thus the remuneration may not reflect the occurrence of the acquisition.

The change in remuneration variable, ΔREM_i, was calculated as the average of $\Delta REM_{i,t+1}$ and $\Delta REM_{i,t+2}$. The averaging of two years might better reflect the longer-term impact of the acquisition on remuneration. ΔREM_i was calculated for the highest-paid director and the chairperson.

Directors' Shareholdings

The UK Companies Act 1967 requires that directors' shareholdings in their firms be disclosed in the Annual Report. The holdings of each individual director are published. The impact of the takeover on the value of these stockholdings is assessed as the abnormal return in the week of the announcement of the bid, multiplied by the value of the director's shareholding in the week prior to the bid. The numbers of shares owned by the managing director and the chairperson were taken to be the average of the beginning-of-year and end-of-year holdings. The change in the managing director's (chairperson's) shareholding wealth, denoted $\Delta STOCK$, was adjusted to 1980 £s.

Senior Management Total Wealth

The takeover is postulated to have a potential impact on both the remuneration and the shareholding wealth of senior management. It is possible that the shareholding wealth aspect could offset the gains achieved in remuneration, and so a total wealth variable is needed to measure the overall impact on senior management. The $\Delta STOCK$ variable captures the change in the manager's stockholding wealth due to the takeover and the ΔREM variable averages the changes in remuneration for years $t+1$ and $t+2$ following the acquisition. In order to capitalize the impact of the takeover on a manager's annual emoluments, a tenure of six years beyond the acquisition date is assumed. A factor of 5.242 was used to multiply the ΔREM variable. The factor 5.242 is the annuity value of £1 for 6 years and discounted at 4%. This admittedly arbitrary factor is similar to that used by Lambert and Larcker

(1987).[4] The $\Delta WEALTH$ variable is calculated as $\Delta WEALTH_i = \Delta STOCK_i + 5.242 \Delta REM_i$, and one calculation is done for the chairperson and one for the managing director (it is assumed that the highest-paid director is the managing director).

RESULTS

The residuals surrounding the takeover announcement were calculated using the well-known market-model methodology of Fama *et al.* (1969). The parameters of the market model were estimated using 60 weeks of data ending twelve weeks prior to the announcement of the takeover. The significance test is based on Patell's (1976) Z-test, which examines whether the scaled squared abnormal return is different from unity. The abnormal return for the successful acquirors in week 0, the week surrounding the announcement, was −0.042 and was statistically significant at the $\alpha = 0.05$ level. More than two thirds of the acquiring companies suffered negative abnormal returns. Abnormal returns in other weeks were close to zero, and Table 1 gives the details. The average increase in size due to the takeover was 23%. For the companies experiencing positive abnormal returns the figure was 24% and, for the negative category, 23%. The direction (sign) of the abnormal returns appears to be independent of the size of the bid.

The impact of the takeover announcement on the value of the managing director's and the chairperson's shareholdings in their own firm was measured. On average, there was a decline in the market value of their wealth amounting to −£2237.[5,6] Within this aggregate the average (median) market value gain of those 47 firms who experienced positive abnormal returns was £2006. The corresponding median gain for the chairperson was £2746. For those firms that experienced negative abnormal returns the average (median) market value decline amounted to −£3845. The corresponding median loss for the chairperson was −£2068. The results from Firth (1980) indicated that the higher the personal wealth that senior management invest in their own firm, the more circumspect they are in making acquisitions. In a similar way, Amihud *et al.* (1990) concluded that high managerial ownership was associated with more positive abnormal returns. In order to examine whether this empirical finding holds true in the current study, abnormal returns were correlated with the value of the managing director's (chairperson's) shareholdings prior to the takeover announcement. The correlation coefficient was 0.32 (0.29 for the chairperson) and statistically significant, thus indicating that the greater the senior management's personal investment in their own firm, the higher the abnormal return. This result is consistent, therefore, with previous findings.

The median change in remuneration (ΔREM) of the highest-paid director and of the chairperson subsequent to the takeover is shown in Table 2. ΔREM is partitioned on the basis of whether the abnormal returns are positive or negative. As can be seen, the median remuneration increases substantially after the takeover and ΔREM is statistically different from zero for both partitions (using the Wilcoxon Matched Pairs Signed-Ranked Test). The

Table 1. Abnormal Returns and Cumulative Abnormal Returns Accruing to Acquiring Firms Centred at the Takeover Announcement Week (Week 0)

Week	Abnormal returns	Number of positive abnormal returns $n=171$	Cumulative abnormal returns
−4	−0.007	82	−0.007
−3	0.007	87	0.000
−2	0.009	90	0.009
−1	−0.001	85	0.008
0	−0.042[a]	47	−0.034
1	−0.008[a]	73	−0.042
2	0.007	89	−0.035
3	0.002	86	−0.033
4	−0.001	84	−0.034

[a] Statistically significantly different from zero at $\alpha = 0.05$.

Table 2. Change in Remuneration (ΔREM) for the highest-paid Director and the Chairperson following a Takeover Bid.

(a) Successful bids	Highest-paid director median	Chairperson median
For firms experiencing positive abnormal returns	£4832[a]	£4169[a]
For firms experiencing negative abnormal returns	£3917[a]	£3263[a]

(b) Unsuccessful bids	Highest-paid director Median	Chairperson Median
	£122	−£179

[a] Statistically different from zero at $p < 0.05$ (Wilcoxon Matched Pairs Signed-Rank Test).

change in remuneration for those firms experiencing positive abnormal returns was greater than that for those experiencing negative abnormal returns, although the difference was not statistically significant ($p > 0.10$, Wilcoxon and Mann–Whitney tests). Although the change in the remuneration is highest for takeovers that benefit stockholder returns, the highest-paid director and chairperson of firms associated with negative abnormal returns also receive substantial increases in their remuneration. This result contrasts with that of Lambert and Larcker (1987), whose US-based research found no statistically significant increase in compensation for the senior management of firms making acquisitions that resulted in negative returns to stockholders.

Panel (b) of Table 2 shows the ΔREM for those bidding firms that did not successfully complete the acquisition. The change in remuneration was small and not statistically different from zero at any meaningful level of significance. Absent a takeover, the $PREREM_i$ model appears to give good predictions of actual remuneration.

The $\Delta WEALTH$ variable measures the overall impact on the total wealth of the highest-paid director/managing director and chairperson. It is an aggregate of $\Delta STOCK$ and the capitalization of ΔREM (6 years of ΔREM discounted at 4%). The median $\Delta WEALTH$ for firms that experienced positive abnormal returns (and hence positive $\Delta STOCK$) was £26 217 for the managing director and £24 718 for the chairperson. This is statistically different from zero ($p < 0.05$). For those companies both the stockholders and the senior management appear to prosper from the takeover. Of more interest is the $\Delta WEALTH$ number for firms that experience negative abnormal returns. Here the $\Delta STOCK$ variable is negative and the ΔREM is positive (from Table 2). The median $\Delta WEALTH$ is positive £15 472 for managing directors and positive £15 198 for the chairpersons. Both of these variables were statistically significantly different from zero. While stockholders lost wealth because of the takeover, the managing director and chairperson of the acquiring company fared well. In contrast to this result, Lambert and Larcker (1987) found that, in the USA, managers of bidding companies who made unprofitable acquisitions actually suffered a reduction in personal wealth; this reduction was, however, not statistically significant at $\alpha = 0.10$. Lambert and Larcker's conclusion that senior management did not increase their wealth by

making acquisitions that had an adverse impact on shareholders is not confirmed in this study of UK data.

A comparison of the positive and negative abnormal return partitions showed that $\Delta WEALTH$ was greatest for the positive group and this was statistically significant ($p < 0.10$ Wilcoxon and Mann–Whitney U-test). The evidence indicates that to engage in 'profitable' (that is, positive abnormal return) acquisitions results in higher monetary returns to senior management. The evidence also shows, however, that to make an 'unprofitable' acquisition is better than making no acquisition at all as far as the senior management's overall wealth is concerned. In addition, there is no evidence that the managing director and chairperson suffered increased job-tenure risk because of the takeover.

CONCLUSIONS

While there have been numerous empirical studies examining the consequences of takeovers using both accounting numbers and stock market data, there has been relatively little research into managerial motives and consequences for making acquisition decisions. Two motives have been promulgated as explanators of takeover decisions, one being to maximize stockholder returns and the other to maximize managerial perquisites. These two motives can lead to differing outcomes for the stockholders in the acquiring company. In particular, the managerial perquisites hypothesis may lead to a desire to increase firm size, even at the expense of lowering stock prices. (Presumably, stock price considerations could not be ignored altogether, because if prices fell far enough the acquiring firm

---

Table 3. Change in Total Wealth ($\Delta WEALTH$) for the Highest-paid Director/Managing Director and the Chairperson following Acquisition

	Highest-paid director/ managing director	Chairperson
For firms experiencing positive abnormal returns	£26 217[a]	£24 718[a]
For firms experiencing negative abnormal returns	£15 472[a]	£15 198[a]

[a] Statistically different from zero at $p < 0.05$ (Wilcoxon).

itself would attract takeover bids with the consequent increased probability of management losing their job. In addition to the takeover threat, stockholders are also likely to vote against extension of management contracts if the stock price fell substantially.)

Empirical evidence in the UK has revealed that many takeovers result in negative abnormal returns for the acquiring firm, and this suggests that stockholder wealth maximization might not be an important motive in some of these acquisition decisions. Instead, increasing managerial returns could be a strong motivating factor, and so the current research set out to examine the impact of takeovers on senior managers' remuneration and wealth. Data availability limited the analyses to examining the remuneration and stock wealth of just the highest-paid director/managing director and the chairperson.

The results showed that to make acquisitions that are well received by the stock market (i.e. those with positive abnormal returns) leads to significant increases in managerial rewards. Even acquisitions that are met with negative abnormal returns appear to be rewarding to senior management. The acquisition process leads invariably to an increase in managerial remuneration, and this appears to be predicated on the increased size of the company. The evidence therefore is consistent with takeovers being motivated by managers wanting to maximize their own welfare. Shareholder wealth maximization appears, on the basis of the results reported here, to be a weaker motivation in many acquisitions.

Acknowledgement

The author would like to thank the referee for helpful comments on an earlier version of the paper.

NOTES

1. Firth (1976) found no significant relationship between stock price performance and the ratio of stock market capitalization to stockholders' equity in his study of UK takeovers and mergers.
2. The importance of size and the relative non-importance of growth and profitability has been found in prior studies of executive pay in the UK (Meeks and Whittington, 1975; Yarrow, 1972).
3. *ACTREM* was also modelled by including profitability and growth in size as explanatory variables. The

conclusions did not change with this formulation, and so are not reported.
4. The analysis effectively uses inflation-adjusted data as ΔREM_i is taken to be constant over the six years. For this reason, a 'seemingly low' discount rate of 4% is used. The conclusions from the ensuing analyses are still valid if a discount rate of 10% is employed.
5. No information is available on whether the managing director and chairperson held any shares of the acquired firm.
6. The averages are the median figures. The distribution is heavily skewed to the right, and the median gives a better notion of central tendency than does the mean.

REFERENCES

Y. Amihud and B. Lev (1981). Risk reduction as a managerial motive for conglomerate mergers. *Bell Journal of Economics* 12, 605–17.
Y. Amihud, B. Lev and N. Travlos (1990). Corporate control and the choice of investment financing: the case of corporate acquisitions. *Journal of Finance* 45, June, 603–16.
W. J. Baumol (1959). *Business Behavior, Value and Growth*, New York: Macmillan.
A. Cosh (1975). The remuneration of chief executives in the United Kingdom. *Economic Journal* 85, March, 75–94.
P. Dodd (1976). Company takeovers and the Australian equity market. *Australian Journal of Management* 1, 15–35.
P. Dodd (1980). Merger proposals, management discretion, and stockholder wealth. *Journal of Financial Economics* 8, June, 105–37.
E. Fama, L. Fisher, M. Jensen and R. Roll (1969). The adjustment of stock prices to new information. *International Economic Review* 20, February, 57–70.
E. Fama (1980). Agency problems and the theory of the firm. *Journal of Political Economy* 88, April, 288–307.
M. Firth (1976). *Share Prices and Mergers*, Westmead, Farnborough: D. C. Heath.
M. Firth (1979). The profitability of takeovers and mergers. *Economic Journal* 89, June, 316–28.
M. Firth (1980). Takeovers, shareholder returns, and the theory of the firm. *Quarterly Journal of Economics* 94, March, 235–60.
R. Lambert and D. Larcker (1987). Executive compensation effects of large corporate acquisitions. *Journal of Accounting and Public Policy* 6, Winter, 231–43.
L. Lang, R. Stulz and R. Walkling (1989). Managerial performance, Tobin's Q, and the gains from successful tender offers. *Journal of Financial Economics* 24, 137–54.
W. Lewellen and B. Huntsman (1970). Managerial pay and corporate performance. *American Economic Review* 60, September, 710–20.
W. Lewellen, C. Loderer and A. Rosenfeld (1985). Merger decisions and executive stock ownership in acquiring firms. *Journal of Accounting and Economics* 7, April, 209–31.

P. Malatesta (1983) The wealth effects of merger activity and the objective functions of merging firms. *Journal of Financial Economics* **11**, April, 155–81.

G. Mandelker (1974). Risk and return: the case of merging firms. *Journal of Financial Economics* **1**, December, 303–35.

H. Manne (1965). Mergers and the market for corporate control. *Journal of Political Economy* **73**, April, 110–20.

R. Marris (1964). *The Economic Theory of Managerial Capitalism*, London: Macmillan

J. McGuire, J. S. Y. Chui and A. Elbing (1962). Executive income, sales and profits. *American Economic Review* **52**, September, 753–61.

G. Meeks and G. Whittington (1975). Directors' pay, growth and profitability. *Journal of Industrial Economics* **14**, September, 1–14.

G. Meeks (1977). *Disappointing Marriage: A Study of the Gains from Merger*, London: Cambridge University Press.

R. Morck, A. Shleifer and R. Vishny (1990). Do managerial objectives drive bad acquisitions? *Journal of Finance* **45**, March, 31–48.

D. Mueller (1969). A theory of conglomerate mergers. *Quarterly Journal of Economics* **83**, November, 643–60.

J. Patell (1976). Corporate forecasts of earnings per share and stock price behavior. *Journal of Accounting Research* **14**, Autumn, 246–76.

R. Reich (1983). *The Next American Frontier*, New York: Times Books.

D. Roberts (1956). A general theory of executive compensation based on statistically tested propositions. *Quarterly Journal of Economics* **70**, May, 270–94.

R. Roll (1986). The hubris hypothesis of corporate takeovers. *Journal of Business* **59**, April, 197–216.

R. Shick and F. Jen (1974). Merger benefits to shareholders of acquiring firms. *Financial Management* **3**, Winter, 45–53.

A. Shleifer and R. Vishny (1986). Large shareholders and corporate control. *Journal of Political Economy* **94**, 461–88.

A. Shleifer and R. Vishny (1988). Value maximization and the acquisition process. *Journal of Economic Perspectives* **2**, Winter, 7–20.

M. Utton (1974). On measuring the effects of industrial mergers. *Scottish Journal of Political Economy* **21**, February, 13–28.

O. Williamson (1964). *The Economics of Discretionary Behavior: Managerial Objectives in a Theory of the Firm*, Englewood Cliffs, NJ: Prentice-Hall.

G. Yarrow (1972). Executive compensation and the objectives of the firm. In *Market Structure and Corporate Behaviour* (edited by K. Cowling), London: Gray-Mills.

[19]

THE ACCOUNTING REVIEW
Vol. LXI, No. 2
April 1986

The Merger/Bankruptcy Alternative

Victor Pastena and William Ruland

ABSTRACT: Considerable research has examined the ability of accounting information to predict bankruptcy. Bankruptcy, however, represents only one of many possible outcomes for the distressed firm. A timely merger can serve as a bankruptcy alternative. The study compares a sample of distressed firms that merged to a sample of distressed firms that entered bankruptcy. Theory suggests that the owners of distressed firms should prefer merger. The managers, however, may feel that their interests are better served through bankruptcy. The examination focuses upon both firm-related characteristics and the personal interests of owners as determinants of the merger/bankruptcy choice. A probit analysis was used to test the importance of three firm-related variables—revenues, financial leverage, and the magnitude of tax carryforwards in explaining the merger/bankruptcy decision. The examination shows that the distressed firms that merge have lower financial leverage and are larger than firms that enter bankruptcy. Tax carryforwards are not important in the model. We also examined the association of ownership concentration with the merger/bankruptcy choice. The tests reveal that distressed firms with high ownership concentration (or owner control) show an increased tendency to merge rather than to declare bankruptcy. The results suggest that the self-interest of managers, rather than just the interests of shareholders and creditors, seems to help motivate the merger/bankruptcy choice.

T HE association of accounting relationships and financial distress has been examined extensively in the accounting literature. Early studies including Beaver [1967], Altman [1968], and Deakin [1972] examined the ability of accounting ratios to identify the financially distressed firm. A closely related line of research has examined alternatives to bankruptcy, including the merger alternative. Altman [1971] and Stiglitz [1972], among others, have noted the use of mergers as substitutes for bankruptcy. More recently, Bulow and Shoven [1978] and Shrieves and Stevens [1979] have examined the timely decision to merge as a bankruptcy alternative. This paper seeks to integrate the previous research by examining the extent to which accounting information seems to explain the merger/bankruptcy decision.

THE ALTERNATIVES

A number of alternatives are available to managers of firms in financial difficulty. These alternatives include:

- Bankruptcy with the possibility of business termination;
- Continued operation in expectation of future solvency, perhaps in conjunction with restructuring debt, re-

We wish to acknowledge helpful comments from two anonymous reviewers.

Victor Pastena and William Ruland are Professors of Accounting, both at Baruch College of the City University of New York.

Manuscript received October 1984.
Revision received June 1985.
Accepted August 1985.

288

ducing wages, selling productive assets, or anticipating improvement in general economic conditions; and

- Participation in a merger or other form of acquisition.

The concern here is with the two extreme alternatives—bankruptcy and merger. The merger and bankruptcy alternatives lead to very different implications for the shareholders, creditors, and management of the distressed firm. The alternatives also have important social consequences in that they affect customers, suppliers, the community, and other outside parties.

The next section of the paper examines the impact of the bankruptcy and merger alternatives upon the firm. Following this is an examination of influences on management's choice of the merger/bankruptcy alternatives. We then report on an empirical study of conditions under which management seems to opt for merger as an alternative to bankruptcy.

Bankruptcy

The term bankruptcy refers to a variety of circumstances. One is the condition of negative net worth—where the market value of assets is less than total liabilities. Another is the inability to pay debts as they come due. The term bankruptcy also applies to a legal condition under which a firm continues to operate under court protection. The legal definition is the one adopted for use in this study.

Bankruptcy has multiple objectives. One objective is to protect the rights of creditors. A second objective is to provide time for the distressed business to improve its situation. Bankruptcy prevents creditors from taking additional action to collect on debts or to foreclose on property. A third objective in extreme cases is to provide for the orderly liquidation of assets.

Bankruptcy can be initiated either by the firm or its creditors. Creditors, for example, can petition for bankruptcy on showing that the corporation is not paying its bills. In a bankruptcy the court may appoint an independent trustee to manage the firm's property or may permit the previous management to continue operating the business. The concerned parties then make recommendations for business operations or for the distribution of assets.

The Merger Alternative

There are numerous motivations for merger including growth, synergy, diversification, and control objectives [Halpern, 1983]. With respect to the distressed business merger, the merger of a distressed and a healthy business provides the distressed business with a source of capital and consequently permits continuation in business with less risk of failure.

The literature suggests that generally the distressed firm's shareholders should benefit more from merger than from bankruptcy. The shareholders continue to hold stock with some positive value as a result of the merger. In contrast, the shareholders often receive nothing in a bankruptcy.[1] Shrieves and Stevens [1979] set forth a number of possible reasons for preferring merger over bankruptcy. These include:

- Avoidance of bankruptcy legal and administrative costs;
- Possible loss of tax carryforwards of the loss firm on liquidation (examined later);
- Going-concern value in a merger greater than liquidation value if the bankruptcy progresses to liquidation; and
- Adverse effects of bankruptcy on sales and income due to customer

---

[1] Clark and Weinstein [1983] report that the stock value declined to zero for 66 of the 162 bankrupt firms examined in their study.

fears of inability to honor contracts, provide replacement parts, etc.

Bulow and Shoven [1978] demonstrate that avoiding bankruptcy should always benefit creditors as a whole and that in theory, bankruptcy occurs only because of disagreement between the concerned parties. The literature treats merger as a substitute for bankruptcy under the presumption that the distressed firm should be able to find a merger partner at some price as long as the net asset value is positive and under the assumption of a well-functioning market for information. As the situation deteriorates toward a condition of negative net asset value, the possibility of merger is reduced.

In theory, we might expect the distressed firm to take the initiative in trying to arrange a merger. Empirically, however, this is difficult to test.[2] For example, a possible scenario might involve the distressed firm's quietly mentioning its availability to its bankers with no public announcement. Some time later, a potential acquiring firm formally and publicly demonstrates interest in an acquisition. In this case, the newspaper announcements would not accurately reflect which party initiated the acquisition. This study is concerned with the conditions under which merger seems to be an attractive alternative to bankruptcy, and with management's incentives to merge rather than declare bankruptcy. The interest is limited to whether or not the distressed firm merges and the issue of determining which firm initiates the merger is not addressed.

Merger seems preferred to bankruptcy from the shareholder's view. Even if the discontinuance of operations is contemplated, the ability of the acquiring corporation to benefit from tax loss carryforwards should result in more value in a merger than in a sale of assets in liquidation. When the interests of managers

are considered, however, the situation changes. The next section illustrates that while merger may be beneficial to the equity shareholders, the distressed firm's managers may not view a merger as desirable.

INFLUENCES ON MANAGEMENT CHOICE

This study examines management's merger/bankruptcy decision as a joint function of the characteristics of the distressed firm's ownership and of the distressed firm itself. The expected relationship of ownership in the distressed firm and the merger/bankruptcy choice is examined in the following section. We then examine firm-related characteristics.

Management's Interests

Although merger of the distressed firm should best serve unsecured creditors and shareholders, top managers may feel that their interests are better served through bankruptcy. Jensen and Ruback [1983, p. 31] assert that "since target managers replaced after takeovers lose power, prestige and the value of organization-specific human capital, they have incentives to oppose a takeover bid even though shareholders might benefit substantially from acquisition." Similarly, Baron [1983] suggests that management may resist tender offers because of their "preference for control" to preserve jobs, perquisites, and any agency costs they are appropriating. The results of an empirical study by

[2] We examined *Wall Street Journal* articles published for the year prior to the bankruptcy announcement to obtain insights regarding merger negotiations. Analysis of the bankrupt firms included in our sample revealed evidence of prior merger negotiations in only 15 percent of the cases. The newspaper articles did not indicate which party actually initiated the merger proposal. We have no indication of the number of unreported negotiations or whether the reported negotiations were meaningful. We also searched for announcements of merger negotiations for the merger firms. These announcements did not usually indicate which party initiated the proposal.

Pastena and Ruland   291

Ang and Chua [1981] suggest that managers of acquired firms may lose jobs more rapidly than managers of firms that go bankrupt and successfully emerge from bankruptcy. Corporations sometimes emerge from bankruptcy with the same managers. If the distressed firm's management optimistically anticipates this outcome, management may prefer bankruptcy to merger.

When the firm is controlled by equity shareholders rather than by managers, we expect that the shareholder interests will prevail. Previous work by Williamson [1964] and Monsen and Downs [1965], among others, suggests an association between ownership concentration and management decisions. With respect to the merger/bankruptcy choice, shareholders should prefer merger to bankruptcy because in a merger the equity shareholders receive stock while in bankruptcy they frequently end up with nothing. Jensen and Ruback [1983], in a review of previous studies, note that in tests including both healthy and distressed firms, target firms in successful takeovers experience abnormal stock price increases of 20 percent. Clark and Weinstein [1983], in an examination of distressed firms, report that stock prices decrease substantially when troubled firms file for bankruptcy. They find that this stock price reduction is in addition to previous stock price reductions associated with market awareness of financial distress.

The preceding discussion suggests that the extent of ownership concentration should influence the merger/bankruptcy choice. If ownership is concentrated among a few shareholders, these shareholders will tend to exercise control. An associated possibility is that high management stock ownership is partly responsible for the high owner concentration and that in this case, the interests of managers and shareholders will be more congruent. In

either case we expect that distressed corporations with large ownership concentration ratios will merge rather than declare bankruptcy. On the other hand, if ownership is not concentrated, we expect managers to exercise more control and act in their own interest rather than in the interest of owners. In this event, managers may opt for bankruptcy.[3]

Ownership concentration information is published in a number of sources including proxy statements provided in accord with Securities and Exchange Commission (SEC) Rule 403 and SEC 10-K Statements. For purposes of this study we used a secondary data source, the Standard and Poor's *Corporate Records*. The *Corporate Records* contain financial information including ownership data on most larger publicly held firms. Use of this source resulted in a substantially larger sample than would be possible through relying on proxy statements, which are not readily available for the 1970s.

Ownership concentration is measured as the total percentage of voting stock owned by managers, directors, and other parties. This concentration measure is similar to that used by Dhaliwal, Salamon and Smith [1982] in a study of control and accounting methods. The measure used here differs primarily in that concentration is measured continuously rather than as a dichotomous variable. A high concentration ratio implies owner rather than manager control of the business and is expected to be associated with the merger

---

[3] Conceivably a manager can invest a high percentage of individual wealth in the firm's shares while the manager's stock ownership as a percentage of total shares outstanding still remains relatively low. In this case, the manager's preferences might resemble those of shareholders, even though the observed concentration ratio is low. It seems more likely to us, however, for a low relative concentration measure to be associated with a low relative importance of ownership to the manager. In other words, we assume that low ownership concentration, in general, implies small amounts of management stock ownership.

option. Low concentration implies a high degree of management control and should be associated with the bankruptcy alternative.

As an alternative, we could have examined the percentage or value of stock owned by managers. The concentration measure was used because it seems to better represent control and because we could not always determine the effective management stock ownership. In some cases, the disclosures indicated only the total percentage ownership of both managers and directors. In other cases, individuals with the same family names as the managers owned stock, or trusts owned large percentages of stock with managers voting these shares. Use of the concentration measure avoided arbitrary determinations in these cases.

Firm-Related Variables

A number of firm-related variables also are expected to be associated with the merger/bankruptcy alternative. These include financial leverage, the availability of tax carryforwards, the size of the firm and the severity of financial distress. The study examines these variables in evaluating the association of ownership concentration and the merger/bankruptcy decision.

Financial Leverage. Other things equal, we expect that highly leveraged firms. should make less desirable acquisition candidates. One reason is that if a low-leverage firm acquires a high-leverage firm, the leverage of the new firm will be higher than for the original firm and the borrowing capacity will be reduced. While one might argue that the buyer can take debt into consideration in determining the offering price, it seems more likely that potential buyers will avoid the highly leveraged firm. Empirical support is provided by Stevens [1973], who found that acquired firms were significantly less lev-

eraged than nonacquired firms. Other factors equal, with higher leverage, the distressed firm's shareholders' interests should be advanced more through merger than through bankruptcy. Our expectation, however, is that the dominant factor will be the reduced demand for highly leveraged acquisitions. Consequently, we expect that high leverage will be associated with bankruptcy rather than merger. Leverage is measured here as the ratio of total debt to total assets.

Tax Carryforwards. Many firms in financial distress possess operating loss carryforwards. Tax legislation provides for the carryback of operating losses against taxable income of the three previous years. When tax losses exceed available carryback eligibility, the business obtains carryforward entitlement. The carryforward entitlement reduces taxable income in future profitable years. Currently the legislation prescribes a 15-year carryforward period for operating losses.

Potentially valuable carryforwards also arise from unused investment tax credits. The investment tax credit reduces taxes payable by ten percent of the cost of qualifying investments in most personal property. Since the zero income corporation will likely not pay taxes, the investment tax credit will not provide immediate tax benefit. The legislation also provides for the carryforward of unused investment tax credits.

Carryforwards are of interest to the merger/bankruptcy decision because they have value only if the firm remains in business. If the firm terminates operations, the carryforwards are lost. On the other hand, if the financially distressed business is acquired it may be possible to retain the carryforwards. (The business press frequently cites tax carryforwards as rationale for an acquisition.) Consequently, we expect that financially distressed firms with loss carryover eligibility will tend to merge rather than enter bankruptcy. The carryforward variable is measured as the amount of the carryforward (including investment tax credit carryforward) as a percentage of total revenues. Measurement of the carryforward relative to the size of the firm provides an indication of the relative importance of the carryforward compared to other considerations. If carryforwards provide incentives for merger rather than bankruptcy, we expect carryforwards to be positively correlated with merger.

Total Revenues. We also test for the effect of size because large firms and small firms differ in many respects and size empirically explains differences in many previous accounting studies. Collins, Rozeff and Dhaliwal [1981], for example, suggest that size is an all-inclusive variable that can act as a surrogate for the many variables not specifically included in the study. The direction of the possible association of size and the merger/bankruptcy choice is not clear. Size is measured here as the natural logarithm of total revenue adjusted for changes in the Consumer Price Index. The indexing reduces possible distortions resulting from examining events occurring up to 14 years apart. No direction is hypothesized for the influence of this variable.

The Severity of Financial Distress. The relative severity of financial distress is expected to affect both the attractiveness of the firm as a merger candidate and management's incentive to merge. The literature generally assumes that merger is an alternative to bankruptcy for the distressed firm or at least for firms in the early stages of financial distress. We expect that increased distress will increase the desirability of merger for the distressed firm and at the same time, decrease its attractiveness as a potential merger partner. In the extreme case of negative net market value, it should be difficult for the distressed firm to obtain a merger partner at any price. While our ex-

pectation is that financial distress will be associated with bankruptcy rather than with merger, the interest is in testing for the importance of distress differences in our study design rather than in including distress as an explanatory factor in a model.

Firms classified as financially distressed vary greatly with respect to the degree of financial distress. In some cases the issue of whether or not a firm is distressed and the nature of the distress is not very clear. For example, a reasonably healthy firm may appear distressed due to temporary factors. In other cases, the severity of the situation will be obvious to most observers and the firm will likely have difficulty finding a merger candidate (unless substantial tax carryforwards are available). We expect, other factors equal, that the greater the financial distress, the greater the probability of bankruptcy rather than merger.

Ideally, for the purpose of attributing causality to the ownership concentration variable, the degree of financial distress for the period prior to the bankruptcy or merger event should be the same for the bankruptcy and merger samples. Although the sample selection procedure does not expressly control for financial distress, the study design does test for significant differences in financial distress between the merger and bankruptcy firms.

Financially distressed merger firms are identified using the model developed by Altman [1968].[4] Altman used multiple discriminant analysis to classify firms as bankrupt and nonbankrupt using the following relationship:

---

[4] We selected the Altman [1968] model because the data were readily available, it is relatively easy to use, it seems to be reasonably well understood and, applied on an ex-ante basis, it may work as well as other models proposed to date. Some alternatives such as the Altman, Haldeman and Narayanan [1977] Zeta procedure are more subjective and would have increased study complexity since the model was used to select distressed merger firms from the entire Compustat population.

294

$$z_j = 1.2*X1_j + 1.4*X2_j + 3.3*X3_j + 0.6*X4_j + 1.0*X5_j,$$

where

j is the firm index,
$X1_j$ is working capital/total assets,
$X2_j$ is retained earnings/total assets,
$X3_j$ is earnings before interest and tax/total assets,
$X4_j$ is market value of equity/book value of total debt, and
$X5_j$ is sales/total assets.

The value of the dependent variable, z_j, is compared to the critical cutoff value to identify the bankrupt and nonbankrupt firms. The model incorporates financial relationships for the time period immediately preceding the date of filing for bankruptcy. The discriminant analysis then produces a cutoff or z-score to differentiate between firms filing for bankrupt and nonbankrupt firms. Altman's critical or cutoff z-score was 2.675 with lower z-scores indicating financial distress. A number of subsequent empirical studies have confirmed the success of this model. The present study applies the Altman model and cutoff scores to obtain a z-score for each firm included in the sample.

We expect to find a positive association between financial leverage and financial distress and do not include financial distress in the multivariate model for this reason. We should note that leverage and distress do not necessarily measure the same phenomenon. Financial distress as indicated by the z-score considers profitability and a number of other factors in addition to leverage.

THE SAMPLE

A sample of troubled firms was obtained for the 14-year period beginning in 1970 and ending in 1983. The Bankruptcy Reform Act of 1978 significantly modified the ability of firms to reorganize in bank-

ruptcy [White, 1983; Altman, 1983], and we were initially reluctant to go beyond the 1979 effective date of the Act. The sample size using just pre-1979 data, however, proved to be smaller than expected. To expand the sample we conducted the study first using the entire sample and then using just the pre-1979 data.

The sample of firms was obtained from the 1983 Compustat Annual Industrial Research Tape. This tape shows all firms deleted from Compustat with financial data up to one or two years prior to the year of deletion. The sample of distressed firms was selected using the model developed by Altman [1968]. Previous examinations of this model have indicated high predictive ability for control group firms not included in the sample used to obtain the discriminant function. There are also indications that the model is robust over time. Altman and McGough [1974], for example, examined periods subsequent to that tested in Altman [1968] and concluded that the parameters of the model classified cases with a high degree of accuracy in these later time periods. Consequently, the present study identifies troubled merged firms using the Altman discriminant function parameters and critical cutoff described earlier.

We restricted the sample to manufacturing firms since the Altman model was not developed for banks, insurance companies, or other nonmanufacturing businesses. The Research Tape contains 531 manufacturing firms that merged during the study period. The Altman model was then run on each firm for the last year of data availability. The z-scores suggest that 83 manufacturing firms were distressed. Of these, 15 were not publicly traded, were not listed in Standard and Poor's *Corporate Records*, were missing key Compustat data for several years prior to the merger date, or were operated as subsidiaries and merged through long-

Pastena and Ruland   295

TABLE 1
SUMMARY STATISTICS FOR INDEPENDENT VARIABLES

Variable	Merged Firms		Bankrupt Firms	
	Mean	Standard Deviation	Mean	Standard Deviation
Concentration	0.333	0.226	0.271	0.211
Leverage	0.386	0.163	0.525	0.187
Tax	0.107	0.291	0.116	0.142
Log Size	3.802	1.294	2.690	1.066
Distress	1.980	0.657	1.650	1.478

term creeping acquisition. A sample of 68 distressed manufacturing firms that merged remained for study.

The Compustat research tape includes 95 bankrupt firms, of which 56 are manufacturing firms. Fourteen firms were deleted for data availability reasons, and 42 firms remained for study. (The Altman model classified 33 of these 42 firms as bankrupt as of the latest annual financial data available prior to bankruptcy.) The final sample contains 110 distressed firms that either merged or entered bankruptcy.

The ownership concentration and tax carryforward data were obtained from Standard and Poor's *Corporate Records* using information for the reporting period just prior to the announcement of bankruptcy or merger. All other financial data were taken from Compustat using the most recent financial information available on the bankruptcy or merger announcement date.

THE DISTRIBUTION OF INDEPENDENT VARIABLES

The summary statistics for the independent variables are presented in Table 1. The data show that ownership concentration is substantially higher for merged firms. This is consistent with the hypothesis that firms with low ownership concentration (manager control firms) tend to act in the interest of managers and choose bankruptcy rather than merger. The summary statistics also indicate that distressed firms entering bankruptcy are more highly leveraged, are smaller, have slightly larger tax carryovers, and have somewhat lower Altman z-scores (indicating high financial distress) compared to the merged firms. We consider these relationships in more depth in the following multivariate analysis.

MULTIVARIATE ANALYSIS

We first present data relating to the correlations between independent variables. We then introduce the probit model, present results, and test the predictive ability of the variables.

Cross-Correlations

The degree of cross-correlation between independent variables is summarized in Table 2. Correlation coefficients are relatively low except for the leverage/financial distress relationship. The leverage/financial distress relationship is consistent with the expectation that high z-score (low distress) firms should have less debt. The high correlation was responsible for excluding the distress variable from the probit model.

TABLE 2

CORRELATION MATRIX OF INDEPENDENT VARIABLES

	Concentration	Leverage	Tax Carryforward	Size	Distress
Concentration	1.000	−0.006	−0.123	−0.148	0.134
Leverage		1.000	0.135	−0.192	−0.425
Tax Carryforward			1.000	0.006	−0.190
Size				1.000	0.142
Distress					1.000

Probit Analysis

The joint ability of the independent variables to explain the merger/bankruptcy choice was examined using both probit analysis and multiple discriminant analysis. Multiple regression analysis requires a dependent variable with an interval scale— an assumption not met with the merger/ bankruptcy measure. Probit analysis is less restrictive in that it assigns a distribution to the dependent variable under the assumption that the underlying distribution is approximately normal. An advantage of probit over multiple discriminant analysis is that it provides significance tests for the individual independent variables as well as for the overall classification. Kaplan and Urwitz [1979] and Hagerman and Zmijewski [1979] provide more detailed comparisons of alternative models.

The form of the classification model is:

$$M_j = a + b1*CON_j + b2*LEV_j + b3*TAX_j + b4*SIZE_j + e_j.$$

where

j is the firm index,

M_j is 0 if the result is bankruptcy; 1 if a merger,

CON_j is the percentage of outstanding shares owned by major shareholders as reported in Standard

and Poor's *Corporate Records*,

LEV_j is the ratio of total debt to total equity,

TAX_j is the ratio of available tax loss carryforwards (including investment tax credit carryforwards) to total revenues, and

$SIZE_j$ is the natural logarithm of total revenue adjusted for changes in the Consumer Price Index.

The intercept a and the terms $b1$ through $b4$ are coefficients obtained by fitting the model, and e_j is the unexplained error term.

The probit model results are presented in Table 3. The percentage of variance explained (adjusted R^2 statistic) by the model is 53.2 percent. The model correctly classifies 73.6 percent of the cases. The accuracy of the probit model classification was compared to the accuracy of the best naive model using a standard test of proportions. This test reveals that the classification results are significant at the 0.01 level. The chi-square statistic of 40.9 with four degrees of freedom is significant at the 0.01 level.

The analysis of each independent variable as summarized in Table 3 indicates that ownership concentration, financial leverage, and size are all significant at the 0.01 level. The tax carryover variable does not exert any important influence

TABLE 3
PROBIT ANALYSIS OF MERGER/BANKRUPTCY CHOICE MODEL

	Adjusted R^2		53.2 percent	
	Percent of cases predicted correctly		73.6 percent	
	Chi-square statistic (4 d.f.)		40.9 (.01 significance)	

Independent variables	CON	LEV	TAX	SIZE
Expected sign of independent variables	POS	NEG	POS	—
Maximum likelihood estimate	1.671	−3.036	0.861	0.619
t-statistic	2.396	−3.400	0.830	4.064
Significance level	.01	.01	.40	.01

upon the ability to explain the merger/bankruptcy choice after the effects of ownership concentration, financial leverage, and size are considered.

We note that the results may understate the role of financial leverage since leverage is one variable used in the Altman model to select the sample of merged firms. We expect that the merger sample used here will tend to have high-leverage firms and since we also expect high leverage for bankruptcy firms, the ability of financial leverage to explain the merger/bankruptcy choice may be greater than that indicated by this model.

With respect to the owner concentration variable, the probit model results differ from those suggested in Table 1. The Table 1 data do not suggest substantial differences between ownership concentration for the merger and bankruptcy samples. The probit analysis, however, shows that after adjusting for the effects of leverage and size, concentration adds to the ability of the model to explain merger/bankruptcy choice.

The univariate examination showed that the merger and bankrupt firms have slightly different distress measures and consequently did not seem to be in identical circumstances just prior to bankruptcy. As indicated previously, financial distress was not included in the multivariate model due to high correlation with the financial leverage variable. We repeated the probit analysis with the distress variable included and obtained very similar results to those reported in Table 3. These findings suggest that the observed differences in distress measures between the two samples were not responsible for the study results.

The data seem to demonstrate that owner-controlled and manager-controlled firms act differently. Previous research showed the relationship between ownership control and the choice of accounting alternatives. The present study suggests that ownership control is also associated with merger/bankruptcy choice. Since owner and manager control firms seem to make different economic decisions, ownership structure should be important to investors, lenders, and other financial statement users. Consequently, the results seem to support the SEC proxy statement

298   The Accounting Review, April 1986

TABLE 4
DISTRIBUTION OF SAMPLE BY YEAR

Year	Number of Merged Firms	Number of Bankrupt Firms
1970	0	2
1971	5	1
1972	3	3
1973	3	3
1974	2	3
1975	2	3
1976	6	6
1977	7	2
1978	8	6
Subtotal	36	29
1979	15	2
1980	1	4
1981	9	1
1982	3	4
1983	4	2
Subtotal	32	13
Total sample	68	42

requirements for ownership concentration disclosure.

The 1978 Bankruptcy Act

The 1978 Bankruptcy Act, as indicated earlier, substantially changed bankruptcy procedures and may have influenced the merger/bankruptcy decision. The analysis so far has considered the entire sample including both the pre-1979 and post-1979 periods (see the distribution of events by year shown in Table 4). To examine the possible influence of the 1978 Act upon study results, we repeated the analysis using only pre-1979 data. The sample size was reduced to 65 firms.

The distribution of independent variables was similar to that reported in Table 1 for the complete sample. The probit model classification, however, is even more powerful than with the larger sample. The percentage of variance explained by the probit model increases to 74.3 percent from 53.2 percent for the full sample, and the percent of cases predicted correctly increases to 83 percent from 73.6 percent. The apparent ability of the model to fit the pre-1979 period better (than for the entire observation period) may be due to a variety of factors including the effect of the new legislation.

Discriminant Analysis

As a consistency check, we conducted a multiple discriminant analysis to test the predictive power of the variables considered in the merger/bankruptcy choice. First we discuss the ability of the model to classify observations. The results summarized in Table 5 reveal that for the full sample of firms, the discriminant function correctly classified 86.8 percent of the mergers and 57.1 percent of the bankruptcies for an overall classification rate

Pastena and Ruland   299

TABLE 5

MULTIPLE DISCRIMINANT ANALYSIS OF MERGER BANKRUPTCY CHOICE MODEL

Standard Multiple Discriminant Analysis:

Group	Percent Correct	Classification	
		Merger	Bankrupt
Merger	86.8	59	9
Bankrupt	57.1	18	24
Total	—	77	33
Average	75.5	—	—

Lachenbruch Holdout Sample Technique:

Group	Percent Correct	Classification	
		Merger	Bankrupt
Merger	80.9	55	13
Bankrupt	54.8	19	23
Total	—	74	36
Average	70.9	—	—

of 75.5 percent. For the reduced sample of 65 pre-1979 firms, the classification rates for mergers, bankruptcies, and combined sample were 72.2 percent, 82.8 percent, and 76.9 percent, respectively. The difference in classification accuracy for the merger and bankruptcy groups is due at least in part to statistical properties of the classification model. Analysis of correct cases requires priors regarding the expected distribution. With unequal probabilities, the model assigns proportionately more observations to the larger group [Pinches, 1980].

The Lachenbruch jackknife holdout sample procedure then was applied to test the predictive accuracy of the discriminant function. The jackknife technique avoids the problem of testing the model on the same data used to fit the model. It is also distribution-free and does not require multivariate normality, equal dispersion matrices, and other restrictive assumptions of multiple discriminant analysis. This approach correctly predicted 80.9 percent of the mergers and 54.8 percent of the bankruptcies for an overall prediction rate of 70.9 percent. An overall prediction accuracy of 76.9 was achieved when the discriminant function was developed using only pre-1979 data. The results of the jackknife model predictions exceeded those achieved by the best naive model at the 0.01 significance level.

SUMMARY AND CONCLUSIONS

Numerous corporate bankruptcies occur every year despite the apparent attractiveness of merger as a possible alternative to bankruptcy for some distressed firms. This study examined factors associated with the merger/bankruptcy choice. Analysis of the

300   The Accounting Review, April 1986

literature suggested that variables to be considered include ownership concentration, financial leverage, tax carryovers, and size. The results show that size, leverage, and ownership concentration dominate the explanatory model. The tax carryover variable was not significant.

The results are consistent with the hypothesis that the self-interest of managers seems to be at least partly responsible for the merger/bankruptcy choice. Previous research by Dhaliwal, Salamon and Smith [1982] revealed the importance of ownership control as a determinant of accounting method choice. This study suggests that ownership control is also associated with the merger/bankruptcy alternative. One potentially important accounting implication is that proxy disclosure of ownership concentration appears to be potentially useful to investors for providing a basis for predicting future management behavior.

REFERENCES

Altman, E., *Corporate Bankruptcy in America* (Lexington Books, 1971).
———, "Discussion of Bankruptcy Costs and the New Bankruptcy Code," *Journal of Finance* (May 1983), pp. 517–523.
———, "Financial Ratios, Discriminant Analysis and the Prediction of Corporate Bankruptcy," *Journal of Finance* (September 1968), pp. 587–609.
——— and T. McGough, "Evaluation of a Company as a Going Concern," *Journal of Accountancy* (December 1974), pp. 50–57.
———, R. Haldeman and P. Narayanan, "Zeta Analysis: A New Model to Identify Bankruptcy Risk of Corporations," *Journal of Banking and Finance* (June 1977), pp. 29–54.
Ang, J. and J. Chua, "Corporate Bankruptcy and Job Losses Among Top Level Managers," *Financial Management* (Winter 1981), pp. 70–74.
Baron, D., "Tender Offers and Management Resistance," *Journal of Finance* (May 1983), pp. 331–342.
Beaver, W., "Financial Ratios as Predictors of Failures," *Journal of Accounting Research* (Supplement, 1967), pp. 71–111.
Bulow, J. and J. Shoven, "The Bankruptcy Decision," *The Bell Journal of Economics* (Autumn 1978), pp. 437–456.
Clark, T. and M. Weinstein, "The Behavior of the Common Stock of Bankrupt Firms," *Journal of Finance* (May 1983), pp. 489–504.
Collins, D., M. Rozeff and D. Dhaliwal, "The Economic Determinants of the Market Reaction to Proposed Mandatory Accounting Changes in the Oil and Gas Industry: A Cross Sectional Analysis," *Journal of Accounting and Economics* (March 1981), pp. 37–71.
Deakin, E., "A Discriminant Analysis of Predictors of Business Failure," *Journal of Accounting Research* (Spring 1972), pp. 167–179.
Dhaliwal, D., G. Salamon and E. D. Smith, "The Effect of Owner versus Management Control on the Choice of Accounting Methods," *Journal of Accounting and Economics* (July 1982), pp. 41–53.
Hagerman, R. and M. Zmijewski, "Some Economic Determinants of Accounting Policy Choice," *Journal of Accounting and Economics* (August 1979), pp. 141–161.
Halpern, P., "Corporate Acquisitions: A Theory of Special Cases? A Review of Event Studies Applied to Acquisitions," *Journal of Finance* (May 1983), pp. 297–317.
Jensen, M. and R. Ruback, "The Market for Corporate Control," *Journal of Financial Economics* (April 1983), pp. 5–50.
Kaplan, R. and G. Urwitz, "Statistical Models of Bond Ratings: A Methodological Inquiry," *Journal of Business* (April 1979), pp. 231–263.
Monsen, R. and A. Downs, "A Theory of Large Managerial Firms," *The Journal of Political Economy* (June 1965), pp. 231–236.
Pinches, G., "Factors Influencing Classification Results From Multiple Discriminant Analysis," *Journal of Business Research* (December 1980), pp. 429–456.

Pastena and Ruland   301

Shrieves, R. and D. Stevens, "Bankruptcy Avoidance as a Motive for Merger," *Journal of Financial and Quantitative Analysis* (September 1979), pp. 501–515.

Stiglitz, J., "Some Aspects of the Pure Theory of Corporate Finance: Bankruptcies and Take-Overs," *The Bell Journal of Economics and Management Science* (Autumn 1972), pp. 458–482.

Stevens, D., "Financial Characteristics of Merged Firms: A Multivariate Analysis," *Journal of Financial and Quantitative Analysis* (March 1973), pp. 149–158.

White, M., "Bankruptcy Costs and the New Bankruptcy Code," *Journal of Finance* (May 1983), pp. 477–488.

Williamson, O. E., *The Economics of Discretionary Behavior: Managerial Objectives in a Theory of a Firm* (Prentice-Hall, 1964).

[20]

Journal of Financial Economics 25 (1989) 163–190. North-Holland

ORGANIZATIONAL CHANGES AND VALUE CREATION IN LEVERAGED BUYOUTS
The Case of The O.M. Scott & Sons Company*

George P. BAKER and Karen H. WRUCK

Harvard University, Boston, MA 02163, USA

Received December 1989, final version received February 1990

This study documents the organizational changes that took place at the O.M. Scott & Sons Company in response to its leveraged buyout. Our findings confirm that both the pressure of servicing a heavy debt load and management equity ownership lead to improved performance. Equally important at Scott, however, and undocumented in large-sample studies, are debt covenants restricting how the cash required for debt payments can be generated. the adoption of a strong incentive compensation plan, a reorganization and decentralization of decision making, and the relationship between managers, the leveraged buyout sponsors, and the board of directors.

1. Introduction

1.1. A brief history of the company

In December 1986, the O.M. Scott & Sons Company (Scott), the largest producer of lawn care products in the U.S., was sold by the ITT Corporation (ITT) in a divisional leveraged buyout. Scott, located in Marysville, Ohio, was founded in 1870 by Orlando McLean Scott to sell farm crop seed. Beginning in 1900, the company began to sell weed-free lawn seed through the mail, and in the 1920s, introduced the first home lawn fertilizer, the first lawn

*We would like to thank everyone at the O.M. Scott & Sons Company and Clayton & Dubilier who gave generously of their time and made this study possible: Lorel Au, Richard Dresdale, Martin Dubilier, Richard Martinez, Lawrence McCartney, Tadd Seitz, John Smith, Robert Stern, Homer Stewart, Henry Timnick, Kenneth Tossey, John Wall, Craig Walley, and Paul Yeager. In addition, we would like to thank Kenneth French (the referee), and Robin Cooper, Robert Eccles, Leo Herzel, Michael Jensen, Steven Kaplan, Kenneth Merchant, Krishna Palepu, Richard Ruback, G. William Schwert, Eric Wruck, the participants in the Financial Decisions and Control Workshop and the Organization Behavior and the Theory of the Firm Workshop at the Harvard Business School, and the participants in the Conference on the Structure and Governance of Enterprise sponsored by the *Journal of Financial Economics* and the Harvard Business School for their helpful comments and suggestions. Support from the Division of Research, Harvard Business School, is gratefully acknowledged.

164   *G.P. Baker and K.H. Wruck, Creating value in LBOs: The case of O.M. Scott*

Table 1

Financial performance and divestiture and acquisition activity of ITT Corporation, 1978–1986.[a]

Year	Units acquired[b]	Units divested[b]	Earnings per share	Dividends per share	Stock return	Market return
1978	2 [$198]	0 [$0]	$4.66	$2.05	−6.1%	9.0%
1979	9 [$35]	17 [$74]	2.65	2.25	4.1	22.3
1980	2 [$35]	17 [$564]	6.12	2.45	27.5	30.5
1981	4 [$13]	9 [$82]	4.58	2.62	11.2	−3.5
1982	3 [$38]	7 [$498]	4.75	2.70	19.7	20.2
1983	3 [$26]	11 [$126]	4.50	2.76	45.7	21.4
1984	NA	8 [$638]	2.97	1.88	−30.5	5.9
1985	NA	23 [$1455]	1.89	1.00	31.9	27.9
1986	NA	12 [$597]	3.23	1.00	39.1	17.0

[a]Acquisition and divestiture activity as reported in ITT 10-K reports, NA indicates not available in these reports. Acquisitions for 1984–1986 were not reported by year, but the total amount is $208 million. Stock returns are annual returns. The market return is the CRSP value-weighted return.

[b]Number of units and value in $millions given in brackets.

spreader, and the first patented bluegrass seed. In fiscal 1988, Scott had sales of $197 million and employed 792 people.

Scott was closely held until 1971, when it was purchased by ITT. Scott became a part of the consumer products division of the huge conglomerate, and operated as a wholly owned subsidiary for 14 years. In 1984, ITT began a series of divestitures, prompted by a decline in financial performance and rumors of takeover and liquidation. Table 1 presents a summary of ITT's financial performance and of the number of companies it bought and sold from 1978 to 1986. In January 1985, ITT announced that it would divest $1.7 billion in assets. The object of these sales was to 'streamline ITT into a telecommunications, insurance, and high technology company'. On January 17, 1985, an article in the *Wall Street Journal* identified Scott as one of the businesses that 'could be included among the certain companies' ITT wanted to sell. On November 26, 1986, ITT announced that the managers of Scott, along with Clayton & Dubilier (C&D), a private firm specializing in leveraged buyouts, had agreed to purchase the stock of Scott and another ITT subsidiary, the W. Atlee Burpee Company. The deal was closed on December 30, 1986, and represented 25% of ITT's total dollar divestitures for the year.

Table 2

Financing of Clayton & Dubilier's purchase of O.M. Scott & Sons Company from ITT Corporation, 12/31/86, sources and uses of funds.

Sources of Funds		
Bank revolving credit agreement ($137 million available)	$77,000,000	37%
Bank working capital loan	$44,000,000	21%
Subordinated notes	$50,300,000	24%
Subordinated debentures	$19,600,000	9%
Common stock	$20,000,000	9%
Total	$210,900,000	100%
Uses of Funds		
Purchase of Scott and Burpee	$151,000,000	72%
Repayment of indebtedness to ITT	$52,600,000	25%
Transactions fees	$5,000,000	2%
Working capital	$2,300,000	1%
Total	$210,900,000	100%

Clayton & Dubilier secured financing for the sale. Table 2 describes the financial structure of Scott after the buyout. Bank loans and the sale of notes and debentures raised $190.9 million. Another $20 million was raised through the sale of equity: 61.4% of the shares were held by the C&D partnership, 20.6% by debtholders, 17.5% by Scott management and employees, and 0.4% by Joseph Flannery, a board member who had been involved in another C&D deal. Immediately following the buyout, Scott's capital structure consisted of 91% debt.

Large-sample studies of leveraged buyouts have documented median levels of post-buyout management equity ownership and leverage strikingly similar to those at Scott. Kaplan (1989), Muscarella and Vetsuypens (1989), and Smith (1989) analyze leveraged buyouts and post-buyout operating performance for samples of 76, 72, and 58 firms, respectively. Kaplan and Smith document median post-buyout equity ownership by management of 22.6% and 16.7%, respectively, and median post-buyout leverage of about 90%.

Scott's operating performance improved dramatically following the buyout. See table 3. Between the end of December 1986 and the end of September 1988, earnings before interest and taxes increased by 56%. Over the same period, sales were up 25%. These increases were not caused by a reduction in spending on research and development, or spending on marketing and distribution: R&D spending increased by 7%, and marketing and distribution spending by 21%. Capital spending increased by 23% after the buyout. Largely through attrition, average annual full-time employment dropped by about 9%. Average working capital requirements were reduced by a total of $23.1 million over this same 21-month period, falling from 37.5% to 18.4% of sales. All three large-sample studies cited above find that over two to four

Table 3

Financial and operating data for O.M. Scott & Sons Company [$000,000s].

	Pre-buyout: Year ended 12/30/86	Post-buyout: Year ended 9/30/88	Percent change
Income Statement			
EBIT	$18.1	$28.2	55.8%
Sales	$158.1	$197.1	24.7%
Research & development	$4.1	$4.4	7.3%
Marketing & distribution	$58.4	$70.7	21.1%
Balance Sheet[a]			
Average working capital	$59.3	$36.2	−39.0%
Total assets	$243.6	$162.0	−33.5%
Long-term debt	$191.0	$125.8	34.1%
Adjusted net worth	$20.0	$38.3	91.5%
Other			
Capital expenditures	$3.0	$3.7	23.3%
Employment	868	792	−8.9%

[a]Balance sheet figures are reported at the close of the buyout transaction. Adjusted net worth is GAAP net worth adjusted for accounting effects of the buyout under APB no. 16. In Scott's case the bulk of the adjustment is adding back the effects of an inventory write-down of $24.7 million taken immediately after the buyout.

years following the buyout operating income increases by an average of 40%. Smith examines changes in accounting line items and finds no evidence that repair and maintenance expenditures are postponed, or that research and development expenditures are reduced. In addition, she provides evidence that firms manage working capital more closely after a buyout, documenting a significant reduction in both days receivables and inventories during the post-buyout period.

1.2. Purpose of our study

By the objective measures used in the large-sample studies, Scott appears to be a typical buyout: its post-buyout leverage, equity ownership, and operating performance are close to the median values reported in those studies.[1] The authors interpret their results as being consistent with an agency theory of the firm in which high leverage and managerial equity ownership lead to improved incentives and consequently improved operating

---

[1]Scott's increase in capital expenditures appears atypical, given Kaplan's result that on average capital expenditures fall by 20% after a leveraged buyout.

Table 4

Titles of the individuals interviewed as a part of the data collection process.

At O.M. Scott & Sons Company
President and Chief Executive Officer, Board Member
Chief Financial Officer
Assistant Treasurer and Head of Working Capital Task Force (now Treasurer)
General Counsel
Director of New Process Development
Vice President, Associate Relations
Assistant Vice President, Associate Relations
Manager of Contract Operations
Plant Manager

At Clayton & Dubilier
Chairman of the Board of O.M. Scott and Clayton & Dubilier Partner
Member of the Board, Liaison to O.M. Scott, Clayton & Dubilier Partner

performance. The studies do not, however, actually document any organizational changes resulting from an LBO. They cannot, therefore, explore the organizational links between buyouts and improved operating performance. Documenting these organizational changes is essential if researchers are to understand the mechanisms by which changes in a firm's financial structure affect organizational performance.

This study documents the organizational changes that took place at Scott in response to its LBO. The structure of the Scott organization and the way managers made decisions changed radically after the buyout. Our analysis of the data leads us to conclude that the organizational changes at Scott were a response to three factors: i) the constraints imposed on the organization by high leverage, ii) changes in the way managers were compensated, and iii) changes in the way Scott's top managers were monitored and advised.

The factors that led to improved operating performance are examined in detail below. Each of the next three sections covers one of the factors crucial to organizational change at Scott: the constraints of high leverage, changes in incentives and compensation, and changes in the monitoring of top managers. Section 5 summarizes the organizational changes that took place, and section 6 presents our conclusions.

Our analysis focuses on the effect of each factor on the alignment of incentives across the firm's claimants. The combination of equity ownership and close monitoring by the board of directors aligns managers' interests with those of the firm's shareholders. The large debt burden and incentive compensation based on cash measures of performance give managers the incentive to operate the firm in a way that generates cash, while the debt covenants and equity ownership prevent managers from taking actions that would damage firm value in the long run.

1.3. Data collection

The data used in this study are drawn from both public and private sources, including extensive interviews with C&D partners and managers at all levels of the Scott organization, confidential internal documents, prospectuses, ITT 10-K reports, and the *Wall Street Journal*. Table 4 lists the titles of all the individuals we interviewed. The confidential data (both quantitative and interview quotations) presented in this study were released by the company for publication here. We had access to other data that are too sensitive for publication. Where applicable we describe the conclusions from our analysis of these data, though we are unable to publish the data themselves.

2. Constraints of high leverage

2.1. Cash requirements for debt service

Scott's senior debt consists of floating-rate working capital loans and borrowings against a $137 million revolving credit agreement. A group of six major banks, headed by Manufacturers Hanover Trust, provides this capital, as well as a standby letter of credit for up to $2 million. The interest rate on the loans is either the agent's reference rate plus 1.5% or LIBOR plus 3.5%, with interest periods of one, three, or six months, both at Scott's option. There is a repayment penalty of 2.5% if the loans are repaid with other than internally generated funds or the proceeds of a public equity offering. These loans are secured by substantially all of Scott's assets. After the buyout, Scott hedged some of its floating-rate obligations by entering into an agreement with lenders that limited the interest rate adjustment to a maximum increase of 2%. The rate of interest has averaged 10.25% over the post-buyout period. In addition to interest payments, the credit agreement includes a principal repayment schedule that requires the principal amount to be repaid by the end of calendar 1994.

Scott's subordinated debt consists of unsecured 13% notes to mature in 1996, and unsecured $13\frac{1}{2}$% debentures to mature in 1998. The notes are senior to the debentures, but junior to the bank debt. The subordinated debt was originally sold to 16 financial institutions. These institutions sold the debt to the public in February of 1988. Sinking-fund payments are required for both the notes and the debentures. By maturity two-thirds of the principle amount of the notes and three-fourths of the principle amount of the debentures will have been set aside.

The amount of cash required to service the debt was substantially greater than Scott's prebuyout cash flow. In the first year after the buyout interest expense was $15 million, in the second year it was $18.5 million. Additional cash is required to pay down bank borrowings and make sinking-fund payments as follows:

1989:	$ 7.9 million,
1990:	$ 9.0 million,
1991:	$ 9.0 million,
1992:	$ 9.0 million,
1993:	$ 9.0 million,
1994:	$28.0 million,
1995:	$22.0 million,
1996:	$ 5.0 million,
1997:	$ 5.0 million.

In 1986, the year before the buyout, Scott's *EBIT* (earnings before interest and taxes) was only $18.1 million. Table 3 presents a summary of Scott's income statement and balance sheet before and after the buyout.

2.2. Debt covenants

With so much pressure on the organization to generate cash, managers may be tempted to take actions that help service the debt but do damage to the value of the firm. Such actions are detrimental to all of the firm's claimholders, including the debtholders. Debtholders are interested in the firm's ability to generate cash over the life of the debt agreement.[2] Debt covenants serves as a contract that restricts managers' ability to use value-reducing methods to generate cash or take other actions that reduce debtholder value.

If a firm defaults, managers are forced to negotiate with lenders to resolve the situation, or if no agreement can be reached to seek protection from creditors under Chapter 11. Resolution of a default or Chapter 11 generally involves replacing debt claims with equity claims, leading to a substantial dilution of the existing equity. A default is costly not only to equityholders, but to managers, since it may force them to surrender control of the company to a bankruptcy court. There is also a risk to managers of losing their jobs. Gilson (1989) finds that 44% of the CEOs of firms in financial distress lose their jobs as a part of the recovery process.

Restrictive covenants can also help control potential conflicts of interest between equityholders and debtholders. In highly leveraged organizations such as Scott the benefit to equityholders of taking actions that reduce debtholder wealth, for example paying themselves a liquidating dividend

---

[2]This assumes that the value of the debtholder's claim on the organization as a going concern is generally higher than the value of the claim in liquidation. Jensen (1989) argues that in a highly levered firm this is likely to be true and that creditors will therefore tend to work out default situations rather than force Chapter 11 or liquidation.

from the proceeds of a loan or making a 'lottery ticket' investment, can be large.[3]

The covenants in Scott's debt agreements are summarized in table 5. They restrict certain economic and financial activities and require the maintenance of certain levels of accounting-based measures of performance. With the exception of priority, the covenants of the subordinated issues are similar and are therefore discussed collectively. The accounting-based covenants are defined in terms of audited figures. Each year Scott's financial statements are prepared in compliance with Generally Accepted Accounting Principles, and audited by Coopers & Lybrand. This is done to assure the credibility of the reports to debtholders, to assure the ability to continue to raise funds in the debt market, and to have an audited track record should the company be taken public again in the future.

Scott's bank credit agreement restricts the firm's investment and production decisions. Managers are allowed discretion in the choice of specific projects, but annual capital expenditures are restricted to specific dollar amounts set forth in a schedule. Scott can dispose only of assets that are worn out or obsolete and have a value of less than $500,000. No changes in the corporate structure, for example mergers or the acquisition of assets, are allowed. Hence, although Scott's credit agreement does not dictate production decisions, the firm is indirectly required to continue in the same economic activity. Cash dividends to stockholders are prohibited, as is the issuance of additional debt other than the debt securities outstanding at closing.

The subordinated debt covenants define restrictions on many of the same items restricted in the credit bank agreement, but the covenants are looser. Dividends, for example, are not prohibited, but a complex set of conditions must be met for dividends to be allowed. Similarly, control changes are not prohibited, but all subordinated debentures are required to be redeemed in the event of a change in control. Redemption also becomes mandatory if Scott's net worth falls below a specified level. Asset sales are not prohibited, but the covenants require that 75% of the proceeds from the sale of a business segment be applied to the repayment of debt in order of priority.

The overall effect of the covenants is to restrict both the source of funds for scheduled interest and principal repayments and the use of funds in excess of this amount. Cash to pay debt obligations must come primarily from operations or the issuance of common stock. It cannot come from asset liquidation, stock acquisition of another firm with substantial cash balances, or the issuance of additional debt of any kind. Excess funds can only be spent

---

[3]The role of debt covenants in controlling the conflict of interest between debtholders and equityholders is developed in Smith and Warner (1979). They classify the actions that equity-holders can take to benefit themselves at the expense of debtholders as i) asset substitution, ii) claim dilution, iii) underinvestment, and iv) dividend payout.

Table 5

Summary of debt covenants of Scott borrowings to finance the buyout.

	Bank debt restriction	Subordinated debt restriction
Economic Activities Restricted		
Sale of assets	· Only worn-out or obsolete assets with value less than $500,000 can be sold	· 75% of proceeds must be used to repay debt in order of priority
Capital expenditures	· Restricted to specific $ amount each year debt is outstanding	· None
Changes in corporate structure	· Prohibited	· Mandatory redemption if change in control · No acquisition if in default · Must acquire 100% equity of target · Must be able to issue $1.00 additional debt without covenant violation after acquisition
Financing Activities Restricted		
Issuance of additional debt	· Capitalized leases: max = $3,000,000 · Unsecured credit: max = $1,000,000 · Commercial paper: max = amount available under revolving credit agreement	· Additional senior debt: max = $15,000,000 · For employee stock purchases: max = $4,250,000 · Pre-tax cash flow/interest expense: min = 1.0 for four quarters preceding issuance
Payment of cash dividends	· Prohibited	· Prohibited if in default · Prohibited if adjusted net worth < $50,000,000
Accounting-Based Restrictions		
Adjusted net worth[a]	· Specific min at all times, min increases from $20.5 million in 1986 to $43.0 million after 1992	· If adjusted net worth falls below $12.0 million then must redeem $17.0 million notes and $5 million debentures both at 103
Interest coverage	· Min 1.0 at end of each fiscal quarter	· None
Current ratio	· Min 1.0 at end of each fiscal quarter	· None
Adjusted operating profit	· Min at end of each fiscal quarter, min increases from $22.0 million in 1987 to $31.0 million after 1990	· None

[a]Adjusted net worth and adjusted operating profit are the GAAP numbers adjusted for accounting effects of the buyout under APB no. 16. In Scott's case the bulk of the adjustment is adding back the effects of an inventory write-down of $24.7 million taken immediately after the buyout.

on capital goods in accordance with the schedule, and cannot be spent on
acquisitions or dividends to shareholders. Therefore, once the capital expenditure limit has been reached, excess cash must be either held, spent in the
course of normal operations, or used to pay down debt ahead of schedule.
Assuming the capital expenditure limits are set appropriately, the high
leverage in conjunction with the debt covenants serves to reduce the free
cash flow problem in a way that is not damaging to the long-run viability of
the firm's operations.[4]

Additional bank agreement restrictions require Scott to maintain specific
levels of consolidated net worth and the current ratio at all times. A required
level of adjusted operating profit and interest coverage must be attained at
the end of each fiscal quarter. These restrictions can be viewed as indicators
of potential future problems. Even if Scott is currently able to service its debt
obligations, the firm can still violate one of these accounting-based constraints. Such violation constitutes a technical default and brings managers
and bankers together to renegotiate the terms of the loan.

The constraints imposed by the covenants can be relaxed at the discretion
of the lender, though it is likely that the lender will be able to negotiate
better terms in exchange. For example, if lenders can be convinced that a
particular default was not the result of a financial problem, or that a new
project prohibited by the covenants would increase firm value, they have an
incentive to waive the default because it increases the value of their claim. In
fact, despite the covenant that prohibits mergers and the acquisition of
assets, Scott's lenders have recently agreed to allow Scott to acquire
Hyponex, a garden and lawn products company, for $111 million.

3. Changes in incentives and compensation

3.1. Management equity ownership

The final distribution of equity in the post-buyout Scott organization was
the product of negotiations between C&D and Scott management. ITT took
no part in these negotiations, nor were Scott managers able to negotiate with
C&D prior to the close of the sale. ITT sold Scott through a sealed bid
auction in which the winner would own 100% equity in the former subsidiary.
Eight firms bid for Scott, and although bidding was open to all types of

---

[4]Jensen (1986) defines free cash as cash generated by the firm in excess of what is required to
fund all positive NPV projects. The most valuable use of these funds is to pay them out to
investors.

potential buyers, seven of the eight bidders were buyout firms. The parent was interested primarily in obtaining the highest price for the division.

Scott managers did not participate in the buyout negotiations, and therefore had no opportunity to extract promises or make deals with potential purchasers prior to the sale. Scott managers had approached ITT several years earlier to discuss the possibility of a management buyout at $125 million. At that time ITT had a no-buyout policy. The stated reason for this policy was that a management buyout posed a conflict of interest.

Each potential bidder spent about one day in Marysville and received information on the performance of the unit directly from ITT. Prior to Martin Dubilier's visit, Scott managers felt that they preferred C&D to the other potential buyers because of its reputation for working well with operating managers. The visit did not go well, however, and C&D fell to the bottom of the managers' list. According to Tadd Seitz, president of Scott:

> To be candid, they weren't our first choice. It wasn't a question of their acumen, we just didn't think we had the chemistry. But as we went through the controlled bid process, it was C&D that saw the greatest value in Scott.

There is no evidence that ITT deviated from its objective of obtaining the highest value for the division, or that it negotiated in any way on behalf of Scott managers during the buyout process. C&D put in the highest bid. ITT did not consider management's preferences and accepted this bid even though managers were left to work with one of their less favored buyers. If ITT paid little attention to management's preferences in selecting a buyout firm, the distribution of common stock ownership after the sale clearly received no attention from the parent company.

Immediately following the closing, Clayton & Dubilier controlled 79.4% of Scott's common stock. The remaining shares were packaged and sold with the subordinated debt. C&D was under no obligation to allow managers equity participation in Scott, and clearly managers' funds were not required to consummate the deal. On the basis of their experience, C&D partners viewed management equity ownership as a way to provide managers with strong incentives to maximize firm value. Therefore, after Clayton & Dubilier purchased Scott, it began to negotiate with managers concerning the amount of equity they would be given the opportunity to purchase. C&D did not sell shares to managers reluctantly, in fact, it insisted that managers buy equity and that they do so with their own, not the company's, money. The ownership structure that resulted from the sale can be viewed as the ownership structure that C&D felt gave managers optimal incentives.

Table 6 presents the distribution of common stock ownership across investors and managers. There were 24,250,000 shares outstanding, each of

Table 6

Owners of common stock of O.M. Scott & Sons Company after the leveraged buyout, as of 9/30/88.[a]

	Number of shares [000's]	Percent of shares outstanding
Clayton & Dubilier private limited partnership	14,900	61.4%
Subordinated debtholders	5,000	20.6%
Mr. Tadd Seitz, President, CEO	1,063	4.4%
Seven other top managers (250,000 shares each)	1,750	7.2%
Scott profit sharing plan	750	3.1%
Twenty-two other employees	687	2.8%
Mr. Joseph P. Flannery, Board Member	100	0.4%
Total	24,250	100.0%

[a]All shares were purchased by owners at $1 per share. Percentages don't foot due to rounding error.

which was purchased for $1.00. As the general partner of the private limited partnership that invested $14.9 million in the Scott buyout, Clayton & Dubilier controlled 61.4% of the common stock. The Clayton & Dubilier partners who are responsible for overseeing Scott operations own shares of Scott through their substantial investment in the C&D limited partnership. Subordinated debtholders owned 20.6% of the equity.

The remaining 17% of the equity was distributed among Scott's employees. Eight of the firm's top managers contributed a total of $2,812,500 to the buyout and so hold as many shares, or 12% of the shares outstanding. Tadd Seitz, president of Scott, held the largest number of shares (1,062,500, or 4.4% of the shares outstanding). The seven other managers purchased 250,000 shares apiece (1% each of the shares outstanding). As a group, managers borrowed $2,531,250 to finance the purchase of shares. Though the money was not borrowed from Scott, these loans were guaranteed by the company. The purchase of equity by Scott managers represented a substantial increase in their personal risk. Bob Stern, vice-president of Associate Relations,[5] recalled that his spouse sold her interest in a small catering business at the time of the buyout; they felt that the leverage associated with the purchase of Scott shares was all the risk they could afford.

Top management had some discretion over how common shares were distributed and, although C&D did not encourage it, issued shares to Scott's employee profit-sharing plan and other employees of the firm. Although they allowed managers to distribute the stock more widely, C&D partners felt

[5]Scott refers to all of its employees as 'associates'. Stern's position, therefore, is equivalent to vice-president of human resources or personnel.

that the shares would have stronger incentive effects if they were held only by top managers. As Craig Walley, Scott's General Counsel, described it:

> We [the managers] used to get together on Saturdays during this period when we were thinking about the buyout to talk about why we wanted to do this. What was the purpose? What did we want to make Scott? One of our aims was to try to keep it independent. Another was to try to spread the ownership widely. One of the things we did was to take 3% of the common stock out of our allocation and put it into the profit-sharing plan. That took some doing and we had some legal complications, but we did it. There are now 56 people in the company who own some stock, and that number is increasing. Compared to most LBOs that is really a lot, and Dubilier has not encouraged us in this.

A group of 11 other managers bought an additional 687,500 shares (2.84% of the total) and the profit-sharing plan bought 750,000 shares (3.09%). These managers were selected for the right to purchase stock not by their rank in the organization, but because they would be making decisions considered critical to the success of the company.

The substantial equity holdings of the top management team, and their personal liability for the debts incurred to finance their equity stakes, led them to focus on two distinct aspects of running Scott. One was the need to avoid even technical default on the company's debt, for although such default was unlikely to lead to liquidation, it very likely would have led to a reduction in the managers' fractional equity holdings (due to dilution in a debt-for-equity conversion), and thus a significant reduction in the managers' wealth. Thus the equity ownership served to bond managers to honor the debt covenants.

A second important effect of equity ownership was to encourage managers to make decisions that increased the value of the company, whether or not the violation of a debt covenant was imminent. Because managers owned a capital value claim on the firm, they had an incentive to meet debt obligations and avoid default in a long-term value maximizing way. Short-sighted decision making would reduce the value of the managers' equity, and thus reduce their wealth.

Under this combination of incentives, value-reducing behavior will not occur unless the only way to avoid default is to make suboptimal decisions *and* the cost to managers of default is greater than the loss in equity value from poor decision making. Here, because default is so costly to managers, they may, for example, reduce investment in brand-name advertising, or cut back on research and development or the maintenance of plant and equipment to meet debt obligations. As evidenced in table 3, none of this type of activity was observed at Scott: the company's high leverage combined with covenants and management equity ownership provided managers with the incentive to generate the cash required to meet the debt payments without bleeding the company.

3.2. Changes in incentive compensation

Among the first things Clayton & Dubilier did after the buyout was to selectively increase salaries and begin to develop a new management compensation plan. A number of managers who were not participants in the ITT bonus plan became participants under the C&D bonus plan. The new plan substantially changed the way managers were evaluated, and increased the fraction of salary that a manager could earn as a bonus. While some of these data are confidential, we are able to describe many of the parameters of C&D's incentive compensation plan and compare it with the ITT compensation system.

3.2.1. Salaries

Almost immediately after the close of the sale the base salaries of some top managers were increased. The president's salary increased by 42%, and the salaries of other top managers increased as well. Henry Timnick, a C&D partner who works closely with Scott, explains the decision to raise salaries:

> We increased management salaries because divisional vice-presidents are not compensated at a level comparable to the CEO of a free-standing company with the same characteristics. Divisional VPs don't have all the responsibilities. In addition, the pay raise is a shot-in-the-arm psychologically for the managers. It makes them feel they will be dealt with fairly and encourages them to deal fairly with their people.

In conversations with managers and C&D partners it became clear that C&D set higher standards for management performance than ITT. Increasing the minimum level of acceptable performance forces managers to work harder after the buyout or risk losing their jobs. Indeed, managers did work harder after the buyout; there was general agreement that the management team was putting in longer hours at the office. Several managers used the term 'more focused' to describe how their work habits had changed after the buyout. Therefore, an increase in base salary may have been necessary to make managers equally well off before and after the buyout.

The increase in compensation also serves as remuneration for increased risk bearing. As reported earlier, Scott managers borrowed substantially to purchase equity in their company. Requiring managers to hold equity and using strong incentive compensation in addition increases managers' exposure to firm-specific risk. Because they cannot diversify this risk away, managers will require an increase in the level of pay as compensation.

Finally, C&D may have increased salaries because Scott managers are more valuable to C&D than they were to ITT. Consistent with this, managers at Scott felt that ITT was much less dependent on them than Clayton & Dubilier. One Scott manager noted: 'When ITT comes in and buys a company, the entire management team could quit and they wouldn't blink.' C&D was not, however, completely dependent on incumbent managers to run Scott. Several Clayton & Dubilier partners had extensive experience as operating managers. These partners were available to run Scott if necessary, and had on several occasions stepped in to run C&D buyout firms. They did not, however, have the specific knowledge about the Scott organization that incumbent managers had. If part of the value created by the buyout results from giving managers an incentive to use their specific knowledge about the firm more efficiently, then Scott managers would be preferred by C&D to its own operating partners. We believe that this is the case.

ITT had created a control system that allowed headquarters to manage a vast number of businesses, but did not give managers the flexibility or incentive to use their specialized knowledge of the business to maximize the value of the division. C&D relied much more heavily on managers' firm-specific knowledge, hence the incumbent management team was more valuable to the buyout firm. C&D was willing to pay managers more to reduce the risk of the managers quitting, and depriving Scott and C&D of this valuable knowledge.

3.2.2. Bonus

The bonus plan was completely redesigned after the buyout. The number of managers who participated in the plan increased, and the factors that determined the level of bonus were changed to reflect the objectives of the buyout firm. In addition, both the maximum bonus allowed by the plan and the actual realizations of bonus as a percentage of salary increased by a factor of two to three.

After the buyout 21 managers were covered by the bonus plan. Only ten were eligible for bonuses under ITT. The maximum payoff under the new plan ranged from 33.5% to 100% of base salary, increasing with the manager's rank in the company. For each manager, the amount of the payoff was based on the achievement of corporate, divisional, and individual performance goals. The weights applied to corporate, divisional, and individual performance in calculating the bonus varied across managers. For division managers, bonus payoff was based 35% on overall company performance, 40% on divisional performance, and 25% on individual performance. Bonuses for corporate staff managers weighed corporate performance at 50%, and personal goals at 50%.

Table 7

Bonus paid to top ten managers at O.M. Scott & Sons Company as a percentage of year-end salary, listed by rank in the organization before (1985–1986) and after (1987–1988) the buyout.

	Before the buyout		After the buyout	
	1985	1986	1987	1988
	18.3%	26.6%	93.8%	57.7%
	14.0%	23.4%	81.2%	46.8%
	12.8%	18.8%	79.5%	46.0%
	13.3%	20.6%	81.2%	48.5%
	11.2%	19.4%	80.7%	46.8%
	10.5%	17.1%	76.5%	46.0%
	7.1%	10.8%	29.6%	16.6%
	6.1%	22.9%	78.0%	46.7%
	4.6%	6.3%	28.7%	16.8%
	5.1%	6.6%	28.4%	16.4%
Mean	10.3%	17.3%	65.8%	38.8%

At the beginning of each fiscal year performance targets (or goals) were set, and differences between actual and targeted performance entered directly into the computation of the bonus plan payoffs. All corporate and divisional performance measures were quantitative measures of cash utilization, and were scaled from 80 to 125, 100 representing the attainment of target. For example, corporate performance was determined by dividing actual earnings before interest and taxes (*EBIT*) by budgeted *EBIT*, and dividing actual average working capital (*AWC*) by budgeted *AWC*, and weighting the *EBIT* ratio at 75% and the *AWC* ratio at 25%. The resulting number, expressed as a percentage attainment of budget, was used as a part of the bonus calculation for all managers in the bonus plan.

The plan was designed so that the payoff was sensitive to changes in performance. This represented a significant change from the ITT bonus plan. As Bob Stern, vice-president of Associate Relations, commented:

> I worked in human resources with ITT for a number of years. When I was manager of staffing of ITT Europe, we evaluated the ITT bonus plan. Our conclusion was that the ITT bonus plan was viewed as nothing more than a deferred compensation arrangement: all it did was defer income from one year to the next. Bonuses varied very, very little. If you had an average year, you might get a bonus of $10,000. If you had a terrible year you might get a bonus of $8,000, and if you had a terrific year you might go all the way to $12,500. On a base salary of $70,000, that's not a lot of variation.

Table 7 presents actual bonus payouts for the top ten managers as a percent of salary for two years before and two years after the buyout. Fig. 2

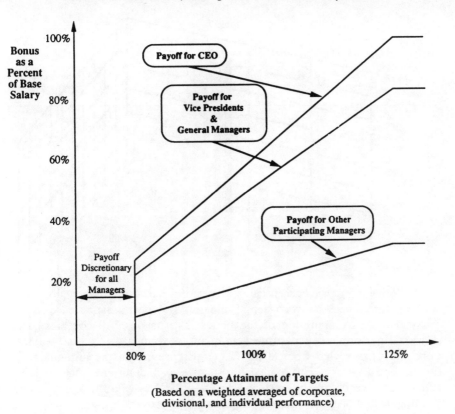

Fig. 1. Bonus payoff function under the post-buyout incentive compensation plan for three levels of management.

graphically illustrates these data. The new bonus plan gives larger payouts and appears to generate significantly more variation in bonuses than occurred under ITT. Average bonuses as a percent of salary for the top ten managers increased from 10% and 17% in the two years before the buyout to 66% and 39% in the two years after, a period during which operating income increased by 42%. There also appears to be a bigger cross-sectional variation in bonus payout across managers within a given year. In the two years prior to the buyout, bonus payout ranged from 5% to 27% of base salary, whereas over the two years following the buyout, it ranged from 16% to 94% of base salary.

In addition to measures that evaluated management performance against quantitative targets, each manager had a set of personal objectives that were tied into the bonus plan. These objectives were set by the manager and his or her superior, and their achievement was monitored by the manager's supe-

180 G.P. Baker and K.H. Wruck, Creating value in LBOs: The case of O.M. Scott

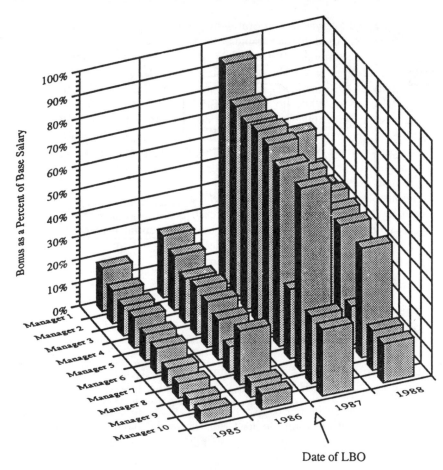

Fig. 2. Bonuses for top ten managers in the two years before and the two years after the LBO.
Data source: Table 7.

rior. Personal objectives were generally measurable and verifiable. For instance, an objective for a personnel manager was to integrate the benefits package of a newly acquired company with that of Scott within a given period. An objective for the president of the company was to spend a fixed amount of time out of Marysville. talking to retailers and salespeople. At the end of the year, the manager's superior would evaluate whether the manager had achieved these objectives, and would quantify the achievement along the same 80–125 point range. This rating was then combined with the quantitative measures to come up with a total performance measure.

The weighted average of corporate, divisional, and personal target achievements was then used to determine total bonus payoffs. Fig. 1 shows how payoffs were determined. If a manager achieved an 80% weighted average attainment of target goals, the payoff varied from about 30% of salary for the CEO to about 10% for lower-level managers. At 125% attainment, bonuses varied from about 100% to about 30%. Between 80% and 125%, bonus payouts as a percentage of salary varied linearly with target attainment. Below 80%, payments were at the discretion of the president and the board.

The combination of equity ownership by eight top managers, and a much more highly 'leveraged' bonus plan for thirteen more, changed the incentives of the managers at Scott substantially. For those managers who held equity, the bonus plan, with its emphasis on *EBIT* and working capital management, served to reinforce the importance of cash generation. Those who did not hold equity, and were thus unaffected by the potential loss in equity value that would attend a violation of the debt covenants, were still induced to make the generation of cash a primary concern.

4. The monitoring of top managers

4.1. Purpose and composition of the board

The purpose of Scott's board of directors was to monitor, advise, and evaluate the CEO. As Henry Timnick describes it:

> The purpose of the board is to make sure the company has a good strategy and to monitor the CEO. The CEO cannot be evaluated by his management staff, so we do not put the CEO's people on the board. Scott's CFO and the corporate secretary attend the meetings, but they have no vote. The outside directors are to be picked by the CEO. We will not put anyone on the board that the CEO doesn't want, but we [C&D] have to approve them. We do not view board members as extensions of ourselves, but they are not to be cronies or local friends of the CEO. We want people with expertise that the CEO doesn't have. The CEO should choose outside directors who are strong in areas in which he is weak.

At the close of the buyout Scott's board had five members. Only one, Tadd Seitz, was a manager of the firm. Of the remaining four, three were C&D partners; Martin Dubilier was the chairman of the board and voted the stock of the limited partnership, Henry Timnick was the C&D partner who worked most closely with Scott management, and Alberto Cribiore, the third C&D partner, was a financing specialist. The outside director was Joe Flannery, then CEO of Uniroyal, which had been taken private by Clayton & Dubilier in 1985. Later, Flannery left Uniroyal and became a C&D partner. He stayed on the Scott board, becoming an inside, rather than outside, director.

Over the next few years three new directors were added; one was an academic, one was a consumer products expert, and one, Don Sherman, was the president of Hyponex, the company acquired by Scott. The academic, Jim Beard, was one of the country's leading turf researchers. Henry Timnick described the process of putting him on the board.

> Our objective was to find the best turf specialist and researcher in the country. We wanted someone to keep us up with the latest developments and to scrutinize the technical aspects of our product line. We found Jim Beard at Texas A&M. It took Jim a while to be enthusiastic about being on the board, and it took Tadd a while to figure out how to get the most out of Jim. After Jim was appointed to the board, we encouraged Tadd to have Jim out on a consulting basis for a couple of days. Now Tadd is making good use of Jim.

Seitz and Timnick were considering an individual with extensive experience in consumer products businesses to be the second outside director. They chose Jack Chamberlain, who had previously run GE's Consumer Electronics Division, Lenox China, and Avon Products. All board members were stockholders; upon joining the board they were given the opportunity to purchase 50,000 shares at adjusted book value. All the directors chose to own stock.

This board structure was typical for a C&D buyout. Martin Dubilier explains:

> We have tried a number of board compositions and we found this to be the most effective. If you have too many insiders the board becomes an operating committee. Outsiders fortify the growth opportunities of the firm.

The board of directors met quarterly. A subset of the board, the executive committee, met monthly. The executive committee was made up of Martin Dubilier, Tadd Seitz, and Henry Timnick. In their meetings they determined policy, discussed personnel matters, and tested Seitz's thinking on major issues facing the firm. The board meetings were more formal, usually consisting of presentations by members of the management team other than Seitz.

4.2. The operating partner

In each of C&D's buyouts a partner with extensive operating experience serves as the liaison between the firm's managers and C&D. The operating partner functions as an advisor and consultant to the CEO, not a decision maker. Henry Timnick was Scott's liaison partner. He had been CEO of a division of Mead that was purchased through a leveraged buyout and had since worked with several of C&D's other buyout firms. Timnick spent several weeks in Marysville after the buyout closed. Following that he was in touch with Seitz daily by telephone and continued to visit regularly.

Timnick would advise Seitz, but felt it was important that Seitz make the decisions. When he and Seitz disagreed, Timnick told him: 'If you don't believe me, go hire a consultant, then make your own decision.' Initially, Seitz continued to check with Timnick, looking for an authorization for his decisions. Henry Timnick explains:

> Tadd kept asking me 'Can I do this? Can I do that?' I told him, 'You can do whatever you want so long as it is consistent with Scott's overall strategy.'

This consultative approach to working with Scott managers was quite different from ITT's approach. Martin Dubilier explains:

> ITT challenges managers not to rock the boat, to make budget. We challenge managers to improve the business. Every company takes on the personality of its CEO. Our main contribution is to improve his performance. All the rest is secondary.

Scott managers confirmed Dubilier's assessment. Meetings between ITT managers and Scott managers were large and quite formal, with as many as 40 members of ITT's staff present. Scott managers found the meetings antagonistic, with the ITT people working to find faults and problems with the operating unit's reported performance. By meeting the formal goals set by ITT, Scott could largely avoid interference from headquarters. Avoiding such interference was an important objective. As Paul Yeager, CFO, describes it:

> Geneen [then CEO of ITT] said in his book that the units would ask for help from headquarters; that the units came to look at headquarters staff as outside consultants who could be relied upon to help when needed. I have worked in many ITT units, and if he really thought that, then he was misled. If a division vice-president went to headquarters for help, in effect he was saying, 'I can't handle it.' He wouldn't be a vice-president for very long.

5. Organizational changes and changes in decision making

The organizational changes and changes in decision making that took place at Scott after the buyout fall broadly into two categories: improved working capital management and a new approach to product markets. These changes were not forced on managers by C&D. The buyout firm made some suggestions, but the specific plans and their implementation were the responsibility of Scott managers. Few of the changes in managerial actions represent keenly innovative or fundamentally new insights into management problems. As one observer noted: 'It ain't rocket science.' These changes, however, led to dramatic improvements in Scott's operating performance.

Management's ability did not change after the buyout, nor did the market or the assets they were managing. The only changes were in the incentive structure of the firm, as described in sections 2 through 4, and in the management control systems. According to Scott managers, the biggest difference between working at Scott before and after the buyout was an increase in the extent to which they could make and implement decisions without approval from superiors. ITT maintained control over its divisions through an inflexible formal planning and reporting structure. Changing a plan required approval at a number of levels from ITT headquarters, and a request for a change was likely to be denied. In addition, because ITT was shedding its consumer businesses, Scott managers found their requests for capital funds were routinely denied. After the buyout, Seitz could pick up the phone and propose changes in the operating plan to Timnick. These changes were likely to be accepted. This, of course, improved the company's ability to respond quickly to changes in the marketplace.

5.1. The working capital task force

Shortly after the buyout, a task force was established to coordinate the management of working capital throughout the company. The members of the task force were drawn from every functional area. The group was charged with reducing working capital requirements by 42%, or $25 million, in two years. They exceeded this goal, reducing average working capital by $37 million. The task force helped Scott managers learn to manage cash balances, production, inventories, receivables, payables, and employment levels more effectively.

5.1.1. Cash management

Before the buyout, Scott's managers never had to manage cash balances. John Wall, assistant treasurer and chairman of the working capital task force, describes how cash was controlled under ITT:

> Under the ITT system, we needed virtually no cash management. The ITT lock box system swept our lock boxes into Citibank of New York. Our disbursement bank would contact ITT's bank and say we need $2 million today and it automatically went into our disbursement account.

To control cash flow in its numerous businesses, ITT established a cash control system that separated the collection of cash from cash disbursements.

Receipts went into one account and were collected regularly by ITT's bank; once deposited, these funds were not available to divisional managers. Cash to fund operations came from a different source, through a different bank account. This system allowed ITT to centrally manage cash and control divisional spending.

When Scott was a division of ITT, cash coming into Scott bore little relation to the cash Scott was allowed to spend. In contrast, after the LBO, all of Scott's cash was available to managers to spend. They needed to establish a system to control cash so that operations were properly funded, and to meet debt service requirements. Wall describes the process:

> In the first six months after the LBO we had to bring in a state-of-the-art cash management system for a business of this size. We shopped a lot of treasury management systems and had almost given up on finding a system that would simply let us manage our cash. We didn't need a system that would keep track of our investment portfolios because we had $200 million borrowed. Finally, we found a product we could use. Under the LBO cash forecasting has become critical. I mean cash forecasting in the intermediate and long range. I don't mean forecasting what is going to hit the banks in the next two or three days. We could always do that, but now we track our cash flows on a weekly basis and we do modeling on balance sheets, which allows us to do cash forecasting a year out.

5.1.2. Production and inventories

Between 1986 and 1988, the efforts of the task force increased the frequency at which Scott turned over its inventory from 2.08 to 3.20 times per year – an increase of 54%. During this period both sales and the number of products produced increased. Because Scott's business is highly seasonal, inventory control was always a management problem. Large inventories were required to meet the spring rush of orders; however, financing inventories was a cash drain. Scott's production strategy under ITT exacerbated the inventory problem. Before the buyout, Scott produced each product once a year. Slow-moving products were produced during the slow season, so that long runs of fast-moving products could be produced during the busy season. Before the spring buying began almost an entire year's worth of sales were in inventory.

The old production strategy took advantage of the cost savings of long production runs, but under ITT, managers did not consider the tradeoff between these cost savings and the opportunity cost of funds tied up in inventory. The cash requirements of servicing a large debt burden, the working capital-based restrictions in the debt agreements, and the inclusion of working capital objectives in the compensation system gave managers a strong incentive to consider this opportunity cost. As Wall explained it:

> What the plant managers had to do was to figure out how they could move the production of the slow-moving items six months forward. That way the products we used to make in May or early June would be made in November or December. Now [instead of producing long runs of a few products] production managers have to deal with setups and changeovers during the high-production period. It requires a lot more of their attention.

Managing inventories more effectively required that products be produced closer to the time of shipment. Because more setups and changeovers were necessary the production manager's job became more complicated. Instead of producing a year's supply of one product, inventorying it, then producing another product, managers had to produce smaller amounts of a variety of products repeatedly throughout the year.

Inventories were also reduced by changing purchasing practices and inventory management. Raw material suppliers agreed to deliver smaller quantities more often, reducing the levels of raw materials and finished goods inventories. Through close tracking, Scott managed to reduce inventory levels without increasing the frequency of stock-outs of raw materials or finished goods.

5.1.3. Receivables and Payables

Receivables were an important competitive factor, and retailers expected generous payment terms from Scott. After the buyout, however, the timing of rebate and selling programs was carefully planned, allowing Scott to conserve working capital. Scott also negotiated with suppliers to obtain more favorable terms on prices, payment schedules, and delivery. Lorel Au, manager of Contract Operations, stated:

> Within two months of the LBO, the director of manufacturing and I went out to every one of our contract suppliers and went through what a leveraged buyout is, and what that means. We explained how we were going to have to manage our business. We explained our new goals and objectives. We talked about things like just-in-time inventory, talked terms, talked about scheduling. Some suppliers were more ready to work with us than others. Some said, 'OK, what can we do to help?' In some cases, a vendor said, 'I can't help you on price, I can't help you on terms, I can't help you on scheduling.' We said: 'Fine. Good-bye.' We were very serious about it. In some cases we didn't have options, but usually we did.

The company succeeded in getting suppliers to agree to extended terms of payment, and was able to negotiate some substantial price cuts from major suppliers in return for giving the supplier a larger fraction of Scott's business.

Scott managers felt that the buyout put them in a stronger bargaining position vis-a-vis their suppliers. Wall states:

> One reason we were able to convince our suppliers to give us concessions is that we no longer had the cornucopia of ITT behind us. We no longer had unlimited cash.

The suppliers understood that if they did not capitulate on terms, Scott would have to take its business elsewhere or face default.[6]

5.1.4. Employment

Scott had a tradition of being very paternalistic toward its employees and was a major employer and corporate citizen in the town of Marysville. Some have argued that an important source of cash and increasing equity value in buyouts is the severing of such relationships.[7] There is no evidence of this at Scott. Scott's traditional employee relations policies were maintained, and neither wages nor benefits were cut after the buyout. Scott continues to maintain a large park with swimming pool, tennis courts, playground, and other recreational facilities for the enjoyment of employees and their families. The company also continues to make its auditorium, the largest in Marysville, available for community use at no charge.

The company did begin a program of hiring part-time employees during the busy season, rather than bringing on full-time employees. This allowed Scott to maintain a core of full-time, year-round employees who enjoyed the full benefits plan of the company, while still having enough people to staff the factory during busy season. Largely through attrition, average annual full-time employment has dropped by about 9% over the first two years after the buyout.

5.2. Approaches to the Product Markets

Scott is the major brand name in the do-it-yourself lawn care market, and has a reputation for high-quality products. Ed Wandtke, a lawn industry

---

[6]Schelling (1960) supports the idea that increased bargaining power can occur as the result of a precarious financial situation. He states: 'The power to constrain an adversary may depend on the power to bind oneself. ... In bargaining, weakness is often strength, freedom may be freedom to capitulate, and to burn bridges behind one may suffice to undo an opponent. ...[M]ore financial resources, more physical strength, more military potency, or more ability to withstand losses ... are by no means universal advantages in bargaining situations; they often have a contrary value.'

[7]Shleifer and Summers (1988).

analyst and partner of All Green Management Consultants Inc., states:

> O.M. Scott is ultra high price, ultra high quality. They absolutely are
> the market leader. They have been for some time. No one else has the
> retail market recognition. Through its promotions, Scott has gotten its
> name so entrenched that the name and everything associated with
> it – quality, consistency, reliability – supersede the expensive price of
> the product.

In 1987, Scott had a 34% share of the $350 million do-it-yourself market.
Industry experts report, however, that the market had been undergoing major
changes since the early 1980s. Indeed, Scott's revenue fell by 23% between
1981 (the historical high at that time) and 1985. The buyout allowed Scott
managers the flexibility to adapt to the changing marketplace, assuring a
future for the company.

The do-it-yourself market was shrinking because an increasing number of
consumers were contracting with firms to have their lawns chemically treated.
Seitz had proposed that Scott enter this segment of the professional lawn
care market for years, but ITT continually vetoed this initiative. Among the
first actions taken after the buyout was the creation of a group within the
professional division whose focus was to sell to the commercial turf maintenance market. Within two years, the segment comprised 10% of the sales of
the professional division, and was growing at a rate of almost 40% per year.

Scott's position in the do-it-yourself market was challenged by the growth
of private label brands that were sold at lower prices and a shift in volume
away from Scott's traditional retailers – hardware and specialty stores – to
mass merchandisers. Under ITT Scott managers did not try to develop new
channels of distribution. Timnick described it as too 'risky' an experiment for
ITT. The company's post-buyout acquisition of Hyponex gave Scott access to
the private label market. Wandtke argues:

> With Hyponex, Scott will capture a greater percentage of the home
> consumer market. Hyponex is a much lower priced product line. It
> gives them [Scott] access to private labeling, where they can produce
> product under another label for a lesser price. ...This will improve
> their hold on the retail market.

The acquisition of Hyponex represented a major response to the changes
taking place in Scott's product markets. Hyponex was a company virtually the
same size as Scott, with $125 million in sales and 700 employees, yet the
acquisition was financed completely with bank debt. The successful renegoti-
ation of virtually all of Scott's existing debt agreements was required to
consummate the transaction. Because the new debt was senior to the existing
notes and debentures, a consent payment of $887,500 was required to
persuade bondholders to waive restrictive covenants. That such an ex-
pansionary acquisition was possible only $2\frac{1}{2}$ years after the buyout

demonstrates the flexibility of the LBO as an organizational form. It also demonstrates the ability of the contracting parties to respond to positive NPV projects that might appear to be blocked by the post-LBO company's capital structure.

6. Conclusions

Our findings confirm the results of large-sample studies – that the pressure of servicing a heavy debt load and management equity ownership lead to improved performance. Equally important in the Scott organization, how-ever, and undocumented in large-sample studies, are the debt covenants that place restrictions on how the cash required for debt payments can be generated, the adoption of a strong incentive compensation plan, a reorgani-zation and decentralization of decision making, and the relationship between Scott managers, the Clayton & Dubilier partners, and the board of directors.

We attribute the improvements in operating performance after Scott's leveraged buyout to changes in the incentive, monitoring, and governance structure of the firm. Managers were given strong incentives to generate cash and were allowed more decision-making authority, but checks were estab-lished to guard against behavior that would be damaging to firm value. In the Scott organization, high leverage was effective in forcing managers to gener-ate cash flow in a productive way largely because debt covenants and equity ownership countered short-run opportunistic behavior. Value was created by decentralizing decision making largely because managers were closely moni-tored and supported by an expert board of directors who were also equity-holders.

We view this study as a first step toward the development of a theory of how organizations respond to radical changes in their financial structure and how these changes affect managerial behavior. Our results are applicable to organizations with other combinations of high leverage, management equity ownership, and active boards of directors, such as venture-backed high-tech-nology firms or public companies that undertake leveraged recapitalizations. For example, if counterbalancing incentives are important, we should observe restrictive covenants and management equity ownership in leveraged recapi-talizations. If it is important to couple a strong bonus plan with equity ownership to motivate managers, then why do we not observe such bonus plans in venture-backed startup companies? Further research can help us determine the relative importance of these factors and their interactions in determining optimal organizational forms.

References

DeAngelo, H., L. DeAngelo, and E. Rice, 1984, Going private: Minority freezeouts and stockholder wealth, Journal of Law and Economics XXVII, 367–401.

190   G.P. Baker and K.H. Wruck, Creating value in LBOs: The case of O.M. Scott

DeAngelo, L.E., 1986, Accounting numbers as market valuation substitutes: A study of manage-
    ment buyouts of public stockholders, The Accounting Review LXI, 400–420.
Gilson, S., 1989, Management-borne bankruptcy costs: Evidence on executive turnover during
    corporate financial distress, Working paper (University of Texas, Austin, TX).
Jensen, M.C., 1986, Agency costs of free cash flow, corporate finance, and takeovers, American
    Economic Review 76, 323–329.
Jensen, M.C., 1989, Active investors, LBO's, and the privatization of bankruptcy, Journal of
    Applied Corporate Finance 2, 35–44.
Jensen, M.C., S. Kaplan, and L. Stiglin, 1989, Effects of LBO's on tax revenues of the U.S.
    Treasury, Tax Notes 42, 727–733.
Jensen, M.C. and K. Murphy, 1989, Performance pay and top management incentives, Journal of
    Political Economy 98, forthcoming.
Kaplan, S., 1988, Management buyouts: Efficiency gains or value transfers?, Graduate School of
    Business working paper (University of Chicago, Chicago, IL).
Kaplan, S., 1988, Sources of value in management buyouts, Graduate School of Business thesis
    (Harvard University, Boston, MA).
Kaplan, S., 1989, Management buyouts: evidence on taxes as a source of value, Journal of
    Finance 44, 611–632.
Kaplan, S., 1989, Management buyouts: Evidence on post-buyout operating changes, Graduate
    School of Business working paper (University of Chicago, Chicago, IL).
Kirkland, L., 1989, Testimony before the House Ways and Means Committee on leveraged
    buyouts, 89–3.
Lehn, K. and A. Poulsen, 1989, Leveraged buyouts: Wealth created or wealth redistributed?, in:
    M. Wiedenbaum and K. Chilton, eds., Public policy toward corporate mergers (Transaction
    Books, New Brunswick, NJ).
Lichtenberg, F.R. and D. Siegel, 1989, The effect of takeovers on the employment and wages of
    central-office and other personnel, Graduate School of Business paper (Columbia University,
    New York, NY and National Bureau of Economic Research).
Marais, L., K. Schipper, and A. Smith, 1988, Wealth effects of going private for senior securities,
    Journal of Financial Economics 23, 155–191.
Muscarella, C. and M. Vetsuypens, 1988, Efficiency and organizational structure: A study of
    reverse LBO's, Graduate School of Business working paper (Southern Methodist University,
    Dallas, TX).
Schelling, T., 1960, The strategy of conflict (Harvard University Press, Cambridge, MA).
Schipper, K. and A. Smith, 1988, Corporate income tax effects of management buyouts,
    Graduate School of Business working paper (University of Chicago, Chicago, IL).
Shleifer, A. and L. Summers, 1988, Breach of trust in hostile takeovers, in: A. Auerbach, ed.,
    Corporate Takeovers: Causes and consequences (University of Chicago Press, Chicago, IL).
Smith, A., 1989, Corporate ownership structure and performance: The case of management
    buyouts, Graduate School of Business working paper (University of Chicago, Chicago, IL).
Smith, C.W. and J.B. Warner, 1979, On financial contracting: An analysis of bond covenants,
    Journal of Financial Economics 7, 117–161.

[21]

Journal of Financial Economics 24 (1989) 363–403. North-Holland

INFORMATION DISCLOSURE, METHOD OF PAYMENT, AND TAKEOVER PREMIUMS
Public and Private Tender Offers in France*

B. Espen ECKBO

University of British Columbia, Vancouver, BC, Canada V6T 1Y8

Herwig LANGOHR

INSEAD, 77305 Fontainebleau Cedex, France

Received July 1985, final version received August 1989

In 1970, France introduced disclosure rules governing public tender offers without changing an existing four-week minimum offer period. We document a substantial increase in total offer premiums thereafter. Post-1970 premiums are also significantly higher in public than in private tender offers, where information disclosure is not required, and in all-cash than in all-stock offers. The impact of the payment method is evident in minority buyouts as well as in offers for voting control. The component of the total premium reflecting the value of the option to tender appears to be unaffected by either disclosure regulations or the payment method.

1. Introduction

The expected return from acquisition activity depends on whether the bidder's initial information advantage can be maintained throughout the bidding process. If the resources needed to generate takeover gains are available to potential rival bidders, the information in the initial bid will stimulate competition for the target shares, increasing the price necessary for success. This possibility underlies the concern that disclosure regulations deter acquisition activity, potentially undermining the efficiency of the corporate

*We are grateful for the comments and suggestions made by Nathalie Dierkens, Pierre Hillion, Bruno Husson, Ronald Masulis, John McConnell, seminar participants at INSEAD, the University of Alberta, the University of California at Los Angeles, the University of British Columbia, the University of Oregon, the University of Southern California, the American, the European, and the French Finance Association meetings, and, in particular, Michael Jensen and Richard Ruback (the editors), and Wayne Mikkelson (the referee). We thank the French stockbroker association (CAC), Slimane Echihab, and Martine Delcour for assistance in collecting the data. Financial support from INSEAD and the Ministry of Finance and Corporate Relations of the Province of British Columbia is also gratefully acknowledged. This research was in part performed while Eckbo was a Fellow of the Batterymarch Financial Management Corporation.

0304-405X/89/$3.50 © 1989, Elsevier Science Publishers B.V. (North-Holland)

sector.[1] In the first part of this study, we provide new empirical evidence on the effect of disclosure rules on offer premiums and abnormal stock returns based on cash tender offers for control of publicly traded target firms in France.

Rational bidders, facing the risk that information in the initial offer will stimulate competing bids, may react by implementing offer strategies designed to protect their information advantage. Such strategies may involve attempting to acquire a foothold in the target before launching the takeover, negotiating with target management, presenting a two-tiered offer designed to overcome free-rider problems when the target is widely held,[2] and, of particular interest in this paper, selecting a particular payment method (cash and/or securities in the bidder firm). There is theoretical support for the proposition that the means of payment can play a strategic role in deterring competition and signal the true value of the bidder firm under asymmetric information.[3] Evidence is also growing that both the level and division of takeover gains are systematically related to the payment method.[4] In the second part of this paper, we provide new empirical tests of the impact of the payment method on offer premiums and abnormal stock returns in both tender offers for control and minority buyouts.

In their study of the impact of disclosure rules on takeover bids, Jarrell and Bradley (1980) find that the average premium over the pre-offer price in cash tender offers increased from 32% to nearly 53% after the passage of the U.S. Williams Act in July 1968.[5] Schipper and Thompson (1983) report that a sample of frequent acquirers on average earned significantly negative abnormal returns over the months surrounding announcements related to the introduction of the Williams Act. This is consistent with market expectations that the Williams Act would be costly for bidder firms, which is also the conclusion of Jarrel and Bradley (1980). Asquith, Bruner, and Mullins (1983), and Bradley, Desai, and Kim (1988) report significantly lower average abnor-

---

[1] '[T]ake-overs, like bankruptcy, represent one of Nature's methods of eliminating deadwood in the struggle for survival. A more open and more efficiently responsible corporate society can result,' Samuelson (1970, p. 505).

[2] Grossman and Hart (1980a), Comment and Jarrell (1987).

[3] Hansen (1987), Fishman (1989), Eckbo, Giammarino, and Heinkel (1988). Jensen (1986) argues that the payment method may in part be driven by agency cost considerations.

[4] Wansley, Lane, and Yang (1983), Travlos (1987), Huang and Walkling (1987), Eckbo (1988), Eckbo, Giammarino, and Heinkel (1988), Asquith, Bruner, and Mullins (1988), and Franks, Harris, and Mayer (1988).

[5] The disclosure provisions of the Williams Act require the bidder in cash tender offers for 10% or more of voting stock to disclose any plans to liquidate the target firm, merge it, or make any changes in its basic corporate structure. In 1970, these requirements were extended to securities exchange (stock for stock) offers and 5% acquisitions. Smiley (1975) estimates that the disclosure requirements have raised direct transaction costs of a tender offer by as much as 25%.

mal returns to bidder firms after 1968, which further supports the proposition that the Williams Act has increased competition among bidders.[6]

The studies above do not show that the *disclosure provisions* of the Williams Act are the only – or the most important – factor explaining this evidence. The Williams Act also increased the minimum tender offer period from zero to ten days, in itself an economically important change. A substantial delay in the execution of the tender offer gives potential rival bidders valuable time to collect the information needed to construct competing offers. Thus, the delay requirements permit production of information that may generate higher-valued bids during the auction for the target shares.[7] An analogous argument is made by Jarrell (1985), who reports that delaying the execution of a tender offer by suing the bidder on average substantially increases the final offer price received by successful targets.

Disclosure regulations similar to those in the Williams Act were introduced in France in 1970. These regulations, however, left unchanged a four-week minimum tender offer period in effect since 1966. Thus, our French institutional setting permits tests of the proposition that disclosure regulations increase offer premiums when existing regulations already give potential rival bidders ample time to counterbid. In our sample of successful cash tender offers for control, we document a statistically significant increase in the average offer premium over the pre-offer target share price after 1970, from 34% to 73%. We also present evidence on the two components of this premium: the offer-induced revaluation of the target shares and the premium over the post-expiration price, reflecting the value of the option to tender. Empirically, the increase in the premium over the pre-offer price is driven entirely by the offer-induced revaluation of the target shares; there is no evidence of a change in the value of the option to tender.

An increase in the cost of public tender offers (due to disclosure regulations) causes bidders to substitute toward privately negotiated block trades, if the voting power in the target is such that a single block trade can transfer control. Apparently, there was an increase in the number of such private tender offers in France after 1970, prompting their regulation in 1973. Since then, privately negotiated controlling-block trades must be followed by a mandatory fifteen-day offer for the remaining (any or all) target shares at the block price. The

---

[6]As argued by Nathan and O'Keefe (1989), it is also possible that the post-1968 increase in average offer premiums and decrease in average bidder gains are driven by (yet unspecified) factors unrelated to the Williams Act. Examining the annual time-series behavior of average offer premiums, they find no substantial increase until after 1972, i.e., some time following the passage of the Williams Act.

[7]The auction is open since the Williams Act also specifies that target shareholders who have tendered their shares to one bidder firm can withdraw them should a higher-valued offer be made by another firm before the minimum offer period for the initial offer has elapsed. Further, any upward revision in an outstanding offer must be applied to those shareholders who have already tendered at the previous terms.

bidder in a private tender offer is, however, exempted from the disclosure regulations governing the public tender offer procedure. On this basis it is interesting to find that the average offer premium in control-oriented cash takeover bids in the post-1970 period is significantly higher in public than in private tender offers (73% versus 27%).

Bidder abnormal returns are on average indistinguishable from zero both before and after 1970. Since the average gains to targets are significantly higher after 1970, this suggests that total takeover gains are larger after the regulatory change. This outcome is consistent with the argument that disclosure regulations have deterred offers that, on average, produce lower total gains than offers that survive mandatory information disclosure.[8]

In examining the impact of the payment method, we argue that any compensation for the realization of a personal capital-gains tax liability should be reflected in the value of the option to tender, while the information effect of the payment method will cause an offer-induced revaluation of the target shares. In a sample of public tender offers for voting control after 1970, we find that the offer-induced revaluation is significantly higher when the payment is all cash than all stock in the bidder firm. The average premium over the post-expiration target share price, however, is indistinguishable across the two payment methods, a result that fails to support the hypothesis that all-cash offers compensate for a relative personal tax disadvantage. Bidder firm abnormal returns are on average indistinguishable from zero in both all-cash and all-stock offers. This result is similar to recent evidence on takeover bids in Canada [Eckbo (1988)] and the U.K. [Franks, Harris, and Mayer (1988)], but it contrasts with the significantly negative average market reaction reported for all-stock mergers in the U.S. [Travlos (1987) and Asquith, Bruner, and Mullins (1988)].

Through a sample of minority buyouts, we also examine whether the superior performance by targets in all-cash offers is limited to transactions involving transfer of control. The bidders in our minority buyouts all control enough of the target voting shares (on average 80%) to put in place the preferred production/investment policy without the formal consent of minority shareholders. Interestingly, we find that the average offer-induced revaluation in minority buyouts shows the same systematic dependence on the payment method we observe for control-oriented takeover bids.

The rest of the paper is organized as follows. Section 2 summarizes the institutional characteristics of public and private tender offers for publicly traded target firms in France. Sample characteristics and estimation procedures are detailed in section 3. Section 4 presents average abnormal returns

---

[8]A similar inference is made by Jensen and Ruback (1983, p. 29) in their review of studies of the Williams Act.

based on the total samples of successful and unsuccessful public tender offers for control, private tender offers, and minority buyouts, thus providing a perspective on the overall valuation effects of French tender offers. The effect of disclosure regulations on tender offer premiums in cash offers for control is presented in section 5. Section 6 estimates the effect of the payment method on offer premiums. Section 7 concludes the paper.

2. Tender offers in France: Institutional characteristics

The French stock market is an auction market operating under the general rule that all trades must be executed through a broker at the final auction (floor) price.[9] Before 1966, the rule made no exception for public takeover bids, preventing tender offers at a premium over the market price, with the predictable result that no such bids took place.[10] To encourage public tender offers, the French Minister of Economics and Finance and the French Stock Brokers' Association (CAC) established in 1966 a procedure under which *cash tender offers for control*, conditional on prior authorization by the CAC, can be executed off the exchange floor with the CAC acting as an auctioneer.[11] The CAC determines control as a de facto situation, unless control is explicitly defined under French corporate law.[12]

The CAC can reject the bidder's application to use the tender offer procedure if it views the offer price and the number of target shares sought as unreasonable.[13] The offer starts when the CAC announces its terms. During

---

[9] The auction market operates as follows: from the opening of the exchange until twelve noon, brokers collect buy and sell orders. At noon, the specialists, who are responsible for clearing the markets for their respective securities, determine the price at which the maximum number of transactions can be executed. Any excess demand or supply is then cleared in an auction that lasts until the exchange closes. Each specialist auctions out one company's shares at a time, so the number of simultaneous auctions equals the number of specialists in the market. Brokers participate in the auctions exclusively as agents and are not allowed to intervene as principals. The auction system prevents the broker from executing an order at a price different from the floor price.

[10] See Bradley (1980) and Grossman and Hart (1980a) for a discussion of the necessary conditions for a tender offer to succeed.

[11] The appendix provides a chronology summary of the rules and regulations discussed in this section, and includes relevant references.

[12] French corporate law determines the number of corporate voting rights needed to implement certain changes in a firm's organization, including replacement of members of the board of directors and merging with another firm. Two-thirds (plus one) of the voting rights constitutes absolute control, a rule that historically has *not* been altered by means of corporate charter supermajority provisions such as those seen in the U.S. A simple majority (50% of the votes plus one) is sufficient to replace the board of directors, whereas a two-thirds majority is needed for a merger with another firm. See, e.g., Fleuriet (1977) for a survey of the French corporate law in effect during our sample period.

[13] Historically, the CAC has occasionally refused to authorize a tender offer on the grounds that the offer price was too low.

the offer period, which is required to be at least four weeks, the CAC monitors the auction. Shareholders can transmit sell orders to financial intermediaries until the offer expiration date. After this date, the CAC collects the sell orders and corresponding share certificates from brokers and counts the total number of shares tendered. After the final count is reached, the CAC publicly announces the offer outcome. For more than 90% of the tender offers in our sample the announcement came two weeks after the expiration-day week. The time between the expiration date and the CAC's announcement is sometimes used to solicit additional target shares if the initial response is unsatisfactory.

The bidder is allowed to increase the offer price once by at least 5% during the first twenty days of the offer period (all tendered shares automatically participate in the price increase) but is not allowed to extend the offer expiration date, which is announced by the CAC at the beginning of the offer period. Rival bids exceeding the initial offer price by at least 5% are permitted during the offer period, in which case all prior sell orders are cancelled and the initial bidder is allowed to respond.[14] Rules introduced in 1978 prohibit a bidder from making another public offer to acquire additional target shares during the twelve months immediately following expiration of the initial offer period.

In 1970, the public tender offer procedure was made available for *control-oriented security exchange offers*, in which the bidder pays target shareholders in stocks and/or bonds, and for *complete minority buyouts*, in which the bidder's prior holdings in the target are at least 50%. Further, to increase the costs of speculating on the outcome of the offer, regulations introduced in 1970 require that the CAC be informed daily of insider or principle share-holder trades in the bidder and target securities during the offer period. While the offer is outstanding, margin requirements for target share trades are raised to 100%, private trades in the target shares are prohibited, and target share forward and options transactions are suspended.[15]

The 1970 regulations also impose substantial disclosure requirements on both bidder and target firms. For the first time, the two firms must disclose 'all important facts' for target shareholders to make 'informed decisions', includ-ing the bidder's prior ownership in the target, the rationale behind – and financing of – the offer, shareholdings of members of the target's board of directors, and the target board's evaluation of the offer. Additional, relatively minor disclosure requirements were subsequently introduced in 1973 and 1978. As of 1973, bidders are required to disclose a detailed justification for the offer

---

[14]As of 1978, rival bids are permitted only during the first ten days of the one-month offer period.

[15]In France, short-selling of shares takes place by means of forward contracts that expire or are marked to market at the end of each month. Thus the short seller does not physically deliver the shares until month-end. A relatively small fraction of all French publicly listed companies trade in this forward market, and for the remaining companies short-selling is impossible.

price or exchange ratio as well as the ownership structure, research policy, business policy orientation, production/investment strategy, and forecast end-of-year sales and earnings for every firm represented by a security given to the target firm in an exchange offer. The target firm must disclose similar information about itself. As of 1978, the bidder firm must also disclose the identity of any shareholder owning more than 5% of its common stock, and a detailed description of its subsidiaries' business activities. The target board must disclose its vote structure concerning the tender offer, and target board members who are also shareholders must disclose their intended response to the offer.

In 1973 a rule was implemented that effectively converts a *successful private tender offer* involving a controlling block of shares into a public tender offer for 100% of the target's shares. According to this new regulation, the size of the block, the block price, and the identity of the buyer and seller must be publicly disclosed the same day the block trade is executed. Further, during the fifteen days following the block trade, the buyer must be prepared to accept all additional shares tendered to him at the block trade price. The parties involved in the controlling-block trade are otherwise exempt from the disclosure requirements governing public tender offers.

Between 1970 and 1978, the public tender offer procedure was gradually made available to a broader spectrum of acquisitions. For example, in 1972 a 'simplified' procedure was introduced to complete buyouts of relatively small minority shareholdings that has fewer disclosure requirements than the regular tender offer procedure. Further, the CAC does not centralize the sell orders or declare the outcome of the offer. The minimum offer period is twenty trading days and no competing bids or changes in the initial bid are allowed while the offer is outstanding.[16] As of 1973, it is also possible to use the public tender offer procedure to become a minority holder in the target firm, provided the minority holding is at least 15%. In 1975, the public tender offer procedure was made available to bidders who own a majority of the target's shares and who seek to reinforce the majority position by acquiring an additional 15% (but not all) of the shares.[17]

---

[16] Under the 1972 rules, a bidder may use the simplified procedure if two of the following three conditions are met: (1) the bidder holds at least 90% of the target shares; (2) the number of target shares not held by the bidder is 15,000 or less; (3) the market value of the target shares not held by the bidder does not exceed two million francs. In 1975, the 15,000-share rule was changed to 20,000: the two million franc maximum was increased to five million; and dealer transactions in the target shares during the offer period were prohibited. In 1978, the 90% rule was relaxed to two-thirds of all target shares, and the required amount of information disclosure was further reduced.

[17] The regulations summarized above concern the tender offer *process*. Before October 1977, no French institution had the authority to prevent an acquisition on the basis of the possible impact of the takeover on product market competition. As of that date, however, the bidder must also be prepared to submit proof that the aquisition does not 'harm competition'.

3. Data and estimation procedures

3.1. Sample characteristics

Our sample period starts with the first cash public tender offers for control of a French target firm in 1966 and ends in 1982. Information on control-oriented security exchange offers as well as minority buyouts became publicly available with the regulatory reform in 1970, and data on private tender offers became available just prior to their regulation in 1973. A total of 306 public and private tender offers for voting control and minority buyouts took place over the 1966–1982 sample period.[18] The population of 306 assumes that an offer that has successive price increases by the initial bidder, or that receives competing bids, is counted as one offer only. During the 1966–1982 period, tender offers were only rarely contested: in our data base there are less than ten contests with multiple bidders, and none in which the target management openly resisted the takeover bid. Of the 306 takeover bids, 256 offers qualify for inclusion in our data base. Seven offers are excluded because of missing information on one or more offer parameters, which include the offer price and the numbers of target shares held, sought, tendered, and purchased;[19] 27 cases are excluded as a result of our minimum restriction on the availability of stock prices necessary to estimate abnormal stock returns; and 16 offers are excluded because we lack information on the payment method in the transaction.

Table 1 lists the annual distribution of the sample of exchange-listed bidder and target firms, classified by the type of offer. The target firms (which are all publicly traded) are listed on the Paris Stock Exchange in 211 of the 256 cases; the remaining targets are listed on either the Lyon Exchange, the Marseille Exchange, or the Lille Exchange. Of the 256 bidders, 139, representing 100 firms, are listed at the time of the offer.[20]

Of the 119 public tender offers for voting control, 70 are all-cash and 49 are securities exchange offers. Of the 44 minority buyouts, in which the bidder's

---

[18]*Source*: CAC, Année Boursière Exercises 1965–1982, and Commission des Opérations en Bourse (COB) 1er–15ème Rapport au Président de la République Exercises, Journal Officiel de la République Francaise, 1968–1982.

[19]Data sources for the various offer parameters are CAC, Année Boursière Exercises 1965–1982, vols. 5–20; CAC, Décision et Avis de la Chambre Syndicale 1965–1982; COB, 1er–15ème Rapport au Président de la République Exercises, Journal Officiel de la République Francaise, 1968–1982; CAC, Service Statistique, 1984 (fiches individuelles d'entreprise); DAFSA, Les Microfiches sur les Actionnaires et les Participations 1976–1982; and DAFSA, Les Liasions Financières, vols. 1–2, 1966–1977.

[20]The source of the stock exchange listing is CAC, Cote Officielle, Cours Officiel et Authentique, 1966–1983.

B.E. Eckbo and H. Langohr, Tender offers in France   371

Table 1

Annual distribution of public and private tender offers for control and of minority buyouts for the total sample of 256 publicly traded French target firms, 1966–1982. The sample is classified by the outcome of the transaction and by the method of payment (cash versus securities in the bidder firm).

Year of offer	212 offers for control[a]						44 minority buyouts[b]	
	119 public offers				93 private offers		All public	
	90 successful[c]		29 unsuccessful		All successful[c]		All successful	
	Cash	Securities[d]	Cash	Securities[d]	Cash		Cash	Securities[d]
1966	1	0	1	0	0		0	0
1967	3	0	4	0	0		0	0
1968	5	0	4	0	0		0	0
1969	4	0	2	0	0		0	0
1970	1	7	2	0	0		3	0
1971	1	2	0	0	0		2	3
1972	6	2	1	2	3		4	0
1973	3	9	0	1	8		1	0
1974	4	4	0	0	7		2	2
1975	4	3	1	2	7		4	1
1976	4	4	0	0	9		1	2
1977	3	5	2	1	9		4	2
1978	2	2	0	0	9		1	3
1979	4	0	2	0	9		2	0
1980	0	2	4	0	12		1	1
1981	2	0	0	0	9		3	1
1982	0	3	0	0	11		1	0
1966–82	47	43	23	6	93		29	15

[a]An offer to transfer control is one in which the bidder owns less than 67% (voting control) of the target shares before the offer and seeks to acquire voting control.

[b]In a minority buyout the bidder seeks 100% of the target and owns 67% or more of the target before the offer.

[c]A 'successful' offer is one in which the bidder firm purchases at least the minimum number of shares specified as a condition for buying any shares at all. If no minimum is specified, an offer is 'successful' if the bidder purchases at least 50% of the maximum number of shares sought. For the private tender offers, we count the block traded as the minimum number of target shares sought by the bidder firm. Thus, all the private offers are by definition successful.

[d]In a securities offer the bidder pays for the target shares using one or more types of securities (possibly in combination with a cash payment). Of the 64 securities offers in the total sample, 49 involve exchanging bidder shares for the target shares, while in 15 cases the bidder offers to exchange straight or convertible bonds. In 11 of the 64 securities offers the payment is a mix of cash and securities. All the private tender offers are cash offers.

prior holding in the target exceeds 66%, 29 are all-cash.[21] The 93 private tender offers for voting control are all-cash offers. Thus, of the 256 offers in

[21]Footnote 12 above motivates the 66% threshold used to define a minority buyout. In our sample, the mean percentage of the target shares held by the bidder before the offer is 79 in the group of minority buyouts and 21 in the group of control-oriented public tender offers.

Table 2

Average market value of total equity eight weeks before the tender offer announcement, the percentage of the target shares held by the bidder before the offer, the percentage tendered and the percentage purchased, for the total sample of 227 successful public and private tender offers for publicly traded French target firms, 1966–1982.

	90 successful public offers for control[a]				Private offers		44 minority buyouts	
	All-cash offers 1/66–12/69 (N=13)	All-cash offers 1/70–12/82 (N=34)	Common-stock offers[b] 1/70–12/82 (N=31)	Bond offers[c] 1/72–12/82 (N=12)	All-cash for control 1/72–12/82 (N=93)	All-cash offers 1/70–12/82 (N=29)	Common-stock offers 1/70–12/82 (N=12)	Bond offers 1/70–12/82 (N=3)
(I) *Market value of total equity of publicly traded bidder and targets (million franc)[d]*								
Target firms	39.7	48.1	130.0	445.7	115.5	99.7	123.1	252.0
Listed bidder firms	490.7 (N=7)	1413.6 (N=12)	595.1 (N=26)	1869.2 (N=7)	1870.0 (N=45)	9413.3 (N=15)	1146.1 (N=9)	n.a.[e]
Bidder/target	12.3 (N=7)	29.4 (N=12)	4.6 (N=26)	4.2 (N=7)	16.2 (N=45)	94.4 (N=15)	9.3 (N=9)	n.a.[e]
(II) *Percent of target shares held, tendered and purchased*								
Percent held	14.0	23.0	21.2	16.4	12.6	79.5	78.4	70.1
Percent tendered	57.9	66.1	71.2	66.4	59.0	16.4	24.5	24.1
Percent purchased	56.1	59.0	67.2	59.0	59.0	16.4	20.9	24.1
Purchased/tendered	0.97	0.89	0.94	0.89	1.00	1.00	0.85	1.00

[a] In the sample of 29 unsuccessful public offers for control (1/66–12/82), the average equity value of the bidder and target firms are 930.1 and 173.0 million francs, with a ratio of bidder-to-target value of 5.4, where 18 of the 29 bidders are publicly traded firms. Furthermore, for this category of offers, the average percentage of the target shares held before the offer is 10.5, the percentage tendered is 13.5, and the percentage purchased is 11.3, respectively. The average maximum percentage of the target shares sought by the bidder in these unsuccessful offers is 84.1.

[b] In 5 of the 31 stock offers, the total compensation also involves a small cash component.

[c] In 4 of the 12 bond offers, the total compensation also involves a small cash component.

[d] Number of publicly traded bidders in parentheses.

[e] None of the three bidders are publicly traded firms. Thus, the information is not available.

the data base, 192 are all-cash offers and in the remaining 64 cases the bidders offer to exchange securities (stocks and/or bonds) in their own firms for the target shares.[22]

We define a 'successful' offer as one in which the bidder (i) purchases at least the minimum of target shares sought, or (ii) if no minimum was specified, purchases at least 50% of the maximum number of target shares sought. Although condition (ii) is somewhat arbitrary it is not restrictive, as the percentage of the target shares actually purchased in unsuccessful offers is small in comparison with the percentage purchased in successful offers (on average 12% versus 60% in public offers for control). With this definition, 29 of the 256 offers in the data base, all control-oriented public tender offers, are unsuccessful. Since our sample contains nearly the entire population, a reasonable estimate of the *ex post* success rate is therefore 76% (90 of 119) for control-oriented public tender offers over the 1966–1982 period. All the private tender offers are necessarily classified as successful, since only those transactions that actually took place appear in our data sources. Further, table 1 overstates the success rate for the minority buyouts, since our sample selection criteria eliminated seven buyouts that would have been classified as unsuccessful under the definition above.

Table 2 shows the average values of the bidder and target firms' total equity, the percentage of the target shares held by the bidder before the offer, and the percentage tendered and purchased for eight subsamples of the total data base. The ratio of the average bidder-to-target equity value is higher after January 1970 and generally higher in cash offers than in securities exchange offers. The average percentage of the target shares held by the bidder before the tender offer rises from 14% before January 1970 to 23 afterward. On average, the bidder ends up holding more than 70% of the target shares in all categories involving tender offers for control. The oversubscription in public offers is generally small, with an average of 80% or more of the tendered shares purchased. The typical offer attracts less than 100% of the target shares, even when the bidder is prepared to purchase any or all of the outstanding target shares, e.g., as in private tender offers during the mandatory fifteen-day offer period following the controlling-block trade.

3.2. Estimation of offer premia and abnormal stock returns

Information on stock prices, dividends, and other distributions needed to compute offer premiums and security returns are not readily available in

---

[22] Of the 64 exchange offers, 43 are public offers for control. Of these, 31 are stock-exchange offers (five mixed with cash) and 12 are bond offers (four mixed with cash). Of the 15 minority buyout exchange offers, 12 involve common stock and in three cases bonds are the means of payment.

France and were collected from several sources.[23] For every offer in the sample, we recorded weekly (Friday to Friday) prices from week -53 relative to the week the offer was made through week 52 relative to the week of the expiration of the offer, i.e., roughly one year of weekly data on either side of the total offer period. Adjustments were made in the returns for cash dividends as of the ex-dividend week and for splits and rights issues.[24]

Define P as the offer price and P_h as the market price of the target shares before any information about the tender offer is revealed to the market. We refer to $P - P_h$ as the 'premium over the pre-offer price'. This total premium can be written as the sum of two components,

$$P - P_h = (P - P_e) + (P_e - P_h),$$ (1)

where P_e is the postexpiration target share price. We refer to $P - P_e$ as the 'premium over the post-expiration price', and $P_e - P_h$ as the 'total offer-induced revaluation'. In France, all oversubscribed offers must be executed pro rata, so the before-tax value to tendering target shareholders of the premium over the post-expiration price is $\alpha(P - P_e)$, where $0 \leq \alpha \leq 1$ is the expected fraction of the tendered shares the bidder will purchase. We refer to $\alpha(P - P_e)$ as the (ex post) 'value of the option to tender'.

A cash bid states the franc value of the offer price, while we use an estimate of the market value of securities the bidder offers in exchange for the target shares.[25] Define week a as the week of the offer announcement and week e as

---

[23] First, we used the 1982 and 1984 versions of the data tape issued by the CAC, that covers weekly stock returns to firms listed simultaneously on the Paris forward and spot markets between 1967 and 1982. This tape, which also contains a small sample of firms listed exclusively on the spot market, covers only a small number of the firms in our data base. The tape does not maintain a record of delisted securities. Second, we obtained data from a tape maintained by the CAC since 1977 and which covers all officially listed securities and preserves the historical record of delisted securities. Third, and most importantly, information was collected manually from various issues of CAC, Cote Officielle, Cours Officiels et Authentique, 1965–1982, and CAC, Année Bourisière Exercises, 1966–1982.

[24] Since the bulk of the stock return data had to be hand-collected, and given our objective of analyzing a comprehensive set of takeover transactions, we chose to work with weekly rather than daily stock returns. Daily returns have an advantage when longer return intervals 'hide' the market reaction to the event under study. Given the large and significant abnormal returns reported below, however, this is not likely to be an important consideration in this paper. This suspicion is confirmed by the results reported by Husson (1986), which are based on daily stock returns and approximately half of the takeovers in our data base.

[25] Specifically, in a stock-exchange offer, we use the stock price on the last trading day before expiration of the offer to construct the offer price. If the stock is not publicly traded, we use the value of the bid as stated in the data sources listed above. The value of bidder bonds offered as means of payment is estimated using the following algorithm:

$$\hat{B} = (B + T_1 C)e^{-rT_1} + T_2 C,$$

where B is the first observed market price of the bond after expiration of the offer; C is the bond's coupon; T_1 is the number of days from the offer expiration date through the date B is observed divided by 365; T_2 is the number of days of (unpaid) coupon accrued at the offer expiration day the offer expiration week. Our event window runs from week $a - 8$ through week $e + 8$, which, given the minimum four-week offer period in public tender offers, typically spans a period of five months.[26] The price at the beginning of this event period, P_{a-8}, is used as a proxy for P_h. The ending price, P_{e+8}, is sufficiently removed from the offer expiration to qualify as a post-expiration price. The ratio of the number of shares purchased, N_p, to the number of shares tendered is used as a proxy for the value of α.[27]

The total offer-induced target revaluation is measured either as the relative price change over the event window, $(P_{e+8} - P_{a-8})/P_{a-8}$, or as the market-adjusted abnormal stock return (including dividends) over the same period. Abnormal return estimates are based on return observations from week $a - 52$ through week $e + 52$ and the following market model:

$$r_{jt} = \alpha_j + \alpha'_j d_{jt} + \beta_j r_{mt} + \beta'_j r_{mt} d_{jt} + \sum_{n=1}^{6} \gamma_{jn} d_{nt} + \varepsilon_{jt}, \tag{2}$$

$$t = a - 52, \ldots, e + 52,$$

where

r_{jt} = continuously compounded rate of return to firm j over week t,
r_{mt} = continuously compounded rate of return to the value-weighted market portfolio over week t,
d_{jt} = a binary variable that takes a value of one in the estimation period after the offer expiration week and zero otherwise,
d_{nt} = a binary variable that takes a value of one if t is in event period n (defined below) and zero otherwise, and
ε_{jt} = a mean zero distribution term assumed normally, identically and independently distributed.

The coefficients α'_j and β'_j are estimated to control for a possible post-offer change in the firm's expected return and only if the firm has at least ten return

---

divided by 365; and r is the daily (annualized) averageovernight interbank interest rate. In our data base, B is either observed within the offer expiration month or in the subsequent month. If B is observed within the offer expiration month, then r is the average interest rate for this month. If B is observed in the month following the expiration month, then r is the weighted average of the monthly averages in the two consecutive months.

[26] For 90% of the public tender offers in the sample, the tender offer period equals the mandatory minimum of four weeks, while the mean offer period in this sample is 4.3. The average offer period in the sample of private tender offers is 2.2 weeks, i.e., slightly above the fifteen-day mandatory minimum for this offer category. None of the targets in the data are delisted before week $e + 8$.

[27] There is virtually no change in the empirical results if we use the number of shares sought, instead of N_p, in constructing the proxy for α, as these two quantities are in most cases virtually identical.

observations in the estimation period after the event period. While no adjustment is made for missing return observations in the estimation period outside of the total event window $[a - 8, e + 8]$, missing price observations inside the event window are replaced assuming an abnormal return of zero. This substitution is based on parameter values of α_j and β_j estimated using observations in the pre-event period $[a - 53, a - 9]$ only. This return substitution allows estimation of the total abnormal return over the event period $[a - 8, e + 8]$. The CAC typically suspends trading in the bidder and target shares during the announcement week. Since we replace the resulting missing price observation with an estimate assuming zero abnormal return, most of the announcement effect shows up in week $a + 1$, the first week of trading after the announcement.[28]

The event parameter γ_{jn} ($n = 1, \ldots, 6$), multiplied by the number of weeks w_n in the event period, is the abnormal stock return to firm j over event period n. The six event subperiods are nonoverlapping and cover the total event window $[a - 8, e + 8]$. The first event subperiod is $[a - 8, a - 1]$, i.e., γ_{j1} captures pre-offer leakage of information and, in general, any nonzero stock price performance before the offer. The second and third subperiods are week a and week $a + 1$, capturing the announcement effect of the offer. The fourth and fifth subperiods cover the interim offer period, $[a + 2, e - 1]$, and the week the offer expires and the following week, $[e, e + 1]$. The sixth subperiod covers the seven-week period $[e + 2, e + 8]$ following offer expiration.[29] Finally, the abnormal return over the total event window $[a - 8, e + 8]$, computed as $\sum_{n-1}^{6} w_n \gamma_{jn}$, is our market-adjusted measure of the total offer-induced target revaluation.

In a sample of N firms, the equal-weighted cross-sectional average abnormal return for the nth event period is computed as

$$AAR_n = \frac{w_n}{N} \sum_j^N \gamma_{jn}. \tag{3}$$

AAR_n represents the average continuously compounded return from a strategy of investing an equal dollar amount in each of the N securities at the beginning of event period n with no further rebalancing over the event period

---

[28]For all offers in the data base, a trading price is available in week $a + 1$.

[29]Since the intercept dummy d_{jt} overlaps with the abnormal return dummy d_{6t}, the estimated value of γ_6 could understate the true abnormal return in the post-expiration period. As it turns out however, none of our conclusions are altered if one starts the intercept dummy after event week $e + 8$, or if this dummy variable is eliminated.

(a buy-and-hold strategy). Under the null hypothesis of zero abnormal return, and presuming the N events are independent, it follows that

$$z_n = \frac{1}{\sqrt{N}} \sum_{j=1}^{N} \frac{\gamma_{jn}}{\sigma_{\gamma_{jn}}} \sim N(0,1),$$ (4)

where $\sigma_{\gamma_{jn}}$ is the standard deviation of γ_{jn}. Replacing the true values of γ_{jn} and $\sigma_{\gamma_{jn}}$ with their ordinary least-squares estimates, this z-statistic is approximately standard normal for large N.[30]

4. Abnormal returns: Total sample results

Tables 3 and 4 report average abnormal stock returns in French takeover bids without specific reference to disclosure regulations or the payment method. The two tables partition the total data base into successful and unsuccessful public tender offers for control, private tender offers for control, and minority buyouts. First, targets of successful and unsuccessful tender offers realize similar significant gains over the event window (13.5% versus 12.4%). Using U.S. data, Bradley, Desai, and Kim (1983) show that initial offer-induced gains to targets in unsuccessful tender offers are reversed on average unless a subsequent bidder wins control within two years of the initial bid. We are unable to repeat this test, because none of the 29 unsuccessful targets in our sample received subsequent offers. Of course, if one equates the low *ex post* frequency of repeat offers with the market's expectations *ex ante*, it also follows that the gains to unsuccessful targets shown in table 3 are unrelated to anticipations of a change in control through a future takeover bid. If so, the gains could represent an information effect (causing the revaluation of previously undervalued resources), or gains from anticipated changes in target management following the unsuccessful takeover bid.

Second, in the vernacular of Bradley (1980), the evidence in table 3 does not support the 'corporate raiding' argument that holds that the average successful bidder is expected to transfer wealth from *ex post* minority shareholders. In contrast, the evidence shows that target shareholders earn significantly positive abnormal returns from successful control-oriented offers – both public and

---

[30]Since the event period dummies in eq. (2) are orthogonal, the z-value for the sum of two event parameters that measures abnormal return over periods of different length, e.g., γ_1 and γ_2, is computed as

$$z_{1+2} = \frac{1}{\sqrt{N}} \sum_{j=1}^{N} \frac{w_1 \gamma_{j1} + w_2 \gamma_{j2}}{\sqrt{\sigma_{\gamma_{j,1+2}}^2}} \quad \text{where} \quad \sigma_{\gamma_{j,1+2}}^2 = w_1^2 \sigma_{\gamma_{j1}}^2 + w_2^2 \sigma_{\gamma_{j2}}^2.$$

Table 3

Percent average abnormal return for 256 French *target* firms, 1966–1982.

Abnormal return for firm j over event period n is based on the OLS estimates of the coefficients γ_{jn} ($n = 1,\ldots,6$) in the following market model:

$$r_{jt} = \alpha_j + \alpha'_j d_t + \beta_j r_{mt} + \beta'_j r_{mt} d_t + \sum_{n=1}^{6} \gamma_{jn} d_{nt} + \epsilon_{jt}, \qquad t = a - 52,\ldots,e + 52,$$

where r_{jt} and r_{mt} are the continuously compounded weekly rates of return to firm j and the value-weighted market index, d_t is a dummy variable that takes on a value of one in the estimation period and zero otherwise, and the six dummy variables d_{nt} take a value of one in each of six nonoverlapping event periods defined in relation to the offer announcement (week a) and offer expiration (week e) and zero otherwise.

(Z-value and percent of the sample with positive abnormal return are given in parentheses.)

Event period[a]	Successful public tender offers for control (N = 90)	Unsuccessful public tender offers for control (N = 29)	Successful private tender offers for control (N = 93)	Successful public tender offers, minority buyouts (N = 44)
a: Offer announcement week				
e: Offer expiration week				
n = 1: Pre-offer period [a − 8, a − 1]	2.96 (1.26; 61.4)	1.70 (0.71; 62.1)	3.32 (2.00; 53.8)	3.13 (1.23; 54.5)
n = 2: Offer announcement[b] [a, a]	0.77 (2.11; 44.3)	0.33 (0.28; 41.4)	3.46 (8.83; 54.8)	0.14 (0.25; 50.0)
n = 3: Offer announcement + 1[b] [a + 1, a + 1]	16.48 (37.57; 72.7)	15.68 (18.10; 72.4)	9.47 (22.28; 60.2)	22.26 (34.18; 79.5)
n = 4: Interim period [a + 2, e − 1]	2.26 (0.87; 47.7)	1.75 (−0.08; 55.2)	−1.21 (−0.96; 33.3)	1.33 (1.05; 61.4)
n = 5: Offer expiration [e, e + 1]	−2.55 (−5.23; 16.4)	−2.34 (−2.33; 37.9)	−2.65 (−4.90; 22.6)	−0.20 (−0.08; 43.2)
n = 6: Post-expiration period [e + 2, e + 8]	−6.37 (−2.99; 40.9)	−4.75 (−1.77; 41.4)	−3.87 (−2.58; 46.2)	−3.50 (−0.84; 36.4)
Total event period [a − 8, e + 8]	13.54 (5.13; 65.9)	12.36 (2.64; 62.1)	8.53 (4.31; 54.8)	23.16 (6.47; 79.6)

[a] Missing returns in the total event period (week $a - 8$ through week $e + 8$) are replaced assuming zero abnormal performance based on estimates of α and β from the period week $a - 52$ through week $a - 9$ relative to the offer announcement. Since γ_{jn} represents the weekly abnormal return over event period n, the firm's total abnormal return is found by multiplying γ_{jn} by the number of weeks in period n. The number of weeks is identical across firms except in the interim period (event period $n = 4$). 90% of the public offers for control have a four-week offer period (which is the mandatory minimum), while the average offer period is 4.3 for this sample. The private tender offers have a minimum fifteen-day (two-week) offer period, and the average offer period in this sample is 2.2 weeks.

[b] The stock exchange commission typically suspends trading in the bidder and target shares in the week of the offer announcement. Since we replace the resulting missing price observation assuming an abnormal return of zero, the announcement effect almost uniformly shows up in week $a + 1$, the first week of trading after the announcement. For all cases in our data base, a trading price is available in week $a + 1$.

Table 4

Percent average abnormal return for 139 French *bidder* firms, 1966–1982.

Abnormal return for firm j over event period n is defined based on the OLS estimates of the coefficients γ_{jn} ($n = 1,...,6$) in the following market model:

$$r_{jt} = \alpha_j + \alpha'_j d_t + \beta_j r_{mt} + \beta'_j r_{mt} d_t + \sum_{n=1}^{6} \gamma_{jn} d_{nt} + \epsilon_{jt}, \quad t = a - 52, ..., e + 52,$$

where r_{jt} and r_{mt} are the continuously compounded weekly rates of return to firm j and the value-weighted market index, d_t is a dummy variable that takes on a value of one in the estimation period after the expiration of the offer and zero otherwise, and the six dummy variables d_{nt} take on a value of one in each of six nonoverlapping event periods defined in relation to the offer announcement (week a) and offer expiration (week e) and zero otherwise.

(Z-value and percent of the sample with positive abnormal return are given in parentheses.)

Event period[a] a: Offer announcement week e: Offer expiration week	Successful public tender offers for control (N = 52)	Unsuccessful public tender offers for control (N = 18)	Successful private tender offers for control (N = 45)	Successful public tender offers, minority buyouts (N = 24)
n = 1: Pre-offer period [a − 8, a − 1]	−0.73 (0.27; 56.6)	2.92 (1.26; 50.0)	−2.15 (−0.93; 44.4)	−0.89 (−0.30; 48.0)
n = 2: Offer announcement[b] [a, a]	0.16 (0.04; 52.8)	0.87 (1.07; 62.5)	0.82 (1.52; 55.6)	−0.54 (−0.52; 44.0)
n = 3: Offer announcement + 1[b] [a + 1, a + 1]	−0.29 (0.18; 47.2)	1.08 (1.53; 37.5)	0.14 (0.40; 46.7)	−0.96 (−1.13; 36.0)
n = 4: Interim period [a + 2, e − 1]	−1.23 (−1.25; 49.1)	−5.06 (−2.05; 37.5)	1.57 (1.73; 57.8)	−2.40 (−1.24; 52.0)
n = 5: Offer expiration [e, e + 1]	−0.37 (−0.87; 39.6)	−0.75 (−1.11; 37.5)	0.94 (1.50; 55.6)	1.66 (1.54; 44.0)
n = 6: Post-expiration period [e + 2, e + 8]	−0.75 (−0.53; 43.4)	0.13 (0.22; 50.0)	−0.42 (−0.60; 42.2)	−1.45 (−1.15; 44.0)
Total event period [a − 8, e + 8]	−3.21 (−0.79; 35.8)	−0.82 (0.35; 50.0)	0.90 (0.19; 53.3)	−4.58 (−1.32; 36.0)

[a] Missing returns in the total event period (week a − 8 through week e + 8) are replaced assuming zero abnormal performance based on estimates of α and β from the period week a − 52 through week a − 9 relative to the offer announcement. Since γ_jn represents the weekly abnormal return over event period n, the firm's total abnormal return is found by multiplying γ_jn by the number of weeks in period n. The number of weeks is identical across firms except in the interim period (event period n = 4). 90% of the public offers for control have a four-week offer period (which is the mandatory minimum), while the average offer period is 4.3 for this sample. The private tender offers have a minimum fifteen-day (two-week) offer period, and the average offer period in this sample is 2.2 weeks.

[b] The stock exchange commission typically suspends trading in the bidder and target shares in the week of the offer announcement. Since we replace the resulting missing price observation assuming an abnormal return of zero, the announcement effect almost uniformly shows up in week a + 1, the first week of trading after the announcement. For all cases in our data base, a trading price is available in week a + 1.

private – and from minority buyouts (event window abnormal returns are 13.5%, 8.5%, and 23.1%, respectively).

Third, the results contradict the 'inside information' argument that the bidder typically sets the offer price below his private postexpiration target share value, as proponents of disclosure regulations often argue. The significant decline in the target share price with the expiration of the offer (event parameters γ_5 and γ_6) implies that the bidder on average incurs a loss on the shares purchased. This, of course, does not mean that acquiring firms do not profit from the tender offer. For example, in synergistic offers, the underlying synergy is presumed to have a value-increasing effect on the shares of both firms.

Fourth, table 4 fails to uncover statistically significant gains or losses to bidder firms in any of the four offer categories. The significantly negative value of γ_4 in the sample of 18 unsuccessful bidders is indirect evidence that takeovers are valuable to bidder firms, thus the negative price adjustment as the market (presumably) starts to realize that the offer will fail. There is no direct confirmation of this hypothesis, however, as the abnormal returns to the 52 successful bidders in public tender offers for control are indistinguishable from zero.[31]

Fifth, targets in successful public and private tender offers experience a statistically significant average price decline in the event period $e + 2$ through $e + 8$ (event parameter γ_6, table 3). Closer inspection reveals that this price drop coincides with the CAC's announcement of the offer outcome. In our estimation procedure, week e represents the offer expiration date announced by the CAC at the beginning of the offer period. However, week e is not necessarily the final offer week. After week e but before the CAC formally announces the offer outcome, a period that typically lasts two weeks,[32] the bidder frequently enlists the aid of the CAC, financial intermediaries, and brokers to attract additional target shares. The exact length of the period between the expiration date and the offer outcome announcement date is not known by the market until the CAC formally announces the outcome. As a result, the negative impact of the offer expiration is reflected in the average values of both γ_5 and γ_6. Since we use P_{e+8} as a proxy for the post-expiration equilibrium price P_e, the empirical results presented below fully reflect the impact of the expiration of the offer.

---

[31]As shown in table 2, the bidder is typically more than ten times the size of the target. Since the power of stock returns to register a given dollar gain decreases with the size of the bidder, it is possible that the generally insignificant abnormal returns reflect a measurement problem due to relative size. Eckbo (1988) reports evidence consistent with the presence of a size-related measurement problem when measuring gains to bidder firms in a large sample of U.S. and Canadian acquisitions.

[32]In our sample, the outcomes of 64% of the public tender offers were announced in week $e + 2$, 20% in week $e + 3$, and 10% in week $e + 4$. One outcome was announced in week $e + 7$.

5. Offer premiums and disclosure regulations

Disclosure regulations raise the direct transaction costs of making a bid and reduce the expected return from acting on private information that the target resources are undervalued. As a result, the regulations are expected to deter some otherwise marginally profitable bids.[33] In addition, the regulations can affect the division of the total takeover gains between the bidder and target shareholders in offers that survive mandatory information disclosure. Previously undisclosed information that the target resources are undervalued in their current or best alternative use creates expectations of higher-valued offers, increasing the offer-induced target revaluation. Alternatively, the bidder and target firms may be locked in a bilateral monopoly, in which case greater knowledge of the source of the takeover gains gives the target additional bargaining power. To the extent that disclosure regulations produce this information, we expect to see an increase in the premium over the post-expiration target share price, reflecting additional rents from the supply of control.[34]

We first provide empirical estimates of the average total offer premium and its two components based on cash public tender offers for control before and after the 1970 disclosure regulations. We subsequently compare these estimates with the average offer premium in private offers after 1970. As in the public offers, the bidder in private offers pays with cash and acquires voting control of the target. As mentioned earlier, however, the bidder in a private offer is not required to disclose substantive information.

5.1. Public cash tender offers before versus after January 1970

Table 5 shows that the average (median) public tender offer premium over the pre-offer price increased from 33.8 (31.9)% in 1966–1969 to 73.3 (59.0)% over the 1970–1982 period. In franc values, the average premium increased from 7.5 million to 15.2 million (median values of 2.1 and 8.8 million). The table also reveals that the bulk of the premium increase occurred in the offer-induced target revaluation rather than in the premium over the post-expiration price. The former increased from 17.0 to 46.7% (median values of 19.0 and 35.8%) and the latter from 15.2 to 23.7% (median values of 13.6 and 16.1%). The increase in the average value of the tender option from 14.7 to 21.1% (median value virtually unchanged at 13.3 and 13.3%) is somewhat less than the increase in the premium over the post-expiration price, reflecting in

---

[33] Disclosure regulations can also *increase* the information advantage for some bidder firms because antifraud provisions, backed by significant penalties on material misstatements and omissions, generally increase the credibility of information the bidder discloses. A more credible signal can improve the bidder's bargaining position with the target as well as reduce the possibility of costly, uninformed bidding by rival firms. See also Grossman and Hart (1980b).

[34] See DeAngelo and Rice (1983) for discussion of the conditions under which tendering target shareholders may be able to extract a control premium from the bidder firm.

382   *B.E. Eckbo and H. Langohr, Tender offers in France*

Table 5

Mean (median) offer premiums and abnormal returns in 140 successful, all-cash public and private tender offers for control of publicly traded French target firms in the period before and after the January 1970 change in disclosure regulations.

Definition of offer premium		Public tender offers		Private tender offers
a: Offer announcement week e: Offer expiration week		1/66–12/69 ($N = 13$)	1/70–12/82 ($N = 34$)	1/72–12/82 ($N = 93$)
(I) *Premium over pre-offer price*[a]				
$(P - P_{a-\aleph})/P_{a-\aleph}$	(%)	33.8 (31.9)	73.3 (59.0)	27.4 (18.3)
$N_p(P - P_{a-\aleph})$	(million franc)	7.5 (2.1)	15.2 (8.8)	1.6 (2.9)
(II) *Premium over post-expiration price*[b]				
$(P - P_{e+\aleph})/P_{e+\aleph}$	(%)	15.2 (13.6)	23.7 (16.1)	14.6 (5.6)
$\alpha(P - P_{e+\aleph})/P_{e+\aleph}$	(%)	14.7 (13.3)	21.2 (13.1)	14.6 (5.6)
$N_p(P - P_{e+\aleph})$	(million franc)	4.1 (1.0	9.4 (4.4)	1.4 (0.7)
(III) *Total offer-induced target revaluation*				
$(P_{e+\aleph} - P_{a-\aleph})/P_{a-\aleph}$	(%)	17.0 (19.0)	46.7 (35.8)	18.7 (6.5)
$N_p(P_{e+\aleph} - P_{a-\aleph})$	(million franc)	3.4 (1.1)	5.8 (4.9)	0.2 (0.7)
(IV) *Percent average abnormal stock return (Z-value; percent positive)*[c]				
Target firm	Week $a + 1$	16.2 (13.7; 100.0)	28.1 (41.8; 82.4)	9.5 (22.3; 60.2)
	Weeks $a - 8$ through $e + 8$	15.3 (2.3; 75.0)	28.5 (6.4; 79.4)	8.5 (4.3; 54.8)
Bidder firm[d]	Week $a + 1$	1.0 (1.2; 71.4)	0.6 (1.3; 66.7)	0.1 (0.4; 46.7)
	Weeks $a - 8$ through $e + 8$	−0.2 (0.1; 42.9)	−0.1 (0.1; 41.7)	0.9 (0.2; 53.3)

[a]P is the offer price, $P_{a-\aleph}$ is the target price eight weeks before the offer announcement (week a), and N_p is the number of target shares purchased by the bidder.

[b]$\alpha(P - P_{e\cdot\aleph})/P_{e+\aleph}$ is the *ex post* value of the option to tender, where $\alpha = F_p/F_t$, F_p is the fraction of the target shares purchased, F_t is the fraction of the target shares tendered, and $P_{e+\aleph}$ is the target share price eight weeks after the expiration of the offer (week e).

[c]Abnormal returns are computed using the market model described in table 3. The abnormal return in week $a + 1$ is represented by γ_3 in the market model regression, while the abnormal return over the total event period $[a - 8, e + 8]$ is given by the sum of the six event parameters weighted by the total number of weeks in each of the six subperiods of the total event window.

[d]These average abnormal returns are based on a total of 7 publicly traded bidders in the sample of 13 public offers prior to 1970, 12 bidders in the sample of 34 public offers after 1969, and 45 bidders in the sample of 93 private offers after 1971.

part the slight post-1970 increase in the rate of oversubscription.[35] In sum, we find that the January 1970 disclosure regulations were followed by a substantial increase in the average offer-induced target revaluation and only a moderate increase, if any, in the average premium over the post-expiration price. The statistical significance of these sample differences is confirmed by cross-sectional regressions discussed below.

Table 6 reports the annual time-series behavior of the mean total offer premium in the sample of 47 successful cash public tender offers. The average premium in the post-1969 period is relatively evenly distributed, with the single largest premium occurring in the one case that took place in 1970. As noted in the table, the maximum offer premium was 42% in 1967, 36% in 1968, and 53% in 1969. Thus, the offer premiums associated with the two cases in 1970 and 1971 both exceed the maximum in the sample of thirteen offers before 1970. Moreover, the average premium over the pre-offer price associated with the eleven offers in 1970–1973 is 88.4%, which is significantly higher than the 33.8% average for the thirteen cases in 1966–1969 but indistinguishable from the average over the entire post-1969 period. Thus, although the average offer premiums in 1972 and 1974 are relatively moderate, the evidence supports the hypothesis that the January 1970 disclosure regulations had an immediate impact.

Table 7 reports the results of cross-sectional regressions of offer premiums on offer characteristics. The regression model is estimated across the total sample of 163 cash tender offers for control and includes the natural log of the target's total equity value ($\ln V_T$); the fraction of the target shares held by the bidder before the offer (F_h) and the fraction purchased (F_p); and dummy variables for the pre-1970 period ($D_{-70} = 1$), private tender offers ($D_{PRIV} = 1$), and unsuccessful offers ($D_{FAIL} = 1$). The size variable is included to capture the scale of the offer, and is expected to have a negative effect on the *percentage* offer premium. The bidder realizes an offer-induced gain on his prior holding in the target which, in the presence of competition, tends to be transferred to target shareholders. Thus, F_h is predicted to have a positive effect on offer premiums in bids for control. If target shareholders have heterogeneous expectations about the post-offer target share price, or if they face different potential capital-gains tax liabilities, the supply curve of tendered target shares will be upward-sloping.[36] An upward-sloping supply curve is consistent with the fact that less than 100% of the target shares are tendered in the typical tender offer (table 2) despite the substantial average offer premium. Thus, we expect F_p to have a positive effect on offer premiums.

---

[35] The percentage of the tendered target shares purchased by the bidder declined from 97 before 1970 to 89 in the sample period of January 1970 (table 2).

[36] Rosenfeld (1982) and Bradley, Desai, and Kim (1988) analyze the supply curve of tendered target shares (the former study in the context of share-repurchase offers).

384   *B.E. Eckbo and H. Langohr, Tender offers in France*

Table 6

Annual average offer premiums, measured relative to the target price eight weeks prior to week of offer announcement, in the total sample of 47 successful, cash public tender offers for publicly traded French targets, 1966–1982.[a]

(Median values are given in parentheses.)

Year of offer	Number of offers	Premium over pre-offer price $(P - P_{a-8})/P_{a-8}$ (%)
(I) *Period without disclosure regulations*[b]		
1966	1	19.0
1967	3	30.8
1968	5	28.7
1969	4	46.3
1966–69	13	33.8
		(31.9)
(II) *Period with disclosure regulations*		
1970	1	141.7
1971	1	62.5
1972	6	41.6
1973	3	107.6
1974	4	40.3
1975	4	61.4
1976	4	127.2
1977	3	98.6
1978	2	96.4
1979	4	60.4
1980	0	—
1981	2	34.8
1982	0	—
1970–82	34	73.3
		(59.0)

[a] P is the offer price and P_{a-8} is the target share price eight weeks before the week of the offer announcement (week a).
[b] In 1967, 1968, and 1969, the maximum premium was 42%, 36%, and 53%.

The dependent variables of the three regressions in panel I are the premium over the pre-offer price, the premium over the post-expiration price, and the total offer-induced target revaluation. The first regression shows that the premium over the pre-offer price (i) decreases with $\ln V_T$, (ii) is essentially unrelated to both F_h and F_p, (iii) is significantly lower for pre-1970 offers and for private tender offers, and (iv) is as high in unsuccessful as in successful offers. The significant impact of D_{-70} confirms the picture provided earlier by the sample averages in tables 5 and 6. The regression is significant with an R^2 of 0.20 and an F-statistic of 6.24. Regressions 2 and 3 reveal that this

Table 7

Ordinary least-squares estimates of the effect on offer premiums and abnormal stock returns of the size of the target's total equity, the fractions of the target shares held prior to the offer and purchased by the bidder, whether the offer is made before or after the January 1970 change in disclosure regulations, whether the offer is public or private, and whether the offer is successful or fails, for the total sample of 163 cash tender offers of publicly traded French target firms, 1966–1982.[a]

$$Y = a_0 + a_1 \ln V_T + a_2 F_h + a_3 F_p + a_4 D_{-70} + a_5 D_{PRIV} + a_6 D_{FAIL}.$$

(t-values are given in parentheses.)

Dependent variable	a_0	a_1	a_2	a_3	a_4	a_5	a_6	R^2	F-value
(I) Offer premium									
1. Premium over pre-offer price, $(P - P_{a-8})/P_{a-8}$	2.31 (4.09)	-0.11 (-3.47)	-0.11 (-0.48)	0.24 (1.12)	-0.34 (-2.66)	-0.40 (-4.13)	0.02 (0.11)	0.20	6.24
2. Premium over post-expiration price, $(P - P_{e+8})/P_{e+8}$	-0.14 (-0.26)	0.01 (0.21)	0.21 (0.93)	0.37 (1.81)	-0.04 (-0.32)	-0.06 (-0.71)	0.09 (0.52)	0.03	0.77
3. Total offer-induced target revaluation, $(P_{e+8} - P_{a-8})/P_{a-8}$	2.55 (4.28)	-0.11 (-3.49)	-0.46 (-1.88)	-0.26 (-1.15)	-0.35 (-2.56)	-0.28 (-2.71)	-0.06 (-0.34)	0.14	4.01
(II) Abnormal stock return									
4. Listed bidder firms (N = 76), week $a+1$	0.01 (0.15)	0.00 (0.08)	-0.02 (-0.55)	-0.01 (-0.26)	0.01 (0.30)	-0.01 (-0.34)	0.01 (0.39)	0.04	0.45
5. Listed bidder firms (N = 76), weeks $a-8$ through $e+8$	-0.49 (-1.60)	-0.02 (-1.34)	-0.16 (-1.88)	-0.22 (-0.94)	-0.06 (-0.01)	-0.00 (-0.36)	-0.03 (-0.20)	0.10	1.22
6. Target firms, week $a+1$	0.97 (3.44)	-0.04 (-2.94)	0.01 (0.06)	0.05 (0.44)	-0.06 (-0.96)	-0.16 (-3.28)	-0.02 (-0.19)	0.14	4.03
7. Target firms, weeks $a-8$ through $e+8$	1.32 (2.11)	-0.07 (-2.04)	0.08 (0.33)	0.07 (0.28)	-0.04 (-0.26)	-0.14 (-1.29)	-0.00 (-0.01)	0.05	1.29

[a]
P = offer price.
P_{a-8} = target share price eight weeks before the offer announcement week (week a).
P_{e+8} = target share price eight weeks after expiration of the offer (week e).
$\ln V_T$ = log of the value of the target firm's total equity in week $a-8$.
F_h = fraction of the target shares held by the bidder prior to the offer.
F_p = fraction of the target shares purchased by the bidder.
D_{-70} = dummy variable that equals one if the offer is made before the January 1970 change in disclosure regulations and zero otherwise,
D_{PRIV} = dummy variable that equals one if the offer is a private tender offer and zero otherwise
D_{FAIL} = dummy variable that equals one if the offer failed (as defined in table 1) and zero otherwise.

significance is driven almost exclusively by the total offer-induced target revaluation.

The premium over the post-expiration price (regression 2) is essentially unrelated to all the explanatory variables (with the possible exception of F_p), and produces an R^2 of 0.03 and an F-value of 0.77. When the total target revaluation is used as dependent variable (regression 3), however, the values of the estimated coefficients are again significant and almost identical to the parameter values emerging from the regression with the premium over the pre-offer price. This regression is also significant with an R^2 of 0.14 and an F-value of 4.01. In sum, the regression results of panel I of table 7 confirm that the increase in the premium over the pre-offer price after the January 1970 change in disclosure regulations is statistically significant and driven by an increase in the total offer-induced revaluation.

Panel II of table 7 reports cross-sectional regressions of abnormal stock returns to bidder and target firms over week 1 and weeks $e - 8$ through $e + 8$. Regressions 4 and 5, which use the abnormal return to bidder firms as the dependent variable, are both insignificant (F-statistics of 0.45 and 1.22). This confirms the total sample findings of table 4, as well as those in table 5, that the average abnormal return to bidder firms is uniformly indistinguishable from zero.

Regressions 6 and 7 use the abnormal return to the target firm as the dependent variable. Regression 6 is significant (R^2 of 0.14 and F-value of 4.03) but does not capture any association between week 1 abnormal return and the time period of the offer, coefficient a_4. Regression 7 is insignificant (R^2 of 0.05 and F-value of 1.29). In evaluating the discrepancy between the results in panels I and II, note that the abnormal return over week 1 (regression 6) is conceptually different from the offer-induced revaluation used in regression 3.[37] Moreover, while the abnormal return to the target firm over the total event period (regression 7 in table 7) is conceptually equivalent to the offer-induced revaluation used in regression 3, the general lack of power of regression 7 suggests that its dependent variable is a relatively noisy estimate of the simple measure of the offer-induced revaluation used in regression 3, with the additional variability reflecting noise in the estimated market model parameters.

The evidence on the abnormal return to bidder firms fails to reject the proposition that competition on average grants most (if not all) of the takeover gains to targets both before and after the introduction of disclosure regula-

---

[37]The abnormal return over week 1 reflects both the offer-induced revaluation and the value of the tender option, attenuated by any prior leakage of information about the forthcoming offer. Panel IV of table 5 shows an increase in the average abnormal returns to targets from approximately 16 to 28% after January 1970.

tions.[38] The logical implication is that disclosure regulations that increase the cost of takeovers will deter some bids (a truncation effect). The evidence further shows that the sample mean of the distribution of offer-induced target revaluations is significantly higher after the introduction of disclosure rules. Jointly with the evidence on bidder firms, this is consistent with the proposition that tender offers deterred by disclosure rules on average produce lower total gains than tender offers that survive disclosure (i.e., truncation of marginally profitable takeovers).[39]

5.2. Public versus private cash tender offers after January 1970

Referring back to table 5 (panel IV), bidders in private as well as public tender offers earn on average statistically insignificant abnormal returns, both over week 1 and over the total event period $a - 8$ through $e + 8$. Thus, the abnormal performance of successful bidder firms does not provide any evidence that the 1970 change in disclosure regulations has materially affected the distribution of bidder gains in private versus public offers. There is some indication, however, that the 1970 regulation of public offers led to an increase in the frequency of the alternative, private offer procedure. Although data on private tender offers are not publicly available before 1972, we base this conjecture on official statements indicating that the subsequent 1973 regulation of private offers was intended to make substitution of the private for the public offer procedure less attractive.[40]

Table 5 also shows a significant difference between the average gains to targets in public and private cash tender offers after 1970. The average premium over the pre-offer price in the sample of 93 private tender offers is 27.4 (median 18.3)%, which contrasts with the 73.3% average for public offers. The lower total premium in private offers reflects primary a lower offer-induced revaluation of the target shares, which averages 18.7 (median 6.5)%. This offer-induced revaluation is indistinguishable from the 17.0 (median 19.0)% average revaluation in *public* tender offers *before* 1970, but signifi-

---

[38] The z-values in table 5 for event period $a + 1$ is 1.2 for bidders before 1970 and 1.3 for bidders after 1969, both of which fail to reject the null hypothesis of zero average abnormal returns. Note, however, that 71.4% of the bidders before 1970 and 66.7% after 1969 have positive abnormal returns. Under the null, the expected fraction of firms with positive abnormal returns is 0.5 with variance $(0.5)(0.5)/N$. Reflecting the small sample sizes ($N = 7$ before 1970 and $N = 12$ after 1969), a two-sided t-test based on the percentage positive also fails to reject the null hypothesis.

[39] While not reported in table 5, this proposition is supported when looking at the franc value of the sum of the average abnormal return to bidder and target firms as well.

[40] The two-week mandatory price-support period imposed on private tender offers in 1973 was intended to (translated) 'favour the increased use of the *public* tender offer procedure', COB, 1974, Sixième Rapport au Président de la République Année 1973, p. 150 (emphasis added).

cantly less than the 46.7 (median 35.8)% average in public offers after disclosure regulations took effect.

In contrast, the average premium over the post-expiration price is 14.6 (median 5.6)%, which is indistinguishable from the corresponding premium in public tender offers before 1970 (average 15.2%, median 13.5%) and somewhat smaller than the average value of 23.7 (median 16.1)% in public offers from 1970 onward. Interestingly, the latter indicates that, after 1970, the seller of a controlling block of shares typically extracted a *smaller* control premium in a private tender offer than what is typically paid in a public offer. A similar conclusion emerges from a comparison of the values of the tender option, $\alpha(P - P_e)/P_e$, which controls for the fact that only public offers can be oversubscribed. For private offers, the average (median) option value is 14.6 (5.6)%, compared with 14.7 (13.3)% in the sample of public offers before 1970 and 21.2 (13.1)% in public offers from 1970 onward.

The sign and significance of the regression coefficient a_5 in table 7, which multiplies the dummy variable for private offers, give partial support to the above conclusions. In panel I, a_5 is negative and significant in regressions 1 (where the dependent variable is the premium over the pre-offer price) and 3 (total offer-induced revaluation) but insignificant in regression 2 (premium over post-expiration price). Target firm abnormal returns are also significantly lower in private than in public offers during week 1 (coefficient a_5 in regression 6) but not over the total event period (regression 7).

Since the evidence fails to reject the hypothesis that bidders earn zero abnormal returns in either private or public offers, the significantly smaller target returns in private offers are consistent with the proposition that total takeover gains are on average smaller in private than in public offers.[41] If public offers deterred by disclosure regulations tend to move to the private offer procedure, this evidence further supports the earlier conclusion that disclosure regulations have probably deterred offers with relatively small total gains.

It is also interesting that the evidence of lower target gains in the average private tender offer appears in spite of the substantially higher target ownership concentration in this offer category.[42] This finding runs somewhat counter to the argument that, in diffusely held targets, competition among shareholders for the control premium tends to induce individual shareholders to tender 'too soon' in relation to a perfectly coordinated response.[43] On the other hand, recall that private tender offers are offers for any-or-all of the target shares

---

[41]A similar conclusion follows from an analysis of the franc value of the sum of the average abnormal return to bidder and target firms.

[42]Although we do not have direct evidence on ownership structure, recall that all targets of private tender offers are controlled by a single blockholder.

[43]See, e.g., DeAngelo and Rice (1983).

over a mandatory fifteen-day period after the controlling-block trade has been executed. In other words, the bidder in a private offer does not have the option to restrict the number of target shares purchased. This option is valuable when the bidder needs only a majority of the target votes to implement the intended post-offer change in the target. In these cases, the risk of excess supply of target shares at the controlling-block price reduces the equilibrium offer price in a private relative to a public offer.[44]

6. Offer premiums and the payment method

There are several reasons to expect that the level and division of gains in corporate takeovers depend on the method of payment. In France, target shareholders pay capital-gains tax if the shares are tendered for cash, whereas payment in securities allows deferral of taxes.[45] Thus, in a cash offer, the bidder must offer extra compensation equal to the difference between the immediate tax liability and the present value of future (deferred) taxes. This tax hypothesis depicts that the before-tax value of the premium over the post-expiration target share price, which dictates the incentive to tender, is higher in cash offers than in securities exchange offers.[46] Furthermore, the choice of financing may have nontax-related valuation effects. For example, Myers and Majluf (1984) show that the use of equity can convey unfavorable information, while Jensen (1986) argues that the use of cash can increase value by obviating potential agency problems associated with excessive retention of cash ('free cash flow'). Hansen (1987), Fishman (1989), and Eckbo,

[44] Formally, for a given post-expiration price P_e, the bidder seeking only a controlling block of shares is indifferent between a public tender offer price of P and a private tender offer price of $P_p = \alpha P + (1 - \alpha) P_e$, which implies that $P_p < P$ if the offer is expected to be oversubscribed ($\alpha < 1$). The condition $P_p < P$ is also acceptable to the controlling-block seller provided collusion with minority shareholders is ruled out.

[45] If the tendering shareholder is a corporation and if the corporation purchased the target shares within two years prior to the offer, the realized capital gain is treated as general business revenue and taxed at the 50% corporate income tax rate. If the shares have been held for more than two years, the realized capital gain is considered long-term and taxed according to a flat rate of 15%. If the tendering shareholder is an individual, any capital gains realized before December 31, 1978 are fully tax-exempt. After this date (and throughout the rest of our sample period), the taxation of realized capital gains depends on the total value of the securities sold. If the total value is less than 150,000 francs, any capital gain is free. If the value exceeds this limit, the tax rate is a flat 15%. There is an exception to this rule if the individual realizes gain from what is considered 'speculative selling' (a term referring in particular to short-selling). In this case, if the individual's portfolio turnover ratio (i.e., the ratio of the value of the shares sold to the total value of the portfolio) exceeds 2.6, the individual must choose between a 30% flat tax rate and the individual's marginal tax rate on ordinary income.

[46] During our sample period, cash and securities exchange offers were given identical accounting treatment for the purpose of *corporate* taxes. Thus, accounting-related tax benefits on the corporate level, e.g., such as those discussed in Carleton, Guilkey, Harris, and Stewart (1983) and Gilson, Scholes, and Wolfson (1988) in the context of takeover bids in the U.S., are not a determinant of the payment method in our French sample.

Table 8

Mean (median) offer premiums and abnormal returns in 84 successful public tender offers for control and minority buyouts in France, classified by the payment method, 1970–1982.

Definition of offer premium a: Offer announcement week e: Offer expiration week	Offers for control			Minority buyouts	
	Payment in cash only[a] (N = 34)	Payment in common stock (N = 31)	Payment in bonds (N = 12)	Payment in cash only (N = 29)	Payment in common stock (N = 12)
(I) Premium over pre-offer price[b]					
$(P - P_{a-8})/P_{a-8}$ (%)	73.3 (59.0)	17.2 (19.0)	34.9 (55.2)	38.3 (35.6)	9.0 (17.1)
$N_p(P - P_{a-8})$ (million franc)	15.2 (8.8)	6.9 (5.4)	38.2 (15.4)	6.0 (0.8)	57.0 (4.0)
(II) Premium over post-expiration price[c]					
$(P - P_{e+8})/P_{e+8}$ (%)	23.7 (16.1)	22.5 (20.0)	38.5 (33.7)	9.2 (6.1)	3.2 (14.5)
$\alpha(P - P_{e+8})/P_{e+8}$ (%)	21.2 (13.1)	21.2 (17.0)	34.3 (30.9;)	9.2 (6.1)	2.7 (12.0)
$N_p(P - P_{e+8})$ (million franc)	9.4 (4.4)	12.4 (4.8)	54.1 (46.2)	1.4 (0.2)	6.9 (1.4)

(III) Total offer-induced target revaluation

$(P_{e+8} - P_{a-8})/P_{a-8}$ (%)	46.7 (35.8)	-1.1 (0.4)	-1.8 (0.3)	27.8 (22.0)	7.4 (7.5)
$N_p(P_{e+8} -)P_{a-8}$ (million franc)	5.8 (4.9)	-5.5 (0.1)	-15.9 (0.1)	4.5 (0.7)	-1.2 (1.3)

(IV) Percent average abnormal stock return (Z-value; percent positive)[d]

Target firm Week $a+1$	28.1 (41.8; 82.4)	5.4 (6.6; 54.8)	12.1 (7.1; 60.0)	28.7 (36.7; 85.7)	12.1 (8.0; 66.7)
Weeks $a-8$ through $e+8$	28.5 (6.4; 79.5)	3.9 (1.2; 54.8)	-0.0 (-0.2; 60.0)	33.2 (7.4; 89.2)	5.6 (0.7; 66.7)
Bidder firm[e] Week $a+1$	0.6 (1.3; 66.7)	-0.9 (-0.9; 34.6)	-1.2 (-1.2; 28.6)	-0.8 (-0.5; 40.0)	-1.1 (-1.1; 33.3)
Weeks $a+1$ through $e+8$	-0.1 (0.1; 41.7)	-3.6 (-0.7; 34.6)	-11.8 (-1.3; 14.3)	-5.6 (-1.0; 40.0)	-1.0 (-0.6; 33.3)

[a] This column repeats column 2 of table 5.

[b] P is the offer price, P_{a-8} is the target price eight weeks prior to the offer announcement (week a), and N_p is the number of target shares purchased by the bidder.

[c] $\alpha(P - P_{e+8})/P_{e+8}$ is the ex post value of the option to tender, where $\alpha = F_p/F_t$, F_p is the fraction of the target shares purchased, F_t is the fraction of the target shares tendered, and P_{e+8} is the target share price eight weeks after the expiration of the offer (week e).

[d] Abnormal returns are computed using the market model described in table 3. The abnormal return in week $a+1$ is represented by γ_3 in the market model regression, while the abnormal return over the total event period $[a-8, e+8]$ is given by the sum of the six event parameters weighted by the total number of weeks in each of the six subperiods of the total event window.

[e] These average abnormal returns are based on a total of 12 publicly traded bidders in the sample of 34 all-cash offers for control, 26 bidders in the sample of 31 all-stock offers, 7 bidders in the sample of 12 bond offers, 15 in the sample of cash minority buyouts, and 9 in the sample of 12 stock minority buyouts.

Giammarino, and Heinkel (1988) also demonstrate that the choice of payment method can convey information under conditions of asymmetric information. Although we do not attempt to distinguish empirically between these nontax-based valuation arguments, they lead us to expect a higher offer-induced revaluation in cash than in stock offers, for both the bidder and the target firm.

Below, we first compare offer premiums and abnormal returns in public, all-cash and all-securities offers for control. We subsequently make the same comparison for minority buyouts. The sample period is restricted to 1970–1982, the period for which securities exchange offers and minority buyouts are available for study (table 1).

6.1. Public tender offers for control

The two first columns of table 8 list the average and median offer premiums and abnormal returns in the samples of 34 all-cash and 31 all-stock offers after 1970.[47] The table reveals a striking difference in the offer premiums in the two samples. The average (median) premium over the pre-offer price is 17.2 (19.0)% when the payment is all stock, compared with 73.3 (59.0)% for all-cash offers. The average franc value of the total offer premium, multiplied by the number of target shares purchased, is 15.2 million in all-cash offers versus 6.9 million in stock-exchange offers.

Table 8 also shows that the average premium over the post-expiration price is almost identical across the two payment methods: 22.5 and 23.7 (medians 20.0 and 16.1)%, respectively. Thus, the difference in the offer premiums over the pre-offer price across all-cash and securities-exchange offers is driven by a difference in the total offer-induced revaluation in the two offer categories. The average (median) total revaluation is −1.1 (0.4)% in stock offers and −1.8 (0.3)% in bond offers, compared with the 46.7 (35.8)% for the all-cash offers.

While surprising, our finding of an approximately zero total offer-induced target revaluation in securities-exchange offers appears to hold with alternative definitions of the post-expiration price P_e. Wansley, Lane, and Yang (1983), in the context of takeovers in the U.S., argue that a relatively small offer-induced target revaluation in a securities-exchange offer can simply reflect a measurement problem. That is, while a cash offer can be executed over a relatively short time, the U.S. Securities and Exchange Commission requires that securities offered in exchange for the target shares be registered before the transaction is completed. A lengthy pre-registration process can cause information

---

[47]Column 1 reproduces, for convenience, the information in column 2 of table 5. In five of the 31 all-stock offers, the means of payment is a mixture of cash and common stock. The cash component in each of these five offers represents less than 50% of the total compensation given target shareholders. Because of the small sample, we do not present separate results for mixed offers. See Eckbo, Giammarino, and Heinkel (1988) for a theoretical and empirical analysis of mixed cash-stock offers.

about the forthcoming offer to leak to the market, which attenuates the abnormal returns measured in relation to the offer announcement. Although this may be a problem when comparing abnormal stock returns in all-cash and securities-exchange offers in the U.S., we do not observe a materially different registration period for all-cash than for securities offers in France. Also, French law explicitly requires the regulatory agencies to keep information about a forthcoming offer secret until the offer has been formally approved and announced. Thus, this particular regulatory argument does not confound our comparison of cash and securities exchange offers in France.

Also, shareholders of bidder firms in France can refuse to authorize the issuance of stocks promised in a securities exchange offer *after* the offer has been made by management and target shareholds have accepted. That is, the securities exchange commission grants the bidder management the right to offer target shareholders yet-to-be authorized common stock in order to avoid leakage of information about a forthcoming takeover bid from the stock authorization process itself. In principle, one would expect bidder shareholders to exercise this *ex post* veto right in accepted offers when they believe management is overpaying for the target. The relatively low offer premiums in stock offers are, however, almost certainly not explained by the existence of this veto right: first, the average offer premium over the pre-offer price in the six unsuccessful (and potentially vetoed) exchange offers in our data base is only 15%, i.e., lower than the average offer premium of 22.5% in successful bids. Second, as seen from table 8, the abnormal stock returns to bidders in both cash and stock offers are indistinguishable from zero.[48] There is no evidence that bidders in all-stock offers perform better than bidders in all-cash offers.

To further analyze these findings, table 9 reports the results of cross-sectional regressions of the offer premiums and abnormal returns for the total sample of 139 public tender offers during 1970–1982. The regression model includes the natural log of the target's total equality value ($\ln V_T$) and dummy variables for payment with common stock in the bidder firm or a combination of cash and stock ($D_{STOCK} = 1$), minority buyouts ($D_{MBO} = 1$), and unsuccessful offers ($D_{FAIL} = 1$). As regression coefficient a_2 in panel I shows, the payment method is statistically significant, with a t-value of -5.08 in regression 1 (with the premium over the pre-offer price as dependent variable) and -4.86 in regression 3 (with the total offer-induced revaluation as dependent variable). The parameter estimate is virtually identical in the two regressions,

---

[48] The z-values in table 8 for event period $a + 1$ are 1.3 for the 12 listed bidders in the sample of 34 all-cash offers and -0.9 for the 26 listed bidders in the sample of 31 all-stock offers, both of which fail to reject the null hypothesis of zero average abnormal returns. Moreover, 66.7% of the bidders offering cash and 34.6% of the bidders offering stock have positive abnormal returns. The hypothesis that either one of these two percentages equals the expected value of 50 cannot be rejected at the 10% level of significance. On the other hand, there is some indication that the two percentages are different from each other; the t-value of the difference (66.7 − 34.6) is 1.84, which is significant at the 10% level.

Table 9

Ordinary least-squares estimates of the effect on offer premiums and abnormal stock returns of the size of the target's total equity, the payment method, and whether the offer is for control or a minority buyout, for the total sample of 139 public tender offers for publicly traded French target firms, 1970–1982.[a]

$$Y = a_0 + a_1 \ln V_T + a_2 D_{STOCK} + a_3 D_{MBO} + a_4 D_{FAIL}.$$

(*t*-values are given in parentheses.)

Dependent variable	a_0	a_1	a_2	a_3	a_4	R^2	F-value
(I) *Offer premium*[b,c]							
1. Premium over pre-offer price, $(P - P_{a-8})/P_{a-8}$	1.30 (2.73)	−0.04 (−1.33)	−0.39 (−5.08)	−0.21 (−2.81)	−0.17 (−1.66)	0.23	9.84
2. Premium over post-expiration price, $(P - P_{e+8})/P_{a-8}$	−0.26 (−0.74)	0.03 (1.40)	−0.00 (−0.03)	−0.14 (−2.39)	−0.14 (−1.81)	0.08	2.74
3. Total offer-induced target revaluation, $(P_{e+8} - P_{a-8})/P_{a-8}$	1.42 (3.04)	−0.06 (−2.12)	−0.37 (−4.86)	−0.10 (−1.32)	0.05 (0.46)	0.24	10.36
(II) *Abnormal stock return*							
4. Listed bidder firms ($N = 82$), week $a + 1$	0.02 (0.27)	−0.00 (−0.17)	−0.02 (−1.35)	−0.01 (−0.78)	0.00 (0.09)	0.03	0.61
5. Listed bidder firms ($N = 82$), weeks $a - 8$ through $e + 8$	0.37 (1.32)	−0.02 (−1.30)	−0.06 (−1.29)	−0.02 (−0.38)	0.02 (0.25)	0.05	1.09
6. Target firms, week $a + 1$	0.55 (2.17)	−0.02 (−1.15)	−0.18 (−4.30)	0.05 (1.32)	−0.03 (−0.47)	0.20	8.08
7. Target firms, weeks $a - 8$ through $e + 8$	0.92 (2.21)	−0.04 (−1.57)	−0.21 (−3.05)	0.06 (0.85)	−0.13 (−1.46)	0.14	5.41

[a] P = offer price.

P_{a-8} = target share price eight weeks before the offer announcement week (week a),
P_{e+8} = target share price eight weeks after expiration of the offer (week e),
$\ln V_T$ = log of the value of the target firm's total equity in week $a - 8$,
D_{STOCK} = dummy variable that equals one if the payment method is common stock in the bidder firm or a combination of cash and stock and zero otherwise,
D_{MBO} = dummy variable that equals one if the offer is a minority buyout and zero otherwise,
D_{FAIL} = dummy variable that equals one if the offer failed (as defined in table 1) and zero otherwise.

[b] When the regression is restricted to the sample of minority buyouts only, excluding D_{MBO} and D_{FAIL}, coefficient a_2 becomes −0.32 (*t*-value of −2.44) when the dependent variable is the premium over pre-offer price (regression 1), −0.03 ($t = 0.33$) with the premium over post-expiration price as dependent variable (regression 2), and −0.29 ($t = 2.72$) with the total offer-induced target revaluation as dependent variable (regression 3). Thus the negative value of a_2 shown in this table is driven by the minority buyouts as well as by the tender offers for control.

[c] When the regression is restricted to successful cash offers only, excluding D_{STOCK} and D_{FAIL}, coefficient a_3 becomes −0.36 (*t*-value of −3.12) in regression 1 (premium over pre-offer price), −0.14 ($t = -2.31$) in regression 2 (premium over post-expiration price), and −0.20 ($t = -1.70$) in regression 3 (total offer-induced target revaluation).

and indistinguishable from zero in the regression with the premium over the post-expiration price as the dependent variable (regression 2). Overall, regressions 1 and 3 explain a significant portion of the total variation in the dependent variables with R^2s of 0.23 and 0.24 and F-statistics of 9.84 and 10.36, respectively. Since the premium over the post-expiration price is statistically indistinguishable for the two payment methods, we cannot conclude that the larger premium over the pre-offer price in all-cash offers is driven by compensation demanded by target shareholders for giving up the option to defer capital gains taxes. The sample of twelve bond offers in column 2 of table 8 also provides evidence against the tax hypothesis. Like stock offers, payment in bonds of the bidder firm allows target shareholders to continue to defer capital gains taxes on the sale. The average premium over the post-expiration price in bond offers is 38.5 (median 33.7)%, i.e., somewhat higher than in the comparison sample of all-cash offers.

Although the average abnormal return to bidder firms is indistinguishable from zero in both offer categories, the average franc value of the total offer premium, multiplied by the number of target shares purchased, is 15.2 million franc in all-cash offers versus 6.9 million in all-stock offers. The total gains in all-cash offers are thus larger than the total gains in all-stock offers. This finding is consistent with both the information-signaling and agency-cost hypotheses referred to above. The evidence does not provide strong support for these hypotheses, however, since we have failed to identify a significant signaling benefit to the average bidder firm, and since our tests do not incorporate information on the existence of free cash flow in either the bidder or the target firm.

6.2. Minority buyouts

As shown in the last two columns of table 8, the average (median) offer premium over the pre-offer price is 38.3 (35.6)% for the sample of 29 all-cash minority buyouts and 9.0 (17.1)% for the 12 stock-exchange buyout offers. The average (median) premium over the post-expiration price is 9.2 (6.1) and 3.2 (14.5)% for the two offer categories, while the total offer-induced revaluation is 27.8 (22.0) and 7.4 (7.5)%, respectively. The premium over the pre-offer price and the total revaluation are both significantly higher in all-cash buyouts, whereas the premium over the post-expiration price is statistically indistinguishable across cash and stock-exchange buyouts (see footnote 2 of table 9 for the respective t-values).[49]

---

[49]Our estimate of the offer-induced revaluation in minority buyouts is comparable to the evidence reported by Dodd and Ruback (1977) for their sample of 19 'clean-up' offers (which they define as offers where the bidder owns at least 50 percent of the target prior to the offer). Targets in their 'clean-up' offers on average earn 17.4% abnormal return over the offer announcement month, compared to an average of 20.8% for targets in 136 tender offers for control.

Thus the payment method effect observed for control-oriented tender offers carries over to minority buyouts. This finding suggests that the difference in payoff structures between cash and securities-exchange offers is relevant in developing an optimal bidding strategy. As before, however, there is no direct support for this conjecture from the average performance of bidder firms. In minority buyouts, as well as in control-oriented tender offers, the abnormal performance of bidder firms is indistinguishable from zero regardless of the means of payment in the transaction.

Finally, for all-cash offers, the total offer premium is significantly lower in minority buyouts than in control-oriented offers (38.3 versus 73.3%). This time, however, the premium over the post-expiration price appears to drive the difference. The minority buyout regression coefficient a_3 in panel I of table 9 is statistically significant, with a t-value of -2.81 in regression 1 (with the premium over the pre-offer price as dependent variable) and -2.39 in regression 2 (with the premium over the post-expiration price as the dependent variable). It is insignificantly different from zero with a t-value of -1.32 in regression 3 (where the total offer-induced revaluation is the dependent variable).[50]

7. Conclusions

This paper presents empirical estimates of the effects of disclosure regulations and the payment method on offer premiums and abnormal stock returns in public and private tender offers in France over the period 1966–1982. Disclosure regulations governing public tender offers were introduced in 1970 without changing the four-week minimum tender offer period in effect since 1966. In the sample of successful cash tender offers in which the bidder acquires voting control of the target firm, we find a statistically significant increase in the average premium over the pre-offer target share price from 34 to 73% following the 1970 disclosure regulations. This increase is driven primarily by an increase in the total offer-induced revaluation of the target shares. There is no evidence that the regulations have changed the component of the offer premium that reflects the value of the option to tender (as measured by the premium over the post-expiration price). Our evidence also fails to reject the hypothesis that bidder firms earn zero offer-induced abnormal stock returns both before and after 1970. Overall, our results are consistent with the hypothesis that disclosure regulations have deterred tender offers

---

[50]As stated in footnote d of table 9, identical conclusions emerge when the cross-sectional regression is restricted to successful cash offers only, excluding dummy variables D_{STOCK} and D_{FAIL}.

that, on average, produce lower total gains than offers that survive mandatory information disclosure.

An increase in the cost of public offers (due to disclosure requirements) causes bidders to substitute toward privately negotiated controlling-block trades, provided a single target shareholder can transfer control. As of 1973, privately negotiated controlling-block trades must be followed by a public offer to purchase any-or-all target shares at the block price over a fifteen-day period. On the other hand, the bidder in a private tender offer is not required to disclosure substantive information. We find that the average premium over the pre-offer price in private bids after 1970 is 27%, which is significantly lower than the 73% average in public offers. This finding lends further support to the proposition that the French disclosure requirements for public offers have deterred some public offers with below-average total gains, some of which have sought the alternative, private offer procedure. Gains to bidder firms in private offers are statistically indistinguishable from zero.

We also document that the average premium over the pre-offer price is significantly higher in all-cash than all-stock exchange offers (73 versus 17% in public tender offers for voting control). Again, the difference is driven by the offer-induced revaluation of the target shares. The average premium over the post-expiration price is virtually identical across offers with the two payment methods (24 versus 23%), which suggests that the payment method effect does not stem from a need to compensate target shareholders for a potential capital-gains tax liability. Bidder firm abnormal returns are on average indistinguishable from zero in both all-cash and all-stock offers.

Finally, our evidence challenges the proposition that a larger revaluation of the target shares in cash offers necessarily reflects relatively large synergy gains in this particular category of bids. 'Synergy gains' is typically used as a generic term for the value created by the improvement in the firm's production/investment strategy after the takeover. It is natural to assume that the bidder must acquire voting control of the target to implement a substantial change in the firm's operating policy. In this context, it is interesting that the average offer premium in the minority buyouts in our data base exhibits the same systematic dependence on the payment method we observe for control-oriented tender offers. In our sample of minority buyouts, the bidder's prior holding in the target is on average 80% of the voting shares, and no less than 67%, which in France constitutes absolute voting control. If we interpret the target revaluation in minority buyouts as an information (rather than a synergy) effect, this evidence supports the hypothesis that the bidder's choice of payment method depends partly on the information asymmetry between the bidder and the target before the tender offer, and that the payment method *per se* conveys information to the market.

Appendix

Table 10

Summary of major regulatory changes governing public and private tender offers to purchase shares of publicly traded firms in France, 1966–1982.[a]

Offer procedure	Date of regulatory reform m/d/y	Summary of major restrictions
		(I) Restrictions on the use of alternative tender offer procedures
1.1 Regular tender offer (not available prior to 4/4/66)	4/4/66[b]	Bidder must (i) hold less than 20% of the target shares prior to the offer, (ii) seek control over the target (as defined by CAC), and (iii) pay in cash.
	1/23/70[c]	Bidder is allowed to pay in securities.
	3/15/73; 10/10/73[d]	Bidder's prior holding in target can be greater than 20%. However, the bidder must acquire a majority of the target shares or control.
	5/2/75[c]	Bidder must seek control and a minimum of 15% of the target shares.
	8/13/78; 11/13/78[f]	Bidder must seek control and *either* (i) at least 10% of the target shares and 5 million francs worth of target shares *or* (ii) at least 20 million francs worth of target shares.
1.2 Minority buyouts using regular tender offer procedure (not available prior to 1/23/70)	1/23/70[c]	Bidder must (i) hold at least 50% of the target shares prior to the offer and (ii) seek 100% of the target shares.
1.3 Minority buyouts using simplified tender offer procedure (not available prior to 2/22/72)	2/22/72[g]	Prior to the offer the bidder must (i) hold at least 90% of the target shares *or* (ii) hold all except at most 15,000 of the target shares, *or* (iii) hold all except at most 2 million francs worth of target shares. The bidder must seek 100% of the target.
	5/2/75[c]	Restrictions (ii) and (iii) above are changed from 15,000 shares to 2,000 shares and from 23 million francs to 5 million francs.
	8/13/78; 10/3/78[f]	Restriction (i) above is changed from 90% to 67% and restrictions (ii) and (iii) are dropped entirely.
1.4 Purchases of up to a minority interest using the regular tender offer procedure (not available prior to 3/15/73)	3/15/73; 10/10/73[d]	Bidder acquires (i) a minimum of 15% of the target shares and (ii) at most a minority interest in the target.

1.5	Privately negotiated controlling-block trades (no restrictions prior to 3/15/73)	8/13/78; 10/3/78[f]	Restriction (i) above is changed from 15% to at least 10% and 5 million francs or at least 10 million francs worth of target shares. Use of securities as method of payment is ruled out.
		3/15/73; 10/10/73[d]	Any private tender offer executed through a block trade is converted to a public tender offer for 100% of the target shares at the block trade price.

(II) *Restrictions in effect while the tender offer is outstanding*

2.1	Regular tender offer procedure	4/4/66[g]	Minimum offer period is one month.
		1/23/70[c]	Bidder has the option to increase the value of the initial bid once by a minimum of 5% during the first twenty days of the offer period. Competing bids are allowed up to the day before the expiration day of the initial offer, in which case the initial bidder is allowed to counterbid. Competing bids and counterbids must exceed the initial offer by at least 5%. The initial bidder cannot extend the initial expiration day. Initial bidder can withdraw from offer only if competing bid materializes. Target shareholders can withdraw already tendered shares only if competing bid materializes. During the offer period, target forward and options quotations are suspended and margin on target share forward trades is lifted to 100%.
		3/15/73; 10/10/73[d]	Target share limit orders expire with offer; dealer transactions are not permitted during offer period; dealers must close existing positions before expiration of offer; target share trade secrecy is repealed, all insider trades and trades involving 5% or more of the target shares are published.
		5/2/75[c]	The target firm may not trade during the offer period to 'significantly reinforce' its position in the takeover (i.e., significant share repurchases are excluded).
		8/13/78; 10/3/78[d]	Competing bids are generally allowed during the first ten days of the initial offer period. After the expiration of the initial bid, the initial bidder must wait at least one year before launching another bid for the same target shares.

Continued overleaf

Table 10 (continued)

	Offer procedure	Date of regulatory reform m/d/y	Summary of major restrictions
			(II) Restrictions in effect while the tender offer is outstanding
2.2	Minority buyouts using the regular tender offer procedure	1/23/70[c]	Same rules as those governing the regular tender offer procedure in general.
2.3	Minority buyouts using the simplified procedure	2/22/72[g]	No competing bids are allowed during the offer period; the bidder cannot increase his own bid; no restrictions on trades in the target shares during the offer period.
2.4	Purchases of up to a minority interest using the regular tender offer procedure	3/15/73	Same rules as those governing the regular tender offer procedure in general.
2.5	Privately negotiated controlling-block trades	3/15/73; 10/10/73[d]	None of the restrictions governing the regular tender offer procedure, except that the target share margin requirement is raised to 100% during a fifteen-day mandatory price support period that starts the day of the block trade. During the price support period, the buyer of the block must accept all additional target shares tendered at the block price.
			(III) Disclosure rules[h]
3.1	Regular tender offer procedure	1/23/70[c]	*Bidders*: must disclose 'all important facts' for shareholders' choice, including the exact motive behind and financing of the offer. *Targets*: must disclose 'all important facts' for shareholders' choice, including the board's recommendation concerning the offer.
		3/15/73; 10/10/73[d]	*Bidders*: must disclose the issue status of securities offered in an exchange bid, and, for each security offered, the capital structure, investment policy over next five years, principal markets and market shares, subsidiaries and shareholdings, management compensation schemes, business policy orientation, and sales and earnings forecasts of underlying business operation. *Targets*: must disclose the same information about its capital, ownership structure, and operations as the bidder must disclose for each security offered in exchange offer.

		Date	Description
		8/13/78; 10/3/78[f]	*Bidders*: regardless of the method of payment, must disclose its principal activities and products, share ownership of more than 5%, a five-year financial report, and sales and earnings forecast.
			Targets: no additional requirements (beyond the 1973 rules).
3.2	Minority buyouts using regular tender offer procedure	1/23/70[c]	Same disclosure requirements as those governing the regular tender offer procedure in general.
3.3	Minority buyouts using the simplified offer procedure	2/22/72[g]	Same disclosure requirements as those introduced for the regular tender offer procedure in 23/1/70.
		3/15/73; 10/10/73[d]	Same disclosure requirements as those introduced for the regular tender offer procedure.
		8/13/78; 10/13/78[f]	Simplified minority buyouts essentially exempted from the additional disclosure requirement imposed on the regular tender offer procedure.
3.4	Purchases of up to a minority interest using the regular tender offer procedure	3/15/73; 10/10/73[d]	Same disclosures rules as those governing the regular tender offer procedures in general.
		8/13/78; 10/3/78[f]	Essentially exempted from all the major disclosure rules governing the regular tender offer procedure in general.
3.5	Privately negotiated controlling-block trades	3/15/73; 10/10/73[d]	No disclosure requirements.

[a] Institutions involved in enforcing the regulations described in this table include the French Stockbrokers' Association ('Compagnie des Agents de Change' or CAC) and the Stock Exchange commission ('Commission des Operations de Bourse' or COB). For all types of offers discussed here, the bidder must obtain prior authorization to go ahead with the offer from CAC and COB who verify that the offer complies with existing regulations. CAC judges whether an offer constitutes an attempt to acquire 'control'. CAC generally plays the role of auctioneer in the public tender offer, and publicly announces the identity of the bidder and target firms, the terms of the offer (including revised or competing bids), and (with the exception of privately negotiated controlling-block trades and simplified minority buyouts) the outcome of the offer.

[b] Letters of April 4, July 6, and November 29, 1966, between CAC and the French Minister of Economics and Finance.

[c] COB. General ruling on public tender offers, Journal Officiel de la République Francaise (henceforth Journal Officiel), January 23, 1970; CAC. Addendum to CAC general regulation, Journal Officiel, January 23, 1970.

[d] CAC. Addendum to CAC general regulation, Journal Officiel, March 15, 1973; COB. Note on the interpretation and application of COB. General ruling on public tender offers, COB Monthly Bulletin 46. February 1973; COB. General ruling on controlling-block trades, Journal Officiel, March 17, 1973; CAC. CAC general regulation, Journal Officiel, August 24, 1973; COB. General instruction on information schedule, October 1973.

[e] COB. General ruling on public tender offers, Journal Officiel, May 1, 1975.

[f] COB. General ruling on public cash and exchange offers, Journal Officiel, August 13, 1978; COB. Instruction concerning the application of rule D5 of COB general ruling on public tender offers, October 3, 1978.

[g] CAC. Addendum to CAC general regulation, Journal Officiel, February 11, 1972.

[h] Disclosure regulations are enforced by assigning the bidder and target management certain fiduciary responsibilities vis-a-vis their shareholders. The rules impose an *ex post* penalty on attempts to release misleading information.

References

Asquith, P., R. Bruner, and D. Mullins, 1983, The gains to bidding firms from merger, Journal of Financial Economics 11, 121–140.

Asquith, P., R. Bruner, and D. Mullins, 1988, Merger returns and the form of financing, Unpublished paper (Harvard University, Cambridge, MA).

Bradley, M., 1980, Interfirm tender offers and the market for corporate control, Journal of Business 53, 345–376.

Bradley, M., A. Desai, and E.H. Kim, 1983, The rationale behind interfirm tender offers: Information or synergy?, Journal of Financial Economics 11, 183–206.

Bradley, M., A. Desai, and E.H. Kim, 1988, Synergistic gains from corporate acquisitions and their division between the stockholders of target and acquiring firms, Journal of Financial Economics 21, 3–40.

Carleton, W.T., A.K. Guilkey, R.S. Harris, and J.F. Stewart, 1983, An empirical analysis of the role of the medium of exchange in mergers, Journal of Finance 38, 813–826.

Comment, R. and G. Jarrell, 1987, Two-tier and negotiated tender offers: The imprisonment of the free-riding shareholder, Journal of Financial Economics 19, 283–310.

DeAngelo, H. and E.M. Rice, 1983, Antitakeover charter amendments and stockholder wealth, Journal of Financial Economics 11, 329–360.

Dodd, P. and R. Ruback, 1977, Tender offers and stockholder returns: An empirical analysis, Journal of Financial Economics 5, 351–374.

Eckbo, B.E., 1988, Gains to bidder firms: Methodological issues and U.S.–Canadian evidence, Unpublished paper (University of British Columbia, Vancouver, BC).

Eckbo, B.E., R. Giammarino, and R. Heinkel, 1988, Asymmetric information and the medium of exchange in takeovers: Theory and tests, Unpublished paper (University of British Columbia, Vancouver, BC).

Fishman, M., 1989, Preemptive bidding and the role of the medium of exchange in acquisitions, Journal of Finance 44, 41–57.

Fleuriet, M., 1977, Pouvoir et finance d'enterprise droit et practiques (Dalloz, Paris).

Franks, J.R., R.S. Harris, and C. Mayer, 1988, Means of payment in takeovers: Results for the U.K. and U.S., in: A. Auerbach, ed., Corporate takeovers: Causes and consequences (NBER, University of Chicago Press, Chicago, IL).

Gibson, R.J., M.S. Scholes, and M.A. Wolfson, 1988, Taxation and the dynamics of corporate control: The uncertain case for tax-motivated acquisitions, in: J.C. Coffee, Jr., L. Lowenstein, and S. Rose-Ackerman, eds., Knights, raiders and targets: The impact of the hostile takeover (Oxford University Press, New York, NY).

Grossman, S. and O. Hart, 1980a, Takeover bids, the free rider problem, and the theory of the firm, Bell Journal of Economics 11, 42–64.

Grossman, S. and O. Hart, 1980b, Disclosure law and takeover bids, Journal of Finance 35, 323–334.

Hansen, R.G., 1987, A theory for the choice of exchange medium in the market for corporate control, Journal of Business 60, 75–95.

Huang, Y.-S. and R.A. Walkling, 1987, Target abnormal returns associated with acquisition announcements: Payment, acquisition form, and managerial resistance, Journal of Financial Economics 19, 329–349.

Husson, B., 1986, The gains from take-over operations: The French case, Unpublished paper (C.E.S.A. de Jouy-en-Josas, Paris).

Jarrell, G.A., 1985, The wealth effects of litigation by targets: Do interests diverge in a merge?, Journal of Law and Economics 28, 151–177.

Jarrell, G.A. and M. Bradley, 1980, The economic effects of federal and state regulations of cash tender offers, Journal of Law and Economics 23, 371–407.

Jensen, M.C., 1986, Agency costs of free cash flow, corporate finance and takeovers, American Economic Review 76, 323–329.

Jensen, M.C. and R. Ruback, 1983, The market for corporate control: The scientific evidence, Journal of Financial Economics 11, 5–50.

Myers, S.C. and N.S. Majluf, 1984, Corporate financing and investment decisions when firms have information that investors do not have, Journal of Financial Economics 13, 187–221.

Nathan, K.S. and T.B. O'Keefe, 1989, The rise in takeover premiums: An exploratory study, Journal of Financial Economics 23, 101–119.

Rosenfeld, A., 1982, Repurchase offers, information-adjusted premiums and shareholder response, MERC monograph, Series MP-8201 (University of Rochester, Rochester, NY).

Samuelson, P., 1970, Economics, 8th ed. (McGraw-Hill, New York, NY).

Schipper, K. and R. Thompson, 1983, Evidence on the capitalized value of merger activity for acquiring firms, Journal of Financial Economics 11, 85–119.

Smiley, R., 1975, The effect of the Williams amendment and other factors on transactions costs in tender offers, Industrial Organized Review 3, 138–145.

Travlos, N.G., 1987, Corporate takeover bids, method of payment, and bidding firms' stock returns, Journal of Finance 42, 943–963.

Wansley, J., W. Lane, and H. Yang, 1983, Abnormal returns to acquiring firms by type of acquisition and method of payment, Financial Management 12, 16–22.

[22]

8 Means of Payment in Takeovers: Results for the United Kingdom and the United States

Julian R. Franks, Robert S. Harris, and Colin Mayer

8.1 Introduction

Many aspects of corporate acquisitions have received extensive investigation, but there has been little analysis of their means of financing. This omission is notable in view of the substantial expenditures involved in takeovers. An earlier paper (Franks and Harris 1986b) records that in 1985 acquisitions represented 6 percent of the capital stock extant in the United Kingdom. By any account these are substantial investments whose method of financing warrants careful scrutiny. This paper provides a detailed empirical assessment of acquisition financing.

Although a descriptive analysis of acquisition finance is interesting in itself, there are more fundamental reasons for pursuing the subject. Over the past few years several theories of acquisition finance have appeared. As in other areas of research on corporate finance, these

Julian R. Franks is National Westminster Bank professor of finance at the London Business School and a visiting professor at the University of California, Los Angeles. Robert S. Harris is professor of finance at the University of North Carolina at Chapel Hill. Colin Mayer is the Price Waterhouse Professor of Corporate Finance at City University Business School, London England.

The authors thank Claude Wolff, Richard Boebel, and Pat Rowan for collecting some of the data, and Nick Grattan and Ed Bachmann for programming assistance. They also acknowledge financial support from the Leverhulme Trust and the Frank Hawkins Kenan Institute for Private Enterprise. Colin Mayer is supported by the Centre for Economic Policy Research project "An International Study of Corporate Financing". In addition to being presented at the NBER conference on which this volume is based, this paper was presented at seminars at UCLA, UNC at Chapel Hill, Oxford University, the London Business School, and the University of Colorado. The authors thank the participants for their comments and suggestions, including Michael Brennan, Elizabeth Callison, Jennifer Conrad, Robert Conroy, Eugene Fama, Michael Fishman, Mark Flannery, Mark Grinblatt, David Hirshleifer, Paul Marsh, Stanley Ornstein, Eduardo Schwartz, Sheridan Titman, Walter Torous, and Fred Weston. The authors are especially grateful for suggestions made by Artur Raviv and Richard Ruback.

theories have emphasized the influence of taxation and information asymmetries. To date, however, little empirical work has examined their validity. An examination of these theories may be of value not only in understanding the acquisition process but also in assessing the relevance of information and tax considerations to more general issues of corporate capital structure.

We have chosen to make international comparisons between the United States and the United Kingdom in the analysis that follows because there are well-documented differences between the two countries in the response of share prices to the announcement of new issues of equity. One interesting question is whether similar differences are observed in equity-financed acquisitions. The two countries also exhibit significant institutional differences in regulations affecting corporate financing activities and taxation, regulations that should affect the preferred means of payment for acquisitions. For example, the U.S. government has demonstrated a much more liberal attitude toward share repurchases than has the U.K. government over most of the period under study here. As a consequence, at least one set of theories would anticipate different financing patterns between the two countries.

Following a preview of this paper's results in the next section, section 8.3 surveys theories of acquisition financing, and section 8.4 summarizes existing empirical studies. The data set and methodology are described in section 8.5. Spanning the period 1955–85, the data include over 2,500 acquisitions in the United Kingdom and the United States, forming probably one of the largest corporate data sets employed in an analysis of acquisitions.

Section 8.6 examines the forms of financing that were used in acquisitions over the 30 years of the study. These financing patterns are related to salient tax and institutional considerations. Section 8.7 describes share price responses around the announcement date of the acquisition and also reports the wealth gains to bidders and targets in cash- and equity-financed acquisitions. Previous studies have recorded performance variations by class of acquisition. For example, bid premia have been observed to be greater in tender offers than in mergers. Here we assess whether these differences can be attributed to the forms of financing or to the type of acquisition. Section 8.8 reports postmerger performance for up to two years after the acquisition. Finally, section 8.9 summarizes the results and discusses how the limitations of the methodology employed here can be avoided in a broader cross-sectional study.

8.2 A Preview of the Results

In view of the length of this paper, we provide a preview of the results to help focus our description of the theory and the hypotheses.

223   Means of Payment in Takeovers

8.2.1 Means of Payment

1. Just over half of the sample of U.K. acquisitions were either "all equity" or "all cash" bids, with an approximately equal distribution between the two. Almost two-thirds of the U.S. acquisitions were either all equity or all cash.

2. The higher proportion of "mixed bids" in the United Kingdom is in part accounted for by the provision of cash alternatives to equity offers. Those cash alternatives are frequently underwritten.

3. In the latter half of the 1960s approximately half of the U.S. acquisitions were effected by an offer of convertibles, although their use dropped significantly by the 1970s.

4. Cash acquisitions in the United States increased from a negligible proportion of all acquisitions during the 1950s to just under 60 percent by number during the 1980s.

5. There has not been a similar discernible upward trend in the use of cash in the United Kingdom.

8.2.2 Returns around the Announcement of a Merger

1. Returns to bidder shareholders were similar in cash- and equity-financed acquisitions in the United Kingdom during the six months before (but not including) the announcement month. U.S. acquirers offering equity slightly outperformed those offering cash in the prebid period.

2. Bid premia to target shareholders in cash acquisitions were significantly in excess of those accruing to shareholders in equity acquisitions in both countries.

3. In the United Kingdom neither cash nor equity acquisitions displayed significant abnormal returns to bidder shareholders in the month of an acquisition. Gains to acquisitions thus accrue to target shareholders.

4. In the United States there are significant positive gains to bidder shareholders in cash acquisitions and significant losses in equity acquisitions.

8.2.3 Postmerger Returns

1. Postmerger returns (measured two years after the merger was finalized) were not significantly different from zero in cash acquisitions in either country.

2. There is evidence that U.S. shareholders sustained abnormal losses in the two years after an equity acquisition.

8.2.4 Results Relating to Capital Gains Tax Theories

1. The larger gains accruing to target shareholders in cash acquisitions than in equity acquisitions may be consistent with the theory that

target shareholders have to be compensated for the capital gains taxes levied on cash but not on equity acquisitions.

2. Nevertheless, differences in bid premia in cash- and equity-financed acquisitions in the United Kingdom existed before 1965, when a capital gains tax was introduced. Bid premia can therefore at best only be partly explained by capital gains tax.

3. Furthermore, this proposition is not supported by other evidence showing the means of payment to be unresponsive to appreciable changes in capital gains tax rates in the United Kingdom.

8.2.5 Results Relating to "Trapped Equity" Theories

1. Theories that treat acquisitions as a tax-efficient method of making distributions to shareholders predict a reduction in cash acquisitions when the costs of alternative forms of distributions (such as dividends) fall (King 1986). The proportion of acquisitions financed with cash was not affected by the 1973 introduction of the imputation tax system in the United Kingdom, which reduced the costs of dividend payments.

2. Despite the fact that repurchases of shares were not feasible in the United Kingdom over the period of the study, the proportion of acquisitions financed with cash in that country was less than in the United States in recent years. Since repurchases are as tax efficient as cash acquisitions, trapped equity theories would predict a greater use of cash in the United Kingdom. The availability of a stepped-up basis on depreciable assets may have provided a tax incentive for the higher use of cash in the United States.

8.2.6 Results Relating to Information and Agency Theories

1. The proposition that cash is used in high-value acquisitions to preempt competing bids (Fishman 1986) is consistent with the finding of larger bid premia paid in cash than in equity acquisitions.

2. Nonetheless, the evidence that cash was more commonly employed in contested bids is not consistent with the view that cash is preemptive.

3. The abnormal losses incurred by shareholders of bidding companies (in the United States, at least) upon announcements of equity acquisitions, and the postmerger abnormal losses associated with equity acquisitions, are consistent with the proposition that asymmetries in information encourage the issue of overvalued equity by acquirers.

8.2.7 Explaining Previous Results

1. A significant proportion of the difference in bid premia between tender and non-tender offers is attributable to the greater use of cash in tender offers.

225   Means of Payment in Takeovers

2. Negative postmerger performance by the firm, which has been observed in some previous studies, appears to be closely associated with the use of equity.

8.2.8   International Comparisons

1. In the U.S., acquirers using equity incur abnormal losses on the bid announcement, whereas those using cash make abnormal gains. In the U.K., in contrast, no significant gains or losses are incurred by bidders using cash or equity. These results are similar to those found in event studies of new (seasoned) equity issues in the United Kingdom and United States, respectively.

2. Underwriters in the United Kingdom played a much more important role in acquisition finance than did their counterparts in the United States. Not only did they play a role in financing acquisitions where the bidder lacked cash, but also where the bidder required external validation of the valuation of its offer.

8.3   Theories of Means of Payment in Acquisitions

In complete markets with symmetric information and in the absence of taxes, shareholders should be indifferent to the means of payment used in acquisitions: share price responses should reflect only the changes in fundamental values induced by the merger. But the tax system and specific features of the capital market do encourage the use of particular forms of finance. This section surveys theories of the choice of acquisition financing. We first discuss the tax-based models and then agency and information theories.

8.3.1   The Influence of Taxation on the Medium of Exchange

The choice of a means of exchange affects the tax liabilities of the acquired firm's shareholders. In an equity acquisition the investor's acceptance of the stock of the acquiring company avoids the realization of any capital gain and does not therefore impose an immediate capital gains tax liability on the investor. These taxes are deferred until the investor sells the shares. In a cash purchase the investor's gain must be realized immediately for tax purposes, thus creating a tax liability at the capital gains tax rate. In the absence of other considerations, we would not expect to observe cash acquisitions. Nonetheless, the payment of capital gains taxes depends on the tax status of the investor, and the full capital gains tax rate may be mitigated by exemptions and allowances. The rate will be smallest for targets with "marginal" investors that are tax exempt or have unused allowances. For these investors personal tax considerations will bear little relation to the desired means of payment.

Where a capital gains tax liability is created, additional considerations must justify the use of cash. For example, under the U.S. tax code a cash acquisition permits the acquiring company to "write up" certain assets of the acquired firm to their fair market value. This write-up produces higher tax deductible depreciation allowances not available in all equity bids. This corporate tax advantage of cash bids is somewhat tempered by the recapture taxes due on the written-up values of tangible assets when the acquisition is consolidated by the acquirer. Thus, the U.S. code can provide an incentive for cash bids in cases in which market values exceed book values of the acquired firms' assets. Such a "stepped up" basis is not available in the United Kingdom. For target shareholders to be indifferent to the use of cash and nontaxable forms of payment, cash purchases must create pretax gains, as measured by bid premia, that are larger than those associated with equity purchases. The net gain to the bidder is then the value of the "write up," less the increment to the bid premium. Thus:

HYPOTHESIS 1. *Bid premia are higher in cash-financed than in equity-financed acquisitions. Other things equal, the use of cash in acquisitions is inversely related to the capital gains tax rate of the acquired firms' shareholders and directly related to the potential for writing up depreciable assets.*

The above-mentioned disincentives to use cash in acquisitions may be offset by considerations of the tax position of the acquiring firm's shareholders. Cash acquisitions may afford tax savings because dividend payments are taxed at shareholders' personal income tax rates. Thus, cash acquisitions may be more tax efficient than dividend payments if capital gains taxes are smaller than personal income taxes on dividend income. According to the models of Auerbach (1979) and King (1977), under conditions in which a firm's marginal valuation ratio (referred to below as q) is less than unity but more than the value of a unit dividend distribution to shareholders, there are disincentives to paying cash dividends. Distributions to shareholders could be achieved at a lower tax cost by share repurchases or voluntary liquidation (see Edwards and Keen 1985). In the United Kingdom share repurchases have been permitted only since 1985. In the United States share repurchases were permitted for the period of our study and have now become widespread (see Shoven and Simon 1987). It is possible, however, that even in the United States restrictions on the tax status of repurchases may favor alternative routes of distributing cash—through, for example, acquisitions. Thus:

HYPOTHESIS 2. *The incentives to use cash in acquisitions are greater in circumstances where share repurchases are prohibited or costly.*

227   Means of Payment in Takeovers

King (1986) has further specified the tax incentive to make cash acquisitions. He argued that, in the absence of share repurchases, cash acquisitions are a tax-efficient way of distributing trapped equity to stockholders. Companies make cash acquisitions because the cost of purchasing assets traded in the corporate sector is less than that of purchasing (equivalent) assets in the unincorporated sector. The difference in cost is accounted for by the tax wedge between income taxed in the corporate and personal sectors.

More formally, let C_a and C_i be the costs of adjustment associated with a unit purchase of capital through acquisition and capital investment, respectively. Equality at the margin of the cost of purchases through cash acquisition and investment requires that:

$$(1) \qquad q + C_a = 1 + C_i,$$

if we assume that financial markets place a value of q on an additional unit of capital (which costs \$1 to purchase in the absence of adjustment costs) once it is in the corporate sector. King's model focuses on the implications of having \$1 in the corporate sector (generated from, say, previously profitable investments) that is worth q^* in financial markets; q^* may be less than unity because of the double layers of corporate and personal taxes. As these dollars are used to purchase capital (at a cost of $1 + C_i$), equality at the margin requires that

$$(2) \qquad q = q^* (1 + C_i).$$

Substituting (2) into (1) and simplifying yields

$$(3) \qquad C_a = q((1/q^*) - 1).$$

If profits in the corporate sector are taxed more heavily than those in the personal sector, q^* is less than unity, and the expression on the righthand side of equation (3) is increasing in q. Thus, under reasonable descriptions of the cost of adjustment function, C_a, acquisitions are increasing in q. For example, letting A represent dollars spent on acquisitions and K the capital stock, the quadratic costs of adjustment are described as $C_a = \beta_0 + \beta_1 (A/qK)$. Substituting this into equation (3) yields

$$(4) \qquad A/K = -(\beta_0 q/\beta_1) + (1/\beta_1)q^2[(1 - q^*)/q^*]$$

The driving force behind King's description of acquisitions is the undervaluation at the margin of \$1 in the corporate sector—the so-called trapped equity model of acquisitions. For example, if the corporate tax rate is t and the personal tax rate is m, then under a classical system of taxation, $q^* = (1 - t)$, and under an imputation system with an imputation rate of m, $q^* = (1 - t)/(1 - m)$, which creates an incentive to acquire so long as $t > m$.[1] Thus:

HYPOTHESIS 3. *The tax incentive to make cash acquisitions is increasing in the value of the tax wedge $(1 - q^*)$ and the square of the marginal valuation of capital ratio, q.*

8.3.2   Information and Agency Models

If all parties to an acquisition are not equally well informed about future prospects, the choice of a means of finance may be influenced by considerations other than taxation. In particular, asymmetries in information encourage the pursuit of opportunistic gains. In acquisitions two types of asymmetries in information might be anticipated: either the acquirer has superior information about valuations of its assets, or the acquiree has superior information about its assets. In the former case the acquirer has an incentive to undertake equity acquisitions during periods in which its shares are overvalued—or at least not undervalued. In the latter case the acquiree has an incentive to accept offers during periods in which its equity is perceived to be overvalued.

Myers and Majluf (1984) have examined the influence of misvaluations on the incentives for firms to make new equity issues. They argued that there is a disincentive for firms to use new equity as a means of funding new investments. If managers have superior information about the value of the firm's existing assets and investment opportunities, they will want to restrict sales of shares to periods when current and prospective investments are not undervalued by new investors. New shareholders in turn appreciate this incentive to sell overvalued equity, and as a result they downgrade their valuation of firms that make new equity announcements. Furthermore, since firms have an alternative form of financing available (say, cash or debt) that avoids the adverse selection problem, any new issues of equity must be prompted by overvaluation.[2] Riskless securities will be issued in preference to equity, thereby creating the "pecking order" hypothesis of Myers (1984), according to which retentions are used in preference to debt, which is in turn issued in preference to equity. Smith (1986) reviewed studies demonstrating negative average price effects when a new stock issue is announced.

In the context of acquisitions the Myers and Majluf model has two principal implications. The first is that the use of equity will be discouraged in circumstances in which bidders are better informed about their own asset valuation. The second is that bidders will be discouraged from buying shares in targeted companies if the targets are better informed about their own valuations than are bidders. In sum, asymmetries in information about the value of targets discourage acquisitions, and asymmetries in information about the value of the bidder discourage the use of equity finance. These information asymmetries give rise to the following share price response:

HYPOTHESIS 4. *The announcement of equity as the medium of exchange in an acquisition leads to a fall in the share price of the bidder (the issuer), while the use of cash leads to a rise in share price.*

Changing one's assumptions about the information structure leads to rather different predictions. If information about the quality of the acquirer or acquiree becomes evident only after the bid announcement, revaluations will subsequently occur and managers will have incentives to use particular types of finance. The literature discusses three possibilities.

First, if the acquirer is better informed about the value of its own equity and misvaluations are revealed only after the acquisition, the acquirer has an incentive to use equity during periods of overvaluation. When equity is undervalued, acquirers will offer cash (Myers and Majluf 1984).

Second, if the acquiree is better informed about its own value, and its true valuation is revealed only after the acquisition, equity offers will be preferred to cash when equity is believed to be undervalued (Hansen (1984, 1987)). Acquirees prefer to retain an equity participation in the merged firm in order to capture some of the subsequent gains when the undervaluation is revealed.

Third, if premerger appraisals make the acquirer well informed about the high value of the acquiree, it will offer cash in the acquisition. This follows from the desire of the acquirer to capture the benefits of high value acquisitions and to avoid sharing these gains with the acquiree. Conversely, when it is uncertain about acquiree valuations, the acquirer will wish the acquiree to retain an equity holding. This diminishes the adverse selection problems associated with better informed acquirees (Fishman 1986).

Fishman has also argued that cash will be associated with high offers and high bid premia provided by the acquirer. He assumed some fixed costs for collecting information about the value of the prospective target, which encourage acquirors who establish high-value acquisitions to make preemptive bids.[3] These preemptive bids deter other companies from paying for information and initiating competing offers. Cash offers should therefore be associated with high bid premia for the target, low levels of competition, and positive abnormal performance for the bidder after the bid announcement.

In sum, theories of acquisition finance offer some explicit hypotheses about the means of payment, bid premia, and share price movements after a bid announcement. In the remainder of the paper we examine how well each of the theories explains the empirical results.

8.4   Previous Empirical Work

8.4.1   Means of Payment

Two previous studies have investigated the choice of financing method used in U.S. acquisitions, incorporating, at least to some extent, personal tax considerations. Applying a conditional logit model, Carleton et al. (1983) examined the financial accounts of acquired firms to study the probability of three events: being acquired in a cash offer, being acquired in a securities exchange, and not being acquired. In their sample of companies from the years 1976–77, they found (p. 825) that "lower dividend payout ratios and lower market-to-book ratios increase the probability of being acquired in a cash takeover relative to being acquired in an exchange of securities." The authors concluded that on the assumption that book values measure the basis on which capital gains liabilities are calculated, the finding on market-to-book ratios is consistent with a personal tax disadvantage to cash offers. They also discussed the possibility that a market-to-book ratio may proxy for other effects such as inefficient management of the target. The authors found no satisfactory explanation for their findings on dividend payout.

Niden (1986) has provided an extensive discussion of tax issues in U.S. takeovers. She examined the choice between taxable (essentially all-cash) and nontaxable (mainly equity) forms of payment based on an analysis of variables proxying for the tax position of each of the combining firms. Although her logit models had small explanatory power, Niden found no relationship between the tax paying status of target shareowners and the form of payment.

8.4.2   Bid Premia

A recent study by Asquith, Bruner, and Mullins (1986) focused directly on the impact of the form of financing on merger returns. Using a sample of 343 U.S. mergers over the years 1975–83, the authors found that equity offers were associated with significantly smaller returns to both bidders and targets than were cash offers. For targets they reported bid premia of 27.5 percent for cash bids and 13.9 percent for equity bids. For bidders, those using cash earned 0.2 percent and those using equity earned −2.4 percent, although for relatively large targets the figures were 0.95 percent and −5.39 percent, respectively. Abnormal losses were positively related to the relative size of the acquisition. The findings suggested that differences in merger returns between alternative forms of financing can completely explain the differences recorded between returns in mergers and those in tender offers.

Controlling for whether a merger was horizontal or conglomerate in nature, Wansley, Lane, and Yang (1983) found acquiree bid premia of 31.5 percent in 102 cash bids and 16.8 percent in 87 securities offers. They concluded that higher bid premia are required in cash acquisitions to compensate for capital gains tax liabilities. Niden (1986) also uncovered higher bid premia to acquirees in taxable acquisitions . Dividing U.S. acquisitions over the years 1963–77 into 230 taxable (largely all-cash) and 318 tax-free (mainly all equity) acquisitions, she reported bid premia of 25.4 percent and 11.9 percent, respectively.

No similar studies of the United Kingdom have been undertaken. Nevertheless, Eckbo and Langohr (1986), in a study of bid premia in French takeovers from 1966 to 1980, found that the average offer premia were significantly higher in the 50 cash offers (53 percent) than in the 49 exchanges of securities (20 percent).

The most consistent result to emerge from these previous studies is that bid premia are significantly higher in cash acquisitions than in equity offers. We provide further evidence on this below.

8.5   Data and Methodology

8.5.1   Sample

Our sample contains data from both the United Kingdom and United States, constructed in parallel fashion. For the U.K. data we started with an exhaustive set of almost 1,900 acquisitions as recorded in the London Share Price Database (LSPD) for the period January 1955 to June 1985 (see Franks and Harris 1986a). The LSPD includes all U.K. companies quoted in London since 1975 and approximately two-thirds of the companies quoted before 1975, with a bias in favor of larger companies. For each acquisition we then gathered data on the means of payment from the Stock Exchange Year Book, which reports information from offer documents only where the acquirer is quoted. Financing data existed for 954 of the acquisitions.

For the U.S. data we extracted information on all firms, recorded in the Chicago Research in Security Prices (CRSP) files, that disappeared through acquisition during the period January 1955 to December 1984. The CRSP files cover all companies on the New York and American Stock Exchanges since 1962 and all firms on the NYSE since 1926. We obtained data on means of payment from *The Capital Changes Reporter*. Our final U.S. sample contains 1,555 acquired firms with financing data, and 850 bidders. Using the *Wall Street Journal Index*, we classified takeovers as tenders or mergers based on when control first passed to the bidder. Thus, if the bidder purchased 60 percent of the target's shares via tender and the remaining shares via merger, the bid would be classified as a tender.

In cases where several acquisitions were made by the same bidder, the bidder was counted separately by each acquisition made.

8.5.2   Merger Dates

For each U.K. acquisition we have up to four key dates. The *first approach date* is the date when the Stock Exchange is first informed that merger talks are under way. The *first bid date* gives the date of the first formal merger offer. This is followed by an *unconditional date* when a sufficient proportion of shares has been pledged to the acquiring company to guarantee legal control. Finally, the *LSPD date* shows the last date for which stock returns data are available for the target, usually the delisting date. The first three dates are taken from records of the EXTEL Company, which collects and records such data. Not all acquisitions had four distinct dates. For example, the first bid date may not be preceded by a formal announcement of talks.

For each U.S. acquisition we obtained three key dates. The first mention of an acquisition in *The Wall Street Journal Index* was taken to be the *announcement date*. This date is often the actual bid date but may also be a positive indication of a forthcoming bid. We record dates of bid revisions, as well as the *final bid date*, the date of the bid that was ultimately successful. Finally, we record the *delisting date* for the acquiree's stock.

8.5.3   Share Price Data

Monthly rates of return are taken from the LSPD and CRSP files. In the United Kingdom these are calculated using jobbers' (market makers') price quotes (the average of the bid and the asking price) at the end of the final trading day of the month. Although traded prices are available, the order of prices during a day is not, thereby prohibiting identification of end-of-day traded prices. Jobbers' quotes may not be available on the last day of the month, either because the company's stock has been suspended or because the shares were not traded that day. If there were no jobbers' quotes on the last day of the month, we calculated the returns using a randomly selected traded price on the day of the month when the stock was last traded. The results were not appreciably affected when we used traded prices only instead of the price quote.

8.5.4 Abnormal Returns and Tests

To assess the effects of mergers on share prices, we use variations of event study methodology. Specifically, for any company j we define an abnormal return (ar_{jt}) as

$$(5) \qquad\qquad ar_{jt} = r_{jt} - c_{jt},$$

where r_{jt} is the continuously compounded realized return (log form) in month t (dividends plus capital gains), and c_{jt} is a control return that estimates shareholder returns in the absence of a merger. Time, t, is defined relative to an event date. For the U.K. mergers we use the first available of either the first approach, first bid, unconditional or LSPD dates; for the U.S. mergers we use the announcement date. Since specification of the control returns is controversial, we define control return in three alternative ways as described later in this section.

Company abnormal returns are then aggregated to form a portfolio abnormal monthly return (AR_t) defined as

$$(6) \qquad\qquad AR_t = \frac{1}{N} \sum_{j=1}^{N} ar_{jt},$$

where N is the number of companies in a particular portfolio, for example, the portfolio of acquirees. The statistical significance of AR_t is assessed with the statistic $TAR_t = AR_t/\sigma$, where σ is the standard deviation of the AR_t terms (assumed to be normally distributed) for a time period assumed to be unaffected by the merger. In the results reported here σ is calculated for the period $t = -71$ to $t = -12$. Given these procedures, TAR_t is distributed according to student's t- (distribution with 59 degrees of freedom. This procedure provides a crude adjustment for cross-sectional dependence, as discussed by Brown and Warner (1980). Alternatively, the statistical significance of AR_t is tested nonparametrically using the percentage of the ar_{jt} terms that are positive. This is accomplished by comparing the positive percentage to a binomial distribution when the probability of a positive return is 0.50.

To measure returns over a number of months, we calculate a cumulative abnormal return, CAR_t, as

$$(7) \qquad\qquad CAR_t = \sum_{i=t_b}^{t} AR_i,$$

where t_b is the month at which the cumulation begins. Under the assumption that the AR_t estimates are independent, the significance of CAR_t can be assessed using the statistic $TCAR_t = CAR_t/\sigma_{CAR}$ where $\sigma_{CAR} = \sigma\sqrt{t - t_b + 1}$ and σ is estimated as described above. $TCAR_t$ is approximately a standard normal variate under the null hypothesis that CAR_t has a zero mean.

Although *CAR* is frequently used for assessing multiperiod returns, it can be unsatisfactory when companies disappear from the analysis because of nontrading or because companies are delisted or suspended close to the bid date. As an alternative to *CAR*, we construct company-specific multiperiod returns. These company "bid premia," bp_{jt}, are aggregated into portfolio bid premia, BP_t, defined as

$$(8) \qquad BP_t = \frac{1}{N}\sum_{j=1}^{N} bp_{jt} = \frac{1}{N}\sum_{j=1}^{N}\sum_{i=t_b}^{t} ar_{ji},$$

where the cumulation process begins at time t_b and includes those monthly abnormal returns which are observed up to and including month t. For example, if in month $+1$ two companies obtain an average residual of 10 percent and in month $+2$ only one survives (or is traded) and obtains a residual of 5 percent, the *CAR* for the two months according to equation (7) is 15 percent, and 12.5 percent according to equation (8). We assess the statistical significance of *BP* using the statistic $TBP = BP/\sigma_{BP}$, where $\sigma_{BP} = \sigma\sqrt{T}$, and T is the average (across companies) number of months for which return data are available to form *BP*. *TBP* is the analogue of $TCAR_t$ shown above.

The calculations of *TBP* and *TCAR* both use σ specified as the standard deviation of abnormal returns for some time period removed from the merger. It can be argued that there are transitory (or permanent) risk shifts associated with mergers that might not be captured by our calculation of σ. As an alternative procedure, we calculated statistics based on the cross-sectional standard error of company-specific bid premia (bp_{jt}). This "cross-sectional" t is calculated as BP/SE, where $SE = SD/\sqrt{N}$, and *SD* is the cross-sectional standard deviation of the bid premia for the N companies averaged to get *BP*. In general, the results using these cross-sectional t-statistics are quite comparable to those using *TBP* and *TCAR* discussed above.

8.5.5   Control Returns

Brown and Warner's (1980, 1985) simulation results on both monthly and daily data suggest that relatively straightforward procedures are as powerful as more elaborate tests in detecting abnormal returns (see also Brown and Weinstein 1985). To see whether the specification of control returns affects our results, we use three alternate models to determine c_{jt} using the following equation:

$$c_{jt} = \alpha_j + \beta_j rm_t.$$

In the first model, the market model, values for α and β are estimated by regressing r_{jt} on rm_t for the 60-month period beginning at $t = -71$. Because of the documented effects of infrequent trading in the United Kingdom on estimated parameters (Dimson and Marsh (1983)), α and

235   Means of Payment in Takeovers

β for the United Kingdom companies are adjusted for thin trading using Dimson's (1979) method for the same 60-month period.[4] In the second model we set $\alpha = 0$ and $\beta = 1$ for all firms. The third model is based on the capital asset pricing model and sets $c_{jt} = rf_t + \beta_j (r_{mt} - r_{ft})$, where β is from the market model and rf_t is the yield on a government obligation. For the United Kingdom we use the yield on three-month Treasury obligations converted to a one-month yield basis. For the United States we use yields on one month Treasury bills.

8.6 Forms of Financing in U.K. and U.S. Acquisitions

We first describe the different forms of financing used in our samples of U.S. and U.K. acquisitions, the importance of each form, and the trends over the 30-year period. We then assess whether these patterns of financing are consistent with the predictions of the theories reviewed in section 8.3.

8.6.1 Means of Payment

Table 8.1 shows that all-cash offers and all-equity offers were the two most widely used means of payment in both countries. Together these two types of offers constituted almost one-half of the successful U.K. takeovers and over two-thirds of the U.S. offers. In the United Kingdom an additional one in five acquisitions involved either a combination of cash and equity or the seller's option to receive either all cash or all equity. In the "all cash or all equity" case, each shareholder of the target may elect to receive all cash or all equity. The bidder will provide the cash from its own resources or through an underwriter. In the latter case, shareholders of the target tender their shares to the bidder, which then issues new shares to the underwriter (on the basis of the bid terms); the underwriter then remits the amount prescribed by the cash alternative to the tendering stockholders.

These "all cash or all equity" offers have become increasingly prevalent since 1979. One reason is that they provide shareholders who are liable to pay capital gains taxes on realized gains (if they receive cash) with an equity alternative, and others, who do not want the bidder's paper in their portfolio, with cash. The offer is tax and transaction cost efficient. The role of the underwriter may be twofold: It simply provides a source of cash for a cash-hungry bidder; and it provides a signal to the market of the value of the bidder's equity from an informed (or partially informed) trader. This informed trader must agree to purchase any shares at a predetermined price whenever a target shareholder elects to take the cash alternative. This role may be especially important where the acquisition is relatively large and where there is great uncertainty as to the value of the offer to the bidder.

236   Julian R. Franks, Robert S. Harris, and Colin Mayer

Table 8.1   Mediums of Exchange in U.K. and U.S. Acquisitions, in
                   Proportions, 1955–85

	U.K.	U.S.
A. Method of Payment		
All cash	.253	.306
Cash *or* debt	.016	.003
All debt	.014	.014
All cash or (cash plus equity)	.035	.001
Cash plus equity	.101	.009
Cash *or* equity*a*	.100	.013
Convertibles	—	.118
Equity plus debt	.048	.003
Equity plus convertibles	—	.073
All equity	.246	.371
Other*a*	.189	.090
Total	1.00	1.00
*B. Use of Cash, Equity and Debt*b		
At least some equity*c*	.660	.601
At least some cash or some debt	.633	.404
At least some cash	.538	.356

*a*The "*or*" denotes that the seller has the option to receive either form of payment. The
option to receive "cash or equity" has become increasingly popular since 1978. Before
then the ratio of "all equity" to "all cash or all equity" was 3.27, but during 1978–84
it fell to 1.17. The "other" category includes various mixtures of cash, equity, and debt,
as well as other types of payment (such as preference stock). In the U.K. sample the
largest single category involves mixtures subsequent to recapitalizations (.083).

*b*Categories are not mutually exclusive so that percentages sum to more than 100. The
data include mixture offers after recapitalizations.

*c*For purposes of this tabulation, securities convertible into common equity are treated
as equity.

Unlike in the United Kingdom, the cash alternative and cash-equity
combinations have not been significant in the United States. All debt
offers were rare in both countries, and combination offers involving
debt are infrequent, though more common in the United Kingdom. A
striking contrast between the two countries is in the use of convertibles
securities. In the United States 11.8 percent of takeovers involved full
payment with convertibles (such as convertible preferred stock), and
an additional 7.3 percent were combinations of equity and convertibles.
In the United Kingdom the use of convertibles was negligible.

Panel B shows that a larger proportion of U.K. takeovers than U.S.
takeovers involved at least some cash or some debt. In addition, a
slightly larger proportion of U.K. offers involved at least some equity.
These figures reflect the greater use of combination offers in the United
Kingdom.

Table 8.2 divides the entire 30-year period into five-year blocks, and
figure 8.1 displays the results by year. In the United States all-cash

237   Means of Payment in Takeovers

Table 8.2   Time-Series of the Forms of Payment in U.K. and U.S. Takeovers,
                 Using an Equally Weighted Basis

		U.K.			U.S.		
Period	N	All Cash	All Equity	N	All Cash	All Equity	Some Use of Convertibles[a]
1955–59	65	.354	.354	69	.000	.768	.072
1960–64	89	.292	.404	121	.008	.669	.248
1965–69	156	.186	.244	386	.013	.381	.500
1970–74	139	.230	.237	177	.192	.599	.107
1975–79	247	.336	.231	373	.491	.247	.070
1980–84	205	.205	.190	429	.585	.228	.054
1985	53	.094	.170	—	—	—	—
Average[b]	954	.253	.246	1,555	.306	.371	.191

Note: Entries are proportions of the sample (N) with a type of offer.
[a]These are offers that are equity plus securities convertible into equity or which are solely convertible.
[b]Averages are weighted by the number of mergers.

takeovers were not observed in our sample until 1965, but after that they became increasingly important.[5] At the same time, all-equity offers fell from three-quarters of U.S. takeovers in the late 1950s to less than one-quarter in the 1980s. This striking increase in the use of cash occurred over a period in which the Williams Act (1968) and its extension (1970) imposed more stringent requirements on cash offers. In contrast, in the United Kingdom financing proportions fluctuated considerably over the 30 years of the study.

Table 8.2 also demonstrates that the heavy use of convertibles in the United States was largely a phenomenon of the 1960s. Over the years 1965–69 fully one-half of United States bids involved convertible securities. By the 1980s the proportion had fallen to only 5.4 percent. The downturn in takeover financing with convertibles was probably due to changes in U.S. tax law and accounting standards. Enactment of Section 279 of the tax code in 1969 eliminated the tax deductibility of interest payments on convertible debt expressly issued for acquisitions. In addition, Accounting Principles Board Opinion 15, issued in 1969, required the reporting of earnings per share on a fully diluted basis. This change may have reduced the incentive to issue convertibles because of the impact of earnings dilution on contractual arrangements, for example, in bond covenants. Also, managers and investment bankers may have been apprehensive about investor reaction to even only cosmetic reductions in earnings per share.

The proportions in both tables 8.1 and 8.2 were calculated on an equally weighted basis. Table 8.3 provides the proportions of all-cash

238   **Julian R. Franks, Robert S. Harris, and Colin Mayer**

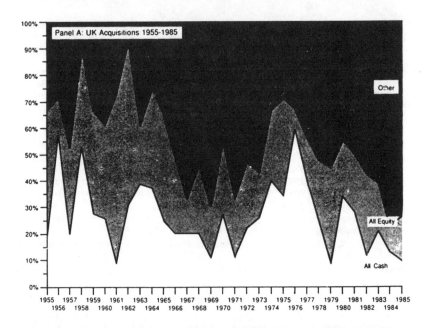

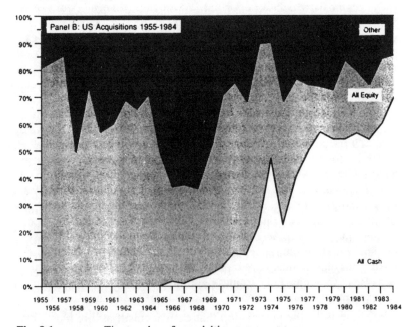

Fig. 8.1   Time-series of acquisition payment type

239   Means of Payment in Takeovers

Table 8.3   Forms of Payment in UK and US Takeovers, on a Value-
                   Weighted Basis

	U.K.		U.S.	
	All Cash	All Equity	All Cash	All Equity
1955–59	0.23	0.67	0.0	0.84
1960–64	0.08	0.67	0.0	0.61
1965–69	0.08	0.26	0.01	0.37
1970–74	0.28	0.12	0.21	0.60
1974–79	0.38	0.30	0.38	0.28
1980–84	0.35	0.14	0.39	0.38

Note: Entries are a proportion of the total. Weights are based on market value of the shares of the acquired company.

and all-equity offers based on the market value of the acquisitions. In the United States the proportion of bids that were all cash on a value-weighted basis was almost identical to the equally weighted proportion for the period 1955 to 1974. After 1974 cash offers constituted a smaller proportion on a value-weighted basis than on an equally weighted basis, suggesting that cash offers were used more frequently in smaller acquisitions. For all equity offers the equally weighted and value-weighted results are very close, except for during the years 1980–84.

In the United Kingdom the proportion of all cash offers on a value-weighted basis was appreciably lower than that on an equally weighted over the years 1955–69. The converse was true for the years 1970–84. Over the entire 30-year period the proportion of bids that were all cash was 0.25 on both an equally weighted basis and a value-weighted basis. For the all-equity figures there was no consistent relationship between the value and equal weightings. In aggregate the all-equity proportion on a value-weighted basis was 0.20, whereas it was 0.25 on an equally weighted basis.

8.6.2 Theoretical Predictions and the Evidence

The data shown in tables 8.1 through 8.3 provide some support for the prediction of hypothesis 1 that the use of cash in acquisitions should be inversely related to the capital gains tax rate. The introduction of capital gains taxes in the United Kingdom in 1965 coincided with a decline in the proportion of cash-financed acquisitions from an average of 29.2 percent in 1960–64 to 18.6 percent in 1965–69. This decrease was short-lived, however, and by 1975–79 the proportion had returned to 33.6 percent.

Hypothesis 2—the proposition that cash acquisitions are most prevalent in an environment, such as the United Kingdom, where share

240   **Julian R. Franks, Robert S. Harris, and Colin Mayer**

repurchases are prohibited—is contradicted by the finding that the proportion of all-cash bids was greater in the United States than in the United Kingdom. But in large part cash acquisitions in the United States began only in the 1970s. Their marked growth may reflect more widespread election of stepped-up basis. Rising inflation in the 1970s increased the benefits of raising the basis for determining depreciation allowances from historic to current prices. Since the stepped-up basis was not available in the United Kingdom, an equivalent trend did not occur there.

The U.K. financing proportions reported here are most informative about the trapped equity hypotheses. Since the trapped equity model is a description of the incentives to make cash distributions through acquisitions, it is worth recalling that a high proportion of acquisitions use "all equity"—in fact, the proportion is as large as that of "all cash". The theory cannot explain the all-equity class of acquisitions. More strikingly, the cycles of merger activity that have been widely observed, and which are an important component of the empirical relationship that King (1986) estimated between the value of acquisitions and stock market prices, do not appear to coincide with peaks in cash-financed acquisitions. According to figure 8.1 the particularly pronounced U.K. merger booms of 1968 and 1972 did not coincide with large upswings in the proportion of cash-financed acquisitions.

Still more troublesome for the trapped equity hypothesis is the poor association between the tax disincentive for dividend distributions and the level of acquisitions using cash. Recall from hypothesis 3 that the incentive for cash acquisitions is increasing in the tax wedge. Over the period under study a number of important tax changes in the United Kingdom should have affected this wedge. Most obviously, the introduction of the corporation tax in 1965 was associated with an increase in the tax price of retaining assets in the corporate sector. The incentive to distribute cash thus rose appreciably in 1965. But figure 8.1 shows that this coincided with a period during which the proportion of cash-financed acquisitions declined. Moreover, the introduction of the imputation tax in the United Kingdom in 1973 should have, in theory, lessened the tax price of retaining assets in the corporate sector. Imputation is a tax credit attributed to shareholders for the payment of corporation tax on the profits underlying a distribution. In 1973, 35 percent of the 52 percent corporation tax was imputed to investors' personal income tax. The corporate tax wedge was therefore only 17 percent, 23 percentage points lower than it was before 1973. Figure 8.1 records, however, that the introduction of imputation was associated with a period in which the proportion of cash acquisitions sharply increased, peaking in 1976.[6]

To summarize, the financing proportions provide little support for the trapped equity model but offer some tentative support for an influence from capital gains tax. The appreciable rise in cash-financed acquisitions in the United States over the period studied can be attributed, at least in part, to tax benefits from stepped-up basis.

8.7 Wealth Effects for Bidder and Target around the Announcement Date

In this section we examine bid premia associated with different means of payment. We discuss, in turn, bid premia around the announcement date in all-cash and all-equity offers; share price changes before the announcement; results for "mixed bids"; the effects of other characteristics of takeover, namely, whether the bids are revised or contested and whether they are tender offers; and finally a cross-sectional regression controlling for these bid characteristics.

8.7.1 Bid Premia in All-Cash and All-Equity Offers

Table 8.4 presents data on bid premia for all-cash and all-equity offers in both countries. Since the results are essentially the same using all three models of control returns, we report only those for the market model. Panel B shows that U.S. acquirers were more than seven times larger than targets in all-cash offers and almost nine times larger in all-equity offers. U.K. acquirers were more than twelve times larger than targets in all-cash offers and more than six times larger in all-equity offers.

Target Shareholders

Panel A in table 8.4 shows that in both countries the bid premia for target shareholders were markedly higher in all-cash offers than in all-equity offers. The month 0 results for the United Kingdom, for example, indicate targets with all-cash offers earned a 30.2 percent bid premium, which was significantly higher than the 15.1 percent premium in all-equity offers. The t-statistic[7] comparing the two figures is 9.49. The differences in the United States are even more dramatic, with the month 0 premium of 11.1 percent in all-equity offers being less than half the all-cash figure of 25.4 percent. We thus find strong evidence that target shareholders receive larger wealth gains in all-cash takeovers than those involving all equity. This observation is consistent with hypothesis 1, the capital gain tax thesis that higher bid premia are required in cash offers to compensate for the capital gains tax liability; with hypothesis 4, the Myers and Majluf argument that there are negative

242   Julian R. Franks, Robert S. Harris, and Colin Mayer

Table 8.4   **Bid Premia and Market Capitalization in All-Cash and All-Equity Offers**

| | A. Bid Premia[a] | | | |
| | Month 0 | | Months −4 to +1 | |
	U.K.	U.S.	U.K.	U.S.
Acquirees				
All cash	.302	.254	.305	.363
	(28.07)	(42.29)	(11.56)	(24.67)
All equity	.151	.111	.182	.156
	(12.88)	(25.90)	(6.34)	(14.86)
Acquirers				
All cash	.007	.020	.043	.026
	(.75)	(3.56)	(1.98)	(1.89)
All equity	−.011	−.009[b]	.018	.006
	(−.95)	(−2.23)	(.63)	(.61)

| | B. Market Value (in millions)[c] | | | |
| | U.K. | | U.S. | |
	All Cash	All Equity	All Cash	All Equity
Acquirees	£ 11.1	£10.6	$ 144.4	$ 134.8
Acquirer	136.1	64.3	1,019.0	1,177.0

Note: Entries are bid premia; *t*-statistics in parentheses.
  Cross-sectional *t*-values for bidder wealth gains are:

| | Month 0 | | Months −4 to +1 | |
	U.K.	U.S.	U.K.	U.S.
All cash	.95	2.99	3.05	2.05
All equity	−1.27	−2.14	.97	.67

where the *t*-value is calculated as BP/SE and where $SE = SD/\sqrt{N}$ and SD is the cross-sectional standard deviation.

[a]Bid premia are calculated using the market model. In the United Kingdom month 0 is the earliest available of the first approach, first bid, unconditional, or LSPD date. In the United States month 0 is the announcement date as defined in the text.

[b]For U.S. acquirers with all-equity offers, where the bid premia are −0.009 for month 0, only 45.7 percent of the 443 acquisitions were positive. The results using a model with $\alpha = 0$ and $\beta = 1$ were virtually identical.

[c]The market value of equity prior to takeover.

signals associated with equity offers; and with the Fishman argument that cash offers coincide with high-value acquisitions.

A comparison of the results for the two countries over the six-month period suggests all-cash bids coincided with slightly higher bid premia in the United States than in the United Kingdom (.363 versus .305), and the differences were statistically significant at better than the .10 level ($t = 1.92$). Comparing the month 0 and month -4 to $+1$ results, we find a greater proportion of the U.S. bid premia in all-cash offers appear to have come prior to month 0. Turning to the all-equity bids, we find the U.K. bid premia were somewhat higher than the U.S. premia (.182 versus .156), though not statistically so when measured over the six-month period ($t = 0.85$).

Bidder Shareholders

Shareholders in the U.K. acquirers earned negligible returns in the bid month for both all-cash and all-equity offers. Over the six-month period, however, small (statistically significant) gains accrued for the all-cash offers. Whether this gain was a result of the bid or of the bidder's timing the offer to correspond to favorable developments in its stock price is uncertain. There is no evidence, however, of significant losses to bidders in U.K. takeovers around the merger announcement date. The results for all-equity offers are similar to those found by Marsh (1979) for the month following the rights issue announcement (results showing small abnormal losses at the time of the announcement).

The difference between the performance of all-cash and all-equity acquisitions in the United States is striking. In all-cash offers the bidders earned significantly positive gains of 2 percent in month 0. In contrast, in all-equity offers they experienced a significant loss of 0.9 percent. These wealth effects were also significantly different from each another ($t = 4.19$).[8]

Taken together, our U.S. results suggest that equity in acquisitions conveys bad news, while cash conveys good news. This role for the medium of exchange is consistent with theoretical predictions (see, for example, Miller and Rock 1985) and with empirical evidence on new equity issue announcements. Smith (1986), surveying an extensive literature on new equity issues, reported a weighted average loss of 1.6 percent. Our results also strongly support Myers and Majluf's predictions described in hypothesis 4.

Our U.K. results indicate the returns to all-equity bidders in the bid month were negative but not statistically different from zero. It is interesting to consider the institutional differences between the two countries. U.K. underwriters play a much more important role in equity issues than do their U.S. counterparts. For example, virtually all new U.K. equity issues have taken the form of rights issues, and virtually all have been underwritten (see Marsh 1979). According to Heinkel and

244   Julian R. Franks, Robert S. Harris, and Colin Mayer

Schwartz (1985), the underwriter may be able to avoid some of the information problems that would otherwise be associated with equity issues.

Table 8.5 compares U.K. bid premia around the announcement date of acquisitions for the periods 1955–64 and 1965–85. The significance of 1965 is that it was in that year that the government instituted a full capital gains tax. According to hypothesis 1, bid premia in all-cash acquisitions should have differed from those in all-equity acquisitions only in the years after the tax was introduced. The table indicates that although the difference was larger in the later period, bid premia were significantly higher in all-cash offers than in all-equity offers (t = 2.26 in the announcement month) in the earlier period as well. Between 1962 and 1965 there was a short-term capital gains tax on holdings of less than one year. The difference between cash and equity bid premia persists prior to 1962, though the sample is too small to provide meaningful tests of significance. The hypothesis that capital gains taxes can entirely explain differences in the premia of the two kind of offers is therefore rejected.

8.7.2   A Comparison of the Premerger Performance of Bidders Using All Cash and Those Using All Equity

Anecdotal evidence from investment bankers in both the United Kingdom and the United States strongly suggests that they believe the choice of equity or cash is influenced by perceptions of overvaluation of the bidder's shares. We can look to the premerger share price performance of bidders for evidence that the premerger valuation of the acquirer may influence the choice of financing. If overvalued acquirers

Table 8.5   A Comparison of U.K. Bid Premia Before and After 1965

	Month 0		Month −4 to +1	
	1955–64	1965–85	1955–64	1965–85
Acquirees				
All Cash	.185	.327	.260	.317
	(6.28)	(29.26)	(3.60)	(11.60)
All Equity	.108	.166	.194	.177
	(6.39)	(11.17)	(4.67)	(4.86)
Acquirers				
All Cash	.032	.001	.072	.037
	(1.80)	(0.09)	(1.66)	(1.59)
All Equity	.005	−.017	.058	.002
	(0.30)	(1.22)	(1.32)	(0.07)

Note: Entries are bid premia; *t*-statistics in parentheses. Bid premia are calculated using the market model. Month 0 is the earliest available of the first approach, first bid, unconditional, or LSPD date.

245   Means of Payment in Takeovers

choose equity, their premerger performance might be expected to be superior to that of acquirers offering cash.

The table below reports abnormal returns to acquirers for the period beginning six months before the bid and ending one month before the bid. The table shows U.S. bidders offering equity had slightly better performance over the prebid period than did those offering cash. The prebid performance of the two types of bidders was the reverse in the United Kingdom. Only very limited support is thereby provided for the hypothesis that overvaluation can be established from premerger data.

	Bid Premia	N
U.K. Bidders		
All cash	.050	198
	(t = 2.31)	
All equity	.034	150
	(t = 1.28)	
U.S. Bidders		
All cash	−.006	201
	(t = −.45)	
All equity	.024	442
	(t = 2.50)	

8.7.3   Other Types of Offers

In preceding sections the focus was on all-cash and all-equity bids since they are the primary types of bids made in both countries (see table 8.1). Table 8.6 presents additional estimates of the wealth effects of other types of bids.

"Cash or Equity" Offers

Combination offers provide the seller with the opportunity to accept either cash or stock. This option should reduce any detrimental personal tax effects associated with an all-cash offer. As shown in table 8.1, these offers have been made frequently in the United Kingdom but less often in the United States. In the United Kingdom target bid premia in combination offers were quite similar to those found in all-cash offers (table 8.4). For example, the 28.4 percent target bid premium (−4 to +1) in cash-or-equity offers shown in table 8.6 is very close to the 30.5 percent premium shown in table 8.4 for all-cash bids. The small sample size for the U.S. results (N = 20) prevents us from making any definitive statements, although target bid premia appear to be between those for all-cash and all-equity offers (Table 8.4). In neither country did these cash-or-equity offers coincide with significant bidder share price performance.

246   **Julian R. Franks, Robert S. Harris, and Colin Mayer**

Table 8.6   **The Wealth Effects of Other Types of Offers**

	Acquirees		Acquirers	
Type of Offer	0	−4 to +1	0	−4 to +1
1. Cash or equity				
U.K. (N = 95)	.276	.284	.007	.075
	(14.79)	(6.21)	(.49)	(2.26)
U.S. (N = 20)	.180	.266	−.002	−0.010
	(8.41)	(5.07)	(−.09)	(−.18)
2. Cash and equity				
U.K. (N = 100)	.238	.271	.003	.054
	(18.70)	(8.71)	(.23)	(1.63)
U.S. (N = 15)	.099	.212	.057	.015
	(3.24)	(2.83)	(1.88)	(.20)
3. Convertibles only				
U.S. only (N = 184)	.117	.176	.018	.031
	(21.34)	(13.11)	(2.80)	(1.97)
4. Convertibles and equity				
U.S. only (N = 115)	.101	.143	−.004	.009
	(12.50)	(7.23)	(−.42)	(.39)

Note: Entries are bid premia; *t*-statistics in parentheses. Bid premia are calculated using the market model. The months are defined as in table 8.4.

These results are further evidence that personal tax considerations do not satisfactorily explain the higher target bid premia in cash offers since the equity-or-cash option, though tax efficient, led to bid premia comparable to those in all-cash offers. Thus, the evidence contradicts hypothesis 1.

"Cash and Equity" Offers

"Cash and equity" bids provide the seller with a combination of cash and equity and have been used frequently in the United Kingdom. They appear to offer targets smaller bid premia than do cash-or-equity or all-cash bids, but higher premia than all-equity bids. Furthermore, there are no significant wealth effects to bidders in acquisitions involving cash and equity. The pattern in these bids thus appears to be an average of the results for the all-cash and all-equity offers discussed earlier.

Convertibles

Convertibles were extensively used in the United States in the 1960s (see table 8.2). As shown in table 8.5, target premia for bids involving convertibles (either alone or along with equity) coincided very closely with target premia for all-equity bids. For example, in the United States the month 0 target bid premium was 11.1 percent in all-equity bids

247   Means of Payment in Takeovers

(table 8.4), 11.7 percent in all-convertible bids, and 10.1 percent in bids involving both convertibles and equity. A major difference, however, has to do with the bidders. Whereas, as noted earlier, all-equity bids in the United States are associated with a negative wealth effect for acquirers in month 0, all-convertible bids were associated with a significant positive gain (1.8 percent) for acquirers in month 0.

8.7.4   Bid Premia: Further Analysis

Variations over Time

The differences in bid premia between all-cash and all-equity offers shown in table 8.4 may be attributable to variations over calendar years in the performance of acquisitions. This issue is less important in the U.K. data because all-cash and all-equity offers took place over the entire 30-year period in that country.

Table 8.7   Wealth Effects in U.S. Acquisitions, Partitioned by Time and by Tender Versus Nontender

A. Time

Time Period	Offer	Target N	Target BP Month 0	Target (t-stat)	Bidder N	Bidder BP Month 0	Bidder (t-stat)
1970–74	All cash	34	.252	(12.35)	21	.066	(3.41)
	All equity	107	.127	(10.88)	80	.006	(.57)
1975–79	All cash	185	.304	(27.84)	85	.012	(1.31)
	All equity	92	.169	(12.45)	75	−.014	(−1.46)
1980–84	All cash	249	.220	(32.39)	90	.018	(1.73)
	All equity	97	.145	(13.79)	64	−.039	(−3.99)

B. Tender vs. Nontender

Offer	N	Target Month 0	Target Month −4 to +1	N	Bidder Month 0	Bidder Month −4 to +1
Tenders all cash	135	.283	.411	78	.014	.025
		(35.20)	(20.87)		(1.84)	(1.34)
Tenders all equity	29	.201	.243	23	−.019	−.060
		(12.50)	(6.17)		(−1.13)	(−1.46)
Nontender all cash	340	.243	.343	123	.024	.026
		(31.66)	(18.24)		(3.00)	(1.33)
Nontender all equity	548	.106	.151	419	−.008	.009
		(22.75)	(13.23)		(−2.02)	(.93)

Note: Bid premia (*BP*) are calculated using the market model. Month 0 is the announcement date as defined in the text.

248   Julian R. Franks, Robert S. Harris, and Colin Mayer

In panel A of table 8.7 we break our U.S. data into three five-year periods beginning with 1970, the onset of significant use of all-cash offers. As the figures show, the month 0 bid premium estimates for the targets was higher in all-cash offers than in all-equity offers in each of the five-year periods. The same patterns hold for the six-month bid premia (not shown here). In addition, in all-equity offers the wealth effects for bidders were consistently lower than in all-cash offers, and they were negative in both the 1975–79 and the 1980–84 period, though significantly so only in the latter. Panel A shows that differences between the wealth effects of all-equity and all-cash bids in the United States cannot be attributed to a particular time period.

Tender and Nontender Offers

Earlier research on acquisitions in the United States has indicated that shareholder wealth effects may be different in tender offers and mergers. For example, surveying a number of studies, Jensen and Ruback (1983) reported acquiree bid premiums of 30 percent in tenders but only 20 percent in mergers; for acquirers the figures are 4 percent and zero percent, respectively. Panel B of table 8.7 shows the data we used to investigate whether the disparity between wealth effects in all-cash and all-equity can be attributed to a greater use of cash in tenders. The data indicate that all-cash bids resulted in higher acquiree bid premia, whether the takeover was a tender or not. Furthermore, panel B suggests that after having controlled for the medium of exchange, a difference in bid premia remains between mergers and tenders. For example, the 28.3 percent premia in all-cash tenders (in month 0) is significantly higher than the 24.3 percent figure in all-cash offers that are not tenders ($t = 3.60$). Panel B also shows that a high proportion of tenders used cash as the form of financing.

Turning to the results for acquirers in Panel B, we find the announcement month wealth effect to acquirers making all-equity bids was negative in both tenders and nontenders, although the sample size is small for all-equity tenders. In contrast, the announcement month wealth effects were positive in all-cash offers whether the bid was a tender or not. Panel B therefore suggests that the medium of exchange and the response of acquirers' share prices are related.[9]

Revised and Unrevised Bids

In table 8.8 we use the U.S. data to test whether the differences in all-cash and all-equity bid premiums (partitioned by tender and merger) are due to the contested nature of the bids. We have evidence from Franks and Harris (1986a) that bid revisions, even when unaccompanied by contestants, show similar wealth effects to contested bids. As a result we partition offers into those that are unrevised and uncontested and those that are revised or contested.

249   Means of Payment in Takeovers

Panel A shows, for unrevised bids, the target bid premia in all-cash tenders were slightly higher than those in all-cash mergers (with six-month bid premia of .384 and .345, respectively). The target bid premia were significantly higher in all-equity tenders (.258) than in all-equity mergers (.154). For bids that were revised or contested a similar pattern emerges, although the difference between tenders and mergers is larger. We can conclude that all-cash bids still provide much larger premia

Table 8.8   Bid Premia for Multiple Bids (Revised or Contested) versus Single Bids (Unrevised and Uncontested), Partitioned by Tender and Merger, U.S. Data

	Month 0		Months −4 to +1	
	Unrevised and Uncontested	Revised or Contested	Unrevised and Uncontested	Revised or Contested
A. Targets				
Mergers				
All cash	.247	.240	.345	.328
	(29.80)	(19.77)	(21.62)	(11.95)
	N = 297	N = 85	N = 297	N = 85
All equity	.106	.116	.154	.136
	(19.49)	(10.62)	(11.93)	(4.02)
	N = 505	N = 89	N = 505	N = 89
Tenders				
All cash	.267	.265	.384	.466
	(31.43)	(23.88)	(13.97)	(14.52)
	N = 103	N = 74	N = 103	N = 74
All equity	.242	.192	.258	.293
	(11.22)	(9.52)	(3.85)	(.71)
	N = 18	N = 14	N = 18	N = 14
B. Bidders				
Mergers				
All cash	.026	.016	.029	.023
	(3.13)	(.93)	(1.57)	(.61)
	N = 111	N = 32	N = 111	N = 32
All equity	−.005	−.023	.012	−.024
	(−1.12)	(−2.07)	(1.20)	(.95)
	N = 389	N = 68	N = 389	N = 68
Tenders	.016	.011	.026	.045
All cash	(1.96)	(.97)	(1.48)	(1.73)
	N = 67	N = 38	N = 67	N = 38
All equity	−.031	−.021	−.076	−.092
	(−1.19)	(−1.04)	(−1.26)	(−1.18)
	N = 14	N = 12	N = 14	N = 12

Note: Entries are bid premia; *t*-statistics in parentheses. Bid premia are calculated using the market model. Month 0 is the announcement date as defined in the text.

than all-equity bids even after controlling for the form and contested nature of the merger and that tenders still provide larger bid premia than mergers.

Table 8.8 also shows that a larger proportion of all-cash than all-equity bids are revised. If we look at the medium of exchange in the final bid, 28.4 percent of the all-cash bids were contested or revised, whereas only 16.5 percent of the all-equity bids were. From Fishman's model we might have expected the converse: His model predicts that contested bids will occur more frequently in low-value equity bids than in high-value cash bids. In the latter case, the bidder has placed a high value on the target and uses a cash offer to preempt competing bids. In fact, competition appears to be more closely associated with cash than with equity offers. It should be noted, however, that a final cash bid may have evolved from an initial equity bid, although Callison's (1987) data show that of 54 all-cash tenders, only one was preceded by an equity offer.

Panel B of table 8.8 shows the wealth gains for bidders. Gains to bidders appear small, and if anything they were larger in all-cash takeovers than in all-equity bids.

8.7.5   Cross-Sectional Analysis

To investigate further the patterns in acquiree bid premia, we estimate the following cross-sectional regression:

$$BP = a_0 + a_1D_1 + a_2D_2 + a_3D_3 + a_4D_4 + \epsilon,$$

where BP is the estimated bid premium

D_1 = 1 if all-cash offer, 0 otherwise
D_2 = 1 if tender offer, 0 otherwise
D_3 = 1 if contested bid, 0 otherwise
D_4 = 1 if revised bid, 0 otherwise
ϵ = a random error term with zero mean.

Only all-cash and all-equity offers in the United States are included in the regression. Furthermore, since the regression results are qualitatively similar for all three models of forming control returns, we report results for the market model only and bid premiums only for the six-month period around the announcement date. The results are (t-values in parentheses):

$$BP = .163 + .148D_1 + .081D_2 + .038D_3 + .025D_4$$
$$(14.94)\quad(6.43)\qquad(3.15)\qquad(1.66)\qquad(.98)$$

$$R^2 = .08, \ F = 20.8$$

251 Means of Payment in Takeovers

Although the regression has a low R^2, in part due to the measurement error for individual company bid premia, the F value of 20.8 is statistically significant at better than the .001 level. The results show that acquiree bid premia were larger in contested or revised bids and were significantly larger in tender offers (coefficient of .081). Even having controlled for these effects, however, the all-cash offers appear to coincide with larger acquiree bid premia. The coefficient of .148 (14.8 percent) is significantly different from zero at better than the .001 level. In fact, the medium of exchange has a larger impact than any of the other three effects. The regression results thus suggest that in the United States the medium of exchange is significantly related to bid premia and that this result is not an artifact of other commonly studied characteristics of the data.

We found qualitatively similar regression results for the U.K. data after controlling for schemes of arrangement, contested or revised bids, and time period (a series of dummy variables). The coefficient on D_1 was .104 with a t-statistic of 2.74.

8.8 Postmerger Performance

In their review of studies on U.S. acquisitions, Jensen and Ruback (1983) suggested several possible reasons for the common finding of negative returns following merger. They concluded (p.22) that "explanation of the post-event negative abnormal returns is currently an unsettled issue." Table 8.9 reports estimates of postmerger performance in all-cash and all-equity bids. The results are calculated as the average cumulative return—*BP* from equation (8)—over the two-year period covering months $+1$ to $+24$. For the purposes of measuring postmerger performance in the United Kingdom, month 0 is the date when the merger was unconditionally accepted; and for the United States, it is the date of the final bid. Four methods of forming control returns are used to test the robustness of the results.

8.8.1 Results for the United States

Panel A of table 8.9 shows that in the United States there is a marked difference between the postmerger performance of all-cash and all-equity bids. Acquirers using all cash did better after merger than did all-equity bidders, no matter what control return is used. The control returns (benchmarks) do, however, give rise to quite different figures for whether postmerger performance is positive, zero, or negative. These results highlight the importance of forming an efficient benchmark (see Grinblatt and Titman 1986).

252   Julian R. Franks, Robert S. Harris, and Colin Mayer

Table 8.9   Postmerger Performance in All Cash and All Equity Acquisitions

A. United States

	Premerger α, β Market Model[a]	α = 0 β = 1.0	CAPM[b]	Postmerger α, β Market Model[c]
All cash	.028	−.036	−.034	.094
	(.70, 55)	(−1.03, 52)	(−.95, 51)	(1.59, 53)
All equity	−.184	−.179	−.178	−.018
	(−7.73, 36)	(−9.31, 34)	(−8.97, 34)	(−.69, 46)

	α	β	N
All cash			
Premerger	−.003	.99	201
Postmerger	−.007	1.04	127
All equity			
Premerger	.000	.99	442
Postmerger	−.006	.99	392

B. United Kingdom

	Premerger α, β Market Model[a]	CAPM[b]
All cash: N = 221	.017	.175
α = .008, β = 1.07	(.50, 53)	(6.09, 65)
All equity: N = 207	−0.094	.042
α = .011, β = 1.07	(−2.31, 51)	(1.23, 64)

Note: Entries are bid premia for months +1 to +24. For the U.K., results month 0 is the unconditional date of the merger. For the U.S., results month 0 is the date of the final bid. The figures in parentheses are t-statistics and percent positive. For this table, the t-statistic is calculated as BP/SE, where SE is the standard error of the mean.

[a]A market value–weighted average of α and β values for the acquiree and acquirer were also used as parameters in the market model to determine control returns. They showed very similar results as the unweighted parameters.

[b]When β was estimated as the market value–weighted average of betas for the acquiree and acquirer, the results were similar. CAPM is the capital asset pricing model.

[c]The α and β values here are calculated over period t = +25 months to +60 months (with a minimum of 24 months of data).

Using either a market model with "premerger" estimated parameters (calculated from six years to one year prior to the bid) or a simple α = 0, β = 1.0 model, we find postmerger abnormal returns were essentially zero in all-cash offers but significantly negative in all-equity offers. It can be argued, however, that these results reflect the use of an inappropriate benchmark, since there may be shifts in a firm's expected returns and risks associated with acquisitions.[10] We therefore estimated α and β values in the market model from a postmerger period producing essentially zero postmerger returns for all-equity offers and positive (though not statistically significant) postmerger returns in all-cash offers. These changes stem from the noticeable reductions in the estimated α values when going from the premerger (six through one years before the bid) to the postmerger (three through five years after the bid) period. The average postmerger α values are negative for both all-cash and all-equity offers.

In summary, acquirers that made all-cash bids on average did not suffer postmerger losses and did better than the bidders that made all-equity offers. Whether all-equity bidders have postmerger losses depends on the benchmark employed. Compared with premerger performance, postmerger returns are negative. But using a benchmark based on postmerger parameters, we find all-equity acquirers did not experience abnormal losses in the two years after an acquisition, but they did have negative α values three to five years after the acquisition.

Given the heavy use of equity in the 1960s, a possible explanation for these different results for cash and equity offers is that they are due to the date of the takeover rather than the medium of exchange.[11] Nonetheless, we found qualitatively similar results (using premerger parameters) when we divided the post-1970 subsample into five-year subperiods (post 1970). The results suggest that the medium of exchange plays an important role in the postmerger performance of acquiring firms in the United States. We can speculate that this role may be related to information asymmetries that may motivate equity rather than cash bids in situations in which the acquirer's equity is overvalued by the market.

8.8.2 Results for the United Kingdom

Panel B of table 8.9 shows that postmerger performance results in the United Kingdom are highly dependent on the formation of control returns. As in the United States, all-equity offers had significantly worse postmerger performance than did all-cash offers. The difference appears to be in the 11 percent to 15 percent range. For example, using the market model, we find postmerger performance in all-equity offers was -9.4 percent, which is 11.1 percentage points lower than the 1.7 percent return in all-cash offers.

The issue that remains unresolved is whether postmerger performance in all-equity takeovers was less than zero. The significant negative figures resulting from use of the market model were essentially the result of the very high premerger α values for the acquirers in all-equity deals ($\alpha = 0.011$ per month, or over 12 percent per year). If one applies the capital asset pricing model, the all-equity takeovers appear to have had small positive bidder returns after merger, and in all-cash offers the bidders had large positive returns of 17.5 percent.

As was the case in the United States, further exploration of these results will be necessary.[12]

8.9 Conclusion

In this paper we have examined the means of payment used in a large set of acquisitions in the United Kingdom and the United States over the years 1955–85. Using data on financing proportions, bid premia, and postmerger performance we tested the validity of several tax and information hypotheses in the literature. Our findings show that it is difficult to explain many of the results in terms of tax effects. The capital gains tax did not appear to be a primary determinant of financing patterns in the United Kingdom during a period in which there were substantial variations in the tax rate. Our data also show that the "trapped equity" model is inconsistent with financing patterns. We could not reject stepped-up basis as an explanation for the substantial increase in cash-financing proportions in the United States, but our data were insufficient to provide a convincing test.

The second set of empirical results we presented concerned wealth gains around the announcement of mergers. In both countries we observed that the bid premia associated with cash bids were much larger than those associated with equity bids. This finding is consistent with Fishman's model that high-valuing bidders make cash offers, and low-valuing bidders make securities offers. After controlling for the form of finance, we found that much of the difference in bid premia between tenders and mergers disappeared. We also examined whether the effects of revised or contested bids could explain the higher bid premia accruing to targets in cash offers than to those in equity offers. After controlling for the form of takeover (tender versus merger) and the contested nature of the bid, we found that cash offers still provided substantially higher wealth gains to shareholders. Moreover, U.S. bidders that offered all equity suffered significant abnormal losses at the time of the bid announcement, consistent with the findings on the wealth effects of seasoned new equity offerings in the United States. Finally, acquirers that made cash offers had better postmerger performance than did those that made all-equity offers. These results support an overvaluation hypothesis, but they are inconsistent with theories of efficient capital markets.

Our findings suggest at least two directions for future work. First, because our results on postmerger performance were sensitive to the benchmark used, further investigation of this topic is warranted (see Loderer and Mauer, 1986). Second, after focusing on the means of payment in takeovers, we believe further insights into the relationships between financing decisions and acquisition performance could be gained by incorporating detailed information on the capital structures of the merging firms.

255   Means of Payment in Takeovers

Notes

1. King's model contains no feature that distinguishes between acquisitions and new investment.

2. It is crucial to Myers and Majluf's argument that all projects have a zero or positive net present value (see idem., 203–4) If projects could have a negative net present value, giving up a new project and not issuing equity may not be good news.

3. Jensen's (1986) theory of free cash flow could also be used to yield the same prediction, since increasing the debt ratio of the bidder (via a cash offer) enables managers to bond their promise to pay future cash flows. See also Grossman and Hart (1982).

4. For the earliest calendar years of our U.K. analysis, prior data were unavailable to calculate α and β. In these cases companies were assigned $\alpha = 0$, $\beta = 1.0$. Our adjustment for thin trading regresses company returns on the market return and one-month leads and lags on the market. The three coefficients in the multiple regression were summed to obtain β.

5. Data from W. T. Grimm show the same upward trend in the use of cash in U.S. acquisitions (and the same decline in the use of stock) beginning around 1970, although the data also reveal that cash was used in the 1960s (the series begins in 1964). Differences in samples probably account for variations in financing proportions. Grimm's data include acquisitions and divestitures of both public and private companies, whereas our data are limited to acquisitions of exchange-listed companies. The latter are, on average, larger concerns.

6. An examination of Department of Trade and Industry (DTI) data on the financing of acquisitions reveals similar changes in financing proportions around the time of the major tax changes discussed here. These data differ from ours primarily in the population from which their samples are drawn. Our data refer to acquisitions by companies that were quoted on the London Stock Exchange. The DTI data are obtained from reports in the British financial press about mergers and acquisitions. We would argue that there is some merit in using data on quoted companies in a study of the financing of acquisitions, on the grounds that the impediments to the choice of financing are less for quoted than unquoted companies. A comparison of the two samples is outlined below.

Years	Proportion (value-weighted) financed by cash:	
	Our sample	DTI sample
1970–74	0.28	0.32
1975–79	0.38	0.59
1980–84	0.47	0.54†

†Up to the third quarter of 1983 only.

7. Significance tests for the difference between two cell means $(M_1 - M_2)$ are based on a t-statistic calculated as $t = (M_1 - M_2)/SD$, where $SD = \sqrt{\sigma_1^2 + \sigma_2^2}$ and σ is the standard deviation used to calculate the bid premia (BP) for the cell mean; in other words, $\sigma_1 = \sigma_{BP}$ for cell 1.

8. As confirming statistical tests, we examined the percentage of companies with positive returns and an alternate method of calculating a t-statistic. For the 200 acquirers making all-cash bids, 59 percent had positive abnormal returns

256   **Julian R. Franks, Robert S. Harris, and Colin Mayer**

in month 0, whereas only 46 percent of the 442 acquirers in all-equity bids had positive abnormal returns in that month. We also calculated a *t*-statistic defined as the mean abnormal return divided by the standard error of the mean. For month 0 this produced $t = 2.99$ in all-cash bids and $t = -2.14$ in all-equity bids.

9. In our U.K. sample over 90 percent of the acquisitions took a form similar to that for the U.S. tenders (see Franks and Harris 1986a), the remaining 10 percent having been schemes of arrangement that required a shareholders' meeting convened under a court's direction. In schemes of arrangement the merger can be consummated if more than 75 percent of the votes cast by those present and voting are in favor of the proposal. Because of the relatively small number of schemes of arrangement, any differences in results for this type of merger are not likely to have a large effect on our U.K. results. Nonetheless, we partitioned our U.K. data into schemes of arrangement that were all-cash bids and those that were all-equity bids. The target bid premia were significantly lower in all-equity bids than in all-cash bids.

10. For example, the merger is combining two firms and hence may change the business mix of the acquirer (but see notes *c* and *d* of table 8.9). In addition, a cash offer may be accompanied by an increase in financial leverage, thus increasing risk. Providing some support for this is the fact that in all-cash offers the postmerger β (1.04) exceeded the premerger β (.99).

11. We also examined use of a value-weighted market index in measuring postmerger performance in the United States. Using an $\alpha = 0$, $\beta = 1.0$ model with a value-weighted index, we found all-cash acquirers had positive (.06) abnormal returns over the 24-month period ($t = 1.71$), whereas all-equity acquirers still displayed significant negative postmerger performance (of .111, $t = -5.54$). To further examine the role that firm size may play in postmerger performance in the United States, we subdivided the sample into quintiles and measured the postmerger performance of each portion. The smallest acquirers appeared to outperform the largest acquirers when we used both a market model (with postmerger α and β values) and an $\alpha = 0$ and $\beta = 1$ model. The results were:

Ranking by Market Capitalization	$\alpha = 0$ $\beta = 1$ N = 195	Postmerger Market Model	
1 Smallest	−.078	.009	N = 153
2	−.102	.030	N = 164
3	−.135	.063	N = 169
4	−.194	−.104	N = 165
5 Largest	−.174	−.098	N = 145

12. One possible explanation for our postmerger performance results may be related to size effects not captured in our formation of control returns (see Dimson and Marsh 1986). We have some evidence suggesting, however, that such size effects cannot fully explain our results. First, as shown in table 8.4, in the United States the average size of all-equity and all-cash acquirers was quite similar both before and after merger. In the United Kingdom all-cash acquirers were larger than all-equity acquirers. As a result, we cannot explain the poorer postmerger performance of the all-equity acquirers on the basis of

their being larger than the all-cash acquirers. Second, our use of postmerger parameters (α and β) should capture, at least in part, changes in a firm's return-generating process due to an increase in size as of the merger date. (See note 11, above.)

References

Asquith, Paul, R. Bruner, F. Mullins. 1986. Merger returns and the form of financing, photocopy. Boston: Harvard Business School, October.

Auerbach, A. J. 1979. Wealth maximization and the cost of capital. *Quarterly Journal of Economics* 93: 443–46.

Auerbach, A. J., and D. Reishus. 1987. The effect of taxation on the merger decision, photocopy. Cambridge, Mass.: National Bureau of Economic Research.

Brown, S. J., and J. B. Warner. 1980. Measuring security price performance. *Journal of Financial Economics* 8: 205–58.

————. 1985. Using daily stock returns: The case of event studies. *Journal of Financial Economics* 14: 3–31.

Brown, S. J., and M. Weinstein. 1985. Derived factors in event studies. *Journal of Financial Economics* 14: 491–6.

Callison, J. Elizabeth. 1987. An analysis of bid premiums and acquisition offers for *Forbes* 500 firms: 1979–83, Ph. D. dissertation. Philadelphia: University of Pennsylvania.

The Capital Changes Reporter. Chicago: Commerce Clearing House.

Carleton, W., D. Guilkey, R. Harris, and J. Stewart. 1983. An empirical analysis of the role of the medium of exchange in mergers. *Journal of Finance* 38: 813–26.

Dimson, E. 1979. Risk measurement when shares are subject to infrequent trading. *Journal of Financial Economics* 7: 197–226.

Dimson, E., and P. Marsh. 1983. The stability of U.K. risk measures and the problem of thin trading. *Journal of Finance* 38: 735–83.

————. 1986. Event study methodologies and the size effect: The case of U.K. press recommendations. *Journal of Financial Economics* 17: 113–42.

Dodd, P., and R. Ruback. 1977. Tender offers and stockholder returns: An empirical analysis. *Journal of Financial Economics* 5: 351–74.

Eckbo, E., and H. Langohr. 1986. Disclosure regulations and determinants of takeover premiums, working paper. Los Angeles: University of California, May.

Edwards, S. J., and M. J. Keen. 1985. Taxation. investment and marginal Q. *Review of Economic Studies* 52: 665–79.

Fama, E., L. Fisher, M. C. Jensen, and R. Roll. 1969. The adjustment of stock prices to new information. *International Economic Review* 10: 1–21.

Fishman M. J. 1986. Pre-emptive bidding and the role of the medium of exchange in acquisitions, photocopy. Evanston, Ill.: Northwestern University, July.

Franks, J., and R. Harris, 1986a. Shareholder wealth effects of corporate takeovers: The U.K. experience, 1955–85, working paper. London: London Business School; Chapel Hill: University of North Carolina; November.

———. 1986b. The role of the Mergers and Monopolies Commission in merger policy. *Oxford Review of Economic Policy* 2: 58–78.

Grinblatt, M., and S. Titman. 1987. A comparison of measures of abnormal performance on a sample of monthly mutual fund returns, photocopy. Los Angeles: University of California, February.

Grossman, S. J., and O. D. Hart. 1982. Corporate financial structure and managerial incentives. In *The economics of information and uncertainty,* ed. J. McCall, 107–40. Chicago: University of Chicago Press.

Hansen, R. G. 1984. Informational asymmetry and the means of payment in auctions, working paper. Hanover, N.H.: Amos Tuck School, Dartmouth College.

Hansen, R. G. 1987. A theory for the choice of exchange medium in mergers and acquisitions. *Journal of Business* 60: 75–95.

Heinkel, R., and E. Schwartz. 1985. Rights versus underwritten offerings: An asymmetric information approach. *Journal of Finance* 41: 1–18.

Jensen, M. C. 1986. Agency costs of free cash flow, corporate finance and takeovers. *American Economic Review* 75: 323–29.

Jensen, M. C., and R. Ruback. 1983. The market for corporate control: The scientific evidence. *Journal of Financial Economics* 11: 5–50.

King, M. A. 1977. *Public policy and the corporation.* London: Chapman and Hill.

———. 1986. Takeovers, taxes and the stock market, photocopy. London: London School of Economics.

Loderer, C.F., and D. Mauer. 1986. Acquiring firms in corporate mergers: The post merger performance, photocopy. West Lafayette, Ind.: Purdue University.

Marsh, P. 1979. Equity rights issues and the efficiency of the U.K. stock market. *Journal of Finance* 34: 839–62.

———. 1982. The choice between equity and debt: An empirical study. *Journal of Finance* 37: 121–44.

Mikkelson, W., and R. Ruback. 1985. An empirical study of the inter-firm equity investment process. *Journal of Financial Economics* 14: 523–54.

———. 1986. Targeted repurchases and common stock returns, working paper 1707–85. Cambridge: Sloan School of Management, Massachusetts Institute of Technology.

Miller, M., and K. Rock. 1985. Dividend policy under asymmetric information. *Journal of Finance* 40: 1031–51.

Myers, S. C. 1984. The capital structure puzzle. *Journal of Finance* 39: 575–92.

Myers, S. C., and N. S. Majluf. 1984. Corporate financing and investment decisions when firms have information that investors do not have. *Journal of Financial Economics* 13: 187–222.

Niden, C. 1986. The role of taxes in corporate acquisitions: Effects on premium and type of consideration, photocopy. Chicago: University of Chicago.

Roll, R. 1986. The hubris hypothesis of corporate takeovers. *Journal of Business* 59: 197–216.

Shoven, J. B., and L. B. Simon. 1987. Share repurchases and acquisitions: An analysis of which firms participate, working paper. Cambridge, Mass.: National Bureau of Economic Research.

Smith, C., Jr. 1986. Investment banking and capital acquisition process. *Journal of Financial Economics* 15: 3–29.

Wansley, J., W. Lane, and H. Yang. 1983. Abnormal returns to acquiring firms by type of acquisition and method of payment. *Financial Management* 12: 16–22.

259   Means of Payment in Takeovers

Comment   Artur Raviv

Franks, Harris, and Mayer document several very interesting empirical regularities in the means of payment offered in takeovers. The most striking results are:

1. The percentage of all-cash offers in the United States increased over time, from none in 1955–59 to 58 percent in 1980–84. At the same time, all-equity offers declined from 76 percent to 22 percent.
2. The United Kingdom demonstrated the reverse pattern of changes over those years.
3. About one-sixth of the acquisitions in the sample were through a tender offer. Nontender, or "friendly," acquisitions are those obtained by an approving board of directors. The appreciation to the targets of tender offers was higher than to those in nontender acquisitions.

This paper can be best viewed as a fact-finding mission. Although the authors survey several propositions that might explain the empirical regularities, no simple theory can account for all the facts simultaneously. I would find it much easier to evaluate the results if a coherent model had been constructed and then tested by the empirical results. Obviously, this would not be an easy task since the problem attacked by the authors is at the core of the unsolved problems in corporate finance: capital structure, taxation, and corporate control.

In the remainder of my comments I would like to propose an alternative model, which in my view is capable of explaining many of the results given by the authors. This model has been developed by Michael Fishman in a working paper entitled "Preemptive Bidding and the Role of the Medium of Exchange in Acquisitions." Here the key economic difference between a cash offer and an offer of securities is that the value of a cash offer is independent of the future profitability of the acquired target, while the value of a securities offer is not. The willingness to offer or accept a given package of securities may indicate something about the information held by the bidder and the target. In particular, if target managers possess private information regarding the profitability of their firm, they will want to use this information in making their decisions whether to accept a securities offer since the value of this offer depends on the future profitability of the target. Thus, securities offers are a means of making an offer contingent on the target's information. In Fishman's model a bidder learns about the profitability of the target, and if his valuation is high, makes a high, *preemptive* bid in order to eliminate potential competition. This bid is in the form of cash. If the bidder's

Artur Raviv is the Harold L. Stuart Professor of Finance and Managerial Economics at the J. L. Kellogg Graduate School of Management, Northwestern University.

valuation is lower, he will make a securities offer, which will induce an efficient accept/reject decision on the part of the target but may also induce competitors to join the bidding for the target.

The results that can be obtained from such a model are:

1. Cash offers are more frequent in tender offers than in nontender offers. In tender offers target managers do not use their information and therefore there is no need for equity payment. Equity is used in the case of nontender offers.
2. Cash offers are higher on average than equity offers. Equity signals lower value and induces competition.
3. The postmerger performance of the bidder, if the initial offer is for cash, is better than if the initial offer is for equity.
4. The postmerger performance for tender offers (which tend to be for cash) is better than that for nontender offers (which tend to be for equity).

These results are consistent with the Franks, Harris, and Mayer evidence. Additional results implied by Fishman's model and which could be tested by the authors are:

1. Competing bidders appear more frequently in equity offers than in cash offers.
2. Target management will more frequently reject an equity offer than a cash offer.
3. Rejecting an equity offer will result in a reduction in the value of the target's shares, since it indicates that the target's managers believe the target is not as valuable now as it was.

It would be interesting to find out whether these results can be supported by the data the authors have analyzed.

Comment   Richard S. Ruback

Empirical evidence shows that the benefits of takeovers to the target's shareholders are large in mergers and even larger in tender offers. Although mergers and tender offers are substitutes, there are some general differences in the two types of takeover methods:

	Tender Offers	Mergers
Process	Through shares	Through management
Perception	Hostile	Negotiated
Payment	Cash	Stock

Richard S. Ruback is associate professor of finance at the Alfred P. Sloan School of Management, Massachusetts Institute of Technology; a visiting associate professor at the Harvard Business School; and a research associate of the National Bureau of Economic Research.

261 Means of Payment in Takeovers

In Jensen and Ruback (1983) we focused on the process difference to explain the larger measured average returns in tender offers than in mergers. Truncation bias could explain the higher *measured* average premiums in tender offers. Low-value merger bids that are rejected by managers do not become hostile tenders because it is more costly to persuade shareholders in hostile deals than in negotiated deals and because hostile deals are more expensive.

Franks, Harris, and Mayer emphasize the payment differences. In particular, they try to use theories of capital structure choice and theories of takeovers simultaneously.

The good part of this approach is that different takeovers do seem to involve different financing schemes, so that the measured effects of takeovers may include factors that are caused purely by the financial restructurings involved.

The bad part of this approach is that it layers ignorance on confusion. As a corporate finance person who works in both areas, I am afraid this is not a pleasant admission. Unfortunately, we have no accepted theory of the choice of takeover method. In contrast, we have many theories about capital structure choice. But none has survived even simple tests. And the interrelations among the many theories are obscure at best. Saying that the state of the art in capital structure choice is confused would be generous.

It is hard to fault the authors of this paper for the confusion of the theory. My complaint is *not* that the authors fail to develop a new theory of capital structure and merger choice. I am mentioning the lack of theory at the outset because it locates and defines what we learn from the authors. Their paper does not really test any particular theory. Instead, it makes perhaps a bigger contribution by providing numerous interesting facts.

The magnitude of the data collection and integration in this paper is huge and competently done. The sample contains merger and tender offer data for both the United States and the United Kindgom over the years 1955–85, including about 2,000 observations.

The facts that I find most interesting are in table 8.7. There, in panel B, the event month abnormal returns are:

Cash tenders	28%	N = 135
Cash nontenders	24%	N = 340
Equity tenders	20%	N = 29
Equity mergers	11%	N = 548

This ranking suggests that both the type of offer and the medium of exchange are important. The regression tests provide an affirmative statistical test of this proposition.

I cannot resist the temptation to explain the rankings. My hypothesis hinges on asymmetric information. Accept the Jensen and Ruback view that the market for corporate control involves competition between management teams for the rights to manage corporate resources. You would then expect most takeovers to be proxy fights.[1] But this is not true. Why? Because these contests require very "management smart" investors—investors that can evaluate the plans of competing management teams. Stockholders are unlikely to have the expertise or incentives to evaluate the plans accurately. Indeed, clever stockholders are efficient risk bearers: They hold a well-diversified portfolio and cannot remember the names of the firms in the portfolio, never mind how they should be managed.

What's a poor potential competing manager to do? Get somebody smarter to make the decision or simplify the decision. If target managers are cooperative, then a merger is more likely. And the range of payment types possible expands because the target managers certify to the shareholders that the takeover is a good deal.

But suppose the target management decides to oppose the merger. Also assume the deal is worthwhile to the bidder even if it becomes hostile. Then the offer has to be simplified. Bidders should use securities that are easy to value—like cash.

In short, the same forces that make some takeovers mergers instead of tender offers also make most tender offers cash transactions and most mergers stock transactions. This means that, as with any set of correlated variables, the attribution of results to particular variables is very risky.

The facts that confuse me the most are in table 8.8. It shows that there were significant negative abnormal returns in the two years following the offer. The returns were about -17 percent in the United States. I have been confused about this issue because we included a table of postmerger performance in Jensen and Ruback (1983) that had similar results. At the time I was convinced the results were due to selection bias or some simple statistical malfunction. Franks, Harris, and Mayer use almost all mergers, and so the selection bias argument now seems less plausible. They also use different specifications and get similar results. Reluctantly, I think we have to accept this result— significant negative returns over the two years following a merger—as a fact.

Accepting the fact does not mean I have to accept the explanation given. I do not believe there is an explanation for this phenomenon that is consistent with market prices, including the information in the *Wall Street Journal*. We finance folks call it semistrong market efficiency. Economists use the label rational expectations. Whatever you call it, this finding can be used to make money. I can tell when a merger

1. This conceptual framework is explained in more detail in Ruback (1984).

263   Means of Payment in Takeovers

is completed. I can sell short. That gives me supernormal returns. And
that violates market efficiency.

References

Jensen, Michael C., and Richard S. Ruback. 1983. The market for corporate
    control: The scientific evidence. *Journal of Financial Economics* 11(1-4): 5–
    50.
Ruback, Richard S. 1984. An economic view of the market for corporate
    control. *Delaware Journal of Corporate Law* 9 (3): 613–25.

11

Are Acquiring-Firm Shareholders Better Off after an Acquisition?

ELLEN B. MAGENHEIM
DENNIS C. MUELLER

Out of the massive amount of research on acquisitions that has been conducted over the past 20 years, some consensus on major issues has emerged. But perhaps surprisingly, several key issues remain in dispute. On the positive side, early theoretical contributions showed that diversification through mergers was an inefficient method for spreading risks (Levy and Sarnat, 1970; Smith, 1970; Azzi, 1978), and empirical findings have corroborated this result (Smith and Schreiner, 1969; Mason and Goudzwaard, 1976). All observers have found that shareholders of acquired companies enjoy substantial immediate gains from the acquisitions, and no disagreement exists on this point. But the pattern of results with respect to the returns to acquiring-firm shareholders has been varied. One study claims to find positive gains; another records negative returns. Nor do reviewers of this literature reach a consensus (e.g., compare Mueller, 1977, 1980; Scherer, 1980, pp. 138–141; Halpern, 1983; Jensen and Ruback, 1983).

This lack of consensus carries over into the explanations for why acquisitions occur. One group of observers sees acquisitions as a means for improving the allocation of assets by transferring assets to more capable management or achieving other synergistic gains from the transfer of control (Manne, 1965; Mandelker, 1974; Dodd and Ruback, 1977). Adherents to this view claim that the existing evidence indicates that acquiring-firm shareholders are slightly better off or, at minimum, no worse off as a result of acquisitions (Halpern, 1983; Jensen and Ruback, 1983).

Although this interpretation of the evidence, if valid, would appear to vindicate a liberal antimerger policy (acquired-firm shareholders are better off; acquiring-firm shareholders are not worse off), it still raises fundamental questions about the theory of the firm and the market for corporate control, which feed back onto the broader policy issues. Acquired-firm managers may sometimes be unwilling partners to an acquisition, as in a hostile takeover, but acquiring-firm managers need never be. Why do the latter enter so readily into the market for corporate control, given its well-known large risks and apparently modest returns?

Several observers have answered this question by hypothesizing that managers undertake acquisitions which increase their utility but do not necessarily increase shareholder wealth (Mueller, 1969; Firth, 1980; Amihud and Lev, 1981; Greer, 1984). To the extent that these hypotheses are valid, the possibility must be entertained that acquisitions neither enhance acquiring-firm shareholder wealth nor confer broader social benefits. Thus, the issue of what the gains to acquiring-firm shareholders are is central to both the theory of the firm and public policy regarding acquisitions.

For this reason, the seemingly contradictory results regarding the effects of acqui-

172   Evidence on the Gains from Mergers and Takeovers

sitions on acquiring-firm shareholders and the lack of consensus among observers of what the results signify are disconcerting. It is the thesis of this paper that disagreement regarding the impact of acquisitions on acquiring-firm shareholders stems in part from the different methodologies individual studies have used. Measures of the impact of an acquisition on acquiring-firm shareholders are quite sensitive to the choice of methodology. In effect, authors have been asking different questions about the performance of acquiring-firm shares and, not surprisingly, have come up with different answers. We shall show that when one attempts to ask the same question in each study, the results turn out to be far more consistent than was heretofore apparent.

To do so, we reexamine the basic methodology used to measure the effects of acquisitions, placing particular emphasis on the pattern of returns to acquiring-firm shareholders before and after the acquisition (the first section). In the second section, we demonstrate the sensitivity of the results to the choice of methodology, i.e., to the particular question asked, using data for 78 mergers and takeovers in the years 1976 to 1981. In the light of the methodological issues raised in the first two sections, we reexamine the results of several published studies in the third section. Conclusions follow.

METHODOLOGICAL ISSUES IN
MEASURING THE EFFECTS OF
ACQUISITIONS

The basic assumption underlying the use of stock market data to estimate the effects of acquisitions is, of course, that share prices reflect future profit and dividend streams, and that any changes in future profit and dividend streams an acquisition is expected to bring about are reflected in changes in the prices and returns of the company's shares. Granting this assumption, one can test for the *expected* effect of an acquistion on future profit and dividend streams by measuring the change in returns to acquiring-company shareholders accompanying an acquisition. To measure such a change, two questions must be answered: When is the effect of the acquisition on stockholder returns to be measured? How is the effect of the acquisition separated from other coterminous events that affect stockholder returns?

The first question could be easily resolved if all of the relevant information regarding an acquisition were to become public on the day the acquisition is announced and the market could be assumed to adjust fully in that day to the new information. But news of an acquisition is known to leak into the market prior to the first public announcement, and it is unrealistic to assume that the market is capable of predicting the full future consequences of an acquisition immediately upon learning of it. The latter point is a key part of our critique of the existing literature and requires some elaboration.

Robert Shiller (1981) has shown that swings in stock market prices exceed by factors of five and more those which should have occurred given the actual movements in dividend streams that occur. In a bull market, prices rise by far more than subsequent increases in dividends will warrant; in a bear market, they fall too far. The market has historically continually shifted from being too optimistic in bull markets to being too pessimistic in bear markets. Shiller (1984, 1986) hypothesizes that the behavior of individuals in the stock market is best explained through the psychology of fads and bandwagon movements.

Shiller's findings and his explanation of them are particularly relevant to the literature on mergers and takeovers, since it is well known that acquisition activity has been highly correlated with stock market activity.[1] Mergers and takeovers have occured most frequently at times when stock market prices are rising and the market in general is known to be overly optimistic about the future performance of companies. Since acquisition and stock market activity seem to respond to the same underlying economic environment and psychological factors (Geroski, 1984), it is reasonable to suppose, or at least prudent to allow for the possibility, that the stock market might be overly optimistic in its evaluation of acquisitions at the time they are first announced. Shiller's results, combined with the positive correlation of acquisition and stock market activity, suggest the importance of tracing the effects of an acquisition's announcement on a stock's price over a long enough period to ensure that any changes in stock prices are an unbiased reflection of the future effect of the acquisition on profits and dividends.

The second conceptual issue to be resolved is the separation of the effects of the acquisition from other coterminous events, i.e., the prediction of what the return on the firm's shares would have been in the absence of the acquistion, over whatever period is chosen to record this event. The counterfactual can never, of course, be truly predicted. Three approximations have been employed in the literature: (1) to assume the firm's returns postevent would have been the same as its returns preevent in the absence of the acquisition, (2) to select a control group and assume the firm's returns postevent would have been the same as those of the control group firm(s), or (3) a combination of (1) and (2), i.e., to assume that the change in returns of the acquiring firm following the acquisition's announcement would have been the same as the change in returns for the control group firm(s) for the same time period. The difference between this predicted change and the change actually observed is attributed to the acquisition. The third method is obviously the best. If one simply compares a firm's postevent performance to its preevent performance, one ignores all of the other events that may be occurring coterminously with the acquisition and affecting its returns. But if one predicts a firm's returns in the postevent period entirely from the control group (method 2) one ignores any systematic difference between the merging firm(s) and the control group that may exist. This latter point proves to be very important because, as we shall see, there are sizable differences between the performance of acquiring firms and the usually employed control groups over the preevent period.

If all events other than the acquisition that affect a firm's returns have the same effect on the firm's control group, then one should be able to isolate the effect of an acquisition by predicting the *change* in returns for the acquiring firm from the observed change in returns for the control group firms, and calculating the difference between observed and predicted returns as the effect of the acquisition. The most frequently employed control group in acquisition-stockholder returns studies is the market portfolio, the returns on all securities each weighted by its aggregate market value.

More formally, the returns for a given firm i are predicted from the characteristic line

$$E\left(R_i\right) = R_f + \beta_i \left[E\left(R_m\right) - R_f\right] \quad (11.1)$$

where $E(R_i)$ and $E(R_m)$ are the expected returns for firm i and the market portfolio, respectively, R_f is the return on a riskless $(0 = \beta)$ asset, and β_i is the covariance of i's returns with the market portfolio divided by the variance of the market portfolio. Equation (11.1) is one of the central results of the capital asset pricing model (CAPM). It states that the return on any firm i's shares, R_i, varies directly with the return on the portfolio of all shares, R_m, and thus that changes in R_i can be predicted from changes in R_m if β_i is unchanged.[2] The β_i term can be estimated from a time-series regression of R_{it} on R_{mt} or, as is frequently done, from a regression of $(R_{it} - R_{ft})$ on $(R_{mt} - R_{ft})$. By Equation (11.1), the intercept of this equation should equal zero. But if the intercept is not constrained to equal zero, regressions of the following sort typically yield nonzero estimates of $\hat{\alpha}_i$:

$$\begin{aligned}(R_{it} - R_{ft}) \\ = \hat{\alpha}_i + \hat{\beta}_i \left(R_{mt} - R_{ft}\right) + e_{it} \quad (11.2)\end{aligned}$$

Now $\hat{\alpha}_i$ is basically the average residual from the characteristic equation (11.1) for firm i implied by the CAPM. As such, it is a measure of the performance of the company over the sample period used to estimate $\hat{\beta}_i$ (Jensen, 1969), and has been so used in some acquisition studies (e.g., Wes-

174   Evidence on the Gains from Mergers and Takeovers

ton, Smith, and Shrieves, 1972). A company with $\hat{\alpha}_i > 0$ has on average earned higher returns than are predicted by the CAPM. If $\hat{\beta}_i$ were not affected by the acquisition, one way to estimate the effects of the acquisition would be to estimate $\hat{\alpha}_i$ from data from before the acquisition and again from data following its announcement. The *change* in $\hat{\alpha}_i$ between the two periods would then be an estimate of the effect of the acquisition on firm i's returns assuming all other effects are captured through the movement of $(R_{mt} - R_{ft})$ over the two periods. Alternatively, one can estimate (11.2) by using preevent data, and then use the $\hat{\alpha}_i$ and $\hat{\beta}_i$ estimated from the preevent data to predict R_{it} from the postevent R_{mt} and R_{ft}. The difference between the actual and predicted R_{it} based on the preevent $\hat{\alpha}_i$ and $\hat{\beta}_i$ is a second measure of the effect of the acquisition on shareholder returns.

Both $\hat{\alpha}_i$ and $\hat{\beta}_i$ are likely to vary with the choice of time period used to estimate them. If this variation is random, measures of the effects of acquisitions are not biased by the choice of time period for estimating $\hat{\alpha}_i$ and $\hat{\beta}_i$, although the power of the tests is weakened. But there is considerable evidence, reviewed later, that acquiring firms earn substantial, positive abnormal returns over a period running anywhere from 18 to 66 months prior to the acquisition announcements. Given this evidence, the estimates one obtains of the effects of acquisitions are sensitive to how the preevent data are treated when estimating $\hat{\alpha}_i$ and $\hat{\beta}_i$. Studies differ widely as to how they treat the preevent period when estimating the $\hat{\alpha}_i$ and $\hat{\beta}_i$ used in predicting postevent performance, and this difference will be shown to have a significant influence on one's evaluation of the impact of the acquisition on stockholder returns.

Although substantial excess returns for acquiring firms have been estimated over prolonged preevent periods in several studies, little attention has been paid to these returns. Perhaps the neglect of the returns to acquiring firms prior to acquisitions can be explained by the prevailing view among many of those working in this area that it is deficiencies in the *acquired*

firm's performance that precipitate acquisitions. But if managers undertake acquisitions which worsen the performance of their companies' shares, it is logical to assume that they would choose to announce the acquisitions at times when the performance of their shares is above average. Also, the above-normal return performance of acquiring-firm shares prior to acquisitions may signal above-normal profit flows which can be used to finance the acquisitions. Thus, the above-normal performance of acquiring firms' shares over sustained intervals prior to their making an acquisition may explain why these particular firms' managements have chosen to make an acquisition at these particular points in time. Whether or not this conjecture regarding casuality is correct, it seems obvious that one should take into account this preevent performance of the acquiring firms when measuring the change in performance the acquisitions bring about.

We face now three conceptual problems: (1) How does one pinpoint the first arrival of information concerning the acquisition to the market? (2) Over what period should the preevent performance of the firm be measured to determine the change in performance caused by the acquisition? (3) How long a period after this event should one allow to measure the full effect of the acquisition on the acquiring firm's returns?

Somewhat surprisingly, the first question is the easiest to answer. While acquisition announcements do not seem to have had a large, systematic impact on acquiring-firm share prices, they have a predictable and large positive impact on acquired-firm share prices owing to the substantial premiums offered. An individual with nonpublic information of an acquisition will make a more certain and substantial gain by purchasing the shares of the to-be-acquired firm. Thus, the date of the first impact of the acquisition on firm share prices can be determined by examining the share price performance of the acquired firm. The month (day) in which its returns begin the sustained rise that culminates in the acquisition can be taken to be the point in time at which knowledge of the acquisition reaches the market. Most studies seem to indicate that information of an acquisition reaches the market in the month of the announcement or the month before. No study which we have seen presents evidence suggesting that information of the acquisition reaches the market more than four months prior to its announcement. Thus, we should expect to see the effects of acquisitions on acquiring-firm share prices commencing over a short time interval prior to the announcement month.

The question of what preevent period should be used against which to measure postevent performance is obviously somewhat arbitrary. It seems to us more reasonable to judge the effect of an acquisition against the period immediately preceding the market's learning of the acquisition than against a period some distance removed, since the acquiring firm's performance over the three preceding years is more relevant than over the interval four to six years before the acquisition, if one wishes to measure the *change* in performance caused by the acquisition.

If Equation (11.2) estimated on preevent data is used to predict post-acquisition performance, then an improvement in performance upon the market's obtaining information of an acquisition should appear as an upward movement in the residuals one obtains when preevent estimates of $\hat{\alpha}_i$ and $\hat{\beta}_i$ are used to predict postevent performance. Should one observe a systematic rise (fall) in the cumulative residuals from (11.1) commencing around the time of the acquisition, one might reasonably attribute this movement to the acquisition. As long as the cumulative residuals continue the rise (fall), which commenced with the acquisition, one can assume that the market is continuing to reevaluate the expected effects of the acquisition on the acquiring firm's performance. When the rise (fall) stops, the adjustment process is complete.

On the other hand, the market may reevaluate a firm's prospects as a consequence of an acquisition at almost any point in time following its announcement at which new information is received (e.g., a manager leaves; a contract is lost). If all subsequent movements in share prices not caused by the acquisition are assumed to

be random, then a prudent strategy for ensuring that all possible effects on share prices caused by the acquisition are captured is to measure the acquiring firm's postevent performance over as long a period as possible. Here again, as we shall show, one's interpretation of the effects of an acquisition is in some cases sensitive to just how long an interval one allows the market to complete its evaluation after the acquisition.

ESTIMATES OF THE EFFECTS OF ACQUISITIONS ON THE PERFORMANCE OF A SAMPLE OF ACQUIRING FIRMS

In this section, we examine the implications of the methodological issues just discussed for a specific sample of acquiring firms. A description of the sample is presented, and the techniques for measuring returns are discussed. Particular emphasis is placed on the sensitivity of the conclusions to the choice of a time period for measuring the market model, and the length of time over which postevent returns are measured.

Description of the Sample

The sample of 78 acquiring firms is composed of companies completing takeovers valued at $15 million or more. Of the 78 acquiring firms, 51 entered into mergers and 26 into tender offers.[3] All of the firms are listed on the New York or American Stock Exchanges. To ensure data availability, only firms listed on Price-Dividend-Earnings (PDE) tapes are included. The sample period begins in 1976. To ensure three full years of postevent data, we specify 1981 as the end of the sample period. Announcement and completion dates and the mode of acquisition in each case were checked in the *Wall Street Journal*.

These acquisitions span a more recent time period than do samples previously analyzed. We describe here some characteristics of this sample. The distribution of initial bid announcements is reported in Table 11.1. These bids were made within an active market for acquisitions.[4] The

176   Evidence on the Gains from Mergers and Takeovers

Table 11.1 Distribution of Initial
Announcement of Acquisition Bid by Year

Year	Number of Acquisition Bids
1976	9
1977	9
1978	21
1979	18
1980	7
1981	14

$$R_{it} = \alpha_i + \beta_i R_{mt} + e_{it} \qquad (11.3)$$

where

R_{it} = return on stock i at time t

R_{mt} = return on the market portfolio at time t

e_{it} = homoscedastic, normally distributed, serially uncorrelated, zero-mean-error term with variance $\hat{\sigma}(\hat{e}_{it})$

The coefficient on R_{mt}, β_i, measures the sensitivity of the ith firm's return to fluctuations in the market index. The intercept measures the risk-free return plus the average abnormal performance of the firm over the sample period used to estimate (11.3). The error e_{it} measures that part of R_{it} which is due to neither movements in the return on the market portfolio nor to the firm's average abnormal return.

level of acquisition activity intensified in the mid 1970s following a fairly placid period; the end of the sample period coincides with a leveling off in the number of transactions recorded (W. T. Grimm, 1984). This wave of activity coincides with a periodically depressed stock market which makes it an anomaly among acquisition waves.

On average, 16 weeks elapsed between the bid announcement and completion of the transition; the median level is 13 weeks. The length of the interval ranges from 1 week or less in three cases to more than 80 weeks in two cases. The average ratio of the preevent equity value of acquiring to acquired firm is 3.77. The average percentage premium over stock value paid by sample firms is 81%, and the average value of the premium paid to acquired-firm shareholders is $191.58 million.

Each R_{it} is calculated from monthly data taken from the PDE tapes, with stock prices adjusted for splits and dividends. The New York Stock Exchange equally weighted index is used as a proxy for the market portfolio. Monthly residuals for each firm i are calculated as $\hat{e}_{it} = R_{it} - \hat{R}_{it}$. From these monthly residuals for each firm, average abnormal returns are calculated for each time t:

$$AR_t = \sum_{i=1}^{I} \frac{\hat{e}_{it}}{I}$$

where I is the total number of firms and $t = 0$ is the event date, i.e., the month of the initial announcement. This yields, for each time period, a measure of the average divergence between actual and forecast returns, adjusted for each firm's normal level of performance and for marketwide fluctuations. Cumulated average abnormal returns are then calculated as

$$CAR_{xy} = \sum_{t=x}^{y} AR_t$$

where x and y are the start and end dates of the cumulation period. To test the statistical significance of the average and cumulative average abnormal returns, we

Methodology for Measuring Abnormal Returns

To measure the effect of acquisitions on stock price returns, we follow the Fama, Fisher, Jensen, and Roll (1969) event study technique. This technique relies on the use of the market portfolio as a control group to capture the effect of marketwide fluctuations in stock prices. Any remaining unexplained abnormal performance can be attributed to the effect of a specific event—in this case, an acquisition bid announcement.

We estimated the following market model using ordinary least-squares regression.[5]

construct a test statistic following the commonly used procedure (Linn and Mc-
Connell, 1983; Malatesta, 1983).

Results

In this section, the sensitivity of conclusions regarding the effect of acquisitions on
firm returns to the time period used to estimate the market model coefficients and
the length of the postevent measurement
period is shown. We first review what we
define as our basic case; then we show how
results change with the choice of different
estimation periods. To understand these
changes more fully, we examine how $\hat{\alpha}$, the
measure of the firm's abnormal perfor-
mance over the estimation period, varies
with the choice of time period.

To allow for information reaching the
market prior to an acquisition's announcement, all preevent periods are ended four
months prior to the announcement month,
an interval which seems prudent on the
basis of existing studies (see the third section). Consistent with previous research,
we find significant positive gains being
earned in the two years preceding the
event. During the period [−24, −4] acquirers earn returns that are 18.4% in excess of the expected returns based on their
performance over the [−60, −25] period
(Table 11.2). These abnormal returns are
significant at the .05 level. The pattern of
returns for each firm was examined over
this preevent period. Of the 78 firms, 71
experienced a preevent upward trend in
abnormal returns which, on average, began
at $t = -33$. For the 48 merging firms,
this upward trend began, on average, at
$t = -29$; for 21 firms making tender offers
the upward movement begins, on average,
at $t = -36$.

The returns for the [−3, −1] period,
measured by using coefficients estimated
from [−60, −4], introduce a trend of negative but insignificant returns that continues for the two years following the event.
In the third postevent year, however, significant losses of −9% occur. A pattern
emerges in which acquirers earn substantial positive gains until shortly before the

Table 11.2 Cumulative Average Abnormal
Returns: All Sample Firms

Forecast Period	Estimation Period	
	[−60, −25]	[−60, −4]
[−24, −4]	.1839 (3.4161)[a]	
[−3, −1]	—	−.0148 (−.5683)
[0]	—	.0019 (−.3386)
[1, 6]	—	−.0336 (−1.273)
[7, 12]	—	−.0121 (−.6261)
[13, 24]	—	−.0096 (−.3403)
[25, 36]	—	−.0883 (−.2115)
[−3, 36]	—	−.1565 (−1.2364)

[a]The numbers in parentheses are the test statistics which are
distributed standard normal.

event, following which returns begin to
drop.

Breaking the full sample down by type of
transaction, we see similar patterns (Table
11.3). Firms engaging in tender offers and
mergers earn large positive gains prior to
the event; the level ranges from 28% for the
former group to 12.7% for the latter.
Around the event month and over the next
three years, a mixed pattern is observed.
Bidders in tender offers experience a sharp
drop in returns in the second year after the
event, a sharp rise in the third year. In the
third year, [24, 36], acquiring firms in
mergers exhibit a significant decline in returns. Despite these differences, we confine
most of our attention to the combined
sample of 78 acquisitions, since we do not
have enough observations on tender offers
to undertake a meaningful separate analysis for this group. For both groups of acquiring firms the pattern emerges that the
preevent period is one of positive abnormal performance; returns in the postevent
period reflect a lower level of performance.

The high performance in the three years

178   Evidence on the Gains from Mergers and Takeovers

Table 11.3 Cumulative Average Abnormal Returns by Mode of Acquisition

| | Estimation Period | | | |
| | [−60, −25] | | [−60, −4] | |
Forecast Period	Mergers	Tender Offers	Mergers	Tender Offers
[−24, −4]	.1271 (1.9472)[a]	.2804 (2.6400)	—	—
[−3, −1]	—	—	−.0300 (−.9918)	.0122 (.3078)
[0]	—	—	−.0037 (−.6769)	.0138 (.4500)
[1, 6]	—	—	−.0495 (−1.3182)	.0022 (−.1339)
[7, 12]	—	—	−.0252 (−.6257)	.0209 (.0968)
[13, 24]	—	—	.0281 (1.0110)	−.0908 (−1.0091)
[25, 36]	—	—	−.1971 (−3.709)	.1309 (1.7843)
[−3, 36]	—	—	−.2774 (−2.6039)	.0892 (.5633)

[a]The numbers in parentheses are the test statistics which are distributed standard normal.

prior to the event suggests that the treatment of this period in estimation of the market model coefficients may significantly affect the measurement of abnormal returns. Since the intercept measures firm performance over the estimation period, an intercept calculated from this period of above-normal performance is larger than if calculated from a lower-performance period. With a higher benchmark the residuals calculated relative to this "normal" performance level are lower.

Table 11.4 provides evidence of how the performance benchmark embodied in $\hat{\alpha}_i$ varies with differences in the estimation period. The first estimate of mean $\hat{\alpha}$ is

Table 11.4 Average Intercepts by Estimation Period, All 78 Firms

Estimation Period	Mean $\hat{\alpha}$	$\hat{\sigma}_{\hat{\alpha}}$
[−60, −25]	.0091	.0150
[−60, −4]	.0134	.0127
[−36, −4]	.0181	.0189
[−3, 36]	.0107	.0147
[4, 36]	.0080	.0300

.0091, based on [−60, −25]. It is small relative to the estimate of .0134 calculated from the period [−60, −4], reflecting the upward trend in returns that begins approximately three years prior to the event. While the first estimation period stops short of much of the rise in returns, the second period captures most of it. The estimates from [−36, −4] are from a period of almost exclusively higher returns and are much larger. The mean $\hat{\alpha}$ from [−36, −4] is double that estimated over [−60, −25]. The measures in the last two rows are based largely on the postevent periods over which lower average returns are observed. The mean $\hat{\alpha}$ from [−36, −4] is more than double that of the postevent period [4, 36].

These differences in $\hat{\alpha}$ lead one to expect sizable differences in the residuals from the market model depending on the choice of estimation period, and one observes them (Table 11.5). The cumulative residuals are uniformly lower when measured against the last 33 months of the preevent period [−36, −4] than when measured against the last 57 months [−60, −4]. Acquiring-

Table 11.5 Cumulative Average Abnormal Returns Based on Selected
Estimation Periods: All Sample Firms

	Estimation Period		
Forecast Period	[−60, −4]	[−36, −4]	[13, 36]
[−3, −1]	−.0148 (−.5683)[a]	−.0298 (−.7743)	—
[0]	.0019 (−.3386)	−.0028 (−.4784)	—
[1, 6]	−.0336 (−1.2730)	−.0620 (−1.7100)	−.0175 (−.8249)
[7, 12]	−.0121 (−.6261)	−.0508 (−1.5890)	−.0146 (−.7386)
[1, 12]	−.0457 (−1.3429)	−.1128 (−2.3328)	−.0321 (−1.1057)
[13, 24]	−.0096 (−.3403)	−.0940 (−1.5520)	—
[25, 36]	−.0883 (−2.1150)	−.1826 (−4.5930)	—
[−3, 36]	−.1567 (−1.2464)	−.4221 (−4.9307)	—

[a]The numbers in parentheses are the test statistics which are distributed standard normal.

firm shareholders experienced an insignificant decline in returns of 15.67% over the period [−3, 36] as measured against the acquiring-firms' performance over [−60, −4]. They experienced a significant decline in returns almost three times greater than that when returns are measured against performance over [−36, −4].

Table 11.5 reveals that the choice of preevent period against which postevent performance is measured can have a significant effect on one's conclusions as to the change in performance following an acquisition. Several studies measure acquiring-firm postevent performance not against a preevent period, however, but against a subsequent postevent period.[7] But the average performance of acquiring firms in the postevent periods is systematically lower, as measured by $\hat{\alpha}$, as is evident in Table 11.4. Thus, use of postevent-period estimates of the market model yield systematically higher residuals than do preevent estimates. The third column of Table 11.5 reports the cumulative residuals for the first 12 postannouncement months measured against the acquiring companies' predicted performance from [13, 36]. They are an insignificant −3%. In contrast, if the acquiring companies' performance over these 12 months is measured against how they did over the last 33 months of the preevent period, one observes a significant 11% lower return in the first year after the announcements. The differences in estimates of postevent normal returns, depending on choice of base period against which performance is judged, are depicted in Figure 11.1.

Acquiring firms performed substantially better over the period [−24, −4] than they did over [−60, −25]. If we define the latter as normal, then acquiring firms exhibit above-normal performance starting between two and three years before the acquisition announcements, an interpretation which is consistent with that of other studies reviewed later. Assuming this preevent performance is above normal, then acquiring firms must eventually exhibit some worsening of performance postevent. At some point in time, the market must adjust fully to whatever it is that causes the above-normal performance. A key methodological issue in judging the ef-

180   Evidence on the Gains from Mergers and Takeovers

Figure 11.1. Month relative to event month. For all three cases, errors in [−24, −4] are calculated relative to performance in [−60, −25]. For case I, errors in [−3, 36] are based on [−60, −4]; for II, they are based on [−36, −4]. Case III is identical to case I for [−24, 0]; errors for [1, 12] are calculated relative to performance in [13, 36].

fects of acquisitions is the relationship between this point in time and the announcement month.

To begin to answer this question, one must explain why acquiring firms earn above-normal returns long *before* an acquisition. One possible explanation is that managers choose to acquire other companies when their own firms and their shares are doing relatively well. If this assumption is valid, the next question is whether the acquisitions are announced toward the beginning, middle, or end of these periods of above-normal performance. This is the kind of counterfactual question that never can be answered in a merger study. Our acquiring firms exhibit an upward trend in returns for roughly three years prior to the announcements. If the announcements come in the middle of the period of above-normal performance, then comparison of the first three postevent years with the last three preevent years would be appropriate.

Bradley and Jarrell's calculation of postevent performance in their comment (Chapter 15) effectively assumes that the announcements occur at the end of the period of above-normal performance. That the acquiring companies' period of above-normal performance just happens to end around the time the acquisitions are announced strikes us as an unlikely coincidence. Their estimate of the cumulative return to acquiring-firm shareholders over the three postevent years, which is almost identical to our estimate of −15.65% using the [−60, −4] interval as benchmark, we thus regard as an upper-bound measure of acquiring-firm performance. The −42.2% estimate using the interval [−36, −4] as benchmark, which implicitly assumes that the announcements occur in the middle of the above-normal performance period, is perhaps a reasonable lower bound.[8]

Our main results are summarized in Table 11.6, in which we again break out the merger and tender offer subsamples. If one assumes that the market's adjustment to news of an acquisition takes place entirely within the announcement month,

Table 11.6 Cumulative Average Abnormal Returns for Different Time Periods

Cumulation Period	Estimation Period [−60, −4]		
	All Firms	Mergers	Tender Offers
[0]	.0019	−.0037	.0138
	(−.3386)	(−.6769)	(.4500)
[−3, 6]	−.0465	−.0832	.0282
	(−1.4039)	(−1.7776)	(.2070)
[−3, 12]	−.0586	−.1084	.0491
	(−1.4932)	(−1.7885)	(.2229)
[−3, 24]	−.0682	−.0803	−.0417
	(−1.3513)	(−.6900)	(−.4920)
[−3, 36]	−.1565	−.2774	.0892
	(−1.2464)	(−2.6039)	(.5633)
	Estimation Period [−36, −4]		
[0]	−.0028	−.0070	.0065
	(−.4784)	(−.8527)	(.4637)
[−3, 6]	−.0946	−.1144	−.0514
	(−1.8993)	(−1.4770)	(−1.004)
[−3, 12]	−.1454	−.1692	−.0859
	(−2.4746)	(−1.8976)	(−1.2304)
[−3, 24]	−.2394	−.2125	−.2857
	(−2.8866)	(−1.4076)	(−2.7711)
[−3, 36]	−.4220	−.4909	−.2734
	(−4.9307)	(−4.2564)	(−2.1715)

The numbers in parentheses are the test statistics which are distributed standard normal.

then acquisitions have no significant impact on acquiring-firm shareholders. If, however, one allows the market three years following the announcement to evaluate an acquisition's effects, then acquiring-firm shareholders are significantly worse off following an acquisition than they would have been had the acquiring firms continued to perform as they had over the three years (i.e., the [−36, −4] interval) prior to the acquisition. The hypothesis that acquiring-firm shareholders are better off as a result of acquisitions fares better if one uses the longer preevent period [−60, −4] and, in general, if one uses shorter postevent periods.

Studies on this subject vary considerably in their choices of pre- and postevent-period lengths when estimating the effects of acquisitions. We favor a longer postevent period, because we doubt that all relevant information regarding an acquisition's likely effects reaches the market in the announcement month, and that the movements of stock prices in the few months surrounding an acquisition are, necessarily, unbiased estimates of the future consequences of the acquisitions.

Both the merger and tender offer subsamples reveal substantial declines in the stockholder returns over the three years following the announcement month, as judged against the [−36, −4] time-period performance. For the merging firms, the biggest decline occurs in the third year following the announcement; for the tender offer bidders, in the second. We do not place much weight on this difference. Indeed, we anticipate significant changes in stock market values for individual companies at different points of time following the initial announcement as additional information reaches the market. This anticipation is what leads us to favor a relatively long postevent interval for measuring the effects of acquisitions.

182   Evidence on the Gains from Mergers and Takeovers

Jensen and Ruback (1983) stress the importance of differentiating between mergers and tender offers in event studies, and some support for the position is present in our results. Acquiring-firm shareholders are noticeably better off in tender offers than they are in mergers. But the similarities between the two subsamples are also noteworthy. Both groups experience an upward trend in abnormal returns over roughly three years prior to the acquisition's announcement. Commencing roughly with the announcement, the paths of abnormal returns for the two groups are refracted. After another three years, both groups of shareholders are significantly worse off than they would have been had their companies continued to perform in the postevent period $[-3, 36]$ as they had prior to the event $[-36, -4]$.

If our study were the only one to expose such a pattern of returns, one might be inclined to dismiss the substantial differences between the post and preannouncement acquiring-firm share performances as curiosa of our sample. But as we shall now illustrate, the same pattern has been observed in several studies from different time periods and countries.

A REEXAMINATION OF THE LITERATURE

The results of the previous section indicate that, at least for our sample, acquiring firms do earn substantial, positive abnormal returns prior to the market's learning of acquisitions and that acquiring-firm shareholders are not better off, relative to this preevent performance, after information of the acquisition reaches the market. Moreover, whether the acquiring-firm shareholders are judged no better off or significantly worse off depends on both the pre- and postevent periods used in the comparison.

In this section, we further illustrate the importance of these methodological issues by examining results reported in several other studies. While all take inspiration from the CAPM, they actually differ in a surprisingly large number of respects, and

it is not possible to comment on each in detail. We focus upon the general patterns.

Our thesis emphasizes the possible importance of the return pattern both before and after an acquisition, and thus we exclude from consideration studies that leave out entirely or severely truncate these pre- and postevent periods (e.g., Halpern, 1973; Bradley, 1980; Dodd, 1980; Asquith et al., 1983). To facilitate comparisons, we focus upon only those studies that measure returns by months or days surrounding a single-event announcement, i.e., we do not consider studies which measure returns on an annual basis (Hogarty, 1970; Lev and Mandelker, 1972; and those in Mueller, 1980).

The first group of studies we wish to consider measures a firm's return performance in any day or month relative to that of a control group. Bradley (1980), Asquith (1983), and Asquith et al. (1983) use Center for Research in Security Prices excess returns and thus use as a control group companies with $\hat{\beta}$'s similar to those of the acquiring firms. The prediction in these studies is that an acquiring firm would earn a return each day equal to that of firms with similar $\hat{\beta}$'s. Of the three, only Asquith (1983) presents sufficient returns data before and after the announcement date to allow comparison with the other studies in this section.

Table 11.7 summarizes his main results. Asquith reports 22 months of returns data prior to the announcement day. The acquiring firms earn positive cumulative excess returns over this entire preannouncement period. Acquiring-firm shareholders enjoy cumulative abnormal returns above those earned by shareholders in the control group of 14% between the first month in Asquith's data series (-22) and the last month before the market learns of the merger (-2). The cumulative excess returns for acquiring-firm shareholders reach a peak of 14.5% above the control group on press day and level off through the period between announcement and consummation; 30 trading days after the merger a decline begins that continues for as long as Asquith reports figures (roughly 17 months after announcement). An individual who purchased an acquiring firm's shares just prior to the first signs of market knowledge of the merger (-1) and held them throughout the period over which Asquith reports data would have experienced a cumulative return 7.2% *below* that of shareholders of nonacquiring firms with similar β's over the same period.

An analogous procedure to that just described uses Fama-MacBeth residuals. These are calculated from the following equation:

$$e_{it} = R_{it} - \hat{\gamma}_{1t} - \hat{\gamma}_{2t}\hat{\beta}_i \qquad (11.4)$$

where R_{it} and β_i are defined as before. The $\hat{\gamma}_{1t}$ and $\hat{\gamma}_{2t}$ parameters are the cross-section estimates of the intercept and slope from monthly regressions of average portfolio returns on average $\hat{\beta}$. Thus, $\hat{\gamma}_{1t}$ and $\hat{\gamma}_{2t}$ differ from month to month, but for any single month they are the same for all firms. The acquiring firm's predicted return for each period t reflects market factors common to all firms. Thus the use of Fama-MacBeth residuals effectively treats the market portfolio as the control group. Table 11.7 summarizes the main results for three studies which employ Fama-MacBeth residuals (Mandelker, 1974; Ellert, 1976; Kummer and Hoffmeister, 1978). All three studies again exhibit positive premerger returns for acquiring-firm shareholders commencing in Ellert's study with the first month of data, some 100 months prior to the merger. Mandelker's study exhibits a leveling off and slight decline in returns commencing around the time of merger announcement, as Asquith's study did. Ellert's sample is more difficult to interpret, since it consists of firms whose mergers were challenged by the FTC or Justice Department. The firms, which eventually succeeded in consummating the mergers, experienced a very slight decline in returns relative to the market portfolio over the 48 months after the challenge to the merger was settled.

The Kummer and Hoffmeister (1978) results indicate substantial positive abnormal returns for acquiring-firm shareholders in the month the tender offer is

announced, followed by no clear pattern. It is the only study in Table 11.7 for which the acquiring-firm shareholders do better than their control group over the combined announcement-event–postevent period.

The four studies examined so far are similar in that they all measure a firm's excess return in any month relative to a control group's performance. Any inference regarding the *change* in acquiring-firm performance must be drawn by comparing the preevent performance of the acquiring firms relative to their control groups and their postevent performance relative to these control groups.

All four studies report positive, abnormal return performance for acquiring-firm shareholders over periods ranging from 17 to 100 months prior to announcement. All report a poorer relative performance for the acquiring companies' shares over the announcement-event–postevent period than observed for the preevent period. Indeed, only one study reports significant positive gains relative to the control group for this period (Kummer and Hoffmeister), but the abnormal gains they report for the 21 months commencing with an acquisition's announcement are only a third of the abnormal returns the same firms earned over the preceding 28 months. In the Mandelker and Ellert studies, the acquiring firms perform roughly the same as the control group firms following the merger announcements. In Asquith's study, the acquiring firms perform significantly worse than their control group after the mergers, where they had performed significantly better before.

Before turning to the next set of studies, let us briefly reconsider Mandelker's results. Although the general pattern of return performance in Mandelker's study resembles the others, the premerger rise in returns is much smaller. Mandelker's sampling of mergers stops in 1963. Unlike the other three studies, it does not include mergers from the peak years of merger and stock market activity, 1967–1969. Consistent with our earlier arguments that merging firms' returns may be particularly af-

Table 11.7. Before- and After-Acquisition Performance of Acquiring Companies in Nine Studies

Study	Time Period (Country)	Control Group Against Which Preacquisition Abnormal Performance Measured	Month Information of Acquisition Reaches Market (t_j)	Month in Which Cumulative Residuals Begin Upward Trend (t_u)	Cumulative Abnormal Returns at Month t_{j-1}	Control Group Against Which Postmerger Abnormal Performance Measured	Month Following Acquisition in Which Cumulative Residuals Stops (t_f)	Difference Between Cumulative Residuals in t_f and t_{j-1}	Last Month for Which Return Performance Reported (t_e)	Difference Between Cumulative Residuals in t_e and t_{j-1}	Notes
Asquith (1983)	1962–1976 (USA)	Companies with similar βs	−1	−22[a]	14.0	Companies with similar βs	17	−7.2	17	−7.2	Returns reported in days. We have converted to months by dividing by 22 trading days per month. Interval between announcement day and merger completion assumed to equal 6 months.
Mandelker (1974)	1941–1963 (USA)	Fama-MacBeth residuals	−1	−17	3.5	Fama-MacBeth residuals	46	+0.2	46	+0.2	Mandelker's data centered around merger completion. We have assumed announcement is 6 months before completion.
Ellert (1976)	1950–1972 (USA)	Fama-MacBeth residuals	−3	−100[a]	23.6	Fama-MacBeth residuals	82	−3.4	82	−3.4	Ellert's data centered around month a merger complaint is made by antitrust authorities. We assume announcement month is same as complaint month. Premerger returns are for all acquirors; postmerger returns for only those which completed the acquisition.
Kummer and Hoffmeister (1978)	1956–1974 (USA)	Fama-MacBeth residuals	0	−28	17.0	Fama-MacBeth residuals	No systematic movement following merger		20	+5.8	

Study	Time Period (Country)	Control Group Against Which Premerger Abnormal Performance Measured	Month Information of Merger Reaches Market (t_i)	Month in Which Cumulative Residuals Begin Upward Trend (t_u)	Cumulative Abnormal Returns at Month t_{i-1}	Control Group Against Which Postmerger Abnormal Performance Measured	Month Following Merger in Which Fall in Cumulative Residuals Stops (t_f)	Difference Between Cumulative Residuals in t_f and t_{i-1}	Last Month for Which Return Performance Reported (t_e)	Difference Between Cumulative Residuals in t_e and t_{i-1}	Notes
Dodd and Ruback (1977)	1958–1976 (USA)	Acquiring firm's performance relative to market portfolio −73 through −14	−1	−43	10.47	Acquiring firm's performance relative to market portfolio +14 through +73	60	−1.85	60	−1.85	
Franks et al. (1977)	1955–1972 (UK)	Acquiring firm's performance relative to its industry, −29 through +8	−3	No systematic movement prior to merger	−0.3	Acquiring firm's performance relative to its industry, −29 to +8	15	−2.4	40	−0.1	Sample is for acquisitions in brewing and distillery. Returns are measured net of industry index.
Langetieg (1978)	1929–1969 (USA)	Acquiring firm's performance relative to market portfolio and its two-digit SIC industry, −72 to −12	0	−60	13.58	Acquiring firm's performance relative to market portfolio and its two-digit SIC industry, +12 to +72	78	−29.0	78	−29.0	Langetieg's data centered around merger completion month. We have assumed announcement is 6 months before completion based on acquired-firm return performance.
Firth (1980)	1969–1975 (UK)	Acquiring firm's performance relative to market portfolio in 48 preceding months	−1	−48[a]	1.5	Acquiring firm's performance relative to market portfolio in 48 preceding months (omiting −12 to +12)	1	−7.4	36	−4.8	
Malatesta (1983)	1969–1974 (USA)	Acquiring firm's performance relative to market portfolio in 36-month period from −62 to −1	−4 (?)	−60[a] (?)	3.6	Acquiring firm's performance relative to market portfolio in 36-month period in +13 to +60	12	−7.7	12	−7.7	

Notes: Month 0 is the announcement month.

[a] First month for which data are reported.

186   Evidence on the Gains from Mergers and Takeovers

fected by stock market swings, both the more modest premerger increases and postmerger declines recorded by Mandelker may stem from his having employed a merger sample drawn from a more tranquil period of stock market–merger activity.

The last technique for estimating the effect of acquisitions we consider uses the residuals from some variant on Equation (11.5):

$$e_{it} = (R_{it} - R_{ft}) - \hat{\alpha}_i$$
$$- \hat{\beta}_i(R_{mt} - R_{ft}) \quad (11.5)$$

Recall that the value of $\hat{\alpha}$ for the average firm is zero and that $\hat{\alpha}_i$ thus captures a firm's abnormal performance over the time period from which (11.5) is estimated. Thus, if (11.5) is estimated over a period prior to the event's announcement, the residuals from (11.5) at and after announcement do measure the *change* in performance for the firm relative to the preevent period over which (11.5) was estimated. More generally, the inferences one draws from residuals from (11.5) are sensitive to the time period over which it is estimated.

This point is illustrated by the bottom five entries of Table 11.7. We first consider the study of Dodd and Ruback (1977) in some detail, since it clearly illustrates the issues. They estimate Equation (11.5) separately on data from $[-73, -14]$ and $[14, 73]$. If the pre– and post–tender offer performance of acquiring firms in their sample resembles that of the studies just discussed, then acquiring firms exhibit above-normal performance over some part, if not all, of $[-73, -14]$ and normal or below-normal performance over part or all of $[14, 73]$. The $\hat{\alpha}$'s from (11.5) over $[-73, -14]$ will be higher than those for $[14, 73]$.[9] The residuals they report for $[-60, -1]$ are for $\hat{\alpha}$ and $\hat{\beta}$ estimated over $[-73, -14]$ and those for $[0, 60]$ from $[14, 73]$. Thus, the reported residuals for the preevent period are calculated against a benchmark of above-normal performance and are thus smaller than if they had been measured relative to a period of poorer performance. Residuals for the an-

nouncement month and postevent period are calculated against a benchmark of poorer performance than the preevent period and thus are certainly larger than they would be if they were measured against the acquiring firms' preevent performance.

That these inferences are likely to be valid can be seen by an examination of the cumulative residuals for the bidding firms in the Dodd and Ruback study (Figure 11.2).[10] As with the studies using CRSP and Fama-MacBeth residuals, a period of sustained above-normal performance is observed commencing at A some 43 months prior to the initial tender offer month (B), where *normal* is now defined as how these firms did over the period $[-73, -14]$. Since acquiring-firm performance over $[-73, -14]$ is, if anything, above that predicted from the market portfolio and Equation (11.1), these residuals probably understate the extent of abnormal, positive performance of acquiring firms prior to the acquisitions. A period of gradual but sustained decline in share returns commences at C, month 6, about the time the takeovers are probably consummated.[11] It continues through month 60 and conceivably through 73. It is against this period of deteriorating performance $[14, 73]$ that the abnormal returns $[0, 60]$ are calculated. Thus, the level of returns in the interval $[0, 12]$ is judged relative to how the firms did from one to six years after the tender offers, not to how they did before. A comparison of Figures 11.2 and 11.1 reveals that Dodd and Ruback's acquiring-firm residuals pattern resembles the pattern for our sample when a postevent estimation period is used as benchmark (our case III). Had preevent period α's and β's been used by Dodd and Ruback, their postevent residuals probably would have exhibited a steeper decline, as with our cases I and II.[12]

Similar reasoning calls into question Dodd and Ruback's conclusion that acquiring-company shareholders are better off from the acquisitions on the basis of the statistically significant average residual of 2.83% in the announcement month. The rise in "abnormal" returns in month 0 stems in part from the switch at this month from the higher performance period

Acquiring-Firm Shareholders and Acquisitions   187

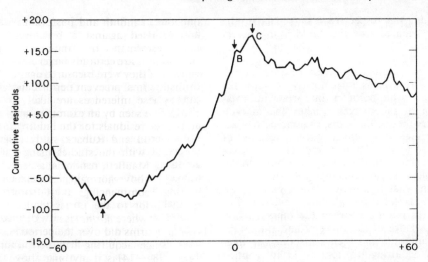

Figure 11.2. Plots of cumulative residuals for successful bidding firms. (*Source:* Dodd and Ruback, 1977.)

$[-73, -14]$ $\hat{\alpha}$'s and $\hat{\beta}$'s to the lower-period $[14, 73]$ estimates. That is, acquiring-firm shares appear to have gained in abnormal performance in month 0 partly because the benchmark of normality has shifted downward.

The importance of the treatment of $\hat{\alpha}$ and thus the choice of time period over which $\hat{\alpha}$ is estimated is further illustrated by Malatesta's (1983) study. Residuals over the period $[-60, -13]$ are calculated by using the first available 36 observations from the preceding 50 months. The cumulative average $\hat{\alpha}$ over $[-24, -4]$ is 10.7, and the forecast error is -1.6. Thus, acquiring firms in Malatesta's sample also were earning significantly higher returns than the market portfolio prior to the market's learning of the mergers. The modest cumulative residuals Malatesta reports for the premerger period relative to the acquiring firms' performance over this period merely indicate that the above-normal performance for the acquiring firms was fairly uniform throughout the entire premerger period $[-62, -1]$ and thus is adequately represented by his $\hat{\alpha}$ estimates.

The residuals for months 1 through 60 are calculated from $\hat{\alpha}$ and $\hat{\beta}$ estimated from the first available 36 months in the interval

$[13, 60]$. The cumulative residuals over $[1, 12]$ are negative and significant even relative to the acquiring firms' subsequent performance in the postmerger period. While Malatesta does not report the $\hat{\alpha}$'s for the postmerger residuals, one presumes from Asquith's results that they would be substantially less than the 10.7% cumulative $\hat{\alpha}$ obtained prior to the mergers. Thus, the acquiring firms probably did even worse during the first 12 months after the announcements, compared with how they were doing before, than is implied by the residuals Malatesta calculates relative to the postmerger period's $\hat{\alpha}$'s and $\hat{\beta}$'s.

The importance of how one treats the $\hat{\alpha}$ estimates from Equation (11.5) is further illustrated by the results of Langetieg's (1978) study. Langetieg estimates a variant on Equation (11.5), which also controls for movements in acquiring-firm returns common to all firms in the acquiring firm's two-digit SIC industry. His measure of abnormal returns for firm i is the sum of $\hat{\alpha}_i$ and $\hat{e}_{it}$. Thus, although Langetieg estimates separate $\hat{\alpha}$'s and $\hat{\beta}$'s for the pre- and postmerger periods, his measures of abnormal returns do not suffer from the same problems as the Dodd and Ruback and Malatesta measures do, because Langetieg in-

188   Evidence on the Gains from Mergers and Takeovers

cludes the respective $\hat{\alpha}$'s as part of the abnormal returns, thus building into his results the systematic change in the intercept.

The cumulative excess returns for the acquiring firms turn positive 60 months prior to the point in time when information of the merger reaches the market. Over these 60 months, shareholders of acquiring firms enjoy excess returns of 13.58% over what one predicts from movements in both the market portfolio and the acquiring firm's two-digit industry.[13]

In what is now a familiar pattern, we witness in Langetieg's data a leveling off of excess returns between the market's first knowledge of the mergers and their consummation, and then a sustained decline. The acquiring-firm returns decline continuously over the 72 months following a merger. A shareholder who bought into an acquiring firm just prior to the market's learning of the merger and held its shares for the next 78 months would experience a cumulative loss relative to the market portfolio and shareholders of other firms in the same industry of 29%.

Firth (1980) calculates the residual at month t from $\hat{\alpha}$ and $\hat{\beta}$ estimates for the 48 months immediately preceding t, when t varies from -48 to -13. Thus, if acquiring firms earned above-normal returns uniformly over a substantial interval prior to the mergers, this fact would not be apparent in the residuals for the premerger period.

The residuals over the entire interval $[-12, 12]$ are calculated by using $\hat{\alpha}$'s and $\hat{\beta}$'s estimated from $[-60, -13]$. Thus, unlike the results in both Dodd and Ruback and Malatesta, the immediate pre- and postannouncement residuals are all calculated relative to the acquiring companies' premerger return performance. As it turns out, in Firth's study this difference does not prove to be important. The market adjusts fully in the announcement month, at which time the acquiring-firm shareholders suffer a significant 6.3% loss relative to premerger performance. The residuals for the postmerger months reveal no distinctive pattern.

The Franks et al. (1977) study of 94 ac-

quisitions by United Kingdom breweries and distilleries is difficult to analyze. They first present, for the combined merging companies, cumulative average residuals which "display a strong upward bias throughout, thus exhibiting effects which cannot be attributed to mergers" (1977, p. 1521). Since the residuals for the acquiring and acquired firms are combined, one cannot determine whether it is the performance of the former or the latter which accounts for this positive abnormal premerger performance. But if it were the acquiring firms that were exhibiting above-normal premerger performance, the Franks et al. results would correspond closely to those of the other studies we have discussed. When they control for industry performance, the acquiring firms exhibit no above-normal returns prior to the merger. But since the acquiring firms are part of the industry index, this choice of control group introduces a bias toward zero in the residual estimates.

Franks et al. estimate Equation (11.5) over the time period $[-29, 8]$, omitting an interval around the announcement, which "is adjusted on the basis of the resulting estimates of abnormal residuals" (p. 1515). Given that the excluded interval varies from firm to firm, it is difficult to determine against what yardstick abnormal performance is being gauged. Nevertheless, returns initially rise (from -4 through 0) and then decline, leaving acquiring shareholders no better off as a result of the mergers. "Indeed since some gain would have been anticipated as a result of premerger interests [of the acquiring firms in the targets], one could argue that there may have been losses exclusive of these interests" (p. 1523).

SUMMARY AND CONCLUSIONS

To acquire another firm, a buyer must pay a substantial premium over the current market value of the target. In our sample, this premium averaged 81% of the target firms' market value. Thus, over the period between the initial decision to acquire and the completion of an acquisition, shareholders of acquired firms enjoy substantial increases in their wealth. The key question for the theory of the firm and for antimerger policy is whether these wealth increases measure net increases in wealth for society as a result of some synergistic efficiency gain, or mere wealth transfers from acquiring-firm to acquired-firm shareholders.

To answer this question, one must measure the effects of the acquisitions on acquiring-firm shareholder wealth. While it is reasonable to assume that the changes in acquiring-firm shareholder wealth related to the acquisition begin about the same time as the changes in acquired-firm shareholder wealth begin, somewhere between the announcement and four months before, it is arguable whether all changes in acquiring-firm wealth caused by the acquisition are complete by the date of its announcement or its completion. Conceivably, new information about its future consequences might reach the market at intermittent intervals for some time after the market's first knowledge of the acquisition. This consideration suggests that a longer-run perspective of the consequences of acquisitions for acquiring-firm shareholders might be appropriate than is warranted for acquired-firm shareholders.

Several studies have measured the performance of acquiring firms relative to the average firm in the stock market or in the acquiring firm's industry, both before and after acquisition announcements.[14] A consistent pattern emerges. Acquiring firms begin to experience significant positive abnormal returns as early as 100 months prior to the acquisition announcements. The cumulative preacquisition gains of acquiring-firm shareholders are inevitably positive and are typically large.[15]

Starting around the time the market begins to learn of an acquisition, or at its consummation, the performance of the acquiring firm's shares begins to deteriorate relative to their preevent performance. In some cases, they exhibit a roughly normal postevent performance (e.g., Mandelker, 1974); in others, a significant relative decline (Langetieg, 1978; Asquith, 1983).[16]

A second set of studies measures an ac-

quiring firm's performance as a result of an acquisition, relative to this performance over another period, controlling for general shifts in the economy by using the basic CAPM equation (11.5). Given that the acquiring firm's performance relative to the market (or its industry) differs significantly over the pre- and postevent time intervals, estimates of "abnormal" returns to acquiring-firm shareholders are sensitive to the choice of time period over which the "normal" $\hat{\alpha}$ and $\hat{\beta}$ of Equation (11.5) are measured. Our own results indicate significant above-normal returns are earned by acquiring-firm shareholders over the immediate two to three years prior to the market's learning of an acquisition, relative to the performance of these firms in the three preceding years. Following the market's receipt of information of the acquisition, the acquiring firms' shareholders experience lower returns than they enjoyed over the preevent period. Moreover, the deterioration in performance is more dramatic if comparison is made with the immediate three years' performance than if comparison is with the five preevent years.

Our findings are consistent with those of other studies using Equation (11.5) and the CAPM, although comparisons are made difficult by the differing choices of time periods for estimating (11.5). A significant decline in acquiring-firm returns is observed by Firth (1980) in the announcement month and perhaps by Franks et al. (1977) in the first few months following the merger announcements. Malatesta (1983) observes a significant decline in acquiring-firm performance in the first 12 months after the announcement, relative to the acquiring companies' performance over a postmerger period; Dodd and Ruback (1977) record a steady decline in performance over 54 months following the acquisition's completion, again measured relative to the acquiring companies' own normal postevent performance. Since acquiring firms perform worse after acquisitions than before, when measured against the market, the decline in returns measured by Malatesta and Dodd and Ruback following the acquisitions is in all likeli-

190   Evidence on the Gains from Mergers and Takeovers

hood considerably smaller than it would have been had these authors measured the decline against the predicted performance of acquiring firms on the basis of their preevent histories.

Thus, the answer to the question posed in the title of this chapter, "Are acquiring-firm shareholders better off after an acquisition than they were before?" seems to be no, if by *before* we mean the three years or so prior to the time information reaches the market, and if by *after* we mean the three years or so after this point in time.

The evaluation of the effects of acquisitions on acquiring-firm shareholders' wealth presented here is considerably more negative than that found in some other parts of the literature. Others have reached more positive conclusions than we in part because they have posed different questions from ours. To the extent that one focuses on the acquiring companies' performance only at the time of the announcement (e.g., Dodd and Ruback, 1977; Bradley, 1980) and makes one's comparison not to the acquiring firms' own preevent performance but to that of the market portfolio (e.g., Mandelker, 1974; Kummer and Hoffmeister, 1978; Bradley, 1980), one obtains a more optimistic assessment of the performance of acquiring-company shares. Halpern (1983) ignores the evidence on postevent acquiring-company returns entirely in his survey; Jensen and Ruback (1983) clearly give more weight to the figures regarding the gains at the time of acquisition in their Table 3 than they do to the figures which include postacquisition performance in Table 4. Neither survey has much to say about the substantial positive abnormal returns acquiring-firm shareholders earn before the market learns of the acquisitions.

The stock market is subject to substantial swings in returns that cannot be justified by an application of the rational-expectations assumption to subsequent dividend streams. Acquisition activity is correlated with stock market activity and is arguably subject to the same underlying psychological factors and motivations. The stock market may be over- or under optimistic about the future consequences of acquisitions at different points in time. Moreover, an acquisition is a sufficiently complex event that it might take the market more than a single month or year to form an accurate estimate of its future effect. These considerations suggest to us the need for a longer-run view of the consequences of acquisitions. But whether or not one agrees with us on this point, we do hope we have achieved our goal of demonstrating that one's answer to the question "Are shareholders of acquiring firms better off after an acquisition than they were before?" is sensitive to both the choice of time intervals over which before and after performance is defined and the choice of benchmark against which performance is measured.

NOTES

1. Nelson (1959, 1966); Melicher et al. (1983); Geroski (1984). Casual observation suggests that this correlation may have weakened in the most recent years. But the cited studies carry the analysis up through the midseventies. Since all of the empirical work discussed in this chapter, save our own, is from the period in which the positive correlation has been found to exist, our point with respect to the existing literature and its interpretation is valid even if it should prove that acquisition activity is no longer strongly correlated with stock market price movements.

2. Recent critiques by Roll (1977) and Levy (1983), among others, call into question some of the assumptions of the CAPM. While these papers pose serious challenges to many of the conclusions drawn from the CAPM, they carry less weight with regard to the literature on the effects of acquisitions. The market portfolio may be a reasonable choice as a control group for predicting changes in an acquiring firm's returns, even if it is not a reasonable portfolio for an individual to hold.

3. The total number of firms exceeds the number of firms involved in mergers and tender offers because one of the firms could not be classified.

4. The pattern of overall acquisition activity during the sample period can be seen in this record of completed acquisitions:

Acquiring-Firm Shareholders and Acquisitions 191

Year	Number of Acquisitions	Percent Change
1976	1145	16.7
1977	1209	5.6
1978	1452	20.1
1979	1564	7.7
1980	1583	1.2
1981	2314	46.2

Transactions counted here are valued at $1 million or more; the list includes partial acquisitions (*Mergers and Acquisitions,* Winter 1984).

5. See Fama (1976) for a full description of the market model.

6. Each firm error $\hat{e}_{it}$ is divided by its standard deviation $\hat{\sigma}(\hat{e}_{it})$, where

$$\hat{\sigma}(\hat{e}_{it}) = \left\{ S_i^2 \left[1 + \frac{1}{T} + \frac{(R_{mt} - \overline{R}_m)^2}{\sum_{\tau=1}^{T} (R_{m\tau} - \overline{R}_m)^2} \right] \right\}^{1/2}$$

and

$S_i^2 =$ error variance calculated from the market model regression for firm i

$\overline{R}_m =$ average return on the market portfolio over the estimation period

$T =$ number of months in the estimation period

The standardized errors $\hat{e}_{it}/\hat{\sigma}(\hat{e}_{it})$ are summed and divided by I, the total number of firms, to obtain AS_t, the average standardized error for each time period. We define z, the test statistic, as $z_t = \sqrt{I_t} (AS_t)$, where z is distributed as approximately a normal variable for large samples. To obtain the test statistic for the null hypothesis that the CAR_{xy} are insignificantly different from zero, we calculate

$$\overline{z} = \sum_{t=x}^{Y} \frac{z_t}{(y - x + 1)^{1/2}}$$

where z is also distributed approximately normally for large samples.

7. The typical justification for choosing a postevent period against which to measure postevent residuals is that the $\hat{\beta}$'s may change as a result of the acquisition. But those studies which test for shifts in the $\hat{\beta}_i$ report no *systematic* shifts in them (see the third section). Nor do we find any. For example, only two of the $\hat{\beta}$'s estimated over $[-3, 36]$ are significantly different from those estimated over $[-60, -4]$, one being larger, the other smaller. The other 76 insignificant changes divide almost evenly between increases and decreases.

8. Michael Jensen also argues that the postevent benchmark should be the normal performance of the acquiring firms, not their above-normal preevent performance. We thank Michael for his comment at the conference, which helped clarify our thinking on this point.

9. Although Dodd and Ruback (1977) report the differences between the $\hat{\beta}$'s for the two periods, they unfortunately do not report the differences in $\hat{\alpha}$'s (p. 358).

10. Dodd and Ruback (1977) do not report the cumulative residual series, so we have added the averages they do report to obtain Figure 11.2. Our Figure 11.2 corresponds to and resembles very closely their Figure 2.

11. Both Mandelker (1974) and Langetieg (1978) center their data around the consummation of the acquisition, not its announcement. Judging from the acquired firms' returns in these studies, information regarding the mergers would appear to reach the market about six months before the mergers are completed. In our sample, four months elapse on average between first announcement and consummation, which corresponds to these other studies if one allows two months for preannouncement information leakage. We assume the gap between announcement and consummation to be six months in the Mandelker, Langetieg, and Asquith studies.

12. The reason Dodd and Ruback (1977) give for using separate $\hat{\alpha}$ and $\hat{\beta}$ estimates from before and after the announcement is that for 34 of the 184 firms in their sample (18%), there is a significant change in $\hat{\beta}$ (pp. 358–359). But changes in $\hat{\beta}$ are equally divided between increases (10 for successful bidders) and declines (9). Thus, no *systematic* shift in residuals should result if preannouncement $\hat{\beta}$'s are used. But if postannouncement $\hat{\alpha}$'s are significantly lower than preannouncement $\hat{\alpha}$'s, postannouncement residuals are systematically raised by their choice of period against which to measure postannouncement performance.

13. Langetieg (1978) reports four sets of similar results (Table 1, p. 373). We quote from only the first set, using an equally weighted industry index.

Langetieg also reports residuals net of the market portfolio, industry index, *and* the performance of a "well-matched non-merging firm" (p. 371). The latter is selected from the acquiring firm's two-digit industry by the criterion that its residuals from the market portfolio regression (11.5) have the highest correlation with the residuals for the acquiring firm. This criterion for selecting a control group firm

192   Evidence on the Gains from Mergers and Takeovers

biases Langetieg's findings for this comparison toward zero. With an infinitely large population from which to select control group firms, one would find for any acquiring firm a nonacquiring firm whose residuals correlate perfectly, leaving nothing to be explained. A two-digit industry is not an infinite population, but it is large enough to introduce serious bias toward zero. Nevertheless, the same preevent-positive-excess-returns, postevent-negative-excess-returns pattern appears even after netting out the movements in the control group returns (see Table 2, p. 377).

14. Since Langetieg (1978) adds $\hat{\alpha}_i$ back into his estimate of abnormal returns, his is really an estimate relative to both the market portfolio and the two-digit SIC industry and should be included with this group.

15. Other studies reporting substantial positive premerger returns for acquiring firms are Lev and Mandelker (1972) and Cosh et al. (1980).

16. Other studies reporting postmerger period declines include Hogarty (1970); Cosh et al. (1980); Dodd (1980); Jenny and Weber (1980); and Mueller (1980).

REFERENCES

Amihud, Y., and L. Baruch (1981). "Risk reduction as a Managerial Motive for Conglomerate Mergers." *Bell Journal of Economics* 12, 605–617.

Asquith, P. (1983) "Merger Bids, Uncertainty, and Stockholder Returns." *Journal of Financial Economics* 11, 51–83.

———, R. F. Bruner, and D. W. Mullins, Jr. (1983). "The Gains to Bidding Firms from Merger." *Journal of Financial Economics* 11, 121–139.

Azzi, C. (1978). "Conglomerate Mergers, Default Risk, and Homemade Mutual Funds." *American Economic Review* 68, 161–172.

Bradley, M. (1980). "Interfirm Tender Offers and the Market for Corporate Control." *Journal of Business* 53, 345–376.

Cosh, A., A. Hughes, and A. Singh (1980). "The Causes and Effects of Takeovers in the United Kingdom: An Empirical Investigation for the Late 1960s at the Microeconomic Level." In *The Determinants and Effects of Mergers: An International Comparison*, ed. D. C. Mueller, 227–270. Cambridge, Eng.: Oelgeschlager, Gunn, and Hain.

Dodd, P. (1980). "Merger Proposals, Management Discretion and Stockholder Wealth." *Journal of Financial Economics* 8, 105–137.

———, and R. Ruback (1977). "Tender Offers and Stockholder Returns: An Empirical Analysis." *Journal of Financial Economics* 5, 351–374.

Ellert, J. C. (1976). "Mergers, Antitrust Law Enforcement and Stockholder Returns." *Journal of Finance* 31, 715–732.

Fama, E. F. (1976). *The Foundation of Finance.* New York: Basic Books.

———, L. Fisher, M. C. Jensen, and R. Roll (1969) "The Adjustment of Stock Prices to New Information." *International Economic Review* 10, 1–21.

Firth, M. (1980). "Takeovers, Shareholder Returns, and the Theory of the Firm." *Quarterly Journal of Economics* 94, 315–347.

Franks, J. R., J. E. Broyles, and M. J. Hecht (1977). "An Industry Study of the Profitability of Mergers in the United Kingdom." *Journal of Finance* 32, 1513–1525.

Geroski, P. A. (1984). "On the Relationship Between Aggregate Merger Activity and the Stock Market." *European Economic Review* 25, 223–233.

Greer, D. F. (1984). "Acquiring in Order to Avoid Acquisition." Mimeo, San Jose State University.

Halpern, P. J. (1973). "Empirical Estimates of the Amount and Distribution of Gains to Companies in Mergers." *Journal of Business* 46, 554–575.

——— (1983). "Corporate Acquisitions: A Theory of Special Cases? A Review of Event Studies Applied to Acquisitions." *Journal of Finance* 38, 297–317.

Hogarty, T. F. (1970). "The Profitability of Corporate Mergers." *Journal of Business* 43, 317–327.

Jenny, F., and A. P. Weber (1980). "France, 1962–72." In *The Determinants and Effects of Mergers: An International Comparison,* ed. D. C. Mueller, 133–162. Cambridge, Eng.: Oelgeschlager, Gunn, and Hain.

Jensen, M. (1969). "Risk, the Pricing of Capital Assets, and the Evaluation of Investment Portfolios." *Journal of Business* 42, 167–247.

———, and R. S. Ruback (1983). "The Market for Corporate Control." *Journal of Financial Economics* 11, 5–50.

Johnston, J. (1972). *Econometric Methods.* 2nd ed. New York: McGraw-Hill.

Kummer, D. R., and J. R. Hoffmeister (1978). "Valuation Consequences of Cash Tender Offers." *Journal of Finance* 33, 505–516.

Langetieg, T. C. (1978). "An Application of a Three-Factor Performance Index to Measure Stockholder Gains from Merger." *Journal of Financial Economics* 6, 365–384.

Lev, B., and G. Mandelker (1972). "The Microeconomic Consequences of Corporate Mergers." *Journal of Business* **45,** 85–104.

Levy, H., and M. Sarnat (1970). "Diversification, Portfolio Analysis and the Uneasy Case for Conglomerate Mergers." *Journal of Finance* **25,** 795–802.

Levy, H. (1983). "The Capital Asset Pricing Model: Theory and Empiricism," *Economic Journal* **93,** 145–165.

Linn, S. C., and J. J. McConnell (1983). "An Empirical Investigation of the Impact of 'Antitakeover' Amendments on Common Stock Prices." *Journal of Financial Economics* **11,** 361–399.

Malatesta, P. H. (1983). "The Wealth Effect of Merger Activity and the Objective Functions of Merging Firms." *Journal of Financial Economics* **11,** 155–181.

Mandelker, G. (1974). "Risk and Return: The Case of Merging Firms." *Journal of Financial Economics* **1,** 303–335.

Manne, H. G. (1965). "Mergers and the Market for Corporate Control." *Journal of Political Economy* **73,** 110–120.

Mason, R. H., and M. B. Goudzwaard (1976). "Performance of Conglomerate Firms: A Portfolio Approach." *Journal of Finance* **31,** 39–48.

Melicher, R. W., J. Ledolter, and L. J. D'Antonio (1983). "A Time Series Analysis of Aggregate Merger Activity." *Review of Economics and Statistics* **65,** 423–430.

Mergers and Acquisitions, 1984 Almanac and Index, p. 21.

Mueller, D. C. (1969). "A Theory of Conglomerate Mergers." *Quarterly Journal of Economics* **83,** 643–659.

——— (1977). "The Effects of Conglomerate Mergers: A Survey of the Empirical Evidence." *Journal of Banking and Finance* **1,** 315–347.

——— (1979). "Do We Want a New, Tough Antimerger Law?" *Antitrust Bulletin* **24,** 807–836.

———, ed. (1980). *The Determinants and Effects of Mergers: An International Comparison.* Cambridge; England: Oelgeschlager, Gunn, and Hain.

Nelson, R. L. (1959). *Merger Movements in American Industry, 1895–1956.* Princeton: Princeton University Press.

——— (1966). "Business Cycle Factors in the Choice Between Internal and External Growth." In *The Corporate Merger,* eds. W. Alberts and J. Segall. Chicago: University of Chicago Press.

Roll, R. (1977). "A Critique of the Asset Pricing Theory Tests." *Journal of Financial Economics* **4,** 129–176.

Scherer, F. M. (1971). *Industrial Market Structure and Economic Performance.* 2nd ed. Chicago: Rand McNally.

Shiller, R. J. (1981). "Do Stock Prices Move Too Much to Be Justified by Subsequent Changes in Dividends?" *American Economic Review* **71,** 421–436.

——— (1984). "Stock Prices and Social Dynamics." *Brookings Papers on Economic Activity,* December, 457–498.

——— (1986). "Fashions, Fads, and Bubbles in Financial Markets." Chapter 3 of this volume.

Smith, K. V., and J. C. Schreiner (1969). "A Portfolio Analysis of Conglomerate Diversification." *Journal of Finance* **24,** 413–427.

Smith, V. L. (1970). "Corporate Financial Theory Under Uncertainty." *Quarterly Journal of Economics* **84,** 451–471.

Weston, J. F., K. V. Smith, and R. E. Shrieves (1972). "Conglomerate Performance Using the Capital Asset Pricing Model." *Review of Economics and Statistics* **54,** 357–363.

Name Index